VOICINGS

TEN PLAYS from
the DOCUMENTARY THEATER

VOICINGS

TEN PLAYS from
the DOCUMENTARY THEATER

Edited and with an Introduction by
ATTILIO FAVORINI

(0)02

THE ECCO PRESS

The Ecco Press
100 West Broad Street
Hopewell, New Jersey 08525
Published simultaneously in Canada by
Penguin Books Canada Ltd., Ontario
Printed in the United States of America

Designed by Debby Jay

FIRST EDITION

Library of Congress Cataloging-in-Publication Data
  Voicings: ten plays from the documentary theater /
Attilio Favorini, editor.
    ISBN 0-88001-397-4
    I. Plays

The text of this book is set in Sabon

Mrea uxori

Acknowledgments

This book is neither a comprehensive history nor a theory of documentary theater, though it manifestly contains elements of both. Rather, it is a response to the documentary impulse in the theater driven by a desire to make accessible plays that have undeservedly fallen from view. I wish to express my genuine gratitude to all the playwrights and publishers whose permissions have made the present publication possible. I also wish to thank the American Society for Theatre Research for permission to reprint a portion of my Introduction, which previously appeared in *Theatre Survey*.

Because the range of interests of documentary playwrights is vast, the list of scholars and colleagues both within and beyond the field of theater research upon whom I have called for help is likewise extensive. Christopher Murray, Peggy Mecham, Barry Witham, Laurence Senelick, Antigone Trimis, Robert Cohen, Tom Gibbons, Peter Koehler, Bernard Cohen, Linda Eller, Cary Mazer, Alan Filewod, Mae Smethurst, James Maher, Colin Chambers, Clive Gehle, Barry Norman, Kathleen George, and Harvey Meieran all answered my questions or volunteered valuable information.

Among my colleagues in the Department of Theatre Arts at the University of Pittsburgh, Kiki Gounaridou and Dennis Kennedy offered more than collegial support, going out of their way to aid and encourage the project. Vladimir Padunov of the Slavic Department was especially generous with his expertise in contemporary Russian theater and film.

Lynda Kaiserman and Rick Whitten facilitated the production of the manuscript at critical stages. At The Ecco Press, Ellen Foos, Vincent Janoski, and Phyllis Berk have been especially helpful. Nor would the publication of this volume have been possible without the support of a grant from the Research Development Fund of the University of Pittsburgh.

I owe a special debt of gratitude to Peter Cheeseman, whose work inspired Gillette Elvgren and me to write our own documentary drama, and to Gillette whose generosity and theater savvy I have benefited from through most of my career. They are chief among the begetters of this book.

In my research I have enjoyed the assistance of Anna Rosenstein, as well as the students in my documentary theater seminar: Gwen Orel, Janet Shum, Kevin Wetmore, David Pellegrini, and Melissa Gibson.

Maria Krol and Richard Korb speeded my work with help in translation from German. Carolyn Kelson and Aleksandr and Helen Prokhorov were both diligent and devoted in translating *Compensation*. To Carolyn I am especially grateful for serving as my ambassador in Moscow, diplomatically making contacts for me that I could not have managed on my own.

To the playwrights Sergei Kurginian (as well as his wife Masha), Molly Newman, Barbara Damashek, Emily Mann, and Mame Hunt my debt of gratitude is considerable. Each took time away from busy schedules and new creative work to sift through memories and scrapbooks in support of this project.

Ellen Kelson, friend, not only planted the seed for this book in a casual conversation but also enlisted the aid of her daughter Carolyn as translator. Ellen spent many hours checking pesky facts and, exactly when needed, cheerleading. I am especially grateful to her.

Both my parents and children continue to be a source of inspiration. Mrea, my loving and thoughtful wife, has been throughout a pillar of patience and understanding, to which this book is both testament and document.

Contents

Introduction

After the Fact: Theater and the Documentary Impulse

"Mnemosyne, not Hephaestus, is the mother of the Muses."
—Walter Ong, S.J.

In Book VI, chapter 21 of what is variously called the "History," "Histories," or "Researches," Herodotus preserves an anecdote relating to the first factual drama of the Western tradition, a play produced within mere decades of the "invention" of the drama by Thespis. The anecdote reports a *succès de scandale* by the playwright Phrynichus, a contemporary of Aeschylus, who wrought his drama out of the fresh horrors of the Persian War. "When Phrynichus produced his play, *The Capture of Miletus,* the whole audience at the theater burst into tears and fined Phrynichus a thousand drachmas for reminding them of a calamity that was their very own; they also forbade any future production of the play."[1] To Herodotus' report we can add relatively little, as neither this nor any other play of Phrynichus has survived. But we know that in the 490s B.C. Themistocles had been unsuccessful in persuading his fellow Athenians to support the Ionian revolt, of which the fall of Miletus was a notorious episode. And if, as seems likely, *The Capture of Miletus* was produced in 492 B.C., only two years after the event, that was the year Themistocles as archon oversaw play selection at the City Dionysia. So there were appar-

ently both political and aesthetic reasons for the production of Phrynichus' play and its censure—thereby setting a pattern for the challenges faced by the documentary playwrights included in this volume.

The Capture of Miletus was followed, at some distance, by two other Persian War plays of which we have knowledge. Phrynichus himself faired better with *The Phoenician Women,* which won first prize in 476 B.C. with Themistocles as *choregos* (producer). Perhaps encouraged by Phrynichus' latter treatment, Aeschylus somewhat inaccurately brought to the stage in 472 B.C. the story of the Battle of Salamis, leaving us the earliest surviving Greek drama, *The Persians.*[2] Though there are very occasional references to other plays of a historical nature down to the third century B.C. and speculations as to a tradition of dramatic commemorations of the Persian War, historical dramas were apparently the exception rather than the rule in Ancient Greece.[3]

---

[1] *Herodotus, The History,* tr. by David Grene (Chicago: University of Chicago Press, 1987), 416–17.

[2] See Rush Rehm, *Greek Tragic Theatre* (London: Routledge, 1992), 22–23, and Edith Hall, *Inventing the Barbarian Greek Self-Definition through Tragedy* (Oxford: Clarendon Press, 1989), 62–69 for the political context of these historical dramas.

[3] See Hall, 63–64 and 74, n. 78.

Why this was so is a complicated issue. In the period between Phrynichus' first historical drama and his second there was a struggle between Themistocles and his political enemy Cimon "expressed in a propaganda battle" (Hall, 66) in which the latter had an interest in celebrating Salamis. The trio of historical dramas evidently were skirmishes in that battle, and perhaps the Athenians wearied of the fray. On the other hand, Phyrnichus and Aeschylus wrote long before Aristotle taxonomized the differences between tragedy and epic, so maybe tragedy was flexible enough in its early stages to admit historical material. Hall cites contemporary forms of epicinian odes and elegaic poetry that celebrated recent military victories. The case of tragedy, however, was probably more like that of vase-painting, which was almost exclusively mythological and absorbed contemporary reference in "the dialectical process by which such epoch-making events as the expulsion of tyrants and the defense of the democracy against Persia acquired stature and theological meaning by being molded along familiar mythopoeic lines" (Hall, 69). That is, historical dramas may have disappeared because a "new ethnocentric ideology" was better served by "the old and familiar mythical conflict" (Hall, 68). Finally, the "pervasiveness of performance" (Rehm, 4) in fifth-century Athenian public life perhaps made it less urgent for the theater to be pressed into service as still another forum to debate contemporary history without the obliqueness afforded by myth.

Equally part of this performance culture was Herodotus, who most often refers to himself as "speaking" rather than "writing" his history, which itself was surely intended to be read aloud, performed. Standing somewhere between Homer and Thucydides, between the poetic and the parascientific, Herodotus claims a territory much later to be occupied by the contributors included here. Like them, he was a poet who nonetheless engaged in a historical discourse.[4]

There appears to have been no sharp break between what Herodotus did and the earlier oral memorialists whose work might take the form of song or prose and whose aim was "to celebrate the achievements of both the heroes of myth and legend and the more recent, tangible figures from the past, for it is likely that they blurred the distinction between the two."[5] The key transition in Herodotus was not from oral to written production but from memorized recitals to readings aloud. Indeed, the evidence is compelling that "the whole of the *Histories* is a ring composition" (Evans, 89) characteristic of oral epics—that is, a nested structure of typical events or encounters, characterized by repeated themes, "runs" or formulaic descriptions, and other sorts of ritual repetitions.[6]

Herodotus' text consequently bears the marks of a certain tension between words heard and words seen, between the choric form and the data the form is meant to convey, perhaps also between the dynamism of his oral traditional sources for the data and the static nature of Herodotus' writing it "down." This tension is not at all unlike that of the theater and suggests that the oral historian and the historical dramatist are parts of a continuum of performance genres whose boundaries were a lot more porous than we may have thought. Without denying the anachronism of applying the phrase "living newspaper" to the work of Herodotus, I nevertheless offer it as close in meaning to the *"Histories apodeixis"* of Herodotus' opening sentence[7] and also as a descriptor of what Phyrnichus crafted so to provoke the Athenians. I thus mean to link ancient Greek and twentieth-century practice not by "influence" but by impulse. When Herodotus, Phyrnichus, and Aeschylus "wrote," "attitudes towards the past still belonged to the oral tradition, and were shaped by the orators and the theatre" (Evans, ix). Documentary playwrights belong to this same shared tradition of historians

---

[4]On Herodotus as poet, see K. H. Waters, *Herodotus the Historian* (London: Croom Helm, 1985).

[5]J.A.S. Evans, *Herodotus, Explorer of the Past* (Princeton: Princeton University Press, 1991), 96.
[6]On ring compositions, see Albert Lord, "Words Heard and Words Seen," in *Epic Singers and Oral Tradition* (Ithaca and London: Cornell University Press, 1991), 15–37.
[7]See Evans, 3, on the difficulties of rendering Herodotus' opening phrase without resorting to anachronism.

and dramatists, particularly in their reliance on oral sources for their work.

While we know nothing of Phyrnichus' and little of Aeschylus' sources for their historical dramas, there is evidence that the latter brought to bear on *The Persians* a passion for research shared by his documentary descendants. Aeschylus was, of course, a war veteran and had seen Persians with his own eyes. He may also have consulted Persian war prisoners. In any case, it is worth noting the "extraordinary aural impact" (Hall, 77) registered by *The Persians*. Evidently, in laboring to create a Persian soundscape (there are no Greek characters in the play and it is set in Persia), Aeschylus did everything he could to make his audience forget they were hearing Greek. Hall identifies among his devices the use of Iranian proper names, cacophonous catalogues, imitation of foreign vocabulary, cries, interjections, repetition, and anaphora designed to suggest barbarian diction, Ionicisms (to lend an eastern feel to the language), and epic terms (76–79).

Whether or nor Aeschylus' ethnographic interests extended thematically to a "sympathetic" treatment of the Persians remains a source of scholarly debate. But even if one acknowledges *The Persians* as the first "file in the archive of Orientalism" (Hall, 99)—that is, the exoticizing and intellectual colonization of Asia[8]—Aeschylus marshaled a powerful array of stage techniques to approach the historically Other. When this effort "begins to give way in the second half of the century to a sophistic examination of the canonical antithesis of Hellene and barbarian" (Hall, 161), it also represents a weakening of the documentary[9] impulse in the theater.

A weakening, not a death. While we can identify relatively few plays between Aeschylus and the

Elizabethans that directly engage contemporary history, there existed a "commemorative culture"[10] continuous from classical times through the late Middle Ages and early Renaissance. This culture encompassed not only a vast oral "literature" of epics and ballads but also a tradition of mnemonic devices, such as memory palaces and memory theaters—all of which are linked in their performative aspects to theater.[11] The persistence of the oral performance of literature and the ubiquity of oral presentations of all sorts—from trials to sermons to scholarly disputations—combined with low literacy rates and the paucity of written texts to make the art of memory central to civilization. Rhetoricians regularly conflated oratory and acting, and their refinement of the canons of memory and of delivery (codifying rules of voice, gesture, and expression) are still relatively unexploited in understanding drama and theater. Recent scholarship,[12] however, makes it ever clearer that the fluidity of performance genres characteristic of Ancient Greece had its medieval equivalent.

In the religious sphere, a continuity existed from the dialogic sermon in church to the mock *sermon joyeux* on the boards, from liturgy to liturgical drama to the mystery plays. In the secular sphere the links are among oratory, debates, mock trials and moot court, dramatic monologues and the various more formally dramatic

---

[8]Edward Said, *Orientalism* (New York: Pantheon, 1978), 56–57 considers *The Persians* in this context.
[9]Ancient Greek theater may have occasionally anticipated the documentary's use of "actuals" if the speculations are true that Xerxes' tent was taken to Athens and used as a backdrop for historical tragedies and that timbers from the Persian fleet were used in the reconstruction of the theater in the early 470s. See Hall, 74 and n. 78.

---

[10]See Eugene Vance, "Roland, Charlemagne, and the Poetics of Memory," in *Textual Strategies,* ed. Josué Harrari (Ithaca: Cornell University Press, 1978), 374–403 for an explication of this notion. Jody Enders, *Rhetoric and the Origins of Medieval Drama* (Ithaca: Cornell University Press, 1992), 53, evokes it in reference to medieval French drama.
[11]On the oral tradition see, e.g., the extensive bibliography in John Miles Foley, *Immanent Art. from Structure to Meaning in Traditional Oral Epic* (Bloomington, Ind.: Indiana University Press, 1991); on the mnemonic tradition see Frances Yates, *The Art of Memory* (Chicago: University of Chicago Press, 1966) and (for the connection to theater) her *Theatre of the World* (Chicago: University of Chicago Press, 1969). Also of relevance are *The Gutenberg Galaxy* (London: Routledge, 1962) and Walter J. Ong, S.J., *Orality and Literacy: the technologizing of the word* (London: Routledge, 1988).
[12]See especially Enders (note 10 above).

medieval genres, such as morality, farce, and *sottie* (satirical fools' play). Exemplary is the case of the Basoche,[13] the society of Parisian law clerks, whose legal histrionics both drew on and contributed to the medieval secular theatrical tradition. Not only was acting part of the young lawyers' training, but Basochien playwrights added substantially to the repertoire of medieval farce. Thus, law and drama formed the hub of a conflictual discourse that regularly trespassed the boundary between staged spectacle and reality, as when mock trials devolved into real brawls (Enders, 102–3). Similarly, if much more harrowing, there are recorded instances of a criminal being cast in the role of Christ in a mystery play, so as to exploit his actual torture and death as part of the spectacle (ibid.). To the medieval sensibility, not only was such a contrivance devotional, but its conflation of reality and representation suited a religious belief system whose key concept was the Real Presence of Christ evoked by the Consecration in the Mass—itself a commemorative re/presentation of Christ's Last Supper actions. ("Do this in memory of me.") Understandably, then, mystery plays were contemporarily classified,[14] along with profane historical dramas (e.g., *La Déstruction de Troye*) and saints plays, as historical representations, squarely within the commemorative culture comprised of works "whose end is to recover, in the name of a collectivity, some being or event either anterior in time or outside of time in order to fecundate, animate, or make meaningful a moment in the present" (Vance, 374). Perhaps less obviously, plays addressing themselves directly to everyday life were classified as "fictions" (Knight, 23). This would have been the case even with a transparently political allegory such as *Jeu du Prince des Sots et de Mère Sotte,*[15] by the pamphleteer and playwright Pierre Gringoire. Presented at the command of

Louis XII on Mardi Gras 1512 at les Halles, the play was designed to swing public opinion against Pope Julius II, who had recently betrayed his French allies. Despite Gringoire's intent to portray the treachery of the pope in a manner corresponding to the facts (as Louis XII conceived them), the play would have been classified contemporarily as a fiction, because the incidents of the three-part drama (farce, morality, *sottie*) were arranged in other than a historical sequence. Thus, while the Middle Ages made a distinction between reality-driven representa-tions and fictions, it was not the same as *our* distinction.

In the Elizabethan era the documentary impulse took two paths in the theater: chronicle plays whose episodic form recalled the medieval mysteries and tragic dramas inspired by contemporary "true crime" stories. While only a handful of the latter has survived, evidence exists that a score or more lost plays were based on contemporary incident, at least one commissioned and begun within a week of a 1603 murder.[16] Clark (137–38) notes that their playwrights often appeal in prologues to the "simple truth," claim to be presenting the facts "naked," or apologize for "this true and homeborne tragedy," though the plays themselves tend to be extremely formulaic.

Practically speaking, the writers of the chronicle plays seemed equally content to alter events to suit the requisites of dramatic form, as Shakespeare did throughout the sequence of plays beginning (in historical time) with *Richard II* and ending with *Richard III*. But Shakespeare's disposition towards conflation, allegorization, analogizing, and creating fables was also shared by Tudor historians who, like Herodotus, were probably bet-

---

[13]The name probably derives from Greek *basochein,* connoting histrionics, playfulness, loquacity—Enders, 131. The Basoche was founded in 1303, but its theatrical activities peaked 1450–1550.

[14]See Alan E. Knight, *Aspects of genre in late Medieval French drama* (Manchester: Manchester University Press, 1983), 19.

[15]The text is to be found in *Oeuvres Completes de Gringoire,* ed. by Charles d'Héricault and A. de Montaiglon (Paris: 1858), I, 199–286. On the circumstances of production and the political background, see L. Petit de Julleville, *Les Comédiens en France au Moyen Age* (Paris: 1858), 97.

[16]See Andrew Clark, *Domestic Drama: A Survey of the Origins, Antecedents and Nature of the Domestic Play in England, 1500–1640.* 2 vols. (Salzburg: Institüt für Englishe Sprache und Literatur, 1975), I, Appendix C.

ter known to their contemporaries in oral form than written.[17] Nevertheless, argues Matthew K. Wikander,[18] "the play of truth and state" represented in the histories justifies serious consideration of Shakespeare as a historian. Wikander finds the history plays fraught with tension between a tendency to moralize and a skepticism as to whether facts made any sense at all; between an Augustinian, providential view of history and a Machiavellian one in which deceit and manipulation predominate; between an open-handed acknowledgment of the fictiveness of the historical endeavor and (in *Henry VIII*) the development of an antihistorical attitude. The effect of these tensions is to create a dialectic in which the audience is required to participate in the effort of interpreting the facts. Thus, even when Shakespeare makes as if to dismantle the history play in *Henry VIII*—subtitling it, ironically, according to Wikander, "all is true"—in so doing he paradoxically turns his audience into historians.[19]

It is in responding to this impulse, rather than in any intention of conformity with the facts of history, that Shakespeare participates in the documentary trope I have been describing thus far. Without question, Shakespeare was more interested in analogizing between the turmoils of Tudor history and contemporary anxieties over the succession (Elizabeth I was in her sixties when Shakespeare commenced the history cycle) than he was interested in reconstructing the past. Similarly, though not exclusively motivated in this respect, was Friedrich Schiller, the most acclaimed

writer of historical drama between Shakespeare and the twentieth century.

Early in his playwriting career, Schiller exalted a romanticized notion of rebellion, epitomized in *The Robbers*. But the reality of the French Revolution and the execution of Louis XVI sobered, even sickened, him.[20] The spectacle of terrifying passions gone awry, of reason unyoked from sympathy, and of political action fueled by rumor and ignorance challenged his political philosophy and undermined his confidence in the social role of theater. Schiller chose to address such issues obliquely through the events of the Thirty Years War in his most celebrated historical drama, the *Wallenstein Trilogy*.

Schiller was a professor of history at the University of Jena and in the early 1790s completed an academic history of the Thirty Years War, later to be his subject in *Wallenstein's Camp, The Piccolomini,* and *The Death of Wallenstein* (1796–99). Scholars generally agree that the academic work, revealing a providentialism and Whiggish bias, is less successful than the plays in revealing the ironies and complexities of 17th-century European politics, as well as Wallenstein's own skills as a *Realpolitiker*.[21] Indeed, in constructing his main character, Schiller was departing both from his previous take on Wallenstein as a betrayer of national interests and from his previous model of the tragic hero driven by an ideal, or *idée fixe*.

Like Shakespeare, Schiller struggled with the relationship between dramatic form and the facts of history. But while in Shakespeare this struggle feels like an absorbing dramaturgical problem or an engaging intellectual issue, in Schiller the struggle is subsumed into a moral debate over the social function of theater and the ethics of history-writing. The sequence of Shakespeare's chronicle plays leaves the impression of a dramatist tailoring Tudor history variously to the forms of tragedy (*Richard II*), comedy (*1 Henry IV*), and epic pageantry (*Henry V*). By contrast, the playwright of the *Wallenstein Trilogy* worries

[17]See D. R. Woolf, "Speech, Text and Time: The Sense of History and the Sense of the Past in Renaissance England," *Albion* 18 (1986): 159–83.
[18]In *The Play of Truth and State: Historical Drama from Shakespeare to Brecht* (Baltimore and London: Johns Hopkins University Press, 1986), 28.
[19]I cannot do justice here to the subtlety of Wikander's analysis of Shakespeare as historian, but see, e.g., his analysis of how in the sequence of II, 5 through III, 2 in *1 Henry IV*, iconic historical images and moralized spectacle are undermined by the comic elements—esp. 24–25.

[20]See T. J. Reed, *Schiller* (Oxford and New York: Oxford University Press, 1991), 70.
[21]See Reed, 70–85, and Wikander, 141–49.

over the deceptions of theater, fears that it will be "put to shame by life's own stage,"[22] and ends his drama in a moral and political ambiguity edging towards irresolution.

In his Prologue, Schiller uses the occasion of the dedication of a refurbished theater and a conventional observation on the evanescence of drama ("And as the sound recedes upon our ears/The moment's quick creation dies in echoes"—ll. 38–39) to speculate on the resemblances between theater and history. Unlike Shakespeare's reference to his "wooden O" (conceivably in Schiller's mind when he wrote), which urges the Elizabethan audience to forget their immediate circumstances, Schiller deliberately alerts his audience to their own place in history and to his own ability to influence their thinking about it. In this context, then, the following apology for versifying the goings-on in *Wallenstein's Camp* may be seen as Schiller's (dis)ingenuous gesture simultaneously disarming and arming the spectators against his blandishments: The highly stylized *Knittelvers* represents, he claims, his Muse "Herself destroying her illusion in/Good faith, not substituting with deceit/The semblances of Truth for Truth itself" (ll. 135–37).

The trilogy plays out this issue in daunting complexity, compelling its audience to thread their way towards "Truth itself" through deceptions, numerous Machiavellian plots, pseudoplots, and counterplots and to choose among competing accounts of Wallenstein's motivations. Furthermore, while it would be difficult to determine how aware Schiller's audience was of the plays' divagations from historical fact (the telescoping of months into four days, the introduction of a nonhistorical pair of lovers, etc.), these inventions cannot but have amplified the overarching theme of the theatricalization of history.

Recent commentators seem anxious to defend Schiller against the charge that he was insufficiently historical. Wikander (158–59) contends that Schiller's audience would have read the trilogy in light of the felicitous Peace of Westphalia

(which resolved the Thirty Years War) and thus would have carried away an impression of the divergence of tragedy (as instanced in Wallenstein's personal fate) and history. Reed (70) cautions that Schiller's apparently reactionary retreat to aestheticism after the trilogy needs to be read against the horrifying excesses of the French Revolution. If to a modern reader the lasting image of the Wallenstein plays is that of a greater man brought down by his inferiors—a conventional and ahistorical tragic pattern—one nevertheless values Schiller's call for his profession to grapple with its own historical moment. In raising vis-à-vis the theater the question of "whether the business to which we are devoting the best part of our mental powers is compatible with the dignity of our spirit,"[23] Schiller sounds a note of high seriousness reechoed in the later docudramas of the German tradition.[24]

Deprived of the luxuries of distance and reflection, French playwrights of the revolutionary period yielded to the documentary impulse with alacrity, if not with accomplishment.[25] A spate of *pièces de circonstance* (patriotic dramas based on contemporary events) accompanied the tumultuous political developments. For a typical example, *L'Ami du peuple ou La Mort de Marat* was offered on 8 August, 1793 by the Variétés Amusantes; Marat had been killed on July 13th (Carlson, 166). At other theaters, irrespective of the nature of the bill of fare, actors stepped forward during entr'actes to report on the number executed that day on the Place de la Révolution.

---

[22]Friedrich Schiller, *Wallenstein*, tr. Charles Passage (New York: Frederick Ungar Publishing Co., 1960), Prologue, l. 69.

[23]Reed, 33, quoting Schiller's 1784 address on the "Effect of the theater on the people."
[24]A tradition of German historical drama, notably personified in Grabbe and Büchner, connects Schiller with the documentary theater of the 1960s. Perhaps as much as one-sixth of *Danton's Tod*, e.g., was transcribed from the histories Büchner used. See Sidney Parham, "The Performance of Fact: A Study of Documentary Drama in Germany During the 1960s" (diss. Tufts University, 1975), chapter 1.
[25]See Graham E. Rodmell, *French Drama of the Revolutionary Years* (London: Routledge, 1990) and Marvin Carlson, *The Theatre of the French Revolution* (Ithaca, N.Y.: Cornell University Press, 1966).

Such exercises appear to have been motivated entirely by political expediency, for in the reaction after Robespierre's death, the switch to anti-Jacobin scripts was almost instantaneous. The speed with which the *pièces* were turned out necessitated a heavy reliance on formula, and it was common to infuse older plays with new political material, as in the example of Laya's reworking of Moliere's *Les Femmes Savantes* into *L'ami des lois.* An innovative exception was Maréchal's propaganda piece *Le Jugement dernier des rois,* which, however, is a fantasy of internationalized revolution, not an event-based play. While some ingredients (e.g., actual events reported in a political context) of a documentary theater are to be found in the theater of the French Revolution, neither historical accuracy nor understanding appears to have been a goal.

Anticipating *Les Miz* by almost exactly two centuries, recreations of the storming of the Bastille were on London stages in the year of the historical event.[26] Here the motive was profit, not politics (though a little jingoistic rabble-rousing was not amiss). In the late eighteenth and nineteenth centuries, Bastille plays took their place alongside battle reconstructions, hippodramas, nautical melodramas, and kindred spectacles regularly drawing on contemporary events and transgressing the boundaries between pantomime, circus, and the "legitimate" theater.[27] On a lesser scale, in the 1830s lurid East End "penny gaffs" (crude productions in hole-in-the-wall houses) sometimes took inspiration from recent murders occurring in the neighborhood of the theater (Booth, 1965, 56). Such efforts stand in relationship to the documentary theater as the tabloids do to journalism: They value pictures more than words and a good story more than verifiable facts. Thousands flocked to, say, *The Battle of Waterloo* (1824) at Astley's not for the facts but for the thrills: "[N]inety horses were on stage at one time

during the performance of the piece" (Saxon, 141). Of course, it would be anachronistic to expect plays to behave like modern newspapers long before standards of journalism were developed, newspapers became universal, and literacy rates rose. The nineteenth-century theaters nonetheless fed a hunger for "news" before the modern technological apparatus of picture and word transmis-sion carried the day.

But what happened in the transition period, "when the advent of the special correspondent and the photographer at the front, and the electric telegraph, dispelled the illusion of apparently factual reporting created by the popular artist?"[28] J. S. Bratton has looked at the twenty-five or so plays dealing directly or indirectly with the Crimean War that reached London stages in 1854–55. He records the struggles of theater managers to keep up with events—announcing then withdrawing plays keyed to battles that failed to take place or proved not to be the sort of triumphs inviting dramatic celebration. Although the majority of Crimean War dramas were formulaic and mostly fictional, "with little regard for actual events" (121), the older melodramatic and comic forms proved fluid and vital enough to allow the substitution of new stereotypes for old (the war correspondent for the cockney opportunist), accommodate fresh battle details, and ride the tide of current feeling without in any way changing the structural underpinnings of spectacle, comedy, or melodrama or challenging the basic reluctance of manager and public alike to deal with the shocking and often antiheroic events generated by the scene of war (Bratton, 135).

Aptly enough, when the challenge came it sprang in response to a still more shocking and horrible war. It may have become a cliché of criticism that conventional artistic means proved inadequate to represent the massive catastrophe wrought by a new technological-industrial complex, but it is

---

[26]See Michael Booth, *English Melodrama* (London: Herbert Jenkins, 1965), 93 ff.

[27]See Arthur Saxon, *Enter Foot and Horse* (New Haven, Conn.: Yale University Press, 1968) on hippodrama (i.e., dramas on horseback) and Michael Booth, *Victorian Spectacular Theatre 1850–1910* (Boston: Routledge, 1981).

[28]J. S. Bratton, "Theatre of War: the Crimea on the London stage 1854–5," in *Performance and Politics in Popular Drama,* ed. by David Brady, Louis James, and Bernard Sharratt (Cambridge, Eng.: Cambridge University Press, 1980), 119.

nevertheless true that artists responded to World War I with profound anxiety about the relevance of their vocation, along with a fresh burst of innovation. Straddling the range of artistic response from Dada to documentary was Erwin Piscator (1893–1966), who in postwar Berlin first tried to tear theater apart with his dadaist friends and then decided to rebuild it from the ground up. Commenting in 1926 on Piscator's experiments, Bertolt Brecht used the term "documentary" for the first time in a theatrical context—the same year John Grierson first applied it to Robert Flaherty's film, *Moana*.[29] The documentary impulse now took expression in a documentary form, though in so putting it I wish to imply neither a deterministic nor an evolutionary model.

In order to appreciate the revolution wrought by Piscator, whose **In Spite of Everything!** (*Trotz Alledem!*) (1925) may rightfully be named the Urtext of documentary theater, it is the (un)likeness of the documentary to historical drama that must be engaged. Crucially, technological developments in the reproduction of voice and image, along with advances in stage machinery, required the exploration of a new relationship between theater and reality. The rise of the modern newspaper; the availability of archives to historians and the raising of standards for the justification of historical description; the wide acceptance of the ideas of Comte, Marx, Darwin, and Spencer, who examined individual behavior in a context bound by social, economic, and physical laws; the embrace of the nineteenth-century scientific model of truth as fact supported by empirical evidence—all these exerted increasing pressure on the theater to represent reality concretely, precisely, and directly. Although this may sound superficially like a rehash of the project of Naturalism or Realism, in practice documentary theater rejected both the emphasis on the clash of personalities, hallmark of the old historical drama, and psychological drama in the realistic idiom. As Piscator himself put it in 1928: "It is not theater we want, but re-

ality. Reality is still the biggest theater. In a world where the real shocks spring from the discovery of a gold field, from petroleum production, and from the wheat trade, of what import to us are the problems of half-insane people!"[30]

Himself a veteran of the war and an early, ardent convert to Communism, Piscator had already placed himself in the service of the Proletarian Theater movement when the German Communist Party (KPD) commissioned him and playwright Felix Gasbarra to create a political revue (*Revue Rotter Rummel*—1924). Pleased with both the propaganda and artistic value of their effort, the KPD employed the same team to create a piece for the opening of the Tenth Party Congress to be held in Max Reinhardt's cavernous Grosses Schauspielhaus. By Piscator's account (q.v. below), he and Gasbarra originally hoped to mount a theatrical panorama composed of "the revolutionary highlights of the history of mankind from the Spartacus rebellion to the Russian Revolution."[31] When this proved unworkable, he settled on recounting the ten-year history of the KPD, taking his title from the slogan of the Communist martyr, Karl Liebknecht. Partly in response to the requirements of producing in a 3,000-seat theater and partly because the material he was working with seemed to demand it, Piscator invented a new kind of theatrical piece composed exclusively from documents, both verbal and visual. His innovation was to create a drama based on the principles of news reportage, constructed in an epic succession of tableaux and stations, and designed to promote direct social action. Presented

---

[29]See John Willet, *The Theatre of Erwin Piscator* (London: Eyre Methuen, 1978), 186, and *The Documentary Tradition: From Nanook to Woodstock,* ed. by Lewis Jacobs (New York: Hopkinson and Blake, 1971), 4–5.

[30]Erwin Piscator, "A letter to the Weltbühne," rpt. in *World Theatre* 17 (1968): 329.
[31]This sounds remarkably like the postrevolutionary spectacles mounted in Soviet Russia, particularly *The Mystery of Freed Labor* (1920), although Piscator denies any knowledge of previous Soviet practice—see page 8. In addition to Piscator's account of the creation of *In Spite of Everything!* see Willet, op. cit.; C. D. Innes, *Erwin Piscator's Political Theatre* (Cambridge, Eng.: Cambridge University Press, 1972), 49–65; Ludwig Hoffman and Daniel Hoffman-Ostvald, *Deutsches Arbeittheater* (Munich: Rogner and Bernhard, 1973), 1, 168–84; and Shiela McAlpine, *Visual Aids in the Productions of the First Piscator-Bühne, 1927–28* (Frankfurt am Main: Peter Lang, 1990).

in a revue format and accompanied by music, political cartoons, moving pictures borrowed from government archives, and photographic projections, *In Spite of Everything!* created an alternative to the capitalist newspaper accounts of the same events.[32]

In the process Piscator discovered the elements of what he would later call "Total Theater," bombarding the emotions with an arsenal of theater technology to achieve maximal audience manipulation. For example, a film sequence of Liebknecht distributing antiwar pamphlets in 1914 "merged into a stage scene reenacting his protest against military preparations in parliament, which was drowned out by a saber-rattling speech by the Kaiser over loudspeakers. This provided a transition to the later vote (which Liebknecht alone opposed) granting the war credit accompanied by photographs of mobilization. Synchronized with the raising of hands in parliament, a film of fighting on the Western Front was projected. Then on two separated stage levels, the reactions of different sections of society to the opening of hostilities was shown simultaneously in a street scene and a munitions factory" (Innes, 52–53). Without at all relinquishing factuality and rational argument, Piscator marshaled powerful kinesthetic effects in order to impart "a dialectical grasp of reality which implies movement rather than stasis, relationships rather than reism" and to convey to his audience that reality was "changing and changeable" (McAlpine, 40–41). A dynamic active theater would naturally produce a dynamic, active body politic.

In Spite of Everything! was thus in line with Piscator's subsequent, if irregular, attempts to bring to theater the directness of political speech, that is, to transform representation into political action. Whether such a thing is possible, desirable, or effective had already been debated by Soviet ideologues and continues to color much discussion of political theater.[33] Here I only wish to point out Piscator's innovation in this context, which was to construct a theater even *metonymically*, that is using "actuals" (verbatim speeches, documentary film footage, some amateur actors) to attract to itself the immanent and extratextual. The idea very likely owes something to Soviet postrevolutionary outdoor spectacles such as *The Storming of the Winter Palace*. But metonymy is also the basic building block of the oral epic—the documentary of preliterate societies—"in which a text or version is enriched by an unspoken context that dwarfs the textual artifact."[34] In thus making reality the object rather than the subject of theater,[35] Piscator is turning the institution "inside out," transforming mimesis into a (re)present/ing of history. This is also the technique of Heinar Kipphardt and Peter Weiss, whose documentary dramas Piscator was to direct at the end of his career.[36]

In 1925, however, the critic of the party paper, *Die Rote Fahne*, (q.v. pages 12–13) identified political shortcomings within the theatrical innovations. The script was *too* documentary: "Comrade director . . . You are simply too true to history"—for example, on the question of when workers' protests were initiated. "Don't be so literal, there's no reason to get so hung up about 'how it was,'" he advised, though complaining that the actor playing Liebknecht was not enough of a "hurricane" and the actress playing Rosa Luxemburg was too loud. Later on, as John Willett shows,[37] Piscator was to be found too political by the administrators of the Volksbühne, where he produced some of his greatest work, and too formalist by Soviet ideologues when he attempted to work in Russia—the latter judgment one which often carried with it, for Piscator's Russian colleagues, a death sentence. In these kaleidoscopic political contexts, Piscator must have sensed that the presentation of documented facts on the stage carried with it the danger of simultaneously establishing—on all sides—an ironic atti-

---

[32]The text of Trotz Alledem! is lost. We have, however, a police report, Piscator's testimony, and reviews, included herein.

[33]See, e.g., Baz Kershaw, *The Politics of Performance: Radical theatre as cultural intervention* (London: Routledge, 1992). Ernst Schumacher, "Piscator's Politi

[34]Foley, 7 (see note 11 above).

[35]I am indebted to Innis, 58, for this phrase.

[36]McAlpine (242) takes note of the metonymic nature of the settings in some of Piscator's later productions at the Volksbühne.

[37]Willett, 55 ff. and 141.

tude towards them. The reaction of the *Die Rote Fahne* to *In Spite of Everything!* must have been particularly vexing to Piscator, as the party critic required the subordination of historical truth to propaganda value, while at the same time nailing him with the standards of the old bourgeois theater for not getting the psychological features of Liebknecht and Luxemburg just right!

Here, at their virtual origin, we confront the paradox that "Documentary modes participate in, indeed are a symptom of, two distinct but interlinked structures of feeling: one is expressive of a faith in facts, grounded upon positivist scientific rationality; the other is expressive of a profound political skepticism which disputes the notion that 'facts=truth.'"[38] And, as is evident even from this fragmentary account of *In Spite of Everything!,* the paradoxical nature of the documentary enterprise places the documentarian on the horns of more than one dilemma. The artist may have to relinquish his identity and freedom by restricting himself to actual rather than invented event. The playwright/historian's obligation to tell the truth may be compromised by the playwright/propagandist's need to persuade. The arc described by Piscator's career is an attempt to straddle these dilemmas by grounding the definitiveness of the theater artist's assertions simultaneously in authenticity and political validity. Piscator's apologetic defense of his formalism in *The Political Theater* (1929), his theoretical inconsistencies, and the misdirections taken in middle career surely bespeak the difficulty of his task. Perhaps, too, he came to realize how slender the evidence was for the political effectiveness of the theater. Yet, his last, lean productions of Kipphardt and Weiss, passional and passionate, remind us that a faith shaken is not a faith lost.[39]

Piscator's practice effectively generates a definition of documentary drama as *plays characterized by a central or exclusive reliance on actual rather than imaginary event, on dialogue, song and/or visual materials (photographs, films, pictorial documents) "found" in the historical record or gathered by the playwright/researcher, and by a disposition to set individual behavior in an articulated political and/or social context.* Such a definition allows us to locate documentary theater in a continuum of reality-driven representations and at the same time distinguish its tendencies from conventional historical drama as follows:

Historical Drama	Documentary Drama
integration propaganda (reshaping behavior for stable social setting)[40]	dialectical propaganda (demystifying a complex situation)
author/ity	authentic/ity
individual	collective
metaphorical	metonymic
character	event
theatricalized history	historicized theater

For Piscator, documentary theater was capable of achieving a special veracity based on its "containment" of reality—a conviction he reiterated very late in his career (1966), celebrating Weiss and Kipphardt for "plays which comply with the factual quality of documents and with the strictness of exact historical analysis."[41] By this time, however, historians had begun to question their own basic premises and to undermine the methodological assumptions permitting such an assertion. Even more profoundly, theorists such as Richard Rorty or Jean Baudrillard have since disputed the reliability of any description of the world to yield a "true" representation of reality.[42] Advancements in the technology of representation, which earlier had so inspired Piscator, have

---

[38]Derek Paget, *True Stories? Documentary drama on radio, screen and stage* (Manchester, Eng.: Manchester University Press, 1990), 17.

[39]See Sidney Parham, chapters 3 and 4, on Piscator's last productions.

[40]See Jacques Ellul, *Propaganda: The Formation of Men's Attitudes* (New York: Alfred A. Knopf, 1966) for a taxonomy of propaganda. Also useful is George Szanto, *Theater and Propaganda* (Austin: University of Texas Press, 1978).

[41]"Post 'Investigation,' " *World Theatre* 17 (1968): 353.

[42]See Richard Rorty, "Realism and Reference," *Monist* 59 (1976): 321–40, and *Philosophy and the Mirror of Nature* (Princeton, N.J.: Princeton University Press, 1980); and Jean Baudrillard, *Simulations* (New York: Semiotext(e), 1983).

caused Baudrillard (11) to posit the idea of non-referential simulation as opposed to representation and to offer a taxonomy in which a representational image progressively stands in ever-greater disconnection from its origin in reality:

This would be the successive phases of the image:

—it is the reflection of a basic reality
—it masks and perverts a basic reality
—it masks the absence of a basic reality
—it bears no relation to any reality whatever; it is its own pure simulacrum.

Considering simulation as part of a "discourse that is no longer true or false" (6) and fancy-free in its rhetoric ("Never again will the real have to be produced"—4), Baudrillard's *Simulations* appears to wallow in the hyperreality it so cleverly describes. It nevertheless challenges historians outside and inside the theater to agree or disagree that the only present alternatives are simulation and "nostalgia, the phantasmal, parodic rehabilitation of all lost referentials" (72). Likewise contributing to this discourse, historians Hayden White and Michel de Certeau make us aware of how the lost referentials of history-writing are refracted through the conventions of narrative and the perspective predicaments of the historian—though we may take note here of de Certeau's explicit objective of facilitating a discourse of facts.[43] It is through such lenses that the history of documentary theater in the twentieth century must inescapably be viewed—without forgetting that such views are themselves representative of a specific moment in history.

Although the German Communist revolution chronicled in *In Spite of Everything!* failed and the Russian one succeeded, each spawned reality-driven theater practices with markedly similar features. While Soviet theoreticians differed in the role of theater in a postrevolutionary society, theater practitioners generally approached the prob-

lem with gusto. Red Army units began reading newspapers aloud on stage for illiterate comrades, and from this practice sprang "animated," "oral," or "living" newspapers, which went beyond reading to rudimentary staging. When satirical commentary was added, the form was embraced by "Blue Blouse" agitprop troupes (initially amateur, then professional), who began to produce full-scale reviews on contemporary issues. Much more ambitious were the mammoth outdoor spectacles, which either commemorated revolutionary events or exhorted the faithful to new triumphs. Sometimes these spectacles were called "mysteries," recalling the similar function served by sacred plays in the medieval theater and linking them to commemorative culture. At the more established theaters, plays were adapted or commissioned in service of the propaganda effort. Meyerhold, for example, incorporated nightly news reports from the front into the Belgian Symbolist play *Dawn* (1920), turning it into a "performance-meeting" in which actors were spread throughout the audience, urging appropriate reactions to one patriotic speech or another. Tretyakov's *Roar, China!* (1926), based on the recent notorious execution of Chinese workers, was deliberately fashioned by the playwright to resemble a newspaper "article." It was influential on the great filmmaker Eisenstein. The Red Army commissioned *First Cavalry* (1929), which, recalling Piscator's innovation, incorporated newsreel film of the Army's heroics.[44]

By the time Piscator himself, fleeing the Nazis, arrived in the U.S.S.R. in 1931, Stalinist antiformal-

---

[43]Michel de Certeau, *The Writing of History,* tr. by Tom Conley (New York: Columbia University Press, 1980), 30. See also Hayden White, *Metahistory: The Historical Imagination in Nineteenth-Century Europe* (Baltimore: Johns Hopkins University Press, 1973) and *Tropics of Discourse: Essays in Cultural Criticism* (Baltimore: Johns Hopkins University Press, 1978).

---

[44]See Konstantin Rudnitsky, *Russian and Soviet Theatre: Tradition and the Avant-garde* (London: Thames and Hudson, 1988); Nikolai A. Gorchakov, *The Theater in Soviet Russia* (New York: Columbia University Press, 1957); Robert Russell, *Russian Drama of the Revolutionary Period* (Totawa, N.J.: Barnes and Noble, 1988); Frantisek Deak, "Russian Mass Spectacles," *TDR* 19, 2 (June 1975): 7–22; *Russian Theatre in the Age of Modernism,* ed. Robert Russell and Andrew Barratt (London: Macmillan, 1990); James von Geldern, *Bolshevik Festivals, 1917–1920.* (Berkeley: University of California Press, 1993).

ism had begun to neutralize some of this ferment. Even so, the energy of Soviet theater attracted a stream of theatrical visitors eager to see how political commitment might be wedded to theatrical verve. Two of these, Hallie Flanagan and Joseph Losey, are closely identified with the first American flourishing of documentary theater: Flanagan as Director of the Federal Theatre Project, bureaucratic parent of the "Living Newspaper Unit," and Losey as the director of the first fully produced Living Newspaper, *Triple A Plowed Under* (1936). Though subsequent anti-Communist pressures caused its originators to disassociate the Living Newspaper from its European forebears, the work of Flanagan, Losey, and Arthur Arent owes much to German and Russian example, both directly and through the intermediary of the American workers' theater movement.[45] Flanagan traveled to Germany and Russia in 1926 and 1927 as a Guggenheim Fellow and returned to Russia in 1931. Before becoming director of the FTP, she had produced her own semidocumentary piece *Can You Hear Their Voices?* (1931) at Vassar. Losey spent January through August of 1935 in Russia where, among other activities, he "laboriously translated Piscator's *Political Theatre*" (Goldman, 70). Losey was largely responsible for introducing Piscator's stage vocabulary into the Living Newspapers, not only the epic scene progression but also his technical innovations: multilevel sets, projections, loudspeakers, and an ironic juxta-

position of live stage image with cool and objective projected image.

Triple A Plowed Under had, in fact, been preceded by an earlier Living Newspaper whose production had been prevented by the direct intervention of Works Project Administration chief Harry Hopkins, perhaps even by Roosevelt himself. Created under the "managing editorship" of Arthur Arent and the regional directorship of Elmer Rice, *Ethiopia* (January 1936) differs from later Living Newspapers in crucial ways. It relies almost exclusively on verbatim excerpts from political speeches of world leaders on the Italian invasion of Ethiopia. (Indeed, it drew the unwanted attention of the Roosevelt administration when a request came from the FTP to the White House for a tape recording of one of Roosevelt's speeches.[46]) It is not heavily interlarded with typical though nonfactual scenes, as were its "orthodox" (McDermott, 89) successors. And it contains neither the "common man" protagonist nor the signature "Voice of the Living Newspaper," the anonymous loudspeaker that became more prevalent and directive as the genre developed.

At sixty years distance from the Ethiopian crisis, we need to be reminded of the cheekiness of the Flanagan/Rice/Arent team in selecting such a subject for their first Living Newspaper. Despite his personal convictions, Roosevelt had made important concessions to the isolationists in the election of 1932 and was up for reelection in 1936. The Neutrality Resolution, forbidding the sale of war materiel to belligerents, had been passed by Congress and signed by Roosevelt in August of 1935. Politically, it was a "no-win" situation for the administration to take sides in the Italo-Ethiopian conflict, which was beginning to raise ugly passions among two of the Democratic Party's prime constituencies, Italian-Americans and African-Americans. Even the Joe Louis vs. Primo Carnera heavyweight title fight seemed like a political contest, with an Italian-American fac-

[45]Douglas McDermott, "The Living Newspaper as a Dramatic Form," *Modern Drama*, 8, 1 (May 1965): 82–94 identifies two American scripts called "living newspapers" prior to the founding of the Federal Theatre Project. On the origins of the FTP Living Newspapers, see Jane de Hart Mathews, *The Federal Theatre, 1935–1939: Plays, Relief and Politics* (Princeton: Princeton University. Press, 1967); Arnold Goldman, "Life and Death of the Living Newspaper Unit," *Theatre Quarterly*, 3, 9 (Jan.–March 1973): 69–82; Malcolm Goldstein, *The Political Stage* (New York: Oxford University Press, 1974), 276–77; Hallie Flanagan, *Arena* (New York: Duell, Sloan and Pearce, 1940), 64–65; Elmer Rice, *Minority Report* (New York: Simon and Schuster, 1963), 356 ff.

[46]As reported by Flanagan, 65. The speech is unidentified but was likely Roosevelt's "State of the Union" address of 3 January 1936, which alluded to the Ethiopian crisis.

tion vowing that Italy would take its revenge in Ethiopia for Carnera's defeat.[47]

Two crisis-related events late in 1935 created a sensation in the United States. On 3 October, after almost a year of posturing, Mussolini invaded Ethiopia. On 9 December news of an Anglo-French diplomatic deal to sell out the Ethiopians was leaked to the press. When in January of 1936 *Time Magazine* featured on its cover Haile Selassie as Man of the Year, the Living Newspaper team must have congratulated itself on having a play on the hottest subject of the day in rehearsal.

Not so the Roosevelt administration. Alerted by the innocent request for Roosevelt's speech, the federal bureaucracy moved to avert any embarrassment or political liability. Most objectionable was the impersonation of heads of state involving the use of the actual words spoken by these individuals. As reported by the *New York Times* (q.v. below), in letters to Hallie Flanagan WPA Assistant Administrator Jacob Baker first insisted that foreign heads of state could not be depicted in a Living Newspaper and then emended his order: "No one impersonating a ruler or Cabinet officer shall actually appear on the stage. If it is useful for you to do so, the words of such persons may be quoted by the others." This was too much for Elmer Rice, who recognized that Baker was, in effect, banning the production and resigned—though not before staging an open rehearsal of the piece for reporters.

Brooks Atkinson's evaluation (see pages 25–26) of the play as "unbiased" appears generally to hold today.[48] Although Ethiopians are depicted as the victims of Italian aggression and the League of Nations vote on sanctions against Italy

is given prominence, the play avoids analyzing the subtleties of U.S. policy; ignores the backdrop of Nazism abroad (Hitler announced Germany's rearmament on 16 March 1935) and Fascist sentiment at home; and restricts comment on the United States' nonmembership in the League to a single line. In two respects, however, *Ethiopia* may have packed some of the Piscatorian punch. In refusing to link the speeches with a coherent narrative and in featuring the Anglo-French deceptions, the script reveals in its silences the vastness of the unknown behind the political screen, how much was untold and awaited to be revealed. And in allowing the eccentric Colonel Julian (an African-American who briefly headed the Ethiopian air force) the opinion that "Ethiopia is not worth civilized nations fighting for," *Ethiopia* opens up a painful issue of America's African policy, which lingers in today's headlines.[49]

The results of the administration proscription against the depiction of foreign statesmen speaking in their own words—which, according to Flanagan's phone log (de Hart Mathews, 65), originated from a discussion between the President and Mrs. Roosevelt—were many. The Living Newspapers which followed avoided international issues entirely. An intended Living Newspaper about the South and discrimination, in which certain senators were to be depicted using their actual words in opposition to an antilynching bill, never took place (ibid. 67). Although some domestic public figures were subsequently characterized with their own words, later scripts relied very little on such devices or invented subterfuges like having members of the Supreme Court appear in silhouette as they spoke (e.g., *Triple A Plowed Under*, Scene 23).[50] Finally, "[t]hough each region was encouraged to develop living newspapers on local problems, few were

---

[47]On the Ethiopian crisis see, e.g., James Dugan and Laurence Lafore, *Days of Emperor and Clown: The Italo-Ethiopian War 1935–36* (New York: Doubleday, 1973); Stephen U. Chukumba, *The Big Powers Against Ethiopia* (Washington, D.C.: University Press of America, 1977); and Brice Harris, *The United States and the Italo-Ethiopian Crisis* (Stanford, Calif.: Stanford University Press, 1964). None mentions the Living Newspaper.
[48]A full production, of course, may have had a different effect.

---

[49]These ideas were suggested to me by Janet Shum in a seminar paper on *Ethiopia*.
[50]Text in Pierre de Rohan, ed., *Federal Theatre Plays: Triple A Plowed Under, Power, Spirochete* (New York: Random House, 1938); see 44–47. *The text of Ethiopia was first published in *Educational Theatre Journal*, 20, 1 (1968).

produced. The national office of the FTP wanted full documentation and proof they were factually accurate," no doubt out of sensitivity to political pressure.[51]

The issue of direct quotations remained problematic for the Living Newspapers. Senator Charles Andrews (D), of Florida complained that while *One-Third of a Nation* portrayed him as opposing a slum clearance bill in debate, it failed to record that he eventually voted for the bill. The script was duly altered, but the harm had been done. This and other political insensitivities eroded support for the FTP, which in four short years was itself history, an early victim of the House Un-American Activities Committee. Testimony before that Committee named all of the Living Newspapers among plays identified as being nothing more than Communist propaganda (de Hart Mathews, 202). But in recalling the Communist objections to Piscator's earlier documentary efforts, we may observe that disparate ideological hegemonies may on occasion share discomfort over strict historical chronology and direct quotations.

Brooks Atkinson's pessimistic forecast, provoked by the banning of *Ethiopia*—"how futile it is to expect the theatre to be anything but a sideshow under government supervision"—proved both harsh and inaccurate as an assessment of the Living Newspapers. In dispelling popular myths (though perhaps disseminating liberal myths) about the topics they engaged, they focused reasoned attention on complex issues. Today, we would be pleasantly surprised if the federal government poured substantial funds into plays about the homeless (*One-Third of a Nation*—1938), the history of sexually transmitted disease (*Spirochete* —1938), and the health-care crisis (*Medicine Show*, an FTP script produced on Broadway in 1940 after the closing of the FTP). It is nevertheless a long way from *Ethiopia*'s implicit questioning of United States neutrality to the endorsement of an administration-sponsored housing bill in *One-Third of a Nation* (which, of course, took its title from a Roosevelt speech). In any case, documentary drama of the more radical sort was a road not taken by the Federal Theatre Project.

British documentary theater of the 1930s, 1940s and 1950s followed the more orthodox American model: politically liberal and problem-solving in orientation, sometimes employing both the "common man" protagonist and the Voice of the Living Newspaper. Two theaters were prominently associated with the genre, the Communist-affiliated Unity Theatre and Theatre Workshop. Unity director Andre van Gyseghem had visited the United States, and Arthur Arent had come to Unity in the mid-thirties, so the linkage to the American tradition was in this case direct. Arent's influence may be seen in *Busmen,* on the 1937 Coronation bus strike, and *Crisis,* on the Czechoslovak appeasement, which opened on 29 September 1938, the day Chamberlain flew to Munich. Mixing documentary material (broadcasts, verbatim speeches, statistics) with fictionalized individual reactions (and the Voice of the Living Newspaper), *Crisis* played through early November and was regularly updated with such developments as Hitler's occupation of the Sudetenland. After World War II, Unity produced *Black Magic* (1947), on the coal industry, and *The Rosenbergs* (1953), based on spy-trial documents and the Rosenbergs' correspondence.[52]

Living Newspaper No. 5, **World on Edge** (1956) proved to be a watershed for Unity and an interesting variation on the form. Written in twelve days and several times revised after its 23 November opening, the play provocatively and courageously (in view of the theater's patrons) links the Suez Crisis (July–December, 1956) with the Hungarian Revolution (23 October–4 November). Although the decision to do the piece in lieu of the usually lucrative Christmas pantomime was financially rewarded with full houses, it ulti-

---

[51]John O'Connor and Lorraine Brown, eds., *Free, Adult, Uncensored: The Living History of the Federal Theatre Project* (Washington, D.C.: New Republic Books, 1978), 14.

[52]I can trace no direct influence on *Inquest* (1970), included herein. The authoritative work on the Unity Theatre is Colin Chambers, *The Story of Unity Theatre* (London: Lawrence and Wishart, 1989).

mately eroded Communist support for the theater and profoundly changed its character. Bearing the marks of its hasty composition, *World on Edge* nevertheless gives us a fascinating glimpse of a theater on the fly, rushing to keep up with events.

In most respects, *World on Edge* is an adequate example of the Living Newspaper, setting down a common-man protagonist intermittently in a political nightmare of sorts. It relies very little on found material (except for a recitation of the United Nations Declaration on Human Rights and an awkwardly introduced U.N. film) and rather more on satire than the American model. Its most interesting feature is highlighted by the subtitle its producers added in newspaper advertisements: "All Your Answers Questioned." In rejecting orthodoxies of both the Right and the Left, *World on Edge* documents most poignantly Unity's own crisis of conscience. The metatheatricality induced by the staged "intrusion" of audience members onto the stage in Act II was only amplified in rowdy postperformance discussions, which engaged Unity's reasons for departing from the Party line on Hungary. Although *One-Third of a Nation* had jocularly introduced its "Little Man" from the audience, the risks and responsibilities of the truth-telling enterprise came to the fore at Unity as never previously in the documentary tradition. What had remained only a subtext or paratext of *In Spite of Everything!* and *Ethiopia*—the role of fact in representational discourse—here literally shares the stage with the ostensible "subjects" of the play, Suez and Hungary. This is Pirandello with a political edge, even if the script exploits its tensions in only a rudimentary fashion, and resolves its "plot" conventionally, with a statement of faith in the United Nations.

Like the Unity Theatre, Theatre Workshop sprang as much from a commitment to Leftist politics as from aesthetic impulses.[53] Its guiding force until 1954 was Ewan MacColl, whose earlier involvement with the Red Megaphones, Theatre of Action, and Theatre Union included agitprop and Living Newspapers. For Theatre Union

MacColl authored *Last Edition* (March 1940), a Living Newspaper covering Munich, the Spanish Civil War, and the Finnish-Soviet War in an inflammatory enough manner to provoke a wartime injunction against its production. After the War, Theatre Union metamorphosed into Theatre Workshop, its 1945 Manifesto (q.v. below) sounding an ambitious, if not a revolutionary, note. MacColl also wrote the documentarylike *Uranium 235*[54] (1946), chronicling the development of atomic energy and weaponry, which was popular enough to remain in Theatre Workshop's repertory until 1952. When MacColl left, Theatre Workshop came under the leadership of Gerry Raffles and Joan Littlewood, the latter associated with the company since the Theatre Union days.

A genuine theatrical legend, Littlewood was largely responsible for the company's prodigious successes in the 1950s, notably a series of outstanding classical revivals and The Hostage, Quare Fellow, A Taste of Honey, and Frank Norman's Fing's Ain't Wot They UsedT' Be. She is also acknowledged to be the "editor-in-chief" of *Oh What a Lovely War* (1963), a Theatre Workshop group creation whose complicated and disputed germination has been authoritatively recorded by Paget.[55] Collective creation had long been part of the Theatre Workshop tradition, out of both aesthetic and political convictions. MacColl had valued an "anonymity" of authorship, which Paget (1990, 250) rightly connects to the oral tradition; Littlewood insisted that actors do their own research on World War I, the production's ostensible subject, as a base for improvisational work.

An actor in the company recalls Littlewood insisting that they were not doing a play "about" World War I, despite the fact that the play was composed of songs of the era, documented statistics, photographic projections of actual battle scenes, and research-based improvisations. It

---

[53]The primary source on Theatre Workshop is longtime company member Howard Goorney, *The Theatre Workshop Story* (London: Eyre Methuen, 1981).

[54]*Uranium* 235 has been published in Howard Goorney and Ewan MacColl, eds., *Agitprop to Theatre Workshop: Political Playscripts 1930–1950* (Manchester, Eng.: Manchester University Press, 1986).
[55]Derek Paget, "'Oh What a Lovely War': the Texts and Their Context," *New Theatre Quarterly*, 6, 3 (Aug. 1990): 244–60.

may even be a distortion to think of *Lovely War* as an antiwar play, though without question it gestured, in 1963, against a backdrop of burgeoning nuclear arsenals and the build-up to the Vietnamese war.[56] Rather, I think the production might take as its epigraph Marx's epigram (after Hegel) that "all facts and personages in world history occur twice, the first time as tragedy, the second time as farce." Or perhaps it would be more accurate to say that the intent of *Lovely War* is to portray history *simultaneously* as tragedy and farce. This is the effect of the jarring montage of nostalgic song and battle statistics, of *commedia* and agitprop, of music hall and epic, of the pastness of the documentary "actuals" and the present/ationalism of performance. That is, the disparate styles of the production add up to a new and powerful historiography, a way of "writing" history that brings one very close to "being there."[57] And, at least for some, the creative collectivity which generated the script manifested itself in performance, offering "a potent theatrical emblem for another sense of collectivity—that which helped to sustain the ordinary soldier of the First World War."[58]

Apart from the international success of *Lovely War,* the mainstream of documentary drama in the 1960s was a German one. Rolf Hochhuth, Heinar Kipphardt, and Peter Weiss form a group not only in their attention to historical fact and left-wing politics, but also because Piscator, after an artistically unsatisfying spell in the United States (1939–62), returned to Berlin to direct their major works. Writing at the same time and place, each may be said to be responding to the complex of conditions accounting for the flourishing of documentary drama in (then) West Germany. These included the Schillerian tradition of the stage as a rostrum or tribunal[59]; the Nazi manipulation of history, particularly in such films as the viciously anti-Semitic *Jud Süss* and the "documentary" *Triumph of the Will;* the presence of former Nazis in industry and the Adenauer government; the German romantic infatuation with *Helden,* "heroes who summed up the traits of the nation"[60]; the legacy of Brecht; and the televised and stage-managed Eichmann trial in 1961, both in its form (court setting, presentation of evidence, etc.) and content (historical accuracy, moral accountability, political responsibility).[61]

Without denying the similarities among these playwrights, it is equally important to register the substantial differences among their works. While Hochhuth's later *Soldiers* (1968) certainly debunks the *Helden* tradition in dealing with Churchill, *The Deputy* (1963) places two tragic heroes at its moral and dramaturgical center, the historical Gerstein and Father Riccardo (based on Fr. Maximilien Kolbe). Despite its lengthy historical appendix, it relies little on found dialogue and its plot is largely composed of invented event. It is, in terms of the distinction made above (23–24), a conventional historical drama—even if written with the political aim of preventing the canonization of Pius XII (in which it has, to date, succeeded).

Similarly, although Kipphardt's *In the Matter of J. Robert Oppenheimer* (1964) relies heavily on verbatim excerpts from the Atomic Energy Commission's transcripts of the Oppenheimer hearings (April 1954), Kipphardt molds this material into one of the familiar categories

---

[56]Paget, 258, notes that there was a stronger "nuclear link" in one of the Urtexts, though this dialogue is dropped from the published version. By the time the production reached the United States in the Fall of 1964, the Vietnam issue had become part of its context.
[57]Charles Marowitz, "Littlewood Pays a Dividend," *Encore* 10 (May–June 1963): 48, took note of the disparate styles and Paget, 253–54, approaches a point similar to mine.
[58]Paget, 245, who saw the West End production.

[59]See A. V. Subiotto, "German Documentary Theatre" (Inaugural Lecture delivered at and published by the University of Birmingham, 1972): 2.
[60]See Parham, 367 ff. This excellent dissertation is sensitive to both the similarities and differences among the German documentary playwrights.
[61]See Jack D. Zipes, "Documentary Drama in Germany: mending the circuit," *Germanic Review* 42 (1967): 60.

of historical drama, the martyr play.[62] Parham's (197 ff.) sophisticated analysis of the text reveals that Kipphardt's chief technique is to create a "nesting" structure in which incremental repetitions reveal biases in the witnesses. Kipphardt also invents some key speeches for Oppenheimer so as to make his story and its background of McCarthyism more analogous to West Germany's attitudes toward the East—that is, Kipphardt wanted to show that the United States' scapegoating of Oppenheimer for reputed Communist sympathies was a typical maneuver of the contemporary German government. Oppenheimer himself (*Washington Post,* 9 November 1964) objected to Kipphardt's rendition of him and subsequently preferred Jean Vilar's *Le Dossier Oppenheimer* (1965). Oppenheimer claimed that he saw the hearings as a farce rather than a tragedy, and his statement points up what we may recognize as the insufficiency of Kipphardt's dramaturgy (compared to Joan Littlewood's) to capture the contradictions of historical events as both farce and tragedy.[63]

If any single playwright may be said to epitomize the documentary theater it would be Peter Weiss, whose praxis has tempted his sympathetic critics to identify him with an ideal of "pure" documentary (e.g., Parham, 375). Such characterizations, even when well intended, are unfortunate, for they represent Weiss and the movement as monolithic, pedantic, and dull. Weiss is also a chief theoretician of the movement, his "Fourteen Propositions for a Documentary Theater" (q.v. below) appearing to stake out the sort of positivist position on historical fact increasingly called into question: "[T]he documentary theater affirms that reality, whatever the obscurity in which it masks itself, can be explained in minute detail."

Although most of Weiss's plays exhibit a keen engagement with history, two are particularly reliant on found materials and explicit in articulating a political context for actual events. *Vietnam . . . Discourse* (1968) virtually does away with character in schematizing the exploitation of Vietnam by outside oppressors; its second act, reminiscent of *Ethiopia,* is composed entirely of political speeches relating to the American involvement in Vietnam. Weiss appended to the German edition a bibliography with 183 entries.[64] *Vietnam . . . Discourse* is generally considered less successful than its documentary predecessor **The Investigation** (1965), derived from the Frankfurt war-crime trials, which Weiss himself attended in 1964.

The relationship of **The Investigation** to its sources is complex enough to have evoked outraged responses from German nationalists and Jews alike, ranging from accusations that the play was nothing but a plagiarism of Bernd Naumann's newspaper reports of the trials to the charge that Weiss had grossly distorted the "truth" about Auschwitz.[65] The extremity and superficiality of the reactions may be attributed to the resentment among Germans at having to confront the Holocaust "once again" and, among Jews, to Weiss's controversial contention (see pages 121–122, "The Song of the Possibility of Survival") that the roles of victim and victimizer might easily have been exchanged. As well, there was among some intellectuals a strong feeling that it was barbaric for art even to attempt a representation of the Holocaust.[66]

---

[62]See Herbert Lindenberger, *Historical Drama: The Relation of Literature and Reality.* (Chicago and London: University of Chicago Press, 1975), 49. Lindenberger is generally unsympathetic to documentary theater and insensitive to its differences from historical drama. Parham (224) identifies the influence of Kipphardt's medical training on the structure of the play as a medical "case history" *(Krankengeschichte).*

[63]If Kipphardt's take on the events as tragedy needs to be played off against's Oppenheimer's own view that they were farce, Kipphardt's *Joel Brand* (1965), which depicts the unsuccessful attempt to trade one million Hungarian Jews for ten thousand armored trucks, might fruitfully be compared to *Schindler's List.*

---

[64]See Erika Salloch, *Peter Weiss' Die Ermittlung: Zur Struktur des Dokumentars Theaters* (Frankfurt: Athenäum Verlag, 1972), 11

[65]For the range of German and foreign reactions see Salloch, 142–61 and Thomas von Vegesack, "Dokumentation zur 'Ermittlung,' " *Kürbiskern* 2 (1966): 74–83.

[66]Epitomized in Adorno's famous "No poetry after Auschwitz"; see also George Steiner, *Language and Silence* (New York: Atheneum, 1967).

Although Salloch's meticulous comparison of the text with its sources will not resolve the larger issues, it nevertheless helps us to evaluate a play that is not only written from documents but itself strives to be one (Parham, 231). Weiss has compressed the testimony of hundreds of witnesses to nine nameless individuals. Tellingly, for example, he has silently incorporated some testimony of Gerstein, one of Hochhuth's protagonists, into the speeches of one of the witnesses—thereby subordinating the aesthetics of individualism informing Hochhuth's text. He has reduced the number of defendants from twenty-two to eighteen named individuals. In allocating speeches to the witnesses, he has sometimes split a historical witness into two stage figures or combined the statements of two different individuals into a single stage speech. "The Song of Lili Tofler," for example, incorporates stories of at least two different women. Weiss regularly makes minor, subtle changes in language for poetic effect or to change tonality slightly or to emphasize the machinelike nature of the camp. Crucially, although the well-documented involvement of German industry with the camps is a leitmotiv of the text and its sources, the assertion that the camps were the "logical" outcome of capitalism is in the form of words put in the mouth of Witness Three[67] by the playwright and not found in the trial transcripts nor other sources. Whether this assertion is "true" or not, Salloch (106) appears to be justified in suggesting that at this point the "witness' has become the supporter of a theory whose praxis is not bodied forth in the drama.

Weiss's open declaration (von Vegesak, 78) in June 1965 of his Marxist-Leninist sympathies caused much critical reaction to the 19 October premiere to focus on whether Weiss had merely created a piece of Communist propaganda. The unprecedented simultaneous openings of The Investigation at fifteen theaters in East and West Germany and in a reading at the Royal Shakespeare Company in London evidently served to increase the embarrassment of most critics at having to deal with it. An equally unfruitful theme running through the criticism questioned

whether Weiss had written a play at all; in following the playwright's instruction to eschew theatricalization and any attempt to represent realistically either the courtroom or the camp, Piscator's Berlin production probably exacerbated the querulousness of the critics (Parham, 246 ff.). Receiving almost no attention was the feature of the play which, leavening the materialist mass of its dread documentation, radiates a numinous energy: that is, Weiss's evocation of Dante's Divine Comedy.[68]

While working on the play, Weiss noted to himself that there were three courses of action transpiring at the trial: one in Auschwitz, one in Frankfurt, and one inside a man (Weiss) who happened to be in Frankfurt (Salloch, 90). If the Auschwitz action is registered in the density of the documentation in The Investigation and the Frankfurt action in its propagandistic thrust, the inner action is Weiss's engagement with Dante. Salloch and Cohen have insightfully pursued Dantesque themes in Weiss and, in particular, structural parallels between the Divine Comedy and The Investigation, subtitled (in the German edition) an Oratorio and divided into "cantos." Neither, however, quite makes the point I wish to emphasize here, namely that the intertextual presence of Dante threatens to deconstruct the Marxist model Weiss simultaneously labors to construct. I cannot agree with Salloch (107) that Weiss's oratorio is wholly of this earth and antimetaphysical, though surely that was Weiss's intent. Weiss sets the Divine Comedy off against Auschwitz rather in the way Littlewood runs commedia right into the statistics of slaughter, critiquing by juxtaposition with metaphor and departure from metaphor. It would be a mistake to suggest that the adduction of Dante aestheticizes Auschwitz and makes it stand vaguely for man's inhumanity to man; rather, Dante and Marx both "accompany" Weiss through Auschwitz, the explanation of each threatening to

[67]Salloch, 103, indicates that only Witness 3 speaks words not in the sources.

[68]The connection with Dante has subsequently been much commented on; see Roger Ellis, Peter Weiss in Exile: A Critical Study (Ann Arbor, Mich.: UMI Research Press, 1987), 46 ff., and Robert Cohen, Understanding Peter Weiss (Columbia, S.C.: South Carolina University Press, 1993), 78 ff.

dissolve that of the other. Ultimately, however, Weiss has made Auschwitz "My Place," as he entitled an essay about his visit to the camp (Salloch, 73 ff). *The Investigation* is not a metaphor of anything, but an instance of moral, political, and legal discourse, a metonym of a process of interrogation, denial, proof, innocence, and guilt, which Weiss's life project kept under constant scrutiny. *The Investigation* begins *in medias res* and ends without a verdict. Like the best documentaries, it throbs with a sense of discovery, of searching for and attempting to fix meaning, and of the elusiveness of meaning and truth: a sense of journey rather than of arrival.

The same year, 1963, which saw productions of *The Deputy* in Germany and *Lovely War* in England, sparking renewed interest in documentary theater in those countries, also brought Martin Duberman's *In White America* to off-Broadway in New York. Duberman's "documentary play" tells the story of racial prejudice from the slave trade to the present (it opens with an actor reading from "today's" newspaper) entirely in historical and contemporary documents read and lightly dramatized by six actors. American dramatists were slow to follow his lead, and whatever flourishing of documentary theater there has been in the United States came in the 1970s—initiated if not inspired by Donald Freed's *Inquest* (1970), a revisionist replay of the espionage trial of Julius and Ethel Rosenberg.

Although receiving somewhat favorable notices from Clive Barnes (*New York Times*), Julius Novick (*Village Voice*), and John Simon (*New York*), *Inquest* (in a shortened, one-act version) brought forth a storm of negative criticism reminiscent of the reaction to the Broadway production of Hochhuth's *The Deputy*.[69] Freed was excoriated not only for being a bad playwright but for "moral pollution" (*Time*), "paranoia" (*Commentary*), and "brainwashing" (*New Yorker*). The production, directed by Alan Schneider and starring George Grizzard and Anne Jackson as the Rosenbergs, closed after eight previews and 28 performances.

The virulence of the critical reaction can be understood in the context (borrowed from Weiss) of the three "courses of action" in *Inquest:* one in the early 1950s, one in 1970, and one inside Donald Freed (the personal "in/quest"). The early action is reflected in a reasoned, if partisan, reevaluation of the case against the Rosenbergs based on the revisionist scholarship of Walter and Miriam Schneir (*Invitation to an Inquest*) and John Wexley (*The Judgment of Julius and Ethel Rosenberg*). It transpired against a cultural backdrop of McCarthyism and "Lucy" laugh tracks. The current action is meant to take the spectator, as Freed puts it in "The Case and the Myth" (q.v. pages 239–242), "from [Judges] Kaufman to Hoffman," that is, from the Rosenbergs' court to that of the Chicago Seven. Its propagandistic intent is to compel an acknowledgment that the conditions that spawned the Rosenberg trial still prevail. The action inside Freed, registered both in the play's rhetorical features and in the playwright's commentary, entails the construction of an antimyth to combat the government's hegemony over the facts relative to the Rosenbergs.

Freed's strategies in this enterprise are so explicitly rationalized in "The Case and the Myth" as to make their recapitulation unnecessary. Yet, there is both a convergence and a collision between his project to exonerate the Rosenbergs and the one to construct an antimyth, which may not be immediately obvious (although the intertextuality between the trial and the transpiring play builds steadily in the text). The "drama" of *Inquest* lies (1) in the creation and manipulation of evidence and (2) in the crucial decision over whether the Rosenbergs should exercise their Fifth Amendment rights against self-incrimination, both at the trial and subsequently to save themselves from execution. In regard to the former, Freed appears to claim for his play a special veracity in announcing (via a projection onstage) that "EVERY WORD YOU WILL SEE OR HEAR ON THIS STAGE IS A DOCU-

---

[69]Among the negatives were *Time* 95 (4 May 1970): 62; *Newsweek* 75 (4 May 1970): 89; *New Yorker* 46 (2 May 1970): 83–85; and *Commentary* 50 (July 1970): 18–25. See, for comparison, Eric Bentley, ed., *The Storm over The Deputy* (New York: Grove Press, 1964). The critical reactions were also bound up with the culture of Broadway, which was on the cusp of changing from New York's regional theater to a tourist attraction.

MENTED QUOTATION FROM TRIAL TRANSCRIPTS AND ORIGINAL SOURCES OR A RECONSTRUCTION FROM ACTUAL EVENTS." In defending this announcement, however, Freed reveals an ambivalence amounting to an admission that he will be manipulating the evidence and compelling his audience to evaluate it as did the Rosenberg jurors. This constitutes, for the documentary playwright, a species of "self-incrimination" that Freed hopes will be replicated in the audience: "You were passive and did not choose when you had the chance and now must undergo everything twice, only now it is forbidden you, that choice, by finitude and time." Not only did the critics resist this invitation to self-incrimination (as did the Rosenbergs), they may also have been reacting against the postmodern miasma over historical "truth" and author/ity stirring in Freed's text.[70]

Broadway has remained unfriendly to documentaries (*Execution of Justice*—New York, 1986), quasi-documentaries (*Zoot Suit*—New York, 1979; *The Song of Jacob Zulu*—1993), and even plays occasionally sounding like documentaries (*The Texas Trilogy*, *The Kentucky Cycle*). Documentaries widely performed in the regional theater, such as *Quilters* (New York, 1984) and *Working* (1978), have characteristically fared poorly in New York. As well, several challenging examples of the form either never came to New York (Sidney Greenberg's *Pueblo,* produced at the Arena in 1971) or received minor productions (Fr. Daniel Berrigan's *Trial of the Catonsville Nine*—1971).[71] Nevertheless, the early 1970s did yield a handful of documentaries, including Eric Bentley's *Are You Now or Have You Ever Been* (1972, on early House Un-American Activity hearings) and Robert Brustein's *Watergate Follies* (1973), which, like most American documentaries, were event-specific.

By contrast, the resurgence of documentary theater in England sparked by *Oh What a Lovely War* generated site-specific documentaries of considerable innovation and variety.[72] While the documentary plays of John Arden and Margareta D'Arcy, John McGrath and Theatre 7:84 (notably *The Cheviot, the Stag and the Black, Black Oil*—1973), and Peter Cheeseman are also driven by political commitment and contemporary event, they retain a provincialism in the best sense, being plain-spoken and rich in regional history. Among these, Cheeseman's work stands out for its radical historiography and longevity.

Cheeseman, the articulate and energetic artistic director of The Victoria Theatre in Stoke-on-Trent, saw Littlewood's production of *Lovely War* in 1964. He immediately started work on a musical documentary of his own entitled *The Jolly Potters* (1964), which told the story of the potteries industry in Stoke-on-Trent and the "five towns," an area noted for its exquisite Royal Doulton, Wedgwood, and Spode china. Its initial success generated yearly docudramas at The Victoria dealing with such topics as the history of Staffordshire during the Civil War (*The Staffordshire Rebels*—1965), the history of the local rail line (*The Knotty*—1966), the federation of the six towns (*Six Into One*—1968), the life of Hugh Bourne, founder of Primitive Methodism (*The Burning Mountain*—1970), and many more.

The distinct character of the Stoke documentaries derives not only from their highly specific and localized subject matter, but also from their creation at the hands of a group, rather than a single author, and the self-imposed rule that "The material used on stage must be primary source material. . . . If there is no primary source material available on a particular topic, no scene can be made about it."[73] Cheeseman's discipline acknowledges in practice what the French historian de Certeau asserts in theory, i.e., that any attempt

---

[70]My analysis of *Inquest* benefited from a seminar paper by Gwen Orel.

[71]On *Pueblo* and *Catonsville Nine,* see Dan Issac, "Theatre of Fact," *The Drama Review* 15, 3a (Summer 1971): 109–35.

[72]See Paget, 1990, and Dan Garrett on "Documentary theatre in the provinces," *New Theatre Magazine* 12, 3 (1973): 2–4.

[73]Peter Cheeseman, "Introduction" to *The Knotty,* "Created by the Victoria Theatre Company working from historical research conducted by Peter Terson under the direction of Peter Cheeseman" (London: Methuen, 1970), xiv.

at representing the real is entangled with the protocol of history-writing: The happenstance of accessible documents determines the course of history. But such an acknowledgment, according to de Certeau's paradox, clears the path for a discourse of facts about real events in the past: "The discourse destined to express what is other remains their [historians'] discourse and the mirror of their own labors. Inversely, when they refer to their own practices and examine their postulates in order to innovate, therein historians discover constraints [e.g., loss of documents; the accidents of their own birth—French rather than English; the time in which one is born; the place one lives] originating well before their own present, dating back to former organizations of which their work is a symptom, not a cause" (35–36). What de Certeau says about history (i.e., the academic praxis issuing in a discourse) applies with particular relevance to the documentary work at Stoke: It is less the effect of personal philosophy than a product of a place, a fabrication bearing the mark of its origins (64).

In contrast with the German documentarians of the 1960s, Cheeseman is concerned with creating an audience of listeners rather than an audience of believers:

> One of the things wrong with our society is that too few people have a sense of history. We have lost in our society the sort of natural structure whereby old men pass down knowledge to the young in a community. . . . In this sort of atmosphere it seems to me that our obligation is to show people . . . that they [do] not stand alone in the present but are part of a historical perspective.[74]

Cheeseman goes so far as to maintain that "You can't write a documentary—it's a contradiction in terms. You can only edit documentary material" (ibid.). Though refusing to accept authorial credit for the plays created under his leadership and

leery of the encroachment of ideology, Cheeseman does not deny that the inevitable arrangement, editing, and abridgment involve subjectivity and personal judgment. But he does intend that the compositional pains taken by his company inoculate his productions against political narrow-mindedness and naiveté. The rule of primary source materials, he asserts, "ensures that a multiplicity of voices are heard" (*The Knotty,* xiv). The collective creation "tends to preserve the contradiction of viewpoint inherent in every historical event" (ibid., xiv–xv). In historical writing, observes de Certeau (94), the plurality of original sources is diminished to the singularity of the historical discourse because the citations do "not assume the form of a dialogue or a collage." Cheeseman, however, does his utmost to preserve the plurality, though the shape of the resulting narrative approximates the constructed "singularity" of the historian.

In most docudramas, projections are used to provide visual variety and convey factual data graphically. Since projections in theater-in-the-round—Cheeseman's stage arrangement—are both technically difficult and expensive, he puts special emphasis on the actor as the direct visual representation of the documentary fact. The actor "must have a totally candid and honest basic relationship with the audience to start with" (*The Knotty,* xviii)—a relationship initiated long before the performance begins. Cannily undermining the distinction between professional actor and member of the community, Cheeseman typically insists that his actors, who come from all over England, steep themselves in the Midlands accent, often going so far as to live with the local residents. All actors performing in a documentary do library research and take oral histories from living personages who might figure in the drama—thereby uniting the tasks of composition and performance as in traditional oral epics. In performance, objectivity is fostered by having any one actor play several different roles, and by having the transformations from character to character made in full sight of the audience. Actor/narrators quote their sources, and taped voices of the real people interviewed are played during the production as "voice-over," with the actor then assuming the role and playing the scene.

---

[74]In an interview with Gillette Elvgren cited in the introduction to Elvgren and Attilio Favorini, *Steel/City: A Docudrama in Three Acts* (Pittsburgh: University of Pittsburgh Press, 1992), xvii. A small portion of the material relating to Cheeseman in the present essay has previously appeared in the Elvgren/Favorini volume.

Training this battery of authenticating techniques upon an issue of vital interest to the community can generate a script of considerable dramatic power and political efficacy. When in 1973 the British Steel Corporation declared its intention to close down inland steel mills, including the newly renovated works in Stoke-on-Trent, the Victoria Theatre, urged on by Ted Smith and Bill Foster of the Shelton Works Action Committee, joined with the local populace in opposing this decision by creating *Fight for Shelton Bar*. Produced in 1974, the documentary provided a colorful and accurate picture of the steel-making process, as well as coverage of the political decisions being made at both local and national levels. Nightly updated with reports documenting the latest developments in the negotiations, the play became a rallying point for the community. Not despite but because of the wonderful hesitancies, digressions, and repetitions in the dialogue, and the start and stop of the action, the script generates tremendous tension and emotion as we hear the early rumors of shutdown, then participate at the meeting when Lord Melchett coldly declares that the plant will be closed, then hear, in Ted's own recorded voice, how he remembered the men who had died in the plant and became inspired to fight back: "And I could hear these voices, mate, and loud and clear they were. You know, men, Tommy Cooper, you know, men 'at'd been killed. . . . And tears *did* roll down my bloody cheeks, mate. Unashamed tears of bloody joy, because I, I was prepared to put my bloody life down the same as they had" (end of Part I).

The through-line of this play's action, to save the community by fighting for Shelton Bar, extends at either end beyond the termini of the dramatic experience: originating in the will of Ted Smith and Bill Foster, passing through the Victoria Theatre (which accepted the mens' suggestion to do a Shelton documentary), and issuing in the galvanization of the community and the reversal of the BSC decision to close the steelworks. The theater and the community had become one.

In theory, the political efficacy of *Fight for Shelton Bar* might be attributable to its participation in the symbolic construction of community by dealing with the "fundamental constitution of the audience's community identity."[75] In practice, it is the natural outcome of a sustained commitment to interpolate the creative process of the theatrical work within its host community. It would be accurate to say that although the topics of the Victoria documentaries change, they share a single action: the making of the Midlands. Thus, while the railroad in *The Knotty* may indeed stand metaphorically for the road men travel, its uniqueness is as a metonym for the making of Stoke, reckoning the gains and losses of "progress" as it goes along. By the same token, both the steel-making process and the negotiating process documented in *Fight for Shelton Bar* are less illustrations than instances of the craft that gives the region its character.

This dense intertextuality was brought about through the application of documentary techniques developed over most of this century and influenced, of course, by successive revolutions in recording technology. In the example just cited we have the spectacle of the actor playing Ted performing for the real individual, who is sitting in the audience watching the actor playing him give way to the recorded voice of the real Ted— all of this transpiring before other witnesses watching other actors portray them and their neighbors, whose stories continue to unfold and develop and change and which are therefore erased and edited and taped over in the course of the run of the show. It is tempting to respond to this occasion with a Baudrillardian shrug about the intangibility of the border between fact and fiction or represented and representation. I prefer, however, to carry away the image of the actor as representative, place-taker, *Stellvertreter* (to borrow the title of Rolf Hochhuth's quasi-documentary)—a term reminding us that the concept of

---

[75]Kershaw, 33. Cheeseman is not the subject of this quote, nor are the Victoria documentaries accorded much attention by Kershaw. In addition to documentaries produced by regional professional theaters, the "community play" movement in Great Britain commissions scripts with a strong documentary component, hiring professional playwrights and directors to create site-specific historical plays acted by amateurs in the community. See Ann Jellicoe, *Community Plays: How to put them on* (London: Methuen, 1987).

representation binds our aesthetic deputies together with our political ones.

The making or crafting that animates so many Victoria documentaries also lies at the heart of Molly Newman and Barbara Damashek's *Quilters* (1982), which is based on *The Quilters: Women and Domestic Art* by Patricia Cooper and Norma Bradley Allen. The action of the play, culminating in a striking *coup de théâtre* at the end, is the quilting of a "Legacy." More specifically, it is woman's legacy, and quilting is woman's way of making: collective, recreative, fecund. Of course, one may "read" this metaphorically ("a woman's life is a quilt"), but the construction of the play, its own patchwork quality, brings a metonym to the fore: quilting as an act of remembering.

The stuff of the play is the fabric of memory. Not a "memory play" like *Glass Menagerie* or *Dancing at Lughnasa,* in which the past and present are filtered through an individual psychology, *Quilters* is instead a "memory theatre." While in Renaissance models the memories were attached to architectural features, in *Quilters* they adhere to scraps of material which, en/gendered female, might otherwise be discarded or lost by the hegemonic culture. That the play is itself stitched together from women's oral histories makes for a particularly satisfying coalescence of matter and form, as the preservation of memory is twice enacted—by characters and playwrights. Not incidentally, it makes the play's feminism feel part of its texture, like shot silk.

The discrepancy between the popularity of the play, which has been regularly in production at regional theaters since its premiere at the Denver Center Theatre, and the condescending, sometimes sexist and almost sneering reaction of the New York critics,[76] fits the pattern of documentary theater in America. As a musical documentary it confounded the critics twice, since neither did it conform to their expectations for a "Broadway" musical nor were its politics easily identifiable with those of the "typical" documentary. What

was one to make of a play that appeared to bring delight equally to radical feminists and the conservative homebodies of Reagan's America?[77] The example of *Quilters* also reminds us that while Americans have produced much regional drama—from the earliest "Yankee" efforts to the ubiquitous "historical" pageants that present fictionalized incident and dialogue and are commercially produced outdoors for a largely tourist audience—documentary dramas in the more restricted sense employed here have been responsive to events rather than communities.[78] An exception is Emily Mann's *Execution of Justice* (1984) which, though driven by the assassination of San Francisco Mayor George Moscone and gay City Supervisor Harvey Milk, bears the vivid marks of its place of origin.

Oskar Eustis of the Eureka Theatre in San Francisco had previously produced Mann's *Still Life* (1980), an interview-based play about a Vietnam veteran, his wife, and his mistress. Mann accepted Eustis's commission for a new work on the condition that the work be specific to his theater and his community.[79] The subject of Supervisor Dan White's 1978 murder of his political opponents naturally suggested itself, as White's light sentence and imminent release on parole kept the painful events alive in the city.

Mann's play is "sculpted" (her word) out of the transcripts of Dan White's trial and from inter-

---

[76]Typical was Frank Rich in the *New York Times,* 26 September 1984.

[77]Audience composition as testified to by the playwrights in separate phone interviews with me, 3 June 1994. See also Joanne Karpinski, "The Shadow Block: Female Bonding in *Quilters,*" *Women and Performance: A Journal of Feminist Theory,* 4, 1 (1988): 6–22, on the play's feminism and some reasons for its failure in New York.

[78]Cheeseman's example of site-specific documentaries has been followed less in the United States than in Canada, which already had a rich documentary tradition. See Alan Filewod, *Collective Encounters: Documentary Theatre in English Canada* (Toronto: University of Toronto Press, 1987). Elvgren and Favorini's *Steel/City* (see note 74) is an American documentary in the Cheeseman mold and, to my knowledge, the first musical documentary in the United States.

[79]My account of the generation of *Execution of Justice* is based on a telephone interview with Mann, 27 January 1994. The interpretation of the play is my own.

views Mann herself conducted. All of the dialogue is thus "found." First fully produced at Actors Theatre of Louisville in February of 1984, the script underwent continual revision in productions at the Empty Space, Berkeley Rep, Center Stage, The Alley, The Guthrie (directed by the playwright), and the Arena (December 1985), where the script stabilized prior to its brief Broadway run (March 1986). In the meantime, White had been released from prison (6 January 1984) and committed suicide (21 October 1985), and the script was altered to accommodate these events. The Arena Theatre production was the first to incorporate film footage and dialogue from *The Times of Harvey Milk* by Robert Epstein and Richard Schmiechen. Included in the present volume are reactions by a San Franciscan (William Kleb) to the Louisville premiere and by (then) *Washington Post* critic David Richards to the Arena production.

The play's inventive departures from the trial format most recall *Inquest,* as do its metatheatricality and disposition to turn the audience into jurors. But unlike Freed, Mann is not impelled chiefly by a desire to expose a misprision of justice. Rather she is driven to examine its "execution": to look at the design by which justice is carried out and fully to reveal its contours. In the play, those contours are the topography of San Francisco. *Execution of Justice* is not "set" at the trial but rather transpires at multiple locations stereochronically across the city. When District Attorney Freitas reveals the prosecution's reluctance to put the "city on trial," he also reveals the playwright's strategy, for that is precisely what she does. But the play's intent is not to assign guilt, nor to indict society; instead, it attempts to restore to events a fullness that the trial attenuated. In the words of White's jailer: "What was left unsaid was what the trial should have been about."

As her cast of characters specifies, Mann was determined to give a hearing to the "uncalled" witnesses, to place White and his actions in an articulated social and geopolitical context. Her play virtually begins with a cop remembering "a time in San Francisco when you knew a guy by his parish" and it ends with White's ironic "I was just trying to do a good job for the city"—an ambition

the playwright herself might admit to. It is undoubtedly true, as Mann observed in conversation, that *Execution of Justice* becomes a different play when performed outside the Bay area. Dan White's character takes more focus and the loss of Mayor Moscone and Supervisor Harvey Milk to the community recedes to the margins. Even so, the play is "civil" and "civic-minded," in ways that bring new excitement to those old notions, reminding us that "theatre is not about something. It is from something, from a given place, from the social and personal forms of life."[80]

The revival of documentary theater in the early 1960s sparked new interest in the genre far beyond Western Europe and the United States and continues to yield ingenious and innovative examples.[81] Augusto Boal's early experiments had a documentary thrust, entailing the dramatic creation of alternative newspapers with audience members.[82] Many respected Japanese playwrights have undertaken documentary dramas, notably Kinoshita Junji, whose *Between God and Man* (1970) engages the Japanese War Crime Trials of 1946–48.[83] And in post-*glasnost* Russia, documentaries have been produced by the controversial Sergei Kurginian at his Moscow Theater Studio "On the Boards"—most notably the provocative **Compensation (A Liturgy of Fact)** (1987), sourced in the Chernobyl nuclear disaster.

Scientist, political theorist, self-styled mystic and director of avant-garde theater, Kurginian brings renewed meaning to the hackneyed phrase

---

[80]Stephen Balint, artistic director of the dis/placed Squat Theatre of Hungary, quoted by Johannes Birringer, "Invisible Cities/Transcultural Images," in *Interculturalism and Performance,* ed. Bonnie Marranca and Gautam Dasgupta (New York: PAJ Publications, 1991), 117.

[81]*World Theatre,* 17 (1968) devoted an entire issue to the documentary theater, noting its robust development in Asia and South America.

[82]See his *Theatre of the Oppressed* (New York: Urizen, 1979).

[83]The play was published in English translation by University of Tokyo/University of Washington Press (Seattle and London: 1979).

"uniquely qualified." His scientific background is in theoretical physics. His politics are pro-Communist and reactionary, allied with the anti-Yeltsin Ruslan Khasbulatov, Chairman of the Supreme Soviet of Russia. His mysticism is Christian, political, and apocalyptic. He believes that Communism expropriated the cult of Christianity, while linking it to a new creed and code, and long predicted the collapse of a barren state ideology: "When you put a salami on the altar, it's funny."[84] His response, however, is not to reject both but to attempt to reconcile them, asserting that for him the understanding of "Red" and "Orthodox" are close to one another. His theater work most resembles that of Grotowski: cultish, based on experimental acting techniques, shorn to the essentials, laboratorylike.

"On the Boards" began as an underground theater and has been shut down fourteen times during its twenty years of operation.[85] During all that time it has produced only two conventional plays, *Boris Godunov* and *Nocturnal Assault* by Alfonso Sastre. Most of the theater's scripts have been created by Kurginian in response to literary texts ranging from Dostoevskii to Jack London. Linking the theater to an older Russian tradition and placing it antithetically to "Soviet" theater, Kurginian's wife (and actress in the company) Masha identifies the work of "On the Boards" as "mystery plays." *Stenographic Report,* a subsequent documentary sourced in a contraband transcript of the 15th Party Congress in 1926 (in which Stalin was pitted against Trotsky), is termed by her a "political mysteria"—a phrase that may also describe *Compensation.*

In the Kurginians' view, Chernobyl was not just a "technical" disaster, but a catastrophe with religious meaning. In Ukrainian the word "Chernobyl" connotes "wormwood," and the Kurginians give this a biblical resonance (Rev. 8:10–11), connecting it with "Anna Bogaslova," a reputed disciple of Christ figuring in Russian Apocalyptica. In *Compensation* this religious dimension takes form in liturgical music, vestmentlike costuming, a doll representing an angel, and an altar-table setting (see Alma Law's account of performance below). The text of the play likewise features the sacrificial actions of the "Liquidators," who gave their lives in attempting to control the damage to the Chernobyl reactor. Furthermore, like the Father Berrigan who was both author of and character in the *Trial of the Catonsville Nine,* Kurginian insists on the status of his work as a religious act.

But this "mysteria" is also political, an interrogation of a historical event so as to make the play's "investigation" of it part of the event itself. In this, as well as in its ambiguous religiosity, it most recalls Peter Weiss. Like *The Investigation, Compensation* alludes to Dante (quoted in the first lines of the Psychologist), and its "episodes" correspond to Weiss's evocation of "cantos." Also as in Weiss, Kurginian's text seems to be pulled between Marxist and religious orthodoxies, between immanence and transcendence.

Coming twenty-five and thirty years after Berrigan and Weiss, however, Kurginian is much more saturated, irradiated, with the mutabilities and disjunctions of postmodernism. His characters are unstable, appearing to change their nature without the mediation of events in the "plot." The Psychologist narrator transforms from a noncommittal observer repeatedly responding "I don't know" to one who identifies sympathetically with the Liquidators. The Voice on the Radio is identified, on the one hand, with a do-nothing bureaucracy: Moscow apartments used to come with a radio in the wall broadcasting the official station, which could not be turned off; he is heard to be slurping tea as the recitation of horror and sacrifice proceeds. On the other hand, the Voice is the creator of the theater piece, to whom the Psychologist came with his files of Chernobyl'tsy. And in the final episode the Voice participates in a reminiscence of a subversive film, his persona almost blending with the Psychologist and First Liquidator. The Liquidators themselves

---

[84]I am drawing here on a profile by Kurginian by "S.R." published in *Kto est kto [Who's Who],* 7 (September 1993) translated by Carolyn Kelson, as well as Lev Anninskii, "*Tabula Rasa:* The Theatre Studio 'On the Boards,'" published in Russian as a booklet introduction to the theater and translated into English by Nancy Condee and Vladimir Padunov (unpublished).

[85]In addition to the previously cited accounts, I am relying on interviews with Kurginian (18 November 1993) and his wife Masha (20 April 1994) conducted on my behalf by Carolyn Kelson.

are simultaneously concelebrants in a liturgy, living survivors of Chernobyl, and the ghosts of the dead heroes.

Grotowski's title for his theater's encounter with human devastation well suits Kurginian's: *Compensation* is an *"apocalypsis cum figuris."* Though its documentary nature grounds it more in the specificities of this world—a hell in which the populace wait in line for irradiated mayonnaise—the power of its religious symbolism is in danger of eroding its historicity. *Compensation* threatens to dismantle its own documentary mechanism and is, like Kurginian's other work, "a drama of disembodiment" (Anninskii) or, in religious terms, a *via negativa*. Here the politics of representation, the actor effecting solidarity, dissolve into the mysticism of representation: "Do this in memory of me." The iridescent discs everywhere on the set of *Compensation* are simultaneously reactor components and angelic halos—perhaps also the Host itself. If, like Rauschenberg's notorious treatment of de Kooning's drawing, *Compensation* is "documentary erased," it is also documentary transubstantiated.

Is the idea of postmodern documentary oxymoronic? One of the pillars of postmodernism is the ineffability of the border between fiction and fact, a principle undermining the very foundation of documentary art. The relentless revelation of the biases that have marginalized the histories of the disenfranchised and the exposure of the rhetorical strategies and simulations of the truth-telling enterprise in all media have, at the least, provoked a deep crisis for the documentarian. In the cinema this crisis has lately been met with the development, according to Paul Arthur, of an aesthetics of failure, in which the inability "to adequately represent the person, event or social situation stated as the film's explicit task functions as an inverted guarantee of authenticity."[86] He cites Michael Moore's popular *Roger and Me* (1989) as a film displaying "a series of

inadequate gestures at empowerment by which fidelity to the Real is simultaneously derided as a goal and instated" (131). The closest theatrical parallel is probably the strongly autobiographical work of performance artist/monologists, such as Spalding Gray. But an aesthetics of representational failure, or at least frustration, also infuses Mame Hunt's *Unquestioned Integrity: The Hill/Thomas Hearings* (1992), carved out of the Senate Judiciary Committee hearings on the nomination of Clarence Thomas to the Supreme Court and centering on the testimony of Anita Hill.

Hunt, currently Artistic Director of the Magic Theatre in San Francisco, has not set out to prove either Thomas or Hill to be the liar on the issue of what sexual conversations ever took place (or did not) between them. Rather, for Hunt the issue seems to be verification itself, the possibility of accurate recollection and reporting, and especially how credibility is fabricated in the electronic age. She hopes to afford her audience the opportunity "to listen more carefully . . . unmediated by news commentary and hype," though her own mediation of the hearing transcripts problematizes this objective, as David Pellegrini's commentary suggests (q.v. pages 414–417).

Do facts represent the truth or can their veracity easily be turned into "garbage," as Anita Hill convincingly insists in repelling the innuendos arising from the manipulation of information about her telephone logs? But if telephone logs can be deceptively manipulated, what about hearing transcripts? One of the most dramatically compelling moments in *Unquestioned Integrity* occurs when Anita Hill rises and crosses to The Senator to emphasize her point that she has made no legal claim of sexual harassment, but brought her information forward so that its veracity might be tested. It is, however, a gestus that manifestly never took place.

This is not at all to imply that Hunt is less reliable than the other documentary playwrights collected here, much less that the definitive realities of race and gender underlying the Senate hearings are obscured in her play. On the contrary, my impression is that she has given a fair "hearing" to all parties involved. But the deconstruction of linear narrative that is central to her dramaturgy

---

[86]Paul Arthur, "Jargons of Authenticity (Three American Moments," in *Theorizing Documentary,* ed. by Michael Renov (New York: Routledge, 1993), 127.

converts the issue of sexual harassment into an emblem for the crisis of representation. In an encounter between two when both see it differently, veracity can be established only by psychological credibility, rhetorical presence, "acting" ability—as Clarence Thomas unintentionally affirms when he declares in the play that "the facts can change, but my denial does not."

Some of the issues featured in *Unquestioned Integrity*—the relationship of "performance" to veracity, irreconcilable conflicts in points of view—inform the work of Anna Deveare Smith, whose Tony-nominated *Twilight: L.A. 1992* (1993) appeared on Broadway for a short run. Two of Smith's documentaries are currently in print, precluding her inclusion here. Her documentary engagement with public figures and high profile events (racial tension in Crown Heights, Brooklyn [*Fires in the Mirror*] and the Los Angeles riots) brings the conventions of 1960s "direct cinema"[87] into tension with the postmodern aesthetics of performance art. Her subjects are social actors, and she consequently constructs social history as verisimiliar portraiture. But her foregrounding of performance virtuosity (she plays all the roles in her plays, which are sourced in interviews she conducts) constantly diverts the referential vector of her presentation. Even so, Smith may be recognized in the context I have outlined here as an oral memorialist, an individual who, in carrying the many and contradictory lives of the populace physically within her, is a living metonym of communitas.

The problem of representing the other, of putting oneself in another's place—arguably the central problem of history-writing, as well—has been and continues to be addressed in characteristic and ingenious ways by the documentary playwright. The problem*atics* of representing the other inscribe the work of both docudramatist and academic historian. We may now observe that in endeavoring to represent the truth, the documentarian simulates the historian's methodology and protocol: collecting data, citing pri-

mary source materials, producing charts and illustrations, employing real-seeming film clips and, via (e.g.) the Voice of the Living Newspaper (or, in film, the invisible camera), approximating the desubjectivized, omniscient, third-person voice of the historian. Inversely, and problematically, an important body of contemporary historiography describes the heavy reliance of the academic historian on the rhetorical strategies of the fiction-maker and theater artist. Herbert Lindenberger cites the affinity of the historian for the theatrical metaphor to affect a sense of continuity (plotting) and dignity, to create with theatrical flair the "panorama" of history (22). De Certeau (xvi) suggests that the historian and artist alike produce a discourse of knots and half-signs, since the way events are handed down to us partakes of literary devices and typologies which, in turn, "dictate our relation to what we construe to be the past." He vigorously contends that the typical historical text narrates more than it reasons (in order to shut off debate), that the plethora of proper names, descriptions, and deictics (the strategies of visuals aids) merely create the illusion of true knowledge of another time, and that the suppression of the author's subjectivity in adopting the third-person is nothing more than a dissimulation designed to convey the illusion of authority (100). Historical writing, de Certeau implies, hankers towards theater in assembling "a coherent set of great units [that is, ideas of period, family, class, or historical constructs such as the industrial revolution or the *ancien regime*] into a structure analogous to the architecture of places and characters in a tragedy" (97). We can therefore observe with some irony that when the historian wants to create the impression of truth s/he draws on the techniques of theater; and when the documentary playwright has the same objective, s/he copies the ceremonial forms of the historian.

Similarly, Hayden White's controversial contention that poetic and historical narratives draw alike on the same fund of structures and conventions both focuses and complexifies the issues surrounding documentary theater. Unquestionably, history is a narrative, tells a story. How is the historian's narrative different from that of, say, the dramatist? According to White, once one acknowledges that historical events differ from fic-

---

[87]On which, see Arthur, ibid.

tive events in that the former have or had space-time locations while the latter are hypo- thetical—a distinction further obscured by documentary theater—similarities in the narrative enterprise are overwhelming. Thus, after distinguishing truth of correspondence (i.e., cor- respondence to "the real") as an objective of history from truth of coherence (i.e., logical relatedness) as an objective of fiction, White demonstrates how both forms of discourse aspire to a judicious mixture of both sorts of truth. Crucially, he asserts that the integrity and coherence brought to historical discourse are genuinely and exclusively discursive—i.e., fashioned by the historian in the course of his representation of the facts.[88]

But even so radical a formulation need not lead to epistemological anarchy or rhetorical absolutism. White himself acknowledges that awareness of and mediation among the available tropes defend the historian against, at the least, their unwitting employment. De Certeau goes further, allowing that the research undertaken by the historian continuously qualifies and interrupts the dramatics of the constructed text: "But the system of this drama is the space where the movement of documentation, that is, of smaller units, sows disorder within this order, escapes from established divisions, and brings about a slow erosion of organizing concepts" (97–8). This erosion of a model of comprehension nevertheless leaves in its wake a discourse of facts. Paradoxically, that is, it can produce a true encounter with the other, glimpsed only in moments of ravishment, in gaps that knowledge cannot rationalize (xvi).

Crucially, the paradigmatic episode of ravishment cited by de Certeau is that of the 16th-century traveler Lery *overhearing* the chant of the Tupis of Brazil, an incident de Certeau identifies as a primal scene for the encounter of speech and writing. While writing, in conquering both distance and time, colonizes the other and is immunized against alterity (216), the delinearizing quality of voice preserves a distortion, a locus of

the other, a ravishment (236). One feels this ravishment in the earliest recorded responses to the documentary impulse, in Herodotus, whose writing preserves an orality already eroding (though not entirely) in Thucydides. One feels it, too, in those documentaries that are most assiduous in preserving the integrity of their spoken word sources. Whether or not originating in transcripts of a legal proceeding, all such documentaries are based in a "hear/ing" and on the most fundamental level dramatize the act of listening itself. Here is the very point where the re/present/ation of the other—heightened by mature historiography or sophisticated technology—apotheoses into solidarity as in *Shelton Bar,* sisterhood as in *Quilters,* or even sacrament as in *Compensation.*

The emphasis on orality in the plays I have included here suggests a genealogy of the documentary that can fill out the conventional account tracing docudramas back through realism, Schiller, and historical drama. Alongside this patrilinear descent stands a matrilinear one in which the symbols of community are less attenuated, including narrative ballads, oral epics, folk and passion plays, and other examples of what Northrop Frye designates the encylopedic forms, back to primitive dramas whose function was "to present a powerful sensational focus for the community."[89] Thinking of the testament of Ted Smith quoted earlier—"I could hear these voices, mate"—and borrowing a term from Walter Ong (14; see above, footnote 11) I designate such plays "voicings," plays which restore to the Western tradition "the old oral mnemonic world of imitation, aggregative, redundant, copious, traditionalist, warmly human, participatory" (Ong, 167). That this world appears to be "antipathetic to the analytic, sparse, exact, abstract, visualist, immobile world of 'ideas'" (ibid) we associate with most political drama testifies both to the flexibility and instability of the form. The historiography of documentaries in which voice predominates may thus be more controlled by the structure of remembrance (as in other oral performances—Ong, 59) than by the structure of the written text. This charac-

---

[88]See especially "The Fictions of Factual Representation" and "The Historical Text as Literary Artifact" in *Tropics of Discourse.*

[89]Northrop Frye, *The Anatomy of Criticism* (New York: Atheneum, 1969), 283.

teristic makes such a documentary, in a way I take to be meaningful, "true"—at least in a limited, adverbial sense of not deviating from the fact or reality that it aims at.

At the extreme other end of the documentary spectrum from the plays I have discussed would be what the television industry calls BOATS ("Based on a True Story") dramatizations and "reality" programming, so prevalent in the mass media, which merely exploit the cachet of fact for commercial advantage and which example the "panic-stricken" reproduction of the real Baudrillard anatomizes so ingeniously: "Today, when the real and imaginary are confused in the same operational totality, the esthetic fascination is everywhere. It is a subliminal perception (a sort of sixth sense) of deception, montage, scenaria— of the overexposed reality in the light of the models . . . " (150). Such dramatizations fall into what Paget terms the recording tradition of documentary, which both tells us about reality and, as

it were, " 'untells' us. While the discourse of factuality is helping to legitimate the fiction, issues are draining away into an exaggerated 'human interest' which is (ultimately) unproductive" (87). Telling true stories in the global village certainly presents new challenges.

The common, and often aggressively uttered expression "That was then; this is now" testifies to the urgency of discriminating the past from the present. The writing of history, de Certeau reminds us, "allows a society to situate itself by giving itself a past through language, and it thus opens to the present a space of its own" (100). Documentary drama participates in this project and thereby serves as the locus of conflicts more profound than any individual subject matter it may take up: the conflict between the assertive and hypothetical tendencies in literature, between the realm of the event and the realm of the word, between endorsement of the power of fact and its subversion, between partisanship and the idealistic impulse to know.

Erwin Piscator and Felix Gasbarra

IN SPITE OF EVERYTHING!

Historical revue of the years 1914 to 1919 in twenty-four scenes with intermittent films

1925

Translated by Richard Korb, with Attilio Favorini

In Spite of Everything! was performed in the Grosses Schauspielhaus, Berlin, on 12 and 14 July 1925. The play was directed by Erwin Piscator. Edmund Meisel was the musical director and John Heartfield designed the stage sets. Piscator and Felix Gasbarra wrote the text. The two-hundred–member cast was made up of professional Berlin stage actors, members of the proletarian community choirs and sports clubs, as well as members of the Red Front action committee and working-class singers.

The text to *In Spite of Everything!* is lost and is here approximated from the program notes, which list the titles and players for the scenes, and in excerpts from a police report in the Archiv des Instituts für Marxismus-Leninismus, Akte 12/70. These data were originally assembled and have been historically annotated by Ludvig Hoffman and Daniel Hoffman-Ostvald in *Deutsches Arbeittheater*, 1, pages 168 to 194.

Scene titles from the program notes are reproduced here in capital letters, the dramatis personae are in italics, and comments from the police report follow in regular type. The German editors' remarks appear in parentheses.

(The Tenth Party Convention of the KPD met from 12 to 17 July 1925. . . . The Leninists at the Tenth Party Convention did not completely succeed in taking over the party leadership from the extreme leftist group led by Fischer-Maslow. However [. . .] only shortly thereafter, at the first Party Workers' Conference held from 30 October to 1 November 1925, the sectarians were excluded from the Central Committee. This conference elected Ernst Thälmann as leader of the KPD. The Tenth Party Convention had helped to prepare this development. The portrayal of the revolutionary traditions of the party as seen in the revue *In Spite of Everything!* promoted the necessary clarification processes within the Party.)

SCENE 1. BERLIN AWAITS WAR —POTSDAM SQUARE

von Wildhagen, von Falkenhausen—Schulze, Lehmann, Franz, Willy, Paul—Newspaper carriers, citizens of Berlin.

A newspaper carrier distributes extra-editions bearing the news: Assassination of the Austrian crown prince in Sarajewo. The public is made up of a mix of Social Democrats and right-wing enthusiasts who discuss the possibilities of an approaching war.

(On 28 June 1914 Crown Prince Franz Ferdinand was murdered by Serbian nationalists while on tour of troops in the Bosnian city of Sarajewo. As a result, on 23 July the Austro-Hungarian government delivered a provocational ultimatum, which amounted practically to a denial of Serbian sovereignty. The Serbian government refused. On 28 July war was declared. [. . .] Wilhelm II and the German government undermined all attempts at reconciliation between Austria and Serbia. . . .)

SCENE 2. MEETING OF THE SOCIAL DEMOCRATIC REICHSTAG FACTION, 25 JULY 1914

Ebert, Landsberg, Scheidemann, David, Legien, Bauer, Haase, Barth, Dittmann, Ledebour, Liebknecht—the party members.

Meeting of the Social Democratic faction of the German Reichstag (25 July 1914) with Ebert, Scheidemann, Landsberg, and Liebknecht, during which the latter speaks decisively against an eventual war.

(That same day, 25 July 1914, the leaders of the SPD formalized a call for a mass demonstration by German workers protesting against the threat of war. The results were antiwar pronouncements in Berlin and in all larger German cities. Four days later, however, the Social Democratic Reichstag deputy Südekam wrote to Imperial Chancellor Bethmann-Hollweg that the party leadership was not planning any actions against the war. He apologized for the radical language that had appeared in *Vorwärts*, the official newspaper of the SPD).

SCENE 3. AT THE IMPERIAL PALACE IN BERLIN—1 AUGUST 1914

Wilhelm II, Imperial Chancellor Bethmann-Hollweg, Minister of War von Falkenhayn, an orderly—proletarians, citizens.

Wilhelm II declares war on Russia and speaks from the balcony of the palace to the people.

(On 1 August 1914, the German Reich declared war on Russia. Simultaneously, the general mobilization order was given. The world was set on fire. . . .)

SCENE 4. MEETING OF THE SOCIAL DEMOCRATIC REICHSTAG FACTION, 3 AUGUST 1914

Ebert, Landsberg, etc. Party members—Proletarians.

(On 3 August 1914 a meeting of the Social Democratic faction of the German Reichstag took place, during which the question of granting credits for the German war effort was discussed and decided upon. In keeping with the solemn peace declarations of international socialist congresses, Karl Liebknecht expressly demanded that the SPD reject the notion of war credits. The reformist majority of the Reichstag faction rejected his proposal. Seventy-eight deputies voted for the acceptance of the credit bill; only 14 voted against the proposal. [. . .] The Social Democratic faction in the German Reichstag voted on 4 August 1914 in favor of granting war credits.)

Newsreel: Mobilization, advance, the killing begins.

SCENE 5. REICHSTAG SESSION OF 2 DECEMBER 1914 (SECOND VOTE ON WAR CREDITS)

Representatives of all parties—Voices: von Bethmann, Reichstag President Kämpf, Liebknecht, Scheidemann, Noske, Ledebour.

(On 2 December 1914, the second credit bill was presented in the Reichstag. Liebknecht once again attempted unsuccessfully to organize a group of deputies against the war credits. The SPD faction prevented him from delivering a separate declaration. In spite of this Liebknecht was the only German Social Democrat to cast a vote against the war credits. . . .)

SCENE 6. IN A BERLIN GRENADE FACTORY

Franz, Willy, Paul, Gustav, the management—radical workers and moderate workers.

Radical workers demand a strike. But the strike never gets off the ground because management threaten to retract exemptions from active duty.

SCENE 7. 1 MAY 1916—POTSDAM SQUARE

Proletarians, Liebknecht. The patrolmen, Becker and Rothke, one police officer.

On the First of May at the Potsdam Square Liebknecht speaks and is arrested by two patrolmen.

(As the result of preparatory agitation by the Spartacus Union, there were massive peace demonstrations in cities throughout Germany on this May Day. The most important rally took place in Berlin. Ten thousand working people poured into Potsdam Square. Karl Liebknecht admonished them with cries of "Down with the war! Down with the government!" He was immediately arrested amidst stormy protests from the crowd.)

SCENE 8. LANDSBERG'S SPEECH ON 11 MAY 1916, CALLING FOR THE SUSPENSION OF LIEBKNECHT'S IMMUNITY

Landsberg—the parliament.

(In the name of the Party, Social Democratic Deputy Landsberg refused to come to the support of the rights of his comrade Karl Liebknecht as a member of the Reichstag. The Reichstag suspended the immunity of Deputy Liebknecht. Thus, on 28 June 1916, it was possible for a war tribunal to sentence Liebknecht as an armed soldier to two and a half years of prison for betraying his country. At a second hearing at the end of August the sentence was increased to four years and one month.)

SCENE 9. LIEBKNECHT STANDS TRIAL BEFORE THE WAR TRIBUNAL, 23 AUGUST 1916

Liebknecht's voice.

Liebknecht speaks before the war tribunal on 23 August 1916. He stated that he would be proud to be permitted to wear the prison uniform; others would advance his work in his absence. He petitioned the Supreme War Tribunal to place his case before the united populace. The entire court should address the people and then give him a chance on his own to do the same; it should then be left up to the people to decide his case.

Newsreel: The Killing Goes On—authentic footage of battles from the World War.

SCENE 10. IN THE GRENADE CRATER

German soldiers, one officer, one French soldier.

Newsreel: But the Proletariat no longer wants to be abused. Russian rebels; Lenin speaks.

(According to the police report, this scene was not performed.)

SCENE 11. THE MUNITIONS WORKERS' STRIKE OF 1918—30 JANUARY—IN TREPTOWER PARK

Paul, Willy, Adolf, Gustav, striking workers—Ebert, Dittmann, police officers, patrolmen.

Ebert speaks to the striking munitions workers, but the workers hiss and boo, shouting him down. 30 January 1918.

(As a direct result of the October Revolution and propaganda efforts of the Spartacus Union, a violent strike broke out among the munitions workers all over Germany at the end of January 1918. More than 500,000 male and female workers went on strike in Berlin. The number of strikers across the country exceeded a million. Mass meetings and demonstrations accompanied the strike. The main issues of the strike were the annexations involved in the peace negotiations at Brest-Litowsk and the continuation of the war. The workers demanded an immediate peace accord without annexations, improved provisioning, introduction of democratic self-determination, and release of political prisoners. The German munitions workers' strike of January 1918 was the largest political mass strike during World War I. This strike could have brought about the end of the war. The right-wing leadership of the SPD caused the strike to falter. Braun, Ebert, Scheidemann and others joined the action committee in order to prevent it from becoming too radical.)

SCENE 12. BERLIN AWAITS THE REVOLUTION—POTSDAM SQUARE

Von Wildhagen, von Falkenhausen, Schulze, Lehmann, Willy, Paul, newspaper carriers, people of Berlin.

Potsdam Square. Extra editions are distributed among the groups discussing the eventuality of a revolution.

(At the beginning of November 1918, the revolutionary crisis had reached its high point in Germany. On 1 October, the national conference of the Spartacists had met in Gotha and set up a program of action for revolutionary rebellion against the . . . war. At the end of October, the German Front broke up. At the same time, Karl Liebknecht and other leaders of the Spartacus Union had to be released from prison as the result of growing public pressure. The actual revolution began with the sailors' mutiny in Kiel on 4 November 1918. The first soldiers' council resulted from this mutiny. The revolt was immediately taken up by groups all over Germany. . . .)

SCENE 13. THE 9TH OF NOVEMBER—IN THE PALACE OF THE IMPERIAL CHANCELLOR

Ebert, Scheidemann, Bauer, Landsberg, Noske. On the street. The demonstrating proletariat, Liebknecht.

Ebert, Scheidemann, Bauer, and Landsberg meet in council in the palace of the imperial chancellor on 9 November 1918. Masses of people march on the streets outside the palace, among them sailors with red flags and guns. Leading the demonstration is Liebknecht, who has just been released from prison. First Scheidemann speaks, then Liebknecht.

(On 7 November announcements were hung on every corner in Berlin forbidding the formation of workers' and soldiers' councils. Simultaneously, all military units within the city were placed on emergency alert. On 8 November the Spartacus Union and the executive committee of the now-outlawed workers' and soldiers' councils called on the workers of Berlin to join in the general strike set for 9 November. The revolt in Berlin began. Even as late as that morning, the leadership of the SPD had attempted to save the monarchy, to prevent the formation of councils, and to keep the workers in the workplaces. Finally, as the workers and the rebelling soldiers took over the streets, the right-wing leadership of the SPD tried to install itself at the head of the movement and to place the councils under their influence. Together with the central-based leaders of the USPD (Independent Party), they negotiated a government, which was unfriendly to the workers. In the meantime, massive numbers of workers joined by the majority of the revolting soldiers were demonstrating in the heart of the capital city. By about noon, the police headquarters, the central telegraph office, the Reichstag, and the city hall were in the hands of the revolutionaries. In a declaration from the steps of the imperial palace, Karl Liebknecht proclaimed a socialist republic. Simultaneously, Philipp Scheidemann proclaimed the "Free German Republic" in order to prevent the masses from following Liebknecht's call.)

SCENE 14. IMPERIAL CHANCELLERY— LANDSBERG'S WORKROOM—5 DECEMBER

Landsberg, Petty Officer Krebs.

Landsberg briefs Petty Officer Krebs: "A Spartacus demonstration has been planned on Chaussee

Street. There will be a shot from the crowd and that will be your sign to commence firing. Use machine guns and fire upon the crowd."

SCENE 15. CHAUSSEE STREET—6 DECEMBER

Spartacus demonstration, the troops called "Rotherz" ("Red-Heart").

The demonstration on Chaussee Street. A shot is fired from the crowd, whereupon soldiers fire into the crowd. 6 December 1918.

(Counterrevolutionary troops attempted their first coup on this day. They attacked a workers' demonstration and fired machine guns at them. Sixteen workers were killed. The counterrevolutionaries attempted to arrest the executive committee of the workers' and soldiers' councils, and to proclaim Ebert president. Additional troops occupied the offices of the *Rote Fahne*, "Red Flag"—the newspaper of the Spartacus Union. The printing facilities were destroyed as troops searched the premises for Karl Liebknecht. The coup was put down by revolutionary workers and sailors from the revolutionary navy. As a result, the right-wing SPD leadership called up more troops to Berlin under the command of General Lequis.)

SCENE 16. *DIE ROTE FAHNE* EDITOR'S OFFICE

Liebknecht, Rosa Luxemburg, Karl Radek, Franz, Willy, one Printer, one Worker.

Liebknecht, Rosa Luxemburg, and Radek meet in the editor's office of the *Rote Fahne* to decide what steps they must take.

(From 16 to 21 December, the first Congress of the National Councils was in session in Berlin. The Spartacus Union had neglected to take part in the preparations for the election of delegates. As a result, the majority of the congress voted to summon a national convention to create a new constitution rather than to proclaim the workers' and soldiers' councils as the highest instrument of

power in the revolutionary dictatorship. The result was that the councils practically eliminated themselves. The most important result of the November Revolution was the founding of the KPD during the national conference of the Spartacus Union held from 30 December 1918 to 1 January 1919. Scene 16 of this revue seems to have dealt with the particulars of these two events.)

SCENE 17. IMPERIAL CHANCELLERY— EBERT'S WORKROOM—9 JANUARY 1919

Ebert, Scheidemann, Braun, Landsberg.

Ebert, Scheidemann, Landsberg take counsel, as well, with regard to what is to be done, since Noske has promised to send the military. 9 January 1919.

(At the beginning of January 1919, the Ebert government made preparations for the final submission of the revolutionary movement. The battles that took place in Berlin in January were orchestrated by Ebert's forces. Emil Eichhorn, the police president of Berlin, who belonged to the left wing of the USPD, was removed from office by the government on 4 January. In his place, the right-wing Social Democrat, Eugen Ernst, was to take office in order to turn the police back into a dependable instrument of reaction and to guarantee that the proletariat should be disarmed. The Berlin workers responded to a joint call from the revolutionary leaders, the USPD, and the KPD asking them to protest this arbitrary measure. Mass demonstrations took place in the heart of Berlin on 5 and 6 January. The buildings of the SPD newspaper Vorwärts and of several middle-class newspapers were occupied on the spur of the moment. The reactionary forces decided the time had come to deal the fatal blow against the revolutionary proletariat. The government assembled troops and volunteer forces in Berlin. The Social Democrat Gustav Noske was ordered to execute the bloody suppression of the resisting workers.)

SCENE 18. IN ALEXANDER SQUARE

Franz, Willy, Paul, armed workers.

Armed workers wait in Alexander Square to learn the results of consultations by their leaders.

(The leadership of Berlin's USPD and of the revolutionary shop stewards proved incapable of establishing clear leadership goals, and they failed to organize the throngs pressing them for action. On the evening of 5 January a Revolution Committee had been formed by representatives from the USPD, the shop stewards, the revolutionary navy, the rail workers, the Berlin garrison, and the KPD. The representatives from the KPD were none other than Karl Liebknecht and Wilhelm Pieck. In endless discussions Liebknecht and Pieck attempted to arrive at clear decisions and to execute decisive action. The KPD, which had only been established itself some days earlier, had neither the organizational strength nor the political experience at this point to lead the revolutionary activities. Thus, the counterrevolutionaries were successful in building up their forces while the armed workers and soldiers steadfastly waited for the command to fire or wasted their meager energy on isolated actions.)

SCENE 19. SESSION OF THE "REVOLUTION COMMITTEE"—11 JANUARY

Rosa Luxemburg, Liebknecht, Ledebour. The revolutionary shop stewards. The Independents.

(Under the influence of the central-based leadership of the USPD, the "Revolution Committee" declared itself ready to negotiate with the Ebert-Scheidemann government. Karl Liebknecht and Wilhelm Pieck protested against this decision. The government had proposed negotiations in order to win time to call up volunteers from Pomerania and East Prussia. These negotiations had a paralyzing and disorienting effect on the revolting workers. The KPD withdrew its representatives from the committee. The Party immediately placed itself at the front of the battle.)

SCENE 20. THE STORMING OF THE POLICE HEADQUARTERS

Willy, Franz—voices.

Storming of the police headquarters. A room in the headquarters, where Spartacus holds out and from which it defends itself. Soldiers storm into the room and shoot the defenders.

(On the morning of 12 January 1919 the police headquarters, the last bastion of the January freedom fighters, was taken by Noske's troops.)

SCENE 21. THE LAST EVENING—15 JANUARY

Rosa Luxemburg, Karl Liebknecht, members of a civil defense corps.

Rosa Luxemburg and Karl Liebknecht are arrested.

(A high price had been offered as a reward for the arrest of Rosa Luxemburg and Karl Liebknecht. The press—including the Social Democratic *Vorwärts*—openly demanded their murder. On 15 January 1919, Rosa Luxemburg and Karl Liebknecht were arrested in an off-limits sector and taken by members of the Garde-Kavallerie defense corps to the Eden Hotel.)

SCENE 22. RECEPTION HALL IN THE EDEN HOTEL—ON THE SAME EVENING

White guards, Hunter Runge, von Pflugk-Hartung—Rosa Luxemburg, Liebknecht.

Reception hall of the Eden Hotel. Hunter Runge is briefed by a lieutenant captain. It is important to the government that Liebknecht and R. Luxemburg be put to death. Runge is instructed to take the two of them by car through the zoological garden. At the lake, he was to pretend he had had a breakdown, to have the two of them get out of the car, and then to shoot them "while attempting to escape."

(Karl Liebknecht was in fact murdered in this fashion. Rosa Luxemburg, who had passed out in the car as the result of brutal beatings by her civil guard captors, was shot in the car. Her corpse was thrown into a canal.)

SCENE 23. ZOOLOGICAL GARDEN—ON THE EDGE OF NEUSEE

Two passersby—voices, Runge, Pflugk-Hartung, Liebknecht.

The car stops on the edge of the lake. Liebknecht gets out of the car, takes two steps and is shot down.

CONCLUDING SCENE

Proletariat demonstration. Liebknecht lives!

Red Front revolutionaries march onto the stage and take position with approximately 50 men and eight flags.

END

"The Documentary Play"
(from *The Political Theatre* [1929] translated by Hugh Rorrison)

The first production in which the text and staging were based solely on political documents was *In Spite of Everything!* (Grosses Schauspielhaus, 12 July 1925).

The play grew out of a mammoth historical revue I was to put on in the spring of that year for the Workers' Cultural Union at a midsummer festival in the Gosen Hills [on the southern outskirts of Berlin—tr.]. The revue—I commissioned Gasbarra to put the text together—was to show briefly the revolutionary highlights of the history of mankind from the Spartacus rebellion to the Russian Revolution, and to be a summary in instructive scenes of the whole development of historical materialism. We planned on a grand scale. There were to be 2000 participants; twenty gigantic spotlights were to light up the natural arena, massive symbolic props would illustrate the separate passages. (A sixty-five-foot battleship would represent British Imperialism.) I had moved nearby to Schmöckwitz to be able to keep a con-

stant eye on the work. The scenario had been worked out and the general outline of the music, again by Edmund Meisel, was ready, when the Cultural Union, prompted by Ernst Niekisch (who is, after several changes of loyalty, currently a pioneer of national "socialism"), suddenly had political reservations. While negotiations were still in progress, the German Communist Party asked us to put on a performance in the Grosses Schauspielhaus for their Berlin Conference. The form and content of the thing had not been determined, but were to be worked out at a meeting at the Central Office the next day. The idea of having this performance stemmed from Ernst Torgler, a Communist member of the Reichstag, and an old friend of ours from the days of the *Red Revue*.

I talked with Gasbarra about what we should do. To transfer our show from the Gosen Hills to the Grosses Schauspielhaus was not feasible. On the other hand, we had gotten so used to thinking on a vast historical scale during the weeks of work on our revue that the idea of using a ready-made play seemed unsatisfactory. Gasbarra suggested that we should take an extract from what we had already put together, perhaps turn the period between the outbreak of war and the murder of Liebknecht and Rosa Luxemburg into a separate revue. The revue took as its title Liebknecht's phrase "In spite of everything" to show that the social revolution continued to take place, even after the terrible disaster of 1919.* The plan caused head-shaking among senior party officials at the meeting, because we intended to have figures like Liebknecht and Rosa Luxemburg portrayed on the stage. Many felt that our plan to include members of the government in the revue (Ebert, Noske, Scheidemann, Landsberg, etc.) was dangerous. They finally consented, because nobody came up with a better suggestion, but remained skeptical—all the more so since we had barely three weeks left till the day of the performance.

The show was a collective effort. The separate tasks of writer, director, musical director, designer and actor constantly overlapped. The scenery was

---

Ed. note: The assassination of Liebknecht and Luxemburg led to the collapse of the Communist revolutionary movement in Germany.

built and the music composed as we wrote the script, and the script itself emerged gradually as the director worked with the group. Different scenes were put together simultaneously in different parts of the theater, sometimes even before a definite script had been worked out. Film was to be combined organically with live action on the stage for the first time. (As planned, but not carried out in *Flags*.)*

The way I combined apparently contrasting art forms features prominently in the critics' discussions and in the general public's appraisal of my work. For my part, I did not consider this aspect of the thing so important. The technique has been rejected out of hand, or praised to the skies, but rarely accurately appraised. The use of film clips followed along the same lines as the use of projections in *Flags*. (Not to mention the fact that the general idea of transforming the stage with film goes back to my time in Königsberg, though the stress then was still on the decorative possibilities.) All I did was to extend and refine the means; the aim stayed the same.

Later it was often maintained that I got the idea from the Russians. In fact, I was quite ignorant of what was happening on the Soviet stage at this time—very little news about performances and so on came through to us. Even afterwards I never heard that the Russians had employed film with the same function I had had in mind. In any case, the question of priority is irrelevant. It would merely prove that this was no superficial game with technical effects, but a new, emergent form of theater based on the philosophy of historical materialism which we shared. After all, what do I consider the essential point of my whole work? Not the propagation of a view of life through formal clichés and billboard slogans, but the presentation of solid proof that our philosophy and all that can be deduced from it is the one and only valid approach for our time. You can make all sorts of assertions, but repeating assertions does not make them more true or effective. Conclusive proof can be based only on scientific analysis of the material. This I can only do, in the language

of the stage, if I can get beyond scenes from life, beyond the purely individual aspect of the characters and the fortuitous nature of their fates. And the way to do this is to show the link between events on the stage and the great forces active in history. It is not by chance that the factual substance becomes the main thing in each play. It is only from the facts themselves that the constraints and the constant mechanisms of life emerge, giving a deeper meaning to our private fates. For this I need some means of showing how human-superhuman factors interact with classes or individuals. One of the means was film. But it was no more than a means, and could be replaced tomorrow by some better means.

The film used in *In Spite of Everything!* was documentary. From the archives of the Reich which were made available to us by one of our contacts, we used authentic shots of the war, of the demobilization, of a parade of all the crowned heads of Europe, and the like. These shots brutally demonstrated the horror of war: flame thrower attacks, piles of mutilated bodies, burning cities; war films had not yet come into "fashion," so these pictures were bound to have a more striking impact on the masses of the proletariat than a hundred lectures. I spread the film out through the whole play, and where that was not enough I projected stills.

For the basic stage I had a so-called "Praktikabel" built, a terraced structure of irregular shape with a raked platform on one side and steps and levels on the other. This structure stood on a revolving stage. I built the various acting areas into terraces, niches and corridors. In this way the overall structure of the scenes was unified and the play could flow uninterrupted, like a single current sweeping everything along with it.

The abandonment of the decorative set was taken a stage further than in *Flags*. The predominant principle was that of a purely practical acting structure to support, clarify and express the action. Freestanding structures, a self-contained world on the revolving stage, put an end to the peep-show world of the bourgeois theater. They can also be set up in the open. The squared stage area is merely an irritating limitation.

The whole performance was a montage of authentic speeches, essays, newspaper cuttings, ap-

---

Ed. note: Piscator directed Paquet's *Flags* at the Volksbühne in 1924.

peals, pamphlets, photographs, and film of the War and the Revolution, of historical persons and scenes. And all this was in the Grosses Schauspielhaus that Max Reinhardt had once used to stage classical (bourgeois) theater. He, too, probably sensed that the masses had to be reached—but he came to them from the other side with foreign wares. *Lysistrata, Hamlet,* and even *Florian Geyer* and *Danton's Death* were no more than circus performances, blown up and coarsened. All Reinhardt did was to inflate the form. Actual involvement of the masses in the audience was not a conscious part of his program, and never amounted to more than a few ingenious touches from the director.

Nor did Karlheinz Martin's use of "Expressionist movement" achieve this, either with classical drama or with *The Machine-Wreckers* (*Die Maschinenstürmer*)—it worked only in *The Weavers.** In our case arena and stage were fused into one. In this there was one decisive factor: Beye had organized block bookings for the trade unions that summer. Class-conscious workers were sitting out front, and the storm broke. I had always been aware that we were not filling the house, and had wondered how we could actually reach this mass audience. Now I had them in my hand—and even today I still see that as the only real possibility for mass theater in Berlin.

For the first time we were confronted with the absolute reality we knew from experience. And it had exactly the same moments of tension and dramatic climaxes as literary drama, and the same strong emotional impact. Provided, of course, that it was a political reality ("political" in the original sense: "being of general concern").

Ed. note (Rorrison): The Machine-Wreckers by Ernst Toller was produced at the Grosses Schauspielhaus (30 June 1922) by Karlheinz Martin. It was based on Cobbett and the Luddite Movement in England. The set was a huge machine with pistons, flywheels, drive shafts and steam vents, devised by John Heartfield. The workers posed and gesticulated in front of this monster. Hauptmann's *The Weavers* is set in Silesia, and the separation of Upper Silesia from Germany was being debated at the time of Martin's production (20 June 1921), so its audience impact was partly political.

I must admit that I myself was tense with apprehension as that evening approached. The tension was twofold: How would the interacting and interdependent elements onstage actually work, and would the effect that I was after come off to any degree?

The dress rehearsal was utter chaos. Two hundred people ran around shouting at one another. Meisel, whom we had just converted to Negro music, was conducting a loud, incomprehensible, fiendish concert with a twenty-man band, Gasbarra kept popping up with new scenes (until I put him in charge of the projectors), Heartfield stuck out his jaw and began to paint every single prop brown from top to bottom, none of the film clips came in on cue, the actors did not know where they were supposed to be half the time, and I myself began to be overwhelmed by the masses of material that still had to be fitted in. People sitting out in the auditorium during that rehearsal went home at 3:00 A.M. with no idea of what had happened on the stage. Even the scenes that were ready no longer pleased us. One thing was missing—the public.

On opening night there were thousands in the Grosses Schauspielhaus. Every seat was taken; steps, aisles, entrances were full to bursting. The living masses were filled from the outset with wild excitement at being there to watch, and you could feel an incredible, willing receptivity out in the audience that you get only with the proletariat.

But this inner willingness quickly turned into active participation: The masses took over the direction. The people who filled the house had for the most part been actively involved in the period, and what we were showing them was in a true sense their own fate, their own tragedy being acted out before their eyes. Theater had become reality, and soon it was not a case of the stage confronting the audience, but one big assembly, one big battlefield, one massive demonstration. It was this unity that proved that evening that political theater could be effective agitation.

The drastic effect of using film clips showed beyond any theoretical consideration that they were not only right for presenting political and social mechanisms, that is, from the point of view of content, but also in a higher sense, right from the formal point of view. The experience we had had with *Flags* repeated itself. The momentary surprise when we changed from live scenes to film was very effective. But the dramatic tension that live scene and film clip derived from one another was even stronger. They interacted and built up each other's power, and at intervals the action attained a *furioso* that I have seldom experienced in theater. For example, when the Social Democratic vote on War Loans (live) was followed by film showing the first dead, it not only made the political nature of the procedure clear, but also produced a shattering human effect, became art, in fact. What emerged was that the most effective political propaganda lay along the same lines as the highest artistic form:

> Grosses Schauspielhaus . . . Main Scene: A plenary session of the wartime Reichstag. . . . Text from the shorthand minutes of the Reichstag. I happened to have been in Berlin on holiday during that session and had witnessed it all. Here Bethmann-Hollweg (in his general's uniform) was on his feet once more, thanking God for endowing our fields so fruitfully again that year. At the end of the session, the Members fought over single bread coupons. The thousands in the theater laugh, shout in contempt, stamp their feet, wave threatening fists. At another point a soldier from the pioneer corps (standing below the rostrum) in shabby battledress shouts down the speaker—Karl Liebknecht. Then we see Liebknecht in the streets distributing pamphlets and speaking against the war. He is arrested, and as the mob lets him be taken away without protest, cries of anguish and self-accusation are heard in the audience.
> —From the *Frankfurter Zeitung,* 1 April 1929 ("How It Began")

Rote Fahne, 14 July 1925: [See complete review following text.]

Jacob Altmeier in the *Frankfurter Zeitung:* "And that was the overall impression it left. With all its exaggeration and tendentiousness, one no longer stepped uncomprehending into the street that night. Jessner might work wonders with *The Death of Wallenstein* or *The Prince of Homburg,* and Reinhardt might spread heaven at our feet with *Twelfth Night,* or with Elisabeth Bergner, and yet when you stepped out into the city after the show, it was a jungle and you were lost. . . . But after a revue like this you felt as if you had had a bath. You had new strength. You could swim and

row in the streets. Traffic and lights, the roar and the machines all made sense."

Neue Berliner 12 Uhr: "For the opening of the Communist Party Conference, workers and actors under the guidance of E. P. are staging dramatized world history in the Grosses Schauspielhaus. Scenes of war and revolution crammed together with a kind of wild power, with a gaping, tattered message, but with an almost unexpectedly moving personal effect, at least when bald, factual events were being shown. Political convictions . . . their fanatical, touching and sacred expression merges to produce something with climaxes which in some mysterious way achieve the same visible result as high dramatic art."

Welt am Abend, 17 July 1925: "And yet it seems to us that it is not the intention but the effect that makes art. Here it must be said that this revue got across to its public and produced dramatic climaxes such as we rarely see, and then usually only in works of dramatic genius."

After the second evening had drawn such a flood of people that hundreds could not get in, I tried to get them to keep the show going for at least fourteen days, if only to cover our costs. And Torgler supported this energetically. Thousands were being spent on propaganda posters which were by now so familiar to people that they had no effect. But the authorities were afraid to take the risk, and so for the umpteenth time it was my bitter experience, in spite of success and approval, in spite of massive audience support that any bourgeois theater might have envied, that even this stage in the development of the political theater achieved no real outward progress.

—Erwin Piscator

Clippings from *Die Rote Fahne*

"IN SPITE OF EVERYTHING!: Behind the Scenes in the Schauspielhaus."

Evening rehearsal in the Grosses Schauspielhaus (Mainstage, Playhouse Theater, Berlin). The final preparations for Sunday. Hammers, shouting, lots of running about. People rehearsing everywhere: in the halls, in the lobby. Floodlights blind you when you walk into the main hall. Suddenly, from far away come strains of singing: the "International." Cheers come closer. "Take it from the top" exclaims Piscator, who is working on the stage, surrounded by an entire staff of co-workers. "I've seen it coming, Fritz; this is the collapse," whines *Scheidemann.* "Courage, courage," soothes *Ebert,* who for the time being is still a likable young actor. "We'll tame the masses." Aha: 9 November. Palace of the Imperial Chancellor. Now, proletarian multitudes flood the stage from both sides. "Long live the Revolution!" "Hurrah for the Republic!" cry the voices. It looks spectacular. But the director is hard to please. The beginning scene must be rehearsed again, and again, and again until it works. Only then does Ebert get a chance to hold his speech in which he divulges his intention to "tame" the masses with "unity."

The masses are somewhat tired. And yet it shoots through everyone like an electric shock when *Liebknecht* storms in at the head of his loyal followers. Alone the name, Liebknecht, has a strong effect. It is as if the whole room were under a spell as his first words are heard loud and clear in the deathly still room: "Workers! Soldiers! A thousand years of servitude is at an end!" The spirit of 9 November; the voice of the Revolution. The director is the only one who doesn't allow himself to be moved by the performance. Every single word must be worked through, repeated, discussed with regard to its political significance. Sometimes, at such moments, the rehearsal turns into a political debate. To many of the participants, the real magnitude of the treachery of the Ebert-Scheidemann-Landsberg government only begins to become clear as the result of this intense engagement with the material. But let's continue! The entire first part including the newsreel, from the beginning of the war on, has to be worked through today. So, let's take it once again from the top. "Clear the stage!"

And then the events roll by, which have been forgotten already by so many: The Reichstag decision of the SPD faction on 24 July: against the war! The Reichstag decision on 2 August: in fa-

vor of the war. In between we see Wilhelm, promising "not to give in again," signing the mobilization act. Following *Liebknecht's speech* to the war tribunal, comes the war newsreel out of some dark, faraway place, as though it were echoing from behind the walls of a prison.

These are probably the most impressive images that had ever been shown on screen: authentic footage of the slaughter of the world war, recalling the entire gruesome barbarism of those days. People being pulverized in the jaws of the "creeping barrage of gun fire" as they fled the tongues of fire leaping out from the giant flame throwers! This is propaganda! The glorious days of August, which called up the "heroes" to that "summer excursion," come back to haunt us. This assemblage of film and dramatic scenes, which had never before been brought together with such effect, results in extraordinary heights and contrasts of emotion.

The revolutionary proletariat can be proud of the fact that it has issued such a new impulse while the bourgeois theater gets bogged down and fails. And search as we may, where can we find any other theater in which this performance could take place? This is no longer art in any middle-class meaning of the word. This is political agitation! There can be no denying, that this performance represents a giant step forward for "political theater" as revolutionary propaganda.

In the meantime it is half past midnight. A couple hours of sleep. Tomorrow morning at 9:30 there's another rehearsal, with orchestra. And so it goes, day after day. Everyone gives his best effort to the cause. There were lots of difficulties to be overcome in the short rehearsal period. Perhaps the most difficult was the timid hesitancy of the party members to take part in the crowd scenes. This is where change must take place. Our theater teaches people how to work in a collective. We should never again have to pay people because our own party members won't cooperate. And so, "in spite of everything!" has become the battle cry here, too!

And what a worthy performance: worthy of the occasion and worthy of the great names Liebknecht and Luxemburg.

—(*Rote Fahne,* 11 July 1925)

• • •

"PROLETARIAN AGITATION THEATER: The Performance in the Grosses Schauspielhaus,"

There was something corruptive about using all the facilities of a large stage trying to create proletarian agitation theater, trying to make *political agitation* lively and effective in a polemical performance.

Did it succeed? We are optimistic and say: Yes, it succeeded in doing something which otherwise has eluded us until now. Workers have made the idea of their own theater come true in an attempt that allows us all to hope we will experience greater and more effective theater very soon, staged by and for the proletariat, here in Germany.

What is it that the Berlin workers undertook in their presentation on the stage of the Grosses Schauspielhaus when they greeted the delegates at the opening of the 10th Party Conference of the KPD? In a manner of speaking, they attempted to bring their own most recent past to life. Truly, a great subject, full of dramatic effect. History captured in sparkling brilliance recapitulated in the highest dramatic tension using the most modern technical resources of the theater. In no fewer than 23 scenes, which the revolving stage of the Grosses Schauspielhaus made possible, the suffering and battles of the Berlin workers since 1914 rolled along in all their vitality before the eyes of the viewers, warning and frightening them, admonishing and firing them up.

The first scenes: "Berlin awaits the war, Potsdam Square"—"Meeting of the Social Democratic Reichstag Faction on 25 July 1914"—"In the imperial palace in Berlin on 1 August 1914." And on and on. The decisive meeting of the Social Democratic Reichstag Faction during which the SPD approves the war credits on 2 December: Landsberg and Liebknecht, *Scheidemann* and *Ebert* right there on stage. Then: "In a Berlin grenade factory." This scene was followed by "The First of May at Potsdam Square: Liebknecht speaks and is arrested."—"Liebknecht stands trial before the war tribunal on 23 August 1916." Scene eleven: "The munitions workers' strike of 1918—30 January—in Treptower Park." . . .

Meanwhile, let us halt for a moment and consider the scene in the theater itself. It often turned into a tribunal. The masses—the tribunal— shoulder to shoulder, thousands upon thousands filling up the Grosses Schauspielhaus clear to the ceiling, feverish at certain moments. Still it was too "disciplined," to openly jump in and take part. For example, when *Scheidemann* summarized, Landsberg dictated, and *Ebert* "embodied" the "completed" disposition, the decision of the party leaders, when he made history before the tribunal on the stage and in the auditorium. These were dramatic moments containing unheard of possibilities for intensifying the mood. They should have brought the masses to a bursting explosion. They could have released a unified scream of embitterment and rage. It just didn't come to that. Was that the fault of the actors, or of this history which has yet to be staged by a proletariat poet? Was it the fault of the tribunal? The masses didn't jump in when Liebknecht was arrested after his fiery speech; it never came to this reaction, onstage nor in the auditorium. The masses remained silent. . . .

But that, of course, would have been fiction. Because back then the masses really were "silent." But what about today?

And then it continued. "Berlin awaits the revolution." . . . Aha! Now everyone became a little more alert, didn't they? And it was certainly high time! Then "9 November in the Imperial Chancellor's Palace." Once again the "incarnated ones," the ones who "freed the people." That disgusting Noske—played with such gentility. (Comrade Piscator: Give Noske a kick. He needs to be fleshed out; please refrain from being "all too historical." You must whisper in Landsberg's ear: You're doing a good job, but even in your mask not so good as your role model then and/or now. And Scheidemann, Comrade Piscator, is just a little bit too melancholy, too stiff. He's really got to be much more versatile, more cunning, the fox.)

Sixteenth scene: "Liebknecht in the editor's office of *Rote Fahne*." Friends, a couple of words about *Liebknecht* and *Luxemburg*. How is Liebknecht portrayed? Surely the best of all: sincerely, with warmth. But Karl was more than this! You're doing a good job. But surely you must have heard Karl speak? Maybe you belonged to the throngs who always followed him around. You've got to put more into your Karl.

On Tuesday, at the second performance, you must embrace this great responsibility, Comrade: Karl wasn't just the product of a noble, sincere interior. He was a hurricane, a fireball, a spirit, a whit, a fury, a fist. Karl, you will, made people shake in his presence, their throats got dry, their tongues became heavy. People got all worked up, they became heated, all of a sudden, when Karl appeared on the scene. Your Karl, just doesn't make them shake, Comrade. . . . A small correction, also for the actress playing Rosa. Rosa was never so "loud," Comrade. She was loud precisely because of her "stillness." She was loud by virtue of the effectiveness of her arguments during the conferences of the editors and everywhere else; she was loud in her calmness, in her circumspection. She never shouted. Rosa never shouted. It was also the other way around: Karl didn't "instruct" Rosa. These are all incidental remarks, Friends, to be understood as constructive criticism. You play your roles well, but you ought to play them even better, give it even more. You can do it! Because, after all, it's for *our* cause.

As a whole: The *combination* of film and theater was superb. *John Heartfield* had a hand in this combination; there is no one better. He also got the most out of the transitions on the stage. But the film itself was the "main event." This war film gave the play its "mood": the illustration, the directness of it, precisely that which one cannot portray just on a revolving stage. The film was the most stimulating element; it stirred us all up, deep down inside. The film was the capstone, it was absolutely necessary. Hopefully, we will see this newsreel again very soon "on its own." It is a powerful propaganda instrument, by itself in its entirety, more than just in these short excerpts.

The music was good, too. Edmund Meisel was at his best. He worked perfectly with the director, in the caricatures, in the ensemble. "The story" itself was to blame for the fact that he had to orchestrate so many "Fatherland Melodies." Maybe this is where the problem lies, Comrade Director. You are simply too true to history. There needs to be more rumbling and grumbling from the masses *right from the start*. For example, I would simply let Wilhelm be hissed and shouted down. Unashamedly. The monarchy! And, of course, Ebert and Scheidemann: These two should get even more rotten tomatoes dumped on their heads. As for the finale, there ought to be more excitement among the masses on the stage. You did a good job, but you've got to reach a higher pitch of excitement in the final scene, Worker Actors: a little more energy, more force. Don't play up the "tragic" conclusions so much. The cries of "Trotz alledem!" rising out of the tragic must be much stronger, more emphatic; they have to ring out! Don't be so literal; there's no reason to get so hung up about "how it was."

It was grand seeing the march of the proletariat as the final apotheosis; the march of the Spartacus Youth, the march of the "Red Front" on the stage. This panorama symbolizes the battle lying ahead of us in the immediate future.

The performance in the Grosses Schauspielhaus has suddenly brought the theoretical discussions about "proletarian theater" and art miles closer to all of us in a practical manner. We extend our best wishes to the Berlin Organization and to the initiators of this cause, Comrades Ernst Torgler and Erwin Piscator.

— Otto Steinicke (*Rote Fahne*, 14 July 1925)

Arthur Arent

ETHIOPIA

1936

Ethiopia received a single performance—an open rehearsal—on 24 January 1936 at the Biltmore Theatre in New York. No director was credited. The cast was drawn from actors employed by the Federal Theatre Project, including members of an African opera company stranded in America. (Whether or not they were Ethiopian is unknown.) Elmer Rice (*Minority Report*, 357) claimed that "all of the speeches used in *Ethiopia* were taken verbatim from dependable news sources without editing or comment, all the factual material was presented objectively, without caricature or innuendo." Source-checking generally corroborates this assertion. For the source of the information supplied below in editorial notes, see Introduction, note 47, page xxiii.

SCENE 1

Teletype:
   WALWAL, ETHIOPIA, DEC. 5, 1934. . . . ITAL-IANS, ETHIOPIANS. CLASH NEAR SOMALILAND FRONTIER:

Ethiopian encampment at Walwal, flat terrain. It is the midday rest, and soldiers in their white shammas are sprawled on the ground, eating, drinking, etc. A few musical instruments are seen on the ground.
   Soon the first few notes of a native song are heard, vague at first, then growing clearer as one instrument after another takes it up. It is a sad, keening sort of air. The song mounts and soon a single plaintive voice is heard. The harmony is picked up by all, pianissimo. Sharply the song ends, and without pause the players start a livelier tune. A soldier starts to dance. The song rises, the tumult increases.
   At its very apex a sudden shot is heard. All stop. The music dies. More shots, nearer and then the sharp rat-a-tat-tat of a machine gun. Pandemonium. The machine gun dies and in its place is heard the regular beat of rifle fire.

SCENE 2*

Teletype:
   GENEVA, SWITZERLAND. . . . LEAGUE OF NATIONS RECEIVES OFFICIAL GOVERNMENT STATEMENTS:

A long table. Various members of the League formally attired. At the head of the table stands the CHAIRMAN. *He holds a sheaf of telegrams. His gavel has carried the beat without a break from Scene 1.*

———

Ed. note: The Ethiopian statement is drawn from telegrams sent to the League on 14, 18 and 24 December 1934. Sir John Simon, British foreign secretary, worked secretly to get Italy to agree to arbitration on the Ethiopian complaint and thereby forestalled League action.

CHAIRMAN: Gentlemen, the official Ethiopian statement to the League is as follows: Addis Ababa, Dec. 20, 1934. Italian aggression occurred at Walwal and Gerlogubi yesterday. The Walwal region is Ethiopian territory which Italian troops have occupied illegally for years. The situation is increasingly serious.

The members talk among themselves excitedly; as he resumes there is a hush.

CHAIRMAN: The official Italian statement: It is denied in the most emphatic terms that our troops have advanced into Ethiopian territory. The town of Walwal has been garrisoned by Italian troops for years. The Ethiopians have committed an act of flagrant aggression!

Commotion. CHAIRMAN has to pound gavel.

CHAIRMAN: I have here, in addition, the statements from certain other member-nations of the League Council. (*Reads.*) London, England. As the disputed ownership of the wells in the region of Walwal had previously given rise to local unrest, I had instructed the British representatives at Rome and Addis Ababa, prior to the present incident, to recommend the desirability of early demarcation of the frontier.... Signed, Sir John Simon. (*Before the members have a chance to react he continues.*) Paris. France is determined that Ethiopia shall get a fair hearing and stands pledged with Great Britain and Italy to respect the territorial rights of King Haile Selassie's domain. Moscow, USSR. It is well known that ancient Rome treated her victims as an inferior race, as barbarians, whose destiny it was to be eternally enslaved to the superior race, TO ROME! But what came of it? The result was that the barbarians united against a common enemy, against Rome, and overthrew it!

The members' voices rise in a terrific clamor as the lights fade.

SCENE 3

Teletype:
GERLOGUBI BOMBED—WOMEN AND CHILDREN SLAIN, CHARGES KING OF KINGS:

The corner of a mud hut at Gerlogubi. Before it are seated Ethiopian charwomen washing corn in huge gourds. Suddenly the terrific roar of a bomb is heard nearby. Also a plane. Another blast. The women are panic-stricken, race about madly. More bombs. Two women fall, wounded. The bombing continues. Blackout.

SCENE 4*

Teletype:
ADDIS ABABA, ETHIOPIA.... HAILE SELASSIE DEFIES IL DUCE:

Lights up on HAILE SELASSIE seated at desk. His manner is calm, scholarly.

SELASSIE: As a sovereign state recognized by the League of Nations ours is the right to do anything we please in our own territory, of which Walwal is a part. We intend to follow the example of our fathers in safeguarding the integrity of this territory. Ethiopia will never accept proposals capable of injuring her liberty, and to this end we place our hope especially in England and France. We will make no concessions to Italy! It is not for Ethiopia to institute the practice of offering bribes in order to induce potential aggressors to refrain from making war. With this in mind I saw it is far better to die on the field of battle, a free man, than to live as a slave!

Blackout.

Teletype:
ROME, ITALY.... IL DUCE "MUST PROCEED WITH MILITARY MEASURES":

Ed note: Haile Selassie's speech is drawn from his statement of 19 July 1935. Foreign Secretary Hoare's speech to the House of Commons was given 11 July. (Hoare had been appointed to replace Simon by the new Prime Minister, Stanley Baldwin, in June.) Secretary of State Hull's statement is from a press conference 11 September. The speech attributed to Mussolini was actually delivered by Aloisi, Italian representative to the League of Nations, to the League Council on 4 September—though Aloisi was clearly voicing Mussolini's will. League discussions continued through 17 September.

Lights up on MUSSOLINI *standing behind desk. He wears the uniform of a corporal of the Fascist Militia. Down left stand three officers in full uniform (army, navy, air force) and two members of his civil cabinet.*

MUSSOLINI: Italy can and will present a whole library of documents and photographs bearing out our claims against Ethiopia. . . . But the accelerated pace of Ethiopian military preparations renders it necessary for us to proceed with further measures of a military character. We might have reached an agreement if certain European nations had not worked against us. . . . But we shall go forward until we have founded a Fascist Empire! England may storm and threaten, but we will achieve our purpose despite her! The road before us has been traced out. It is the one road, the right road, the only road! Italy is for peace, I am for peace, BUT WHAT I HAVE STARTED I WILL FINISH!

Blackout.

Teletype:
LONDON, ENGLAND. . . . SIR SAMUEL HOARE EXPLAINS BRITISH STAND:

Light up on HOARE, *standing behind the small wooden railing of the House of Commons.*

HOARE: England stands for peace. She will never abandon any reasonable chance that may offer itself for helping to prevent a disastrous war. For this we have no ulterior motive, but a motive of peaceful settlement. Are the facts that Italy needs expansion and that complaints have been made against the Ethiopian government sufficient cause for plunging into war? I THINK MUCH LESS OF WHAT THE LEAGUE OF NATIONS HAS OR HAS NOT DONE IN THE PAST THAN WHAT IT MAY DO IN THE FUTURE IF IT IS GIVEN A CHANCE!

Blackout.

Teletype:
PARIS, FRANCE. . . . PREMIER PIERRE LAVAL SPEAKS TO DEPUTIES:

Light up on LAVAL.

LAVAL: I speak in the name of France, which does not follow any egotistical ends. France has her legitimate desires for protection, for security, but she intends to undertake her part in the necessary work of reconciling the differences of these two nations.

Blackout.

Teletype:
WASHINGTON, D.C. . . . SECRETARY HULL WARNS AGAINST CONFLICT:

Light up on HULL *reading statement.*

HULL (*reads*): With goodwill toward all nations the American government asks of these countries which appear to be contemplating armed hostilities that they weigh most carefully the declaration and pledge given in the pact of Paris, which pledge was entered into by all the signatories for the purpose of safeguarding peace and sparing the world the incalculable losses and human suffering that inevitably follow in the wake of warfare.

Blackout.

Teletype:
GENEVA, SWITZERLAND. . . . LEAGUE COUNCIL DISCUSSES ETHIOPIA:

Light up on LEAGUE SECRETARY. *As he speaks he plays with the gavel in his hand.*

SECRETARY: The League of Nations has shown the world it can respond to present needs. . . . Will this Council assume the responsibility in the eyes of the world for allowing preparations to continue unchecked for the MASSACRE OF A PEOPLE WHICH CONSTITUTES A MENACE TO NONE?

As he reaches the final peroration he bangs his gavel, the lights fade and in the dark, picking up exactly where he left off and in the same tempo, is heard the rhythmic beat of a tomtom.

SCENE 5*

Teletype:
ADDIS ABABA. . . . KING OF KINGS MOBILIZES:

Ed. note: Ethiopian mobilization took place on 28 September 1935.

A flagstoned courtyard of the Emperor's palace. In a position of great prominence stand three huge war drums, covered with lion skins. Above is the balcony used for state occasions. On it is a thronelike chair. A gigantic warrior stands beside a smaller tomtom used to signal the approach of the Emperor. In the courtyard, the warriors wait, all wearing their native white shammas, some accompanied by their wives and families. They carry guns and spears. There is a group of native musicians carrying biblical harps (herars). In each group there sits a tribal chief in bright uniform and lion's mane headdress. . . . Each tribe has its drummer beating a small tomtom which has taken the beat right through from the previous scene. As the curtain rises, there is an intense, electric atmosphere. Suddenly, a single clear voice rings out, singing one of the psalms of David. The melody is taken up by the musicians, and then the entire multitude. At the topmost note, the melody suddenly stops dead. There is a pause, and then a witch doctor steps forward, fantastically dressed. She emits weird, blasting cries, starting a dance of incantation. The tomtoms beat more furiously; the voices become hysterical. The entire scene becomes a saturnalia. . . . At this point the warrior on the balcony pounds his tomtom, signalling the entrance of the Emperor! Immediately everybody freezes. Slowly HAILE SELASSIE appears on the balcony. With him stands CHANCELLOR HAILE WOLDEROUFE. The kind of kings sits. WOLDEROUFE begins to read the mobilization speech.

WOLDEROUFE (*reading*): Soldiers of Ethiopia. . . . Today is the Day of Days. Today you must go forth, united under your chieftains, obeying them with one heart, that the enemy who comes to invade our native land may be repulsed! Soldiers, the opinion of the entire world is revolted by this unprovoked aggression against Ethiopia. . . . And so I say, to the strong, to the young, to the brave—be ready! To the old, the infirm, the feeble, I say—help us in this sacred struggle with your prayers. God will be with us! (*Pause, then*) Long live the Emperor of Ethiopia!

The mob breaks out into shouts. Guns are fired. Suddenly the balcony tomtom again silences them.

WOLDEROUFE: Now sound the war drums! Let each chief step forward and give the signal that will be picked up on every mountain crag, on every arid desert, and there sent on to the farthest extremes of the Empire, from Egypt to Kenya, from Somaliland to the Sudan! LET THE DRUMS SPEAK!

Three or four of the chiefs step out from their men, and one by one go up and take a whack at the drums. Silence. After a moment the drum beat is taken up from a distance. The curtain slowly falls.

SCENE 6*

Teletype:
   MUSSOLINI CALLS TO ARMS EVERY MAN,
   WOMAN AND CHILD:

The balcony of the Piazza Venezia. There are microphones and loud speakers. A strong shaft of light picks up MUSSOLINI. He is standing on the balcony, alone. In the darkness below are massed his countrymen. The blackness is pierced here and there by a torch.

MUSSOLINI: Citizens of Rome, a solemn hour is about to strike. Twenty million Italians are gathered in the squares of Italy with one heart, one will, one decision. We are not only an army, we are forty million Italians marching because the blackest injustice is being attempted against us—that of taking from us our place in the sun. . . . When, in 1915, Italy threw in her fate with the Allies, how many were the cries of admiration, how many the promises! But after the great victory which cost Italy 600,000 dead, 400,000 lost, 1,000,000 wounded, when peace was being discussed around the table, only the crumbs of the rich colonial booty were left for us to pick up. For thirteen years we have been patient while the circle tightened around us. And now, instead of recognizing the rights of Italy, the League of Nations dare talk sanctions. But until there is proof to the contrary I refuse to believe that the

---

*Ed. note: Mussolini's speech was given 2 October 1935, on the eve of the Italian invasion of Ethiopia.

people of France and the people of Britain will want to spill blood and send Europe to its catastrophe for the sake of a barbarian country unworthy of ranking among civilized nations! . . .

Cries of viva! etc.

MUSSOLINI: Nevertheless, we cannot afford to overlook the possible development of tomorrow. To economic sanctions we shall answer with our discipline, our sacrifice, our obedience. To military sanctions we shall answer with acts of militarism. To acts of war we shall answer with acts of war! Never as at this historical hour, have the people of Italy revealed such force of character, and it is against this people of heroes, of poets, of saints, of navigators, of colonizers, that the world dares threaten sanctions! . . . Italy! Italy!! Entirely and universally Fascist! The Italy of the Black Shirt Revolution, rise to your feet! Let the cry of your determination reach out to the skies and fall on the ears of our soldiers in East Africa! Let it be an encouragement to our friends, and a warning to our enemies! FOR IT IS THE CRY OF ITALY WHICH GOES BEYOND THE MOUNTAINS AND THE SEAS! IT IS THE CRY OF JUSTICE AND VICTORY!

A wild tumult of cheering. Then the church bells start to ring, first the great full tones of St. Peter's.

SCENE 7

Teletype:
ADOWA, ETHIOPIA, OCT. 6, 1935. . . . ITALIANS WIPE OUT DEFEAT OF 1896

The principal square of the city, dominated by a huge stone shaft, a monument to those who died in 1896. This monument is veiled with a white sheet, stands three feet square at the base and extends into an obelisk; it is set upon a square pedestal much broader than itself. It bears the inscription "Per perduti de 1896." At the left, a huge head of Mussolini. To the right of the statue stands GENERAL VILLASANTA looking very impressive on this auspicious occasion. There is a platoon of men, a military band. Scattered about are the leading citizens of the town, Coptic and Moslem priests, etc. The priests are advancing in single file, presenting their crosses in token of submission. They are saluted in the European fashion by VILLASANTA. When the last priest has taken his place, the General steps forward.

VILLASANTA: In the name of Victor Emanuel, I declare this, the shrine of Adowa, where ten thousand of our Italian fathers went to a glorious death, forever a part of the Kingdom of United Italy.

There is a roll of the drums; the veil drops from the monument.

VILLASANTA (*reading the inscription*): To the fallen heroes of Adowa, 1896!

The band breaks into "Giovinezza." The soldiers join in at the top of their lungs, the natives stand about making earnest, if futile, attempts at the fascist salute, and the lights dim out.

SCENE 8*

Teletype:
GENEVA, SWITZERLAND, OCT. 7, 1935. . . .
LEAGUE VOTES ECONOMIC SANCTIONS AGAINST ITALY:

Same as Scene 2.

CHAIRMAN: Gentlemen, the League Council, after giving much careful thought to the statements of the representatives of Italy and Ethiopia, has arrived at a conclusion. (*Dramatic pause. . . . He reads.*) It is the opinion of this council that the Italian Government has resorted to war in disregard of its agreement under Article XII of the Covenant of the League, and has thereby committed an Act of War against all other members. . . .

Much excitement. . . . BARON ALOISI jumps up.

CHAIRMAN: The member from Italy has the floor.

*Ed. note: This scene conflates League discussions which took place 7 through 18 October 1935, when sanctions were voted.

ALOISI (*excitedly*): Gentlemen: Italy had a treaty of friendship with Ethiopia and she kept that treaty. Ethiopia did not. My statement declared that there is no more treaty, no more friendship with Ethiopia . . . and I appeal to the conscience of the whole world to witness that Italy is being wronged. Why are you so quick to act and so determined with Italy when you were so slow and faltering in Manchuria and Chaco!

An excited buzz of conversation as TECIA HAWARIATE *jumps up.*

CHAIRMAN: The member from Ethiopia has the floor.

HAWARIATE: I thank the members of the Council for this decision, and I wish to remind them that meanwhile, at this very moment, the Italian Government is rolling up the most highly perfected engines of death and destruction that have been imagined by the most advanced civilization, engines of whose existence the people of Ethiopia never even dreamed . . . and that day after day, thanks to these instruments of carnage, the Italian Government issues bulletins of victory which, in the strong light of truth, can only be considered bulletins of massacre! Nevertheless, I wish to repeat, ETHIOPIA IS DETERMINED TO DEFEND ITS INDEPENDENCE TO THE DEATH!

Same excitement. Three or four members jump up.

CHAIRMAN: The chair recognizes Mr. Eden of Great Britain.

EDEN: Gentlemen: The League is now faced by a great task. Action must be taken at once, the first objective of which is to STOP THIS WAR! . . . It is my duty to state that Great Britain . . .

There is applause. LAVAL *jumps up.*

CHAIRMAN: The chair recognizes M. Laval of France.

LAVAL: I wish to affirm the statement of my colleague from Great Britain. France, too, fully intends to discharge every one of her obligations under the League Covenant. She will also continue passionately to seek a solution by conciliation!

CHAIRMAN: The member from the Union of Soviet Socialist Republics has the floor.

LITVINOV: The Union of Soviet Socialist Republics will cooperate without exception in the undertakings provided by the League Covenant!

Enter a clerk with memo which he gives SECRETARY *who scans it a moment and then raps his gavel.*

SECRETARY: Gentlemen: I have here the results of the balloting on the three questions propounded this morning. . . . These results are: Fifty-six nations embracing every country in the world except Japan, Brazil, Albania, Iceland, Costa Rica, Hungary, and Arabia will refuse to supply arms to the aggressor nation, Italy, under any circumstance, at any price! . . . Fifty-three nations, embracing every creditor country except the United States, whose government, however, will not protect such loans, will refuse to give the aggressor nation, Italy, even a single day's credit! . . . And finally, fifty nations, constituting seventy percent of Italy's trade, undertake to purchase nothing more from the aggressor nation, Italy!

Silence. The Italian delegate, BARON ALOISI, *rises and totters off. The lights fade.*

SCENE 9*

Teletype:
LONDON, ENGLAND. . . . BALDWIN, HOARE, BACK LEAGUE IN CAMPAIGN:

Speaker's stand in a typical English election rally. It is a street corner. There are a few stragglers and a few banners reading: VOTE THE CONSERVATIVE PARTY, WE STAND BEHIND THE LEAGUE OF NATIONS, *etc.*

BALDWIN: . . . I say England is a member of the League, a loyal member, and we are basing our policy on the agreements we made in the name of the League. We do, however, realize that the fulfillment of these policies may involve risks,

---

*Ed. note: British elections were held 14 November 1935. These campaign speeches were belied by the revelation of secret negotiations enacted in Scene 11.

but we believe that therein lies our duty, and that only by giving the League of Nations our full support can we make progress to the rule of law and order and peace for which the League was created! . . . In being true to our pledged word we would also like to preserve an old friendship with Italy. But loyalty to our pledge is foremost and inescapable! . . . Finally, the League has desired France and ourselves to do what we can to bring peace—to find a solution satisfactory to both Italy and Ethiopia. This attempt will be welcomed by all who seek peace as giving greater security to the world, as assuring the world that we stand by our pledges and as a promise of fuller and more effective cooperation in the work of creating a great and lasting peace!

Applause. BALDWIN *steps down and his place is taken by* HOARE.

HOARE: Although our policy is simple and straightforward to the utmost degree, it is travestied by defamers into a policy of dishonesty and intrigue. . . . If you believe that we are letting down the League, that we are not abiding by its judgments, then my answer is, "If you believe that you will believe anything!" . . . As to the fantastic suggestion that we are determined to deprive the League of its coercive powers, what better answer could there be than that day after day, week after week, Mr. Eden and I have been doing our utmost to strengthen the hands of the League, and to make its collective action really successful! . . . Remember, nothing is farther from our minds than to make an agreement that is not acceptable to all three parties concerned, for let us not forget, THERE ARE THREE PARTIES CONCERNED, THE LEAGUE, ITALY, AND ETHIOPIA!

Blackout.

SCENE 10*

Teletype:
NEW YORK, DEC. 15. COL. HUBERT JULIAN, THE BLACK ACE, COMES HOME:

Ed. note: On Julian, see Introduction above, page xxiii.

The deck of the Acquitania. PHOTOGRAPHERS *are busy with the* COLONEL, *posing him in different positions, etc. Standing about are five* REPORTERS. *After some commands by the* PHOTOGRAPHERS *("This way, Colonel," "Smile, Colonel," etc.), the* PHOTOGRAPHERS *exit and the* REPORTERS *advance in a body.*

COLONEL: Now, gentlemen, what would you like to know?

1ST MALE REPORTER: Colonel, how long have you been in Ethiopia?

COLONEL: Gentlemen, there is something I'd like to have strictly understood. I want to be called Mister, plain Mister, after this. No colonel anymore. I've been in Ethiopia for ten months.

1ST MALE REPORTER: Why did you leave?

COLONEL: I left because the Ethiopians are savages, just plain savages, that's all. It is an act of God that Italy should go in there and take over the land.

2ND MALE REPORTER: Of course, you're not prejudiced in any way, this is really your honest opinion . . . ?

COLONEL: Mister, I'm like an umpire at a ball game, I calls 'em as I sees 'em. And I have come to the unanimous conclusion that Ethiopia is not worth civilized nations fighting for. Boy, what a backward country!

3RD MALE REPORTER: Why did you go to Ethiopia in the first place, Colonel?

COLONEL: I made the trip to offer my services as an air fighter to the Emperor. I had left my brand new plane at the factory in Delaware, which I intended to present to Haile Selassie.

1ST MALE REPORTER: Why didn't you?

COLONEL: Because I couldn't keep up the payments on it!

1ST FEMALE REPORTER: Tell us about some of your experiences, Colonel.

COLONEL: Well, I arrived in Addis Ababa expecting a good hot time for myself and the colored pilots who had promised to come and do or die for Old Ethiopia. I was given a Commander's uniform and I walked around like a debutante that had been stood up by her boyfriend—all dressed up and no place to go. But I couldn't find any airplanes! Then I learned that the Ethiopian Chiefs were all very jealous of me and my reputation, so I asked one of my orderlies when I would get a chance to fly and he said "Yellem!"—that means, "You no go." . . . Well, it all came to me as plain as day: The Emperor was so fond of me that he was playing the old army game, not telling me that there weren't any airplanes. So I was sent to Ambo, a distant village, to instruct the tribesman in modern warfare, but when I arrived there they received me in a very commonplace manner—not too cool, but not so hot.

3RD MALE REPORTER: I see. Tell me, Colonel, is there anything else that stands out in your mind about Ethiopia?

COLONEL: Yes, sir! I was particularly impressed with the slipshod manner of the Ethiopian Government in the matter of pay checks. . . . when an officer is employed.

2ND GIRL REPORTER: Colonel Julian, there's a rumor to the effect that you had a romance with the Emperor's daughter . . .

COLONEL: Christopher Columbus! That's the silliest story I ever did hear! A romance with the Emperor's daughter! . . . Of course, she's a very fine and charming young lady—but if they offered her to me on the condition of remaining in Ethiopia I'd reject the offer. Incidentally, I'm a married man.

1ST GIRL REPORTER: Colonel, my paper would appreciate just one final statement on your attitude toward Ethiopia.

COLONEL: Well, for the wind-up I repeat: I am just playing the part of a young intern who saw the patient—Ethiopia—and am reporting to my superior, the public, what is the matter with the patient. (Slowly.) He is very, very, very sick. But I make no indictment. I offer no remedy. I CAME! I SAW! I QUIT!

Blackout.

SCENE 11*

Teletype:
    PARIS, DEC. 8. . . . HOARE AND LAVAL REACH
    PEACE "DEAL":

———

*Ed. note: Details of the backdoor negotiations became public on 9 December 1935.

The Conference Room at the Quai D'Orsay. . . . There is a small table at which sit LAVAL and HOARE. Standing behind each is a retinue of two advisers. In the center, between HOARE and LAVAL, stands a male STENOGRAPHER with a sheaf of notes in his hand.

STENOGRAPHER (reads): . . . and the government of Great Britain and France, meeting in the persons of Sir Samuel Hoare and Pierre Laval, at Paris on December 8th, have, after due deliberation, evolved the following plan as a means of calling a halt to the present conflict and insuring the perpetuation of world peace:

   1. In the North, Italy shall receive from Ethiopia all of the province known as Eastern Tigre, including the cities of Adowa and Makalo already in the hands of Italian troops.

   2. In the South, Italy shall receive from Ethiopia a territory 250 miles wide and 700 miles long, extending from the British Somaliland frontier as far west as Lake Rudolf, and including all of the provinces of Ogaden, Bale and Boran.

   3. In fair and equitable exchange for these territories Ethiopia shall receive from Italy (Pause . . . he stops and coughs.) the city of Assab and the use of a corridor leading to that city. (Another pause.) We do therefore sincerely recommend the acceptance of these terms which embody, in our opinion, a just and equitable settlement to both the nations concerned—a settlement which is born of the spirit of fairness to all, of fair play and equal consideration to the great and the small, the powerful and the weak!

LAVAL and HOARE rise. They shake hands on a good day's work. As the lights begin to dim, the music suddenly roars out—a furious, seething, portentous motif.

SCENE 12*

Teletype:
    "BETRAYED!" CRIES BRITISH PUBLIC:

———

*Ed. note: British public reaction is accurately portrayed. See Daniel Waley, British Public Opinion and the Abyssinian War (London: Maurice Temple Smith Ltd., 1974).

The music dies gradually until it becomes a kind of running commentary underneath the various speeches. A searchlight sweeps, at the conclusion of each speech, from one speaker to the next.

Teletype: (*continuing*)
LONDON LONDON LONDON LONDON LONDON:

Trafalgar Square: An AGITATOR *on a soap box. Beside him is a British flag.*

AGITATOR (*Cockney*): . . . They comes before us and says, "Vote for Baldwin and the Conservative Party because the Conservative Party stands behind the League of Nations and the League will see that every nation gets a square deal," that's what they says. . . . And what do we do? We does what we're told like good little boys and girls and we votes them in with a majority of twelve million. TWELVE MILLION! And THEN what happens? They proceed to forget every rotten plank in their platform and they get up a peace plan which is nice and sweet and fair and square for everybody—except Ethiopia—which has to give up half its territory so Italy won't make war on it any more. . . . We've been betrayed, BETRAYED!

Blackout

Teletype:
LIVERPOOL LIVERPOOL LIVERPOOL LIVERPOOL LIVERPOOL:

Another soap box, another agitator—well-dressed middle-aged WOMAN.

WOMAN (*calmly and dispassionately*): Look: The League decides that Italy is guilty of aggression, of unprovoked assault on Ethiopia. They apply economic sanctions as a further emphasis of this guilt. So far so good. But what does Sir Samuel Hoare do? He decides to re- ward Italy for this aggression, for this unprovoked assault, by giving her practically everything she asks and more than she expected—while Ethiopia, a nation that has been fairly judged to be the injured party, is stripped of al- most everything it's got that's worth taking! AND THAT, MY FRIENDS, IS EXACTLY WHAT THE HOARE-LAVAL PEACE PLAN IS!

Teletype:
MANCHESTER MANCHESTER MANCHESTER MANCHESTER:

Another street scene: The speaker is a GIRL.

GIRL: . . . So Mister Baldwin says this is the only way a world war can be averted, does he? Well, what I say is this: What good is the League of Nations if the only way you can stop a war from coming on is by giving the guilty nation everything it wants? What's the League for anyhow? . . . Didn't I read about some agreement in the Covenant which says that all the nations should support each other in outlawing an aggressor? And if this outlawing leads to a war of everybody concerned against this aggressor—well then, I say didn't they think it meant that when they established the League? Didn't they? . . . WE'VE BEEN BETRAYED!

Blackout.

Teletype:
SHEFFIELD SHEFFIELD SHEFFIELD SHEFFIELD SHEFFIELD:

Light up on another street scene, SPEAKER, *soap box, etc.*

SPEAKER: . . . and what do you think everybody else is going to say about this—all the little countries like Rumania, Greece, Turkey, Yugoslavia, Poland, and the rest of them? What are they going to think of British diplomacy and the League of Nations now? . . . I'll tell you what's they're going to think! Suppose it was our country that was being invaded—Rumania, Greece or Turkey? Why, we'd be getting the same kind of raw deal that Ethiopia is getting now—that's what they'll say. And they'll wash their hands of the whole dirty business and then you can throw the WHOLE LEAGUE OF NATIONS INTO THE SCRAP HEAP AND CIVILIZATION WILL BE PUT BACK ANOTHER TWENTY YEARS. . . . WE'VE BEEN BETRAYED!

Blackout.

SCENE 13*

Teletype:
  SIR SAMUEL HOARE RESIGNS:

A section of the benches in the House of Commons. SIR SAMUEL *stares straight out, a little weary. He rises slowly.*

HOARE: The House always gives a sympathetic and generous hearing to a former Minister who explains the reasons for his resignation. About a fortnight ago it was clear that a situation was about to be created by oil sanctions. That Italy would regard an oil embargo as a military action or an act involving war against her. Let me make our position clear; we had no fear whatever, as a nation, of any Italian threat. Whatever Italy's conduct, we should retaliate—and judging from our past history, with full success! (*Pause.*) It was in these circumstances, then, that I went to Paris. It was a moment of great urgency. Within five days the question of oil sanctions was to come before the League. It was a moment in which, while most of the member nations had taken part in economic sanctions, none except ourselves had taken any military precautions. There is a British fleet in the Mediterranean. There are British reinforcements in Egypt, Malta, and Aden. No ship, no gun, no man has been moved by any other member of the League. It was, at this moment, then, I went to Paris. (*Pause.*) Now that these proposals suggested by Premier Laval and myself have failed we must have something more than general protestations of loyalty to the League. Let the House remember the conditions of modern warfare. The aggressor had a great advantage. He is ready to strike and he strikes with appalling speed! This makes it all the more necessary that all the member states

Ed. note: The text of Hoare's speech was published in the *New York Times*. 20 December 1935.

should make themselves ready not for an event that may take place three or four months ahead, but for AN EVENT THAT MAY TAKE PLACE AT ANY MOMENT! It is a choice between full cooperation or the kind of unsatisfactory compromise Mr. Laval and I drew up in Paris! (*Pause.*) I come now to the conclusion of the matter as far as it concerns me. . . . I ask myself whether I have a guilty conscience or whether my conscience is clear. (*His voice rises slightly.*) I say that with all humility to the House that my conscience is clear! That despite the fact that the great body of public opinion is intensely critical of the course I have adopted I cannot honestly recant, and I sincerely believe that the course I took was the only course possible in the circumstance. . . . It may be that many in the House disagree. In any case, there is the hard fact that I have not got the confidence and approval of a great body of people behind me, and since I realize that fact, without any suggestion from anybody, I asked the Prime Minister to accept my resignation. . . . (*The voice fades.*)

Blackout.

SCENE 14

Teletype:
  WAR DRUMS BEAT OVER EUROPE:

The figures as they speak are lit up by pin spots and blacked out. They are all dressed in uniforms of the countries they represent. There is a projection of marching feet, and the tramp, tramp, tramp is amplified on the sound system.

ENGLAND: Home Fleet in the Mediterranean!
ITALY: 300,000 troops in Africa!
ETHIOPIA: A rifle for every man!
FRANCE: Half a million under arms!
RUMANIAN: More planes!
POLAND: More soldiers!
JAPAN: More troops to China!
GERMANY: More money for guns!
RUSSIA: One million men in uniform!
ENGLAND: Oil sanctions!
ITALY: Sanctions mean war!

ETHIOPIA: 200 killed today!
FRANCE: France fights beside Britain!
RUMANIA: Rumania backs France!
POLAND: Rearm!
JAPAN: Naval parity!
GERMANY: Heil Hitler!
RUSSIA: Down with Fascism!
ENGLAND: Watch Italy!
ITALY: Watch Britain!
ETHIOPIA: Fight to the death!
FRANCE: Watch Germany!
RUMANIA: Be ready!
POLAND: More bullets!
JAPAN: Watch Russia!
RUSSIA: Watch Japan!
GERMANY: Der Tag!

The single word "war" is passed right down the line, from England to Germany, the music blares out in a mounting climax, the feet tramp louder. Blackout.

END

"Banned on Broadway": Clippings from the *New York Times*

"RICE QUITS IN ROW OVER WPA DRAMA: Resigns as Regional Director of Theatre Project in 'Ethiopia' Dispute."

MUSSOLINI A CHARACTER:
Administrator Baker Objected to Showing State Heads in 'Living Newspaper.'

Elmer Rice resigned last evening as the regional director of the Federal Theatre Project in this city. He did so in a dispute over the subject-matter in what was to be the project's first play—"The Living Newspaper." The WPA authorities felt that the government's shows could not rightly picture the heads of other nations—as was to be done in a sketch called "Ethiopia"—but Mr. Rice apparently felt otherwise.

The Federal Theatre Project is a subject that has enlivened Broadway all Winter, and the disasters attendant on the living newspaper's career form only the climax. The idea behind that particular unit was to provide the theatre with something similar to the radio and screen's "March of Time." Playwrights and members of the Newspaper Guild were to write the scripts, taking their subjects from current events of the day, and the first number was given over to the Ethiopian dispute. Mussolini and Emperor Haile Selassie were two of the figures shown. The play was scheduled for the Biltmore Theatre next Wednesday evening.

Yesterday morning Jacob Baker, the assistant Federal administrator of the WPA, came to town, and it was revealed that last Saturday he had suggested that some of the subject matter of "Ethiopia" might not be satisfactory. At that time he sent to Mrs. Hallie Flanagan, the national director of the Theatre Project, a note saying that "this will direct that no issue of the 'The Living Newspaper' shall contain any representation of the head, or one of the Ministers, or the Cabinet of a foreign State."

During the course of the afternoon Mr. Baker went to the Biltmore Theatre and saw a rehearsal of "Ethiopia." Coming away afterward, he sent another note to Mrs. Flanagan.

"This will modify my memorandum of Jan. 18 as to the performance of 'Ethiopia,'" it said. "No one impersonating a ruler or Cabinet officer shall actually appear on the stage. If it is useful for you to do so, the words of such persons may be quoted by the others. I very much hope that the script is susceptible of such modifications as to enable you to present it."

Mr. Rice called on Mr. Baker and received a copy of the above note, also one addressed to himself. That said:

"When difficulties have arisen in the past in connection with the operation of the Federal Theatre Project within the framework of the governmental structure, you have proposed either to resign or to take the difficulties to the press. Now that a problem has arisen in connection with a dramatization that may affect our international relations, you renew your proposal of resignation in a telegram to Mr. Hopkins. This time I accept it, effective upon receipt of this letter. In your telegram to Mr. Hopkins, you suggest that you wish to make a statement to the press. I should be glad to have you include this letter with any statement that you make."

Mr. Baker also thanked Mr. Rice for the "energy, enthusiasm, imagination and the hard work that you have put into this project."

Mr. Rice, however, could not be reached last evening for comment, nor could Mr. Baker, although he was reported to be still in the city. The Biltmore Theatre was dark, and there was no rehearsal going on. Mrs. Flanagan visited the local offices of the Theatre Project at Eighth Avenue and Forty-fourth Street in company with Philip Barber, the production assistant to Mr. Rice, but she declined to comment. She was asked whether the question of free speech in the project plays were involved whether she, too, would resign. She declined to say.

What would become of "Ethiopia" remains an open question. It was scheduled first to open last Wednesday evening, but the Project was unable to obtain technical equipment from the government in time to do so. Whether the whole sketch would be dropped, or would be amended along the lines suggested by Mr. Baker, could not be learned. According to Morris Watson, the director of The Living Newspaper, "Ethiopia" will be shown this noon at the Biltmore to invited guests, and Mr. Rice is expected to make a statement at that time.

—(*New York Times*, 24 January 1936)

. . .

" 'Ethiopia,' the First Issue of The Living Newspaper, Which the Federal Theatre Cannot Publish."

Apart from the questions of free speech involved in the withdrawal of "Ethiopia," let us attempt to look at it dispassionately as a play. It was put on yesterday noon at the Biltmore Theatre as a rehearsal before an audience of WPA workers and newspaper men. Let this correspondent say at once that he felt proud of the newspaper men who had written it and the actors and directors who put it on the stage; and he shared with them the desolate feeling that comes when good work is denied its logical reward.

What they have done in this forty-five-minute show is to skeletonize the long story of the Ethiopian disaster which has been echoing around the world. It opens with a casually sketched impression of Ethiopia before the war—the natives, impersonated by Negro actors, singing and dancing to the vibrant beating of drums. Then "Ethiopia" touches briefly on the salient points of the dispute by skipping over Europe after the manner of a newsreel, showing as factually as possible how an isolated war stirs up repercussions everywhere—in the League of Nations, on the streets of England, in Parliament as well as in Italy and Ethiopia. Mussolini, Haile Selassie, Baldwin, Laval, Hoare, Eden, Litvinoff are all represented by actors who speak lines taken from actual speeches; and by way of humor a ship news scene is thrown in with an actor impersonating the grandiloquent Colonel Hubert Julian. In the concluding scene the war drums beat over Europe and the curtain descends on the ominous thunder of marching feet.

"Ethiopia" is no masterpiece. But as a living newspaper account of a breach of peace that is happening under our nose it is sobering and impressive—even frightening. Although this correspondent had no genuine expectations of the project for dramatizing the news, the result amply justifies the hard work that has gone into it. It was acted yesterday without scenery, with only a few cheap costumes, and the props used consisted of a few spears, chairs and tables. But the acting was crisp, earnest and selfless; the Negro scenes were particularly stirring. Among other things, the writing and staging showed that in the large ranks of the jobless there is an abundance of first-rate talent. To sit in the audience before a bare rehearsal yesterday was to realize how much eagerness has gone into this plain production. All questions of policy and wastefulness aside, "Ethiopia" proves that the human principle of the WPA art projects is sound. The keenest privation of the unemployed artist is the lack of professional expression.

As far as this correspondent can see, "Ethiopia" is an unbiased dramatic account; and any unbiased account that is also complete includes the League of Nations' verdict that characterizes Italy as the aggressor, and it involves the decisive vote on sanctions. "Ethiopia" has suppressed none of the essential news.

To come at last to the point of free speech involved in WPA's withdrawal of "Ethiopia" from public performances, any one can understand the government's unwillingness to sponsor out of public funds a play that would certainly be misinterpreted in Italy. The international situation is dangerously sensitive; officially we are neutral. Although "Ethiopia" is factual and objective and entirely above-board, it would be misconstrued in Italy as evidence of American animosity, subsidized by the government, and it would provide another irritant in diplomacy.

But the theatre is reduced to innocuous commonplaces when it has to conform to diplomatic manners. This episode, which is silly in itself, shows how futile it is to expect the theatre to be anything but a sideshow under government supervision. Mrs. Flanagan and Mr. Rice took office last Autumn with definite assurance that the Federal Theatre Project would be free from official censorship. The first crisis shows, what many of us foresaw, that a theatre paid for out of public funds cannot enjoy the freedom normal in private ventures.

Since Mr. Rice has stood aggressively for freedom of artistic expression for a number of years, he cannot change face now, and he has resigned as director of the New York project. It has been a thankless job, entangled with red tape and plagued by all sorts of external resistance; and the fact that WPA was organized as a temporary relief measure has been almost forgotten. But over the past four months Mr. Rice has done well something that had to be done under the most trying circumstances, and he deserves more thanks than he is likely to get. What we all know now is that a free theatre cannot be a government enterprise.

—Brooks Atkinson (*New York Times,*
25 January, 1936)

Eric Paice and Roger Woddis

WORLD ON EDGE
A Living Newspaper
1956

World on Edge premiered at Unity Theatre on 23 November 1956. In addition to Paice and Woddis, others contributing to the script included Howard Goorney of Theatre Workshop, Reggie Smith of the BBC, and American director Charles Marowitz. André van Gyseghem directed. The script printed here does not include some (lost) scenes referred to in various reviews nor other manuscript scenes indicated as "cut."

ACT ONE

Overture of war sounds, bombs exploding, etc., fade and hold under. A woman REFUGEE *from Eastern Europe walks on stage with bundle. She looks around for a moment, stunned. From S.R. another* REFUGEE, *a man from Egypt also walks on. They meet.*

1ST R: Which way?
2ND R: I don't know.
1ST R: Is it bad there?
2ND R: I can't describe it.
1ST R: There must be some place.
2ND R: Where?
1ST R: Where, where. . . .

They walk off together. EDITOR *of Living Newspaper enters.*

ED: Where? Where are any of us going? I don't know. Do you? (*To audience.*) But I do know this. We've got to find out, and find out quickly. We must be honest with you, we don't know all the answers, but we know that if this crisis is to be solved at all, it must be by reason and clear thinking. And that goes for everybody.

We are going to present you with certain facts tonight—illuminate certain aspects—and let you draw your own conclusions. We have tried to select these facts as fairly as possible. We shall present no dogma except one—that war is no solution to the world's problems. With the world hovering on the brink of catastrophe. . . . Excuse me. . . .

TELEGRAM BOY *enters and goes over to* ED. *Hands him telegram.*

ED (*reads*): REF UNITY THEATRE'S GRAVE HAND-OUT STOP ADVISE BRINKMANSHIP STOP EXPLA-NATION SOONEST STOP DUSTER FOLLIES.*

Spot in on FOLLIES. *Reads.*

DUSTER FOLLIES: The art of brinkmanship is the art of the Statesman who is perpetually on the brink. That is to say, the art of maintaining

*Ed. Note: The reference is to American Secretary of State, John Foster Dulles.

equilibrium on the edge of a precipice—brink-wise.

Politicwise and likewise strategicwise, it is vital to maintain a delicate balance between falling offwise and staying putwise. It is, if you like, a form of fencesquattingmanship. Now from this vantage point it is impossible for your opponent to know whether you are peacewise, warwise or otherwise. It is equally important that you don't know either. Let not your right buttock know what your left buttock is doing—backwise. Thus, everyone is taken by surprisewise. . . .

ED: Yes, well, with that timely warning, let us now open our living newspaper—"World on Edge."

Spot up on EDEN.

EDEN: All my life I have been a man of peace, working for peace, striving for peace, negotiating for peace. But . . . there are times for courage, times for action—and this is one of them—in the interests of peace. . . .

Enter NEWSBOY *with newsbill.*

NEWSBOY (*walks across stage*): Crisis . . . Troops Massing . . . Ultimatum . . .

CROWD *follow on excitedly buying newspapers. Argue among themselves.*

CROWD:
—About time too.
—We'll show 'em we can't be kicked around.
—Ain't it terrible.
—Hope my Harry don't get called up.
—Let's get it over with quick, that's what I say.
—Where's it all going to end.

ED: Where indeed? That is the question everyone is asking. The whole world is in turmoil. . . .

CROWD *reenter. One is carrying a banner:* "Free Hungary." *Shouts and demonstration in support.*

ED: And in a packed House of Commons. . . .

Spot on LABOR M.P.

M.P.: Does the Prime Minister realize that this aggressive act in the Middle East has dismayed and shocked our friends—split the common-wealth—torn up a solemn treaty and threat-ened the very foundations of the United Nations?

Shouts of "Here, here," "Resign," "Nonsense, shut up," "etc."

M.P.: The whole world is waiting for the Government to answer. . . . What is the Government going to do!

UPROAR. *Yells of* "Answer," "Get Out," *etc. Spot out.*

ED: And in Mayfair too, they are asking. . . .

Fade in to smart YOUNG MEN *drinking.*

1ST YM: What do you feel like doing tonight, old man?

2ND: I don't really know, old man. What do you feel like doing tonight? (*Pause.*)

1ST: I say, old man, isn't there a Top Hat and Lingerie Party at Penelope Boulanger's?

2ND: Isn't she rather a bore, old man?

1ST (*sipping wine*): Hmm. (*Pause.*) I say, they're holding a Champagne and Footwash spree at Clifford's after Bunny's affair.

2ND (*without enthusiasm*): Are they?

1ST: Yes . . . of course, we could join Fiona and Fenella.

2ND: Fiona and Fenella?

1ST: They're cruising down the Wapping Canal.

2ND: Expensive?

1ST: God no, 2,000 . . . starts at midnight.

2ND: When does it finish, old man?

1ST: Friday morning, old man.

2ND: Reasonable, old man, reasonable—for four days slumming?

1ST: Ye-e-e-s.

2ND: Still, old man, four days with Fiona (*grimaces with disgust*) . . . and Fenella, old man. Remember last June? (*Winces, pause.*)

1ST: What do you feel like doing tonight, old man?

2ND: I don't really know, old man. What do *you* feel like doing tonight?

Cross-fade into CROWD *reentering, angrily arguing amongst themselves.*

CROWD:
—Well, if you're so ruddy keen on fighting, why don't you go and join up. . . .

—I did my bit in the last war, madam. . . .
—And I lost my old man. Now they're taking young Jimmy. . . .
—Yes, but Nasser's got to be stopped. . . .
—And the Russians. . . .
—So has your gab. . . .
—This is a free country. . . .
—Prove it. . . .
—Go back to Russia. . . .
—Go and get stuffed. . . .

Scuffles break out. SERGEANT MAJOR *enters and mounts rostrum.*

S.M.: Attention! (*They all automatically jump to attention.*) Now boys and gels, get fell in. Come on then. Jump to it. We haven't got all day. That's the idea. . . . Right. (*They all shuffle into line except one* MAN.) Come on then, you heard me, when I give an order I expect it to be obeyed at the double.
MAN: But I don't want to go to war. (*Murmurs of assent.*)
S.M.: You don't want to go to . . . this ain't a war, this is a police action.

He takes off cap and puts on Policeman's helmet.

MAN: Whatever it is, I don't want to go.
S.M.: Now that's a good slogan. Come on everybody. We don't want to go. (*They take it up raggedly.*) Louder. . . .
ALL: We don't want to go.
S.M.: That's the ticket! We don't want to go. . . . By the Right! We don't wanner go. (*He marches them off in military fashion with umbrellas at the slope.*) We don't wanner go! (*Into the wings.*)

Fade marching feet and lights. Fade up opposite side and train noise. Lights in on bowler-hatted GENTS. *One straphanging and both swaying slightly as if in a tube train.*

2ND GENT (*takes off his bowler*): Now take this as the Western Hemisphere. We need a base here, and a base there. (*He takes off his friend's bowler hat.*) Excuse me. (*He puts the two together to make a globe.*) Now if this is the Eastern Hemisphere, we shall need a base here. . . .
1ST GENT (*points with umbrella*): And a base there . . . and strengthen this base here, because

they've got a base over there, and then we've got them by the short and curly . . . eh?

Fade. Enter FRED *from the other wings. He is a disheveled, sleepless man in pajamas and slippers. He looks out bewildered in the direction of the audience. Then says to himself:*

FRED: It's terrible. It's getting worse. They're everywhere. I'm so worried I can't sleep. I'm afraid to go out. I'm afraid to stay in. I'd better keep moving. Daren't stay still. They'll get me. (*This takes him off.*)

NEWSBOY *in again. He has a newsbill which he keeps turning round. On one side is the word* "Suez," *on the other* "Hungary."

NEWSBOY (*Calls*): Suez! Budapest! Egypt! Hungary! Suez! Budapest! (*He walks straight across and offstage.*)

Fade. NEWSBOY *enters again.*

NEWSBOY: Russians attack Budapest! Allies attack Egypt! Hungary! Suez! Suez! Hungary!

(*He goes off opposite side.*)
Spot on COMMUNIST.

COM: Fascism was threatening to return to Hungary! I support the action of the Red Army.

Spot on WOMAN TORY.

WOMAN: He had to act, and act quickly! Sir Anthony Eden deserves our gratitude.

Spot on SECOND COMMUNIST.

2ND COM: I have been a member of the party for twenty years. But this is too much.

He slowly tears up party card. Spot on SECOND WOMAN TORY.

2ND TORY: As a Conservative I am horrified by what our Government is doing. I have only one course of action. . . . (*Screws up copy of* The Times.)

Fade in to two MEN *with pints. Miming darts.*

1ST MAN: Double top.
2ND MAN: Double top it is.
1ST MAN: Think they'll start something?

They take darts and change places.

2ND MAN: Who?

1ST MAN: The Russians.

2ND MAN: Dunno. Can't tell.

1ST MAN: They've got 200 divisions.

2ND MAN: And the H-bomb.

1ST MAN: Think they'll use it?

2ND MAN: You never know.

Cross-fade to two RUSSIANS *playing chess.*

1ST RUSS (*moves piece*): Check.

2ND RUSS: Do you think they will?

1ST RUSS: Check. Who?

2ND RUSS: The West.

1ST RUSS (*after contemplative pause*): It's possible.

2ND RUSS: They've got the bases.

1ST RUSS: And the H-bomb. (*He moves a piece.*)

2ND RUSS: Stalemate.

Cross-fade in to oblong table downstage. At each end is a General. ONE GENERAL *is East and the* OTHER GENERAL *West. They are moving flags on a map and facing one another. Upstage at the foot of each rostrum is a Sentry.* ONE SENTRY *holds a yellow pennant, the* OTHER SENTRY *a green.*

1ST GEN (*to himself*): Now if we support the Syrians against the Assyrians . . .

2ND GEN (*to himself*): . . . er . . . if we back the Arabians against the Bessarabians . . .

1ST GEN: And if we then form an alliance with the Zonians . . . (*Leans over to reach a flag on the other side.*)

2ND GEN: Now we draw up an alliance with the Amazonians. . . . (*Leans over to reach a flag on the other side, bringing them so that their foreheads are almost touching. They suddenly become aware of this and look up.*)

1ST GEN (*with a look of stupefaction*): You've taken my Zonians.

2ND GEN: You've taken my Amazonians.

1ST GEN: I'm warning you!

2ND GEN: Hands off!!

1ST GEN: If you want trouble . . .

2ND GEN: . . . You can have it.

1ST GEN (*erect to attention*): Right!

2ND GEN (*ditto*): Right!

1ST GEN: Left, right, left. (*Marches across and upstage to opposing rostrum.*)

2ND GEN: Right left, right. Right left right.

They arrive at their respective rostra. 1ST GEN. *takes the rifle from the* SENTRY *and pushes the man down.* 2ND GEN. *stands there for a moment, then seizes rifle of the* SENTRY *at the foot of his rostrum and pushes him down. The two Generals stand glaring at one another as the lights cross-fade and* FRED *enters through half-drawn tableau curtains in extreme agitation.* FRED *is caught in the limelight so his shadow is cast behind him.*

FRED: They're all out to get me. They've been trying for years. (*Leans forward to audience.*) It's the Jews . . . and the blacks . . . and the Yanks . . . and the woman upstairs . . . and the cyclists. They're all in it together. They're trying to do me down. There's millions of them! (*He looks furtively around and suddenly sees his own shadow; lets out a strangled cry.*) There's one of 'em now! (*Runs across the stage, turns and still sees the shadow.*) Won't let me alone. They're always following me. (*Runs back across the stage, whips round on the shadow.*) See! (*Takes a swipe at the shadow.*) Go on, go away, go away. (*Backs into the wings and exits.*)

SCIENTIST, GENERAL, *and* STOCKBROKER *sing "Stock Exchange Rock" to tune of "Rock around the Clock."*

GENERAL:
One little incident flares up;
Two little incidents flare up;
Three little incidents flare up;
We're gonna Rock around the Stocks and Shares.

ALL:
So let's unblock that old canal,
Although the whole thing looks somewhat banal.

STOCKBROKER:
We're gonna Rock around the Stocks and Shares—
We're gonna take old UNO unawares.
It may be unorthodox,
But how it Rocks those Stocks and Shares.

GENERAL:
On your marks!;   (ALL: On your marks)
Get set;   (ALL: Get set)
All ready?   (ALL: Ready)

ALL:
GO
Ev'rybody wipe those wogs out!

Ev'rybody wipe those reds out!
Ev'rybody wipe those blacks out!
Ev'rybody wipe those . . .
Hey! Where is ev'rybody?

SCIENTIST:

There's a guided missile
And an atom bomb behind the white door.
And it looks like this'll
Bring the bombs out from behind the white
    door.
Let the whole world whistle—
There's a panic on behind the white door.

ALL:

White door—what's that secret you're keep-
    ing?
White door—please forgive us for peeping.
We've sown—now we're ready for reaping!
WHITE DOOR . . . OPEN UP!

Sound effects: door creaking open followed by massive explosion.

STOCKBROKER:

Steel and oil, and oil and steel,
Just watch those prices roll and reel,
We're gonna Rock around the Stocks and
    Shares,
We're gonna play hepcats and bulls and bears,
It kinda puts back the clock . . .
But how it ROCKS THOSE STOCKS AND
    SHARES!!

STOCKBROKER walks out of number to cutout petrol pump. GARAGE HAND.

STOCKBROKER: The chauffeur's bringing the Siddeley 'round in five minutes. Can you fix me up with five gallons?

GGE. HAND: You'll be lucky sir, we've had a big run on juice today, people are hoarding petrol.

STB: Still, never mind. We've all got to do our bit. The lads in Egypt probably need it more than we do. (*Confidentially.*) You couldn't make it ten gallons could you? . . .

Cross-fade to GIRL reading letter to her MOTHER.

GIRL (*reads*): I can't tell you where I am or when I got here, but I am allowed to say it's ruddy hot. It was a bit rough while it lasted but I'm all right, so don't worry. I hope the money's come through by now and you'll be able to manage.

How's Mum, I hope her back hasn't been playing up. Any news about the hospital yet. Don't be afraid to have a bash about it because I will when I get back . . . which I hope will be soon. . . . (*Fade.*) All my love to you and . . .

MOTHER walks into LADY ALMONER's desk. She goes to sit in vacant chair.

ALMONER: I'm sorry Mrs. Palmer, but there's just no bed vacancy yet.

MOTHER: Well, how long do you think it'll be. It kept me awake all last night again.

ALMONER: I'm very sorry, Mrs. Palmer. The moment there's a vacancy I'll write to you straight away.

MOTHER: Yes, well, I don't want you to think I'm worrying you, but my doctor said a year ago I ought to be in here.

ALMONER: I want you to try and understand that there is a tremendous waiting list for operational beds. . . .

MOTHER: Yes, but where does it all go to—the money I mean, the six and nine we pay. . . .

ALMONER: I'm afraid that's a question I can't answer. . . .

Cross-fade to CABINET MINISTER leaning against rostrum.

CAB. MIN.: . . . and a cut of half a million pounds in hospital. And so, Mr. Speaker, with these and other economies—which we sincerely trust are only temporary—we have been able to reduce Government expenditure to more realistic proportions. . . .

Opposing cries of "Here, here" and "Shame."

SCOTTISH VOICE FROM OFF: What about the fifteen hundred million on armaments!

CAB. MIN. (*blandly*): The honorable member is aware that this is the minimum we dare permit ourselves on defense and I think it highly improper to raise this matter when reports now coming in from certain parts of the world prove the vital need for strengthening our defenses.

Deep gruff cries of "Here, here." Cut to WAR CORRESPONDENTS on separate stage areas.

1ST CORR (*man*): Since early this morning we've heard the reverberating thunder of heavy tanks firing into the town, broken only by the occasional whine of a sniper's bullet and the crash of falling masonry.

2ND CORR (*woman*): From where I'm standing I can actually see one of these tanks slewed across the road with its track torn away. Beside it lie three blood-spattered bodies.

1ST CORR: Almost overnight barricades have been thrown up—barricades often little more than an overturned tram, or a pile of household furniture.

2ND CORR: Behind the barricades civilians and soldiers together are fighting this grim battle. For the past two days we have seen hundreds of refugees, without food and carrying their pitiful bundles, streaming out into the suburbs.

1ST CORR: Where these people will go, or how far they will get, no one knows. They are the eternal victims of war.

2ND CORR: By now the tanks are breaking into the main square. Resistance is being steadily reduced to isolated strongholds.

1ST CORR: It is expected that by nightfall all resistance will be at end.

2ND CORR: This is Jane Geddes reporting to you from Budapest. . . .

1ST CORR: This is Thomas Currie signing off from Port Said. . . .

Fade both. Fade up sound of gunfire. Walk on two REFUGEES *from beginning of play. They sit down on rostrum without looking at one another. He takes out crust of bread and breaks off half, which he gives to her. They chew almost mechanically, staring dumbly out into auditorium.* EDITOR *walks on and leans up against proscenium. Long pause.*

EDITOR: Do you know what I think? I think we're all mad—no, I mean it—not just a figure of speech, but we're really going round the bend. None of us want war—we do the fighting and the dying and the suffering—but we still have it. Why? If we're not mad, why do we allow it? Look at the world today—right on the edge. It just wants a little push, and—that's it. No, let's not say we're mad—let's just say we've lost the power to reason. I mean, reason individually. Because if we can still reason, then there must be an answer, and if there's an an-

swer, we're going to find it—if we have to stay here all bloody night!

END OF ACT I

ACT TWO

EDITOR *discovered downstage left behind desk. He is wearing eye shade, is in short sleeves and going through copy. Seated next to him is* GIRL SECRETARY *opening envelopes, of which there is a large pile. He looks up and speaks directly to audience.*

ED: Right. We're away from the bombs and the noise and the political passions. Let's see if we can examine this appalling situation with a reasonable amount of calm. Easier said than done? Maybe, but we'll have a shot at it anyway. Perhaps the best way to do it is in the form of a readers' forum. You know the sort of thing—readers' questions answered. Only, we're going to reverse the process. Some of you may think you know the answers already, so we're going to let you have your say, then *we'll* do the asking. In other words—*all your answers questioned.* Our first 'answer' comes from—

Spot on WOMAN *on rostrum.*

WOMAN: Housewife, North London. I think we were quite right to go in to Egypt on our own because the U.N. wasn't doing its job and needed waking up.

Spot fades on WOMAN *and lights up on* ED.

ED: A valid argument? Well, now, let's see how it might be used in another context. . . .

Fade out on ED. *Spot on* BURGLAR *in cutout of dock,* POLICEMAN *and* MAGISTRATE.

P.C.: . . . I was proceeding down the High Street at 2:38 A.M. this morning, when I observed the defendant helping himself to a quantity of rings, watches and other valuables through a large hole in the window of a jeweler's establishment. I approached him and asked him for an explanation of his actions. His reply was not satisfactory, whereupon I apprehended him and escorted him to the station, where he was later charged with shopbreaking and being in possession of half a brick with felonious intent.

MAG: Thank you, Constable. Does the defendant plead guilty or not guilty, as charged?

BURGLAR: Well, your honor, I do—and then again, I don't.

MAG: You do and you don't? Perhaps you had better explain yourself to the Court, Mr. Sykes.

BURGLAR: Well, I admit to having the half brick and busting the window and lifting the sparklers, but I don't admit to the felonious intent.

MAG: Oh?

BURGLAR: No your Honor. You see, the rozzers round here are dead slack, and people's property ain't safe, so I done what I done as a good citizen—*to remind the force of its duty to the public!*

Cross-fade back to EDITOR.

ED: Our next letter also deals with Egypt, though in a somewhat stronger tone. It begins . . .

Spot on FIERY-LOOKING GENTLEMAN.

F.L.G.: Sir! You are a blackguard! Our sole motive in intervening in the Middle East struggle was—in words of the Prime Minister—"to separate the combatants."

Spot on two BOXERS *sitting in their corners.* REF *comes forward to introduce* BOXERS.

REF: Ladies and Gentlemen! The main event tonight is for the welterweight championship of the Middle East! On my left—Harry the Mauler. (*HARRY gets up and moves center, acknowledging cheers with arms upraised.* REF *holds nose and gestures "thumbs down."*) On my right—BENNY THE KID! (*REF leads cheers as BENNY comes forward.* REF *speaks to boxers while examining their gloves.*) Now boys, I want a clean fight, stop at the bell, and no holding in the clinches. (*As he examines HARRY's gloves, he ties laces together. To audience*—) And by the way, I want to dispel an ugly rumor that I've got a coupla quid on Benny the Kid. Right, boys—(*Winks at BENNY, bell goes, he steps back.*)

Boxers start weaving, HARRY *discovers gloves are tied together. He tries in vain to hit BENNY, but*

only succeeds in brushing him lightly. REF *dashes forward.*

REF: Foul!

He throws bucket over HARRY's head, grabs arms from behind and holds them over HARRY's head. BENNY *hits HARRY hard in his exposed midriff.* REF *pushes HARRY aside and holds up BENNY's arms.*

REF: The winner!

Blackout. Back to EDITOR.

ED: We have a couple of letters here with two viewpoints on the same subject. They are the sort of letters I like to get—they are reasoned, they are honest, and they come from the heart. . . .

Fade ED. *Spot on* FIRST FACTORY WORKER *on rostrum.*

FIRST W.: As much as I was against the Government sending troops into Suez, because I think it's bad for other countries to see us as an aggressor—once the lads are out there, well—there's a couple of boys from my factory who have gone—and I think it's our job to back them up.

Spot on SECOND WORKER *on opposite rostrum.*

SECOND W.: I can understand your feeling like that, but there *is* another way of looking at it. My husband is a member of the Labor Party, and though I don't go much on flags and demonstrations and that, we went along to Trafalgar Square when the trouble broke out. I was really amazed to see the thousands of people there, and, to see how strongly they felt about stopping the War. No one was more surprised than me, when we *did* stop it—for the time being, anyway. My point is, if a thing is wrong, you don't make it right by supporting it—you only make it worse.

Spot off. Fade back to EDITOR.

ED: The next letter I have from the top of the pile deals with . . .

VOICE FROM AUDIENCE: Hungary!

ED (*pretending he hasn't heard*): . . . This letter deals with . . .

VOICE: What about Hungary?

ED: Now quiet please, we deal with that when we come to it.

VOICE: You deal with it now!

ED (*fumbling*): Now look. . . . Look. . . . We're trying to be fair and present everybody's point of view. . . .

VOICE: Why are you frightened to say anything about Hungary!

ED: We're not frightened to say anything. . . . We're trying to say . . .

VOICE: Why are you frightened to say anything about Hungary!

ED (*gets up from his desk and goes center stage*): You've got a lot to say for yourself, why don't you come down here and say it. (*There is silence from the circle.*) Come on then, come down here and say it. . . . (*Still silence.*) Come on then. Come on! (*EDITOR turns to prompt corner.*) Dick!

DICK (*putting his head around proscenium*): Yes?

ED: Put the house lights up.

House lights are brought in.

ED: Come on, then. Come up on the stage and say what you want to say!

INTERRUPTER, a man, stands up in circle.

INTER: All right I will! (*He leaves the circle, comes down the stairs, through the stalls doors and down the center aisle. He reaches the pit.*)

ED (*As INTERRUPTER is coming down the stairs, turns to wings*): All right, all right. Leave it to me. (*Calls to LIGHTS BOX.*) LIGHTS! Let's have some light on the stage!

LIGHTS BOX (*over the monitor*): Which lights do you want?

ED: All of them!

LIGHTS BOX: Is this plotted?

ED: No, it doesn't matter, hold the next cue. (*INTERRUPTER should, by now, be at the foot of the stage.*)

ED (*to INTERRUPTER*): Come on. The stage is yours. (*INTER. comes up on stage rather reluctantly. EDITOR retires to his desk.*)

INTER (*to EDITOR*): Well, all I'm saying is, this is supposed to be a what-you-call-it "Living Newspaper" and dealing with things that are happening now; but so far, all you can talk about is Suez. Hungary is what everybody's talking . . .

ED: Well, don't tell me, tell the audience.

INTER (*to audience*): Well, I'm going to say, in case they don't want to say it here, what I think, and there's thousands, there's millions of people think the same. Everybody I've talked to—thinks it's terrible what Russia's done in Hungary. As bad as Hitler. They go in there with tanks. They shoot down women and children, and you call that Communism, Socialism, whatever you like to call it. I call it murder.

2ND VOICE FROM AUDIENCE: Quiet!

INTER: Why should I be quiet? I've got a right to speak, this chap asked me.

2ND VOICE: Nobody wants to hear you!

INTER: You're afraid to let them hear what I've got to say—

2ND VOICE: Why don't you go home?

INTER: Shoot me, go on! If you had a gun you'd shoot me, wouldn't you? (*To audience.*) That's what they call Free Speech.

2ND VOICE (*getting up from seat near front of stalls and coming down to stage*): I didn't pay 3 and 6 to come and listen to you. (*Climbs up on stage.*)

ED (*getting up*): I think you'd better get off and go back to your seat.

2ND VOICE: I will, I will, but I want to say something first. He's told you what he thinks about Hungary. I'll tell you what *I* think—I think the Red Army was absolutely right to go into Budapest! If they hadn't, there'd be a fascist government there by now! It's a class question and you can't expect Russia to stand by while an anti–working-class gang gets in. . . .

INTER: What about shooting women and children?

2ND VOICE: I'm a Socialist. . . .

INTER: You're a Communist. . . .

2ND VOICE: I'm a Socialist, and I stand by the Soviet Union, yes, I stand by the Soviet Union! Seven million of them gave their lives fighting against Hitler!

INTER: They're a lot of murderers!

ED: All right, hold it, you two.

Various members of cast have come onto stage from both wings.

INTER: This is supposed to be a working-class theatre. What's Unity coming to?—You let people like this come and shoot their filthy mouths off—

ED: Calm down, we've had enough of this. . . .

MALE ACTOR: He's right, we shouldn't allow chaps like that. . . .

GIRL SECRETARY: He's not right—the Russians are doing terrible things in Hungary. Why shouldn't we say so?

2ND ACTOR: What are you acting in Unity Theatre for? If you don't understand—

GIRL SECRETARY: I didn't come here to study politics—I just want to act, but if it's going to mean putting over some Party Line that I don't agree with—

3RD ACTOR (*other side of stage*): Here, here. I voted against this show going on in the first place. We should have had the Burlesque—

ACTRESS: Don't talk rubbish!

2ND ACTRESS: It's not rubbish—look what it's started! Nobody's clear about anything—

4TH ACTOR: I didn't like that bit about tearing up Party Cards—

Then a babble from everyone, very quick and overlapping each other.

SEVERAL OF CAST:
   —Why shouldn't he tear up his Party Card? It's what's happening—!
   —We should have treated Hungary differently—!
   —I still say the Burlesque—!
   —You're up the creek—!
   —We let Eden off too lightly—!
   —We shouldn't be afraid to say what we think—!

INTER (*topping it*): You Reds are all the same! If Russia does it, it's all right!

2ND VOICE: Go on talking! You'll never smash the Soviet Union!

ED (*trying to make himself heard*): QUIET everybody—Quick now—PLEASE! (*He gets up on rostrum.*) SHUT UP! SHUT UP! EVERYBODY! (*They do so reluctantly.*) Right. That's better. All right, now, everyone off stage—everyone. Hurry up now. And you two (*To* INTERRUPTERS) go back to your seats—and try and control yourselves for the rest of the evening.

The cast go off and INTERRUPTERS *climb down from the stage and return to seats.*

ED: Now perhaps we can carry on. I'm sorry for that interruption, but in a way I'm not. It might almost be a sort of prelude to the next scene. (*Calls into prompt corner.*) DICK! We'll take it from a ticker tape—O.K.!

DICK (*off*): O.K.

ED (*calls to* LIGHTS BOX): We're going from the beginning of the ticker tape scene, all right Tom?

LIGHTS BOX (*over monitor*): O.K. Whenever you're ready.

ED: We're ready.

Lights go down on rest of stage. Spot on EDITOR's *corner. The* SECRETARY *reads off ticker tape, sound of tape coming over speaker.*

SECRETARY: French Communist paper *L'Humanité* attacked by large crowd—Premises smashed and set on fire—Three Communists beaten to death—Police take no action. . . .

Over speaker comes chant of crowd, rising and dying away—"Soviet Assassins! Soviet Assassins!" in French. As it dies away:

SECRETARY: Students besiege Russian embassy in London—Break through Police guard—Scale walls and break window. . . .

Over speaker—"Down with the Reds! Down with the Reds!" Light fades on EDITOR's *corner. English and French crowds come on from opposite sides still chanting their slogans. They mill around, the mood rising almost to one of hysteria. At its peak, a young* RED ARMY MAN *holding rifle at the ready appears in a spot on the rostrum. The crowds see him and surge forward yelling:*

SEVERAL VOICES:
   —Murder!
   —String him up!
   —Lynch him!

The RED ARMY MAN *watches them warily. A middle-aged working-class* WOMAN *comes on, sees the screaming crowds, and forces her way through them until she reaches a point just below the* RED ARMY MAN. *She turns and stands between him and the mob.*

WOMAN: Leave him alone!

The crowd quiets somewhat and the light on them fades a little, leaving her and RED ARMY MAN *in the spot. She speaks to him as though the others were not there.*

WOMAN: Are you surprised? After what you've done? Oh yes, I suppose you can justify it—find reasons—or will you turn around tomorrow and say it was all a "terrible mistake"? I never thought I'd say this to you, but I'll say it to you now—*I'm ashamed of you—sick ashamed!* When the other side does what you did I expect it. But *you*—somebody I—I . . . (*She falters, unable to go on.*) I brought up my kids to believe in you—you were something to love and live up to. What are you now? Don't you see? They don't believe in you anymore. All the wonderful things you've done—40 years of—of—splendor—blown away overnight. Well, I'm not going to take away their hopes, I'm not going to let them forget—what you were and what you *can* be! I'll *never* let them forget—however hard you make it for me!

She is almost crying now with anger and shame. She hits him hard around the face. He claps his hand to his cheek and stares at her, stunned. The crowd goes mad. They start screaming louder than ever.

SEVERAL VOICES:
—That's right! Let him have it!
—Kill the swine!
—Kill him—Kill him—Kill him!

The WOMAN *whips around on them and cries out in a voice from the depths of her being:*

WOMAN: No! I am the only one that's got the right to hit him!

Blackout. INDIAN *walks down into spot.*

INDIAN: My name is (*actor's name*). I am an actor here, and like all of us I have an opinion. Of course, it is not only my own. Millions of my countrymen share it. Millions of people here in Great Britain share it. So all I perhaps need to do tonight is to remind you of it. (INDIAN *walks down.*) In 1945, after the most frightening and devastating war we have known, a child was born. The child was called the United Nations. At its birth and at its christening were the representatives of all the nations of the world. It was agreed and signed by charter that this child should be appointed to speak and arbitrate for all nations, great or small, and that all nations should be equal before it. In Paris, in December 1948, the infant issued this appeal to the world, an appeal breathtaking in it's beauty, simplicity and courage. It was called "The Declaration of Human Rights."

Spot in on WOMAN *dressed in white on rostrum.*

WOMAN: Whereas recognition of the inherent dignity and of the equal and inalienable rights of all members of the human family is the foundation of freedom, justice and peace in the world . . .

SECOND WOMAN moves into spot.

2ND WOMAN: Whereas disregard and contempt for human rights have resulted in barbarous acts which have outraged the conscience of mankind, and the advent of a world in which human beings shall enjoy freedom of speech and belief and freedom from fear and want has been proclaimed as the highest aspiration of the common people . . .

1ST WOMAN: Whereas it is essential, if man is not to be compelled to have recourse as a last resort to rebellion against tyranny and oppression, that human rights should be protected by the rule of law . . .

*Third figure—*MAN*—moves into spotlit area.*

MAN: Now, therefore, the General Assembly proclaims this universal declaration of human rights as a common standard of achievement for all peoples and all nations, to the end that every individual and every organ of society shall strive by teaching and education to promote respect for these rights and freedoms and by progressive measures, national and international, to secure universal recognition and observance, both among the peoples of member states themselves and among the peoples of territories under their jurisdiction. . . .

Fade area lights—back to INDIAN.

INDIAN: The child was appointed five* guardians, representing the balance of great powers then existing in the world. These guardians, The United States of America, the Soviet Union, Britain and France, in order to effect and protect the decisions of the United Nations, formed themselves into the Security Council. One great danger was realized, that in the event of disagreement, any combination of three or four members of the Security Council, might, by combination, invoke the power of the United Nations to intimidate or attack the other. To safeguard themselves, they invoked what they termed the "right of Veto"; in other words, they agreed that if they speak at all, they must speak with one voice, and if they could not reach agreement that they should appeal to the General Assembly of all nations for a decision. It was here, around the right of veto, that the young United Nations had its first lesson in the . . . tortuous resources of the human intellect.

Fade to Security Council scene. Fade in to four men seated around a circular table. They are IVAN IVANOVITCH, PIERRE DUBOIS, SMEDLEY CAVENDISH, *and* JOE BLOW.

JOE: Gentlemen, the reason for our meeting today is a serious one. The decisions to reach in this room will have worldwide repercussions. As you know, the International Police Force is now a fact. Before long, over a million uniformed men will be marching in the ranks, and they will all be subject to our commands. Gentlemen, consider deeply before you reply, and remember, our decision will influence every man in that force. Gentlemen (*leaning forward earnestly*), what color shall the uniform be?

IVAN: Mister Chairman. My country has been debating this question for many months. At first we felt the uniform should be painted green and the helmets black; after much discussion it was felt that the uniform should be painted black and the helmets green. Some sug-

gested making the helmets and uniforms black and painting the soldiers green. Eventually it was decided that the only proper color for the uniform of the United Nations Police Force, should be . . . Red. And I respectfully submit that color in the form of a revolution.

JOE: Uh. What?

IVAN: I mean resolution. I say, Red.

JOE: Mr. Ivanovitch, although I do not disagree with your choice, I point out a very great danger in such a move. Should the Police Force be summoned to a Police Action, let us say, and should they by some remote chance be caught in gunfire . . . and perhaps wounded, the blood of their wounds would fuse with the color of their uniforms and it would be impossible to tell who was hurt and who was not. I would like to suggest therefore, Fellow Delegates, that though Red is a trifle dangerous, Red, White, and Blue is a fetching color scheme. It would have a marvelous psychological effect on our troops.

SMEDLEY: Here, here.

JOE: And that the Red appear in the form of 48 stars in the top right hand. . . .

PIERRE: Gentlemen, please, let us not be chauvinistic about this. May I suggest instead that a more aesthetic color scheme for uniforms is polka-dot blue. It puts our soldiers in a merry frame of mind. It makes them forget they're being sent on Police Actions.

IVAN: Polka-dot blue! Why don't you dress them in skirts and pinafores?

PIERRE: There's no need to be rude, Mr. Ivanovitch.

SMEDLEY: Gentlemen, if I might make a point. Most men are averse to Military Service because the apparel tends to discourage their interest. There is nothing fetching or attractive about uniforms. Therefore, I suggest, in place of uniforms, we clothe our troops in evening wear; nothing fancy, a dinner jacket and white trousers, perhaps for the tropical forces—pin-striped trousers for the continental troops. Something that will make them feel they are not warriors at all, but guests at a tea party. I assure you we would get a much greater percentage of volunteers through such a scheme. And it would go a long way towards making war respectable.

*Ed note: China was the fifth member of the Security Council but, unaccountably, does not appear in the scene.

JOE: Gentlemen, consider the expenses. After all, this has to be borne by our respective governments. As it is, we can take existing uniforms and dye them whatever color we finally agree upon. Now I have a motion before the meeting. I propose Red, White and Blue as the colors for the new uniform. Do I heard a second? Mr. Cavendish, I said, do I hear a second?

SMEDLEY: Oh yes, yes, certainly I second it.

PIERRE: I third it.

IVAN: I veto it.

JOE: You what?

IVAN: I veto it.

PIERRE: In that case, I propose the color be polka-dot blue. Do I hear a second?

JOE: In view of the veto on the first proposition I second this one. All in favor say aye.

All say "aye" except IVAN.

JOE: The motion is carried.

IVAN: I veto it and propose the color be Red.

PIERRE: Impossible. Red is a disastrous color, and completely demodé.

IVAN: But it is the color of your best wines, Mr. DuBois. Think what a worldwide advertisement it could become for Vin Rouge.

PIERRE: Excellent point. I second it.

IVAN (*to* SMEDLEY): And the flag of St. George, Mr. Smedley? Is it not a bold red cross?

SMEDLEY (*taking the hint*): St. George and the Dragon. Yes, a rather apt simile. Providing it is overlaid with a pattern of small heraldic dragons—I vote for Red.

IVAN: The motion is carried. Red it is.

JOE: I veto it.

IVAN: What?

JOE: I veto it.

IVAN: I veto your veto.

SMEDLEY: Just a moment, I veto your veto of his veto.

PIERRE: I veto the whole business. Let's break and have some wine.

IVAN: I veto wine. We'll break and have vodka.

JOE: Vodka, hell! We'll have a Coke.

SMEDLEY: A Coke at three in the afternoon, unthinkable. I veto that suggestion. How about some tea?

IVAN: Vetoed.

SMEDLEY: Scotch.

PIERRE: Vetoed.

SMEDLEY (*meekly*): Some milk perhaps?

PIERRE: Mendes France in Mollet's clothing. I veto milk.

SMEDLEY (*weakly*): A little chocolate.

JOE: Vetoed, I want Coke.

IVAN: Vodka!

SMEDLEY: Tea!

PIERRE: Wine!

IVAN: Red!

JOE: Red, White and Blue!

PIERRE: Polka-dot blue!

SMEDLEY: Evening clothes!

They all chant together: "Veto! Veto! Veto!" *Fade on scene. Fade up on* INDIAN.

INDIAN: Nevertheless, despite its infinite problems, despite the tendency of this modern ziggurat to become a Tower of Babel, the work went on, quietly, unpublicized by a world hungry for sensation, the work of the Economic and Social Council, with it's own subcommittees. The World Health and Food Organizations in Geneva and Rome have already set an example to the world that puts our politicians—and ourselves—to shame.

Cut into film of UNESCO work. Duration 12 to 15 minutes. At end of film, EDITOR *comes on.*

EDITOR: Ladies and gentlemen, what (*actor's name*) has just presented to you is not, we feel, a panacea for all the world's ills. The United Nations is not a godhead, not a father figure for our political guidance—I think we have been suffering from too many father figures as it is. More important, like all man-made things, it *is* capable of considerable abuse. "What crimes may be permitted in thy name?" Nevertheless, it is all we have. As (*actor's name*) has told us, it is still a child. But it's a child whose upbringing lies in our hands. (FRED *walks onstage front of black curtains.*) Hullo! Are you still wandering around? Why don't you go and get some sleep, you're beginning to look like a scriptwriter.

FRED: I've been trying to sleep. I went up in the Green Room for a kip. But as soon as I dropped off, I had the most horrible dreams. I dreamt I was in Hungary—and I was just going to be shot by the Russians. Then, somehow or other, I don't know how it happened, but I was on the other side. I was a Security Guard and the mob was going to hang me from a tree. I no sooner got out of that when I was surrounded by British paratroops. Then the Egyptians were after me—then the Israelis—then the woman upstairs—all fighting. . . . I told somebody in the bar just now, you know what they said?

EDITOR: No.

FRED: They said I should go to the United Nations. Do you reckon I should?

EDITOR: We could arrange it.

FRED: There's one snag.

EDITOR: What's that?

FRED: I don't trust 'em. No, that's a fact, I don't trust any of 'em.

Lights fade on FRED *and* EDITOR. *Black tableau curtains and lights in on four U.N.* DELEGATES *seated around table. In front of each is card reading "USA," "UK," "France," "USSR."*

USSR: The proposals I now wish to place before you are as follows: (1) Within two years the armed forces of the USSR, the USA, and China to be reduced to between one and one and-a-half million men of each country, and the forces of Britain and France to 65,000 men for each country. (2) Production and use of hydrogen and atom bombs be banned. (3) A cut of one-third be made in 1957 in the Soviet, French, and British forces in Germany. Aerial photography be permitted up to 500 miles each side of the East-West frontier in Europe. Finally, a summit disarmament conference be called between the powers represented here and including India.

USA: I am gratified to hear that the proposals put forward by my Government for "open skies" have been accepted—at least in part. Nevertheless, there are certain problems, previously raised, which have yet to be solved—in particular, the question of the banning of nuclear weapons. It is one thing to agree that they should be banned; it is quite another thing to ensure that they are indeed banned.

UK: Gentlemen, our experiences in the past have been rather unfortunate in this respect. Our discussions here might have advanced much further, could we be sure that the words of some nations could be taken at more than their face value.

FRANCE: I would go further. Unless the nations here can be trusted to carry out both the spirit and the letter of United Nations agreements, then the proposals we have heard become devoid of meaning.

USSR: Such a pious statement comes strangely from the lips of delegates whose nations have, during the past few weeks, flouted the authority of the United Nations in the Middle East.

USA: I take it you include the USSR in that remark—or are recent events in the Balkans to be considered outside the scope of this organization?

USSR: If you are referring to Hungary, that is a matter to be settled by the Hungarian Government.

UK (*blandly*): Which Hungarian Government?

Enter FRED, *still in pajamas. He walks down towards table.*

FRED (*hesitantly*): Excuse me—

USA: Who are you?

FRED: I was told to come here and tell you about my complaint.

USA: Where are your credentials?

FRED: My credentials are that I've got a terrible problem. I can't sleep.

UK (*terribly blasé*): I must say, old chap, I sympathize with you there.

FRANCE: It is impossible to work in this atmosphere. (*He storms out.*)

UK: I entirely agree. (*He goes out.*)

USSR: . . . (*shrugs shoulders and goes out.*)

USA: I am sorry we abandoned isolationism! We never had this trouble with Coolidge! (*He goes.*)

FRED is alone. The spot on him dwindles.

FRED: Thank heaven they've gone. Now I can have a bit of peace and quiet. (*He takes a cigarette from a box on table, lights it and leans back in a chair with his feet on the table.*) That's better—ah, quiet at last. . . . It *is* quiet isn't it. (*He eases himself off table.*) I've never known it so quiet—I wonder where they've all gone—Oh well, good riddance any way. (*Light goes down further.*) Perhaps I can get a bit of sleep now—but it's too quiet to sleep—I'm not used to it. (*He stabs cigarette and gets up.*) I bet if I were to shout, nobody would hear me. A bloke could die here, nobody would know. Funny being alone in the dark—the things you hear and see. Those shadows—lucky I haven't got an imagination—I'd think they were all sorts of things. I'd think they were moving! (*He whistles tunelessly, the whistle finally fading away as his panic grows.*) It's terrible being alone—all sorts of terrible things could happen—murders and wars and famines—nobody would know, nobody would see! It's not natural. I've got to have people 'round me—anybody—even my worst enemy would be better than nobody at all. At least you could see him and know what he's up to! (*Suddenly crying out.*) *Where are they? Where have they gone?* (*Calls off stage.*) Come back!—all of you!—*Any* of you!—*Please!* (*The* FRENCH DELEGATE *backs into the spot, turns and sees* FRED. FRED *almost clutches him.*) Oh, thank heavens, you're back.

The lights go up and spread. All the DELEGATES *walk in, take their seats. The* UK DELEGATE *looks up from his papers.*

UK: Now gentlemen, to continue. . . .

Tableau curtains close on them.

END

"Edgy in London": Clippings from the *Daily Worker, New Statesman and Nation, What's On in London,* and *Peace News*

"WHERE'S THE EDITOR!"

It is an old and wise maxim of Press procedure that the Editor's decision is final. The trouble with London Unity Theatre's newly opened living newspaper *World on Edge* is that we are left without any editorial decision.

Courageously scrapping a burlesque which would have been ill-timed in the present tragic situation, the Labour movement's theatre decided instead to speak, and speak quickly, on Suez and Hungary.

A living newspaper was the only possible form, despite the difficulty that this theatrical method of presenting social and political criticism has not been used in Britain for at least ten years.

No trouble here, however. Unity shows that it can handle the form; production and staging are competent.

Points are swiftly and slickly made, as when two Tory ladies have their telephone quarrel about Eden from opposite corners of the stage.

The deadly imbecility of H-bomb politics is grilled to a turn in the Rock 'n' Roll number.

But all this is in the first act. In the second, chaos takes over.

It will not do to give us an "Editor" without a mind of his own.

We can accept the fact of a Communist tearing up his card, for that is news. But we cannot take the Unity Theatre company beating its breast in public.

The stage "Editor," introducing a readers' letters column, cannot shrug off responsibilities with the slick line:

"You have heard of 'Your Question Answered.' Our column will be different. 'Your Answers Questioned.'"

Seeking for something to believe in the company plumps for the Food and Agriculture Organisation of the United Nations.

It is the corny old retreat of the do-gooders of the '30s, dismayed by the impotence of the League of Nations, and pointing in timid hope to a League sub-committee's success in curbing a little opium smuggling.

Unity invites people to send in their own contributions to the "Readers' Forum."

I am sure they will get scores, even hundreds, and that these will help the production. I would like to make mine here. You have a show which will bore nobody. You rightly decided to deal with the most critical issues of the day, and I recognise that you have set yourself a difficult task.

But a newspaper must take a stand. Abdication of responsibility has never yet saved an editor or a newspaper.

If you think Soviet troops should get out of Hungary, come out and say so. Equally, if you think not, say so.

"This is what our readers say" is no substitute.

—(EDWARD ARMITAGE, *Daily Worker,*
27 November 1956)

. . .

"LONDON DIARY"

When you have worshipped a god who turns out not only to have feet of clay but to be an ogre who devours your friends, your reactions are likely to be violent. How deeply the Russian massacre of Hungarian workers has lacerated the minds and hearts of British Communists is best shown by the present revue at the Unity Theatre called *World on Edge*. It pulls no punches; it even shows a C.P. member tearing up his party card in angry disillusion. The Soviet representative on the Security Council is a figure of ridicule and contempt. The theme is the unhappy predicament of an ordinary citizen. He is shown as a pathetic dim-wit, wandering around unable to sleep, finally driven to a reluctant dependence on the U.N. The excitements come after the performance. It ends on a note of "It's no longer up to Them; it's up to Us—and You." And then, when you are expecting the final curtain, the house lights are flooded and the audience is integrated with the cast. General discussion follows. A guest from outside is introduced on to the stage to start the argument. Last Saturday it was Jim Cameron, who tells me that he was warned to look out for some rough and edgy treatment; he got it, but less than he expected. A wild, wholly despairing ex-Communist jumped onto the stage and violently denounced Moscow. Someone else leapt up and shouted that he was an unashamed party man and would defend the C.P. to the death. Unity was accused of having been the "mouth-piece of King Street," which was passionately denied. Indeed, it was explained, its quarrel with King

Street had led it to sacrifice its usual profitable Christmas burlesque, with the result that the company is already £1,700 in debt. "Somehow someone has got to stop the *killing*," they said. The usual troop of idealistic opinions were all expressed. The argument might have gone on all night. Cameron ended it by saying that thank goodness there was somewhere in the London theatre where actualities were being taken seriously. The outsider at next Saturday's roustabout is to be Sydney Silverman.

—(*New Statesman and Nation,*
15 December 1956)

. . .

"THEATRE"

There is, of course, no reason in all the world why, in political matters, the opinion of a reviewer of theatrical entertainments should be any more sensible or valuable than that of your barber, and it is doubtless very proper that such things should be ignored by this department; as, indeed, they usually are. This week, though, I have no choice but to emerge from the grease-paint vacuum to discuss *World on Edge!* a display at the Unity Theatre which is entirely political. I shall do so, I hope, with the same chilly detachment that invariably guides these notices; which means almost certainly that I am about to enrage both Right and Left.

The Unity offering is described as "A Living Newspaper" and has the provocative headline, "All Your Answers Questions." I went to it uncertain of what I might find. This particular theatre club has always been unashamedly Russophile and its membership is heavily laced with enthusiastic Communists. If *their* answers were to be questioned, it was conceivable that a lively evening was in store. Or if, conversely, Unity was to stick by the Party line, the evening promised to be no less lively—in view of recent defections among the faithful, and the resignation of the *Daily Worker* correspondent whose despatches from Budapest were suppressed by his employers. The only chance of a dull time lay in the possibility of shilly-shallying, and I'm sorry to say that that is largely what came to pass.

There were two issues on the agenda, and you will guess that these concerned Egypt and Hungary. The people on the stage, at first reporting and later discussing, devoted a great deal of time to the Anglo-French assault on the former country and it seemed hardly possible to quarrel with their point of view which was, naturally, that this was in flagrant defiance of the United Nations. There was a jocular sketch in which a criminal pleaded in court that he had only broken into the jeweller's shop to keep the constabulary on its toes.

At this point the management evidently anticipated irritable interruptions from an audience anxious to get on to more controversial ground, and a stooge planted in the circle demanded to know, "What about Hungary?" He was invited on to the stage to voice his indignation. A second heckler then came down to reply in standard Party terms, but I don't think his contention that the Red Army was in Budapest to quell a Fascist uprising was expected to be taken seriously. The Unity view seemed to be the one delivered by a sad-faced woman who addressed herself to an armed Russian soldier thus: "When the *other* side does what you did, I expect it—but you—*you*—I brought up my kids to believe in *you*—forty years of splendour—blown away overnight!"

It occurred to me that this melancholy outburst might have been more appropriately addressed to our own armed Forces, but it was plain that it was the Soviet aggression that we were intended to regard as a unique lapse from the path of virtue. And this, I think, is how the rot really set in. Hungary was altogether too hot a potato for the comrades to handle. Whenever it was brought up, it was cooled off by a comparison with the other outbreak of violence in the Middle East, and I could not but remark the disparity in the vehemence with which Soviet and British actions were deplored. The former were chided sorrowfully, the latter with a keen and ill-concealed glee.

A naïve little woman stood up and said earnestly, "I feel that the key to this lies in disarmament," and much was made of the recent Soviet proposals in this connection. There was also

a long digression in which the lofty phrases of the U.N. Charter were recited, together with a documentary film devoted to the work of its Food and Agriculture Organisation.

It was, as I've already noted, an evening of shilly-shallying. The writers, when driven to the wall, were prepared to say that the operations in Egypt and Hungary were alike in being shameful and indefensible. They were not prepared to dwell on the gulf that separated them in terms of brutality and barbarity, nor to call unequivocally for United Nations action against *all* the invaders.

(KENNETH A. HUTTEN, *What's On in London,*
30 November 1956)

• • •

"WAR IS NO SOLUTION"

World on Edge! (at the Unity Theatre, Goldington Street, N.W.1) is a courageous, lively and remarkably balanced dramatic examination of the wars in Egypt and Hungary, that will appeal to all who "place loyalty to Christian and moral standards above sectional and personal interests."

Its "only dogma" is that "war is no solution to the world's problems."

"The art of Brinkmanship" and "Stock Exchange Rock" are wittily written:—

> "We're going to rock around those stocks and shares,
> "We're going to take UNO unawares."

—and follow the sight of Communists and Tories resigning from their Parties, and a realisation of the stalemate when East and West hold H-bombs.

A long waiting list for hospital beds, the allocation for which has been cut by £500,000 by the Government, is contrasted with £1,500,000,000 expended on armaments.

We see refugees in Budapest and Port Said; and the editor of this "Living Newspaper" says, "I think we're all mad. None of us want war, yet we allow it. The world is on the edge. It wants one push and that's that."

The explanations of "police action," "separating combatants" and "fascist counterrevolution" are amusingly dramatised and fairly discussed.

 Though US expenditure of up to one hundred million dollars on methods of liberation which may include terror is quoted, shame is strongly expressed at the Soviet's killings in Hungary.

"No one has the right to impose government by armed force." We hear too of three French Communists beaten to death by an anti-Soviet crowd.

"What are we going to do to dispel fear?" The Declaration of Human Rights is read and the work of FAO and WHO "which put politicians and ourselves to shame" perfectly illustrated from Rotha's "World of Plenty."

Mayor La Guardia stresses, "We've never had a surplus of food, only more in one country than the people of that country can afford to buy."

Lord Boyd-Orr emphasises that the cost of feeding the world is nothing compared with the cost of war. We have to plan our world so as we have enough of the foods we need and which are good.

"Whatever our race or religion we want peace and plenty. If we pay the price we can have both."

After showing the abuse of the Veto at UN, the performance concludes with an appeal to reason, to try again.

It is a production which merits the support of all sane-minded readers at once.

—(RONALD MALLONE, *Peace News*,
7 December 1956)

Peter Weiss

THE INVESTIGATION
1965

Translated by Ulu Grosbard and Jon Swan

The Investigation opened simultaneously in fifteen theaters on 19 October 1965. The premiere production is considered to be that of the Freie Volksbühne in West Berlin, directed by Erwin Piscator, scenery by Hans-Ulrich Schmückle, music by Luigi Nono. The cast included Dieter Borsche, Günther Pfitzmann, Horst Niendorf, Kurt Mühlhardt, O. A. Buck, Robert Dietl, Angelika Hurwitz, Hilde Mikulicz, Peter Capell, Hugo Schrader, Martin Berliner, Hans Deppe, Heinz Giese, Tilo von Berlepsch, Emmerich Schrenk, Gerd Martienzen, Erich Goetze, Hellmut Gerhard Schinschke, Walter Holetzko, Peter Schiff, Otto Måchtlinger, Lother Koster, Jochen Sehrndt, Alexander Ponto, Carlo Kluge, Günter Glaser and Manfred Meurer. Other productions were East Berlin (dir. Manfred Wekwerth et al.), Dresden (dir. Heinz Pietzsch), Essen (dir. Erich Schumacher), Gera (dir. Jürgen Kern), Köln (dir. Joachim Mühsam), Leuna (dir. Klemm et al.), London (dir. Peter Brook), Meiningen (dir. Dieter Gross), Munich (dir. Paul Verhoeven), Neustrelitz (dir. Rainer Lange), Potsdam (dir. Peter Kupke), Rostock (dir. Hans Anselm Perten), Stuttgart (dir. Peter Palitzsch) and Weimar (dir. Helmut Pollow).

AUTHOR'S NOTE

In the presentation of this play, no attempt should be made to reconstruct the courtroom before which the proceedings of the camp trial took place. Any such reconstruction would, in the opinion of the author, be as impossible as trying to present the camp itself on the stage.

Hundreds of witnesses appeared before the court. The confrontations of witnesses and the accused, as well as the addresses to the court by the prosecution and the replies by the counsel for the defense, were overcharged with emotion.

Only a condensation of the evidence can remain on the stage.

This condensation should contain nothing but facts. Personal experience and confrontations must be steeped in anonymity. Inasmuch as the witnesses in the play lose their names, they become mere speaking tubes. The nine witnesses sum up what hundreds expressed.

The variety of experiences can, at most, be indicated by a change of voice or bearing.

Witnesses 1 and 2 are witnesses who worked with the camp administration.

Witnesses 4 and 5 are female, the rest male witnesses from the ranks of the surviving prisoners.

Each of the 18 accused, on the other hand, represents a single and distinct figure. They bear names taken from the record of the actual trial. The fact that they bear their own names is significant, since they also did so during the time of the events under consideration, while the prisoners had lost their names.

Yet the bearers of these names should not be accused once again in this drama.

To the author, they have lent their names which, within the drama, exist as symbols of a system that implicated in its guilt many others who never appeared in court.

CHARACTERS

JUDGE
PROSECUTING ATTORNEY
COUNSEL FOR THE DEFENSE
1ST WITNESS
2ND WITNESS
3RD WITNESS
4TH WITNESS
5TH WITNESS
6TH WITNESS
7TH WITNESS
8TH WITNESS
9TH WITNESS
ACCUSED #1   ADJUTANT MULKA
ACCUSED #2   BOGER
ACCUSED #3   DR CAPESIUS
ACCUSED #4   DR FRANK
ACCUSED #5   DR SCHATZ
ACCUSED #6   DR LUCAS
ACCUSED #7   KADUK
ACCUSED #8   HOFMANN
ACCUSED #9   MEDICAL ORDERLY KLEHR
ACCUSED #10   SCHERPE
ACCUSED #11   HANTL
ACCUSED #12   S.S. CORPORAL STARK
ACCUSED #13   BARETZKI
ACCUSED #14   SCHLAGE
ACCUSED #15   BISCHOF
ACCUSED #16   BROAD
ACCUSED #17   BREITWIESER
ACCUSED #18   BEDNAREK

THE SONG OF THE PLATFORM*

(I)

---

* *Editors note*: The English translation printed here retains the lack of punctuation in the German text. It also preserves the slight rhythmic variations the author made in transferring the spoken original to the stage.

JUDGE:
The witness
was stationmaster of the railroad station
where the trains arrived
How far was the station from the camp
1ST WITNESS:
A mile and a quarter from the old army
    camp
About three miles from the main camp
JUDGE:
Did your work take you into the camp
1ST WITNESS:
No
I only had to make sure
that the tracks in use were in good condition
and that the trains arrived and departed
according to schedule
JUDGE:
Were you in charge of
setting up the train schedules
1ST WITNESS:
No
I only had to take care of technical measures
related to scheduling the shuttle traffic
between the station and the camp
JUDGE:
The record contains scheduling orders
bearing your signature
1ST WITNESS:
It's possible that in the absence
of the officer in charge
I occasionally had to sign one
JUDGE:
Were you aware
of the purpose of the transport
1ST WITNESS:
I wasn't informed on that matter
JUDGE:
You knew
that the trains were loaded with people
1ST WITNESS:
All we were told
was that it had to do
with relocation transports
carried out under government orders
JUDGE:
Didn't it seem strange to you
that the trains returning
from the camp were always empty

1ST WITNESS:
  The people forwarded
  had been relocated there
PROSECUTING ATTORNEY:
  At present
  you hold a high executive position
  in the management
  of the government railways
  Therefore we may assume
  that you are acquainted with the equipment
  and loading capacity of trains
  How were the trains
  that arrived in your station
  equipped and loaded
1ST WITNESS:
  The trains in question were freight trains
  According to the bills of lading
  some 60 persons were forwarded in each car
PROSECUTING ATTORNEY:
  Were the cars freight cars
  or were they cattle cars
1ST WITNESS:
  Some of the cars were the kind
  used to ship cattle
PROSECUTING ATTORNEY:
  Were there any sanitary installations
  in the cars
1ST WITNESS:
  I don't know
PROSECUTING ATTORNEY:
  How often did these trains arrive
1ST WITNESS:
  I couldn't say
PROSECUTING ATTORNEY:
  Did they arrive frequently
1ST WITNESS:
  Yes
  Sure
  It was a very busy terminal
PROSECUTING ATTORNEY:
  Didn't it strike you
  that the trains
  came from almost every country in Europe
1ST WITNESS:
  We had so much to do
  There wasn't any time to worry about
  things like that
PROSECUTING ATTORNEY:
  Did you ever wonder about

what was going to happen
to the people in those trains
1ST WITNESS:
  We heard they were being shipped in
  for supplementary labor
PROSECUTING ATTORNEY:
  But there weren't only people fit for work
  but whole families
  with old people and children
1ST WITNESS:
  I didn't have time
  to check the contents of the trains
PROSECUTING ATTORNEY:
  Where did you live
1ST WITNESS:
  In the town
PROSECUTING ATTORNEY:
  Who else lived there
1ST WITNESS:
  The town had been cleared
  of its original population
  Camp officials lived there
  and personnel from surrounding industries
PROSECUTING ATTORNEY:
  What kind of industries were those
1ST WITNESS:
  They were branch plants
  of I-G Farben
  Krupp and Siemens
PROSECUTING ATTORNEY:
  Did you see the prisoners
  who had to work there
1ST WITNESS:
  I saw them
  when they marched to work and back
PROSECUTING ATTORNEY:
  What condition were they in
1ST WITNESS:
  They marched in step and they sang
PROSECUTING ATTORNEY:
  You didn't hear anything
  about conditions in the camp
1ST WITNESS:
  There were so many insane rumors going
      around
  you never knew what to think
PROSECUTING ATTORNEY:
  You heard nothing
  about the annihilation of people there

1ST WITNESS:
  How could anybody believe a thing like that
JUDGE:
  The witness was responsible
  for the delivery of the freight
2ND WITNESS:
  All I had to do was
  turn the trains over to the shunting crew
JUDGE:
  What were their duties
2ND WITNESS:
  They hitched the switch engine onto the trains
  and took them on into the camp
JUDGE:
  How many people would you estimate
  were there in each car
2ND WITNESS:
  I can't provide you with any information
  on that matter
  We were strictly forbidden
  to examine the trains
JUDGE:
  Who prevented you
2ND WITNESS:
  The guards
JUDGE:
  Were there bills of lading
  for all the transports
2ND WITNESS:
  In most cases there were
  no bills attached
  There was only the number
  chalked up on the freight car
JUDGE:
  What were the numbers
2ND WITNESS:
  60 or 80 head
  It varied
JUDGE:
  When did the trains arrive
2ND WITNESS:
  Mainly at night
PROSECUTING ATTORNEY:
  What impression did you get
  of the freight
2ND WITNESS:
  I don't understand the question
PROSECUTING ATTORNEY:
  As superintendent

of the government railroads
you are undoubtedly familiar
with travel conditions
Didn't you get some idea of conditions
by looking in through air vents
or by hearing sounds coming from the cars
2ND WITNESS:
  Once I saw a woman
  holding a small child up to the air vent
  and calling out
  over and over
  for some water
  I got a pitcher of water
  I started to lift it up to her
  when one of the guards came over
  and said
  if I didn't leave at once
  I would be shot
JUDGE:
  How many trains would you estimate
  arrived in the station daily
2ND WITNESS:
  On the average a train a day
  When the pressure was on
  two or three
JUDGE:
  How long were the trains
2ND WITNESS:
  They had up to 60 cars
JUDGE:
  Were you ever
  in the camp
2ND WITNESS:
  I went in with the switch engine once
  because there was something
  to clear up in the bill of lading
  Just back of the entrance gate I got off
  and went into the camp office
  I almost didn't get out of there either
  because I didn't have my pass with me
JUDGE:
  Did you see anything of the camp
2ND WITNESS:
  Nothing
  I was just glad to get out of there
JUDGE:
  Did you see the chimneys
  at the end of the platform
  or the smoke and glare

2ND WITNESS:
  Yes
  I saw smoke
JUDGE:
  And what did you think
2ND WITNESS:
  I thought
  those must be the bakeries
  I had heard
  they baked bread in there day and night
  After all it was a big camp

                (II)

3RD WITNESS:
  We traveled five days
  On the second day
  our provisions were used up
  There were 89 of us in the freight car
  Our suitcases and bundles besides
  We relieved ourselves
  in the straw
  Many were sick
  and eight were dead
  At the stations along the way
  we could look out through the air vents
  and see the women personnel
  handing food and coffee up to the guards
  Our children had stopped crying
  when on the last night we were switched
  off the main track onto a siding
  We passed through a flat region
  lit up by searchlights
  Then we came up along a very long
  building like a shed
  There was a tower
  and under it an archway
  The locomotive whistled
  before we went in under the arch
  The train stopped
  The freight-car doors were pulled open
  Prisoners in striped uniforms appeared
  and yelled in at us
  Out
  Move
  Fast
  Fast

It was four feet down the ground
The ground was broken rock
The old people and the sick fell
onto the sharp stones
The dead and the luggage
were thrown out of the cars
Then we heard
Leave everything where it is
Women and children there
Men on the other side
I lost sight of my family
All around
people were shouting for
their families their relatives
They were being beaten with clubs
Dogs were barking
Searchlights and machine guns were trained
at us from the observation towers
At the end of the platform was the sky
glowing red
The air was full of smoke
The smoke had a sweet singed smell
From then on
this smoke was always there
4TH WITNESS:
  I could still hear my husband
  calling me
  We were lined up
  and were not permitted to change places
  We were a group
  of 100 women and children
  We stood five in a row
  Then we had to walk past some officers
  One of them held his hand at chest level
  and pointed his finger
  left then right
  The children and old women
  went to the left
  I went to the right
  The left group had to cross the tracks
  to get over to a road
  I saw my mother for just a second
  She was in the group with the children
  That made me feel a bit easier
  and I thought
  we'll manage to get together again
  A woman next to me said
  They're going to a rehabilitation camp

She pointed to the trucks
parked on the road
and a Red Cross car
We could see
them being loaded into a truck
and we were glad they could ride again
The rest of us had to go
down the muddy road on foot.

5TH WITNESS:
I held my sister-in-law's child
by the hand
My sister-in-law
was holding her smallest child
in her own arms
Then one of the prisoners came up to me
and asked if the child was mine
when I said it wasn't
he said I should give it to its mother
I did and I thought
perhaps mothers got special consideration
They all went off to the left
I went to the right
The officer who divided us
was very friendly
I asked him
where the others were going
and he said
They're just going to shower now
You'll see them again in an hour

JUDGE:
Does the witness
know who this officer was

5TH WITNESS:
I found out later
that his name was Dr Capesius

JUDGE:
Can the witness tell us
which of the accused is Dr Capesius

5TH WITNESS:
When I look at their faces
I find it hard to tell
whether I recognize them or not
But that man there
looks familiar to me

JUDGE:
What is his name

5TH WITNESS:
Dr Capesius

ACCUSED #3:
The witness must have confused me
with someone else
I never took part in the selections
on the platform

6TH WITNESS:
I had known Dr Capesius from my hometown
I was a doctor
and before the war
he used to call on me frequently
as a representative of the Bayer concern
On the platform I greeted him and asked
what was going to happen to us
He said
Everything's going to be fine here
I told him
my wife was not well
Then she should stand over there
he said
She will receive medical attention there
He pointed to the group
of old people and children
I told my wife
You go over there and get in line
She went over with her niece
and a couple of other relatives
to where the sick stood
They were all taken away in trucks

JUDGE:
There is no doubt in your mind
that that man was Dr Capesius

6TH WITNESS:
No
I spoke with him
At the time it was a great pleasure for me
to see him again

JUDGE:
Accused Capesius
do you know this witness

ACCUSED #3:
No

JUDGE:
Were you present on the platform
for the arrival of transports

ACCUSED #3:
I was only there
to receive the medical supplies
from the prisoners' luggage

I had to store these supplies
in the dispensary
JUDGE:
Whom else among the accused
did you see on the platform
6TH WITNESS:
Him
I remember his name
His name is Hofmann
JUDGE:
Accused Hofmann
what were your duties on the platform
ACCUSED #8:
I was there to keep peace and order
JUDGE:
How did you do that
ACCUSED #8:
The people were lined up
Then the doctors decided
who was fit for work
and who wasn't
Sometimes there were more
and sometimes less
The percentage was decided beforehand
It was determined by the need
for manpower at the time
JUDGE:
What happened to those
who were not used for work
ACCUSED #8:
They were gassed
JUDGE:
What percent of the people
was fit for work
ACCUSED #8:
On the average
one third of a transport
When the camp was overloaded
transports went straight through
without being opened
JUDGE:
Did you yourself
carry out any selections
ACCUSED #8:
All I can say
is that sometimes
when they begged me to
I pushed some of the unfit
over to the fit group

JUDGE:
Were you allowed to do that
ACCUSED #8:
No
It was against regulations
but we closed our eyes to it
JUDGE:
Were special rations issued
for men assigned to platform duty
ACCUSED #8:
Yes
We got bread
a portion of sausage
and a half pint of brandy
JUDGE:
In the performance of your duties
did you ever need to resort to force
ACCUSED #8:
There was always a lot of confusion
and naturally sometimes
somebody had to be straightened out
or slapped
I only did my duty
Whatever I'm assigned to do
I do my duty
JUDGE:
How did you get this assignment
ACCUSED #8:
By accident
It was like this
My brother had an extra uniform
I could use
So it didn't cost me anything
Then there were business reasons
My father had a restaurant
that a lot of party members used to come to
When I was sent off
I had no idea
where I would end up
When I got to the camp I asked
Am I really in the right place
They told me
You're in the right place here all right
PROSECUTING ATTORNEY:
Did you know what would happen
to the people who were selected
ACCUSED #8:
Mr Prosecutor
I personally didn't have anything

against those people
There were some like them at home too
Before they were taken away
I always used to tell my family
You go right on buying from them
After all they are human too
PROSECUTING ATTORNEY:
Was that still your attitude
when you were doing platform duty
ACCUSED #8:
Well
except for small troubles
like you get whenever
you have a lot of people in a small place
and except for the gassings
which naturally were terrible
still
everybody had a chance to survive
Personally
I always behaved decently
Anyway what could I do
Orders are orders
And now just because I obeyed
I've got this trial hung on my neck
Mr Prosecutor
I've always tried to live in peace
just like everybody else
and then suddenly I'm hauled out
and everybody starts yelling about Hofmann
That's the one that's Hofmann
they say
What do they want from me
7TH WITNESS:
When we were all lined up
one of the guards came and asked
Does anyone have any physical handicap
A few people stepped forward
They thought
they would get easier work that way
They were sent over to those
who had to go to the left
When the guard led them off
there was a disturbance
and he started shooting
Five or six people were killed
JUDGE:
Does the witness see
the person he has been speaking of
in this room

7TH WITNESS:
Your Honor
it has been many years
since I last stood in front of them
and I find it hard
to look them in the face
That one looks like him
That could be him
His name is Bischof
JUDGE:
Are you sure
or do you have any doubts
7TH WITNESS:
Your Honor
I could not sleep at all last night
COUNSEL FOR THE DEFENSE:
We question the credibility
of the witness
It may be assumed
that he recognized the face of our client
from pictures published in the press
Certainly the exhaustion of the witness
is in itself no proof
of the validity of his testimony
JUDGE:
Would the accused Bischof
care to take a stand
in regard to the accusation
ACCUSED #15:
I frankly can't understand
just what the witness is trying to say
I don't understand either
why he says
five or six
If he had said five
or if he had said six
one or the other
then I could understand it
JUDGE:
Were you assigned to platform duty
ACCUSED #15:
All I had to do
was to organize the prisoners into groups
I never did any shooting
Your Honor
all I would really like to do here
is make a clean breast of everything
It has been troubling me deeply for years
I have developed heart trouble

from all the worry
And then they have to foul up
the last years of my life
with this whole stinking mess

PROSECUTING ATTORNEY:

What stinking mess is
the accused referring to

JUDGE:

The accused is excited
Certainly he can scarcely be referring to
the proceedings
initiated by the attorney general

THE ACCUSED laugh

8TH WITNESS:

As a prisoner
I belonged to the cleanup detail
Our job was
to carry off the luggage of the arrivals
The accused Baretzki
took part in the selections on the platform
and he accompanied
the trains to the crematoriums

JUDGE:

Do you recognize the accused

8TH WITNESS:

That is Barrack-leader Baretzki

ACCUSED #13:

I only belonged to the guard unit
For a guard to do the selecting
was out of the question
A barrack-leader could not select the unfit
on his own
Only a doctor could do that

JUDGE:

Were you aware of the purpose
of the selections

ACCUSED #13:

We heard about it
I was deeply shocked
Once when I was home on leave
I told my mother about it
She wouldn't believe it
That's impossible
she said
Anyway people don't burn
because you can't burn flesh

8TH WITNESS:

I saw

how Baretzki pointed out the people
with his swagger stick
Things never went fast enough for him
He always tried to speed them up
Once a train loaded with 3000 people
came in
Most of them were sick
Baretzki yelled at us
You've got 15 minutes
to get them out of there
A baby was born during the unloading
I wrapped it in a piece of cloth
and set it down by the mother
Baretzki came at me with his stick
and beat me and the woman
What are you doing with that garbage there
he yelled
and he kicked the baby
so it flew about 10 yards
Then he ordered
Bring that shit over here
By then the child was dead

JUDGE:

Can you swear to that

8TH WITNESS:

I can swear to that
Baretzki had a special way of hitting
He chopped
He was known for it

JUDGE:

What was it like

8TH WITNESS:

He did it with the flat of his hand
Like so
Against the aorta
In most cases
it resulted in death

ACCUSED #13:

But the witness just got through saying
that I had a stick
Now if I had a stick
surely
there was no need for me
to hit with my hand
And if I used my hand
then I wouldn't need the stick
Your Honor
the whole thing is a slander
I didn't have any special chop at all

THE ACCUSED laugh

(III)

JUDGE:
  Who else did you see on the platform
8TH WITNESS:
  All the doctors were out on the platform
  The selections were part of their work
  Dr Frank was there
  Dr Schatz and Dr Lucas
COUNSEL FOR THE DEFENSE:
  Where were you
  while the selections were being made
8TH WITNESS:
  At various points on the platform
  picking up suitcases
COUNSEL FOR THE DEFENSE:
  Can you give us a description
  of the platform
8TH WITNESS:
  The platform was behind the entrance gates
  To the right of the platform
  was the men's camp
  To the left the women's camp
  At the end of the ramp
  right and left
  the new crematoriums
  numbered II and III
  At the switch
  the trains were usually
  shunted onto the track to the right
COUNSEL FOR THE DEFENSE:
  How long was the platform
8TH WITNESS:
  About 850 yards long
COUNSEL FOR THE DEFENSE:
  How long were the trains
8TH WITNESS:
  They usually took up about two thirds
  of the platform
COUNSEL FOR THE DEFENSE:
  Where were the selections carried out
8TH WITNESS:
  In the middle of the platform
COUNSEL FOR THE DEFENSE:
  Where did the people line up
8TH WITNESS:
  At both ends of the platform

COUNSEL FOR THE DEFENSE:
  How wide was the platform
8TH WITNESS:
  About 30 feet wide
COUNSEL FOR THE DEFENSE:
  There the people stood
  in two groups next to each other
  each group lined up in rows of five
  We doubt very much that
  in that crowd
  the witness could have stood
  near the selecting officers
  for any amount of time
JUDGE:
  Accused Dr Frank
  did you take part
  in the selection procedure
ACCUSED #4:
  I was sometimes assigned
  to platform duty
  as a replacement
  My assignment was
  to remove equipment
  from arriving dentists
  for use in the camp's dental station
  I also registered the dentists
  and dental technicians
  and saw to it that they were issued clothing
  When someone claimed to be a dentist
  but in fact wasn't
  I did not send him back
  After all
  we had to have somebody around
  to clean up
JUDGE:
  Did you ever try
  to have yourself released
  from platform duty
ACCUSED #4:
  I reported to Dr Wirth at headquarters
  for that very reason
  The only answer given was
  Camp duty is front-line duty
  Any refusal
  will be regarded as desertion
  and dealt with accordingly
JUDGE:
  Did you escort
  transports to the gas chambers

ACCUSED #4:
No
Escort duty was the responsibility
of the guards
I myself did all I could
to help the prisoners
In my ward
I made their stay
as pleasant as possible
They could wear suits that fit
and they didn't have to shave their heads
JUDGE:
Accused Dr Schatz
did you take part in the selections
ACCUSED #5:
I never had anything to do with them
When I was ordered to the platform
to receive medicines
or medical instruments
I did all I could to get out of it
I came to the camp
under protest
I was ordered there
from an infantry dental station
Furthermore I would like to point out
that I enjoyed an unusually cordial
relationship with the prisoners
JUDGE:
Accused Dr Lucas
what did you do on the platform
ACCUSED #6:
I never did anything there at all
Time and again I said
My job as a doctor is to save lives
not destroy them
Also as a Catholic
I cannot take any other position
When attempts were made to force me I said
I was physically unable
I feigned various illnesses and tried
to get transferred back to the army
as soon as possible
I approached my old commanding officer
who said
I should do my best
to avoid making myself
unpleasantly conspicuous
Once on leave I even went so far
as to speak to an archbishop

a friend of mine
and to a prominent lawyer as well
Both told me
that illegal orders need not be obeyed
but that this should not be carried
to the extreme
where one's own life might be endangered
We were at war
and all sorts of things
were going on
PROSECUTING ATTORNEY:
Dr Lucas
what kind of illnesses did you simulate
when you were ordered to take part
in the selections
ACCUSED #6:
I feigned biliary colic
or some kind of stomach upset
PROSECUTING ATTORNEY:
Didn't anyone ever find it odd
that your attacks of colic
occurred only
when you were assigned to platform duty
ACCUSED #6:
There was never any trouble
Passive resistance
was the only way
for me to have as little to do
with those things as possible
I still don't see even now
how else I could have acted then
PROSECUTING ATTORNEY:
And when you did have to participate
what did you do
ACCUSED #6:
Only in three or four cases
my excuses didn't work
I was ordered
to the platform
under the threat
of being taken away then and there
if I did not obey
The meaning of the threat
was unmistakable
PROSECUTING ATTORNEY:
And then you took part in the selections
ACCUSED #6:
All I had to do
was choose people who were fit for work

and the way I chose
many who were obviously unfit
also came into the camp
PROSECUTING ATTORNEY:
    And the others
ACCUSED #6:
    They were led aside
PROSECUTING ATTORNEY:
    When the selection was over
    what happened to the luggage
8TH WITNESS:
    It was taken to the personal-effects camp
    sorted there and stacked
PROSECUTING ATTORNEY:
    How large was the personal-effects camp
8TH WITNESS:
    It consisted of 35 barracks
PROSECUTING ATTORNEY:
    Could you estimate
    the amount and value
    of the goods seized
8TH WITNESS:
    Before deportation
    the prisoners had been advised
    to take with them
    as many objects of value as possible
    sheets clothing money and tools
    The reason given was
    that where they were going
    they wouldn't be able to obtain anything
    Thus
    they brought every last thing
    they could
    Much had already been taken from them
    on the platform
    even before the selection began
    The doctors in charge took
    not only medical instruments
    but also suitcases
    full of currency and jewelry
    Then the guards and the trainmen
    took their share
    For us
    too
    there was always something left over
    which we could use to trade with
    later on
    Still when the final inventory
    was drawn up in the personal-effects office

the total value amounted to millions
PROSECUTING ATTORNEY:
    Could you give us any particulars
    about the value of the goods
    taken from the prisoners
8TH WITNESS:
    According to the final inventory
    covering the period from April 1 1942
    to December 15 1943
    the value of the currency
    stocks precious metals and jewels seized
    amounted to 33 million dollars
    In addition 1900 freight-car loads of textiles
    valued at 12 million dollars
    This does not include the final year
    in which the biggest transports
    were yet to come
PROSECUTING ATTORNEY:
    Who received these assets
8TH WITNESS:
    The goods were forwarded
    to the treasury
    or in some cases to the Department of Finance
JUDGE:
    Were there ever any attempts at resistance
    on the platform
    The arrivals greatly outnumbered
    the guards
    They were being separated from their families
    Their possessions were being taken from them
    Did they not resist
9TH WITNESS:
    They did not resist
JUDGE:
    Why not
9TH WITNESS:
    The arrivals were starved
    and exhausted
    Their only desire was
    to rest at last
JUDGE:
    Did they have no idea
    of what was in store for them
9TH WITNESS:
    How could they foresee
    that practically speaking
    they had ceased to exist
    Each one of them still believed
    he could survive

THE SONG OF THE CAMP

(I)

4TH WITNESS:
When we had crossed the tracks
and were lined up
in front of the camp gate
I heard
a prisoner say to one of the women
That Red Cross truck takes gas
to the crematoriums
Your relatives will be killed there
The woman began to scream
An officer who had overheard the prisoner
turned to the woman
and said
But my dear woman
how can you believe
what a prisoner tells you
They're all either criminals
or insane
Look at the way their ears stick out
and their shaved heads
How can you listen to such people

JUDGE:
Do you recall
who the officer was

4TH WITNESS:
I saw him again later
I was his secretary
in the Political Section
His name is Broad

JUDGE:
Can you point out
the accused Broad

4TH WITNESS:
That is Mr Broad

THE ACCUSED BROAD *nods amiably to the* WIT-
NESS

JUDGE:
What happened to the prisoner

4TH WITNESS:
I heard
he was sentenced to 150 strokes
for spreading reports of atrocities

He died from it

JUDGE:
Does the accused Broad
have anything to say to this

ACCUSED #16:
I don't recall the case
But 150 strokes
We never ordered that many

3RD WITNESS:
Even though our luggage was left behind
and we were separated
from our families
we still walked unsuspecting
through the gate between the barbed wire
We thought
our wives and children
were going to be fed on the other side
and that we would be allowed
to see them again soon
But then we saw
hundreds of ragged figures
many of them starved down to skeletons
We lost all hope

6TH WITNESS:
One of them came up to us
and shouted
Prisoners
See that smoke behind the barracks
That smoke
is your wives and children
And for you too now that you're in here
there's only one way out
Up through the soot in the chimneys

3RD WITNESS:
We were pushed into a washroom barrack
Guards and prisoners came
with stacks of papers
We had to strip
and everything we still had on us
was taken away
Watches rings papers pictures
were registered in personal files
Then numbers were tattooed
on the left forearm

JUDGE:
How was this done

3RD WITNESS:
The numbers were pricked into our skin
with a needle stamp

then ink was rubbed in
Our hair was cut off
and we had a cold shower
After that we got our clothes

JUDGE:
What clothes were you given

3RD WITNESS:
A pair of shorts full of holes
an undershirt
a torn jacket
a pair of patched pants
a cap
and a pair of wooden shoes
Then we set off at the double
to our barrack

JUDGE:
What did your barrack look like

3RD WITNESS:
A wooden barrack without windows
A door in the front and one in the back
Small skylights up under the roof
Right and left
three-decker bunks
the bottom level on the ground
the bunks supported by partition beams
Length of the barrack about 130 feet

JUDGE:
How many prisoners
were quartered there

3RD WITNESS:
It was built to hold 500 people
There were 1000 of us

JUDGE:
How many such barracks were there

3RD WITNESS:
More than 200

JUDGE:
How wide were the bunks

3RD WITNESS:
About six feet
Six men to a bunk
They had to keep shifting from
their right side over to their left

JUDGE:
Was any bedding provided

3RD WITNESS:
Some of the bunks had straw
The straw was rotten
and it sifted down from the top

onto the lower bunks
There was one blanket for each bunk
The men who lay on the outside
kept trying to pull the blanket
over their way
The strongest lay in the middle

JUDGE:
Were the barracks heated

3RD WITNESS:
There were two stoves
The stovepipes went into a chimney
in the middle of the barrack
They were bricked over
and the top of the brickwork
served as a table
The stoves were hardly ever heated

JUDGE:
Were there sanitary installations
in the barracks

3RD WITNESS:
There were wood troughs for washing
in the washroom barracks
A pipe with holes in it ran over the troughs
Water dripped out of the pipe
In the latrine there were long cement troughs
covered with boards with round holes in them
200 people could use them at one time
The latrine detail saw to it
that nobody sat there too long
They clubbed the prisoners right and left
to drive them out
Many of the prisoners
simply couldn't get done that quick
Part of their rectum stuck out from the strain
As soon as they had been driven out
of the latrine
they got back in line
There wasn't any paper
Many people tore pieces off their clothes
to wipe themselves with
or stole
pieces from each other's clothes at night
to have some in reserve
You had to relieve yourself in the morning
After that you couldn't
Anybody caught trying
was locked up
Water from the washroom barracks drained
into the latrine

to carry off the filth on the floor
The latrines kept getting stopped up
because the water pressure was too low
Then the shit detail came in
to pump it out
The stink from the latrines
mixed in with the smell
of the smoke

4TH WITNESS:

The bowls we were given
served three different functions
to wash in
to get our supper in
and to relieve ourselves in at night
In the women's camp
the only place you could get water
was right next to the latrine
At that thin trickle of water
that ran off into the vats full of excrement
women stood and drank
and tried
to collect enough water in their bowls
so they could wash
Those who gave up washing
had given up

5TH WITNESS:

Even as I jumped out of the freight car
into that confusion on the platform
I knew that what mattered here was
to look out for yourself
to try to work your way up
to make a good impression
and to keep away from anything
that might drag you down
When they made us lie down on the tables
in the reception room
and inspected our rectums
and our sexual organs
for concealed valuables
every last remnant
of our usual life
vanished
Family
home
occupation
and possessions
were ideas
that were wiped out
when the number

was stamped into your arm
And already we had started to live
with a new set of values
and to adjust to this world
which for anyone
who wanted to survive in it
became a normal world
The supreme commandment was
to stay healthy
and to show you were physically strong
I stuck close to those
who were too weak
to eat their rations
so I could take their food
at the first opportunity
I didn't take my eyes off
those who were dying
if they had a better sleeping place than I
Our way up in this new society
started in the barrack
which was our home now
From starting out sleeping
on the cold mud floor
we fought our way up
to the warm places on the top bunks
When two had to eat
out of the same bowl
they stared at each other's throats
to make sure
the other wasn't swallowing
an extra spoonful
It was normal
that everything had been stolen from us
It was normal
that we stole too
Dirt sores and diseases
were what was normal
It was normal
that all around us people were dying
and it was normal
to live in the face of one's own death
Our feelings grew numb
and we looked at corpses
with complete indifference
and that was normal
And it was normal
that there were some among us
who helped those who stood over us
to beat us

The woman who became
the Barrack-elder's maid
had come up in that world
and those who managed
to ingratiate themselves
with the Barrack-leader
rose even higher
Only the cunning survived
only those who every day
with unrelenting alertness
took and held their bit of ground
The unfit
the retarded
the slow
the gentle
the bewildered and the impractical
the ones who mourned and the ones
who pitied themselves
were crushed

6TH WITNESS:

The first morning
we lined up for roll call
It was raining
We stood there for hours
Behind the barbed wire
on the other side of the platform
the women were being beaten
and shoved into trucks
They were naked and they screamed
at us
They wanted us to help them
and we couldn't help them

4TH WITNESS:

I walked into a barrack
that was full of corpses
I saw
something move a little among the dead
It was a young girl
I pulled her out of the barrack
into the street
and asked
Who are you
How long have you been here
I don't know
she said
Why were you lying in there
with the dead
I asked
I can't be with the living any more

she said
She died that night

5TH WITNESS:

We were sent out to dig graves
Many of the women collapsed
trying to shovel the mud out
We were up to our hips in water
The guards stood by looking on
They were very young
One of the women turned to the captain
Captain
she said
I can't work this hard anymore
I'm pregnant
The guards laughed
and one of them pushed her
down with a shovel
and kept her under the water
until she drowned

7TH WITNESS:

I heard
a guard talking through the barbed wire
to a nine-year-old boy
You know a lot for a boy your age
he said
The boy answered
I know that I know a lot
and I also know
I'm not going to learn any more
He was loaded into a truck
with a group
of about 90 children
When the children started
screaming and struggling
the boy yelled
Get in here
Get in the truck
Stop your crying
You saw the way
your parents and grandparents
went
Climb in
they you'll get to see them again
And as they were being driven off
I heard
him shout back to the guard
You won't be forgiven
anything

(II)

8TH WITNESS:
  In the morning we got
  a pint of coffee substitute
  and a fifth of an ounce of sugar
  Some of us
  still had a piece of dry bread
  saved up from the night before
  At noon we got soup
  It was made out of scraps of potatoes
  turnips and cabbage
  a minimum of meat or fat
  and a mealy nutrient
  that gave the soup
  its typical taste
  Sometimes there were pieces of paper
  or rags in the soup
  Prisoners fought
  to get not to the head of the line
  but as near the end as they could
  The top third of the soup
  was water
  Only toward the bottom
  was there anything nourishing
  In the evening after roll call
  each of us got his piece of bread
  from 10 to 12 ounces
  and various supplements
  about ¾ of an ounce of sausage
  an ounce of margarine
  or a teaspoonful of turnip jelly
  On Friday we sometimes got
  five or six potatoes
  Often these extra rations
  were cut in half
  or weren't given out at all
  because the camp personnel
  from the guards on
  up to the commanding officer
  helped themselves
  to the prisoners' food supply store
  as much as they wanted
PROSECUTING ATTORNEY:
  How many calories
  did the daily rations contain
8TH WITNESS:
  About 1000 to 1300 calories
  At rest

the body uses 1700
At hard labor
it requires about 4800
Since all the prisoners worked hard
their last reserves were quickly consumed
Movements grew progressively slower
according to the various stages of hunger
until there was no strength left
to keep the body in motion
Drowsiness and apathy
were characteristic symptoms
of weakness
Emaciation of the body
was accompanied by an exhaustion of
    mind
which terminated in a complete loss
of interest in all external events
In this condition
a prisoner could no longer
concentrate his thoughts
His memory was so greatly weakened
that frequently he could not
even remember his own name
On the average
a prisoner could not hold out
longer than three months
COUNSEL FOR THE DEFENSE:
  How then did you
  manage to survive
8TH WITNESS:
  Those who survived
  were only those
  who in the first few weeks managed
  to get some kind of inside position
  either because of their specialized skills
  or by being assigned to special duties
  in the camp work
  A special-duty prisoner
  who knew how to
  exploit the privileges of his position
  could obtain practically anything
COUNSEL FOR THE DEFENSE:
  What privileged position did you hold
8TH WITNESS:
  I was a prisoner doctor
  At first in the quarantine camp
  Later in the infirmary
JUDGE:
  What were the conditions there

8TH WITNESS:
    In the quarantine camp there were rats
    They bit not only the corpses
    but also the critically ill
    In the morning the feet of the dying
    were often bleeding from rat bites
    At night the rats took the bread
    out of the prisoners' pockets
    The prisoners frequently accused each other
    You stole my bread
    But it was the rats
    Fleas infested the camp
    by the million
    Those who had boots got rid of them
    because the fleas
    made those precious possessions unbearable
    With socks and rags
    you could at least scratch
    Conditions in the prisoners' infirmary
    were better
    There were crepe-paper bandages
    cellulose
    a keg of ichthyol ointment
    and a barrel of talcum powder
    All wounds were treated with the ointment
    and barber's itch was covered with talcum
    so it wouldn't show
    We had a few tablets of aspirin
    They were strung up on thread
    Patients with fever under 100 degrees
    were allowed one lick
    Patients with fever over 100 degrees
    could lick twice

JUDGE:
    What were the most common illnesses

8TH WITNESS:
    Aside from general weakness
    and bodily injuries caused by ill treatment
    we had spotted fever and paratyphoid fever
    abdominal typhus erysipelas and tuberculosis
    as well as the characteristic camp disease
    incurable diarrhea
    Furunculosis flourished in the camp
    Guards clubbed abscesses open
    until the skin peeled off to the bone
    In the camp I saw diseases
    I never dreamed I would see
    diseases
    one only reads about in medical texts

    There was Noma for instance
    a disease that occurs
    only in completely debilitated people
    eating holes through the cheeks
    until you can see
    right through to the teeth
    Or phemphicus
    an extremely rare disease
    which detaches the skin
    in blisters
    and after a few days
    results in death

9TH WITNESS:
    After the evening roll call
    the Barrack-elder
    picked some of us out for exercise
    We had to hop like frogs
    He kept shouting
    Jump faster faster
    and if somebody didn't keep up
    he pounded them with a footstool
    until they collapsed

JUDGE:
    What was this Barrack-elder's name

9TH WITNESS:
    His name was Bednarek
    I can point him out

ACCUSED #18:
    I never heard of anybody being beaten
    during the exercise period

JUDGE:
    What did take place
    during the exercise period

ACCUSED #18:
    Prisoners who attracted attention
    had to do some light exercises
    To the left
    To the right
    That was all

9TH WITNESS:
    In winter Bednarek made
    prisoners stand under the cold shower
    for half an hour
    until they were numb with cold
    Then they were thrown out into the yard
    where they died

ACCUSED #18:
    These accusations are simply made up
    I couldn't possibly

have done that sort of thing
I was a special-duty prisoner myself
I had the Kapo over me
the work supervisor
and the Camp-elder
I myself
and I can say it with pride today
let prisoners sleep in my room
and in our block after supper
we always had a good time

9TH WITNESS:
After Bednarek
had beaten a prisoner to death
he went into his room
and prayed

ACCUSED #18:
It's true
I'm a religious man
But as for praying I didn't dare
There were too many informers for that
And I never killed anybody
At the most
there was maybe a slap now and then
when I had to break up an argument

3RD WITNESS:
More than any of the others
there was one who was first
when it came to beating or killing
His name was Kaduk
Kaduk we all knew what that name meant

JUDGE:
Could the witness
point out the accused Kaduk

3RD WITNESS:
That is Mr Kaduk

THE ACCUSED grins at the WITNESS

3RD WITNESS:
The prisoners called him
Professor
or
the Holy Doctor Kaduk
because he carried out
selections on his own
With the crook of his walking stick
he fished out his victims
by the neck or leg

ACCUSED #7:
Mr Chairman

that statement is not true

3RD WITNESS:
I was there
when Kaduk had hundreds of prisoners
hauled out of the hospital
They had to strip in the laundry barrack
and then run past Kaduk
in single file
He held his walking stick out
about a yard off the ground
in front of him
They had to jump over it
If they touched the stick
they were taken off to be gassed
If they cleared it without touching it
they were beaten until they collapsed
Now try it again
Kaduk shouted
But the second time
nobody cleared it

ACCUSED #7:
I selected no prisoners
I made no decisions
I had no such authority

JUDGE:
What was within your authority

ACCUSED #7:
I had to be on hand
during the selections
I watched like a hawk
to make sure nobody
from the selected group slipped over
into the work-fit group

JUDGE:
Did you have any other duties
on the platform

ACCUSED #7:
Yes
I had to organize
the group traffic

JUDGE:
How did you do that

ACCUSED #7:
Everybody out
Baggage on the platform
Fall in columns of five
Forward march

3RD WITNESS:
Kaduk fired

at random
into the crowd
ACCUSED #7:
    I never even thought of
    firing at random
    If I had wanted to shoot
    I would have hit
    whoever I was aiming at
    I was strict
    I'll admit that
    But I only did
    what I had to do.
JUDGE:
    And what did you have to do
ACCUSED #7:
    Make sure that the operation ran smoothly
    It was regulations that children
    were immediately set aside
    also mothers who didn't want
    to be separated from their children
    Everything went without a hitch
    The transports rolled in
    like a line of sausages
    There wasn't any need to rough anybody up
    They all took it very well
    They didn't resist
    since they could see
    resistance would have been pointless
6TH WITNESS:
    Once Kaduk hit one of the prisoners
    in our work detail
    knocked him down
    then laid his walking stick
    down across his throat
    put one foot on each end of the stick
    and rocked from side to side
    until the man choked to death
ACCUSED #7:
    Lies
    Lies
JUDGE:
    Sit down Kaduk
    You will not shout at the witness
ACCUSED #7:
    Mr Chairman
    What he says there
    simply isn't true
    All I care about here is the truth
    No prisoner was ever killed

that way in our camp
We had orders
to go easy
with the work force
Sometimes though I'd only lift my hand
and somebody would fall over
pretending he had fainted

THE ACCUSED laugh

ACCUSED #7:
    Mr Chairman
    we weren't interested in beating anybody
    We were on our feet
    from 5:30 in the morning
    and then at night we
    still had to go on platform duty
    That was enough for us
    Mr Chairman
    all I want is to live in peace
    These last years have proved that
    I was a hospital attendant
    and my patients loved me
    They can bear me out on that
    Papa Kaduk
    that's what they called me
    Doesn't that tell the whole story
    Why should I have to pay now
    for what I had to do then
    Everybody else did it too
    So why of all people
    did they arrest me

(III)

4TH WITNESS:
    The more you managed to push down
    whoever was under you
    the more secure your own position was
    I could see the whole face
    of our Barrack-elder change
    when she talked to a superior
    She was cheerful and friendly then
    and behind that you could feel her fear
    Sometimes her supervisor
    treated her like her best friend
    and she enjoyed many privileges
    But if the supervisor
    had had a bad night just once

then she would be done for
from one minute to the next
And she had already been through everything
she had seen her relatives shot down
she had been forced to watch
as they murdered her children
she had grown completely numb
like the rest of us
She knew
that once she went under
nobody would help her
and whoever took over
would go on beating
so she beat us
because she wanted
to stay on top at any price

5TH WITNESS:
The questions
of right and wrong
didn't exist any longer
The only thing that counted
was what was immediately useful
Only our masters could afford
to have moods
and even to show how moved they were
or to be sympathetic
and make plans for the future
The camp doctor Dr Rohde
let me work in his ward
He found out
we had gone to school in the same city
and asked me
if we hadn't perhaps met each other
at the Ritter
where he frequently stopped in
for a glass of wine
and I thought
Fine if that's the way you want it
I'll go along with you
and so I reminded him of his youth
and he said
After the war we'll meet there again
for a glass of wine
Dr Mengele sent flowers to a pregnant woman
and the wife of the camp commander
sent her best regards
and a baby sweater she had knitted herself
to the children's barrack
where somebody had thought

it would be a nice idea
to paint dwarfs on the walls
and set up a sandbox
The paths to the crematoriums
were carefully raked after each batch
of prisoners had gone by
The bushes along the way were trimmed
and flower beds had been planted
in the grass that grew
over the underground chambers
Mengele used to arrive smartly dressed
his thumbs stuck in his belt
He would nod pleasantly to the children
who called him Uncle
before they were cut up in his laboratory
But there was another man I remember
His name was Flacke
Nobody starved to death in his ward
and the prisoners there all wore
clean clothes
I asked him once
Sir who are you doing this for
Someday
we will all have to be done away with
because not a single witness
can be left behind
He said
there will be enough of us here
who will find a way to prevent that

PROSECUTING ATTORNEY:
Do you mean to say
that each one of the men in charge
could take a stand
against conditions in the camp
and change them

5TH WITNESS:
That is exactly what I was trying to say

1ST WITNESS:
Normal reactions
were possible only in the first few hours
After one had been there for a time
it was impossible
Once you fell into the routine
you were caught
and had to cooperate

PROSECUTING ATTORNEY:
As a doctor
you were assigned to prevent
the spread of epidemics

1ST WITNESS:
  Cases of spotted and typhoid fever
  had broken out among some
  of the camp personnel and their families
  I was ordered
  by the Health Institute
  to report to the camp
PROSECUTING ATTORNEY:
  Then your presence there had nothing to do
  with treating the prisoners themselves
1ST WITNESS:
  No
PROSECUTING ATTORNEY:
  Did you get an impression
  of conditions in the camp
1ST WITNESS:
  Shortly after I arrived
  the doctor in charge of the laboratory
      said
  I realize this is all new to you
  but it's not half so bad
  We don't have anything to do
  with the liquidation program here
  and it's none of our business either
  If after two weeks
  you decide you don't want to stay here
  you can leave
  With the intention to leave the camp
  after two weeks
  I went to work
  A few days later
  the chief camp doctor Dr Wirth
  ordered me to take part
  in the selections on the platform
  When I told him
  I don't want to have anything to do
  with that
  he said
  You won't have much to do there
  But I still refused
PROSECUTING ATTORNEY:
  What happened when you refused
1ST WITNESS:
  Nothing
  I didn't have to take part
  in the selections
PROSECUTING ATTORNEY:
  Did you leave the camp
  after your first two weeks

1ST WITNESS:
  No
  I decided to stay after all
  and see if I couldn't do something
  about the contagious diseases
  I felt that I could
  at least in a few cases
  prevent things
  without exposing myself
  As a result of my work the threat
  of the epidemic was ended
PROSECUTING ATTORNEY:
  Among the camp personnel that is
  Not among the prisoners
1ST WITNESS:
  Yes
  That was my assignment
JUDGE:
  You were at that time in charge
  of the sentry units both within
  and outside the camp
  also of the guard units
  attached to the work details
  What did that involve
2ND WITNESS:
  My assignment was
  to keep an eye on the guards
  to see they carried out their charge
  diligently and faithfully
JUDGE:
  What regulations were they under
2ND WITNESS:
  When a prisoner tried to escape
  the guard was required to call out three times
  before firing a warning shot
  If the prisoner still didn't halt
  he was to be shot
  to prevent further flight
JUDGE:
  Were any prisoners shot
  for this reason
2ND WITNESS:
  Not under my command
JUDGE:
  Did prisoners
  run up against the electrically charged
  barbed wires
2ND WITNESS:
  Not under my command

JUDGE:
  Did it ever occur
2ND WITNESS:
  I heard it happened sometimes
JUDGE:
  Did guard details
  obey regulations
2ND WITNESS:
  As far as I know
  Yes
  On my word of honor
JUDGE:
  Do you know anything about cap shooting
2ND WITNESS:
  About what
JUDGE:
  Shooting caps
2ND WITNESS:
  I've heard about it
JUDGE:
  What did you hear
2ND WITNESS:
  They said
  caps were thrown up
  and then they shot at them
JUDGE:
  Who threw the caps
  whose caps
  and who did the shooting
2ND WITNESS:
  That I don't know
JUDGE:
  What were you told then
2ND WITNESS:
  Yes
  Well
  A prisoner was ordered
  to take off his cap
  and throw it away
  and then
  Move
  run and get your cap they'd say
  and when he started to run
  they'd shoot him down
JUDGE:
  And if he didn't run
2ND WITNESS:
  They they'd shoot him too
  because that was refusal to obey an order

PROSECUTING ATTORNEY:
  Were special rations
  or special leaves granted
  as a reward for
  shooting prisoners attempting escape
2ND WITNESS:
  I never heard of that happening
  I don't believe it either
  To be rewarded for such behavior
  would degrade a soldier's reputation
PROSECUTING ATTORNEY:
  The court has in its possession
  documents which show
  that in a number of instances
  sentries were rewarded for
  shooting prisoners attempting escape
  Furthermore lists of prisoners
  shot while attempting escape
  were posted and periodically
  brought up to date
2ND WITNESS:
  That's news to me
PROSECUTING ATTORNEY:
  According to our information
  you are currently
  director of an insurance company
COUNSEL FOR THE DEFENSE:
  We object to
  these irrelevant interjections
  by the prosecution
PROSECUTING ATTORNEY:
  We take it for granted
  that the witness
  realizes the significance
  of a signature
2ND WITNESS:
  Certainly
PROSECUTING ATTORNEY:
  Some of these lists
  bear your signature
2ND WITNESS:
  It's possible
  that on some occasion
  I had to sign as a matter of routine
  I can't remember

THE SONG OF THE SWING

(I)

JUDGE:
　As a prisoner
　you were employed
　in the Political Division
　What did you do there
5TH WITNESS:
　At first I was stenographer and typist
　in the administrative office
　then because of my knowledge of languages
　I was made interpreter
JUDGE:
　Who assigned you to this position
5TH WITNESS:
　Mr Boger
JUDGE:
　Do you recognize
　Boger among the accused
5TH WITNESS:
　That is Mr Boger

THE ACCUSED BOGER greets the WITNESS amiably

COUNSEL FOR THE DEFENSE:
　Where precisely
　was the Political Division located
5TH WITNESS:
　It was a wooden barrack
　directly behind the entrance
COUNSEL FOR THE DEFENSE:
　Behind which entrance
5TH WITNESS:
　Just to the left behind the entrance
　to the old camp
COUNSEL FOR THE DEFENSE:
　How far was the old camp
　from the main camp
5TH WITNESS:
　About two miles
COUNSEL FOR THE DEFENSE:
　Where were your living quarters
5TH WITNESS:
　In the women's camp
COUNSEL FOR THE DEFENSE:
　Could you describe for us
　the way you took to your office

5TH WITNESS:
　We had to leave camp
　every morning
　and walk along the side of the fields
　The road crossed the tracks
　where the switch engines
　shunted the freight cars
　We frequently had to wait at the barrier
　On the other side of the tracks
　there were more fields
　and a couple of empty farmhouses
　Then we went through a barred gate
　There were trees
　and the old crematorium
　Next to it was the Political Division
COUNSEL FOR THE DEFENSE:
　Was the Political Division
　within the camp proper
5TH WITNESS:
　It was outside the camp
　First
　there were the administration buildings
　Then the two barbed-wire fences
　and the observation towers
　Behind that were the barracks
　where the prisoners lived
COUNSEL FOR THE DEFENSE:
　What did the Political Division barrack
　look like
5TH WITNESS:
　It was one story high
　and painted green
COUNSEL FOR THE DEFENSE:
　What did the administrative office look like
5TH WITNESS:
　There were flower pots on the window sills
　and there were curtains
　and on the walls
　pictures and mottoes
COUNSEL FOR THE DEFENSE:
　What kind of pictures and mottoes
5TH WITNESS:
　I can't remember anymore
COUNSEL FOR THE DEFENSE:
　Who supervised the work in the office
5TH WITNESS:
　Mr Broad
　We typists always had
　to look our best

We were allowed to let our hair grow
We wore kerchiefs
and civilian clothes and shoes
We spat on our shoes in the morning
and polished them with our hands

COUNSEL FOR THE DEFENSE:
How did Mr Boger treat you

5TH WITNESS:
Mr Boger always treated me decently
Frequently he gave me his mess kit
with the leftovers
He saved my life once
when I was about to be transferred
to a penal company
A Kapo had reported me
for doing a careless job of dusting
Mr Boger revoked the sentence.

JUDGE:
How many typists worked
in the Political Division

5TH WITNESS:
We were 16 girls

JUDGE:
What did you have to do

5TH WITNESS:
We had to keep the death lists up to date
We had to enter the particulars
relating to date and cause of death
This was called the Discharge
Mr Broad grew furious
if he found a single mistake in our typing

JUDGE:
How was the filing organized

5TH WITNESS:
There were two tables
On one table
were the card-index boxes
with the numbers of the living
On the other the boxes
with the numbers of the dead
By looking at these we could see
how many from a given shipment
were still alive
Out of a 100 after a week
there were two dozen

JUDGE:
Were all deaths
that occurred within the camp
recorded there

5TH WITNESS:
Only prisoners
who had received a number
were kept on the books
Those who were taken directly
from the platform to the gas
were not entered on any list

JUDGE:
What were the causes of death
that you entered

5TH WITNESS:
Most of them
were fictitious
For instance we were not allowed to write
Shot while attempting escape
but had to write heart attack instead
Instead of malnutrition we wrote
dysentery
We had to make sure
no two prisoners died at the same minute
and that the cause of death
corresponded to their age
Therefore no 20-year-old could die
of a weak heart
In the beginning letters were still sent
to the next of kin

PROSECUTING ATTORNEY:
Can you recall the text of these letters

5TH WITNESS:
In spite of all medical treatment
it has unfortunately been impossible
to save the life of the detained
We extend our deepest sympathies
to you for this great loss
At your request the urn
will be sent to you
COD at a cost of three dollars

PROSECUTING ATTORNEY:
Were the ashes of the deceased
actually in these urns

5TH WITNESS:
The ashes of many dead
were in those urns
We could see out of the windows
the dead piled up
in front of the old crematorium
They were dumped there by the truckload

PROSECUTING ATTORNEY:
Could you give us an idea

of the number of the dead
entered in your office
5TH WITNESS:
  We worked 12 to 15 hours a day
  on the official books of the dead
  It came to about 300 dead per day
PROSECUTING ATTORNEY:
  Were any of those deaths
  caused directly
  by the Political Division
5TH WITNESS:
  Prisoners died there daily
  either by mistreatment or execution
COUNSEL FOR THE DEFENSE:
  Where were the prisoners executed
5TH WITNESS:
  In the camp in Barrack 11
COUNSEL FOR THE DEFENSE:
  Were you allowed to enter the camp
5TH WITNESS:
  No
  but we knew of everything that went on
  Every memorandum and report
  related to the camp
  passed through our office
  Boger said to us
  What you hear and see here
  you have neither heard nor seen
JUDGE:
  How were the interrogations
  in the Political Division carried out
5TH WITNESS:
  Boger always began very calmly
  He came up close to the prisoner
  and asked the questions
  that I had to interpret
  If the prisoner didn't answer
  he shook a bunch of keys
  in front of the man's face
  If the prisoner still didn't answer
  Boger hit him in the face with the keys
  Then he went up even closer
  and said
  I have a machine
  that will make you talk
JUDGE:
  What sort of machine was this
5TH WITNESS:
  Boger called it his talking machine

JUDGE:
  Where was it
5TH WITNESS:
  In the next room
JUDGE:
  Did you ever see the machine
5TH WITNESS:
  Yes
JUDGE:
  What did it look like
5TH WITNESS:
  It was made out of poles
COUNSEL FOR THE DEFENSE:
  Are you sure
  you remember this correctly
5TH WITNESS:
  It was a frame
  They were hung on it
  We heard the beating and the screaming
  After an hour
  or after several hours
  they were carried out
  They were unrecognizable
JUDGE:
  Were they still alive
5TH WITNESS:
  If they weren't dead then
  they seldom lived much longer
  Once Boger saw me crying
  He said
  This is no place for personal feelings
JUDGE:
  For what reasons were prisoners
  subjected to such punishment
5TH WITNESS:
  Sometimes it was because somebody
  had stolen a piece of bread
  or because he was too slow
  in responding to an order to work faster
  Frequently it was enough that an informer
  had denounced somebody
  There was an informer's box
  Anybody could drop a note in
ACCUSED #2:
  I had nothing to do
  with that kind of nonsense
  In the Political Division we dealt
  exclusively with resistance problems
  within the camp

JUDGE:
How often did the witness herself see
prisoners die
after being taken down from the machine

5TH WITNESS:
At least 20 times

JUDGE:
You can vouch for the fact
that in at least 20 cases
prisoners died in your presence

5TH WITNESS:
Yes

JUDGE:
Did you ever see
the punishment being carried out

5TH WITNESS:
Yes
I saw a man hanging there once
with his head down
Another time a woman was
strapped up on the poles
Boger forced us
to go in and look

ACCUSED #2:
It is true
that the witness was an interpreter
However she was never present
at any of the intensive interrogations
On such occasions
ladies were never permitted

5TH WITNESS:
Ladies

ACCUSED #2:
I think I can say that now

THE ACCUSED *laugh*

JUDGE:
Did the witness
see any of the accused present
take part in the beatings

5TH WITNESS:
I saw Boger in his shirt sleeves
holding his whip
and I often saw him
come out spattered with blood
Once I heard Broad say to Lachmann
another member of the Political Division
You know Gerhard
he spouted blood like a pig

Then he handed me his coat
to clean
They always made a big point
of cleanliness
Broad liked to look at himself in the mirror
looking very pleased
especially after he was promoted
to private first class
and I had sewed
his stripe on for him
I had to clean Boger's boots once

JUDGE:
Yes

5TH WITNESS:
A truckload of children
drove by outside
I saw it through the office window
A small boy jumped off the truck
He was holding an apple
Boger came out the door
The child stood there with his apple
Boger went over to the child
grabbed him by the ankles
and smashed his head
against the barrack wall
Then he picked up the apple
called me out and said
Wipe that off the wall
Later at an interrogation
I saw him eat the apple

COUNSEL FOR THE DEFENSE:
You made no mention of this
at the preliminary hearings

5TH WITNESS:
I couldn't speak about it

COUNSEL FOR THE DEFENSE:
Why not

5TH WITNESS:
For personal reasons

COUNSEL FOR THE DEFENSE:
Could you tell us
what those reasons are

5TH WITNESS:
Since that time
I have never wanted to have
a child of my own

COUNSEL FOR THE DEFENSE:
How is it
that you can speak about it now

5TH WITNESS:
Now that I see him again
I must speak
JUDGE:
What does the accused Boger
have to say in reply
to these accusations
ACCUSED #2:
They are completely made up
a poor way for the witness to repay me
for the trust
I placed in her in those days

(II)

7TH WITNESS:
I was brought into the interrogation room
of the Political Division
together with some other prisoners
JUDGE:
Can you describe this room
7TH WITNESS:
There were expensive rugs on the floor
that had come off
one of the transports from France
Boger's desk
was set at an angle across from the door
He was sitting on the desk when I came in
The interpreter sat behind the desk
JUDGE:
Who else was present in the room
7TH WITNESS:
The head of the Political Division
Grabner
and the accused Dylewski and Broad
JUDGE:
What did they say
7TH WITNESS:
Boger said
We are the Political Division
We don't ask questions
We listen
You ought to know what you have to say
JUDGE:
Why had you been brought there
7TH WITNESS:
I didn't know
I didn't know what

I was supposed to say
and I asked them to question me
I was beaten senseless
When I came to I was lying in the hall
Boger was standing there
He said
Get up
But I couldn't get up
He came toward me
I pulled myself up against the wall
I saw I was bleeding
The floor and my clothes
were covered with blood
My head was split open
My nose was broken
All that afternoon and most of the night
I had to stand with my face to the wall
There were several others standing there
Anybody who turned
had his head knocked against the wall
The next day I was interrogated again
I was brought into the room
with the other prisoners
JUDGE:
What did they want to find out
7TH WITNESS:
The whole time I didn't know
what it was all about
A couple of times they
put something around my head
some kind of metal band I think
Then I was taken back to the hall
and Boger took the man next to me
into the room
His name was Walter Windmuller
JUDGE:
Do you know what happened to him
7TH WITNESS:
He was in there for about
two or three hours
I stood in the hallway
with my face to the wall
Then Windmuller came out
He had to stand next to me
Blood was running down his legs
He fell over several times
We had learned
how to talk without moving our lips
When I asked him what had happened

he said
They smashed my balls in there
He died the same day
JUDGE:
  Was Boger responsible
  for this prisoner's death
7TH WITNESS:
  I am convinced that
  if Boger didn't do the killing himself
  he certainly helped kill him
JUDGE:
  Does the accused Boger
  have anything to say
ACCUSED #2:
  Mr Chairman
  if I may be allowed to explain
  that's not the way it happened
JUDGE:
  How did it happen
ACCUSED #2:
  Mr Chairman
  I didn't kill anybody
  I just had to carry out my interrogations
JUDGE:
  What kind of interrogations were they
ACCUSED #2:
  Occasionally
  they were intensive interrogations
  conducted
  according to standard operating procedures
JUDGE:
  What was the reason for these procedures
ACCUSED #2:
  In the interest of camp security
  it was essential
  to take vigorous measures
  against traitors and other harmful elements
JUDGE:
  Accused Boger
  as a criminal investigator
  didn't you know
  that a man
  subjected to such an interrogation
  will say anything you want him to say
ACCUSED #2:
  That's not the way I see it at all
  and especially not in view of
  our specific task
  If a prisoner proved stubborn

force was the only way
to make him confess
8TH WITNESS:
  When I was called into Boger's room
  I saw
  a plateful of herrings on his desk
  Grabner asked me if I was hungry
  I said no
  But Grabner said
  I know how long it's been
  since you've eaten
  Today you're going to see
  how nice I can be
  I'm going to give you something to eat
  Boger's made a salad for you
  He ordered me to eat
  I couldn't
  because my hands were handcuffed
  behind my back
  Then Boger pushed my face into the plate
  I had to eat the herrings
  They were so salty that I threw up
  I had to lick up
  the vomit together with the herrings
  I still had some in my mouth
  and Boger shouted
  Watch him to make sure he doesn't
  spit any of it out in the hall
  Then they took me to Barrack 11
  and up to the loft
  My hands were tied behind me
  I was hung from a pole by my hands
  That was called pole-hanging
  They hung you up just high enough
  so that the bottom of your feet
  barely touched the floor
  Boger pushed me back and forth
  and kicked me in the stomach
  There was a pail of water in front of me
  Boger asked me if I wanted to drink
  He laughed and twisted me
  one way and then the other
  When I lost consciousness
  they threw water over me
  My arms grew numb
  My wrists almost snapped
  Boger questioned me
  but my tongue was so swollen
  I couldn't speak

Then Boger said
We still have another swing for you
I was
taken back to the Political Division
COUNSEL FOR THE DEFENSE:
    Were you subjected to a session
    on that swing too
8TH WITNESS:
    Yes
COUNSEL FOR THE DEFENSE:
    Then it was possible
    to survive it after all

(III)

8TH WITNESS:
    I remember one morning
    in the spring of 1942
    A platoon of prisoner police
    marched up in front of the barrack
    of the former post office
    where the Political Division
    had been installed
    At the head of the column were prisoners
    carrying two wooden supports
    built like the sides of a hurdle
    Behind them were guards
    armed with submachine guns
    and behind them
    the heads of the Political Division
    They had their briefcases
    and especially prepared dried-out bullwhips
    that they used for corporal punishment
    Those supports
    were the frame for the new swing
JUDGE:
    Was that the first time
    the apparatus was used
8TH WITNESS:
    It had existed before
    in a simpler form
    At first it was just a pipe
    laid across two tables
    and the prisoners was strapped to the
        pipe
    Since the pipe turned when the prisoner
    was beaten
    this new frame was made to keep it stable

COUNSEL FOR THE DEFENSE:
    Would the witness
    tell us how he happens to know this
8TH WITNESS:
    Nothing happened in our part of the camp
    that we didn't know about
    In the old camp everything took place
    at close quarters
    The whole camp wasn't more than
    about 200 yards wide and 300 long
    From any one of the 28 barracks
    you could see the whole camp
JUDGE:
    What was the reason for your being
    brought in for interrogation
8TH WITNESS:
    I was assigned to the work detail
    that put in the drainage ditch
    around the outside of the camp
    On the job I helped a fellow prisoner
    get together with his mother
    who was in the women's camp
    The prisoner's name was Janicki
    They took him
    into the interrogation room first
    When they were done with him
    they threw him out into the hall
    He was still alive
    He opened his mouth
    and stuck out his tongue as far as he could
    He started to lick the floor
    he was so thirsty
    Boger came up and turned his head
    with the toe of his boot
    Then he said
    It's your turn now
    If you don't tell us the truth
    the same thing will happen to you
    Then they strapped me up on the swing
JUDGE:
    Would you
    describe the procedure
8TH WITNESS:
    First the prisoner had
    to sit down on the floor
    and draw up his knees
    His hands were tied in front
    and then pushed down over his knees
    Then they shoved the pipe in the space

between the arms and knees
Then the pipe was raised
and set into the wood frame
JUDGE:
Who took care of these preparations
8TH WITNESS:
Two special-duty prisoners
JUDGE:
Who else was in the room
8TH WITNESS:
I saw Boger there
and Broad and Dylewski
Boger asked the questions
but I couldn't answer
I hung with my head down
and the two special-duty prisoners
swung me back and forth
COUNSEL FOR THE DEFENSE:
What questions were you asked
8TH WITNESS:
They asked me for more names
JUDGE:
Were you beaten during the question
8TH WITNESS:
Boger and Dylewski took turns
with the bullwhip
COUNSEL FOR THE DEFENSE:
Wasn't it the prisoners
who did the beating
8TH WITNESS:
I saw Boger and Dylewski
with the whips in their hands
JUDGE:
Where did they beat you
8TH WITNESS:
On the buttocks
back legs
hands feet
and the back of the head
But they concentrated on
the sexual organs
They especially aimed for them
I lost consciousness three times
and they poured water on me
JUDGE:
Accused Boger
do you admit
to having mistreated this witness

ACCUSED #2:
There is only one answer to that
a loud and definite no
8TH WITNESS:
I still have the scars from it
ACCUSED #2:
But not from me
JUDGE:
In the course of your interrogation
did you ever make use
of the instrument here described
ACCUSED #2:
There were times
when I had to arrange for its use
The punishment
was carried out by special-duty prisoners
under my supervision
JUDGE:
Do you regard
the witness's description
as untruthful
ACCUSED #2:
The description leaves out a great deal
and in many respects fails
to conform to the truth
JUDGE:
What was the truth
ACCUSED #2:
The moment the prisoner confessed
punishment was discontinued
JUDGE:
And if the prisoner did not confess
ACCUSED #2:
He was beaten until he bled
That was it
JUDGE:
Was a doctor present
ACCUSED #2:
I never saw an order
requiring the presence of a doctor
nor was it necessary
because the instant blood began to flow
I stopped
The purpose of the intensive interrogation
was achieved
when blood ran down their pants
JUDGE:
You felt you were fully justified

in carrying out these
intensive interrogations
ACCUSED #2:
They were clearly in line
with the duties and responsibilities
of my command
What's more it is my opinion
that even now corporal punishment
if administered
by juvenile courts for instance
would soon put a stop to a good deal
of delinquent behavior
COUNSEL FOR THE DEFENSE:
It has been stated by the witness
that no one could survive
the swing
From all appearances
this claim would seem to be exaggerated
8TH WITNESS:
When they took me down from the swing
Boger said
Now we've got you in shape
for a very pleasant heavenly ascension
I was taken to a cell in Barrack 11
I expected to be shot
at any time
I don't know
how many days I spent in there
The sores on my buttocks were festering
my testicles were blue and green
and tremendously swollen
Most of the time I was unconscious
Then I was taken to the washroom
with a number of other prisoners
We were told to strip
and our numbers were written
on our chests
with indelible ink
I knew that this
meant the death sentence
While we were standing there naked
the chief clerk came in and asked
how many prisoners should be crossed out
as executed
When he had left we were
recounted
There was one too many
I had learned always to be the last in line

Somebody kicked me
and I got my clothes back
I was to be taken back to the cell
to wait until the bunker was emptied again
but a prisoner orderly
took me with him to the infirmary
Sometimes
one of us did survive
and I
am one of those few who did

THE SONG OF THE POSSIBILITY OF SURVIVAL

(I)

3RD WITNESS:
The mood of the camp changed
from one day to the next
It depended on the mood
of the commanding officer
the adjutant
and the Barrack-leader
and it depended
on how the war was going at the time
At the beginning
when they were still winning
we were shoved around treated with contempt
but they could still joke when they hit us
But as the number of retreats
and defeats mounted
camp operations were stepped up
Still you never knew
what was going to happen
An order to fall out could mean anything
standing there for nothing
or getting harassed
In the infirmary
prisoners could get treatment until
they were well again and even
be put on a special diet
only to be sent up through the chimney
as soon as they had recovered
One of the prisoner orderlies was
beaten up by the camp doctor

because he had left out some minor detail
from a patient's chart
Meanwhile
the patient had already been killed
It was only by accident
that I
escaped the gassing
The ovens happened to be stopped up
that night
On the way back from the crematorium
the doctor who accompanied us found out
I was a medical student
and he found a place for me in his ward
JUDGE:
What was this doctor's name
3RD WITNESS:
Dr Vetter
He was a very well-bred man
Dr Schatz and Dr Frank
were also friendly to the prisoners
they delivered up to be killed
They did not kill out of hatred
or conviction
They killed only because they had to
and there was no point in discussing that
Only a few killed with passion
Boger was one of them
I saw prisoners
when they were called into Boger's room
and I saw them
when they came out
And when they were taken out to be shot
I heard Boger say with pride
These are mine
One prisoner who had been shot
was taken to the hospital
with an order from Boger
That man's life must be saved
so he can be hung
But the prisoner died in the hospital
JUDGE:
Does the accused Boger
recall this case
ACCUSED #2:
It was standard procedure that
prisoners wounded while attempting escape
were taken to the hospital
so they could be interrogated
when they had recovered

To that extent the witness's statement can
be considered absolutely correct
In this case I passed on the order
that the prisoner should be kept alive
I said
He must be saved
so he can be interrogated
JUDGE:
Was he to be hanged after that
ACCUSED #2:
That's possible
but that was not within my jurisdiction
6TH WITNESS:
Boger and Kaduk
carried out hangings on their own
Once 12 prisoners were
to be executed
as a reprisal for the escape of a prisoner
Boger and Kaduk
put the noose
over the prisoners' heads
COUNSEL FOR THE DEFENSE:
How do you know that
6TH WITNESS:
We stood on the assembly ground
We were ordered to watch
The prisoners shouted something
Boger and Kaduk went wild with rage
They started to kick
and slap them
then they hung on the prisoners' legs
and pulled them down
ACCUSED #2:
All I recall of this incident
is that one of the sentenced
broke away
while he was being taken out
under strict guard
to be executed
He lunged at me
so hard he broke one of my ribs
He was overpowered
He was bound
and I read the sentence
JUDGE:
Did the witness
hear the reading of a sentence
6TH WITNESS:
No sentence was read

ACCUSED #2:
 Of course it was hard to hear the sentence
 because the prisoners were shouting
PROSECUTING ATTORNEY:
 What were they shouting
ACCUSED #2:
 Political slogans
PROSECUTING ATTORNEY:
 Of what kind
ACCUSED #2:
 They were inciting the prisoners against us
COUNSEL FOR THE DEFENSE:
 How did the prisoners react
ACCUSED #2:
 There were no observable incidents
 The sentence was executed
 as were all sentences
 I did not carry out
 the execution myself
 That was done by special-duty Kapos
COUNSEL FOR THE DEFENSE:
 Isn't it possible
 that the witness simply failed to hear
 the reading of the sentence
6TH WITNESS:
 The execution took place
 immediately after the escape
 There was no time
 for the case to be considered
 by a central office
 and for a sentence to be handed down
JUDGE:
 Was the commanding officer
 or his adjutant present
6TH WITNESS:
 Ranking officers were always present
 at public executions
 They wore white gloves
 on such occasions
 I can't say definitely
 whether the adjutant was present
 Still it can be taken for granted
 since he was responsible
 for the execution of all orders
 within this area of command
JUDGE:
 Does the witness
 recognize the adjutant
 among the accused

6TH WITNESS:
 That one is Mulka
JUDGE:
 Accused Mulka
 were you
 present at this or any other hanging
ACCUSED #1:
 I had nothing to do
 with any killing
 of any kind
JUDGE:
 Did you hear of the orders in question
 or did you ever pass such orders on
ACCUSED #1:
 I did hear of such orders
 but I personally never passed them on
JUDGE:
 When faced with such orders
 what did you do
ACCUSED #1:
 I was careful
 not to trouble my superiors
 with questions about the legality
 of prisoner executions
 that were brought to my attention
 Ultimately of course
 I had a responsibility
 to my family
 and to myself
PROSECUTING ATTORNEY:
 Accused Mulka
 did you ever see the gallows
ACCUSED #1:
 I beg your pardon
PROSECUTING ATTORNEY:
 I asked whether you ever saw the gallows
ACCUSED #1:
 No
 I never set foot in the camp
PROSECUTING ATTORNEY:
 You mean to say
 that you
 as adjutant to the commanding officer
 were never in the camp
ACCUSED #1:
 That's the absolute truth
 The nature of my work was exclusively
 administrative
 I stayed strictly

within the administrative-office area
PROSECUTING ATTORNEY:
    Where was this
ACCUSED #1:
    In the army barracks
    outside of the camp proper
PROSECUTING ATTORNEY:
    Couldn't you see
    into the camp from there
ACCUSED #1:
    I don't believe you could
PROSECUTING ATTORNEY:
    Could the witness
    give us an idea of how the outer buildings
    were situated in relation to the camp
6TH WITNESS:
    All the back windows
    in the administrative buildings
    looked out onto the camp
    Directly behind the administration buildings
    were the concrete posts
    with the electrically charged barbed wire
    Ten yards from the posts was the first barrack
    Right behind that one
    the other barracks in three rows
    The three rows 10 yards apart at the most
    The view up the long streets
    was unobstructed
PROSECUTING ATTORNEY:
    Where were the gallows
6TH WITNESS:
    On the assembly ground
    in front of the camp kitchen
    Just to the right
    as you come in through the main gate
    onto the main street
PROSECUTING ATTORNEY:
    Would you describe the gallows
6TH WITNESS:
    Three poles
    with an iron rail across the top
PROSECUTING ATTORNEY:
    Accused Mulka
    you lived in close proximity to the camp
    According to camp regulations
    your position entailed
    reporting to the commanding officer
    all important events within the camp
    and processing all coded material

as well as instructing all guard units
as to the larger significance
of their assignment
Holding such a position
were you not aware of the punishments
carried out in the camp
ACCUSED #1:
    Only once did I see
    some sort of signed and dated order
    authorizing corporal punishment
PROSECUTING ATTORNEY:
    You were never required
    to investigate
    the reasons for the hangings and shootings
ACCUSED #1:
    It wasn't my job
    to concern myself with them
PROSECUTING ATTORNEY:
    As adjutant to the camp commander
    what were your duties then
ACCUSED #1:
    I calculated operating costs
    charted the distribution of the labor
        supply
    and processed personnel files
    I was also required to accompany
    the commanding officer to receptions
    and command the honor guard
PROSECUTING ATTORNEY:
    When was the honor guard used
ACCUSED #1:
    On ceremonial occasions
    and for burials
    A funeral procession
    was trooped for the burials
PROSECUTING ATTORNEY:
    Whose burial
ACCUSED #1:
    The burial of an officer
PROSECUTING ATTORNEY:
    Who was notified
    of deaths among the prisoners
ACCUSED #1:
    I don't know
    Perhaps the Political Division
PROSECUTING ATTORNEY:
    Weren't you informed
    that from 100 to 200 prisoners
    died daily in the camp

ACCUSED #1:
    I don't recall
    ever having seen
    comparative daily reports
    of the camp population
    On any given day
    10 or 15 discharges might be reported
    but numbers in the amount
    mentioned here
    I never heard
PROSECUTING ATTORNEY:
    You didn't know about the mass killings
    in the gas chambers
ACCUSED #1:
    I didn't know anything about them
PROSECUTING ATTORNEY:
    You never noticed the smoke
    from the chimneys of the crematoriums
    smoke that was visible for miles
ACCUSED #1:
    After all it was a big camp
    with its natural rate of discharge
    and they had to be burned
PROSECUTING ATTORNEY:
    You never noticed
    the condition of the prisoners
ACCUSED #1:
    It was a penal camp
    People weren't there for their health
PROSECUTING ATTORNEY:
    As adjutant to the camp's commanding officer
    weren't you interested in
    how the prisoners were fed and quartered
ACCUSED #1:
    I never heard of any complaints
PROSECUTING ATTORNEY:
    Didn't you ever discuss
    occurrences in the camp
    with your commanding officer
ACCUSED #1:
    No
    There were no exceptional occurrences
PROSECUTING ATTORNEY:
    From your point of view
    what was the purpose of the camp
ACCUSED #1:
    The purpose of a protective-custody camp
    was to educate enemies of the state
    to a different way of thinking

    It was not my job
    to question this purpose
PROSECUTING ATTORNEY:
    Did you know
    the significance of the designation
    special treatment
ACCUSED #1:
    That was a government secret
    of the highest priority
    I couldn't know anything about it
    Anyone who spoke of it
    risked the death penalty
PROSECUTING ATTORNEY:
    Nevertheless you did know about it
ACCUSED #1:
    I cannot answer that
PROSECUTING ATTORNEY:
    What did you do for the troops
ACCUSED #1:
    There was a theater and a movie house
    and entertainment evenings
    Mr Knittel took care of that
    and also held evening classes
    for the officers
PROSECUTING ATTORNEY:
    Was he trained to do that
ACCUSED #1:
    He was a high-school teacher
    and if I am correctly informed
    he is presently a principal
    at a school somewhere
    a man obviously suited
    for the teaching profession
PROSECUTING ATTORNEY:
    And you instructed
    the troops in ideological matters
COUNSEL FOR THE DEFENSE:
    We advise our client
    that he need not reply
    to questions put to him
    by the assistant prosecuting attorney
PROSECUTING ATTORNEY:
    The decision on this matter
    rests solely
    with the accused
    By intervening at this point
    the defense grossly exceeds
    its legitimate authority
    It is obvious

that by resorting to such tactics
the defense is attempting to prevent us
from determining the truth
COUNSEL FOR THE DEFENSE:
  In reply to this astonishing performance
  we must vigorously protest
  At this point it becomes quite clear
  that the prosecution
  is not familiar with the rules obtaining in
  these present proceedings
  that they simply don't know the law
  The prosecution
  initiated these proceedings
  already prejudiced

THE ACCUSED *laugh nodding in agreement*

(II)

3RD WITNESS:
  The power
  of any member of the camp personnel
  was unlimited
  They were free
  each one of them
  to kill
  or to save
  I saw Dr Flage standing by a fence
  with tears in his eyes
  looking at a trainload of children
  being taken to the crematorium
  He did nothing to stop me
  from holding on to the files
  of patients already selected
  and thus preventing their death
  Camp Doctor Flage showed me
  it was possible
  to see the one living person
  among the thousands
  He showed me
  that it would have been possible
  to influence the course of the camp operation
  if there had been others
  like him
COUNSEL FOR THE DEFENSE:
  As a prisoner doctor
  did you have the power to determine
  whether your patient

should live or die
3RD WITNESS:
  I could occasionally
  save a life
COUNSEL FOR THE DEFENSE:
  Yet weren't you also required
  to select patients to be killed
3RD WITNESS:
  There was nothing I could do
  about changing the required quota
  That was set by the camp administration
  Still it was possible
  to alter the lists
COUNSEL FOR THE DEFENSE:
  When it came to choosing
  between one patient and another
  what determined your choice
3RD WITNESS:
  We had to weigh
  which of the two was more likely
  to survive his illness
  Then there was the far
  more difficult question
  which of the two would be useful
  to the internal affairs of the prisoners
COUNSEL FOR THE DEFENSE:
  Were some especially preferred
3RD WITNESS:
  Politically active prisoners
  naturally stuck together
  supported and helped each other
  as much as they could
  Since I belonged to the resistance movement
  within the camp
  I of course did all I could
  to keep others in the movement alive
COUNSEL FOR THE DEFENSE:
  What could the resistance movement
  accomplish in the camp
3RD WITNESS:
  The chief aim of the resistance
  was to keep alive our sense of solidarity
  Furthermore we documented
  everything that went on in the camp
  and buried our evidence
  in tin cans
COUNSEL FOR THE DEFENSE:
  Did you have any contact with partisans
  or any connection with the outside world

3RD WITNESS:
   Prisoners assigned to factory work
   could occasionally establish contact
   with partisans
   and they were able to give us reports
   about the situation at the various fronts
COUNSEL FOR THE DEFENSE:
   Were preparations made
   for an armed rising in the camp
3RD WITNESS:
   We managed to
   smuggle in dynamite later on
COUNSEL FOR THE DEFENSE:
   Was the camp ever attacked
   from the outside or by any groups inside
3RD WITNESS:
   In the last winter of the war
   the special commandos
   that worked in the crematoriums
   revolted
   The revolt was unsuccessful
   That was the only active attempt
   From the outside
   no attempt was made
COUNSEL FOR THE DEFENSE:
   Did you ever request aid
   through your contacts
3RD WITNESS:
   Reports on conditions in the camp
   were smuggled out time and again
COUNSEL FOR THE DEFENSE:
   What did you hope would come
   of getting these reports out
3RD WITNESS:
   We hoped for an air raid
   on the gas chambers
   or that the railroad tracks
   leading
   into the camp
   would be bombed
COUNSEL FOR THE DEFENSE:
   When you saw
   that you were left quite alone
   every form of military assistance denied you
   how were you able to sustain
   your will to resist
3RD WITNESS:
   Considering our situation
   it was resistance enough

just to keep alert
   and never give up the thought
   that someday there would come a time
   when we could speak out
   and tell what we had seen
   and lived through
COUNSEL FOR THE DEFENSE:
   How did you
   justify what you had to do
   with the oath you had taken as a doctor
PROSECUTING ATTORNEY:
   We object to this question
   which the defense has raised
   solely to blur the distinction between
   witness and accused
   The accused killed of their own free choice
   The witness was forced
   to be present at the killings
3RD WITNESS:
   I would like to reply to the question
   Those prisoners who
   by their privileged position in the camp
   managed to postpone their own death
   had at least to some degree
   defied their masters
   In order to maintain the possibility of sur-
      vival
   they were forced
   to give the appearance of cooperating
   I saw that demonstrated very clearly
   in the infirmary
   I soon became bound to the staff doctors
   not only because of our professional relation-
      ship
   but also through my complicity
   in the workings of the camp system
   Every prisoner
   from those who held the most privileged posi-
      tions
   down to those who were dying
   was part of that system
   The difference
   between us and the camp personnel
   was less than what separated us
   from those who were outside
COUNSEL FOR THE DEFENSE:
   Do you mean to say
   there was an understanding
   between the administration and the prisoner

3RD WITNESS:
  When we talk of our experience nowadays
  with people who never were in a camp
  there is always something
  inconceivable to them about it
  And yet they are the same people
  who in the camp were prisoners and guards
  Since such a great number of us
  came into the camp
  and since the number of those
  who brought us there was also great
  one would think that what happened then
  would still be comprehensible today
  Many of those who were destined
  to play the part of prisoners
  had grown up with the same ideas
  the same way of looking at things
  as those
  who found themselves acting as guards
  They were all equally dedicated
  to the same nation
  to its prosperity
  and its rewards
  And if they had not been designated
  prisoners
  they could equally well have been guards
  We must drop the lofty view
  that the camp world
  is incomprehensible to us
  We all knew the society
  that produced a government
  capable of creating such camps
  The order that prevailed there
  was an order whose basic nature
  we were familiar with
  For that very reason
  we were able to find our way about
  in its logical and ultimate consequence
  where the oppressor
  could expand his authority
  to a degree never known before
  and the oppressed
  was forced to yield up
  the fertilizing dust
  of his bones
COUNSEL FOR THE DEFENSE:
  We utterly reject
  theories of this kind

theories that reflect
  a completely distorted
  ideological point of view
3RD WITNESS:
  It is true
  most of the prisoners
  spilling out of the freight cars
  onto the platform
  had no time to comprehend
  what was happening to them
  Baffled and speechless
  they walked that final path
  and let themselves be killed
  because they understood nothing
  We call them heroes
  but their death was pointless
  We can see them before us
  these millions
  lit by searchlights
  standing in a din of curses
  and barking dogs
  Today the outside world wonders
  how they could have
  let themselves be destroyed that way
  We
  who still live with these pictures
  know that millions could stand again
  waiting to be destroyed
  and that the new destruction
  will be far more efficient
  than the old one was
COUNSEL FOR THE DEFENSE:
  Was the witness
  politically active
  even before being sent
  to the camp
3RD WITNESS:
  Yes
  It was our strength
  that we knew
  why we were there
  It helped us
  preserve our identity
  But even that strength
  sustained only a handful
  to the moment of their death
  They could be broken too
7TH WITNESS:

There were 1200 of us
who were led off to the crematoriums
We had to wait a long time
since there was another shipment
ahead of us
I was standing a little to one side
A prisoner walked by
He was very young
He whispered
Get away from here
I picked up my shoes and walked off
I went around a corner
There was another prisoner there
Where are you going
he asked
They sent me away
I answered
Then come with me
he said
So I got back into the camp

COUNSEL FOR THE DEFENSE:
Was it that simple
You could just walk away
7TH WITNESS:
I don't know how it was with others
I walked off
and went into the infirmary
The prisoner doctor asked me
Do you want to live
I said yes
He looked at me for a while
then he found a place for me there
COUNSEL FOR THE DEFENSE:
And so you survived
your stay in the camp
7TH WITNESS:
I came out of the camp
yes
but the camp is still there

(III)

JUDGE:
The witness
spent several months
in women's Barrack Number 10
Medical experiments

were made there
What can you tell us about them
4TH WITNESS:
(*Remains silent*)
JUDGE:
The court can well understand
that you must find it difficult to speak
and that you prefer to remain silent
Yet we request you
to search your memory
for anything that may
shed light on the events
under consideration here today
4TH WITNESS:
There were about 600 of us there
Professor Clauberg directed the research
The rest of the camp doctors supplied him
with the subjects he worked on
JUDGE:
Could you describe the experiments
4TH WITNESS:
(*Remains silent*)
COUNSEL FOR THE DEFENSE:
Does the witness
suffer from lapses of memory
4TH WITNESS:
I have been ill
since my time in the camp
COUNSEL FOR THE DEFENSE:
What are the symptoms of your illness
4TH WITNESS:
Dizzy spells and nausea
Earlier I had to throw up in the bathroom
because it smelled of chlorine
Chlorine was poured over the corpses
I can't stand to be in locked rooms
COUNSEL FOR THE DEFENSE:
No loss of memory
4TH WITNESS:
I would like to forget
but I keep seeing it
I would like to have the number on my arm
removed
In the summer
when I wear sleeveless dresses
people stare at it
and I always see the same look
in their eyes

COUNSEL FOR THE DEFENSE:
What look
4TH WITNESS:
Scorn
JUDGE:
Does the witness
feel she is still being persecuted
4TH WITNESS:
(*Remains silent*)
JUDGE:
What experiments
does the witness recall
4TH WITNESS:
There were girls there
17 or 18 years old
They were chosen
from the healthiest prisoners
They were used for X-ray experiments
JUDGE:
Could you describe these experiments
4TH WITNESS:
The girls were placed
in front of the X-ray machines
A metal plate was attached
to their stomachs and buttocks
The X-rays were directed at their ovaries
which were burned out
Burns and running sores developed
on their stomachs and buttocks as a
    result
JUDGE:
What was done with these girls
4TH WITNESS:
Within the next three months
they were operated on
a number of times
JUDGE:
What kind of operations were these
4TH WITNESS:
Their ovaries and gonads
were removed
JUDGE:
Did the patients die
4TH WITNESS:
If they didn't die during the experiment
they died soon after
After a few weeks the girls
had changed completely
They looked like old women

JUDGE:
Could you
tell us if any of the accused present
took part in these experiments
4TH WITNESS:
All the doctors came together daily
in their quarters
It would seem likely that at the least
they knew what was going on
COUNSEL FOR THE DEFENSE:
We strenuously object
to loose allegations of this kind
The mere fact that our clients
were in the vicinity when these events occurred
by no means
implicates them as accessories
JUDGE:
Would the witness
tell us what other experiments were under-
    taken
4TH WITNESS:
(*Remains silent*)
COUNSEL FOR THE DEFENSE:
It is our opinion
that because of the witness's obvious ill health
she is incapable
of providing the court with credible evidence
PROSECUTING ATTORNEY:
Could you
describe for the court other experiments
which you witnessed yourself
4TH WITNESS:
A syringe
with a tube attachment
was used to inject a fluid
into the womb
JUDGE:
What kind of fluid was it
4TH WITNESS:
It was a cement paste
that burned and hurt like labor pains
The women could only walk stooped
to the X-ray table
where a picture was taken
JUDGE:
What was the purpose of the injection
4TH WITNESS:
The fallopian tubes would be glued together
to prevent conception

JUDGE:
    Were the same patients
    subjected to repeated experiments
4TH WITNESS:
    After the injection of the paste
    a contraction fluid
    was injected for X-ray observation
    Then the paste
    was pumped in once again
    This process
    might be repeated many times
    at three- to four-week intervals
    Infection of the womb
    or of the stomach lining
    caused most of the deaths
    I never saw anyone sterilize
    medical instruments
    between treatments
JUDGE:
    How many such experiments would you esti-
        mate
    were carried out
4TH WITNESS:
    During the six months
    I spent in Barrack Number 10
    400
    In connection with these experiments
    there were others
    in artificial insemination
    If a woman got pregnant
    an abortion was induced
JUDGE:
    In what month of the pregnancy was that
    done
4TH WITNESS:
    In the seventh month
    A variety of X-ray experiments were made
    throughout the pregnancy
    After the abortion
    if by any chance the child was still alive
    it was killed and dissected
COUNSEL FOR THE DEFENSE:
    Are the witness's statements
    based on hearsay
    or on firsthand knowledge
4TH WITNESS:
    I speak from personal experience
COUNSEL FOR THE DEFENSE:
    What saved you then

4TH WITNESS:
    The evacuation of the camp

THE SONG OF THE DEATH
OF LILI TOFLER

(I)

JUDGE:
    Is the name of Lili Tofler
    familiar to the witness
5TH WITNESS:
    Yes
    It is
    Lili Tofler was an unusually
    pretty girl
    She was arrested
    because she wrote a letter
    to a prisoner
    When she tried
    to smuggle it in to the prisoner
    the letter was found
    Lili Tofler was interrogated
    They wanted the prisoner's name
    Boger was in charge of the interrogation
    At his order
    Lili Tofler was taken to the prison bunker
    There she was stood up naked
    against the wall
    They went through the whole procedure
    time and again
    exactly as if she was going to be shot
    All the orders were called out
    but they didn't shoot
    Finally she got down on her knees
    and begged them to shoot her
JUDGE:
    Was she shot
5TH WITNESS:
    Yes
6TH WITNESS:
    I was under bunker arrest
    when Lili Tofler was brought in
    with two other prisoners
    who had been involved
    in the smuggling of the letter

Once during that time
Jakob
the special-duty prisoner
in charge of the bunker
let me use the washroom
I saw the girl lying dead on the floor
Boger killed the other prisoners later
out in the courtyard

JUDGE:
Accused Boger
are you familiar with this case

ACCUSED #2:
That Lili Tofler was executed
is true
As a typist in the Political Division
she had access to confidential files
and was forbidden all contact
with other prisoners
I had nothing to do
with her being killed
I was as shaken to hear of her death
as the Bunker-Jakob
whose face was covered with tears

JUDGE:
Can you tell us
what was in the letter

ACCUSED #2:
No

JUDGE:
Does the witness
know what was in the letter

5TH WITNESS:
In the letter Lili Tofler asked
if they would ever be able
to go on living
after the things they had seen
and experienced there
I remember too
that she went on to ask her friend
if he had gotten her previous letter
She also wrote about some encouraging news
she had heard

COUNSEL FOR THE DEFENSE:
How did you come to know this

5TH WITNESS:
Lili Tofler was a friend of mine
We lived in the same barrack
She talked to me about the letter
Later I saw the letter

I worked in the Camp Registry Office
Lili Tofler's death certificate
was sent there
The letter was attached

JUDGE:
Did you know the prisoner
to whom the letter was addressed

5TH WITNESS:
Yes

JUDGE:
Did Lili Tofler betray his name

5TH WITNESS:
No
The prisoners had to line up
on the assembly ground
Lili was supposed to pick him out
I remember exactly
even now
how she stood in front of him
looked into his eyes
and then went on
without saying a word

COUNSEL FOR THE DEFENSE:
Were you required to appear
for the lineup too

5TH WITNESS:
Yes

COUNSEL FOR THE DEFENSE:
Where was the assembly ground

5TH WITNESS:
It was the street and the open space
in front of the kitchen barracks
in the old camp

COUNSEL FOR THE DEFENSE:
Would you describe the assembly ground

5TH WITNESS:
To the right of the gallows
was the small guardhouse
where officers stood
to take the roll call
Its walls were wood
painted to look like stone
On top of the pitched roof
was a weathervane
It looked like a toy house
There were poplars on both sides of the street
The prisoners stood in the street
and in between the barracks
Lili Tofler was led along in front of them

It was on that same day
that I saw
what was painted on the kitchen roof
It was painted in large letters
THERE IS ONE WAY TO FREEDOM
ITS MILESTONES ARE
OBEDIENCE DILIGENCE CLEANLINESS
HONESTY TRUTHFULNESS
AND LOVE OF COUNTRY
JUDGE:
   Was the prisoner
   to whom the letter was addressed
   ever discovered
5TH WITNESS:
   No

(II)

JUDGE:
   You were in charge
   of the agricultural operations of the camp
   At the time of her arrest
   Lili Tofler was working
   in one of the offices
   under your supervision
   What did she do there
1ST WITNESS:
   She did drafting
   or typing
   I can't remember which
JUDGE:
   Had she been transferred to you
   from the Political Division
1ST WITNESS:
   It's been so long now I couldn't say
   Our operation had no direct connection
   with the camp
   We were under the jurisdiction
   of the S.S. Office of Economy
   Since we were growing rubber plants
   our operations were essential
   to the war effort
   Basically my duties
   were of a purely scientific nature
JUDGE:
   Do you recall
   the arrest
   of Lili Tofler

1ST WITNESS:
   As I remember
   it had something to do with a letter
JUDGE:
   Do you know
   that Lili Tofler was arrested
   because of this letter
1ST WITNESS:
   I believe
   the letter was found in a shipment of carrots
JUDGE:
   What was the shipment for
1ST WITNESS:
   They were carrots we grew
   for the medical section
JUDGE:
   For what purpose
1ST WITNESS:
   I assume
   they were used for special diets
   Professor Clauberg had ordered them
JUDGE:
   What did you know
   about Professor Clauberg's work
1ST WITNESS:
   They carried out research there
   commissioned by various
   pharmaceutical concerns
JUDGE:
   What kind of research
1ST WITNESS:
   That I don't know
   All I knew about the camp
   was that it had to do with
   a large industrial complex
   and that its various branches
   employed prisoners as labor supply
PROSECUTING ATTORNEY:
   To which of these branches
   did your operation belong
1ST WITNESS:
   We were a subdivision of the Buna Works
   of I-G Farben
   We were engaged in war production
PROSECUTING ATTORNEY:
   Were you aware
   that prisoners had been projected
   as the labor supply
   when these industries were established

1ST WITNESS:
Yes
naturally
PROSECUTING ATTORNEY:
Did the industries
pay wages for prisoner labor
1ST WITNESS:
Of course they did
There were established rates
PROSECUTING ATTORNEY:
What were the rates
1ST WITNESS:
For a skilled worker a dollar a day
For an unskilled 75 cents
PROSECUTING ATTORNEY:
How long was the work day
1ST WITNESS:
11 hours
PROSECUTING ATTORNEY:
To whom were the wages paid
1ST WITNESS:
To the camp administration
After all
they had to provide for the prisoners
PROSECUTING ATTORNEY:
Didn't you know
that the prisoners were
used up and then killed
1ST WITNESS:
I always tried to help the prisoners
more so in fact than I had any right to
I suffered
when I saw
how the prisoners assigned to my operation
had to walk all those miles every day
from their barracks over to the work camp
I made use
of every available emergency measure
to ensure that our prisoners
got better care
and a good pair of shoes
PROSECUTING ATTORNEY:
How many prisoners were employed
in your operation
1ST WITNESS:
500 to 600
PROSECUTING ATTORNEY:
Didn't you ever notice
the frequent turnover

in the makeup of the work details
1ST WITNESS:
I did what I could
to hold on to my people
PROSECUTING ATTORNEY:
Did any of them get sick
1ST WITNESS:
Naturally
I knew of course about the epidemics
that afflicted the prisoners in the camp
PROSECUTING ATTORNEY:
You didn't notice
that prisoners on the sick list
never returned
1ST WITNESS:
No
Frequently they did come back
from the infirmary
PROSECUTING ATTORNEY:
Did you hear of any mistreatment in the
camp
1ST WITNESS:
Heard about it
yes
PROSECUTING ATTORNEY:
What did you hear
1ST WITNESS:
I heard
they were beaten
PROSECUTING ATTORNEY:
Who beat them
1ST WITNESS:
I don't know
I never saw it happen
I just heard about it
PROSECUTING ATTORNEY:
Did you know about
the extermination program
1ST WITNESS:
If you were there three years
naturally something leaked out
You knew what was going on
but later on
when I heard the numbers involved
I simply couldn't grasp it
PROSECUTING ATTORNEY:
You never saw any of the transports
1ST WITNESS:
A couple of times at the most

PROSECUTING ATTORNEY:
  Do you know any of the accused present here
1ST WITNESS:
  I know some of them
  Mainly the group leaders
  We used to meet
  in their club
  on a purely social basis
PROSECUTING ATTORNEY:
  Today you hold a high
  advisory position in the government
  Did you meet these men again
  after the war
  when most of them
  had returned to civilian life
1ST WITNESS:
  I may have met one or another of them
PROSECUTING ATTORNEY:
  On such occasions
  did you ever talk about
  the events of those days
1ST WITNESS:
  Mr Prosecutor
  we were all concerned with
  one thing
  winning the war
PROSECUTING ATTORNEY:
  The court has summoned as witnesses
  three former directors
  of factories attached to the camp
  One of these witnesses
  has submitted to the court a sworn affidavit
  stating that he is blind
  and therefore cannot appear
  The second suffers from a fractured spine
  Only one former chairman of the board
  has come
  Would the witness
  tell us if he is still connected
  with the firms
  which formerly employed prisoners
COUNSEL FOR THE DEFENSE:
  We object to this question
  which has no other motive
  than to undermine public confidence
  in our industrial concerns
2ND WITNESS:
  I am no longer actively engaged
  in business

PROSECUTING ATTORNEY:
  Do you receive a pension
  from these concerns
2ND WITNESS:
  Yes
PROSECUTING ATTORNEY:
  Does this pension amount to
  75,000 dollars a year
COUNSEL FOR THE DEFENSE:
  We object to the question
PROSECUTING ATTORNEY:
  Now that you live in your castle
  and are no longer engaged
  with the business of your concern
  which has only changed by changing its name
  what do you do
2ND WITNESS:
  I collect porcelain
  paintings and engravings
  as well as various objects of folk art
COUNSEL FOR THE DEFENSE:
  Questions of this nature
  are entirely irrelevant
  to the stated purpose of these proceedings
PROSECUTING ATTORNEY:
  As a representative of the camp industries
  you were directly responsible
  for assigning prisoners to the factories
  What can you tell us about the agreement
  arrived at between these industries
  and the camp administration
  relating to prisoners
  no longer fit for work
2ND WITNESS:
  I know nothing about that
PROSECUTING ATTORNEY:
  The court has in its possession
  weekly reports which deal with prisoners
      found
  by the management of these industries
  to be too weak to do their work
2ND WITNESS:
  I don't know anything about that
PROSECUTING ATTORNEY:
  Didn't you ever notice the physical condition
  of the prisoners
2ND WITNESS:
  I personally did everything
  I could to prevent the utilization

of a labor force
composed of asocial
or politically unreliable elements
PROSECUTING ATTORNEY:
   The court has in its record
   a letter which mentions
   the happy and prosperous friendship
   existing between your firm
   and the camp administration
   Among other things
   the letter goes on to say
   At dinner
   we made further use of the occasion
   to draw up measures
   advantageous to the Buna Works
   that relate to the merger
   of the truly outstanding
   operations of the camp
   What were those measures
2ND WITNESS:
   I simply had to do my duty
   and to see to it
   that government requisitions
   were met
PROSECUTING ATTORNEY:
   Will you not
   speak out clearly
   to corroborate
   what a previous witness pointed out
   the system of exploitation
   that existed in the camp
   By the limitless grinding down of people
   you
   as well as the other directors
   of the large firms involved
   made profits
   that annually amounted to billions
COUNSEL FOR THE DEFENSE:
   Objection
PROSECUTING ATTORNEY:
   Let us once more bring to mind
   that the successors to those same concerns
   have ended up today in magnificent condition
   and that they are now in the midst of
   as they say
   a new phase of expansion
COUNSEL FOR THE DEFENSE:
   We call upon the court

to make a record
of this slander

(III)

JUDGE:
   What do you know of the arrest
   of Lili Tofler
1ST WITNESS:
   I don't know what happened
   All I remember is
   that she was taken away
   I asked what was going on and heard
   they were still investigating the matter
   Later I heard
   they had killed her
JUDGE:
   Who killed her
1ST WITNESS:
   I don't know
   I wasn't there
JUDGE:
   You were at that time a brigadier general
   which meant you ranked
   between a colonel and a major general
   Was there no way you could have intervened
   when one of your workers was taken away
1ST WITNESS:
   I wasn't
   sufficiently informed about the case
JUDGE:
   You made no inquiries
   about the cause of her arrest
1ST WITNESS:
   That was beyond my jurisdiction
JUDGE:
   Yet that constituted a gross interference
   in your personal sphere of activity
   A person whom you needed
   for work essential to the war effort
   was simply removed from your laboratory
1ST WITNESS:
   Lili Tofler was not an outstanding worker
JUDGE:
   But you greatly outranked
   any man in the Political Division
   Why did you tolerate this invasion

of your own area of responsibility

1ST WITNESS:

Mr Chairman
there was an unwritten law then
that applied to everybody
It was
Take care about doing favors for prisoners
You could go just so far
but no further

JUDGE:

The court calls as witness
the prisoner
to whom Lili Tofler
wrote the previously mentioned letter
Would you tell us
how you managed to survive

9TH WITNESS:

A few days after she had been
taken to the bunker
I was brought there too
I thought
Lili had betrayed me
but I was just one of many
that had been brought in as hostages
I heard there
that every morning and every afternoon
Lili had to stand in the washroom for an hour
The whole time she was in there Boger kept
a pistol pressed against her head
That went on for four days
Then I was taken out
with a group of 50 prisoners
to be shot
All that time I thought
Boger must know
the letter was meant for me
I saw the clerk put a cross
next to my name on the list
On paper I was already dead
The prisoners were taken out to the yard
and shot
Only two
for some reason
were left behind
I was one of them
I was still in the hallway
when suddenly the Bunker-Jakob came
and pulled me back out into the yard

I thought
Now I'm going to be shot
But he just showed me the pile
of dead comrades
On top lay the two prisoners
who had smuggled the letter into the camp
Over to one side was Lili
with two holes in her heart
I asked Jakob
who had shot her
He said
Boger

JUDGE:

Accused Boger
do you have anything to add

ACCUSED #2:

No
thank you

JUDGE:

Where did Lili Tofler originally come from

5TH WITNESS:

I don't know where she came from

JUDGE:

What was she like

5TH WITNESS:

Whenever I met Lili
and asked her
How are you Lili
she said
Fine
I am always fine

THE SONG OF
S.S. CORPORAL STARK

(I)

8TH WITNESS:

The accused Stark
was in charge of the Reception Squad
I was assigned to the squad as a clerk
Stark was 20 years old then
In his free time
he used to study for his high-school finals
To test himself on the subjects

Stark enjoyed putting all sorts of questions
to the college graduates among the prisoners
On the evening
the Polish woman with the two children
was brought in
he was discussing
aspects of humanism in Goethe with us

JUDGE:
What was the reason
for their being brought in

8TH WITNESS:
We only found that out later
The eight-year-old boy
had picked up a rabbit and given it
to the woman's two-year-old daughter
to play with
The rabbit belonged to a camp official
So all three
were to be shot
Stark
carried out the execution

JUDGE:
Could you see the execution

8TH WITNESS:
Executions were carried out
in the old crematorium in those days
The crematorium was directly
behind the reception barrack
Through the window
we could see Stark
with the woman and two children
go into the crematorium
He had his rifle slung over his shoulder
We heard a series of shots
Then Stark came out alone

JUDGE:
Accused Stark
does this description correspond to the facts

ACCUSED #12:
I completely reject it

JUDGE:
What was your rank in the camp

ACCUSED #12:
I was Barrack-leader

JUDGE:
How did you come there

ACCUSED #12:
I was assigned to camp duty

along with a group
of other noncommissioned officers

JUDGE:
Were you made Barrack-leader
right from the start

ACCUSED #12:
That's what we were meant for
that's what we were used for

JUDGE:
Were you trained
for this assignment

ACCUSED #12:
We had our leadership course behind us

JUDGE:
Were you given any general instructions
for your task in the camp

ACCUSED #12:
Only a short indoctrination period

JUDGE:
What happened when you arrived at the camp

ACCUSED #12:
There was a reception commission

JUDGE:
Made up of whom

ACCUSED #12:
The commanding officer and the adjutant
the protective-custody camp leader
and the chief clerk

JUDGE:
What assignment were you given

ACCUSED #12:
I was first assigned to a prisoner barrack
Most of them were young
High-school and university students

JUDGE:
Why were they in camp

ACCUSED #12:
I believe
it was because of their contact
with the resistance movement
It was a collective sentence
They had been transferred there
by Security Police Command Headquarters

JUDGE:
Did you see their admission orders

ACCUSED #12:
No
It wasn't any of my business either

JUDGE:
   What did you have to do then
ACCUSED #12:
   I had to see to it
   that the people got to work on time
   and that the numbers checked out
JUDGE:
   Were there any attempts to escape
ACCUSED #12:
   Not under my command
JUDGE:
   Were the people adequately provided
      for
ACCUSED #12:
   They each got their quart of soup
JUDGE:
   What happened
   if the people could not
   or would not work
ACCUSED #12:
   That didn't happen
JUDGE:
   Didn't you ever have cause to take action
   when prisoners broke rules
ACCUSED #12:
   That never came up
   I never had to turn in a report
JUDGE:
   You never struck anyone
ACCUSED #12:
   I never had to
JUDGE:
   When were you transferred
   to the Reception Section
   of the Political Division
ACCUSED #12:
   May 1941
JUDGE:
   What was the reason
   for your being transferred
ACCUSED #12:
   I used to go riding
   One of the men I got to know that way
   was the chief of the Political Division
   Lieutenant Grabner
   He asked me what I was by profession
   When I told him I was a student
   studying for my final exams

he said
they were looking for people like me
A few days later
I received my transfer orders
JUDGE:
   What were your duties
   in the Reception Section
ACCUSED #12:
   The first thing I had to do
   was to familiarize myself
   with the registration
   Incoming prisoners were
   provided with a number
   After that
   personnel records had to be set up
   and index cards filled out
JUDGE:
   How did the prisoners arrive
ACCUSED #12:
   They were marched in
   trucked in
   or they came by train
   Trains arrived every Tuesday
   Thursday and Friday
JUDGE:
   What was the reception procedure
ACCUSED #12:
   I had to stand by
   when transports were announced
   First
   prisoners were assembled
   in front of the camp entrance
   then the transport leader
   handed over the transport papers
   to Reception
   Prisoners fell in for the count
   and were issued their numbers
   At that time
   numbers were not yet tattooed
   Each prisoner was issued a number
   in triplicate on cardboard
   One number he kept
   one went with personal effects
   one was attached to valuables
   He had to retain his cardboard number
   until he was issued a cloth one
JUDGE:
   What was your part in this procedure

ACCUSED #12:
I handed out the numbers
and conducted the prisoners
to the personal-effects barrack
There prisoners were stripped
showered and dressed
Their hair was cut
Then they were received
by Reception

JUDGE:
What did that entail

ACCUSED #12:
Personnel records were filled out
Questionnaires made up for Reception
were taken to the Reception office
An admissions list was then drawn up
listing the different categories
political prisoners
criminal prisoners
and racial prisoners
This list was then circulated
to the various sections

JUDGE:
To which sections

ACCUSED #12:
To the protective-custody camp leader
to headquarters
to the Political Division
and to the doctors
Twelve copies went out for distribution
with the daily dispatches

JUDGE:
Did you have anything more to do
with the prisoners

ACCUSED #12:
After Reception
for me they were over and done with

PROSECUTING ATTORNEY:
Accused Stark
were you on hand
for the arrival of all transports

ACCUSED #12:
It was my duty to be present

PROSECUTING ATTORNEY:
When transports arrived
what were your duties

ACCUSED #12:
All I had to do there
was manage the record traffic

PROSECUTING ATTORNEY:
What does that mean

ACCUSED #12:
Some of the prisoners were held over
These I had to enter in the book

PROSECUTING ATTORNEY:
And the others

ACCUSED #12:
The others were transferred

PROSECUTING ATTORNEY:
What was the difference

ACCUSED #12:
Prisoners held over
went to the camp
Transferred prisoners
were neither received
nor admitted
That is the difference
between held over
and transferred

PROSECUTING ATTORNEY:
What happened to the transferred prisoners

ACCUSED #12:
They were taken directly
to the small crematorium
for extermination

PROSECUTING ATTORNEY:
Was this before the construction
of the big crematoriums

ACCUSED #12:
The big crematoriums in the outer camp
first went into operation
in the summer of 1942
Until then the crematorium
in the old camp was used

PROSECUTING ATTORNEY:
How were the prisoners transferred

ACCUSED #12:
Lists were compared
and names crossed out
Prisoners who were not
to be received into the camp
were marched into the small crematorium

PROSECUTING ATTORNEY:
What were they told

ACCUSED #12:
They were informed
that they were going to be disinfected

PROSECUTING ATTORNEY:
  Weren't they uneasy
ACCUSED #12:
  No
  They went in quietly

(II)

8TH WITNESS:
  We knew exactly how Stark would behave
  when he came back from a killing
  Everything in the room
  had to be in order and absolutely clean
  and we had to chase the flies out
  with handkerchiefs
  If he spotted a fly
  he would go into a rage
  Even before he took off his cap
  he would wash his hands in a basin
  his flunky always had ready for him
  on a stool next to the door
  When he had washed his hands
  he pointed at the dirty water
  and the flunky had to run out
  for more
  Then he handed us his jacket to be cleaned
  and washed his hands and face again
7TH WITNESS:
  I see Stark always
  all the time
  I can hear him call
  Move
  get in
  move you pigs
  And then we had to go into the chamber
JUDGE:
  What chamber
7TH WITNESS:
  The chamber in the old crematorium
  Several hundred
  women and children
  lay there like packages
  There were prisoners of war in there too
  Move
  Get their clothes off
  Stark yelled
  I was 18 years old
  and I had never seen a corpse before

  I just stood there
  Then Stark started beating me
JUDGE:
  Were there wounds on the dead
7TH WITNESS:
  Yes
JUDGE:
  Were they bullet wounds
7TH WITNESS:
  No
  They had been gassed
  They were heaped up stiff
  on top of each other
  Sometimes when we pulled
  their clothes ripped
  Then we were beaten again
JUDGE:
  Weren't the people required
  to undress first
7TH WITNESS:
  That was later
  in the new crematoriums
  where there were rooms for that
JUDGE:
  Was Stark present there too
7TH WITNESS:
  Stark was always present
  I can hear him shouting
  Move
  Get those rags
  Once a small man hid himself
  under a pile of clothes
  Stark found him
  Come here he shouted
  and pushed him up against the wall
  He shot him first in one leg
  and then in the other
  Finally he slid down on a bench
  and then Stark shot him dead
  He always like to shoot the legs first
  Once I heard a woman scream
  Captain
  I didn't do anything
  He yelled
  Get up against the wall Sarah
  The woman begged him not to kill her
  Then he started shooting
JUDGE:
  When did you

first see the accused Stark
at these killings
7TH WITNESS:
In the fall of 1941
JUDGE:
Were these the first killings
by gas
7TH WITNESS:
Yes
JUDGE:
Would you describe the old crematorium
7TH WITNESS:
It was built of concrete
It had a thick square chimney
The walls were covered by
sloping embankments
The chamber was about 20 yards long
and five yards wide
You had to pass through a small anteroom
first
On the other side of the chamber
a door led to the first oven
and a second door to a room
with the two other ovens
JUDGE:
Accused Stark
how large were the groups
you had to conduct to the crematoriums
ACCUSED #12:
On the average
150 to 200 head
JUDGE:
Were women and children among them
ACCUSED #12:
Yes
JUDGE:
Did you think it right
that women and children
should be part of these transports
ACCUSED #12:
Yes
The Family Liability Laws
were in effect then
JUDGE:
You did not question
the guilt of these women and children
ACCUSED #12:
We had been told
they had actively participated

in poisoning springs and wells
blowing up bridges
and other acts of sabotage
JUDGE:
Did you also see prisoners of war
among these people
ACCUSED #12:
Yes
Those prisoners had
by issued order
lost all claim to decent treatment
PROSECUTING ATTORNEY:
Accused Start
in the fall of 1941
a large number of Soviet
prisoners of war
were brought to the camp
According to court records
you were instrumental
in processing these contingents
ACCUSED #12:
In connection with these transports
I only followed instructions
PROSECUTING ATTORNEY:
What did that mean
ACCUSED #12:
I simply had to march them off
take over their cards marked
for execution
destroy their identification tags
and enter their numbers in the file
PROSECUTING ATTORNEY:
What reason
was given for the execution
of these prisoners of war
ACCUSED #12:
We were dealing with the annihilation
of an ideology
With their fanatical political orientation
these prisoners constituted a threat
to camp security
PROSECUTING ATTORNEY:
Where were the executions carried out
ACCUSED #12:
In the courtyard of Barrack 11
PROSECUTING ATTORNEY:
Did you take part in the executions
ACCUSED #12:
In one instance

yes

PROSECUTING ATTORNEY:

What was the procedure

ACCUSED #12:

The roll was called
and the formalities concluded
They were taken out to the courtyard
one after the other
It was almost over
Then Grabner said
Stark you carry on
Up to then the other corporals
had been taking turns

PROSECUTING ATTORNEY:

How many did you shoot

ACCUSED #12:

I can't remember

PROSECUTING ATTORNEY:

More than one

ACCUSED #12:

Yes

PROSECUTING ATTORNEY:

More than two

ACCUSED #12:

Four of five possibly

PROSECUTING ATTORNEY:

Did you try
to get out of taking part in the execution

ACCUSED #12:

But it was an order
It was my duty as a soldier

PROSECUTING ATTORNEY:

Did you participate
in any other executions

ACCUSED #12:

No
I was given leave
to complete my studies

PROSECUTING ATTORNEY:

When did your leave begin

ACCUSED #12:

In December 1941

PROSECUTING ATTORNEY:

When did you complete your studies

ACCUSED #12:

I passed my examinations
in the spring of 1942

PROSECUTING ATTORNEY:

Did you then

return to the camp

ACCUSED #12:

For a short time yes

COUNSEL FOR THE DEFENSE:

We would like to call
to the attention of the court
the fact that our client
was 20 years old
when he was ordered
to camp duty
As witnesses have substantiated
our client had keen intellectual interests
and his whole personality
made him utterly unfit
for the task assigned him
We would like to call attention to the fact
that one year after completing
his secondary schooling
our client
was granted a further period of leave
to study law
In the last year of the war
he was wounded in front-line action
Immediately after the war
as soon as he was able to settle down
in more normal conditions
he went on to develop in exemplary fashion
He studied agriculture
passed his assessor's examination
was an expert
with the Economic Advisory Council
and until his arrest
was an instructor
in an agricultural school

PROSECUTING ATTORNEY:

Accused Stark
did you take part in the first gassings
which were carried out
on Soviet prisoners of war
in the first weeks of September 1941

ACCUSED #12:

No

PROSECUTING ATTORNEY:

Large-scale extermination
of Soviet prisoners of war began
in the fall and winter of 1941
These resulted in the death of 25,000 men
You processed these prisoners
You knew of their death

you consented to their death
and you performed
essential parts of the operation
COUNSEL FOR THE DEFENSE:
We strongly protest
these attacks on our client
Such wholesale accusations
are completely meaningless
Only clear-cut proofs of criminal acts
or conspiracy in committing such acts
in relation to the charges of murder
are relevant to these proceedings
Wherever there is the slightest doubt
the benefit must be given to the accused

THE ACCUSED *laugh nodding in agreement*

(III)

JUDGE:
Accused Stark
you never once took part in the gassings
ACCUSED #12:
There was one time I had to
JUDGE:
How many prisoners were involved
ACCUSED #12:
Somewhere around 150
Four truckloads anyway
JUDGE:
Who were the prisoners
ACCUSED #12:
It was a mixed transport
JUDGE:
What was your job
ACCUSED #12:
I stood outside by the stairs
after I had led them
into the crematorium
The medical orderlies
in charge of the gassing
had locked the doors
and were making the necessary preparations
JUDGE:
What kind of preparations
ACCUSED #12:
They got out the cans

and put on their gas masks
Then they went up the embankment
to the roof deck
Usually it took four men to do the job
This time there were only three
and they called back
they needed somebody to help them out
Since I was the only one around
Grabner said
Move
give them a hand
Then the camp leader came over
and said rather sharply
If you don't go up there
in you go
So I had to go up
and help pour
JUDGE:
Where was the gas thrown in
ACCUSED #12:
Through vents in the deck
JUDGE:
What did the people in the chamber below
do then
ACCUSED #12:
I don't know
JUDGE:
You didn't hear anything
of what was going on down there
ACCUSED #12:
They screamed
JUDGE:
For how long
ACCUSED #12:
Around 10 or 15 minutes
JUDGE:
Who opened the chamber afterward
ACCUSED #12:
One of the orderlies
JUDGE:
What did you see in there
ACCUSED #12:
I didn't take a very close look
JUDGE:
Did you see anything wrong
with what you saw there
ACCUSED #12:
No

not at all
Only the way it was done
JUDGE:
    What do you mean
ACCUSED #12:
    If they had been shot
    it would have been one thing
    But the use of gas
    was unmanly and cowardly
JUDGE:
    Accused Stark
    during the course of your duties
    didn't you ever have any doubts
    about your conduct in the camp
ACCUSED #12:
    Your Honor
    I would like to explain that
    Every third word we heard
    even back in grammar school
    was about
    how they
    were to blame for everything
    and how they
    ought to be weeded out
    It was hammered into us
    that this would only be for the good
    of our people
    In leadership school
    we were taught above all
    to accept everything
    without question
    If anybody did raise a question
    they were told
    What is being done
    is done strictly according to the law
    It's no use saying
    the laws are different now
    We were told
    You've got to study
    You've got to have an education
    It's more important than food
    Your Honor
    we weren't supposed to think for ourselves
    There were others around
    to do our thinking for us
Assenting laughter from THE ACCUSED

END OF PART I

THE SONG OF
THE BLACK WALL

(I)

3RD WITNESS:
    Executions were
    carried out in front of the Black Wall
    in the yard of Barrack 11
JUDGE:
    Where was Barrack 11
3RD WITNESS:
    At the far right end
    of the old camp
JUDGE:
    Can the witness
    describe the yard
3RD WITNESS:
    It was between Barrack 10 and Barrack 11
    and took up a whole barrack length
    about 40 yards
    It was closed off at both ends
    by brick walls
JUDGE:
    How did one enter the yard
3RD WITNESS:
    Through a side door from Barrack 11
    or through the gate in the front brick wall
JUDGE:
    Was there any way of seeing into the yard
3RD WITNESS:
    Only through the ground-floor windows
    at the front of Barrack 11
    When the gate was opened
    to remove the dead
    there was a curfew
    All the other windows in Barrack 11
    were bricked up except for a crack at the top
    Windows in the women's barrack
    on the other side
    were boarded up
JUDGE:
    How high was the wall
3RD WITNESS:
    About 14 feet high
JUDGE:
    And where was the Black Wall

3RD WITNESS:
  Opposite the front gate
  against the back wall
JUDGE:
  What did the Black Wall look like
3RD WITNESS:
  It was made out of thick planks
  covered with tarred canvas
  Bullet-proof walls
  came out at an angle from the back
JUDGE:
  How large was the Black Wall
3RD WITNESS:
  About 10 feet high
  13 wide
JUDGE:
  From where were sentenced prisoners
  brought out to the Black Wall
3RD WITNESS:
  They came out through the side door
  of Barrack 11
JUDGE:
  Describe the procedure
3RD WITNESS:
  The Bunker-Jakob led out
  two prisoners at a time
  The prisoners were naked
JUDGE:
  Who was this Bunker-Jakob
3RD WITNESS:
  He was the special-duty prisoner
  assigned to Barrack 11
  He was a big powerfully built man
  a former boxer
JUDGE:
  How were the prisoners brought out
3RD WITNESS:
  Jakob was in the middle
  holding them by the arm
JUDGE:
  Were the prisoners' hands bound
3RD WITNESS:
  Up until 1942 they were
  tied behind the back with wire
  Later they stopped using it
  since experience showed that most prisoners
  went along quietly
JUDGE:
  How far was it from the side door
  to the Black Wall
3RD WITNESS:
  First the six steps down from the door
  then 20 paces to the Black Wall
  Everything went at the double
  When Jakob had brought
  the prisoners to the wall
  he ran back
  to get the next two
JUDGE:
  How were the executions carried out
3RD WITNESS:
  Prisoners were put
  face to the wall
  three to six feet apart
  The executioner went up to the first one
  put his gun against the prisoner's neck
  then fired from about four inches off
  The other prisoner saw it
  As soon as the first had fallen
  it was his turn
JUDGE:
  What kind of weapon
  was used
3RD WITNESS:
  A small-caliber rifle with a silencer
JUDGE:
  Whom did you see
  at the Black Wall executions
3RD WITNESS:
  The camp commander
  the adjutant
  the head of the Political Division Grabner
  and his assistants
  Among others I saw Broad Stark
  Boger and Schlage
  Kaduk was frequently there too
COUNSEL FOR THE DEFENSE:
  Are you sure
  the adjutant was there
3RD WITNESS:
  He was a familiar figure
  We knew the camp commander
  We knew his adjutant just as well
COUNSEL FOR THE DEFENSE:
  During the executions
  what were your duties in the yard
3RD WITNESS:
  As a medical student

I was assigned to the corpse-bearers' detail

JUDGE:
Which of the accused
took part in the executions

3RD WITNESS:
Boger Broad Stark Schlage and Kaduk
I saw them carry out executions on their
    own

JUDGE:
Accused Boger
did you take part in executions
carried out at the Black Wall

ACCUSED #2:
I never fired a shot in the camp

JUDGE:
Accused Broad
did you take part in executions
carried out at the Black Wall

ACCUSED #16:
I was never required to carry out
such assignments

JUDGE:
Accused Schlage
as supervisor of Barrack 11
did you
take part in executions
carried out at the Black Wall

ACCUSED #14:
I was not authorized to do so

JUDGE:
Accused Kaduk
did you take part in executions
carried out at the Black Wall

ACCUSED #7:
I never set foot in Barrack 11
What has been said here about me
is nothing but a lie

JUDGE:
Can the witness tell us
if death sentences
were read out before the executions

3RD WITNESS:
Not usually
When there was a death sentence
a special execution squad appeared
but I can only recall that happening
in a few cases
Generally prisoners were
just hauled out of the cells in Barrack 11

JUDGE:
What condition were the prisoners in

3RD WITNESS:
Most of them were badly injured
after the interrogations
and after their time in the Bunker
Some
had to be carried out to the Wall
on stretchers

JUDGE:
We call as witness
the then-ranking officer
of the accused here present
As head of the Central Office
of the Security Police attached to the
    camp
and presiding officer at its summary court
what did you have to do
with the executions carried out
by the Political Division

1ST WITNESS:
My post had no connection whatsoever
with the functioning
of the Political Division within the camp
I dealt exclusively with cases
relating to partisan resistance
These were brought over to the camp
and trial was held there in a hearing room

JUDGE:
Where was this room

1ST WITNESS:
In one of the barracks

JUDGE:
Was it not in Barrack 11

1ST WITNESS:
That's more than I can remember

6TH WITNESS:
I was the clerk in Barrack 11
My job gave me an idea
of the working of the summary courts
Court sessions were held in a room
on the front left side of Barrack 11

JUDGE:
What was the room like

6TH WITNESS:
There were four windows onto the courtyard
and a long table

JUDGE:
Do you recall this room

1ST WITNESS:
  No
JUDGE:
  Did you ever go into the inner area
  of the old camp
1ST WITNESS:
  That's more than I can remember
JUDGE:
  Did you ever pass through the camp gate
1ST WITNESS:
  It's possible
  I remember a band
  playing there once
JUDGE:
  Were you never in the yard of Barrack 11
1ST WITNESS:
  Once perhaps
  There was said to be a wall there
  I can't remember it though
JUDGE:
  But surely a black wall
  is very noticeable
1ST WITNESS:
  I have no recollection of it
JUDGE:
  You were
  the presiding officer
  at these summary sessions
  Did the defendant have counsel
1ST WITNESS:
  If it was requested
JUDGE:
  Was it ever requested
1ST WITNESS:
  Rarely
JUDGE:
  And when it was
1ST WITNESS:
  Then counsel was provided
JUDGE:
  Who was the defense
1ST WITNESS:
  Somebody from the office staff
JUDGE:
  Were intensive interrogations
  ever employed
1ST WITNESS:
  There was never any need for that
  At least I personally never

heard of any such interrogations
  The facts of the case were so clear
  there was no need
  for intensive interrogation
JUDGE:
  What were the facts of the case
1ST WITNESS:
  They were exclusively
  cases of treasonable activity
JUDGE:
  Did the prisoners confess
1ST WITNESS:
  There was nothing to deny
JUDGE:
  How were these confessions obtained
1ST WITNESS:
  By means of interrogations
JUDGE:
  Who conducted the interrogations
1ST WITNESS:
  The Political Division
JUDGE:
  As a judge
  were you ever troubled
  about how these confessions
  were obtained
1ST WITNESS:
  What can I do
  if one or another of my people
  exceeds his authority
  I strictly and repeatedly
  enjoined my assistants
  that they were to conduct
  themselves correctly
  at all hearings
JUDGE:
  Were witnesses called at interrogations
1ST WITNESS:
  Not as a rule
  We asked if everything was as stated
  and they all said yes
JUDGE:
  Then you only had to deliver death sen-
    tences
1ST WITNESS:
  Yes
  There were practically no acquittals
  Proceedings were instituted only
  when everything was perfectly clear

JUDGE:
Did you ever notice
any marks on the accused
which might have indicated improper treatment
1ST WITNESS:
No
JUDGE:
Were women and children
executed at the Black Wall
1ST WITNESS:
I know nothing about that
6TH WITNESS:
Among the prisoners
brought into the barrack
to be sentenced by the court
there were many women and children
The indictment was for smuggling
or for contact with partisan groups
In contrast to the camp prisoners
who were locked up in the basement
prisoners arrested by the Security Police
were held on the ground floor of Barrack 11
They were taken into the session room
one by one
The judge read the sentence
He only read out the names and then said
You have been sentenced to death
Most of the prisoners sentenced
didn't understand the language
and had no idea
why they had been arrested
From the courtroom
they were immediately taken
to the washroom
where they were told to undress
and from there
out to the courtyard
PROSECUTING ATTORNEY:
As judge of the summary court
how many sentences were you
called upon to deliver
1ST WITNESS:
I cannot remember that
PROSECUTING ATTORNEY:
How often
were your sessions held
1ST WITNESS:
I can't recall

PROSECUTING ATTORNEY:
How long
did a session of the summary court last
1ST WITNESS:
I couldn't say
PROSECUTING ATTORNEY:
You are at present the director
of a large business concern
As such you must certainly be accustomed
to dealing with large numbers
and complex time calculations
How many people
did you sentence
1ST WITNESS:
I don't know
6TH WITNESS:
At a single session of the summary court
an average of 100 to 150 death sentences
was delivered
The session lasted
an hour and a half to two hours
and took place every two weeks
PROSECUTING ATTORNEY:
How many prisoners
all told
would the witness estimate
were shot at the Black Wall
6TH WITNESS:
The death books and our own notes
show
that together
with the usual Bunker clearings
approximately 20,000 people
were shot at the Black Wall

(II)

7TH WITNESS:
Early one morning
in the fall of 1943
I saw a little girl
in the courtyard of Barrack 11
She wore a red dress
and her hair was braided into a long pigtail
She stood alone
her hands at her sides
like a soldier
She bent over once

to dust her shoes off
and then stood still again
Then I saw Boger come into the courtyard
He kept his gun
hidden behind his back
He took the child by the hand
and she went along with him like a good
    girl
and let him stand her
face to the wall
against the Black Wall
The child looked around once more
Boger turned her face to the wall
lifted his gun
and shot her

COUNSEL FOR THE DEFENSE:
How could the witness have seen this

7TH WITNESS:
I was cleaning the washroom
which was next to the door
leading out to the yard

JUDGE:
How old was the child

7TH WITNESS:
Six or seven years old
The corpse-bearers told me later
that the girl's parents
had been shot there a few days before

ACCUSED #2:
Your Honor
I never shot a child
I never shot anyone at all

3RD WITNESS:
I saw Boger by the Black Wall many times
I can still hear him yelling
Head up
and then shooting the prisoner in the neck

JUDGE:
Isn't it possible that the witness
may be confusing Boger with someone else

3RD WITNESS:
We all knew Boger
and the way he waddled when he walked
We used to see him frequently
riding to Barrack 11 on his bicycle
his gun slung over his shoulder
Sometimes he used to pull prisoners
along behind him
like dogs on a leash

JUDGE:
Accused Boger
would you care to reconsider
your statement
that you never fired a shot in the camp

ACCUSED #2:
I stand by my statement today
and a thousand years from now
I will still stand by it
Not that I would have been afraid to shoot
I would only have been carrying out orders

3RD WITNESS:
Executions were carried out
every Wednesday and Friday
On May 14 1943
I saw Boger
kill 17 prisoners
I made a note of the date
because my friend Berger was one of them
He had already been beaten to a pulp
on the swing
Berger shouted
You murderers you criminals
Then Boger shot him
Another prisoner was on his knees
in front of Boger
Boger shot him in the face
When word passed around
Boger's here
we knew what it meant
We called him
the Black Death

ACCUSED #2:
I've had a lot of nicknames besides that one
We all had nicknames
That doesn't prove anything

JUDGE:
Accused Boger
during the course of this trial
witnesses have repeatedly testified
that you
killed people in the camp
Has all this testimony
in your opinion
simply been invented

ACCUSED #2:
I was frequently
present at executions
Most likely

the witnesses are confusing me
with somebody else
They've got Boger
so what do they do
It's natural
They dump all their hate on me
JUDGE:
You didn't shoot once
ACCUSED #2:
I did
once
JUDGE:
You did shoot once
ACCUSED #2:
It was an exception
I was ordered
to take part in an execution
JUDGE:
How did that happen
ACCUSED #2:
At one of the Bunker clearings
Grabner called out the order
Sergeant Boger
will carry on with the shooting
JUDGE:
How many times did you shoot
ACCUSED #2:
Twice
on that one single occasion
Later I refused
to take part in such things
I said
Either I work here
or I work with Identification
I can't
do both jobs at the same time
JUDGE:
Who were the people
you had to shoot
ACCUSED #2:
They belonged to a transport
that hadn't been processed
by Identification
JUDGE:
That means
it was assumed from the start
they were going to die
ACCUSED #2:
I believe so

JUDGE:
Accused Boger
why have you consistently maintained
up until this very moment
that no one in the camp
met his death at your hand
ACCUSED #2:
Your Honor
when you get so much thrown at you
you just can't commit yourself right off
JUDGE:
And you persist in maintaining
that you shot in only two cases
and that no one ever died
as a result
of intensive interrogations
ACCUSED #2:
Yes
On my sacred word of honor
JUDGE:
As one of the corpse-bearers' detail
when were you required to appear
in the courtyard of Barrack 11
3RD WITNESS:
We were called up
about an hour before the execution
JUDGE:
Where were you stationed
3RD WITNESS:
In the Ambulance Barrack
JUDGE:
Where was that
3RD WITNESS:
Across from the Bunker Barrack
on the front right side of the camp
JUDGE:
How were you alerted for duty
3RD WITNESS:
A clerk ran in from Barrack 11
He shouted
Corpse-bearers
one stretcher
two stretchers
If he called for one stretcher we knew
it would be a small execution
If he called for more
it was a big one
JUDGE:
Where did the clerk stand

3RD WITNESS:
    He stayed out in the corridor
    and we ran out to him
    When he told us
    how many were needed
    the Kapo
    picked out the ones to go

JUDGE:
    Where did you have to go then

3RD WITNESS: .
    When the siren had signaled the curfew
    we went out into the courtyard
    through the door in Barrack 11
    We had to line up next to the door
    and stand there with our stretchers ready

JUDGE:
    What sort of stretchers were they

3RD WITNESS:
    Canvas
    with wood shafts
    and metal legs

JUDGE:
    Was a doctor present

3RD WITNESS:
    Only for big executions
    Otherwise just the officers
    of the Political Division

JUDGE:
    Where were prisoners awaiting execution
        kept

3RD WITNESS:
    They were held in the washroom
    and in the hall outside

JUDGE:
    What preparations preceded the execution

3RD WITNESS:
    After prisoners came up from the cellar
    they had to take off their clothes
    in the washroom
    or out in the hall
    Numbers were written on their chests
    with indelible pencil
    A prisoner clerk checked out the numbers
    then crossed them out
    as prisoners
    were taken out to the yard

JUDGE:
    What order was given
    to bring out the prisoners

3RD WITNESS:
    The order was
    Take off
    Then the Bunker-Jakob ran out
    with the first two
    As soon as they stood against the wall
    we too got the order
    Take off
    and we ran out with our stretcher

JUDGE:
    Who gave the order

3RD WITNESS:
    Either the doctor
    or one of the officers

JUDGE:
    Had the prisoners already been shot
    when you got there

3RD WITNESS:
    Usually the first one had fallen
    and the second fell right after
    But sometimes it took longer
    Then we stood behind
    the executioner

JUDGE:
    Why did it sometimes take longer

3RD WITNESS:
    Occasionally a gun jammed
    And we'd wait while the man
    took care of it

JUDGE:
    How did the prisoners
    who were to be executed behave

3RD WITNESS:
    Some prayed
    others sang national
    or religious songs
    Once though
    when a woman started to scream
    I heard the order
    Get that crazy one first

JUDGE:
    How did you remove the dead

3RD WITNESS:
    As soon as they had dropped in the sand
    in front of the wall
    we picked them up by the hands and feet
    laid the first one face up on the stretcher
    the second one face down and reversed
    so he lay with his face

between the legs of the one underneath
Then we ran to the drainage ditch
and tipped them out
JUDGE:
Where was this ditch
3RD WITNESS:
Along the left edge of the courtyard
JUDGE:
What happened then
3RD WITNESS:
While we ran with the stretcher
over to the ditch
the Bunker-Jakob was already running
the next two
out to the wall
and the two other bearers ran
behind him with their stretcher
We laid the dead down in layers
on top of each other
with their heads over the ditch
so the blood could drain off
JUDGE:
Did the prisoners die
immediately after execution
3RD WITNESS:
Sometimes the bullet
only went in through an ear
or through the shin
and they were still alive
when they were carried off
Then we had to put the stretcher down
and the injured would be shot again
this time in the head
The Arrest Supervisor Schlage
always took another look
at the bodies we had dumped
and if any of them still moved
he had him pulled out of the heap
and finished off the kill
Once Schlage said to one
who was still living
Get up
I saw
the man try to pull himself up
Then Schlage said
Stay down
and shot him in the heart
and in both temples
But the man was still alive

I don't know how many more he got
First
one in the throat
The blood that came out was black
Schlage said
That one has as many lives as a cat
JUDGE:
Accused Schlage
have you anything to say to this
ACCUSED #14:
It's a riddle to me
To that
I wouldn't know what to say

(III)

7TH WITNESS:
I saw Schlage in the washroom once
with a family that had been brought in
The father had to get down and duck-walk
and then Schlage shot him in the head
Then it was the child's turn
and after that the mother
He had to shoot the child more than once
It screamed and didn't die right away
COUNSEL FOR THE DEFENSE:
Why did he shoot them in the washroom
when the Execution Wall
was just outside
7TH WITNESS:
Smaller executions
were often carried out in the washroom
because it was simpler
The showers could be turned on
to wash the blood off the floor
COUNSEL FOR THE DEFENSE:
Describe the washroom
7TH WITNESS:
It was a small room with one window
that was covered over with a blanket
The bottom half of the room was tarred
the upper half painted white
There were thick black pipes in the corners
About six feet up
a pipe with shower heads
crossed through the middle of the room
JUDGE:
Accused Schlage

do you still maintain
that you shot nobody in the camp
ACCUSED #14:
    I emphatically deny
    these accusations
    I never took part in any killings
7TH WITNESS:
    Some of the corpses
    brought into the washroom
    had flesh cut out of them
JUDGE:
    What do you mean by that
7TH WITNESS:
    In the summer of 1944
    I saw the first of those mutilated corpses
    A man was unloaded
    whom I had already noticed
    when he stripped for execution
    He was a giant
    I saw him lying in the washroom
    There were men in white coats
    and with surgical instruments
    standing around him
    Flesh had been cut out of his stomach
    At first we thought
    he must have swallowed something
    and they were getting it out
    but later on it happened more often
    that flesh was cut out of corpses
    Afterwards it was mainly the case
    with bodies of the stronger heavier women
3RD WITNESS:
    Once we had to remove
    the corpses of 70 women
    Their breasts were gone
    and there were deep cuts
    in their abdomens and thighs
    The medical orderlies loaded
    potfuls of human flesh
    into the sidecar of a motorcycle
    On the wagon
    we had to cover up
    the corpses with boards
4TH WITNESS:
    In Experimental Research Barrack 10
    I looked through a crack in the window
        boards
    I saw the corpses down in the courtyard
    We had heard a loud hum

It was swarms of flies
The ground was covered with blood
Then I saw
the executioners walking across the courtyard
smoking and laughing

WITNESS points at THE ACCUSED

COUNSEL FOR THE DEFENSE:
    We cannot allow
    these insults to our clients
    to pass unchallenged
    We want the record
    to show our objection

THE ACCUSED express their indignation

THE SONG OF PHENOL

(I)

8TH WITNESS:
    I charge Medical Orderly Klehr
    with the singlehanded killing
    of thousands of prisoners
    by injecting phenol into the heart
ACCUSED #9:
    That is slander
    Only in a very few cases
    was I compelled to supervise injections
    and then
    only with the greatest reluctance
8TH WITNESS:
    At least 30 prisoners were killed
    daily in the infirmary
    Sometimes as many as 200
JUDGE:
    Where were these injections given
8TH WITNESS:
    In the Contagious Diseases Barrack nearby
    That was Barrack 20
JUDGE:
    Where was Barrack 20
8TH WITNESS:
    It was the next-to-the-last building
    on the right-hand side
    of the center barrack row

The last building in that row was 21
the camp infirmary
As a prisoner attendant I had to
take selected prisoners
across the yard
to the Contagious Diseases Barrack
JUDGE:
Was this yard closed off
8TH WITNESS:
Only by low iron railings at each end
JUDGE:
How were the prisoners transferred
8TH WITNESS:
Those able to walk
crossed the courtyard half naked
They held their blanket and wooden shoes
over their heads
Many patients had to be supported
or carried over
They entered Barrack 20
through the side door
JUDGE:
In which room
were the injections given
8TH WITNESS:
In Room 1
That was the doctor's office
It was at the end of the central corridor
JUDGE:
Where did the prisoners wait
8TH WITNESS:
They had to line up in the corridor
The critically ill lay on the floor
Prisoners went into the room two by two
Dr Entress assigned Klehr
a third of the patients
That wasn't enough for him
When Dr Entress had left for the day
Klehr stayed to make additional selections
JUDGE:
You saw this yourself
8TH WITNESS:
Yes
I saw it
Klehr loved round numbers
If the final count didn't satisfy him
he went through the wards
selecting victims to round off the number
He looked over the fever charts

which under his supervision
were meticulously kept
then made his selections accordingly
JUDGE:
What were the round numbers
that Klehr especially favored
8TH WITNESS:
From about 23 on
he would round it off to 30
from 36 to 40
and so on
He ordered selected patients
to get up and follow him
JUDGE:
What order was given
8TH WITNESS:
You come along
you come along
you come along
and you
ACCUSED #9:
Your Honor
this statement is untrue
I was not authorized to make selections
JUDGE:
What were your duties then
ACCUSED #9:
I only had to see to it
that the right prisoners were brought over
JUDGE:
And what did you
have to do when injections were given
ACCUSED #9:
That's something I'd like to know myself
I just stood around
The treatment
was carried out by special-duty prisoners
I kept away from that
I wasn't going to let those
contaminated prisoners
breathe in my face
JUDGE:
As staff orderly
what were your duties
ACCUSED #9:
I was responsible
(a) for discipline and sanitation
(b) for registration
(c) for the patients' nutrition

JUDGE:
  What was their diet
ACCUSED #9:
  In the dietetic kitchen milk-soup was
  prepared for postoperational patients
JUDGE:
  How many patients were in the infirmary
ACCUSED #9:
  On the average some
  500 to 600 patients
JUDGE:
  What were the accommodations
ACCUSED #9:
  They lay on triple-decker bunks
JUDGE:
  How were they registered
ACCUSED #9:
  Every sick report received
  was card-indexed
  Selections among advanced patients
  were then registered
JUDGE:
  What were advanced patients
ACCUSED #9:
  Prisoners
  whose state of health was critical
JUDGE:
  How were the selections made
ACCUSED #9:
  The camp doctor examined the prisoner
  and the index card with the diagnosis
  If he did not return the card
  to the prisoner doctor
  but gave it to the prisoner clerk instead
  it meant
  the prisoner was to receive the injection
JUDGE:
  What happened then
ACCUSED #9:
  The cards were assembled on a table
  and processed
JUDGE:
  What does processed mean
ACCUSED #9:
  The prisoner clerk had
  to compile a list from the cards on
      hand
  This list was then handed over
  to the medical orderly

In accordance with this list
patients were dispatched
9TH WITNESS:
  On Christmas 1942
  Klehr walked into the ward
  and said
  Today
  I am camp doctor
  Today
  I shall take care
  of the advanced patients
  With the stem of his pipe
  he pointed out 40 of them
  and designated them for injection
  After Christmas
  a requisition for special rations
  was put in
  for Medical Orderly Klehr
  I saw the requisition
  It said
  For Special Treatment
  carried out 24 12 1942
  a half-pint brandy
  5 cigarettes 3½ ounces sausage
  is requested
ACCUSED #9:
  That's ridiculous
  I had home leave every Christmas
  My wife can testify to that
JUDGE:
  Accused Klehr
  do you still maintain
  you had no part whatsoever
  in selections and killings
  by means of phenol injection
ACCUSED #9:
  All I had to do
  was supervise standard operating procedures
JUDGE:
  Did you always find
  these procedures justified
ACCUSED #9:
  In the beginning I was astonished
  when I heard
  that patients were injected
  by special-duty prisoners
  But then I realized
  that the patients were incurable
  and endangered the health of the entire camp

JUDGE:
  How were the injections given
ACCUSED #9:
  Special-duty prisoner Peter Werl
  from the Ambulance Barrack
  and another called Felix
  administered the injections
  At first
  they were injected into a vein in the arm
  However due to the undernourished
  condition of the prisoners
  these veins were hard to find
  For that reason phenol was later on
  injected directly into the heart
  The hypo wasn't even empty
  the man was already dead
JUDGE:
  Did you ever refuse
  to be present at these sessions
ACCUSED #9:
  I would have been put up against the wall
JUDGE:
  You never expressed your misgivings
  to the camp doctor
ACCUSED #9:
  I did
  a number of times
  But all I was told was
  I had my duty to do
JUDGE:
  Couldn't you have arranged
  for a transfer to some other post
ACCUSED #9:
  Mr President
  we were all in a straitjacket
  We were nothing but numbers
  just like the prisoners
  With us
  a man began to count for something
  only when he had a degree
  We should have just dared try
  to question anything
JUDGE:
  Were you never compelled
  to give an injection yourself
ACCUSED #9:
  Once when I started to complain
  the camp doctor said
  In the future you'll do it yourself

JUDGE:
  And then you did undertake
  selections and killings
ACCUSED #9:
  In a few cases
  yes
  I was compelled to
JUDGE:
  How often did you give injections
ACCUSED #9:
  Generally twice a week
  to about 12 to 15 men
  But I was only there for two or three months
JUDGE:
  That would come to at least
  200 killed
ACCUSED #9:
  It could have been 250 to 300
  I don't remember exactly
  It was orders
  There wasn't anything I could do about it
8TH WITNESS:
  Medical Orderly Klehr
  participated
  in the killing
  of at least 16,000 prisoners
ACCUSED #9:
  That's preposterous
  I'm supposed to have injected away
  16,000 people
  when there were only 16,000
  in the whole camp
  That wouldn't have left anybody but the band

THE ACCUSED *laugh*

(II)

JUDGE:
  Accused Klehr
  how did you kill the prisoners
ACCUSED #9:
  As prescribed by orders
  with an injection of phenol in the heart
  But I didn't do that all by myself
JUDGE:
  Who else was there
ACCUSED #9:
  I don't remember

9TH WITNESS:
   The accused Scherpe and Hantl
   assisted in the killings by phenol
   Yet their behavior was very different
   from Klehr's
   They were polite to us
   and said Good morning
   when they came into the barrack
   and when they left they said
   Good afternoon
   We often saw Klehr wild with rage
   Scherpe
   on the other hand
   was calm and courteous
   He had a pleasant way
   of treating people
   I never saw Scherpe beat
   or kick anybody
   Patients who came to him
   often had confidence in him
   and believed they were only
   going to be treated for their illness
JUDGE:
   As one of the prisoner doctors
   in the infirmary
   what can the witness tell us
   about the early stages
   of phenol injection
9TH WITNESS:
   It was camp doctor Entress
   who initiated the injections
   He began by using gasoline
   but that proved to be impractical
   since it took three quarters of an hour
   for the patient to die
   A quicker means was sought
   The second to be used was hydrogen
   After that came phenol
JUDGE:
   Whom did you see administer
   these injections
9TH WITNESS:
   At first Dr Entress himself
   then Scherpe and Hantl
   Hantl did it infrequently
   We thought of him as a decent person
JUDGE:
   Did you see
   Klehr kill

9TH WITNESS:
   I did not see it myself
   Both Schwarz and Gebhard
   the two prisoners who had to hold the
      victim
   during the injection
   told me about it
   But we didn't waste much time discussing
      it
   It was such an ordinary event
COUNSEL FOR THE DEFENSE:
   The witness
   mentions different names
   in connection
   with these special-duty prisoners
   Weren't the prisoners named Werl and
      Felix
9TH WITNESS:
   There were many special-duty prisoners
   who had to do this job
COUNSEL FOR THE DEFENSE:
   And didn't these prisoners
   also do the killing
9TH WITNESS:
   In the beginning they had to
COUNSEL FOR THE DEFENSE:
   So the prisoners were killed
   by their own people
PROSECUTING ATTORNEY:
   We protest
   these tactics by which the defense
   seeks to blame prisoners
   for actions carried out
   under the threat of death
COUNSEL FOR THE DEFENSE:
   The troops in the camp
   were subject to the same threat
PROSECUTING ATTORNEY:
   In no instance has it been proved
   that anything was done
   to those who refused
   to take part in killings
COUNSEL FOR THE DEFENSE:
   That is easy enough to say now
   In the eyes of the law a subordinate
   can be held responsible
   only when he knows
   that the order of his superior
   involves the commission of a civil

or military crime
Our clients acted in good faith
and according to the basic principle
of unquestioning execution of their duty
With their oath of allegiance to the death
all submitted to the goals
established by
the then-existing administration
as did also
the Department of Justice
and the Army
PROSECUTING ATTORNEY:
We repeat that anyone
who recognized the criminal intent of an
    order
had the choice
of requesting a transfer
We know
why they did not have themselves transf-
    erred
At the front
their own lives would have been endan-
    gered
So they stayed
where their enemy was defenseless
JUDGE:
The court calls as witness
one of the former
ranking camp doctors
In the course of your duties
did you have anything to do with the accused
Klehr Scherpe and Hantl
2ND WITNESS:
I did not come into contact
with these men
JUDGE:
Weren't you their superior
2ND WITNESS:
Their only superior there
was the camp headquarters doctor
All I did was desk work
JUDGE:
What was your position in the medical profes-
    sion
before being called up for service in the camp
2ND WITNESS:
I was a university professor
JUDGE:
And yet with all your professional training

you had only office work to do
2ND WITNESS:
Occasionally I also
did some work in pathology
JUDGE:
You selected
no prisoners for the accused Klehr
2ND WITNESS:
I refused to do so
JUDGE:
You were never present during selections
2ND WITNESS:
Only to accompany the doctor on duty
PROSECUTING ATTORNEY:
Are you aware
that those
who took part in such actions
were granted special rations
2ND WITNESS:
I find it understandable and natural
that for the hard work they had to do
the men should receive
special rations of cigarettes
and brandy
After all it was wartime
Brandy and cigarettes were hard to come
    by
so of course the men were after them
They saved up their coupons
and then went over with their bottle
PROSECUTING ATTORNEY:
You too
2ND WITNESS:
Yes
Everybody went over
PROSECUTING ATTORNEY:
What was your attitude
in regard to the selections
COUNSEL FOR THE DEFENSE:
We object to this question
This witness has already
served his sentence
and he cannot be tried here again
2ND WITNESS:
I consider myself
innocent even today
The only patients chosen
were those who couldn't have recovered
anyway

PROSECUTING ATTORNEY:
  With your medical training
  you saw no alternative
2ND WITNESS:
  Not with the way things were then
  On the front thousands of our own sol-
      diers
  were bleeding to death
  and people were suffering
  in the bombed-out cities
PROSECUTING ATTORNEY:
  But we are talking here
  of people who
  though they had committed no crime
  were held under arrest
  and murdered
  You must have been aware of that
2ND WITNESS:
  There was nothing I could do about it
  My first day there
  the army doctor said to me
  We're in the asshole of the world here
  and we have to behave accordingly
PROSECUTING ATTORNEY:
  Were you present
  when injections were given
2ND WITNESS:
  Yes
  I had to go in there occasionally
PROSECUTING ATTORNEY:
  What did you see there
2ND WITNESS:
  Klehr put on a doctor's coat
  and said to a girl
  You have heart trouble
  You have to have an injection
  Then he jabbed it in
  and I ran out
PROSECUTING ATTORNEY:
  Was Klehr alone
2ND WITNESS:
  Yes
PROSECUTING ATTORNEY:
  Wasn't the woman held down
2ND WITNESS:
  No
PROSECUTING ATTORNEY:
  The court is in possession of the diary
  you kept during your time in the camp

In this diary we read
For lunch today
roast hare
a thick leg of mutton
with potato dumplings and cabbage
It goes on to say
Six women injected by Klehr
2ND WITNESS:
  I must have heard that somewhere
PROSECUTING ATTORNEY:
  We read further
  Bicycle trip
  wonderful weather
  Then
  Present at 11 executions
  Three women begged for their lives
  Fresh samples taken from liver
  spleen and pancreas
  following injections of pilocarpin
  What does that mean
2ND WITNESS:
  I had orders
  to perform autopsies
  The purpose of this work
  was purely scientific
  I had nothing to do with the killings
PROSECUTING ATTORNEY:
  The people whose flesh you took
  had you picked them for autopsy
  while they were still alive
COUNSEL FOR THE DEFENSE:
  We object
  and remind the prosecution once again
  that this witness has already
  paid his penalty
PROSECUTING ATTORNEY:
  Why did you use human flesh
  for your research
2ND WITNESS:
  Because the guards
  ate the beef and horse meat
  received
  for use in our bacteriological research
JUDGE:
  Where was the phenol
  used for injections
  stored
3RD WITNESS:
  It was stored in the dispensary

JUDGE:
  Where was the dispensary
3RD WITNESS:
  In the maintenance buildings outside the camp
JUDGE:
  Who was in charge of the dispensary
3RD WITNESS:
  Dr Capesius
JUDGE:
  Who came for the phenol
3RD WITNESS:
  The requisition
  written up by Klehr
  was handed over
  to Dr Capesius in the dispensary
  by a messenger from the infirmary
  The messenger was then given the phenol
JUDGE:
  Accused Dr Capesius
  what do you have to say to this
ACCUSED #3:
  I don't know anything
  about such requisitions
JUDGE:
  Did you know that people in the camp
  were killed by injections of phenol
ACCUSED #3:
  I heard about it for the first time
  just now
JUDGE:
  Did you store phenol in your dispensary
ACCUSED #3:
  I never saw any great amount of it there
3RD WITNESS:
  The phenol was stored in a yellow cup-
    board
  in the corner of the prescription room
  Later on there were also big bottles of it
  in the cellar
COUNSEL FOR THE DEFENSE:
  How does the witness
  happen to know this
3RD WITNESS:
  I was assigned to duty in the dispensary
  I saw the new requisition forms
  They had been filled out
  and signed by Dr Capesius
  They called it purified phenol
  But I'm not sure whether

the words PRO INJECTIONE were on the forms
    too or not
JUDGE:
  What quantities were requisitioned
3RD WITNESS:
  Small amounts at first
  Later
  from 4½ to 11 pounds a month
JUDGE:
  How is phenol
  generally used as a medication
3RD WITNESS:
  Mixed with glycerine
  it is used for ear drops
ACCUSED #3:
  That's precisely what the phenol in my
    keeping
  was intended for
JUDGE:
  4½ to 11 pounds of phenol per month
  16 ounces per pound
  each ounce contained hundreds of drops
  You could have cured the ears
  of an entire army

THE ACCUSED *laugh*

JUDGE:
  Accused Capesius
  do you still maintain
  that in your dispensary you never saw
  phenol for injection
ACCUSED #3:
  I neither saw large quantities
  of phenol
  nor knew
  that people were being killed with it
JUDGE:
  Who received the phenol
  obtained from the dispensary
3RD WITNESS:
  The doctor on duty
  He then passed it on to the orderly
  in the doctor's office

(III)

JUDGE:
  Describe the doctor's office

6TH WITNESS:
  It was painted white
  The windows on the courtyard side
  were whitewashed over
JUDGE:
  How was the room furnished
6TH WITNESS:
  There were a few cupboards and closets
  and then there was the curtain
  that divided the room
JUDGE:
  What sort of curtain was it
6TH WITNESS:
  It was about six feet long
  and it hung from a little below the ceiling
  It was greenish-gray
  The clerk who sat in front of it
  crossed off the patients
  as they were brought in
JUDGE:
  What was behind the curtain
6TH WITNESS:
  A small table
  and a couple of stools
  On the wall
  there were rubber aprons
  and pink rubber gloves
  hanging on hooks
COUNSEL FOR THE DEFENSE:
  How does the witness
  know this
6TH WITNESS:
  I was a corpse-bearer
  We sat in the washroom right next
  to the doctor's room
  The door was open
  and we could see everything
JUDGE:
  What happened to the prisoners
  who were to be given
  the phenol injection
6TH WITNESS:
  They were brought in two at a time
  from the corridor
  One of the two special-duty prisoners
  who stood ready behind the curtain
  held one prisoner
  while the injection was given
  The other one had to wait

on the other side of the curtain
Meanwhile the second special-duty prisoner
had filled the hypodermic
JUDGE:
  What kind of syringe was used
6TH WITNESS:
  At first
  when they gave intravenous injections
  they were syringes with a capacity of five
    cc's
  Later
  when injections were made
  directly into the heart
  they used syringes that held only two cc's
  They were fitted with needles
  generally used for making lumbar punc-
    tures
  A supply of syringes was kept in a pouch
JUDGE:
  In what sort of vessel was
  the phenol kept
6TH WITNESS:
  In a bottle
  similar to a thermos
  The phenol was poured out
  into a small basin
  The syringes were filled from this
  The fluid turned red
  because needles were seldom changed
  and they were bloody from the injec-
    tions
JUDGE:
  Did the patients know
  what was going to happen to them
6TH WITNESS:
  Most of them did not
  They were told
  they were going to be inoculated
JUDGE:
  They allowed
  this to be done to them
6TH WITNESS:
  Most of them did as they were told
  Many were in a state of utter exhaustion
JUDGE:
  Whom did you see administer injections
6TH WITNESS:
  Klehr took the syringe

when it had been filled
He wore a rubber apron
rubber gloves and high rubber boots
The sleeves of his white coat
were rolled up

JUDGE:

What happened to the prisoner then

6TH WITNESS:

If he still had a shirt on
he had to take it off
and sit down on the stool
He had to hold his left arm up
and out to the side
and cover his mouth with his hand
That was to smother the scream
and to leave the heart open
The two special-duty prisoners
held him down

JUDGE:

What were their names

6TH WITNESS:

They were called Schwarz and Weiss
Schwarz held the prisoner
by the shoulders
Weiss kept the prisoner's hand
against his mouth
and Klehr jabbed the needle
into his heart

JUDGE:

Did death occur immediately

6TH WITNESS:

Most of them made a faint sound
as if they were exhaling
Generally they were dead then
The death rattle went on in some of them
and stopped only
after they had been taken off
to the washroom
Some were still in their death agony
when we took them off
The rest were dragged out
with a leather thong
we slipped around their wrists
It went very quickly
Often two or three patients
were finished off
inside a minute

JUDGE:

What happened to those

who were still alive
after the injection

6TH WITNESS:

I remember a man
who was tall and powerfully built
He got up to his feet in the washroom
with the injection in his heart
I remember it very clearly
There was a boiler
and next to it a bench
Holding on to the boiler
and the bench
he pulled himself up
Then Klehr came in
and gave him a second injection
Others were sometimes only unconscious
because the needle hadn't gone into the
    heart
and the phenol had entered the lung
When he was done for the day
Klehr always went into the washroom
to look over the stacked-up bodies
If one of them was still alive
he shot him in the back of the neck
Or sometimes he would just say
This one won't make it to the crema-
    torium

JUDGE:

Did it ever happen that living prisoners
were taken out with the dead

6TH WITNESS:

Sometimes
yes

JUDGE:

And they were burned alive

6TH WITNESS:

Yes
Or killed with a shovel
at the ovens

JUDGE:

Did prisoners ever
resist

6TH WITNESS:

Once there was a loud shout
This is what I saw
The two special-duty prisoners
were sitting on top of a bare-chested man
who was smeared all over with blood
The man's head had been split open

A poker was lying on the floor
Klehr stood there
the hypodermic in his hand
Klehr knelt down on top of the man
who was still thrashing violently
and jabbed the needle in
JUDGE:
Accused Klehr
what do you have to say to these accusations
ACCUSED #9:
I know nothing about the case in question
JUDGE:
Do you recognize the witness
ACCUSED #9:
Your Honor
This is important
I don't know this witness
and I knew every single prisoner
employed in the corpse-bearer detail
7TH WITNESS:
On September 28 1942
it was my father's turn
He was brought in
together with another prisoner
Klehr said to him
You're going to be given
a typhus shot now
He quickly injected both of them
in the heart
He was in a hurry
to get back to his rabbit breeding
I held my father
and then carried him out myself
JUDGE:
Accused Klehr
do you know the witness
ACCUSED #9:
That's Weiss
He was weeping at the time
so I asked him why he was weeping
Had he told me
right away that it was his father
I would have let him live
JUDGE:
Why didn't you tell him right away
7TH WITNESS:
I was scared
Klehr would say
Sit down next to him

JUDGE:
Were children among those
killed by injection
7TH WITNESS:
Once in the spring of 1943
more than 100 children were killed
JUDGE:
Who carried out this killing
7TH WITNESS:
The killing was carried out
by staff orderlies Hantl and Scherpe
JUDGE:
Can the witness
provide us with the exact number
of children killed at that time
7TH WITNESS:
There were 119 children
JUDGE:
Do you recall the exact date
7TH WITNESS:
It was the 23rd of February
JUDGE:
How do you know this
7TH WITNESS:
I was the clerk at the execution
It was my job
to cross the children off the list
They were boys from 13 to 17 years old
Their parents had been shot earlier
JUDGE:
Where did these children come from
7TH WITNESS:
They came from the province of Zamos
a region that had been cleared
to make room for settlers
from the home country
JUDGE:
Accused Scherpe
did you take part in this killing
ACCUSED #10:
Mr Chairman
I would like to state categorically
that I never killed a single person
JUDGE:
Accused Hantl
what do you have to say
ACCUSED #11:
That children were shipped in too
is completely new to me

Excuse me
Mr Scherpe
did we ever have anything to do
with children
JUDGE:
You are not permitted here
to put any questions to other accused
What we want to know from you
is whether you took part
in the killings by injection
ACCUSED #11:
All I can say to that
is that these accusations are lies
JUDGE:
Were you present
when the injections were given
ACCUSED #11:
At first I refused
I said
Is it absolutely necessary
for me to be around
a mess like that
Anyway I was only there about
eight or ten times
JUDGE:
How many were killed
the times you were there
ACCUSED #11:
Not more than five to eight people
Then it was over
7TH WITNESS:
Hantl helped
select the patients
and he helped kill them
Injections were given almost daily
The only day they weren't was Sunday
ACCUSED #11:
That really makes me laugh
I never heard such nonsense in my life
I simply can't understand
why this witness
of all people
should single me out
when I was the one who helped him out
when he had committed sabotage
JUDGE:
What had he done
ACCUSED #11:
He had stolen sheets

I always did everything I could
to help the prisoners
I managed to get fuel for them
and radishes too
JUDGE:
And you did not take part in the killings
ACCUSED #11:
No
I did not
JUDGE:
Will the witness
resume his report
concerning the children
7TH WITNESS:
The children had been brought
into the courtyard
They played out there in the morning
Somebody had given them a ball
The prisoners there
knew what was going to happen to them
They gave them the best of whatever they
        had
The children were hungry and anxious
They said they had been beaten
They asked us over and over
Are we going to be killed
Scherpe and Hantl came in the afternoon
During the hours
in which they carried out this action
Barrack 20 was quiet as the grave
JUDGE:
Did the children suspect
what was going to happen
7TH WITNESS:
The first ones screamed
Then they were told
they were going to be vaccinated
Then they went in quietly
Only the last ones
started to scream again
because their friends
hadn't come out again
They were brought in to me
two by two
and then went in singly
behind the curtain
The only sound I heard
was the thump
when their heads and bodies

struck the washroom floor
Suddenly Scherpe ran out
I heard him say
I can't anymore
He ran off somewhere
Hantl took care of the rest
After that
the rumor spread around camp
Scherpe's had a breakdown

JUDGE:
Accused Scherpe
do you have anything to say to this

ACCUSED #10:
The report of the witness
seems greatly exaggerated to me
Anyway
I don't recall any of this

PROSECUTING ATTORNEY:
Altogether
how many people
would the witness estimate
were killed by phenol injections

7TH WITNESS:
Going by figures in the camp books
as well as by our personal calculations
approximately 30,000 people

THE SONG OF
THE BUNKER BLOCK

(I)

8TH WITNESS:
I was sentenced
to 30 times in the standing cell
That meant
punitive hard labor during the day
nights in the standing cell

JUDGE:
Why were you sentenced

8TH WITNESS:
I went through the food line twice

JUDGE:
Where were the standing cells

8TH WITNESS:
At the end of the cellar corridor

in Barrack 11
There were four of them

JUDGE:
How large was a cell

8TH WITNESS:
Three feet square
and about six feet high

JUDGE:
Was there a window

8TH WITNESS:
No
There was an air hole up in the corner
an inch and a half square
The air shaft went out through the wall
It was closed up on the outside
with a perforated tin lid

JUDGE:
And the door

8TH WITNESS:
You had to crawl in at the bottom
through a wooden hatchway
about 20 inches high
Outside was an iron gate
that bolted shut

JUDGE:
Were you alone in the cell

8TH WITNESS:
At first I was alone
The last week
there were four of us standing in there

JUDGE:
Were prisoners
there
day and night

8TH WITNESS:
That was the usual sentence
The method varied
Some prisoners were fed only
every two or three days
Others weren't fed at all
Those had been sentenced to death
by starvation
My friend Kurt Pachala
died in the adjoining cell
after 15 days
Toward the end he ate his shoes
He died the 14th of January 1943
I remember that
because it was my birthday

A prisoner sentenced to
the standing cell without food
could scream and swear
as much as he wanted
The door was never opened
For the fist five nights
he screamed
Then hunger stopped
and thirst took over
He begged
he prayed and he moaned
He drank his urine
and licked the walls
The thirst went on for 13 days
Then no sound came from his cell
It took more than two weeks
for him to die
Corpses had to be scraped
out of the standing cells
with iron rods

JUDGE:
Why
had this man been sentenced

8TH WITNESS:
He had tried to escape
Before he was put in the cell
he had to march past
the prisoners
lined up for evening roll call
He had a sign tied to him that read
HURRAY I'M BACK AGAIN
While he shouted out the words on the
    sign
he had to beat on a drum
Of those sentenced to the standing cell
Bruno Graf was the prisoner
who lasted the longest
Arrest Supervisor Schlage
used to stand at his door sometimes
when Graf was bellowing in there
and I heard Schlage
yell
Why don't you just die
It took Graf a month to die

JUDGE:
Accused Schlage
did you allow prisoners to starve to
    death
in the standing cells

ACCUSED #14:
Mr Chairman
I request permission to say the following
I was
if I may say so
only the lockup man
I received my orders from my superiors
and I was duty-bound to carry them out
For what took place in the Bunker
I was not responsible
The Chief Arrest Supervisor was respon-
    sible

JUDGE:
Who brought food to the prisoners

ACCUSED #14:
Special-duty prisoners did that

JUDGE:
Who locked the cells

ACCUSED #14:
Special-duty prisoners did that too
We Arrest Supervisors
were only responsible
for unlocking the outside gates
when the Political Division arrived

JUDGE:
Did prisoners
die in the Arrest Bunker

ACCUSED #14:
That's possible
But I can't really remember

JUDGE:
Who kept the Death Book
and entered causes of death

ACCUSED #14:
Only special-duty prisoners did all that

JUDGE:
And you had nothing to do

ACCUSED #14:
I had our own people to guard
There were sometimes as many
as 18 of them
I had to make
sure
they didn't try to kill themselves
or do some other dumb thing

JUDGE:
You mean to say
that members of units serving in the camp
were also jailed in the Bunker

ACCUSED #14:
Of course
There was justice for all
Surely Your Honor
every sign of weakness
had to be fought against

(II)

JUDGE:
How large were the other cells
in the Bunker
9TH WITNESS:
The other cells were roughly
eight feet wide
eight feet long
eight feet high
Some were dark cells
The rest had a small window
with a concrete rim
The only air vent was
high up in the wall
It was an opening no bigger
than the palm of your hand
JUDGE:
How many such cells were there
9TH WITNESS:
28 cells
JUDGE:
How many prisoners
could be put in a cell
9TH WITNESS:
In that space
there were often as many
as 40 prisoners
JUDGE:
How long did they have to stay there
9TH WITNESS:
Often for several weeks
The prisoner Bogdan Glinski
was in there for more than 17 weeks
from November 13 1942
till March 9 1943
JUDGE:
How was the cell furnished
9TH WITNESS:
There was only a wooden box
with a bucket in it

JUDGE:
What regulations applied
to prisoners put in these cells
9TH WITNESS:
Here too the sentence was either
overnight confinement
or long-term confinement
And here too confinement
without food was practiced
JUDGE:
Which punishment did you undergo
9TH WITNESS:
I spent two nights in there
JUDGE:
Would you describe what happened
9TH WITNESS:
I had to report at Barrack 11
at 9 o'clock at night
together with 38 other prisoners
The Barrack-elder reported
the count
to the Barrack-leader on duty
Then he took us down to the basement
and locked us into Cell 20
By 10 o'clock
the air was already stifling
We stood crowded against each other
We couldn't sit down
and we couldn't lie down
It was soon so hot
we started taking off our jackets
and pants
Around midnight
we couldn't stand any more
Some collapsed
The others hung on to each other
Most of the prisoners were tense
and restless
and shoved and swore
at each other
The smell
from the men who were suffocating
mixed with the stink
coming out of the bucket
The weak got trampled
The stronger fought
to get up next to the door
where a little air came in
We shouted and pounded on the door

We battered and hammered at it
but it didn't give
Once in a while
the peep hole was opened outside
and the jailer on duty
looked in at us
By 2 o'clock in the morning
most of the prisoners
had lost consciousness
At 5
the door was opened
We were pulled out
into the corridor
We were all naked
Of the 38 who went in
19 were still alive
Of these 19
6 were taken to the infirmary
where 4 died

3RD WITNESS:
I belonged to the corpse detail
that had to clean out the hunger cells
Frequently
the dead in there had bites
in their buttocks and thighs
Often those
who had held out the longest
had some fingers missing
I asked the Bunker-Jakob
who was in charge of cleaning the Bunker
How can you stand it
He said
Praise be
what makes a man hard
Everything's fine with me
I eat their rations
Their death doesn't move me
All this moves me about as much
as that stone in the wall

(III)

6TH WITNESS:
On the 3rd of September 1941
the first experiments
in mass killings
using the gas Cyklon B
were carried out in the Bunker

Staff medical orderlies and guards
brought about 850 Soviet prisoners of
     war
and 220 prisoner patients
to Barrack 11
After they had been locked in the cells
earth was shoveled against the windows
to seal them off
Then the gas
was funneled in
through the air holes
The next day it was ascertained
that some of the prisoners
were still alive
As a result
another portion of Cyklon B
was poured in
On the 5th of September
I was ordered to report to Barrack 11
together with 20 prisoners
from the penal company
We were told
that we were being sent
on a special work assignment
and that the penalty
for revealing what we saw there
was death
We were also promised extra rations
when the work was done
We were issued gas masks
and had to get
the corpses out of the cells
When we opened the doors
the tight pack of people
fell out against us
Even dead they were still standing
Their faces were blue
Many of them had bunches of hair
in their hands
It took us the whole day
to pry them apart
and stack them in the courtyard
That evening the commanding officer
and his staff
came
I heard the commanding officer say
Now I'm relieved
Now that we have this gas
we'll be spared all those bloodbaths

The victims too
will be spared
until the very last moment

THE SONG OF CYKLON B

(I)

3RD WITNESS:
  In the summer and fall of 1941
  I worked in the camp's laundry room
  That's where dirty laundry was taken
  to be fumigated with the gas Cyklon B
  Our superior was
  the fumigator Breitwieser
JUDGE:
  Does the witness
  see this person
  in this room
3RD WITNESS:
  That is Breitwieser

ACCUSED #17 *nods to the* WITNESS *agreeably*

3RD WITNESS:
  On September 3rd
  I saw Breitwieser
  accompanied by Stark
  and some other officers
  from the Political Division
  walking to Barrack 11
  with gas masks and cans
  Then the curfew sounded
  The next morning
  Breitwieser was in a bad mood
  because something had gone wrong
  The place hadn't been sealed off properly
  and the gassing
  had to be repeated
  Two days later
  trucks loaded with corpses
  drove off from the courtyard
JUDGE:
  What time was it when you saw Breit-
      wieser
  on his way to Barrack 11
  on September 3rd

3RD WITNESS:
  About 9 o'clock at night
ACCUSED #17:
  That's impossible
  In the first place
  I was never in the camp at night
  Secondly nobody
  could possibly have recognized me
  at that time of the year
  since a heavy fog
  always came up from the river around then
JUDGE:
  Did you know
  that prisoners were to be gassed
  in Barrack 11 that night
ACCUSED #17:
  Yes
  that had gotten around
JUDGE:
  You did not see
  prisoners being driven into the Barrack
ACCUSED #17:
  Mr President
  our workday was over at 6 PM
  I was never in the camp after 6
JUDGE:
  You never had to issue clothing
  after 6 o'clock
  even if new transports had arrived
ACCUSED #17:
  When prisoners arrived after 6
  special-duty prisoners picked up the key
  to the changing room
  and issued the clothes
JUDGE:
  What were your duties
  as fumigator
ACCUSED #17:
  If I may say so
  I had to give instructions
JUDGE:
  Had you been trained
  for this job
ACCUSED #17:
  In the summer of 1941
  with 10 or 15 others
  I was detailed to the fumigation squad
  Some men from the Degesch Company
  delivered the gas

They also gave us our instructions
They taught us how to use the gas
and how to use the masks
that were equipped
with special headgear

JUDGE:

How was the gas packed

ACCUSED #17:

It came in cans
a pound each
They looked like coffee cans
At first they had gray cardboard tops
The cardboard was usually slightly moist
Later on they had metal lids

JUDGE:

What did the contents look like

ACCUSED #17:

It was a grainy crumbly substance
It's hard to describe
It looked something like starch
bluish white

JUDGE:

Do you know what this substance
was made of

ACCUSED #17:

Hydrocyanic acid
in its chemically bonded form
As soon as the crystals
were exposed to the air
cyanide gas was produced

JUDGE:

What did your work with the gas involve

ACCUSED #17:

Prisoners had to hang up their clothes
in the changing room
Then I and an assistant threw in the gas
After 24 hours the clothes
were taken out
and new ones brought in
and so on
We also had to fumigate living quarters
After the windows had been sealed
the cans were pried open
and a rubber cover quickly slipped on
Otherwise the gas began to escape
and we still had several more cans
that had to be opened
When everything was ready
the stuff was scattered

JUDGE:

Was any warning agent
mixed in with the gas

ACCUSED #17:

No
Cyklon B worked very rapidly
I remember
once Corporal Theurer
went in a house
that had been fumigated
During the night
the ground floor had been aired
and the next morning Theurer
went upstairs to the second floor
to open the windows
He must have breathed in some fumes
because he fell over immediately
rolled down the stairs unconscious
and right on out
to where he got some fresh air
If he had fallen any other way
he never would have gotten out of there

PROSECUTING ATTORNEY:

With your professional experience
were you not called in as an adviser
when Cyklon B began to be used
on prisoners

ACCUSED #17:

I speak nothing but the truth
as a matter of principle
I could not stand the gas
It gave me indigestion
I applied for transfer

PROSECUTING ATTORNEY:

Were you transferred

ACCUSED #17:

Not right away

PROSECUTING ATTORNEY:

When were you transferred

ACCUSED #17:

I don't remember that anymore

PROSECUTING ATTORNEY:

You were transferred in April 1944
Before then you were promoted twice
Your first promotion
was to private first class
then to corporal

COUNSEL FOR THE DEFENSE:

We object

to the prosecution's insinuations
The fact that members of the camp staff
were promoted
must be judged only within the context
of their military duty
In no way does it prove complicity

THE ACCUSED *show their agreement*

(II)

JUDGE:
  Where was the gas stored
6TH WITNESS:
  It was stored in crates
  in the dispensary basement
JUDGE:
  Accused Capesius
  as head of the dispensary
  were you aware that Cyklon B
  was stored there
ACCUSED #3:
  I believe
  the witness is the victim
  of some confusion here
  In regard to those crates in the base-
    ment
  they contained Ovaltine
  They were a shipment from the Swiss
  Red Cross
6TH WITNESS:
  I saw the cases of Ovaltine
  and I saw the crates of Cyklon
  and I also saw the suitcases
  where the accused Capesius
  kept jewelry and gold fillings
ACCUSED #3:
  This is a complete fabrication
6TH WITNESS:
  Where did the money come from
  which made it possible
  for the accused Capesius
  to open his own pharmacy
  and a beauty parlor
  immediately after the war
  Be beautiful
  with beauty treatments by Capesius
  That was his firm's advertisement

ACCUSED #3:
  I obtained this money by taking out a loan
6TH WITNESS:
  And where do the 12,500 dollars come from
  that were offered to me
  and other witnesses
  if we would testify here
  that Capesius
  was only in charge of the dispensary
  and was not in charge of
  the phenol and Cyklon B
ACCUSED #3:
  I don't know anything about that
PROSECUTING ATTORNEY:
  Who made this attempt to bribe you
6TH WITNESS:
  It came from an anonymous source
PROSECUTING ATTORNEY:
  Do you know
  whether any of the legal-aid societies
  of the camp guards
  were behind the bribe
6TH WITNESS:
  I don't know
  However I would like to call
  to the attention of the court
  this letter
  which was sent to me
  The heading of the letter reads
  Working Committee for Justice and Freedom
  The letter itself
  You will soon disappear
  You will die an agonizing death
  Our people are keeping you
  under constant observation
  You can choose now
  Life or death
JUDGE:
  The court will take this matter
  under investigation
COUNSEL FOR THE DEFENSE:
  Can the witness
  tell us what was printed on the crates
6TH WITNESS:
  Caution
  Poison gas
  There was also a warning label
  with a skull and crossbones

COUNSEL FOR THE DEFENSE:
Did you see what was in the crates
6TH WITNESS:
I saw opened crates
with the cans inside
COUNSEL FOR THE DEFENSE:
What was on the labels
6TH WITNESS:
Poison gas
Cyklon
COUNSEL FOR THE DEFENSE:
Was there anything else on the labels
6TH WITNESS:
Caution
Contains no warning agent
To be opened only by experienced personnel
JUDGE:
Did the witness
see these cans actually
being taken to the gas chambers
6TH WITNESS:
We had to load the crates
into the ambulance
that came around to pick it up
JUDGE:
Who rode in that ambulance
6TH WITNESS:
I saw Dr Frank and Dr Schatz
as well as Dr Capesius
They had their gas masks with them
Dr Schatz was wearing his steel helmet
I remember that
because somebody in the car
laughed and said
You look like a little toadstool
COUNSEL FOR THE DEFENSE:
We would like to remind the court
that at certain times during the war
the wearing of gas masks was mandatory
Neither the coming or going of our clients
with gas masks
proves anything about where they had gone
JUDGE:
Did the witness
see delivery receipts
for gas shipments
6TH WITNESS:
When these shipments arrived

I was often assigned
to take the accompanying bills
to the administration
The shipments grew increasingly large
and finally had to be stored
outside the camp in the old theater
The sender was
The Blight Prevention Company
JUDGE:
How were these shipments
forwarded to the camp
6TH WITNESS:
Some were trucked in
directly from the factory
Others came in by rail
on army bills of lading
JUDGE:
Do you recall the amounts declared
6TH WITNESS:
14 to 20 crates
came in at a time
JUDGE:
According to your calculations
how often did these shipments arrive
6TH WITNESS:
At least once a week
In 1944
several times a week
Then trucks from the motor pool
were called in to help out
JUDGE:
How many cans
were in a crate
6TH WITNESS:
Each crate held 30 one-pound cans
JUDGE:
Was the price marked
6TH WITNESS:
The price was 50 cents a pound
JUDGE:
How many pounds
were required for a single gassing
6TH WITNESS:
For 2000 people in one chamber
about 16 pounds
JUDGE:
At 50 cents per pound
8 dollars

(III)

JUDGE:
Accused Mulka
as camp adjutant
you were in charge of the motor pool
Did you write up
the transportation orders

ACCUSED #1:
I wrote no such orders
I had nothing to do with that

JUDGE:
Did you know the meaning of the phrase
Requisitions for Material for Relocation

ACCUSED #1:
No

JUDGE:
Accused Mulka
the court has in its possession orders
for the transportation of Material for
    Relocation
These documents bear your signature

ACCUSED #1:
It is possible
that I may have had to sign
some such order occasionally

JUDGE:
You never found out
that Material for Relocation
was in fact the gas Cyklon B

ACCUSED #1:
As I already said
I wasn't aware of that

JUDGE:
Who issued requisitions for this material

ACCUSED #1:
They came over the teletype
and were then passed on
to the commanding officer
or a protective-custody camp leader
They were sent on from there
to the head of the motor pool

JUDGE:
Weren't you in charge there

ACCUSED #1:
Only in disciplinary matters

JUDGE:
But weren't you concerned
to know

to what use trucks from your motor pool
were being put

ACCUSED #1:
I knew of course
that they were required
for the transport of material

JUDGE:
Were prisoners also
transported in these trucks

ACCUSED #1:
I don't know anything about that
In my time
prisoners walked

JUDGE:
Accused Mulka
the court has in its possession a doc-
    ument
which deals with
the urgently required completion
of the new crematoriums
It also refers to the fact that
the prisoners used for this project
were required to work on Sundays as
    well
The document bears your signature

ACCUSED #1:
Yes
well
I must have dictated it then

JUDGE:
Do you still maintain
you knew nothing
about the mass killings

ACCUSED #1:
All my previous statements
conform to the truth

JUDGE:
The court has summoned as witness
the former chief mechanic
of the motor-pool repair shop
Will the witness tell us
how many trucks there were
in the motor pool

1ST WITNESS:
For heavy duty
there were ten 2½-ton trucks

JUDGE:
From whom did you receive
your transportation orders

1ST WITNESS:
  From the head of the motor pool
JUDGE:
  Who signed the orders
1ST WITNESS:
  I don't know
JUDGE:
  What were the trucks used for
1ST WITNESS:
  For picking up freight
  and transporting prisoners
JUDGE:
  Where were the prisoners taken
1ST WITNESS:
  I can't say for sure
JUDGE:
  Did you take part
  in any of these transports
1ST WITNESS:
  I had to go along once
  as a replacement
JUDGE:
  Where did you go
1ST WITNESS:
  Into the camp
  where they picked them out
  and so on
JUDGE:
  Where did you take them
1ST WITNESS:
  To the far end of the camp
  There were woods over there
  a birch wood
  That's where the people were unloaded
JUDGE:
  Where did they go
1ST WITNESS:
  Into a house
  I didn't see anything else after that
JUDGE:
  What happened to the people
1ST WITNESS:
  I don't know
  I wasn't in there
JUDGE:
  Didn't you find out
  what happened to them
1ST WITNESS:
  Well

yes
They were burned up
right then and there

THE SONG OF THE FIRE OVENS

(I)

JUDGE:
  The witness
  drove one of the ambulances
  that carried
  Cyklon B in its solid state
  to the gas chambers
2ND WITNESS:
  I was originally assigned to the camp
  as a tractor driver
  Later on I had to drive an ambulance
      too
JUDGE:
  Where did you have to drive
2ND WITNESS:
  I had to pick up
  the medical orderlies and the doctors
JUDGE:
  Who were the doctors
2ND WITNESS:
  I can't remember
JUDGE:
  Where did you have to take them
2ND WITNESS:
  From the old camp
  to the arrival platform in the new camp
JUDGE:
  When
2ND WITNESS:
  When transports arrived
JUDGE:
  How were transport arrivals announced
2ND WITNESS:
  By a siren
JUDGE:
  Where did you drive to
  from the arrival platform
2ND WITNESS:
  To the crematoriums

JUDGE:
Did the doctors go with you
2ND WITNESS:
Yes
JUDGE:
What did they do there
2ND WITNESS:
The doctors stayed in the ambulance
or stood around outside
The medical orderlies had to
take care of everything
JUDGE:
What did they have to take care of
2ND WITNESS:
The gassings
JUDGE:
When you got there
were the people already
in the gas chambers
2ND WITNESS:
They were still getting undressed
JUDGE:
Was there ever any trouble
2ND WITNESS:
The times I was there
things always went smoothly
JUDGE:
What could you see
of the gassing procedure
2ND WITNESS:
When the prisoners had been taken
into the chambers
the orderlies went up to the vents
put on their gas masks
and emptied their cans
JUDGE:
Where were these vents
2ND WITNESS:
There was an embankment that went up
and over the underground room
It had four compartments
JUDGE:
How many cans were emptied
2ND WITNESS:
Three or four
in each hole
JUDGE:
How long did this take

2ND WITNESS:
About a minute
JUDGE:
Didn't the people scream
2ND WITNESS:
When one of them realized
what was going on
yes
you could hear a scream
PROSECUTING ATTORNEY:
How far from the gas chamber
was your ambulance parked
2ND WITNESS:
It was on the road
about 20 yards off
PROSECUTING ATTORNEY:
And from there you could hear
what was happening down in the chambers
2ND WITNESS:
Sometimes I got out
to wait around outside
PROSECUTING ATTORNEY:
What did you do there
2ND WITNESS:
Nothing
I smoked a cigarette
PROSECUTING ATTORNEY:
Did you ever get near the vents
above the gas chamber
2ND WITNESS:
Sometimes I walked up and down a bit
to stretch my legs
PROSECUTING ATTORNEY:
What did you hear
2ND WITNESS:
When they took the lids off the vents
I heard a humming from down there
as if a lot of people were underground
PROSECUTING ATTORNEY:
And what did you do then
2ND WITNESS:
The vents were shut again
and I had to drive back
JUDGE:
You were prisoner doctor
in the Special Commando
assigned to duty at the crematoriums
How many prisoners

were in that Commando

7TH WITNESS:

A total of 860 men
Each Special Commando was destroyed
after a few months
and replaced by a new crew

JUDGE:

Under whom did you serve

7TH WITNESS:

Dr Mengele

JUDGE:

How did the delivery of prisoners
to the gas chambers proceed

7TH WITNESS:

A whistle from the locomotive
on its way from the platform to the gate
was the signal
that a new shipment had arrived
That meant
that inside an hour
the ovens had to be fully operational
The electric motors were switched on
These started up the fans
that brought the fire in the ovens
up to the required temperature

JUDGE:

Could you see
the groups coming off the arrival platform

7TH WITNESS:

From the window in my workroom
I could see the upper half of the platform
and the road to the crematorium
The people arrived five abreast
The sick came behind in the trucks
The crematorium area
was closed off by an iron fence
There were warnings posted at the gate
The accompanying guards had to stop
    there
and the Special Commando took over
Only doctors staff orderlies
and members of the Political Division
were allowed in

JUDGE:

Which of the accused
did you see there

7TH WITNESS:

I saw Stark there and Hofmann

also Kaduk and Baretzki

COUNSEL FOR THE DEFENSE:

We call attention to the fact
that our clients
deny having participated in these events

JUDGE:

Will the witness continue his account

7TH WITNESS:

The people
went through the gate slowly and wearily
Children hung on to their mother's skirts
Old men carried babies
or pushed baby carriages
The path was covered with black cinders
and on the grass on each side of the path
there were pipes with water faucets
The people crowded around them
and the Commando let them drink
but hurried them on
There was still about 60 yards to go
before they got to the stairs
that led down to the anteroom

JUDGE:

Was there an unobstructed view
of the crematorium

7TH WITNESS:

It was surrounded by bushes and trees
and was set back about 100 yards away
from the fence surrounding the area
Beyond that fence was the outer fence
with observation towers
Back of them were open fields

JUDGE:

What could be seen
of the crematorium installations

7TH WITNESS:

Only the incineration building
with its large square chimney
Underground it was connected
by a corridor
that led to the gas chambers
and branched off
to the anteroom

JUDGE:

How large was the anteroom

7TH WITNESS:

About 50 yards long
Some 12 to 15 steps led down to it

The room was over six feet high
In the middle
there was a row of supporting columns

JUDGE:
How many people were taken down at a
   time

7TH WITNESS:
From one to two thousand people

JUDGE:
Did they know
what lay before them

7TH WITNESS:
At the head of the narrow staircase
there were signs
that said in various languages
BATH AND DISINFECTION ROOM
That sounded reassuring
and calmed a lot of people
who were still mistrustful
I often saw people
go down there quite happily
and mothers joked with their children

JUDGE:
Was there never any outbreak of panic
with so many people
in such a small place

7TH WITNESS:
Everything always went quickly
and smoothly
The command to undress was given
and while the people were still
looking around bewildered
the Special Commando began to
help them off
with their clothes
There were benches along the walls
with numbered pegs over them
It was repeatedly announced
that clothes and shoes
must be hung on the peg
and that its number
must not be forgotten
to avoid unnecessary confusion
upon return from the bath
In the glaring light of that room
the people took off their clothes
Men and women
old and young
Children

JUDGE:
Did this great number of people
never once
attack their guards

7TH WITNESS:
Only once did I hear
somebody shout
They're going to kill us
But somebody answered
That's impossible
That can't happen
Keep calm
And when children started crying
their parents comforted them
and joked and played with them
as they carried them
in the next room

JUDGE:
Where was the entrance to that room

7TH WITNESS:
At the end of the anteroom
It was a solid oak door
with a peep hole
and a hand-wheel
that screwed the door shut

JUDGE:
How long did the undressing take

7TH WITNESS:
About 10 minutes
Then they were all shoved
into the next room

JUDGE:
Was force ever used

7TH WITNESS:
The men in the Special Commando
   houted
Move step it up
the water's getting cold
Naturally there were also
threats and beatings
or one of the guards
would fire a shot

JUDGE:
Was this other room
equipped with showers
or disguised in any way

7TH WITNESS:
No
There was nothing

JUDGE:
  How big was this room
7TH WITNESS:
  Smaller than the anteroom
  About 30 yards long
JUDGE:
  Certainly with 1000 or more people crowded
  into such a small space
  there must have been some disturbance
7TH WITNESS:
  It was too late then
  The last ones were pushed in
  and the door screwed shut
JUDGE:
  Can the witness
  offer any explanation
  why the people permitted
  all this to happen to them
  Faced with that room
  they must have known
  they were facing death
7TH WITNESS:
  No one had ever come out
  to tell about it
JUDGE:
  Once they were in
  what did they see
7TH WITNESS:
  There were concrete walls
  and some valves on the walls
  In the middle of the room were the pillars
  and on each side two posts
  made out of perforated sheet iron
  There were drains in the floor
  This room too was brightly lit
JUDGE:
  What could be heard
  from the people in there
7TH WITNESS:
  They began to scream
  and they pounded on the door
  but you couldn't hear much
  because of the strong roar
  that came from the cremation room
JUDGE:
  What could be seen
  through the window in the door
7TH WITNESS:
  The people crowded the door

and climbed up the pillars
They began to suffocate
when the gas was thrown in

(II)

7TH WITNESS:
  The gas was poured
  into the sheet-iron posts from up above
  There was a spiral channel
  inside the post
  which spread the substance
  In the moist hot air
  it rapidly turned to gas
  and poured out through the holes
JUDGE:
  How long did it take the gas
  to kill
7TH WITNESS:
  That depended on the amount used
  For reasons of economy usually
  a less than adequate amount was poured
    in
  so that the killing
  could take as long as five minutes
JUDGE:
  What was the immediate effect of the gas
7TH WITNESS:
  It induced dizziness and severe nausea
  and made breathing extremely difficult
JUDGE:
  How long was the room kept under gas
7TH WITNESS:
  20 minutes
  Then the ventilation system was turned on
  and the gas pumped out
  30 minutes later the doors were opened
  But there was still gas
  caught in small pockets
  among the dead
  which caused a dry hacking cough
  For this reason
  the men in the Clearance Detail
  had to wear gas masks
JUDGE:
  Did you
  see this room after the door
  had been opened

7TH WITNESS:
  Yes
  The corpses lay piled on top of each other
  near the door and around the columns
  Babies children and the sick at the bottom
  Women above them
  And at the very top the strongest men
  The reason for this
  was that the people trampled
  and climbed on each other
  because the gas initially spread
  most thickly at floor level
  The people clawing each other
  were stuck together
  Their skin was torn
  Many were bleeding from nose and mouth
  The faces were swollen
  and spotted
  The heaps of people were befouled
  with vomit
  excrement urine and menstrual blood
  The Clearance Detail came in with hoses
  and washed the corpses down
  Then they were pulled
  into the freight elevators
  and taken up to the ovens
JUDGE:
  How large were these elevators
7TH WITNESS:
  There were two of them
  each with a capacity of 25 dead
  When one load was in
  a bell was rung
  to signal the Lugging Detail
  that was standing by with carts
  on the floor above
  They had thongs
  that they slipped over the wrists of the dead
  The corpses where then lugged in the carts
  to the ovens on a special track
  Blood was washed away
  by a steady stream of water
  Before cremation
  men of the Special Commando
  conducted a final search
  Every ornament still
  to be found on the bodies
  was removed
  bracelets

  neck chains
  rings
  earrings
  Then the hair was cut off
  and immediately bundled
  and packed
  Finally
  the teeth extractors set to work
  They were a crew picked
  from first-class specialists
  at Dr Mengele's express command
  Still when they started in
  with their crowbars and tongs
  they tore out not only gold teeth
  and bridges
  but whole chunks of jaw
  These pieces of bone and attached flesh
  were thrown into an acid vat
  to be eaten away
  A hundred men worked continually
  in two shifts
  at the ovens
JUDGE:
  How many ovens were there
  in the crematorium
7TH WITNESS:
  There were five ovens each
  in the big crematoriums II and III
  Each oven had three incinerating cham-
      bers
  Beside these two crematoriums
  at the end of the Arrival Platform
  there were crematoriums IV and V
  each with two four-chambered ovens
  These two were set off about
  800 yards back of the birch grove
  When the operation was going full blast
  46 incinerating chambers
  were fired up
JUDGE:
  How many bodies
  could be put into one chamber
7TH WITNESS:
  From three to five bodies
  could be put in one chamber
  However it was rare
  that all ovens operated at one time
  since they were often damaged
  by overheating

JUDGE:
How long did cremation take
in an oven chamber
7TH WITNESS:
Approximately an hour
Then it could take a new load
In crematoriums II and III
more than 3000 people were cremated
in less than 24 hours
If the ovens were overcrowded
corpses were also burned in a ditch
that had been dug outside the building
These ditches were
about 100 feet long
and 20 feet deep
At each end there were drainage trenches
for the fat
The fat was ladled up in cans
and poured over the corpses
to make them burn faster
In the summer of 1944
when the cremations reached their peak
up to 20,000 people
were destroyed
daily
Their ashes were trucked off
to a river a mile and a half away
and dumped into the water
JUDGE:
What was done with the valuables
and gold fillings
1ST WITNESS:
When the clothes were collected
money and ornaments found among them
were dropped into a slot in the top
of a locked crate
Guards filled their own pockets first
Clothes and shoes
that the prisoners themselves
had carefully bundled together
were sent home
for the benefit of people
bombed out of their houses
Gold fillings were melted down
I was called in as examining magistrate
because packages sent from the camp
containing gold by the pound
had been confiscated
In the course of my investigation

I ascertained that this was dental gold
Calculating from the weight
of a single filling
I came to the conclusion
that thousands of people were required
to supply even one such nugget
JUDGE:
Do you mean
that even in those times
a magistrate was called in from outside
to conduct an investigation in the camp
1ST WITNESS:
Somewhere some idea of justice
still survived
The commanding officer
wanted to combat corruption in the camp
At the time of my visit there
he complained
that the men under his command
frequently failed to rise to the demands
made on them by their hard work
Then he took me to a crematorium installation
where he explained
everything to me in great detail
Inside in the cremation rooms everything
was polished to a shine
There was nothing to indicate
that people were cremated there
There wasn't even a speck of their dust
on the oven panels
The guards in their room sat
on a bench half drunk
and in the service room
women prisoners
especially picked for their beauty
were baking potato dumplings
which they served the men
When I made a search of their lockers
they proved
to contain a fortune
As judge I instituted proceedings
for theft
and some of them were arrested
and sentenced
JUDGE:
How were these proceedings carried out
1ST WITNESS:
It was a mock trial
You could go up only so high

and it was impossible
to institute proceedings
for multiple murder
JUDGE:
As examining magistrate
you saw no means
of making your findings public
1ST WITNESS:
Before what court
could I have brought an action
for the killings of masses of people
and the seizure of their goods and property
by the highest administrative offices
I could not institute proceedings
against the government itself
JUDGE:
Was there no other way
of acting on this matter
1ST WITNESS:
I knew
no one would have believed
what I had to say
I would have been executed
or at the very least
locked up in an asylum
I considered fleeing the country
but I doubted whether
even abroad
anyone would believe me
and I asked myself what would happen
if I were believed
and I were called upon to testify
against my own people
and I could only conclude
that this my people would be destroyed
for its deeds
So I stayed

(III)

JUDGE:
There has been testimony of an uprising
carried out by the Special Commando
When did this uprising occur
7TH WITNESS:
On October 6, 1944
The Commando was to be liquidated
by the guards that day

JUDGE:
Did the Commando know this beforehand
7TH WITNESS:
They all knew
they were going to be killed
Weeks before
they had obtained cans of explosives
from prisoners who worked
in the armaments factory
The plan was
to first take care of the guards
then blow up the crematoriums
and escape
But the crematorium
where the explosives were stored
blew up earlier than planned
and many of the men
went up with it
There was a battle
but they were all overpowered
Hundreds of prisoners lay
face down on the ground
behind the birch grove
The men from the Political Division
shot them in the back of the head
JUDGE:
Which of the accused were present
7TH WITNESS:
Boger was in charge
JUDGE:
Was this crematorium
destroyed by the explosion
7TH WITNESS:
The explosion from four barrels of dynamite
blew up one entire building
JUDGE:
What happened to the other crematoriums
7TH WITNESS:
They were blown up
by staff personnel shortly after
The front was getting close
PROSECUTING ATTORNEY:
Does the witness
find it credible
that the adjutant
of the camp's command officer
was not informed
about what went on in the crematoriums

7TH WITNESS:
No
It was impossible
Each one of the 6000 camp staff personnel
knew what was taking place
and each at his post did
what was required
for the functioning of the whole
Furthermore every locomotive engineer
every switchman
every railroad employee
who had anything to do
with the transportation of the people
knew what went on in the camp
Every telegraph clerk and typist
who passed on the Deportation Orders
knew
Every single one
of the hundreds and
thousands of office workers
connected with the widespread operation
knew
what it was all about
COUNSEL FOR THE DEFENSE:
We object to these statements
which are dictated by sheer hate
Hate must never
form the basis
for a judgment
of the particulars under consideration
    here
7TH WITNESS:
I do not speak from hate
I have no desire for revenge
I am not concerned here
with the individual accused
but only wish to bring to mind
that what they did
could not have been carried out
without the support
of millions of others
COUNSEL FOR THE DEFENSE:
This proceeding is strictly confined
to what can be substantiated by proof
against our clients
General charges
are irrelevant
Especially charges
directed against an entire nation

which at that time was engaged
in a great and sacrificial war
7TH WITNESS:
I only
want to point out if I may
how many spectators lined the way
when we were driven from our homes
and loaded into freight cars
The accused in these proceedings
were only the last
in a long line
PROSECUTING ATTORNEY:
Can the witness
tell us how many people
in his estimation
were killed
in total
in the camp
7TH WITNESS:
Of the 9 million 600 thousand persecuted
who lived in the regions
ruled by their persecutors
6 million have disappeared
and it can be taken for granted
that most of them
were deliberately destroyed
Those who were not shot
beaten to death
tortured to death
or gassed
died of hunger disease and misery
or of being worked to death
Yet to arrive at the sum total
of the defenseless sacrificed
in this war of extermination
we must add to the 6 million
killed for racial reasons
3 million Russian prisoners of war
shot or starved to death
as well as the 10 million civilians
of the occupied countries
who perished
COUNSEL FOR THE DEFENSE:
Even though we all feel
most deeply for the victims
still it is our duty here
to counter and oppose
all exaggerations
and vilification

originating from certain parties
In relation to this camp
not even the sum of 2 million dead
can be conclusively established
Only the death of several hundred thousand
can be proven
The majority of the groups named
ended up in the East
and those seized
and liquidated
as armed units
cannot be counted among the murdered
nor can those who deserted
to enemy armies and fell in battle
During the course of these proceedings
it has become all too clear
which political point of view
has determined
the accusations of the witnesses
accusations which the witnesses certainly
had sufficient time
to work out among themselves

THE ACCUSED *laugh nodding in agreement*

PROSECUTING ATTORNEY:
    This is a willful and conscious expression
    of contempt
    for those who died in the camp
    and for those survivors
    who have appeared here
    to testify as witnesses
    The behavior of the counsel for the de-
        fense
    clearly demonstrates the persistence
    of that same outlook
    of which the accused present were guilty
COUNSEL FOR THE DEFENSE:
    Who is the this assistant prosecutor
    with his unsuitable clothes
    It is I believe a Middle European custom
    to appear in court with a closed robe
JUDGE:
    The court calls for order
    Accused Mulka
    will you now tell us
    what you knew
    about the Extermination Program
    and what orders you issued
    in this connection

ACCUSED #1:
    I issued no orders connected with that
JUDGE:
    You knew nothing
    about the Extermination Program
ACCUSED #1:
    Only toward the end of my time in the service
    I can say now
    that I was filled with revulsion
JUDGE:
    If this was the case
    Why did you not refuse
    to participate
ACCUSED #1:
    I was an officer
    and knew the military penal code
PROSECUTING ATTORNEY:
    You were not an officer
ACCUSED #1:
    I certainly was
PROSECUTING ATTORNEY:
    You were not an officer
    You belonged to a uniformed
    Murder Commando
ACCUSED #1:
    You are attacking my honor
PROSECUTING ATTORNEY:
    Accused Mulka
    we are dealing with murder
ACCUSED #1:
    We are convinced
    that our orders
    were all part of achieving some secret
    military objective
    Mr President I almost broke down
    The whole business made me so sick I
    had to be hospitalized
    But I want to make it clear
    that I only looked on from the outside
    and that I
    kept my own hands out of it
    Your Honor I was against
    the whole thing
    I myself was
    persecuted by the system
JUDGE:
    What happened to you
ACCUSED #1:
    I was arrested

because I had expressed
defeatist opinions
I was in prison for three months
After my release
I was caught in an enemy attack
As an old soldier
I was able to save many lives
by helping with the evacuations
My own son was killed
Mr President at this trial
the millions who also lost their lives
for their own country
should not be forgotten
and what happened after the war
shouldn't be forgotten either
and all the things
that are still being done against us
All of us
I want to make that very clear
did nothing but our duty
even when that duty was hard
and even when it grieved us to do it
Today
when our nation has worked its way up
after a devastating war
to a leading position in the world
we ought to concern ourselves
with other things
than blame and reproaches
that should be thought of
as long since atoned for

Loud approbation from THE ACCUSED

END

"Fourteen Propositions for a Documentary Theater"*

(I)

The documentary theater is a theater of factual reports. Minutes of proceedings, files, letters,

------

*Reprinted from *World Theatre* 17 (1968), 375–89.

statistical tables, stock-exchange communiqués, presentations of balance sheets of banks and industrial undertakings, official commentaries, speeches, interviews, statements by well-known personalities, press-, radio-, photo- or film-reportings of events and all the other media bearing witness to the present form the bases of the production. The documentary theater shuns all invention. It makes use of authentic documentary material which it diffuses from the stage, without altering the contents, but in structuring the form. In opposition to the incoherent mass of information which constantly assails us from every side, it presents a selection which converges towards a precise and generally social or political theme. This choice as well as the criterion which determines the editing of these cuttings from reality guarantee the quality of this dramaturgy of the document.

(II)

The documentary theater is an element of public life, as conveyed to us by the media of mass communication. Criticism at different levels enables us to clarify its objective.

a) Criticism of camouflage: Is the information handed out by press, radio and television slanted so as to serve the interests of those in power? What is hidden from us? What purpose do such exclusions serve? Which are the circles that benefit from this camouflage, from this alteration, from this idealization of certain specific social phenomena?

b) Criticism of the falsification of reality: Why is a historical personage, a period or an entire epoch plunged into oblivion? Who reinforce their own positions by eliminating certain historic facts? Who profit by the intentional alteration of certain striking and memorable phenomena? Which classes of society are bent on dissimulating events of the past? What form do the falsifications in question assume? How are they received?

c) Criticism of lying: What are the effects of a historical lie? How does a contemporary situation based on lies show up as such? What are the difficulties one can expect to encounter when questing for truth? What powerful organizations and what authorities will do their utmost to prevent one of becoming aware of the truth?

(III)

Although the means of communication between men have attained a high degree of development and keep us informed of contemporary events throughout the world, the really important happenings which determine the aspect of both our present and our future are hidden from us together with their origins and their interconnections. The documents in the possession of the responsible parties might elucidate activities of which we only perceive the effects, but the said documents remain inaccessible to us. Should it wish to deal, say, with the assassination of Lumumba, of President Kennedy, of Che Guevara, with the massacres in Indonesia, with secret conventions during the Geneva negotiations on Indochina, with the recent war in the Middle East or with the American government's preparations for the Vietnam war, the documentary theater would find itself up against the artificial obscurity used by those in power as a means of dissimulating their manipulations.

(IV)

The documentary theater is opposed to those circles whose policy consists in blinding the observer and making the object of his studies nebulous; it protests against this tendency of the media of mass communication to maintain the population in a desert of besottedness and cretinism; on the final count, it finds itself in the same position as any citizen who endeavors to pursue his own inquiries, i.e., bound hand and foot and obliged, as a last resort, to make use of the sole means still at its disposal: the public protestation. In the same way as the spontaneous open-air gathering with placards, streamers and slogans shouted in unison, the documentary theater constitutes a reaction against the present state of affairs, of which it demands the clarification.

(V)

Manifesting on the public highway, distributing pamphlets, taking part in protest marches, participating in mass movements: These are concrete actions of immediate efficacy. Their improvised nature gives them a powerfully dramatic character, their developments are unforeseeable, at any moment they can degenerate into ranged battles with the police, and thus bring out the violent contradiction that prevails in social conditions. The documentary theater, which offers concentrated examples of this latently explosive matter, seeks, in its forms of expression, to preserve the factual picture; but when the document is structured in order to turn it into a set performance involving a specific moment in time, a limited area and both performers and spectators, the documentary theater has to use other methods than those suited to direct political intervention. The stage of the documentary theater does not represent reality at a given moment, but the image of a fragment of reality wrested from the continuous flux of life.

(VI)

As long as it refuses to assume the form of a demonstration on the public highway, the documentary theater cannot vie with the reality of an authentic political manifestation. It never succeeds in equaling the dynamism born of the vociferous proclamation of opinions made from the rostra of public life. From the playhouse, it cannot provoke the Government and the Civil Service as is so successfully done on the occasion of manifestations directed against administrative, economic, or military centers. Even if it seeks to free itself of the elements that make it an artistic medium, even when it abandons the aesthetic categories, even if it wishes to be something unfinished, even when it tends to adopt a position and pursue militant action, even when it gives the appearance of spontaneous generation, of proceeding without premeditation, the documentary theater is, in the last resort, an artistic production, which it must remain if it wishes to justify its existence.

(VII)

Indeed, a documentary theater intent on being primarily a political platform, and which gives up being an artistic achievement, calls its own validity into question. In such a case, practical political action in the outside world would be more effective. It is only when it has succeeded, by means of its activity in the fields of analysis, control and criticism, in transforming real-life material and in endowing it with the functions of an artistic medium, that it acquires full validity in the critical debate pursued with reality. On such a stage, the dramatic work can become the instrument of the formation of political thought. It is necessary, however, to indicate the specific forms of expression of the documentary theater, which differ from the traditional artistic concepts.

(VIII)

The power of the documentary theater lies in its ability to build, from fragments of reality, a utilizable example, a "model schema," of contemporary events. It is not placed at the center of these events; on the contrary, it adopts the attitude of an observer and analyzes them with critical aloofness. The techniques of cutting and editing enable it to bring out the clear and eloquent details of the chaotic material provided by outside reality. By confronting the contradictory points, it draws attention to a latent conflict, and thanks to the elements it has assembled, it is then in a position to propose a solution, to launch an appeal, or to pose a fundamental question. The documentary theater concerns itself in an attentive, conscious, and deliberate manner with what, by the improvisation, in the politically slanted "happening," merely leads to a diffuse tension, to an emotive participation, and to the illusion of an engagement in contemporary issues.

(IX)

The documentary theater submits facts to an appraisal. It presents the differentiated manner in which events and declarations are judged. It shows the motivations that account for these differences. One side benefits by an event that is prejudicial to the other. The parties face each other. Stress is laid on the relationship of dependency which unites them. The corruption and blackmail which serve to maintain this dependency become the object of the description. The debit and credit accounts occupy neighboring columns. Those who pocket the profits defend themselves. They claim to be the upholders of order. They explain how they administer their fortunes. Over against them, those who sustain the losses. In their ranks, the traitors who are bent on elbowing their own way up. The others who strive not to lose more than they have already done. The constant clash of inequalities. Glances at these inequalities which the concrete transcription renders unbearable. Injustices so evident that they call for immediate intervention. Situations so fraudulent that only violence can transform them. Contrary opinions regarding the same object. One presents conjointly statements and real situations. Promises and solemn undertaking are followed by contradictory acts. One examines the consequences of actions initiated by the secret planification centers. Whose position is consolidated by them and whom do they hit? One notes the silences and the subterfuges of those implicated. One exposes indices. One draws conclusions from a manifest example. One presents authentic personages as the incarnation of specific social interests. One does not depict individual conflicts but modes of behavior linked to their socioeconomic motivations. The documentary theater, rejecting all outward and quickly outdated scintillation, dwells on the "exemplary" fact: It therefore makes use not of dramatic characters or of evocations of atmosphere, but of groups, of magnetic fields, of tendencies.

(X)

The documentary theater takes sides. The only possible epilogue of many of its themes is a condemnation. For a theater of this type, objectivity—from a certain angle—seems a concept of which those in power make use in order to excuse their acts. Calls for moderation and understanding turn out to be the cries of those, precisely, who are afraid of losing their advantages. The attacks of the Portuguese Colonial Forces against Angola and Mozambique, the interventions of the Republic of South Africa against the native populations, the aggressions of the United States against Cuba, against Santo Domingo, against Vietnam can only be presented as unilateral criminal acts. When one wishes to depict pillage and genocide, it is justifiable to use the "black-and-white" technique without any consideration for the murderers in expressing towards the exploited all the solidarity of which one is capable.

(XI)

The documentary theater can take the shape of a tribunal. In this case it does not pretend to vie in authenticity with the Nuremberg trial, with the Auschwitz trial at Frankfurt, with a hearing before the United States Senate or with a session of the Russell Tribunal; it can, however, take the questions and the litigious points raised in the real courtroom and treat of them in a novel manner. Thanks to the remoteness it enjoys, it can argue from effect to cause and thus complete the hearings from points of view which were not presented at the original trial. The characters included in the action are situated in a historical framework. Conjointly with the description of their acts, one shows the process from which the latter stem and one draws attention to the possible aftereffects. Their activities serve to illustrate the demonstration of the mechanism which continues to exert its influence on reality. One prunes away all fortuitous incidents, every chance excrescence, in order to situate the essential problem. The ensuing loss of surprise effects, of local color, of sensational elements, is made up for by the attainment of a universal value. The documentary theater can also introduce the public into the heart of the proceedings, which is impossible in the real courtroom; it places the spectator on an equal footing with the accused or the accuser; it can enable him to sit in on a Commission of Inquiry; it can contribute to the understanding of

interrelated phenomena or else provoke an attitude of maximum opposition.

(XII)

Some further examples of formal work on documentary material:

a) Reports or fragments of reports can be inserted at intervals of precisely limited duration, so as to create a rhythm. Brief passages comprising a single element, made up of a single exclamation, alternate with long and complex units. A quotation is followed by the description of a situation. By means of a sudden break, a situation is transformed into its contrary. An isolated protagonist faces a host of narrators. The structure is composed of antithetic pieces, of enumerations of analogous examples, of contrasting shapes, of varying relationships of size. Variations on an identical theme. A gradation within a process. The introduction of discordant elements, of dissonances.

b) Stylistic work on documentary material. In the quotations, stress is laid on the typical fact. Personalities are caricatured, the situations drastically simplified in order to make them more striking. Songs are used for the purpose of presenting reports, commentaries, summaries. Introduction of chorus and pantomime. Acting by gestures brings out the ultimate possibilities of action. Utilization of masks and of decorative accessories. Musical accompaniment. Sound effects.

c) Interruption in the presentation of the reports. Insertion of a reflection, of a soliloquy, of a dream, of a flashback, of an example of contradictory behavior. These breaks in the unfolding of the action create an insecurity, can produce a shock effect, show how an individual or a group is hit by events. But such violent inclusions must not generate confusion; on the contrary, they must draw attention to the multiplicity of planes on which the event takes place. The techniques must never be used for their own sake: They present experiences supported by evidence.

d) Bursting the structure asunder. No calculated rhythm; but raw material, compact or in unrestricted stream, for the representation of social struggles, for the description of revolutionary situation, for eyewitness accounts from a battlefield. Transcription of the violence in the collision of forces. But here, too, the riot depicted, the expression of the terror and of the indignation cannot remain without clarification or solution. The more unbearable the document, the more imperative the need for an overall view, for a synthesis.

(XIII)

The attempts of the documentary theater to find a convincing form of expression are bound up with the search for appropriate premises. If the performance takes place in a commercial theater with high-priced seats, the documentary theater subscribes to the system it wishes to combat. If it installs itself outside the establishment, it is condemned to premises frequented, as a rule, by groups which already share its opinions. Instead of exerting a real influence on the situation, it manifests its lack of efficacy in relation on the guardians of the established order. The documentary theater must gain entry into the factories, the schools, the sports grounds, the public halls. And in the same way as it abandons the aesthetic canons of the traditional theater, it must always call its own methods into question and develop new techniques adapted to new situations.

(XIV)

The documentary theater is only possible when it takes the shape of a stable working group, possessing a political and sociological formation, and capable of undertaking a scientific inquiry based on abundant archives. A dramaturgy of the document which draws back before a definition, which contents itself with showing a state of affairs without explaining the reasons for its appearance and the necessity as well as the possibility of its disappearance, a dramaturgy of the document which wastes its time in hopeless combats without touching the enemy, such a dramaturgy depreciates its own value. This is why the documentary theater condemns the dramatic output which makes its own despair and its own anger its central theme, and which refuses to abandon the conception of a world which is not only absurd but offers no way out. The documentary theater affirms that reality, whatever the obscurity in which it masks itself, can be explained in minute detail.

—PETER WEISS

Donald Freed

INQUEST

1970

Based, in part, on Invitation to an Inquest by Walter and Miriam Schneir and The Judgment of Julius and Ethel Rosenberg by John Wexley.

Inquest opened in New York at the Music Box theater on 23 April 1970 in a shortened, one-act version directed by Alan Schneider. (The full text was published by Hill and Wang that year.) Special projections were by Ken Isaacs, settings by Karl Eigsti, costumes by Sara Brook, lighting by Jules Fisher, and sound by Gary Harris. The cast included Anne Jackson, George Grizzard, James Whitmore, Allen Garfield, Abe Vigoda, Mason Adams, Mike Bursten, Michael Lipton, Charles Kindl, David Clarke, Jack Hollander, Ed Bordo, Sylvie Straus, Sylvia Gassell, Phil Leeds, and Hildy Brooks.

DRAMATIS PERSONAE

EMANUEL BLOCH: *A kindly, and in this case fatally gentle, defense lawyer. He spent the last years of his life in futile attempts to have the death sentence of the Rosenbergs commuted.*

ROY COHN: *At the time of the trial, a young man in his twenties His great success in the prosecution of the Rosenbergs led on to his notorious career as counsel and colleague of Senator Joseph R. McCarthy. Recent years have blackened his name and he has become a symbol of* the crisis of confidence in the Government that developed in America in the 1950s.

HARRY GOLD: *A bizarre character called onto the stage of history by the times in which we live. A nonentity whose fantasies tallied with those in power.*

DAVID GREENGLASS: *The always smiling younger brother of Ethel Rosenberg and, with his wife, Ruth, the only witness against her. His wife was never indicted and he served only ten years, though they both confessed to the same crime for which the Rosenbergs received the death penalty.*

RUTH GREENGLASS: *David Greenglass's wife. Poor, fierce, and cunning. The Government depended on her to keep her husband in line and credible. She "confessed" but was not even indicted.*

TESSIE GREENGLASS: *Ethel Rosenberg's mother. An illiterate, embittered woman, hostile to her daughter and everyone else except her son David and his wife.*

IRVING KAUFMAN: *The "boy judge" who led his class at Fordham University and became, because of his espionage trials in the 1950s, a famous federal judge.*

ETHEL ROSENBERG: *From the same deprived environment as the Greenglasses, Ethel Rosenberg was, nevertheless, a socially and aesthetically developed woman. Her life was ordinary in every way until her brother's petty thieving* and psychopathic personality selected her to play an incredible role whose first avatar ended in the electric chair at Ossining Prison on 19 June 1953.

JULIUS ROSENBERG: *He was three years younger than his wife and a man of the Depression. Idealistic and a failure in his one business attempt. He became known as the mastermind of Soviet espionage and the perpetrator of the "crime of the century." He died six minutes before his wife with what the* New York Times *called "amazing calm."*

IRVING SAYPOL: *The senior attorney for the Government in the great espionage cases of the fifties. He was subsequently made a judge.*

ANN SIDOROVICH: *She refused to be intimidated. There were many.*

THE COMPANY *and the* MAN IN THE STREET

Throughout, Judge Kaufman appears as THE COURT, *saypol and* COHN *appear as* THE GOVERNMENT, *and* EMANUEL BLOCH *appears as* THE DEFENSE.

DESIGN FOR THE SIDEWALK AND LOBBY

The experience starts on the street with projectors mounted overhead (under marquee) which throw images down to the sidewalk. Exterior lighting must be muted and sidewalk may have to be painted light gray to receive the images.

These are chosen from the large head shots, demonstration (massive textures of people) shots, maps and the two A-bomb sketches made by Greenglass. The strong central images register well and serve to familiarize the audience with the persons in the play—after seating, the familiarity cuts the distance between actors and audience.

The lobby area is largely a print media area with newspaper pages blown up to a six-foot vertical dimension and mounted on wall panels and doors. The pages bear headlines which appear later in the play. The contextual material from the papers will be strong here . . . creating the atmospheres and vibrations of the fifties.

The right and left walls (as you enter) to be covered with large panels of the gods (Freud, Nietzsche, and Marx)—large head shots six feet high rendered in high contrast photography (i.e.,

the grays are all dropped out and only the black and white portions of the pictures remain to make images like branding irons).

The gods' images will bear their names in cool Helvetica typeface and the whole assembly is the dialectic between the cool, considered mien of the gods and the incredibly momentary statement-structure of the news media. Contemplation, thought, and deep feeling in collision with franticness.

Speakers and tape in the lobby will deliver an audio track composed of sound fragments of the fifties. McCarthy, Eisenhower, Truman, Dewey, Fibber and Molly, Berle, Lucy, laugh tracks—a sound collage that time-machines you back into those years.

If there is enough lobby room there should be a great primary structure hanging from the ceiling. This structure will be designed and patterned to translate the time-continuum of the whole Rosenberg event so the audience can place themselves with relation to the action and also get a fix on three or four salient features of the action. This may keep them from getting lost later.

The time-armature (above) will also provide (when seen overall, in unity) a basic translation of the case without detail. This overview is important.

—KEN ISAACS

PROLOGUE

THE DIALECTIC

Full screen of Supreme Court yearly pictures with entire area blue-gelled except for circle surrounding the head of Justice Felix Frankfurter.

Albert Einstein stamp (8¢) repeated en bloc over whole screen alternates with "United States" as his statement runs.

THE VOICE OF FRANKFURTER: To be writing an opinion in a case affecting two lives after the curtain has been rung down upon them has the appearance of pathetic futility. But history also has its claims.

THE VOICE OF EINSTEIN: From the viewpoint of restoring sanity to our political climate, one must not let this case rest.

THE BOMB

Einstein remains on one screen. Building up around him are the images of the early times of the atom from Los Alamos. Trinity Project ground plan, early atomic pile photos, E = MC² appears on several screens. Mushroom clouds, Oppenheimer at tower, Fermi, Los Alamos Newsletter sheets, Fat Man and Big Boy (Hiroshima and Nagasaki).

Switch from Einstein stamp to real shot of him in above process. Bomb remains in center screen, then changes to red circle—small. Combat shot of B-29 bomber appears on one upper screen above red circle. Lower line of screens has complete horizontal coverage with Hiroshige prints of places, people, and things in color. Includes samurai and full-figure lady dressing. Plane moves off to right, bomb (red spot) enlarges over field, and prints are replaced by frieze of Japanese pedestrians along bottom of screen. Note that open slides in above events are blue for sky translation.

Red disc as the bomb enlarges and the pedestrian frieze goes into very high contrast (like the burned-in shadow on the wall of the building in Hiroshima). Shift to a full heroic screen picture of smiling Japanese children—a texture of nine or ten happy young heads with red and orange gel over (the fire). At this point different but intense gels in red and orange alternate over screens and images.

Zoom back from the kids as they move away from us at awesome speed (by going from full screen to one unit). As they move back and become small, they are also displaced from one screen to another in the central area, popping back. After the kids reach the last position, a heavy black diagonal X covers them.

The gel fire storm rages as slides of the pulverization and rubble texture that is Hiroshima build up on the screen. Contorted faces, mountains of rubble, headlines in ten languages, siren, screams, moans. The climax is the sobbing of one child.

Sound for this event should be men talking (but indistinctly), machinery and metal-to-metal clinks, typewriters, generator whines, and a mannerly boom for the experiment in the desert, plus Geiger counters (this all for Los Alamos). Noise of four engines of plane blunt-cut with country-side bird noises for delivery sequence followed by noises of wind and bomb. Pure electronic sound with structured frequency and volume.

At the zenith the fire storm races across the screen. Silence. Then we hear and see, in the darkness, the gods of the twentieth century—Marx, Freud, Nietzsche—appear and disappear. The "red alert" wail, the atomic "music," rises and falls behind the oracles. The gods appear hypnotically. The MAN IN THE STREET, like survivors of an atom bombing, speaks.

MAN IN THE STREET: Nietzsche, have mercy on us.

THE VOICE OF NIETZSCHE: We live in a period of atoms and atomic chaos, and that terrible apparition—the Nation-State.

MAN IN THE STREET: Freud, have mercy on us.

THE VOICE OF FREUD: Men have brought their powers of subduing the forces of nature to such a pitch that by using them they could now very easily exterminate one another to the last man. They know this—hence arises their current unrest, their dejection, their mood of apprehension.

MAN IN THE STREET: Marx, have mercy on us.

THE VOICE OF MARX: If we set out to discover the impelling forces which stand behind historical figures, and constitute the true final impulses of history, we cannot consider so much the motive of single individuals, as those which set in motion great masses and entire nations.

In slow motion, the atom bomb media resume. Through the flames the time chamber of the 1950s begins to bleed into visibility. First comes the popular cultural axis: Early television laugh tracks vie with the cries of the bomb victims; a song like "Cry" canceling the sirens; sports heroes; the big mouths of expensive cars and Milton Berle and Walter Winchell, etc. Next comes the political axis: The brutal comedy routine shares space with Joseph McCarthy; the political imagery of the American Cold War is established before the last layer of media—the "Atom Spy

Ring" case itself—is firmly imprinted. A dating process is evolved from the rash of headlines. The fallout of sights and sounds slows and drops until only frozen images remain on the various screens.

The Screen:

EVERY WORD YOU WILL HEAR OR SEE ON THIS STAGE IS A DOCUMENTED QUOTATION FROM TRIAL TRANSCRIPTS AND ORIGINAL SOURCES OR A RECONSTRUCTION FROM ACTUAL EVENTS.

Picture of J. Edgar Hoover.

THE VOICE OF J. EDGAR HOOVER: The twentieth century has witnessed the intrusion into its body fabric of a highly malignant cancer—a cancer which threatens to destroy Judaic-Christian civilization. In the final analysis the Communist worldview must be met and defeated by the Christian worldview.

Picture of Richard Nixon.

THE VOICE OF RICHARD NIXON: If the President says the American people are entitled to know all the facts, I feel the American people are entitled to know the facts about the espionage ring which was responsible for turning over information on the atom bomb to the agents of the Russian government.

THE SPY RING

The head of Klaus Fuchs covers the screen. Headlines tell the story of his arrest. On one screen the diagram of the Spy Ring begins. This is a cancer-like network. The "Communist Cancer," of the Hoover worldview, is in the paranoid style.

THE VOICE OF KLAUS FUCHS: There are other crimes which I have committed other than the ones with which I'm charged. When I asked my counsel to put certain facts before you, I did so in order to atone for *these* crimes. They are not crimes in the eyes of the law.

THE VOICE OF J. EDGAR HOOVER: Communist man is a brute, ideologically trained . . . he is immune to the emotions of pity, sorrow or remorse. He is truly an alarming monster, human in physical form, but in practice a cynically godless and immoral machine.

THE VOICE OF RICHARD NIXON: We found that in the last seven years six hundred million people had been lost to the Communists and not a single Russian soldier had been lost in combat. The Communists are nibbling us to death in little wars all over the world.

Picture of Joseph McCarthy.

THE VOICE OF JOSEPH MCCARTHY: I have here in my hand a list of two hundred and five that were known to the Secretary of State as being members of the Communist Party.

THE VOICE OF J. EDGAR HOOVER: The secret of the atomic bomb has been stolen. *Find the thieves!*

Film of HARRY GOLD *being taken into custody. Headlines give information. The diagram of the "Ring" expands, including* GOLD's *head.*

The Screen:

PHILADELPHIA CHEMIST, HARRY GOLD, NAMED BY THE FBI, AS KLAUS FUCH'S AMERICAN CONTACT IN RUSSIAN SPY RING

THE VOICE OF J. EDGAR HOOVER: In all the history of the FBI, there never was a more important problem than this one, never another case where we felt under such pressure. The unknown man simply had to be found.

Film of DAVID GREENGLASS *being taken into custody. Headlines and the diagram of the Ring tell the story. Film of* JULIUS *and* ETHEL ROSENBERG *being arrested. Headlines for the arrest of the* ROSENBERGS *appear on the screen.*

The Screen:

NEW YORKER SEIZED AS ATOM SPY GOT LOS ALAMOS ATOM BOMB DATA FOR SOVIET RING

PLOT TO HAVE GI GIVE BOMB DATA TO SOVIET IS LAID TO HIS SISTER

On opposite corners, in tight spotlight, stand JULIUS *and* ETHEL ROSENBERG.

ETHEL ROSENBERG: . . . after a listless game of handball (played solo, of course), a shower, dinner and an evening of enchanting music, during which you made passionate love to me, I . . . finally succumbed to homesick tears. . . . Oh, darling, how greedy I am for life and living.

JULIUS ROSENBERG: At this moment I'm very lethargic and in a romantic mood. I guess it is the combined effect of a nice long spring day and a natural desire to be with my beloved. . . . Everything seems so unreal and out of focus. . . . It seems like we're suspended somewhere far off, seeing everything that's being done and not being able to do anything even though we are the center of controversy.

On the screen headlines give information. The diagram of the "Ring" expands, including GOLD'S, GREENGLASS'S, *and the* ROSENBERGS' *heads.*

THE VOICE OF J. EDGAR HOOVER: The unknown man simply had to be found!

EMANUEL BLOCH appears in a pool of light on the quiet stage.

EMANUEL BLOCH: In the middle of dinner, the phone rang: A man I had never met named Julius Rosenberg asked if I could see him. We took a little walk, it was a nice night, and I said to him, "Mr. Rosenberg, I don't think you have anything to worry about." I figured it was probably something minor, like a loyalty oath case. So, I was the defense. (*He shakes his head and sighs.*) I had no idea of what was waiting for me. They were arrested in July and August of 1950 and executed in June of 1953—in between was the trial. That's all I know. (*Pause.*) I was the defense but I can't tell you what really happened to those two human beings. Let me put it to you this way—the future determines the past.

Over all the screens and scrims the diagram of Fuchs to GOLD *to* GREENGLASS *to the* ROSENBERGS *spreads and duplicates itself like a cancer or octopus over the* ROSENBERG *memorabilia. In the darkness the juror selection drum begins to glow and spin.*

ACT ONE

The CLERK *is spinning the juror drum. The audience is the jury. Dialogue is directed to them. On the screen is the legend:* UNITED STATES DISTRICT COURT, SOUTHERN DISTRICT OF

NEW YORK
The United States of America v. Julius Rosenberg and Ethel Rosenberg, et al. Before Hon. Irving R. Kaufman, D.J., and a Jury, New York, March 6, 1951, 10:30 o'clock A.M.
Slowly the American flag covers the area.

STAGE A

BAILIFF: No talking, please, or reading or gum chewing. Please rise. Hear Ye, Hear Ye: Facing the flag of our country, acknowledging the principles for which it stands, this honorable United States District Court is now in session. The Honorable Irving R. Kaufman, Judge presiding. All persons having business before this court, draw near and ye shall be heard. God bless this United States District Court. Be seated.

THE GOVERNMENT: The District Attorney moves the case for trial and is ready to proceed.

THE DEFENSE: The defendants are ready to proceed.

THE COURT: To the gentlemen in the jury box and to the ladies and gentlemen in the courtroom, I shall attempt to speak loud enough so that all of you can hear my questions. Do any of you know or have any of you had dealings, directly or indirectly, with Irving H. Saypol, the United States Attorney for the Southern District of New York?

THE GOVERNMENT: Shall I rise?

THE COURT: Mr. Roy M. Cohn, would you rise please? I take it by your silence none of you knows any of these gentlemen who have risen. Does any juror know or has he had any dealings, either directly or indirectly, with Mr. Emanuel Bloch?

THE DEFENSE (*rising*): Representing Julius and Ethel Rosenberg.

THE COURT: Do any of you have any scruples against being a juror in a capital case?

PROSPECTIVE JURORS speak from the audience.

PROSPECTIVE JUROR NUMBER ONE: Your Honor, I am prejudiced somewhat against capital punishment and I have so stated in the Supreme Court of New York.

THE COURT: Very well. We will excuse you. Have any of you or any members of your family been in the armed forces of the United States?

FIRST JUROR: Yes, I had four brothers in the Army.

SECOND JUROR: Well, I had three brothers in the last war.

THIRD JUROR: I served in the Navy during the First World War.

FOURTH JUROR: My brother was in the service in the last war.

FIFTH JUROR: My brother also served in the Navy in the last war.

SIXTH JUROR: Yes, the United States Navy in the First World War.

SEVENTH JUROR: I had two brothers in the last war.

EIGHTH JUROR: I had two brothers and three nephews in the past war.

On the screen is the list of jurors:

THE JURY

No. 1: (*Foreman*) Vincent J. Lebonitte—Residence: White Plains, New York. A manager for an R. H. Macy branch in that suburb.

No. 2: Richard Booth—A caterer for a tennis club in Forest Hills, Long Island, called the Seminole Club.

No. 3: Howard G. Becker—Residence: Ma-maroneck, New York. An auditor for the Irving Trust Company for twenty-four years.

Nov. 4: James A. Gibbons—An accountant for the New York City Omnibus Company for twenty-eight years.

No. 5: Charles W. Christie—An auditor for the Tidewater Associated Oil Company, which had "contracts with the Government" to do war work.

No. 6: Harold H. Axley—A restaurant owner previously employed as a civilian expert in the finance department of the Army from 1942 to 1946.

No. 7: Emanuel Clarence Dean (*Negro*)—Eleven-year employee of the Consolidated Edison Company.

No. 8: Chauncey E. Miller—Residence: Scarsdale, New York. A secretary of the Board of Commissioners of Pilots, an agency of the State of New York, for twenty years. A member of the American Legion.

No. 9: Mrs. Lisette D. Dammas—Served on Bronx County Grand Jury in May, 1950. Son-in-law in National Guard.

No. 10: Charles J. Duda—Residence: Dobbs Ferry, New York. A bookkeeper for Davis and Lawrence Company.

No. 11: James Mitchell—An accountant with Harris, Kerr, Foster and Company. When previously employed by the U.S. Post Office, he was passed by "the Loyalty Probe."

No. 12: James F. Tessitore—Residence: Mount Vernon, New York. An estimator for the Alco Gravure Division of Publications Corporation. During World War II, "printed millions of topics for the Government."

Alternate No. 1: John F. Moore—Residence: Bronx, New York. A business representative for the Consolidated Edison Company.

Alternate No. 2: Emerson C. Nein—Residence: Bronx, New York. An officer and auditor for the Empire State Bank.

Alternate No. 3: Richard Lombardi—Residence: White Plains Road. A Government employee (Post Office).

Alternate No. 4: Mrs. Edna Allen—Residence: Bronx, New York. Husband employed by Consolidated Edison Company. Son in Army's Chemical Corps.

THE COURT (*to the audience*): Thank you. Now has any member of the jury ever been a member of, made contributions to, or been associated in any way with any of the following organizations, which are contained on a list published by the Attorney General pursuant to a Presidential executive order? Mr. Schaefer, would you please read page 33?

THE CLERK (*this is live and in media. The action overlaps.*): Abraham Lincoln Brigade, Abraham Lincoln School, Chicago, Illinois, Action Committee to Free Spain Now, American League against War and Fascism, American Association for Reconstruction in Yugoslavia, Inc., American Committee for Protection of Foreign Born, American Committee for a Democratic Greece, American Council on Soviet Relations, American Croatian Congress, American Jewish Labor Council, American League for Peace and Democracy, American Peace Mobilization, American Polish Labor Council, American Russian Institute of San Francisco, American Slav Congress, American Student Union, American Youth Congress, American Youth for Democracy, Armenian Progressive League of America, Boston School for Marxist Studies, California Labor School, Inc., 216 Market Street, San Francisco, California, Central Council of American Women of Croatian Descent, also known as Central Council of American Croatian Women, National Council of Croatian Women, Citizens Committee of the Upper West Side, New York City, Citizens Protective League, Citizens Committee to Free Earl Browder, Citizens Committee for Harry Bridges, *Comité Coordinador por República Española,* Committee for a Democratic Far Eastern Policy, Commonwealth College, Mena, Arkansas, Civil Rights Congress, and its stage affiliates, Committee to Aid the Fighting South, Communist Party, U.S.A., Communist Political Association, Connecticut State Youth Conference, Congress of American Women, Council on African Affairs, Council for Pan American Revolutionary Writers, Council for Pan American Democracy, Daily Worker Press Club, Dennis Defense Committee, Friends of the Soviet Union, George Washington Carver School, New York City, German-American Bund, Hollywood Writers Mobilization for Defense, Hungarian-American Council for Democracy, Independent Socialist League, International Labor Defense, International Workers Order and affiliated groups, Jefferson School of Social Science, New York City, Jewish Peoples Committee, Joint Anti-Fascist Refugee Committee, Ku Klux Klan, Labor Research Association, Inc., Labor Youth League, League of American Writers, Macedonian-American Peoples League, Michigan Civil Rights Federation, National Committee for the Defense of Political Prisoners, National Committee to Win the Peace, National Council of Americans of Croatian Descent, National Council of American Soviet Friendship, National Federation for Constitutional Liberties, National Negro Congress, Nature Friends of America. Since 1939, Negro Labor Victory Committee, New Committee for

Publication, Ohio School of Social Sciences, Peoples Educational Association, Peoples Institute of Applied Religion, Peoples Radio Foundation, Inc., Philadelphia School of Social Science and Art, Photo League, New York City, Proletarian Party of America, Revolutionary Workers League, Samuel Adams School, Boston, Massachusetts, School of Jewish Studies, New York City, Seattle Labor School, Seattle, Washington, Serbian Vidovdan Council, Silvershirt Legion of America, Slovenian-American Committee for European Workers Relief, Socialist Youth League, Southern Negro Youth Congress, Tom Paine School of Westchester, New York, United Committee for Democratic Rights, United Committee for South Slavic Americans, United Harlem Tenants and Consumer Organization, United May Day Committee, United Negro and Allied Veterans of America, Veterans against Discrimination of Civil Rights Congress of New York, Veterans of the Abraham Lincoln Brigade, Walt Whitman's School of Social Science, Newark, New Jersey, Washington Book Shop Association, Washington Committee for Democratic Action, Wisconsin Conference on Social Legislation, Workers Alliance, Workers Party, including Socialist Youth League, Young Communist League, Institute of Pacific Relations, American-Russian Institute for Culture Relations with the Soviet Union, Inc., National Emergency Conference for Democratic Rights, China Aid Council, International Juridical Association.

There is a pause; THE COURT *resumes.*

THE COURT: Now, in the first place, in the matter of punishment, your function is merely to pass upon the evidence. You add a column of figures; that is what you do. When you are through adding a column of figures you have a result.

To put it another way, the minds of the jurors should be the same as a white sheet of paper with nothing on it, with respect to this case, and you should only take the testimony as it comes from the witnesses and from no other source.

The grand jury has returned the indictment that will be read to you ultimately. I want you to know at the outset that the indictment is not evidence of guilt and should be entirely disregarded by you as evidence.

The defendants are presumed to be innocent until it is established beyond a reasonable doubt that they have offended against the law, as charged in the indictment. The defendants stand before you as any individual.

Do you subscribe to the principle that everyone, regardless of race, color, creed or position in society, and regardless also of his political or religious beliefs, is entitled to a fair trial, according to our laws? (*Pause.*) Has any juror any prejudice, bias or sympathy, based solely upon a person's educational background or personal appearance? (*Pause.*) Does any juror have any prejudice against the atomic bomb or information relating thereto, or object to the method employed by the Government of handling information concerning the atom bomb? (*Pause.*) Does any juror oppose use of atomic weapons in time of war or oppose the Government's continued research and development of atomic weapons? (*Pause.*) The following persons will be called as witnesses for the Government in this case. Mr. Schaefer, would you please read them?

THE CLERK: Dr. J. Robert Oppenheimer, Dr. Harold C. Urey, Dr. George B. Kistiakowsky, Dr. Anoch Lewest, Harry Gold, John Lansdale, Jr., Elizabeth T. Bentley, General Leslie R. Groves, David Greenglass . . .

STAGE B: RECONSTRUCTION (THE GOVERNMENT AND THE PRESS, 1951)

All Reconstructions are titled on the screen throughout. A hurrying and frenetic group.

REPORTER: Mr. Saypol, will you ask the death penalty in this case?

REPORTER: Mr. Saypol, will you have to reveal any top secret information?

THE GOVERNMENT: The Government's case will be documented by unimpeachable witnesses and evidence.

REPORTER: Can you tell us who some of the—

THE GOVERNMENT: There is a list of one hundred and twenty witnesses, and that includes some of this nation's top scientists.

REPORTER: Atomic—

THE GOVERNMENT: Top atomic scientists.

REPORTER: Will Harry Gold be your top witness, Mr. Saypol?

THE GOVERNMENT: There will be many famous names from all over the country.

REPORTER: What about the spy ring?

THE GOVERNMENT: The Rosenberg Spy Ring has been smashed and there will be more arrests.

REPORTER: There will be more arrests?

REPORTER: Mr. Saypol, will it involve—

THE GOVERNMENT: We have the masterminds of the ring and we will definitely go before the grand jury for more indictments as this roundup continues. Thank you, gentlemen.

STAGE A

THE CLERK: Mrs. Ruth Greenglass, Ann H. Sidorovich, Rose Sobell, Louis Sobell, O. John Rogge, Louis Abel.

THE COURT: Now, does any member of the jury know any of the persons whose names were called and who will be witnesses in this case? I gather by your silence that your answer is in the negative. (*Pause.*) Mr. Schaefer will now read to you the indictment in this case.

THE CLERK: The grand jury charges:

1. On or about June 6, 1944, up to and including June 16, 1950, at the Southern District of New York, and elsewhere, Julius Rosenberg, Ethel Rosenberg, David Greenglass, the defendants herein, did, the United States of America then and there being at war, conspire, combine, confederate and agree with each other and with Harry Gold and Ruth Greenglass, named as coconspirators but not as defendants, and with . . .

STAGE B

MAN IN THE STREET (*The voice of the questioner, like that of the gods, is oracular and from the cosmos.*): Do you prefer baseball or football?

ANSWER: Baseball.

ANSWER: Football.
ANSWER: Baseball.
ANSWER: Football.
ANSWER: Decline to state.

STAGE A

THE COURT: Now we will hear the openings and then we will call your first witness. Will you keep your opening statements very brief? Proceed, Mr. Saypol.

THE GOVERNMENT: May it please your Honor, Mr. Foreman, ladies and gentlemen of the jury: The facts, as they are developed before you here, will demonstrate that this case is one of unusual significance, of a conspiracy to commit espionage. It takes on added meaning where the defendants are charged with having participated in this conspiracy against our country at the most critical hours in our history, in time of war, around 1944.

The evidence will show that the loyalty and the allegiance of the Rosenbergs was not to our country, but to communism, communism in this country and communism throughout the world.

THE DEFENSE: If the Court pleases, I object to these remarks as irrelevant and I ask the Court to instruct the District Attorney to desist from making any remarks about communism, because communism is not on trial here. These defendants are charged with espionage.

THE GOVERNMENT: I object to this interruption.

THE DEFENSE: I beg your pardon, Mr. Saypol, but I am forced to do it.

THE COURT: Will somebody permit me to make a ruling here?

THE DEFENSE: That is correct, your Honor.

THE COURT: Mr. Saypol objects to your objection, and you answer his objection, and I can't make a ruling.

THE DEFENSE: I am making my objection.

THE COURT: The charge here is espionage. It is not that the defendants are members of the Communist Party or that they had any interest in communism. However, if the Government intends to establish that they did have an interest in communism, for the purpose of establish-

ing a motive for what they were doing, I will, in due course, when that question arises, rule on that point.

THE GOVERNMENT: That is the purpose of my remarks.

THE DEFENSE: Defendants take exception to your Honor's statement.

THE COURT: Very well.

THE GOVERNMENT (*to the jury*): I am sorry for the interruption.

THE COURT: Excuse me a moment, Mr. Saypol. I said that the charge was espionage; I want to correct that. The charge is conspiracy to commit espionage.

THE GOVERNMENT: Yes.

THE COURT: All right.

THE GOVERNMENT: I have said the evidence will show that the primary allegiance of these defendants was not to our country, but to communism, both national and international.

It will show that this love of communism and the Soviet Union soon led them into a Soviet espionage ring.

You will hear how Julius and Ethel Rosenberg reached into wartime projects and installations of the United States Government to obtain from people in the armed services and from people in positions of trust in our Government secret information, documents and material vital to the national defense of our country, so that they could hand this material directly to agents of the Soviet Union and speed it on its way to Russia. The most important scientific secrets ever known to mankind!

The evidence will reveal to you how the Rosenbergs persuaded David Greenglass, Mrs. Rosenberg's own brother, to play the treacherous role of a modern Benedict Arnold, while wearing the uniform of the United States Army.

STAGE B

MAN IN THE STREET: Do you approve of our involvement in the Korean War?

ANSWER: Who are you?

ANSWER: I think we're fighting for freedom in South Korea.

ANSWER: We should win and get out.

ANSWER: No comment.
ANSWER: No comment.

STAGE A

THE COURT: Mr. Saypol, you have passed your allotted time. Try to rush it along a little bit.

THE GOVERNMENT: We will prove that the Rosenbergs stole, through David Greenglass, the one weapon *that might well hold the key to the survival of this nation, and means the peace of the world—the atomic bomb!* There came a day, however, that a vigilant Federal Bureau of Investigation broke through the darkness of this insidious business and collected the evidence that would bring these culprits before the bar of justice, before an American jury like you. These defendants and their Soviet partners in crime had at their command various amounts of money, with which to finance the escape from American justice into safe havens behind the Iron Curtain of the members of this espionage ring. The evidence of the treasonable acts of these defendants you will find overwhelming.

The evidence will prove to you, not only beyond a reasonable doubt, but beyond any doubt, that these defendants have committed the most serious crime which can be committed against the people of this country.

This evidence will point to only one possible verdict on your part, that of guilty, as charged by the grand jury.

THE COURT: Mr. Bloch.

THE DEFENSE: If your Honor please, I move for a mistrial in this case upon the grounds that the opening statement of the learned United States Attorney was inflammatory in character and introduced an element which is not pertinent to the case or relevant to it, to wit, communism, and made other inflammatory and damaging statements which ware not part and should not be part of an opening.

THE COURT: Your motion is denied.

THE DEFENSE: Exception.

THE COURT: Mr. Block, proceed.

THE DEFENSE: Ladies and gentlemen of the jury, I am going to be very, very brief.

THE COURT: I can't hear you, Mr. Bloch.

THE DEFENSE: What I would like to impress upon you now is to remember at all times the oath you took when you were sworn in as jurors. We ask you, we plead with you, don't be influenced by any bias or prejudice or hysteria.

This is a very grave crime that these defendants are charged with. Very grave. And this trial arises in a rather tense international atmosphere. And I think all of us delude ourselves that we believe that we are completely free from all those pressures and influences that every minute of the day are upon us.

May I repeat, and I hope you forgive me if I repeat, and I hope the Court will forgive me if I repeat at this time; all we ask of you is a fair shake in the American way. We ask you to keep your minds open. We ask you to judge these defendants, American citizens, as you would want to be judged yourself if you were sitting as a defendant.

Finally, I would like you, of course, to pay particular attention to the witnesses that appear here and judge the issues by what comes out of the witnesses' mouths. And in that connection pay very careful attention to the witness. Test yourself by the same standards which guide your conduct in your everyday affairs; is this the kind of person who is telling the truth? What motive has this person to say thus and so? And I want you to focus your attention particularly on these witnesses who we now hear will appear for the Government. One is David Greenglass, who is a defendant here and who had pleaded guilty. And I would like you to pay particular attention to the testimony of Harry Gold.

We come to you and say to you, don't be swayed by emotion. The defendants do not expect you to give a verdict on the basis of sympathy or passion or prejudice. We want you to use your mind and your reason. That is all we have a right to expect of you, but that much we have a right to expect, and we tell you that in our opinion by the time you have heard all of the evidence in this case, you will be convinced that these defendants, as they have contended at all times and as they now contend, are innocent of this crime, for which they are now being charged. So please keep your minds open.

STAGE B

MAN IN THE STREET: As a consumer, do you notice any decline in service?
ANSWER: Well, it's not so bad; I can't complain.
ANSWER: Could you repeat the question, please?
ANSWER: Not bad.
ANSWER: No.
ANSWER: I didn't get the question.

STAGE A

THE CLERK: Call David Greenglass to the stand.

He is sworn. All of the GREENGLASS *questioning is conducted for* THE GOVERNMENT *by* ROY COHN. *The volume and book numbers of the trial transcript from which testimony is quoted are flashed on the screen as each sequence begins. Here the citation is: Volume I, Book II.*

THE GOVERNMENT: Mr. Greenglass, will you try to keep your voice up so the Court and jury can get the benefit of your testimony. Are you the David Greenglass who is named as a defendant in the indictment here on trial?
DAVID GREENGLASS: I am.
THE GOVERNMENT: That indictment charging conspiracy to commit espionage?
DAVID GREENGLASS: Yes.
THE GOVERNMENT: Have you entered a plea to that indictment?
DAVID GREENGLASS: I have.
THE GOVERNMENT: What is that plea?
DAVID GREENGLASS: Guilty.
THE GOVERNMENT: Now, prior to the time you were remanded to the custody of the United States Marshal, what was your home address?
DAVID GREENGLASS: 265 Rivington Street.
THE GOVERNMENT: Here in Manhattan?
DAVID GREENGLASS: Yes.
THE GOVERNMENT: How old are you?
DAVID GREENGLASS: Twenty-nine.
THE GOVERNMENT: When were you born?
DAVID GREENGLASS: March 3, 1922.
THE GOVERNMENT: Are your parents alive?
DAVID GREENGLASS: My father is dead. My mother is alive.

THE GOVERNMENT: Do you have any brothers and sisters?
DAVID GREENGLASS: I have two brothers and one sister.
THE GOVERNMENT: Your sister is the defendant Mrs. Ethel Greenglass Rosenberg, is that correct?
DAVID GREENGLASS: That is true.
THE GOVERNMENT: And another defendant, Julius Rosenberg, is your brother-in-law?
DAVID GREENGLASS: That is true.

STAGE B

The Screen: From the files of Emanuel Bloch, attorney for Julius Rosenberg.

FBI: Do you know that your brother-in-law said you told him to supply information for Russia?
JULIUS ROSENBERG: That couldn't be so; he'd have to be out of his mind to say things like that. Will you bring him here and let him tell me to my face?
FBI: What if we bring him here, what will you do?
JULIUS ROSENBERG: I'll call him a liar to his face. Look, gentlemen, at first you asked me to come down and give some information concerning by brother-in-law David Greenglass about some black market trouble he's supposed to be in. Now, you're trying to implicate me in something. I would like to see a lawyer.
FBI: How about a smoke? Just a few more questions; do you want some gum? Now, when did Greenglass come home on furlough from Los Alamos? You said "winter." Was that when you might have discussed this Russian espionage business?
JULIUS ROSENBERG: No, you're trying to involve me and I want to get in touch with my lawyer.
FBI: All right, a lawyer from Mr. Rabinowitz' office has been on the phone. Your wife must have called him.
JULIUS ROSENBERG: Hello. Yes. I don't know. (*To the* FBI. Am I under arrest? (*An* AGENT *replies* "no.") They say "no." Yes, I understand. Thanks. Good-bye. (*To the* FBI *as he leaves.*) Good-bye, gentlemen.

The AGENTS *look at each other as the lights fade.*

STAGE A

The Screen: Volume I, Book II

THE GOVERNMENT: Is Mrs. Rosenberg older or younger than you are?
DAVID GREENGLASS: Older.
THE COURT: How much older is she?
DAVID GREENGLASS: Six years.

STAGE B: RECONSTRUCTION (ARREST, 1950)

ETHEL ROSENBERG is walking out of the New York City Federal Court House. Two AGENTS appear.

FIRST AGENT: Mrs. Rosenberg, you'll have to come with us—you're under arrest.
SECOND AGENT: Federal Bureau of Investigation, Special Agents.
ETHEL ROSENBERG: What? Do you have a warrant?
FIRST AGENT: We don't need one. Let's go upstairs.
ETHEL ROSENBERG: But I just left the grand jury up there. I was called to testify, that's all. My children are waiting for me. I have a three-year-old.
FIRST AGENT: Let's go.
ETHEL ROSENBERG: Why are you doing this—I came down here today of my own free will. My children are expecting me. (*They walk into another area.*) Listen, I have to phone my neighbor. She's watching the children for me.
FIRST AGENT: All right. Go ahead.
ETHEL ROSENBERG: Hello. Listen, don't show any alarm. Are the boys there? Listen, after I testified, as I'm walking out, two FBI agents meet me and they're holding me in the office here. Mr. Bloch's father is coming over, so maybe I'll know more later. I'll have him call you. Meanwhile, take the children over to my mother's. And listen, let me talk to Michael for a minute. (*Pause.*) Hello, Michael. Are you helping take care of Robbie? Listen, dear, Mommy has to stay downtown a while. What? Michael, do you remember what happened to Daddy? Well, dear—

She tries to block out the scream from the other end.

STAGE A

The Screen: Volume I, Book II

THE GOVERNMENT: Are you yourself married?
DAVID GREENGLASS: I am.
THE GOVERNMENT: Do you have any children?
DAVID GREENGLASS: I have two. One is nine months old and one is four years old.
THE GOVERNMENT: Where were you educated, Mr. Greenglass?
DAVID GREENGLASS: I was educated in New York.
THE GOVERNMENT: Would you tell us briefly the schools which you attended here in New York.
DAVID GREENGLASS: I went to P.S. 4, P.S. 97, Haaren Aviation School, Brooklyn Polytechnic, and Pratt Institute.
THE GOVERNMENT: What field have you pursued since your graduation from public school?
DAVID GREENGLASS: I am a machinist.
THE GOVERNMENT: After you left school and prior to 1943, did you have any practical experience as a machinist?
DAVID GREENGLASS: I did.
THE GOVERNMENT: Here in New York?
DAVID GREENGLASS: In New York.
THE GOVERNMENT: Now, in 1943 did you enter the Army of the United States?
DAVID GREENGLASS: I did.
THE COURT: May I suggest, Mr. Cohn, that you stand back a little bit. It will help the witness to speak up.
THE GOVERNMENT: All right. What rank did you hold?
DAVID GREENGLASS: Private. Eventually I became a T/4 Sergeant.
THE GOVERNMENT: Were you thereafter assigned to work as a machinist while in the Army?
DAVID GREENGLASS: I was.
THE GOVERNMENT: Where was that?
DAVID GREENGLASS: Los Alamos, New Mexico.

STAGE B: RECONSTRUCTION (COURTSHIP, 1938)

Here begins the personal time chamber of ETHEL *and* JULIUS ROSENBERG. *The slate is wiped clean and their story begins. Their lives, their family, children, friends; childhood and youth; schools and synagogues and all the banal imagery and music, politics of everyday life.*

DAVID GREENGLASS: Ethel, whatsisname is here.

ETHEL ROSENBERG: Put on a shirt, please.

DAVID GREENGLASS: Crissake!

JULIUS ROSENBERG (*entering*): Hello, Dave. Hi.

ETHEL ROSENBERG: Did you eat?

JULIUS ROSENBERG: We'll have some chow mein afterward.

ETHEL ROSENBERG: Good, I'll be ready in a minute.

JULIUS ROSENBERG: Hot, huh? Why don't you take off your shirt, Dave? (*Pause.*) How'd the game come out? (*DAVID shrugs.*) So, what are you doing tonight?

DAVID GREENGLASS: If I had any money I'd go to a show.

JULIUS ROSENBERG: If I had any extra I'd sure give it to you, too.

DAVID GREENGLASS: Yeah? How much you got?

JULIUS ROSENBERG: Just enough for the dance and the—

DAVID GREENGLASS: Chow mein. You see, you're all set. You should pay me some rent cause Ethel types all your college papers. Keeps me up all night. Fooling around.

JULIUS ROSENBERG: You're right.

ETHEL ROSENBERG (*enters*): Is Davey at it again?

DAVID squeaks a love song.

JULIUS ROSENBERG: That's a pretty blouse. Listen, isn't there anything for him to take in a show?

ETHEL ROSENBERG: Listen, Dave, I told you there's free folksinging at the center. (*He continues to make noises.*) You act like a child. Now, stop it, David. You know why there's never any money around here, for you or anyone else.

DAVID GREENGLASS (*starts to sing "The International"*): "Arise ye prisoners of starvation. Arise ye wretched of the earth."

TESSIE GREENGLASS (*enters*): Leave the child alone, Ettie. In this house forget all your books, please. Julius dear, you know what I mean?

STAGE A

The Screen: Volume I, Book II.

THE GOVERNMENT: While out at Los Alamos, did you come to learn the identity of any scientist working on atomic energy?

DAVID GREENGLASS: I did get to know a number of scientists and some of world fame, for instance, Dr. Oppenheimer—

THE GOVERNMENT: J. Robert Oppenheimer?

DAVID GREENGLASS: That is right, and there was Niels Bohr, whom I first knew as Baker.

THE GOVERNMENT: Did you know that Dr. Harold Urey was connected with the Manhattan Project?

DAVID GREENGLASS: I did.

THE DEFENSE: Your Honor, I will object to whether or not this witness knew some of the most renowned scientists unless it is related to the issues in this case.

THE GOVERNMENT: I would be glad to state to your Honor that the name of each scientist will be directly related to the defendants in this case.

THE COURT: Very well.

THE GOVERNMENT: Now, did you ever have any discussion with your sister and Julius Rosenberg concerning the relative merits of our form of government and that of the Soviet Union?

THE DEFENSE: Objected to as incompetent, irrelevant, and immaterial, and upon the further ground that this will obviously lead to matters which may only tend to confuse the jury and inject inflammatory matter which will make it difficult or almost impossible for the jury to confine themselves to the real issue in the case.

THE COURT: Objection overruled.

DAVID GREENGLASS: Yes. They preferred socialism to capitalism.

THE COURT: Which type of socialism?

DAVID GREENGLASS: Russian socialism.

THE GOVERNMENT: Mr. Greenglass, I think you told us your wife went out to Los Alamos to visit you in August of 1944. What did she say to you at that time?

DAVID GREENGLASS: My wife said that while she was still in New York, Julius Rosenberg invited her to a wonderful dinner at their home at 10 Monroe Street. She came to dinner and later on there was a conversation between the three present, my wife, my sister and my brother-in-law. It went something like this: Ethel started the conversation by stating to Ruth that she must have noticed that she, Ethel, was no longer involved in Communist Party activities—

THE DEFENSE: Now, if the Court please, this is just what I was afraid of, and I move to strike out any reference to Communist—

THE GOVERNMENT: I object to it being struck out, your Honor, on the ground that it is directly relevant to the charge in this indictment, which will emerge as this conversation unfolds.

THE COURT: I will overrule the objection.

THE DEFENSE: I respectfully except.

THE COURT: The mere fact that the word "communism" is mentioned does not taint all of the testimony and make it inadmissible if it is otherwise relevant.

THE DEFENSE: But apart from the lack of causal connection between Communist affiliations and sympathies . . .

THE COURT: Well, you have already stated your objection. You stated it yesterday, and you stated it, I believe, the day before, too.

THE DEFENSE: I think that is so, your Honor.

THE COURT: And I have your objection and I have made my ruling.

THE GOVERNMENT: Go ahead, Mr. Greenglass.

DAVID GREENGLASS: That they don't buy the *Daily Worker* anymore or attend meetings, club meetings. And the reason for this is that Julius has finally gotten to a point where he is doing what he wanted to do all along, which was that he was giving information to the Soviet Union. And Julius then went on to tell Ruth that I was working on the atomic bomb project at Los Alamos and that they would want me to give information to the Russians. My wife objected to this, but Ethel said . . .

STAGE B: RECONSTRUCTION
(THE FAMILY, 1946)

JULIUS ROSENBERG: Ethel, your mother's here. Hello, Mom.

ETHEL ROSENBERG: Hi, Momma, you're early.

TESSIE GREENGLASS: There's garbage in front of the building. It's filthy. (*Her speech is punctuated with Yiddish idioms.*)

JULIUS ROSENBERG: Is that so? It's usually very clean.

TESSIE GREENGLASS: I wouldn't know. Ethel, you look tired.

ETHEL ROSENBERG: Mother, will you have tea?

TESSIE GREENGLASS: I can't stay. I'm going to eat with David and Ruthie. They insist. I just want to know before I give them the money: Julius, can my David make a living from this new shop? Are you looking after him?

JULIUS ROSENBERG: I hope so. The papers talk about things being—

TESSIE GREENGLASS: Don't talk to me about the papers. I'm asking about my David. Will you treat him like a real partner? He's never had a break, you know what I mean, Julius.

ETHEL ROSENBERG: Mother, sit down. I'll call the kids.

TESSIE GREENGLASS: I can't stay. So what do you think, Julius? Is there something in it for David? They want to have a family too, you know. Ruthie is a wonderful girl. They deserve the best. Julius, you know what I mean?

ETHEL ROSENBERG: Momma, we're all hopeful. The prospects look good if we can get enough capital. David will have to work hard and take the same chances as all the rest of us.

TESSIE GREENGLASS: Yeah. So what classes are you taking now?

JULIUS ROSENBERG: You should hear her play the guitar.

TESSIE GREENGLASS: The guitar? I never even had a class to learn to read. Never had a rest or vacation in forty years. You're telling me about work? And she was always singing somewhere in New Jersey.

ETHEL ROSENBERG: Give David and Ruth my love, Momma.

STAGE A

The Screen: *Volume I, Book II.*

THE DEFENSE: May I ask your Honor to instruct the witness to raise his voice, please?

THE COURT: Yes, we had the same difficulty with the other witness.

THE DEFENSE: I think the acoustics in here are very bad. We had the same difficulty at the last trial.

THE GOVERNMENT: Did you have a furlough January 1, 1945?

DAVID GREENGLASS: I arrived home January 1, 1945.

THE GOVERNMENT: After your arrival in New York did there come a time when you saw the defendant Julius Rosenberg?

DAVID GREENGLASS: It was in the morning and he told me to write up this information at night, late at night, and he would be back the following morning to pick it up. And he told me to write it up, to write up anything that I knew about the atomic bomb.

THE GOVERNMENT: Anything else?

DAVID GREENGLASS: He gave me a description of the atom bomb.

THE GOVERNMENT: Did you do any writing at that time?

DAVID GREENGLASS: I wrote up the information he wanted that evening. It included sketches on the lens molds and how they were used in experiments.

THE GOVERNMENT: Tell us exactly what you gave Rosenberg.

The stage is dark as the sketch goes on the screen. The dialogue continues in darkness.

DAVID GREENGLASS: I gave him a sketch of the lens mold. I marked it *A, B, C,* and I defined what the markings meant.

THE DEFENSE: Are you saying that Government's Exhibit 2 represented a true copy of the sketch that you turned over to Rosenberg?

DAVID GREENGLASS: *A* refers to the curve of the lens; *B* is the frame; *C* shows approximately how wide it is.

THE GOVERNMENT: Your Honor, may I pass it to the jury?

THE COURT: Yes.

The sketch remains on the screen.

THE GOVERNMENT (*Lights cross-fade.*): We have reached a good stopping place, your Honor. In that connection, bearing in mind how conscientious your Honor is with respect to maintaining a continuing calendar, Monday, March 19, my son gets married in the afternoon.

THE COURT: Off the record. (*Discussion off the record.*) Well it sort of goes against the grain of my Scotch soul, but it looks like we have got to adjourn early today, so we will recess until Monday morning at ten thirty. I am going to ask you again, I am going to remind you again, not to discuss this case with anybody, not to permit anybody to discuss it with you. This case apparently will arouse a lot of interest in the newspapers. I know that you must, therefore, redouble your efforts not to read anything about it and not to watch anything on television that concerns itself with it. So we will recess until ten thirty Monday morning. I want to compliment you on your record of promptness, and I hope that you keep it up, and I wish all of you a pleasant weekend.

STAGE B

MAN IN THE STREET: What is your favorite TV show?

ANSWER: I don't have one.

ANSWER: "Milton Berle."

ANSWER: "Berle."

ANSWER: What's her name? "Lucy." No. "Howdy Doody."

ANSWER: Are you kidding?

STAGE A

The Screen: Volume I, Book III.

THE GOVERNMENT: Now, Mr. Greenglass, I think you have already told us that this lens mold, along with other things constructed in your shop, were used in connection with experimentation on the atomic bomb; is that correct?

DAVID GREENGLASS: They were.

THE GOVERNMENT: By the way, did you have any conversation with Rosenberg concerning the writing on the descriptive material?

DAVID GREENGLASS: I did. Julius came to the house and received this information, and my wife, in passing, remarked that the handwriting would be bad, and Julius said there was nothing to worry about, as *Ethel* would type it up—retype the information.

THE GOVERNMENT: Did you have any further conversation with Rosenberg on the occasion when you turned over this material?

DAVID GREENGLASS: Not at—he asked me to come to dinner, my wife and myself, for an evening a few days later—I can't remember—a day or two later.

THE GOVERNMENT: Now, I would like you to tell the Court and jury exactly what happened from the time you entered the apartment on that night until the time you left. By that I mean, tell us who was there, tell us what was said and by whom.

DAVID GREENGLASS: When I got to the apartment with my wife, there was Julius and Ethel Rosenberg and a woman by the name of Ann Sidorovich.

THE DEFENSE: What was that name?

DAVID GREENGLASS: Ann Sidorovich.

THE GOVERNMENT: Now, keep your voice up, Mr. Greenglass, and tell us exactly what happened on that evening, exactly what was said and by whom.

DAVID GREENGLASS: Well, the early part of the evening we just sat around and spoke socially with Ann and the Rosenbergs, and then Ann Sidorovich left. It was at this point that Julius said that this is the woman who he thinks would come out to see us, who will come out to see us at Albuquerque, to receive information from myself.

THE GOVERNMENT: What kind of information?

DAVID GREENGLASS: On the atomic bomb. And she would probably be the one to come out to see us. We then ate supper and after supper there was more conversation, and during this conversation there was a tentative plan brought forth, to the effect that my wife would come out to Albuquerque to stay with me, and when this woman, Ann or somebody, would come out to see us, they would go to Denver, and in a motion picture theater they would meet and exchange purses, my wife's purse having this information from Los Alamos, and of course, that is the way the information would be transmitted.

THE GOVERNMENT: Now, was anything said about the reason for Ann Sidorovich being present at the Rosenbergs' home on that particular night when you were there?

DAVID GREENGLASS: Yes, they wanted us to meet this Ann Sidorovich, so that we would know what she looked like; and that brought up a point, what if she does not come? So Julius said to my wife, "Well, I'll give you something so that you will be able to identify the person that does come."

THE GOVERNMENT: In other words, if Ann Sidorovich would come, she knew what you looked like; you knew what she looked like; but if somebody else would come, this would be mutual identification; is that right?

THE DEFENSE: Mr. Cohn, please don't repeat the answer.

THE GOVERNMENT: If I do so, your Honor, it is for the purpose of clarity. Strange names are coming in. However, I won't do it.

THE DEFENSE: You know why I don't want you to do it, because sometimes reemphasis—

THE GOVERNMENT: I will settle it by saying that I won't do it, your Honor. All right, go ahead.

DAVID GREENGLASS: Well, Rosenberg and my wife and Ethel went into the kitchen and I was in the living room; and then a little while later, after they had been there about five minutes or so, they came out and my wife had in her hand a Jello box side.

THE DEFENSE: Side?

THE GOVERNMENT: Side.

THE DEFENSE: S-i-d-e?

THE GOVERNMENT: That's right. About what size Jello box, the small size?

DAVID GREENGLASS: The kind you buy in your home.

THE GOVERNMENT: Right.

DAVID GREENGLASS: And it had been cut, and Julius had the other part to it, and when he came in with it, I said, "Oh, that is very clever," because I noticed how it fit, and he said, "The simplest things are the cleverest."

THE GOVERNMENT: Now, let me see if I understand that. Your wife had one side; is that correct?

DAVID GREENGLASS: That's right.

THE GOVERNMENT: Who kept the other side?

DAVID GREENGLASS: Julius had the other side.

THE GOVERNMENT: Was there any conversation as to what would be done with these two sides?

DAVID GREENGLASS: Well, my wife was to keep the side she had, and she was to use it for identification with the person who would come out to see us.

THE GOVERNMENT: May this be marked for identification, please? (*Marked Government's Exhibit 4 for identification.*) Your Honor, at this point I would like—this will be quite important—to have the witness take this Jello box and cut the correct side into two parts, just as he remembers it was cut on that night, in January of 1945, and I would like to ask him to indicate to the Court and jury which side he kept and which side Rosenberg kept. May I do that?

THE COURT: All right.

THE GOVERNMENT: Will you take Government's Exhibit 4 for identification and this pair of scissors, and address yourself to the appropriate side and cut it into two pieces? (*WITNESS cuts exhibit.*) The side that was cut was one of the thin sides; is that correct?

DAVID GREENGLASS: That's right; this is the side I had. (*Exhibiting.*)

THE GOVERNMENT: That was the side you had?

DAVID GREENGLASS: That's right.

THE GOVERNMENT: May we have this marked for identification as Government's Exhibit 4-A? (*Marked Government's Exhibit 4-A for identification.*) Where did you last see this other side on that night?

DAVID GREENGLASS: In Julius's hand.

THE GOVERNMENT: May we have the other side marked as 4-B for identification, your Honor? (*Marked Government's Exhibit 4-B for identification.*) Now, Mr. Greenglass, did Ann Sidorovich ever come out to see you?

DAVID GREENGLASS: No, she did not.

STAGE B

ANN SIDOROVICH: My husband and I were at the grand jury and we gave them everything. Well, they had some sort of story all set up—it was the Greenglass story—and if my answers didn't go along with theirs, then I was lying. Well,

they kept pounding on that meeting in January which I could not remember for the life of me. I'm just obstinate enough not to tell them that, unless I remember it myself. We were persecuted for several years by the FBI. We were under twenty-four-hour surveillance for over a year. We lost a great many friends. They would call my husband at work and get him out to the car and show him pictures and talk to him, I think simply to embarrass him. Now, I don't know if they honestly believed it. Maybe they did at first because it was so pat. It was a loose end and they would have felt better if I had confessed to it. Anyway, we were fortunate the people my husband worked with liked him or he would have been jobless for a long time. It was really a miracle his firm kept him on. That was really a miracle.

STAGE A

The Screen: Volume I, Book III.

THE GOVERNMENT: Did somebody else come out to see you?

DAVID GREENGLASS: Yes.

THE GOVERNMENT: Was it a man or woman?

DAVID GREENGLASS: It was a man.

THE GOVERNMENT: And when was this visit?

DAVID GREENGLASS: First Sunday in June, 1945.

THE GOVERNMENT: Did you at that time know the name of this man?

DAVID GREENGLASS: I did not.

THE GOVERNMENT: Do you now know his name?

DAVID GREENGLASS: Yes, I do.

THE GOVERNMENT: What is it?

DAVID GREENGLASS: Harry Gold.

STAGE B

HARRY GOLD (*speaks into a wire recorder*): I had completely forgotten the David Greenglass incident. For the life of me I could not recall Greenglass's name, so here's what the FBI did: A list of twenty names was selected; first we eliminated the least likely ten; then we cut the list further; finally a group of the three most likely was chosen, and lo, Greenglass was at the top. For his wife's name we did likewise, and again, Ruth headed the list.

STAGE A

The Screen: Volume 1, Book III.

THE GOVERNMENT: Will you tell us exactly what happened from the first minute you saw Gold?

The following is acted out on Stage B and echoes the testimony continuing on tape.

DAVID GREENGLASS: There was a knock on the door and I opened it. We had just completed eating breakfast, and there was a man standing in the hallway who asked if I was Mr. Greenglass and I said "yes." He stepped through the door and he said "Julius sent me," and I said "oh," and walked to my wife's purse, took out the wallet and took out the matched piece of the Jello box.

Live testimony resumes on Stage A.

THE GOVERNMENT: Mr. Greenglass, one thing I forgot to ask you about in connection with the meeting up at Rosenberg's apartment when you and your wife went there for dinner. After Ann Sidorovich had left the apartment, did you have a conversation with Mr. and Mrs. Rosenberg?

DAVID GREENGLASS: Well, at this point Mr. and Mrs. Rosenberg told me they were very happy to have me come in with them on this espionage work and that now that I was in it there would be no worry about any money they gave me; it was not a loan, it was money given to me because I was in this work—and that it was not a loan.

THE GOVERNMENT: Did they say anything about the source of that money?

DAVID GREENGLASS: They said it came from the Russians, who wanted me to have it.

THE GOVERNMENT: Now, in September, 1945, after you returned to New York, did you see Julius Rosenberg?

DAVID GREENGLASS: It was the morning after I came to New York.

THE GOVERNMENT: Now, would you tell us what happened? Where did you see him?

DAVID GREENGLASS: He came up to the apartment and he got me out of bed and we went into another room so my wife could dress.

THE GOVERNMENT: What did he say to you?

DAVID GREENGLASS: He said to me that he wanted to know what I had for him.

THE GOVERNMENT: Did you tell him what you had for him?

DAVID GREENGLASS: Yes. And I told him, "I think I have a pretty good—a pretty good description of the atom bomb."

THE GOVERNMENT: The atom bomb itself?

DAVID GREENGLASS: That's right.

The sketch, now marked Government's Exhibit 8, appears on screen while the testimony from a darkened Stage A continues.

THE GOVERNMENT: I show you Government's Exhibit 8 for identification, Mr. Greenglass, and ask you to examine it and tell us whether or not that is a replica of the sketch, a cross-section of the atomic bomb.

DAVID GREENGLASS: It is.

THE GOVERNMENT: And how does that compare to the sketch you gave to Rosenberg in September, 1945?

DAVID GREENGLASS: About the same thing. Maybe a little difference in size; that is all.

THE GOVERNMENT: Except for the size?

DAVID GREENGLASS: Yes.

THE GOVERNMENT: It is the same?

DAVID GREENGLASS: Yes.

THE GOVERNMENT: We offer this in evidence, your Honor.

THE DEFENSE: I object to it on the same ground I urged with respect to Government's Exhibit 2 and I now ask the Court to impound this exhibit so that it remains secret to the Court, the jury and counsel.

THE GOVERNMENT (SAYPOL): That is a rather strange request coming from the defendants.

THE DEFENSE: Not a strange request coming from me at the present.

THE GOVERNMENT: We have discussed that with the Court, as counsel knows, and I think nothing else need be said. If I had said it or my colleague, Mr. Cohn, had said it, there might have been some criticism.

THE COURT: As a matter of fact, there might have been some question on appeal. I welcome the suggestion coming from the defense because it removes the question completely.

THE GOVERNMENT: And I am happy to say that we join him.

THE GOVERNMENT (COHN): By the way, who was present when you handed the written material including this sketch over to Rosenberg?

DAVID GREENGLASS: My wife, my sister, Julius, and myself.

THE GOVERNMENT: By your sister, you mean Mrs. Rosenberg?

DAVID GREENGLASS: That is right.

THE GOVERNMENT: Now during the three years from 1946 until 1949 did you see Rosenberg at business from time to time?

DAVID GREENGLASS: Yes, every day almost.

THE GOVERNMENT: Did you have any conversations with him relating to espionage activities?

DAVID GREENGLASS: I did.

THE GOVERNMENT: Would you tell us those conversations which you recall?

DAVID GREENGLASS: Well, in '46 or '47 Julius Rosenberg made an offer to me to have the Russians pay for part of my schooling and the GI Bill of Rights to pay for the other part, and that I should go to college for the purpose of cultivating the friendships of people that I had known at Los Alamos and also to acquire new friendships with people who were in the field of research that are in those colleges, like physics and nuclear energy.

THE GOVERNMENT: Did he mention any particular institutions which he desired to have you attend?

DAVID GREENGLASS: Well, he would have wanted me to go to Chicago, University of Chicago, because there were people there that I had known at Los Alamos.

THE GOVERNMENT: Did he mention any other institutions?

DAVID GREENGLASS: M.I.T. and then later on N.Y.U.

THE GOVERNMENT: Now, did you ever agree to go to any of these schools?

DAVID GREENGLASS: I said I would try, but I never bothered.

STAGE B: RECONSTRUCTION (MOTHER, 1950)

TESSIE GREENGLASS: Hello? Hello? Hello; is this Mr. Bloch? Who? Alexander Bloch? Is this Mr. Emanuel Bloch? You're his father? Listen, this is Ethel Rosenberg's mother. How should I be? I'm an old woman. I'm not a healthy woman and Ethel's children have been dumped on me. It costs money and I am not well. No, they've been here two days already. What? No, the little one grinds his teeth in his sleep. That's right. He won't move from the window, he's watching all day. And the older one is a *vilde hya*, he's too wild. I just can't stand it. What's that? No, listen, they have to use the toilet on the landing and all the neighbors are complaining about the noise. What? Yes, I know all about it. But what's she doing to Davey? Will she save him? Why is she being so stupid? So what would be so terrible if she backed up Davey's story? She wouldn't be in this mess. What can you do? *Zionisten, Socialisten.* Yes, I know, I know. What? How can I take it easy? I can't do nothing. I'm killed. Somebody should be taking care of *me*. Well, I'm just warning you right now—if you don't get those brats out of my house, I'm going to dump them at the nearest police station.

STAGE B

The Screen: From the files of O. John Rogge, attorney for David Greenglass.

FBI: Let's have this again. You say you met Harry Gold where? Let's look at the picture again. You know he was arrested last month and confessed? There's no need to protect him. He came to see you in Albuquerque in 1945, didn't he?

DAVID GREENGLASS: Albuquerque, New Mexico.

FBI: Now, do you remember when? (*Pause.*) I said, do you remember when?

DAVID GREENGLASS: Not too well.

FBI: In June?

DAVID GREENGLASS: O.K.

FBI: Shall I put that in?

DAVID GREENGLASS: Put it in.

FBI: So he came to your place in Albuquerque in June of '45. But then you told him to come back later. Because you weren't ready yet, isn't that right?

DAVID GREENGLASS: All right. Put that in. But, listen, my wife wasn't in the room when this guy came to see me.

FBI: What did Gold say about who sent him? (*Pause.*) "Julius sent me"—was it something like that? (*Pause.*) Shall I put that in?

DAVID GREENGLASS: Put it in.

FBI: Now back to the Jello box. Do you remember where Gold said he got his half of the Jello box or where you got yours? (*Pause.*) I said, do you remember this Jello box business now? Can you recall it? All right, let's go over it all again. You say you met Gold where?

STAGE B

HARRY GOLD (*appears talking into his wire recorder*): If an attorney is appointed for me I would like him to understand very clearly that I must continue to give information to the FBI freely, that he is to put no restrictions whatever on that . . . regardless whether he thinks it is damaging to me or not.

STAGE A

The Screen: *Volume I, Book III.*

THE GOVERNMENT: Now did Rosenberg ever say anything to you about any reward that he had received from the Russians?

DAVID GREENGLASS: He stated that he had gotten a watch as a reward.

THE GOVERNMENT: Did he show you that watch?

DAVID GREENGLASS: He did.

THE GOVERNMENT: Did he mention anything else that he or his wife received from the Russians as a reward?

DAVID GREENGLASS: His wife received also a watch, a woman's watch, and I don't believe it was at the same time.

THE GOVERNMENT: When were you told about a watch that Mrs. Rosenberg had received, do you remember that?

DAVID GREENGLASS: I don't recall when that was but I do recall that my wife told me of it.

THE GOVERNMENT: You got that information from your wife, is that right?

DAVID GREENGLASS: That is right.

THE GOVERNMENT: Now, was there anything else that they received which they told you about?

DAVID GREENGLASS: I believe they told me they received a console table from the Russians.

THE GOVERNMENT: A console table?

DAVID GREENGLASS: That is right.

THE GOVERNMENT: Did you ever see that table?

DAVID GREENGLASS: I did.

THE GOVERNMENT: At their home?

DAVID GREENGLASS: I did.

THE GOVERNMENT: Did you have a conversation with the Rosenbergs concerning that table?

DAVID GREENGLASS: Yes, I did.

THE GOVERNMENT: Now will you tell us what that conversation was in connection with this console table as best you can recall it?

DAVID GREENGLASS: I admired the table and my wife asked Ethel when she bought a new piece of furniture; she said she had not bought it, she had gotten it as a gift and my wife said it was a very nice gift to get from a friend, and Julius said it was from his friend and it was a special kind of table, and he turned the table on its side to show why it was so special.

THE GOVERNMENT: And what did he show you when he turned the table on its side?

DAVID GREENGLASS: There was a portion of the table that was hollowed out for a lamp to fit underneath it so that the table could be used for photograph purposes, and he said when he used the table he darkened the room so that there would be no other light and he wouldn't be obvious to anyone looking in.

STAGE B: RECONSTRUCTION (LOVE, 1949)

JULIUS ROSENBERG: That was great. Shall I call my mother to check on Michael and Robbie? No, it's too late. Listen, get the guitar. They raised a lot of money tonight, at least $2,500. Come on, E, play my favorite.

ETHEL ROSENBERG (*tunes the guitar*): Boy, is he a good guy. I could listen all night to him. Not too loud now, with your singing.

JULIUS ROSENBERG: With just us I'm not embarrassed. O.K.? (*JULIUS and* ETHEL *sing two verses and the chorus of "Solidarity Forever," to the tune of the "Battle Hymn of the Republic."*) Great. Hey, you're as good as Leadbelly. (*They dance.*) In some ways, you're a lot better. You know what I mean?

ETHEL ROSENBERG: It's like a holiday tonight, Mr. Rosenberg. It's been a long time, Julie.

JULIUS ROSENBERG: I love you honey.

ETHEL ROSENBERG: I love you. (*JULIUS hums, off-key, as he starts to undress her and make love.*) Dear Julie, dear bunny.

STAGE A

The Screen: Volume I, Book III.

THE GOVERNMENT: Mr. Bloch may examine, your Honor.

THE DEFENSE: Do you bear any affection for your brother Bernie?

DAVID GREENGLASS: I do.

THE DEFENSE: Do you bear any affection for your sister Ethel?

DAVID GREENGLASS: I do.

THE DEFENSE: You realize, do you not, that Ethel is being tried for conspiracy to commit espionage?

DAVID GREENGLASS: I do.

THE DEFENSE: And you realize the grave implications of that charge?

DAVID GREENGLASS: I do.

THE DEFENSE: And you realize the possible death penalty, in the event that Ethel is convicted by this jury, do you not?

DAVID GREENGLASS: I do.

THE DEFENSE: And you bear affection for her?

DAVID GREENGLASS: I do.

THE DEFENSE: This moment?

DAVID GREENGLASS: At this moment—

THE DEFENSE: And yesterday?

DAVID GREENGLASS: And yesterday.

THE DEFENSE: And the day before yesterday?

DAVID GREENGLASS: And as far back as I ever met her and knew her.

STAGE B: RECONSTRUCTION (DREAMS, 1949)

ETHEL ROSENBERG: . . . so in the dream, I'm all alone in the Hungarian bakery. That's it—I own the bakery or I have control over it. And that's it, I just walk around. Is this an eating dream? Oh, and my dress is too short, as if it had shrunk. But I don't mind. It's kind of . . . kind of sexy.

A long pause.

THE DOCTOR: What about that?

ETHEL ROSENBERG: This is not an eating dream. We haven't had sex in weeks. I was thinking the other day that if we could just get away. Maybe if I could get the kids into some free day camp in the country. You know what I mean?

Pause.

THE DOCTOR: Do you want to go on?

ETHEL ROSENBERG: It's like the dream. I'm alone in the bakery and I have control. If I didn't have the children I would have—what? Not control . . . no, if I weren't married, I wouldn't have any children and I'd have—what? What? Opportunities? Opportunities! (*She groans.*) You know, my problem is I don't know what my problem is.

THE DOCTOR: What kind of "opportunities"?

ETHEL ROSENBERG: I don't know. "Things." This is crazy; the kids are my whole life. Maybe that's my problem. My outside life used to be so full that I had to write out a schedule every week. I got up at six and practiced my music for an hour; went to work; at lunch hour I studied my scores; at night, lessons, rehearsal. I was really going to be something. (*Pause.*) I'm always saying I'm going to go back to singing or take up guitar, I don't know. I was supposed to be the big singer, an actress . . . everything. (*Pause.*) What does the bakery stand for?

THE DOCTOR: Go on about the "opportunities," if you can.

ETHEL ROSENBERG: The hour's up, isn't it? No, the Hungarian bakery has something to do with you. The dress, the whole thing. Remember, I made fun of your accent that time? That was a big day for me.

THE DOCTOR: Ya, it's very painful for you to show anger.

ETHEL ROSENBERG: It's time, no?

THE DOCTOR: Ya, time. I think this dream has something to it. We see next time.

ETHEL ROSENBERG (*opens her purse*): Good-bye. Oh, by the way, I brought a sample of my poetry. Purely for analytic purposes, as they say. Well, good-bye. Listen, take care of your cold. I'll see you the same time on Tuesday? Right?

THE DOCTOR: Right.

STAGE A

The Screen: Volume I, Book III.

THE DEFENSE: Mr. Greenglass, you were questioned many times without your lawyer, isn't that true?

DAVID GREENGLASS: There were other times my lawyer was present. I don't remember whether it was the third time, fourth time, or the fifteenth time.

THE DEFENSE: Do you remember what you talked about to the FBI?

DAVID GREENGLASS: When I came down to talk to the FBI I talked about a number of things; whatever their interrogation led to, it loosened the springs of my memory and I was able to remember things I had forgotten.

THE DEFENSE: From the time you told your wife you were not interested in this work of espionage, until the next morning, did you consult with anybody?

DAVID GREENGLASS: I consulted with memories and voices in my mind.

THE DEFENSE: Are you aware that you are smiling?

DAVID GREENGLASS: Not very.

THE DEFENSE: Did you believe you were doing an honorable or a dishonorable thing?

DAVID GREENGLASS: Well, I had a kind of hero worship there and I did not want my hero to fail.

THE DEFENSE: You say you had a hero worship? Who was your hero?

DAVID GREENGLASS (*smiling*): Julius Rosenberg.

STAGE B

HARRY GOLD: I am absolutely fascinated by a man with ability and therefore I was fascinated by—or rather, attracted to—Klaus Fuchs. We were kindred souls, as good friends as it is possible for two men to be.

STAGE A

The Screen: Volume I, Book III.

THE DEFENSE: Now, were you given any reference books or textbooks, while you were in jail since your arrest, relating to any scientific matter?

DAVID GREENGLASS: No, I didn't—nobody gave me any.

THE DEFENSE: Did you read any scientific books while you have been in jail?

DAVID GREENGLASS: Just science fiction.

THE DEFENSE: That is, of course, not a basic theoretical journal, is it?

DAVID GREENGLASS: No.

THE DEFENSE: That is a popular kind of scientific periodical?

DAVID GREENGLASS: That's right.

THE DEFENSE: Now, Mr. Greenglass, I believe you testified that you graduated from high school here in New York City?

DAVID GREENGLASS: Yes.

THE DEFENSE: And I think you testified that you went to Brooklyn Polytech?

DAVID GREENGLASS: Right.

THE DEFENSE: How long did you go to Brooklyn Polytech?

DAVID GREENGLASS: Six months.

THE DEFENSE: And how many courses did you take during those six months?

DAVID GREENGLASS: About eight different courses.

THE DEFENSE: And did you fail—

THE GOVERNMENT: I object to that, your Honor. What difference does it make?

THE DEFENSE: I am coming to a new subject now, your Honor.

THE COURT: I assume you are.

THE DEFENSE: Yes, and I wish you will bear with me, because I am going to connect this up.

THE COURT: All right.

THE GOVERNMENT: Well, I will let Mr. Bloch finish his question. That is as far as I will commit myself at the moment, your Honor.

THE COURT: Right.

THE DEFENSE: Did you fail in your subjects?

DAVID GREENGLASS: I was young at the time, about eighteen, and I liked to play around more than I liked to go to school, so I cut classes almost the whole term. Simple.

THE DEFENSE: How many of the eight courses that you took did you fail?

DAVID GREENGLASS: I failed them all.

THE DEFENSE: Did you ever get a degree in science?

DAVID GREENGLASS: I did not get a degree.

THE DEFENSE: Did you ever get a B.S.?

DAVID GREENGLASS: I did not.

THE DEFENSE: Did you ever get an engineering degree?

DAVID GREENGLASS: I did not.

THE DEFENSE: From any recognized institution?

DAVID GREENGLASS: I did not.

THE DEFENSE: Have you pursued any other organized and formal courses, held under the auspices of a recognized educational institution, apart from the Brooklyn Polytech and the Pratt Institute courses that you have mentioned you took?

DAVID GREENGLASS: I did not.

THE DEFENSE: Do you know anything about the basic theory of atomic energy?

DAVID GREENGLASS: I know something about it, yes. I am no scientific—I am no scientific expert, but I know something about it.

THE DEFENSE: Did you ever take courses in calculus?

DAVID GREENGLASS: I did not.

THE DEFENSE: Differential calculus?

DAVID GREENGLASS: No.

THE DEFENSE: Or thermodynamics?

DAVID GREENGLASS: I did not.

THE DEFENSE: Or nuclear physics?

DAVID GREENGLASS: I did not.

THE DEFENSE: Or atomic physics?

DAVID GREENGLASS: I did not.

THE DEFENSE: Or quantum mechanics?

DAVID GREENGLASS: I did not.

THE DEFENSE: Or advanced calculus?

DAVID GREENGLASS: I did not.

THE COURT: What is this all about? I haven't heard anybody—

THE DEFENSE: Why, if the Court please—

THE COURT: I haven't heard anybody testify to your complete list.

THE DEFENSE: I wonder, if the Court please, if this might be a convenient place to stop?

THE COURT: Have you got much more to go, Mr. Bloch?

THE DEFENSE: I am afraid so.

THE COURT: Do you think perhaps if we give you a good substantial lunch period you might shorten it?

THE DEFENSE: I will try.

THE COURT: We will recess for an hour and a half for lunch, Mr. Bloch, and that should give you an opportunity to go over your notes and see whether you can shorten it in any respect. We will recess until two twenty-five.

STAGE B

MAN IN THE STREET: What is your opinion of the addition of the words "under God" to the Pledge of Allegiance?

ANSWER: No comment.

ANSWER: It's about time, you know what I mean?

ANSWER: Since when?

ANSWER: Leave me alone.

ANSWER: I say, God bless us.

STAGE A

The Screen: *Volume I, Book III.*

THE DEFENSE: Now, while you were in business at 370 East Houston Street, did you have any quarrels with your brother-in-law Julius?

DAVID GREENGLASS: Only business quarrels. It didn't amount to anything.

THE DEFENSE: Now let us find out. Julius was the outside man, was he not?

DAVID GREENGLASS: That's right.

THE DEFENSE: He was the one who went out and tried to get orders, right?

DAVID GREENGLASS: That's correct.

THE DEFENSE: You were the machine shop?

DAVID GREENGLASS: That's right.

THE DEFENSE: Working on the machines?

DAVID GREENGLASS: That's right.

THE DEFENSE: And you had a number of employees from time to time, did you not?

DAVID GREENGLASS: That's right.

THE DEFENSE: Now, weren't there repeated quarrels between you and Julius when Julius accused you of trying to be a boss and not working on machines?

DAVID GREENGLASS: There were quarrels of every type and every kind. I mean there was arguments over personality, there was arguments over money, there was arguments over the way the shop was run, there was arguments over the way the outside was run. It was quarrels, just business quarrels—

THE DEFENSE: Did you ever come to blows with Julius?

DAVID GREENGLASS: No, I didn't.

THE DEFENSE: Do you remember an incident when you were sitting in the corner candy store of Houston and Avenue D when your brother Bernie had to separate the both of you?

DAVID GREENGLASS: It slipped my mind.

THE DEFENSE: What slipped your mind?

DAVID GREENGLASS: I mean I didn't remember it.

THE DEFENSE: Do you remember it now?

DAVID GREENGLASS: I do.

THE DEFENSE: *You don't?*

DAVID GREENGLASS: *I do.*

THE DEFENSE: *You do? Did you hit Julius?*

DAVID GREENGLASS: I—I don't recall if I actually hit him.

THE DEFENSE: No more questions.

THE CLERK: Call Ruth Greenglass to the stand.

She is sworn.
The Screen: Volume I, Book IV.

THE GOVERNMENT: Now, Mrs. Greenglass, will you keep your voice up so that all the members of the jury can hear you?

RUTH GREENGLASS: Yes.

THE GOVERNMENT: Where do you live, Mrs. Greenglass?

RUTH GREENGLASS: 265 Rivington Street.

THE GOVERNMENT: And you are the wife of David Greenglass?

RUTH GREENGLASS: I am.

THE GOVERNMENT: Do you know that David Greenglass was named as a defendant in the indictment which is now on trial?

RUTH GREENGLASS: I do.

THE GOVERNMENT: And you know, do you not, that you are named as a coconspirator but not as a defendant in that indictment?

RUTH GREENGLASS: Yes.

THE GOVERNMENT: Now, do you recall a time when your husband was inducted into the Army?

RUTH GREENGLASS: Yes.

THE GOVERNMENT: Now, I call your attention to the time in November, 1944. Were you at that time planning to go out and visit your husband in New Mexico?

RUTH GREENGLASS: Yes, I was.

THE GOVERNMENT: And prior to this time that you left New York did you have a conversation with the defendants Julius and Ethel Rosenberg?

RUTH GREENGLASS: Yes, I did.

THE GOVERNMENT: Now, will you state, as best you can recollect, the substance of that conversation?

RUTH GREENGLASS: Yes, Julius said that I might have noticed that for some time he and Ethel had not been actively pursuing any Communist Party activities, that they didn't buy the *Daily Worker* at the usual newsstand. . . .

STAGE B

MAN IN THE STREET: What do you think of the new "TV dinners"?

ANSWER: Stinks.

ANSWER: Well, they're fast.

ANSWER: What?

ANSWER: I like the chicken pie.

ANSWER: I like the beef.

STAGE A

The Screen: Volume I, Book IV.

THE COURT: Madam, would you sit back?

RUTH GREENGLASS: Yes, I am sorry.

THE COURT: Just speak a little slower, please.

RUTH GREENGLASS: Yes.

THE DEFENSE: Now, Mrs. Greenglass, didn't something happen in 1949 that created hostility between you and the Rosenbergs?

RUTH GREENGLASS: No, there was no hostility.

THE DEFENSE: Did you ever visit the Pitt machine shop in 1949?

RUTH GREENGLASS: Yes. It was near my home. About five blocks. I used to go there with the carriage.

THE DEFENSE: Did you know that your husband and Mr. Rosenberg had had differences about the business that was being conducted there?

RUTH GREENGLASS: I heard that.

THE DEFENSE: Didn't your husband accuse Mr. Rosenberg of not treating him right?

RUTH GREENGLASS: My husband didn't accuse him of anything, Mr. Bloch.

THE DEFENSE: There were arguments, weren't there?

RUTH GREENGLASS: There weren't arguments. There were discussions.

THE DEFENSE: Didn't you complain to your mother-in-law and to other members of your family that your husband was being treated as a menial instead of one of the owners of the business?

RUTH GREENGLASS: I said I didn't think my husband was being paid commensurate with the work done.

THE DEFENSE: Was it on account of this friction that had occurred between your husband and Mr. Rosenberg that you stopped visiting them?

RUTH GREENGLASS: No, Mr. Bloch, there was no friction involved. We had to have money for food and he had to go to work.

THE DEFENSE: Are you hostile to either Mr. or Mrs. Rosenberg?

RUTH GREENGLASS: No.

THE DEFENSE: Are you friendly towards them?

RUTH GREENGLASS: I have friendly feelings.

STAGE B

The Screen: From the files of O. John Rogge, attorney for David Greenglass.

FBI: Mrs. Greenglass, your husband seems to have his stories mixed up again.

RUTH GREENGLASS: My husband lies when there's no reason for it. Sometimes he acts like a character in the movies. Last year he had—the doctor called it—a psychological heart attack. And once, he had a fever; he ran up and down the halls, in the nude, yelling "Lead pants, Elephant."

FBI (*very slowly*): He say he wants to take back some of his confession. . . . You know that'll mean going back out West to New Mexico on that uranium business . . . those stealing charges against him . . . and that's what we want to . . . avoid.

RUTH GREENGLASS: You let me talk to him.

The Screen:
    CONVICTED SPY, GOLD, IS STAR U.S. WITNESS

STAGE A

THE CLERK: Call Harry Gold to the stand. Do you swear to tell the whole truth and nothing but the truth?

HARRY GOLD: I do.

SAYPOL conducts the GOLD questioning.

The Screen: Volume I, Book IV.

THE GOVERNMENT: Now you are the Harry Gold, are you not, that is named as a coconspirator in the indictment which is—in the indictment which includes the Rosenbergs?

HARRY GOLD: Yes, I am.

THE GOVERNMENT: Now do you stand convicted of any crime?

HARRY GOLD: Yes, I do.

THE GOVERNMENT: Of what crime?

HARRY GOLD: I stand convicted of espionage.

THE GOVERNMENT: What was the sentence that was imposed upon you?

HARRY GOLD: I was given a sentence of thirty years in the Federal Penitentiary.

THE GOVERNMENT: Now, did you meet Klaus Fuchs, Dr. Klaus Fuchs, some time in the middle of June, 1944?

HARRY GOLD: Yes, I did.

THE GOVERNMENT: Where did you meet Fuchs?

HARRY GOLD: I met Fuchs in Woodside, Queens.

THE GOVERNMENT: Did you have a conversation with Fuchs at this time? And what was the conversation?

HARRY GOLD: The conversation had to do with the fact that Fuchs had given me further information on the progress of the work going on in New York by a joint American and British project, which project was aimed at producing an atomic bomb.

The Screen:
ATOM BOMB SHELTERS FOR CITY AT COST OF
$450,000,000 URGED

This headline appears and remains until the end of the Act. The media are now beginning to throb with GOLD-*related thematic imagery. The comics and cartoons return.*

THE GOVERNMENT: Who was your Soviet superior at this time?

HARRY GOLD: Anatoli Yakovlev.

THE GOVERNMENT: Now, in May of 1945 did you have a meeting with Yakovlev?

HARRY GOLD: Yes, I did.

THE GOVERNMENT: Now, will you tell the jury what happened on this occasion?

HARRY GOLD: Yakovlev told me that he wanted me to go to Albuquerque, New Mexico. I protested. Yakovlev told me that I didn't understand that this was an extremely important business, that I just had to go to Albuquerque and he said, "That is an order," and that was all. I agreed to go. Yakovlev then gave me a sheet of paper; it was onionskin paper, and on it was typed the following: First the name "Greenglass," just "Greenglass." Then a number "High Street"; all that I can recall about the number is that the last figure—it was a low number and the last figure, the second figure was zero and the last figure was either five, seven, or nine; and then underneath that was "Albuquerque, New Mexico." The last thing that was on the paper was "Recognition signal. I come from Julius." In addition to this, Yakovlev gave me a piece of cardboard, which appeared to have been cut from a packaged food of some sort. It was cut in an odd shape and Yakovlev told me that the man, Greenglass, whom I would meet in Albuquerque, would have the matching piece of cardboard.

THE GOVERNMENT: Now will you tell the jury about your last contact with Yakovlev?

HARRY GOLD: Yakovlev called me and said he would meet me at the Earl Theatre in the Bronx at eight o'clock that night. At exactly eight o'clock I was in the upstairs lounge of the Earl Theatre.

THE GOVERNMENT: What happened there?

HARRY GOLD: There I was accosted by a man. The man who met me was not Yakovlev. He was tall, about six feet two, had blond hair and a very determined feature. He walked with a catlike stride, almost on the balls of his feet. (*He leaves the courtroom. He poses and whispers.*) I first got involved in spying through Tom Black of Jersey City. He was a fantastic man. He coiled a pet snake around his neck and he had a trained crow that he used to pitch marbles to. I got involved in order to get Black off my neck about joining the Communist Party. I didn't want to. I didn't like them—they were a bunch of wacked-up bohemians. Then there was Steve Swartz. A virtual giant; long arms, big feet, big . . . (*All the time axes, from political to personal, are building.*) I recall him distinctly. He was at least six foot—possibly six foot one—and had an extremely savage face, tough-looking face, a plug-ugly.

STAGE B

The Screen: From the files of John D. M. Hamilton, attorney for Harry Gold.

FBI: Didn't you have some recognition sign as between the two of you? Some sign?

HARRY GOLD: Yes, we did. I believe that it involved the name of a man and was something on the order of Bob sent me or Benny sent me or John sent me or something like that.

FBI: Then in this case you would've had to say "Julius sent me," huh?

HARRY GOLD: Who's Julius?

Now the action builds, cross-cuts from whispers to screams at the end.

THE CLERK: Abraham Lincoln Brigade, Abraham Lincoln School, Chicago, Illinois; Action Committee for Free Spain Now, American League against War and Fascism, American Association for Reconstruction in Yugoslavia, Inc.,

American Committee for Protection of Foreign Born, American Committee for a Democratic Greece, American Council on Soviet Relations, American Croatian Congress, American Jewish Labor Council, American League for Peace and Democracy, American Peace Mobilization, American Polish Labor Council, American Russian Institute of San Francisco . . .

HARRY GOLD: First I created a wife I did not have. Then there had to be children to go along with the wife, and they had to grow old—it's a wonder steam didn't come out of my ears sometimes. When I went on a mission for the Russians, I immediately turned a switch in my mind; and when I was done, I turned the switch again and I was once again Harry Gold—just a chemist.

RUTH GREENGLASS: David! David!

She is following a running, nude DAVID GREEN-GLASS.

DAVID GREENGLASS: Lead pants! Lead pants! *Elephant!*

They disappear. JULIUS and ETHEL ROSENBERG stand transfixed in the midst of the rising madness.

THE VOICE OF J. EDGAR HOOVER (*over the action*): The unknown man simply had to be found.

HARRY GOLD: In late January or early February of 1944, I received my instructions. I was to walk on an East Side street; I was to carry an extra pair of gloves in my hand and a book with a green binding. I was supposed to meet a man who would carry a tennis ball in his left hand. This was on a deserted street, alongside an excavation, and I saw a slim, boyish-looking man, wearing horn-rimmed glasses, and that was Klaus Fuchs. We were as close as any two men could be.

KLAUS FUCHS: There are also other crimes I have committed that are not crimes in the eyes of the law. I used my Marxian philosophy to conceal my thoughts in two separate compartments. Looking back at it now, the best way is to call it controlled schizophrenia.

HARRY GOLD: When I was done I turned the switch again and I was once again Harry Gold —just a chemist.

TESSIE GREENGLASS (*This is simultaneous.*): Hello? Hello? Hello; is this Mr. Bloch? Who? Alexander Bloch? Is this Mr. Emanuel Bloch? You're his father? Listen, this is Ethel Rosenberg's mother. How should I be? I'm an old woman. I'm not a healthy woman and Ethel's children have been dumped on me. . . .

THE GOVERNMENT (*We hear or see a reprise of part of the prosecution's opening charge and THE COURT. This is simultaneous action.*): The evidence will come from witnesses and you will see and hear that the witnesses are telling the truth as each link in this chain is forged and put into place, by testimony, by documentary evidence. Testimony and documentary evidence which will point conclusively to one thing and one thing alone—the guilt of the defendants.

ROY COHN appears and the MAN IN THE STREET; they all begin a total recapitulation. All of THE GOVERNMENT evidence is repeated on the screen. JULIUS and ETHEL ROSENBERG stand motionless in the center.

HARRY GOLD: While riding in a trolley car one day in Philadelphia I met and fell in love with a beautiful girl named Helen, who had one brown eye and one blue eye. I tried to court her but a wealthy rival named Frank, whose uncle manufactured peanut-chew candy, beat me out.

THE CLERK: Call Harry Gold to the stand. Do you swear to tell the whole truth and nothing but the truth?

HARRY GOLD: I at one time considered marrying and the girl in question told me one time that she didn't think I was really in love with her. She felt that I was too cold. What she didn't know was that what made me cold all over and especially down here was the thought that if we were married and this thing came to light, what then? But I lost her anyway to someone called Nigger Nate. Later I lost my wife to an elderly, rich, real estate broker. I actually had no wife and two twin children. I was a bachelor and had always been one. (*Screaming.*) It was my mother I lived with. My father's name was Sam and so was my Soviet spy master.

DAVID GREENGLASS: *Elephant!* Lead pants! *Elephant!*

The FBI chases DAVID GREENGLASS. *The* AGENT *shouts repeatedly, "Shall I put that in?"* GOLD *and* FUCHS *talk at once.*

HARRY GOLD: Bob sent me, or Benny sent me, or John sent me . . .

KLAUS FUCHS (*continues to repeat*): There are also other crimes I have committed . . .

THE VOICE OF J. EDGAR HOOVER (*over the action*): The unknown man simply had to be found. . . .

HARRY GOLD (*repeating simultaneously until the end of the Act*): We were as close as any two men could be. Nigger Nate, Nigger Nate. We were as close as any two men . . .

On the screen the formula $E = MC^2$ *alternates with* GREENGLASS'S *sketch (Exhibit 8) until the blackout.*

THE VOICE OF JOSEPH MCCARTHY (*This is heard punctuating the action until the blackout*):
I have here in my hand a list of two hundred and five.
I have here in my hand a list of fifty-seven.
I have here in my hand a list of ten.
I have here in my hand a list of one hundred and sixteen.
I have here in my hand a list of one hundred and twenty-one.
I have here in my hand a list of one hundred and six.

THE VOICE OF J. EDGAR HOOVER (*over* GREENGLASS *and* GOLD, *the voice repeats until blackout*): The unknown man simply had to be found. . . . The bomb has been stolen. Find the thieves, find the thieves, find the thieves. . . .

HARRY GOLD (*kneels and weeps*): I always lent other people money. Even when I didn't know them or even if I had to borrow to do it. (*He screams.*) I was known as Raymond and Martin and Dave from Pittsburgh!

THE VOICE OF JOSEPH MCCARTHY: These young men, these fine young men . . .

This is repeated over and over as the entire vocal chorus rises to the blackout. The lunatic chorus involves, by now, the whole cast. The time capsule roars with imagery. At the apogee, the atom bomb wipes out all sound and imagery. There is dead silence. On the screen there is a close-up of HARRY GOLD.

THE VOICE OF HARRY GOLD: Who's Julius?

The picture freezes in the silence.

BLACKOUT

The Government's Exhibit 8 covers the screen during the intermission. Before the beginning of the second act we again see the disclaimer:

The Screen:
EVERY WORD YOU WILL HEAR OR SEE ON THIS STAGE IS A DOCUMENTED QUOTATION FROM TRIAL TRANSCRIPTS AND ORIGINAL SOURCES OR A RECONSTRUCTION FROM ACTUAL EVENTS.

ACT TWO

The dim siren. On the dark stage the CHORUS *intones and the gods slowly appear to speak and then disappear into darkness.*

STAGE B

MAN IN THE STREET (*in darkness*): Freud, have mercy on us.

FREUD: The state has forbidden to the individual the practice of wrongdoing because it desires to monopolize it itself. The warring state permits itself every misdeed, every act of violence. It practices deliberate lying and deception. The state exacts the utmost degree of obedience and sacrifice from its citizens, but at the same time treats them as children by maintaining an excess of secrecy, and a censorship of news. It leaves its citizens intellectually oppressed and defenseless against every unfavorable turn of events and every sinister rumor. The state makes unabashed confession of its lust for power, and the private individual is called upon to give his sanctions in the name of patriotism. Thus, all men suffer the feeling of blood-guilt.

MAN IN THE STREET (*in darkness*): Nietzsche, have mercy on us.

NIETZSCHE: Liberal institutions cease to be liberal as soon as they are attained: Later on, there are no worse and no more thorough injurers of freedom than liberal institutions. . . . In the political realm hostility becomes spiritual. The new state needs enemies more than friends: In opposition alone does it feel itself necessary, only in opposition does it *become* necessary. And it is the same for the "internal enemy."

Thus all states are now ranged against each other: They presuppose their neighbors' bad faith and their own good faith. . . . If the scientific *spirit* is lost, then all the fruits of science could not prevent a return to a state of superstition and witchcraft.

The whole problem of the Jews exists only in these same nation-states for here their energy and intelligence, their accumulated capital of spirit and will, gathered from generation to generation through a long schooling in suffering, has aroused mass envy and hatred. In all contemporary nations, therefore, the literary obscenity is spreading of leading the Jews to slaughter—as scapegoats of every conceivable public and internal misfortune.

Men are now called "free" so that they may be judged and punished—so that they may be made guilty.

Beware! Political superiority without any true human superiority is a calamity. It is time to make amends, to be ashamed of this false power!

MAN IN THE STREET (*in darkness*): Marx, have mercy on us.

MARX: The binding force of civilized society is the state. The state, that is, of the ruling class. A machine for keeping down the oppressed and exploited class. This state plays on the most sordid instincts and passions of mankind. Naked greed has been the moving spirit of the state from the first day of its existence to the present time.

In the highest form of the state, the democratic republic, wealth exercises its power indirectly, but all the more surely. Thus in the direct corruption of officials, America provides the classic example . . . now there is only one revolutionary emotion—*shame*.

Darkness.

MAN IN THE STREET: Will an increase in the postal rate make any difference to you?

ANSWER: No. . . .

ANSWER: Certainly. . . .

ANSWER: No. . . .

ANSWER: No. . . .

ANSWER: What?

STAGE A

THE CLERK: Call Julius Rosenberg to the stand.

He is sworn.

The Screen: Volume II, Book I.

THE DEFENSE: Now, Mr. Rosenberg, please keep your voice up. Don't make the mistake some of the witnesses made and lower it as you go along. What is your full name?

JULIUS ROSENBERG: Julius Rosenberg.

THE DEFENSE: And how old are you?

JULIUS ROSENBERG: Thirty-three.

THE DEFENSE: Where were you born?

JULIUS ROSENBERG: I was born in New York City.

THE DEFENSE: Will you tell the Court and Jury the schools that you attended?

JULIUS ROSENBERG: I attended Public School 88 on the Lower East Side in Manhattan, and then I attended Public School 96, a junior high school. At the same time I attended Hebrew School, the Downtown Talmud Torah. While I attended Seward Park High School, I attended Hebrew High School on East Broadway, New York. I entered the College of the City of New York in 1934.

THE DEFENSE: Now, are you single or are you married?

JULIUS ROSENBERG: I am married.

THE DEFENSE: To whom are you married?

JULIUS ROSENBERG: I am married to Ethel Rosenberg.

THE DEFENSE: And as a result of that marriage did you have any children?

JULIUS ROSENBERG: Yes.

THE DEFENSE: What are the names of those children?

JULIUS ROSENBERG: The oldest boy's name is Michael Allen Rosenberg.

THE DEFENSE: How old is he?

JULIUS ROSENBERG: He is eight years old. And the youngest, his name is Robert Harry Rosenberg.

THE DEFENSE: And how old is he?

JULIUS ROSENBERG: Four years old.

THE DEFENSE: Now, tell me, Mr. Rosenberg, you received an engineering degree, did you not?

JULIUS ROSENBERG: That is correct.

THE DEFENSE: Did you, in the course of your studies looking toward getting that degree, ever take courses in nuclear physics?

JULIUS ROSENBERG: I did not.

THE COURT: At any time prior to January, 1945, had anybody discussed with you, anybody at all, discussed with you the atom bomb?

JULIUS ROSENBERG: No, sir, they did not.

THE COURT: Did anybody discuss with you nuclear fission?

JULIUS ROSENBERG: No, sir.

THE COURT: Did anybody discuss with you any projects that had been going on in Germany?

JULIUS ROSENBERG: No, sir.

THE COURT: On the atom bomb?

JULIUS ROSENBERG: No, sir.

THE COURT: No?

JULIUS ROSENBERG: No, sir.

THE COURT: Did you ever discuss the respective preferences of economic systems between Russia and the United States?

JULIUS ROSENBERG: Well, your Honor, if you will let me answer that question in my own way, I want to explain that question.

THE COURT: Go ahead.

JULIUS ROSENBERG: First of all, I am not an expert on different economic systems, but in my normal social intercourse with my friends we discussed matters like that. And I believe there are merits in both systems, I mean from what I have been able to read and ascertain.

THE COURT: I am not talking about your belief today. I am talking about your belief at that time, in January, 1945.

JULIUS ROSENBERG: Well, that is what I am talking about. At that time, what I believed at that time I still believe today. In the first place, I heartily approve our system of justice as performed in this country, Anglo-Saxon jurispru-

dence. I am in favor, heartily in favor, of our Constitution and Bill of Rights and I owe my allegiance to my country at all times.

THE DEFENSE: Do you owe allegiance to any other country?

JULIUS ROSENBERG: No, I do not.

THE DEFENSE: Have you any divided allegiance?

JULIUS ROSENBERG: I do not, and in discussing the merits of other forms of government, I discussed that with my friends on the basis of the performance of what they accomplished, and I felt that the Soviet government has improved the lot of the underdog there, has made a lot of progress in eliminating illiteracy, has done a lot of reconstruction work and built up a lot of resources, and at the same time I felt that they contributed a major share in destroying the Hitler beast who killed six million of my coreligionists, and I feel emotional about that thing.

THE DEFENSE: Did you feel that way in 1945?

JULIUS ROSENBERG: Yes, I felt that way in 1945.

THE DEFENSE: Do you feel that way today?

JULIUS ROSENBERG: I still feel that way.

THE COURT: Did you approve the communistic system of Russia over the capitalistic system in this country?

JULIUS ROSENBERG: I am not an expert on those things, your Honor, and I did not make any such direct statement.

THE COURT: Did you ever make any comparisons, in the sense that the Court has asked you, about whether you preferred one system over another?

JULIUS ROSENBERG: No, I did not. I would like to state that my personal opinions are that the people of every country should decide by themselves what kind of government they want. If the English want a king, it is their business. If the Russians want communism, it is their business. If the Americans want our form of government, it is our business. I feel that the majority of people should decide for themselves what kind of government they want.

STAGE B

MAN IN THE STREET: Do you vote for the man or the party?

ANSWER: The man.

ANSWER: The man.

ANSWER: The man.

ANSWER: Decline to state.

STAGE A

The Screen: Volume II, Books I–II

THE DEFENSE: Did you tell Ruth or Dave Greenglass that you were entertaining and spending $50 to $75 a night in connection with your espionage work?

JULIUS ROSENBERG: I didn't tell Dave or Ruth Greenglass or anybody that.

THE DEFENSE: Did you ever entertain anybody for any espionage work?

JULIUS ROSENBERG: I did not, sir.

THE DEFENSE: Tell me, how many suits have you bought for the last eleven years?

JULIUS ROSENBERG: About five suits.

THE DEFENSE: Did you come into court with a coat?

JULIUS ROSENBERG: Yes, sir.

THE DEFENSE: When did you buy that coat?

JULIUS ROSENBERG: I would say it was either 1941 or 1942.

THE DEFENSE: Did you ever buy a winter overcoat since then?

JULIUS ROSENBERG: No, sir. I did not.

THE DEFENSE: How much did you pay for that coat?

JULIUS ROSENBERG: Well, I estimate it was somewhere about $55.

THE DEFENSE: How much do you pay for your suits?

JULIUS ROSENBERG: About $26.

THE DEFENSE: Tell us what clothes you bought for your wife just roughly during this eleven-year period from 1940 to 1950.

JULIUS ROSENBERG: When I got a per diem check once while working for the Government.

THE DEFENSE: When was this?

JULIUS ROSENBERG: I think it was about the same time I bought my coat, I bought her a fur coat.

THE DEFENSE: How much did you pay for it?

JULIUS ROSENBERG: Eighty dollars, and we remodeled it a couple of times and she still has it.

Well, my wife bought her own clothes. I didn't buy her clothes for her.

THE DEFENSE: Do you know about how much she spent on clothes for the last ten years?

JULIUS ROSENBERG: Well, sir, I would estimate a maximum of about $300.

THE DEFENSE: Mr. Rosenberg, you say you were aware of some trouble with stealing from the Army that David Greenglass may have been involved in when he was at Los Alamos in 1944?

JULIUS ROSENBERG: That is correct.

THE DEFENSE: When you heard he was being questioned by the FBI did you think it concerned this stealing?

JULIUS ROSENBERG: I didn't know. It had been years before.

THE DEFENSE: Will you describe what took place when David Greenglass approached you, in June of 1950, for help?

JULIUS ROSENBERG: He asked me to meet him. He was very excited when—

STAGE B

DAVID GREENGLASS: Julie, come on, where've you been? Come on, listen, will you?

JULIUS ROSENBERG: Calm yourself, take it easy. What's troubling you?

DAVID GREENGLASS: Julie, I'm in a terrible jam.

JULIUS ROSENBERG: No—I realize you've been asking for money, you've been telling me to go to my doctor for a certificate, you've been talking about Mexico. What is the trouble, Dave?

DAVID GREENGLASS: I can't tell you everything about it. All I want you to do for me, Julie, is I gotta have a couple of thousand dollars in cash.

JULIUS ROSENBERG: David, I don't have that kind of money on me; I can't raise that kind of money.

DAVID GREENGLASS: Can you borrow it from your relatives?

JULIUS ROSENBERG: No, Dave, I can't do that.

DAVID GREENGLASS: Can you take it from the business for me?

JULIUS ROSENBERG: Dave, I cannot do that.

DAVID GREENGLASS: Well, Julie, I just got to have that money and if you don't get me that money you are going to be sorry.

JULIUS ROSENBERG: Look here, Dave, are you trying to threaten me or blackmail—

DAVID GREENGLASS: I'm warning you.

JULIUS ROSENBERG: Look, Dave, you go home and take a cold shower. You look like you're having an attack. I'm going to the shop.

GREENGLASS leaves, mumbling to himself.

STAGE A

The Screen: Volume II, Book II.

JULIUS ROSENBERG (*cross-fade*): Well, he was very excitable at this time, he was puffing and I saw a wild look in his eyes, and I realized it was time to cut this conversation short. I said, "Look, Dave, you go home, take a cold shower; I have some work to do. I am going to the shop; good-bye," and I left him at that time, and I made up my mind at that point that I wouldn't have anything to do with him, and I was very agitated.

THE DEFENSE: Did you give him any money?

JULIUS ROSENBERG: I did not give him any money.

THE DEFENSE: Did you give him any money at any time?

JULIUS ROSENBERG: No, I didn't.

THE DEFENSE: Mr. Rosenberg, to come back to the testimony that you spent $50 or $75 a night for entertainment: Have you ever been in a nightclub in your life?

JULIUS ROSENBERG: Once.

THE DEFENSE: What nightclub?

JULIUS ROSENBERG: Well, the Federation of Architects had a dinner party at Cafe Society.

E DEFENSE: Was that the only nightclub you were ever at?

JULIUS ROSENBERG: That is the only nightclub I ever attended.

THE DEFENSE: Now, were you in the habit of going to high-class restaurants?

JULIUS ROSENBERG: I don't know what you mean by high class, Mr. Bloch.

THE DEFENSE: All right. Did you ever go to restaurants where the prices were expensive?

JULIUS ROSENBERG: Yes, I did.

THE DEFENSE: How many?

JULIUS ROSENBERG: Well, once when I was taking my wife out, to a place near Emerson Radio called Pappas, and on another occasion I have eaten at a place called Nicholaus on Second Avenue.

THE DEFENSE: Did you ever eat at Manny Wolf's?

JULIUS ROSENBERG: Yes. I remember eating there once.

THE DEFENSE: With whom?

JULIUS ROSENBERG: When I was working as an inspector at Jefferson Travers Radio they had a dinner party and they invited the inspectors down to Manny Wolf's for dinner and then for a show.

THE DEFENSE: Thank you. Your witness.

STAGE B

JULIUS ROSENBERG: Ethel, I was terribly shocked to read that Willie McGee was executed. My heart is sad, my eyes are filled with tears. It seems to me that the federal courts have adopted the medieval practice of the Southern Bourbons, legal lynching of Negroes, and are now attempting, as in our case, to apply this to political prisoners. They must be answered with reason and fact. I am positive growing numbers of people will come to understand our fight, and join with us to win so just a cause. I miss you, Ethel, I love you. Julie

STAGE A

IRVING SAYPOL conducts all of THE GOVERNMENT's questioning of the ROSENBERGS.

The Screen: Volume II, Book II.

THE GOVERNMENT: Did you ever go out and collect any money for the Joint Anti-Fascist Refugee Committee?

JULIUS ROSENBERG: I don't recall collecting any money, but I recall contributing money.

THE GOVERNMENT: Do you remember at the time the agents arrested you? Did you ever see this before? (*He flourishes a can and bangs it down on the jury rail.*) May I read the label to the jury?

THE COURT: Yes.

THE GOVERNMENT: Will it be conceded that this is a can commonly used by solicitors for contributions?

THE DEFENSE: I will so concede.

THE GOVERNMENT: And the can reads on the label, "Save a Spanish Republican Child, *Volveremos,* We will return, Joint Anti-Fascist Refugee Committee, 192 Lexington Avenue, Suite 1501," and there is a notice on the back indicating that the City of New York permits these cans to be used for solicitation. So that perhaps you did a little more than just contribute?

THE DEFENSE: Just a second, if your Honor please.

THE GOVERNMENT: Is that so?

THE DEFENSE: Wait a second: I object to the question. It presupposes a state of facts not proven. The can may have been found—

THE COURT: Hold the question a moment. The witness wanted to say something.

JULIUS ROSENBERG: That is not so, Mr. Saypol.

THE COURT: What did you want to say?

JULIUS ROSENBERG: The date on this can is May 20, 1949. I hold insurance in the International Workers Order, and they sent this can to me to solicit funds. I never solicited funds. I just made a contribution to them.

THE GOVERNMENT: Do you know that the International Workers Order is now the subject of a lawsuit across the way in the Supreme Court?

THE DEFENSE: I object to the question upon the ground it is incompetent, irrelevant, and immaterial and not related to the issues in this case.

THE COURT: What is the International Workers Order?

JULIUS ROSENBERG: An insurance organization, your Honor.

THE COURT: Is it a public insurance company?

JULIUS ROSENBERG: Right, sir.

THE GOVERNMENT: Is it not a fact that it is a Communist organization exclusively?

THE DEFENSE: I object to the form of the question.

THE COURT: The form is all right.

THE DEFENSE: Do you want his opinion on it?

THE COURT: Well, he certainly doesn't want mine.

THE DEFENSE: He acknowledges that he belongs to it.

JULIUS ROSENBERG: That is right, sir.

THE DEFENSE: I think, if the Court please, we are really going off the issue.

THE COURT: Oh, no!

STAGE B

MAN IN THE STREET: What do you consider the greatest threat to our nation, today?

ANSWER: Communism.

ANSWER: Communism.

ANSWER: Creeping socialism.

ANSWER: Atheism.

ANSWER: Decline to state.

STAGE A

The Screen: Volume II, Book II.

THE GOVERNMENT: Now you say you had another watch at some other time?

JULIUS ROSENBERG: That is right, sir.

THE GOVERNMENT: What kind of watch was that?

JULIUS ROSENBERG: I remember the name—

THE GOVERNMENT: Wasn't that name Omega, in a white metal case?

JULIUS ROSENBERG: I believe that is the watch.

THE GOVERNMENT: Is that the one you got from some Russian representative?

JULIUS ROSENBERG: That is the one I got from my father.

STAGE B

JULIUS ROSENBERG: My Dearest Sweetheart, I've been reviewing past events of our lives. I remember when my father, a garment worker, was in a long strike against sweatshop conditions. Because he was a chairman and an active unionist, my father was blacklisted and had quite a pull to make ends meet. The constant battle against rats and vermin is still vivid in my . . .

STAGE A

THE COURT: Do you believe in the overthrow of government by force and violence?

JULIUS ROSENBERG: I do not.

THE COURT: Do you believe—do you believe in anybody committing acts of espionage against his own country?

JULIUS ROSENBERG: I do not believe that.

THE COURT: Did you unhesitatingly express, in substance, the thoughts that you have just expressed about the Soviet government, the American government, to your friends and to your relatives?

THE GOVERNMENT: Well, I submit, if your Honor please, just a moment ago in response to the Court's question the witness answered that he did not know enough about it and never talked to anybody about it.

THE COURT: Well, do you presume to be an expert on government?

JULIUS ROSENBERG: Well, I am not an expert but I talked about these matters.

THE COURT: Have you read books?

JULIUS ROSENBERG: Yes, some books I have read.

THE COURT: Well, did you ever belong to any group that discussed the system of Russia?

JULIUS ROSENBERG: Well, your Honor, if you are referring to political groups—is that what you are referring to?

THE COURT: Any group.

JULIUS ROSENBERG: Well, your Honor, I feel that at this time that I refuse to answer a question that might tend to incriminate me.

THE COURT: Are you—

THE GOVERNMENT: Just a moment. May I clarify that?

THE COURT: It seems to me I have been hearing a lot about that.

JULIUS ROSENBERG: Are you referring to membership in the Communist Party?

THE COURT: Well, I am referring to membership in any political organization like the Communist Party.

THE DEFENSE: And when you answered the Court's question did you have in mind the Communist Party?

JULIUS ROSENBERG: Yes, I did.

THE COURT: Well, now, I won't direct you at this point to answer; I will wait for the cross-examination.

STAGE B: RECONSTRUCTION (DECISION, 1951)

THE DEFENSE: Let's take a minute, folks. I think they're going to push us on tomorrow afternoon.

JULIUS ROSENBERG: Tomorrow?

THE DEFENSE: It's a joke. They never intended to call Oppenheimer or Urey or—What's his name?

ETHEL ROSENBERG: Who?

THE DEFENSE: I'll think of it. Anyway we had to prepare anyway, just in case. Now, look, when we go on the stand; I spent the whole weekend debating what our approach should be. My father feels very strongly about it.

JULIUS ROSENBERG: You mean about the Fifth Amendment?

THE DEFENSE: That's it. Here's the point: This is a *political* trial—

JULIUS ROSENBERG: I agree.

ETHEL ROSENBERG (*smiling*): No.

THE DEFENSE: Absolutely political, so we are going to have to take some chances. "Bring it out!" my father says. They have no evidence (let's keep our voices down), they haven't a thing so they're making communism the issue, right? So you deny Greenglass's lies and they come back—"Now, Mr. Rosenberg, did you ever belong to the Young Communist League a hundred years ago?"—

JULIUS ROSENBERG: Or the Steinmetz Society at school.

ETHEL ROSENBERG: This is ancient history.

JULIUS ROSENBERG: Manny, you know—technically—they absolutely cannot prove any connection; we never actually—

THE DEFENSE: Julie, that's not the point. They're going to try to hang us with the Fifth Amendment. I'm just telling you the advice I'm getting.

JULIUS ROSENBERG: What?

THE DEFENSE: That we should tell them what it was like to be poor in New York; a poor Jew, when you two were growing up. *There are no Jews on this jury!* In the meantime, there's three million Jews in this town, but we can't get a Jew on the jury.

ETHEL ROSENBERG: And one woman. Saypol and Kaufman are—

THE DEFENSE: Kaufman is murder. If I let myself go, I'll go to jail for contempt, I'm telling you. He's ready to admonish me now. So, you go on the stand, we open up your whole lives. Why you believe in some kind of socialism, social justice, whatever. Then if they get cute and start red-baiting, we can call their bluff.

JULIUS ROSENBERG: When did you—

THE DEFENSE: I'm even seriously considering bringing your psychiatrist on, too. No?

ETHEL ROSENBERG: No. I'm sorry, that's out, Manny. But look, maybe Manny's right. With the Fifth Amendment we're damned if we do and we're damned if we don't.

JULIUS ROSENBERG: But we've got to stick to the evidence, phony as it is, don't you understand? If we answer just *one* question, then they can ask anything—

ETHEL ROSENBERG: But the jury might be more convinced if we—

JULIUS ROSENBERG: Honey, please, let's let Manny go over the—

ETHEL ROSENBERG: All right, I'm sorry.

JULIUS ROSENBERG: Please. We've got to destroy *their own* phony evidence. The jury—

THE DEFENSE: Let's look at if from their viewpoint. In a murder case, you know, the jurors might be guided by some damning physical evidence—a gun with fingerprints, clothing stained with the victim's blood. But what do they have here? Nothing. Just a story.

ETHEL ROSENBERG: I thought we were presumed to be innocent until—

JULIUS ROSENBERG: Very cute.

THE DEFENSE: All right. If I had anyone to help me, or any money for investigation or real research, we could go the other way. Maybe we could get Einstein on the stand, I don't know. But we're alone. The left—Ethel's family, for God's sake. We're alone and the country's hysterical. I just don't know which way to go. You wouldn't believe what's going on on the outside. People who knew you—friends—take photographs from over the years and flush them down the toilet! No one wants to testify, people are getting passports.

JULIUS ROSENBERG: But you always said, "We can't open the door." What's the use of a privilege if we don't use it? (*Pause.*) What time is it?

THE DEFENSE: In other words, maybe I'm the wrong man for the case.

JULIUS ROSENBERG: Manny, take it easy, Manny. Not so loud. They've got everybody fighting each other.

ETHEL ROSENBERG: You know, this is all just like a dream to me. It's just rushing past. Rushing past and I don't understand anything. I just want to get it over with. Manny, tell me the truth about the children.

JULIUS ROSENBERG: Lookit, we owe you our lives, but I'm afraid of it. If we don't take the Fifth Amendment, the FBI is going to testify that we were Communists. Who is the jury going to believe? Us or the FBI? But if we take the Fifth they can't pursue it. Can they? And the worst of all is if *I* don't take it, they're going to try to drag every name of everybody I ever knew or went to school with out of me. Not just names; *real people*! They'll make twenty spy rings before they're through. I'm afraid of it, Manny.

ETHEL ROSENBERG: I don't understand a word; I think I'm losing my mind.

THE DEFENSE: That's it. If you take it, then the jury says you're Reds anyway. If you deny membership, they could bring in some professional informer to say he saw you at some meeting and if the jury hears that, you'll be a liar in their eyes and you'll be fin—(*Pause.*) I'm so disgusted, I don't know. Maybe I'm kidding myself. All right, we'll see. Anyway, you and Ethel just be yourselves. Don't worry about anything. I'm working on the situation with the children. *Oi*, Julie, Julie.

ETHEL ROSENBERG: Listen, tell the children what we—

JULIUS ROSENBERG: Listen, you take it easy, will you. You're driving yourself. You're only human, you know.

ETHEL ROSENBERG: What if we—

GUARD: Time.

STAGE A

The Screen: Volume II, Book II.

THE GOVERNMENT: Now, Mr. Bloch asked you the question and this was your answer: "Yes, I will, and in discussing the merits of other forms of government"—now this is you talking—"I discussed that with my friends on the basis of the performance of what they accomplished, and I felt that the Soviet government has improved the lot of the underdog there, has made a lot of progress in eliminating illiteracy, has done a lot of reconstruction work and built up a lot of resources, and at the same time I felt that they contributed a major share in destroying the Hitler beast." Then the Court asked this question—

THE DEFENSE: Would you finish, please?

THE GOVERNMENT: "The Hitler beast who killed six million of my coreligionists, and I feel emotional about that thing." Then later on the Court asked you this question: "Did you approve the communistic system of Russia over the capitalistic system in this country?" And you answered: "I'm not an expert on those things, your Honor, and I did not make any such direct statement." Do you remember having testified that way?

JULIUS ROSENBERG: That's right.

THE GOVERNMENT: Well now, you had said a little while before that you felt that "the Soviet government has improved the lot of the underdog there"; what did you mean by that?

JULIUS ROSENBERG: What I read in newspapers.

THE GOVERNMENT: And what did you read about the improvement of the lot of the underdog in Soviet Russia, as you read it in the newspapers?

JULIUS ROSENBERG: Well, that the worker there, as living standards were increased, his housing conditions were better than at times he lived under the Czar. That is what I mean by increasing the lot of the "underdog."

THE GOVERNMENT: What newspapers did you read that in?

JULIUS ROSENBERG: Various newspapers.

THE GOVERNMENT: You mean the *Daily Worker?*

JULIUS ROSENBERG: On occasion; the *New York Times.*

THE GOVERNMENT: Any others?

JULIUS ROSENBERG: Yes.

THE GOVERNMENT: What others?

JULIUS ROSENBERG: The *Herald Tribune,* the *World Telegram.*

THE GOVERNMENT: The *Wall Street Journal,* perhaps?

JULIUS ROSENBERG: No. I don't read the *Wall Street Journal.*

THE GOVERNMENT: "Has made a lot of progress in eliminating illiteracy"; what did you know about that?

JULIUS ROSENBERG: They built schools.

THE GOVERNMENT: Where?

JULIUS ROSENBERG: From what I read.

THE GOVERNMENT: Where were the schools built?

JULIUS ROSENBERG: In the Russian cities.

THE GOVERNMENT: What cities?

JULIUS ROSENBERG: I don't know, sir.

THE GOVERNMENT: Where did you read that, same newspapers?

JULIUS ROSENBERG: Newspapers.

THE GOVERNMENT: "Has done a lot of reconstruction work"; what did you know about that?

JULIUS ROSENBERG: Well, there are a lot of reporters that go to Russia and report how the cities have been rebuilt, that were destroyed by the Nazis.

THE GOVERNMENT: What cities, for instance?

JULIUS ROSENBERG: Stalingrad, Moscow.

THE GOVERNMENT: What type of reconstruction had been done?

JULIUS ROSENBERG: I wouldn't know the details, sir. That is what I read the newspaper reports on.

THE GOVERNMENT: Has "built up a lot of resources"; tell me about the resources, won't you, please? What kind were they? Where were they? What they are? What were they intended for?

JULIUS ROSENBERG: I wouldn't know everything about it, but I knew they built some large dams. That is what I consider "resources."

THE GOVERNMENT: Dams you consider resources?

JULIUS ROSENBERG: That's right, hydroelectric stations. That is a dam.

THE GOVERNMENT: Did you read anything about the request of Russia for the atomic bomb? Would that be perhaps a resource that you had in mind?

JULIUS ROSENBERG: No, I was talking about a previous period.

THE GOVERNMENT: Did you tell the agents about your suspicions that David Greenglass had stolen uranium?

JULIUS ROSENBERG: Well, when a member of the family is in trouble, Mr. Saypol, you are not interested in sinking him.

THE COURT: Were you interested in protecting him at that time?

JULIUS ROSENBERG: Well, I felt that when a man is in trouble, the one thing his family should do is stick by the man, regardless of the trouble he is in.

THE COURT: Now, Mr. Rosenberg, why should David Greenglass come to you for help when you've testified that you had heated arguments over the business? Isn't it strange that he should come to you?

JULIUS ROSENBERG: I don't think so, your Honor, because in the first place his other brother was tied up with his wife dying in the hospital and—

THE GOVERNMENT: Did you tell us about that before?

JULIUS ROSENBERG: About what?

THE GOVERNMENT: About his wife who was dying and this brother who was out of the country and that is why you thought you would go to him; that it was all right for him to call you to come to him.

JULIUS ROSENBERG: I am only trying to understand why he came to me.

THE DEFENSE: I object to the testimony. There is no testimony about a brother being out of the country.

THE GOVERNMENT: Who was dying?

JULIUS ROSENBERG: Bernie's wife.

THE COURT: I think this subject matter, Mr. Saypol, is amply covered.

THE GOVERNMENT: I never heard about his dying, whoever it was.

JULIUS ROSENBERG: Well, Bernie's wife had Hodgkins' disease and was in and out of the hospital.

THE GOVERNMENT: *Don't give us the gory details.* (*Pause.*) That is all—one question, if I may ask it?

THE COURT: Pardon?

THE GOVERNMENT: One question if I may ask it? Is or was your wife a member of the Communist Party?

JULIUS ROSENBERG: I refuse to answer on the ground it might tend to incriminate me.

THE GOVERNMENT: Very well, I don't intend to press it.

THE COURT: Wait a minute. You are not going to press for an answer?

THE GOVERNMENT: No, I don't think so.

THE COURT: You may step down.

STAGE B

JULIUS ROSENBERG: Hello My Love, You are so close at hand and yet your being in a different corridor separated by so much steel, locked away from my sight and beyond my hearing range the frustration is terrific. Tonight I was able to hear your voice when a few of the high notes of one of your arias was faintly audible. . . . Physically I am fairly comfortable and already in the routine of things. . . . I read about six newspapers a day, I play chess in a numbered board by remote control with another inmate and I am reading *The Old Country* by Sholom Aleichem. . . . Good night, my wife.

STAGE A

THE CLERK: Call Ethel Rosenberg to the stand.

She is sworn.

The Screen: *Volume II, Book II.*

THE DEFENSE: Are you married?

ETHEL ROSENBERG: Yes.

THE DEFENSE: To whom?

ETHEL ROSENBERG: Julius Rosenberg.

THE DEFENSE: The other defendant in this case?

ETHEL ROSENBERG: That is right.

THE DEFENSE: What was your maiden name?

ETHEL ROSENBERG: Ethel Greenglass.

THE DEFENSE: Will you kindly give the jury a brief sketch of your schooling and education?

ETHEL ROSENBERG: Well, I attending Public School 22. And then I attended Public School 12. That was called junior high school. Then I attended Seward Park High School.

THE DEFENSE: What, if any, other educational institutions did you attend?

ETHEL ROSENBERG: I didn't go to any kind of institution but I had a private Hebrew tutor who came to the home. I also had a private piano teacher from whom I took lessons for about two years.

THE DEFENSE: Did you also study voice?

ETHEL ROSENBERG: Yes, I did.

THE DEFENSE: With whom?

ETHEL ROSENBERG: The Carnegie Hall Studios.

THE DEFENSE: Anything else you studied?

ETHEL ROSENBERG: Yes. When my child was about two and a half, I think, my older child, I took a course with the New School of Social Research in child psychology. I also took a course in music for children at the Bank Street School in Greenwich Village, and then sometime in the spring of 1950 I took a course in guitar.

THE DEFENSE: Were these two courses, the one in child psychology and the other in music for children, taken in order to equip and condition you to raise your child?

ETHEL ROSENBERG: Yes, that really was the reason.

THE DEFENSE: How many children have you?

ETHEL ROSENBERG: I have two children.

THE DEFENSE: What are their ages?

ETHEL ROSENBERG: Well, Michael was eight March 10.

THE DEFENSE: He is the older of the two?

STAGE B: RECONSTRUCTION
(CHILDREN, 1952)

On the ark stage we hear only THE VOICES OF THE CHILDREN.

THE VOICE OF MICHAEL: Dear President Eisenhower: My mommy and daddy are in prison in New York. My brother is six years old, his name is Robbie. Please let my mommy and daddy go and not let anything happen to them. If they come, Robbie and I will be very happy. We will thank you very much. Very truly yours, Michael Rosenberg

THE VOICE OF ROBBIE: I want to write one, too.

THE VOICE OF MICHAEL: No, I'm supposed to.

THE VOICE OF ROBBIE: I want to! (*He starts a tantrum.*)

THE VOICE OF MICHAEL: Shut up! O.K. Tell me what you want to say and I'll write it down.

THE VOICE OF ROBBIE: O.K. You better.

Pause.

THE VOICE OF MICHAEL: Well, come on, Robbie.

THE VOICE OF ROBBIE: Shut up.

THE VOICE OF MICHAEL: Then I'm—

THE VOICE OF ROBBIE: Dear Mommy and Daddy—

THE VOICE OF MICHAEL: Robbie, you're supposed to write it to the *President.* (ROBBIE *begins to cry again.*) All right, go ahead then.

THE VOICE OF ROBBIE: Dear Mommy and Daddy . . .

There is a long pause.

STAGE A

The Screen: *Volume II, Book II.*

THE DEFENSE: Now, your brother Dave was the youngest in the family.

ETHEL ROSENBERG: That's right.

THE DEFENSE: What was your relationship?

ETHEL ROSENBERG: Well, he was my baby brother.

THE DEFENSE: Did you love him?

ETHEL ROSENBERG: Yes, I loved him very much.

THE COURT: Did he sort of look up to you?

ETHEL ROSENBERG: Yes.

THE COURT: And your husband? Before the arguments that were discussed here in court!

ETHEL ROSENBERG: He liked us both. He liked my husband.

THE COURT: Sort of hero worship?

ETHEL ROSENBERG: Oh, by no stretch of the imagination could you say that was hero worship.

THE COURT: You heard him so testify, did you not?

ETHEL ROSENBERG: Yes, I did.

THE DEFENSE: And it is not correct, is it, that there was any hero worship there between Julius and your brother or your brother and Julius?

ETHEL ROSENBERG: It certainly is not correct.

THE DEFENSE: No. And when your brother went into the Army in 1943, you corresponded with him?

ETHEL ROSENBERG: Yes.

THE DEFENSE: And you also corresponded on behalf of your mother?

ETHEL ROSENBERG: Yes, I did.

THE DEFENSE: Your mother can't write English very well, can she?

ETHEL ROSENBERG: No, she can just about sign her name.

THE DEFENSE: So you were sort of a secretary on behalf of your mother?

ETHEL ROSENBERG: Of both my mothers, yes.

THE DEFENSE: And when your sister-in-law went to live with her husband, your brother, you continued writing to her?

ETHEL ROSENBERG: Yes, I did.

THE DEFENSE: Now, can you give us an idea of what you wrote about when you did write to your brother and to your sister-in-law?

ETHEL ROSENBERG: Well, I wrote the usual "How are you? We are all right"; and "Take care of yourself"; and "This one had a baby," or "The other one got married," and things of that sort.

THE DEFENSE: Did you ever, in any letter written to your brother or to your sister-in-law, refer to any matter pertaining to information concerning either the atomic bomb or any other instrument manufactured or used for national defense?

ETHEL ROSENBERG: You mean, was there any such correspondence?

THE DEFENSE: Did you ever write in any letter the substance of what I just now said?

ETHEL ROSENBERG: Oh, no; no, I never did.

THE DEFENSE: Tell me, did you ever know a man by the name of Yakovlev?

ETHEL ROSENBERG: No, I never did.

THE DEFENSE: Did you ever know a man by the name of Golos?

ETHEL ROSENBERG: No, sir: I never did.

THE DEFENSE: Did you ever know a woman named Bentley?

ETHEL ROSENBERG: No, I never did.

THE DEFENSE: Did you ever hear of those people at any time before this case broke?

ETHEL ROSENBERG: I read about them in the newspapers.

THE DEFENSE: Did you know a man by the name of Harry Gold?

ETHEL ROSENBERG: No, I did not.

THE DEFENSE: Did you know a man by the name of Fuchs, Dr. Fuchs?

ETHEL ROSENBERG: Not until I saw his name in the newspaper.

THE DEFENSE: And the same thing with Gold, you never knew of him until you read about it in the newspapers?

ETHEL ROSENBERG: That is right.

THE DEFENSE: Please describe the last time you saw your sister-in-law Ruth Greenglass.

ETHEL ROSENBERG: After my brother was arrested, I waited for her one day at my mother's. She had the baby and we began to walk, she and I, with the carriage around the block.

STAGE B

The two women walk around the block as they talk.

RUTH GREENGLASS: Let's not go far. Paper says rain.

ETHEL ROSENBERG: Look, Ruth, I would like to know something: Are you and Davey really mixed up in this horrible mess? You know how I have always felt toward Davey and how I have always felt toward you, although I must say you people haven't always reciprocated, especially in the last year. However, that is beside the point. I want you to know that even if you did do this, and Davey, my attitude toward you won't change. But I am his sister, and I have a right to know.

RUTH GREENGLASS: What are you asking such silly questions for? He's not guilty and of course I'm not guilty and we've hired a lawyer and we're going to fight the case because we're not guilty. Did you think we were?

ETHEL ROSENBERG: Look, I really don't know what to think anymore. There've been reports in the newspapers about confessions and much as I believed, always believed in Davey, I really began to wonder. I had to hear it from your own lips.

RUTH GREENGLASS: Well, now you've heard it and it's the truth. Neither of us is guilty.

ETHEL tries to embrace RUTH.

ETHEL ROSENBERG: I'll do whatever you say, Ruthie, Good-bye.

RUTH rejects her.

STAGE A

The Screen: Volume II, Book II.

ETHEL ROSENBERG: "... You can be sure I will do whatever I can," and with that we reached East Houston Street and I put my arms around her and kissed her. She remained rigid in my arms, didn't return the kiss, said, "Good-bye," coldly, turned on her heel and left.

THE DEFENSE: That was the last talk you had with her?

ETHEL ROSENBERG: That is right.

THE DEFENSE: At the time of the arrest of your husband, where did you live?

ETHEL ROSENBERG: Ten Monroe Street, Manhattan. In Knickerbocker Village.

THE DEFENSE: Where are your children now?

ETHEL ROSENBERG (*beginning to break*): They are at a temporary shelter in the Bronx.

THE DEFENSE: Have you seen them since you were arrested?

ETHEL ROSENBERG: No, I have not.

THE DEFENSE: Your sister-in-law testified that she visited you at your home and that she admired a mahogany console table and she said "it was a very nice gift to get from a friend," and that "Julius said it was from his friend and it was a special kind of table" and thereupon your husband, Julius, "turned the table on its side to show us why it was so special"; did any such thing ever occur?

ETHEL ROSENBERG: No, it did not.

THE DEFENSE: Did your husband ever use any table, console table or any other table, for photograph purposes?

ETHEL ROSENBERG: No, he did not.

THE DEFENSE: Did your husband ever photograph on microfilm or any other substance anything pertaining to any information or secret concerning the national defense, or anything else at all?

ETHEL ROSENBERG: No, he did not.

THE DEFENSE: And did you, since the time you moved to the Monroe Street apartment until the time of your husband's arrest and your arrest, acquire any other tables?

ETHEL ROSENBERG: Yes. We acquired a console table that my husband purchased at R. H. Macy. A very inexpensive table, with a back that you could ... sometimes it would stand up, and other times if we wanted to use it for eating purposes, it folded down.

THE DEFENSE: Did you ever hear Julius say to anyone that he got money from the Russians?

ETHEL ROSENBERG: No, I never heard any such thing.

THE COURT: Are you taking up every conversation that supposedly she had with Julius?

THE DEFENSE: No, your Honor, I won't spend much more than a few minutes more to cover it.

THE COURT: I don't want you to get the impression I am rushing you, but I don't want you to overtry a case, Mr. Bloch.

THE DEFENSE: Did you ever hear from any source that Julius offered your brother and sister-in-law $75 or $100 a week to live on?

STAGE B: RECONSTRUCTION (MONEY, 1946)

JULIUS ROSENBERG (*as ETHEL enters*): Hi, Dodgers won. Did you find anything in chairs, E? What's the matter now?

ETHEL ROSENBERG: They're all way out of our price range.

JULIUS ROSENBERG: Secondhand, too? (*Pause.*) What's the tragedy, Ethel?

ETHEL ROSENBERG: Oh, what's the use? There's not any money for another baby and any new things for this house. (*She looks in the mirror.*) I can't stand this sweater! God's sake, I look twice my age!

JULIUS ROSENBERG: Oh, come on, Ethel. Does everything have to be such a tragedy?

ETHEL ROSENBERG: Stop saying that! Stop treating me like a case. I can't stand it. I don't have any clothes. I hate this place.

JULIUS ROSENBERG: Well, what am I supposed to do about it?

ETHEL ROSENBERG: Oh, shut up, will you?

JULIUS ROSENBERG: Will you stop yelling, for God's sake, you'll wake the child.

ETHEL ROSENBERG: You should never have married me. I'm sorry, Julius. I'm just so depressed over everything. You can't beat the system, that's all there is to it. I am never going to wear any of these sweaters again! (*He goes to her.*) Please, just leave me alone. It's not just furniture and clothes. There's just something wrong.

JULIUS ROSENBERG: Listen, Ethel, money never meant that much to you. I mean, we're beyond that kind of thinking. You're just not getting enough from me. I mean that's it, isn't it? (*Pause.*) Will you please talk to me?

ETHEL ROSENBERG: Oh, Julie, we have problems and I have problems. I have to solve *my* problems. Don't take it personally. (*Pause.*) I'm going to sleep with the child tonight in his room. I'm exhausted. Good night. I'm sorry.

STAGE A

The Screen: Volume II, Book III.

THE GOVERNMENT: Is it not a fact, Mrs. Greenglass, that before the grand jury—

ETHEL ROSENBERG: Mrs. Rosenberg

THE GOVERNMENT: Excuse me, I'm sorry. You are the defendant here.

THE COURT: Do you know, Mr. Saypol, if you could probably stand at the edge of the table there, we could all hear much better.

THE GOVERNMENT: I am trying to save space and time.

THE COURT: Go ahead.

THE GOVERNMENT: Were you asked this question and did you give this answer before the grand jury? "Did you invite your brother David and his wife to your home for dinner? I mean during the period while he was on furlough in January, 1945?" "I decline to answer on the ground that this might incriminate me." Do you remember giving that testimony?

ETHEL ROSENBERG: Yes, I remember.

THE GOVERNMENT: Was it true at the time you gave it? Yes or no.

ETHEL ROSENBERG: It is not a question of it being true.

THE GOVERNMENT: I would like to ask now that I have a categorical answer.

THE COURT: Yes, will you answer that, please?

THE GOVERNMENT: Yes or no.

ETHEL ROSENBERG: What is the question?

THE COURT: Was it true when you said that, that you refused to answer because it would incriminate you?

ETHEL ROSENBERG: I said it might tend to incriminate me.

THE COURT: Was that true?

THE DEFENSE: I wasn't to interpose an objection, your Honor.

THE COURT: Have you thought of another ground for an objection?

THE DEFENSE: I think, your Honor, that the method of trying to import an unlawful act to a person who has asserted the privilege against self-incrimination destroys the privilege and undermines and takes away the person's right under the Fifth Amendment, and I object to this entire line of inquiry because inferences may be drawn which are not warranted under the law or under the facts.

THE COURT: However, when a witness freely answers questions at a trial, the answers to the very same questions to which the witness had refused to answer previously upon a ground assigned by that witness, I ask you, is that not a question then for the jury to consider on the question of credibility? Nobody is seeking to destroy any privilege.

THE DEFENSE: May I just answer it in one sentence? I submit that I disagree with your Honor's conception of the law. What I meant was that the objective effect of it was to vitiate the rights.

THE COURT: But the witness herself has vitiated by giving answers to them at the trial, answers to these very questions.

THE DEFENSE: Well then, I submit, your Honor, that there is a failure to make, and I think I am putting my finger on the heart of this thing— there is a failure here to distinguish between the circumstances where a witness involuntarily appeared before a tribunal and is sworn to testify in response to a subpoena, as in the case here of a grand jury proceeding, and a case where the witness willingly takes—

THE COURT: Where is the witness willingly—

THE DEFENSE: Here. This witness has voluntarily taken the stand here. There was no obligation on her part to take the stand, your Honor.

THE COURT: Proceed.

ETHEL ROSENBERG: My brother had been arrested. My husband had been arrested.

THE GOVERNMENT: On August sixth?

ETHEL ROSENBERG: My husband had been arrested and I had been subpoenaed to come before the grand jury. It was not for me to state what I thought or didn't think the Government might or might not have in the way of accusation against me.

THE GOVERNMENT: What you are saying is that you were under no compulsion to confess your guilt in respect to this conspiracy?

ETHEL ROSENBERG: I had no guilt—

THE DEFENSE: Just a moment, please.

THE COURT: She has answered.

ETHEL ROSENBERG: *I had no guilt to confess!*

THE COURT: But in your own interest I think you ought to think about it and give us some reason.

Pause.

STAGE B

MAN IN THE STREET: What is your opinion on the so-called right of the Fifth Amendment?

ANSWER: No comment.

ANSWER: No comment, who the hell are you?

ANSWER: They must have something to hide. Only the Commies want it.

ANSWER: The what?

ANSWER: No comment.

The Screen:
GRUNEWALD V. U.S., 77 S. CT. 963, OCTOBER 1956 TERM, p. 984 (OPINION OF JUSTICE BLACK CONCURRING WITH JUSTICES WARREN, DOUGLAS, AND BRENNAN):

"I CAN THINK OF NO SPECIAL CIRCUMSTANCES THAT WOULD JUSTIFY USE OF THE CONSTITUTIONAL PRIVILEGE TO DISCREDIT OR CONVICT A PERSON WHO ASSERTS IT. THE VALUE OF THE CONSTITUTIONAL PRIVILEGE IS LARGELY DESTROYED IF PERSONS CAN BE PENALIZED FOR RELYING ON THEM."

"IT SEEMS PECULIARLY INCONGRUOUS AND INDEFENSIBLE FOR COURTS WHICH EXIST AND ACT UNDER THE CONSTITUTION TO DRAW INFERENCE OF LACK OF HONESTY FROM THE INVOCATION OF A PRIVILEGE DEEMED WORTHY OF ENSHRINEMENT IN THE CONSTITUTION."

STAGE A

The Screen: *Volume II, Book III.*

THE GOVERNMENT: Will you please tell me whether the answer, when you gave it to the grand jury, as to whether or not you had spoken to your brother David Greenglass to the effect that the answer might tend to incriminate you, was true then or false?

ETHEL ROSENBERG: It was true, because my brother David was under arrest.

THE GOVERNMENT: How would that incriminate you, if you are innocent?

THE DEFENSE: Just a moment.

ETHEL ROSENBERG: I didn't have—

THE DEFENSE: Wait a second. I object to the form of the question.

THE COURT: Let her give her own reasons to why she answered it that way.

THE GOVERNMENT: I am willing to have her explanation, if the Court please.

THE COURT: Yes.

ETHEL ROSENBERG: It wouldn't necessarily incriminate me, but it might—

THE GOVERNMENT: You mean—

ETHEL ROSENBERG: —and as long as I had any idea that there might be some chance for me to be incriminated I had the right to use that privilege.

THE COURT: At any rate, you don't feel that way about that question today, do you? You have answered when you talked to your brother Dave right here in this courtroom, haven't you?

ETHEL ROSENBERG: But I didn't talk to my brother David.

THE COURT: What was the question there, Mr. Saypol? What was the question, please?

THE GOVERNMENT: I am asking—

THE COURT: No, no, the question you read before the grand jury; I want to know that question.

THE GOVERNMENT (*reading*): "Q. Did you discuss this case with your brother David Greenglass? A. I refuse to answer on the ground that this might tend to incriminate me."

THE COURT: You have no objecting to answering that question here in the courtroom?

ETHEL ROSENBERG: I have already answered that question, that I did not discuss it.

THE COURT: And you don't feel that giving that answer will in any way incriminate you here today; is that right? That is why you have answered it?

ETHEL ROSENBERG: That's right.

THE GOVERNMENT: As a matter of fact, a truthful answer at that time would have been that you hadn't talked to him, would it not?

ETHEL ROSENBERG: Well, but self-incrimination—

THE DEFENSE: Wait—

ETHEL ROSENBERG (continuing): Self-incrimination is not a truthful answer.

THE DEFENSE: Wait. I just want to record my objection.

THE COURT: I will sustain the objection to that particular question.

THE GOVERNMENT: As a matter of fact, at the—

THE COURT: Now, let me ask a question. If you had answered at that time that you had not spoken to David, for reasons best known to you, you felt that that would incriminate you?

ETHEL ROSENBERG: Well, if I used the privilege of self-incrimination at that time, I must have felt that perhaps there might be something that might incriminate me in answering.

THE COURT: All right, proceed.

THE GOVERNMENT: As a matter of fact, at that time you didn't know how much the FBI knew about you and so you weren't taking any chances; isn't that it?

THE DEFENSE: I object to the form of the question.

ETHEL ROSENBERG: I was using—

THE DEFENSE: Wait a second.

THE COURT: Overruled.

THE DEFENSE: I respectfully except.

THE GOVERNMENT: May that question be answered yes or no?

THE COURT: Yes, first answer it yes or no, then you can explain.

ETHEL ROSENBERG: Will you please repeat the question?

THE GOVERNMENT: Mr. Reporter, will you please read the question?

Question read.

ETHEL ROSENBERG I didn't know what the FBI knew or didn't know.

THE GOVERNMENT: Of course you didn't, so you weren't taking any chance in implicating yourself or your husband.

THE DEFENSE: Now, if the Court please—

ETHEL ROSENBERG: I was using my right—

THE DEFENSE: Wait a second. I object to this entire line of questions as incompetent, irrelevant, and immaterial and I now move for a mistrial upon the ground that Mr. Saypol is persisting in asking questions, the import of which can only prejudice this defendant in the eyes of the jury, and it has no probative value whatsoever.

THE COURT: Mr. Bloch, you know the purpose of cross-examination, I take it?

THE DEFENSE: I do.

THE COURT: You know the way questions ordinarily are framed in cross-examination?

THE DEFENSE: I do, sir.

THE COURT: They don't expect a witness to volunteer and the cross-examiner has to phrase his questions in such a way as he thinks, with propriety, he can elicit the information which he thinks should be elicited. I think it is proper cross-examination. Your motion for a mistrial is denied. Your objection is overruled.

THE DEFENSE: I respectfully except, your Honor.

THE GOVERNMENT: Were you asked this question and did you give this answer: "Do I understand you are going to decline to answer all questions that I ask you?" "No, no I won't decline to answer all questions. It depends on the questions." Did you say that?

ETHEL ROSENBERG: Yes, I did.

THE GOVERNMENT: When you said, "It depends on the questions," you meant it depends on whether or not the question and the answer that you gave would tend to incriminate you; is that right?

ETHEL ROSENBERG: That is right.

THE GOVERNMENT: You testified here today in response to questions from your counsel that the first time you saw Harry Gold was in this courtroom; is that so?

ETHEL ROSENBERG: That is right.

THE GOVERNMENT: Do you remember having been asked this question and giving this answer: "Have you ever met Harry Gold?" "I decline to answer on the ground that this might intimidate me, incriminate me, I mean." Did you give that testimony at the time?

ETHEL ROSENBERG: I gave that testimony.

THE GOVERNMENT: Was that truthful?

ETHEL ROSENBERG: When one uses the right of self-incrimination one does not mean that the answer is yes and one does not mean that the answer is no. I simply refused to answer on the ground that the answer might incriminate me.

THE COURT: But you did answer it here in court, isn't that true?

ETHEL ROSENBERG: That is right.

THE COURT: And your answer here was that you never met him until he took the witness stand?

ETHEL ROSENBERG: That is correct.

THE GOVERNMENT: "Did you ever hear your husband, Julius, discuss with Ruth Greenglass the work her husband, David Greenglass, was doing at Los Alamos during the war?" Answer: "I decline to answer on the ground that this might tend to incriminate me." Was that testimony given by you?

ETHEL ROSENBERG: Yes.

THE GOVERNMENT: Was it truthful?

THE COURT: Same answer?

ETHEL ROSENBERG: Same answer.

THE GOVERNMENT: You profess a love for your brother, don't you?

ETHEL ROSENBERG: You mean I once had love for my brother?

THE GOVERNMENT: You mean that that has changed?

ETHEL ROSENBERG: It would be pretty unnatural if it hadn't changed.

THE GOVERNMENT: That will be all. The Government rests.

THE DEFENSE: The Defense rests. . . . May it please the Court, ladies and gentlemen of the jury. Two kinds of evidence came out of that witness box. One kind we lawyers call oral evidence. Then we have another kind that we call documentary evidence and those are what we call exhibits. Now what are the exhibits in this case? As we look through this entire pile of Government exhibits, we find nothing . . . but wait. We do have an exhibit, we have an exhibit here that ties Rosenberg up to the case. Here it is. It's a tin can. No question this came from Rosenberg's house. It says "Save A Spanish Republican Child" and it is issued pursuant to a license from the New York Welfare Department. I don't care whether you are in favor of Franco, and I don't care whether you are in favor of the Loyalists. But can you tell yourself in your conscience that there is anything in this

can from which you can infer that Rosenberg was guilty of conspiracy to commit espionage? And finally, we have one last exhibit that connects the Rosenbergs in this case. It's a nominating petition signed by Ethel Rosenberg in 1941. As you can see, with many others she petitioned that Peter V. Cacchione could be nominated by the Communist Party so that he could run legally for office as a Councilman—to which office, incidentally, he was elected. Does signing that petition tie Ethel Rosenberg up with a conspiracy to commit espionage? Ask yourself that. The FBI stopped at nothing in their investigation to try to find some piece of evidence that you could feel, that you could see, that would tie the Rosenbergs up with this case. And yet this is the complete documentary evidence adduced by the Government. This case, therefore, against the Rosenbergs depends entirely upon oral testimony.

Now, here I want to say something to you. This case is packed with drama. Playwrights and movie scriptwriters could do a lot with a case like this. Now, who are the main actors here in this big drama? There is David Greenglass; there is Ruth Greenglass—that is one team, on this side; and in the other corner of the ring there is Julius Rosenberg and there is Ethel Rosenberg. You know, before I summed up, I went to a dictionary and I wanted to find a word that could describe a Dave Greenglass. I couldn't find it because I don't think that there is a word in the English vocabulary or in the dictionary of any civilization which can describe a character like Dave Greenglass. Now look at that terrible spy. (*He points to* ETHEL.) Look at that terrible spy and compare her to Ruthie Greenglass, who came here all dolled up, arrogant, smart, cute, eager-beaver, like a phonograph record. I say to you that this case started out to be a big, big case. It was going to last months, and it petered out in three weeks.

THE COURT: Your time is up, Mr. Bloch.

THE DEFENSE: I'm winding up now, your Honor. The fate of the defendants is in your hands. I have enough confidence in twelve American jurors to believe that they will bring in an honest verdict. That's all I ask you to do, to show to the world that in America a man can get a fair trial.

THE GOVERNMENT: May it please the Court, Mr. Foreman, ladies and gentlemen of the jury. This case is one of the most important that has ever been submitted to a jury in this country. I feel most inadequate to express to you in words the enormity of the thing. You have heard suggestions that the Federal Bureau of Investigation and my staff and I are silly dupes and we have been befogged, we have been fooled. If there had been any fooling, you will remember that one of the defendants made blanket negatives in denial as to whether she knew Harry Gold, as to whether she had ever talked to David Greenglass about his work at Los Alamos, as to whether she and her husband ever talked about atomic bombs, and yet I showed you that in the grand jury, on the advice of her counsel, she refused to answer those questions on the ground that to answer them would be self-incriminating. In the grand jury: "Did you ever know Harry Gold?" Answer: "I refuse to answer on the ground that it tends to incriminate me." "Did you consult your counsel, Mr. Bloch, before you made that answer?" Answer: "Yes."

I leave it to you as to who may have been fooled. The suggestion that the FBI has been duped? The FBI is never duped. The identity of some of the other traitors who sold their country down the river with Rosenberg remains undisclosed. We know that such people exist because of Rosenberg's boasting to Greenglass. *We don't know all the details because the only living people who can supply the details are the defendants.* But there is one part of the scheme that we do know about. We know that these conspirators stole the most important scientific secrets ever known to mankind from this country and delivered them to the Soviet Union. The description of the atom bomb itself, destined for delivery to the Soviet Union, was typed up by the defendant Ethel Rosenberg. Just so had she on countless other occasions sat at that typewriter and struck the keys, blow by blow, against her own country in the interests of the Soviets. Ladies and gentlemen, every word that David and Ruth Greenglass spoke on this stand about that Jello box meeting was corroborated by Harry Gold. The history of this Jello box side, the greetings from Julius, and Greenglass's whereabouts in Albuquerque, New Mexico, come to us not only from Ruth and David, but from Harry Gold, a man concerning whom there cannot be even a suggestion of motive. He can gain nothing from testifying as he did in this courtroom except the moral satisfaction in his soul of having told the truth. Harry Gold, who furnished the absolute corroboration of the testimony of the Greenglasses, forged the necessary link in the chain that points indisputably to the guilt of the Rosenbergs.

The Screen:
CLIMAX OF TRIAL; JURY BEGINS TO DELIBERATE

STAGE B

JULIUS ROSENBERG: Do you remember George Bernard Shaw's *Saint Joan,* Ethel? When John de Stogumber comes rushing in overcome with remorse for what he's done? "You don't know; you haven't seen; it is so easy to talk when you don't know. You madden yourself with words; you damn yourself because it feels grand to throw oil on the flaming hell of your own temper. But when it is brought home to you; when you see the thing you have done; when it's blinding your eyes, stifling your nostrils, tearing your heart, then—then, oh, God, take away this sight from me! Oh, Christ, deliver me from this fire that is consuming me—She cried to thee in the midst of it: 'Jesus! Jesus! Jesus!' She is in thy bosom, and I am in hell for evermore."

STAGE A

THE COURT: Bring the jury in.
THE CLERK: How say you?
THE FOREMAN: We the jury find Julius Rosenberg guilty as charged. We the jury find Ethel Rosenberg guilty as charged.
THE COURT (*to the audience*): Ladies and gentlemen of the jury, I wish to tender you my deepest gratitude. I wish to congratulate the Government for their fair presentation of this case and again I say a great tribute is due to the FBI and Mr. Hoover for the splendid job that they have done in this case. Now I say to the jurors, I al-

most feel as if I will miss seeing those faces here morning after morning, but I know it has been a tremendous inconvenience to you; it has taken you away from your business. God bless you all.

The ROSENBERGS are brought before the bar for sentencing.

THE COURT: The issue of punishment in this case is presented in a unique framework of history. It is so difficult to make people realize that this country is engaged in a life-and-death struggle with a completely different system. This struggle is not only manifested externally between these two forces but this case indicates quite clearly that it also involves the employment by the enemy of secret as well as overt outspoken forces among our own people. All of our democratic institutions are, therefore, directly involved in this great conflict. I believe that never at any time in our history were we ever confronted to the same degree that we are today with such a challenge to our very existence. . . .

The punishment to be meted out in this case must therefore serve the maximum interest for the preservation of our society against these traitors in our midst. . . .

Certainly to a Russian national accused of a conspiracy to destroy Russia, not one day would have been consumed in a trial. It is to America's credit that it took the pains and exerted the effort which it did in the trial of these defendants.

Julius and Ethel Rosenberg, I consider your crime worse than murder. Plain, deliberate, contemplated murder is dwarfed in magnitude by comparison with the crime you have committed.

The evidence indicated quite clearly that Julius Rosenberg was the prime mover in this conspiracy. However, let no mistake be made about the role which his wife, Ethel Rosenberg, played in this conspiracy. Instead of deterring him from pursuing his ignoble cause, she encouraged and assisted the cause. She was a mature woman—almost three years older than her husband and almost seven years older than her younger brother. She was a full-fledged partner in this crime.

Indeed the defendants Julius and Ethel Rosenberg placed their devotion to their causes above their own personal safety and were conscious that they were sacrificing their own children, should their misdeeds be detected—all of which did not deter them from pursuing their course. Love for their cause dominated their lives—it was even greater than their love for their children.

Your spying has already caused . . . the Communist aggression in Korea, with the resultant casualties exceeding fifty thousand and who knows but that millions more of innocent people must pay the price of your treason . . . by your betrayal you undoubtedly have altered the course of history to the disadvantage of our country . . . by immeasurably increasing the chances of atomic war, you may have condemned to death tens of millions of innocent people all over the world.

What I am about to say is not easy for me. I have deliberated for hours, days and nights. I have carefully weighed the evidence. Every nerve, every fiber of my body has been taxed. I am just as human as are the people who have given me the power to impose sentence. I am convinced beyond any doubt of your guilt. I have searched my conscience—to find some reason for mercy—for it is only human to be merciful and it is natural to try to spare lives. I am convinced, however, that I would violate the solemn and sacred trust that the people of this land have placed in my hands were I to show leniency to the defendants Rosenberg.

It is not in my power, Julius and Ethel Rosenberg, to forgive you. Only the Lord can find mercy for what you have done. The sentence of the Court upon Julius and Ethel Rosenberg is, for the crime for which you have been convicted, you are hereby sentenced to the punishment of death, and it is ordered upon some day within the week beginning with Monday, May 21, you shall be executed according to law.

The Screen: "The Pentagon Patriots."

THE CHORUS:
"Now should this pair outwit the law
And wiggle from death's bloody maw;
An outraged nation with a yell

Shall drag them from the prison cell
    And hang them high
    Beyond life's hope,
    To swing and die
    And dangle from
    The Hangman's rope!
Then, while the buzzard's make a feast
On their Red flesh as on a beast;
Our natives shall rejoice and sing
And shout while these two traitors swing
And freedom's cry shall soar and swell
With songs that echo—'All is well!' "

STAGE B

The GUARDS bring in the ROSENBERGS and lock them up. There are a half dozen PRISONERS. As JULIUS ROSENBERG passes one of the cells, he holds up two fingers and tries, unsuccessfully at first, to say, "Ethel, too." There is a long pause after the ROSENBERGS are put in cells at either end of the cell block.

PRISONER: Don't worry, Julie, you still got the appeal.

GUARD: Rosenberg, the Marshal's office upstairs says they're standing by for a message from Washington to take you up to Sing Sing tonight.

There is a long pause.

JULIUS ROSENBERG (*calling*): Ethel, don't be scared if some clown tells you we may be taken to the death house tonight! Everything will be all right; they can't do that.

There is another pause. Very simply and in true pitch ETHEL ROSENBERG sings "Un bel dì ve-dremo," from Madama Butterfly, *in Italian. The GUARDS and PRISONERS are still after she finishes.*

GUARD (*walks up to the cell of JULIUS ROSEN-BERG. They converse quietly.*): Rosenberg, I don't know about upstairs, but down here you're pretty damn lucky. Because of her.

JULIUS ROSENBERG: Thanks, but you look at it this way. I just got the death sentence because I'm supposed to be the big shot in an espionage ring. I pass out $1,000 here, $1,500 there, toss

$5,000 to my brother-in-law—but I never had the money to train that voice. I never had the money to do anything for her.

The PRISONERS call for encores.

ETHEL ROSENBERG (*begins to sing the "Battle-Hymn of the Republic." JULIUS joins her at the beginning of the next verse; at the same time their cells are clanged open and they are taken in opposite directions as the last phrase is heard and the lights fade.*):
"O, be swift, my soul, to answer Him; be jubilant, my feet!
Our God is marching on."

STAGE A

THE COURT: I want the motions very brief.

THE DEFENSE: Your Honor, tens upon tens of millions of people in this country, in Europe, in Asia, know about this case—

THE COURT: Yes, I want to say that I have been frankly hounded, pounded by vilification by pressurists. I think that it is not a mere accident that some people have been aroused in these countries. I think it has been by design. Yesterday, for instance, I received a barrage of telegrams.

THE DEFENSE: Your Honor, how is it that the Government, with thousands upon thousands of FBI agents, could not uncover one scrap of physical evidence so that you could be absolutely sure that these accusations are true?

THE COURT: Wasn't there some evidence about the table?

The Screen:

ARGUMENT BEFORE JUDGES SWAN, FRIENDLY, AND THURGOOD MARSHALL, DECEMBER 7, 1962, DOCKET NUMBER 27558
U.S. V. MORTON SOBELL,
NUMBER 151, OCTOBER 1962

On the screen like lines of a play. The action is continuous:

JUSTICE MARSHALL: How would we rule today if the case being argued were that of Ethel Rosenberg instead of Morton Sobell?

UNITED STATES ATTORNEY: If Ethel Rosenberg were still alive—the bench would have to reverse her conviction.

STAGE A

THE DEFENSE: There is so much new evidence. We've found the console table if you would only look at it. Judge Kaufman, in your hands you have the fate of two human beings and you must ask why in the shadow of death the Rosenbergs continue to insist on their innocence. You know that they have read the newspapers that we've all read. The newspapers that tell them that if they would only talk, if they would only confess, they would save themselves. What is it that stops them from doing this?

THE COURT: I have pondered that question. I have pondered it over and over again, and the only solution I have to it is to answer that it is the very same thing that drove them into it.

THE DEFENSE: Your Honor, the reason they act this way is because they are innocent. Believe me, they don't want to die; they are in their middle thirties. They have been convicted on accomplice testimony that is highly suspicious to more and more people. Surely there is at least some element of uncertainty, your Honor. We can talk about the jury's verdict being proper; this is not the quantum of proof that I am urging upon you now. And I say, in all deference, that your Honor compounded error when you made statements that I believe you probably would not make today, namely, that it was the Rosenbergs who caused the Korean War and the fifty thousand casualties.

THE COURT: They were a contributing cause.

THE GOVERNMENT: Your Honor, the Rosenberg Spy Ring, and that alone, accounts for the stand which the Russians took in Korea, which caused death and suffering to thousands of American boys, and I submit that these deaths and this suffering and *the rest of the state of the world* must be attributed to the tremendous contribution the Rosenbergs made. Now, if they wanted to cooperate, they could give information that would lead to the detection of any number of people. This is not the time for a court to be soft with hard-boiled spies, when they have showed no repentance and have stood steadfast in their insistence on their innocence.

THE DEFENSE: Your Honor, you must resist this war atmosphere. I will get down on my knees here and now to beg you to spare their lives, not just for their sake, but for their two little boys.

THE COURT: I will reserve decision until later this week.

STAGE B

On the Screen: *Lewisburg Penitentiary*.

HARRY GOLD: I am well. My weight is still at a normal 140 pounds and I don't ever intend to become sloppy fat again. Also a great source of satisfaction has been my work assignment here in medical research. A friend once said with much truth, just put Harry in a laboratory and he's happy. I've been reviewing my mathematics systematically and intensively—as I've intended for many years. I heard some of the World Series games over the radio here and we get football broadcasts over the weekend. Lately my "cup runneth over" since Penn beat Penn State.

STAGE B: RECONSTRUCTION (REUNION, 1951)

JULIUS and ETHEL ROSENBERG in prison, a screen between them.

ETHEL ROSENBERG: How did the kids seem to you, honey?

JULIUS ROSENBERG: When I came in the visiting room Michael was hiding under the table and the little one was asleep.

ETHEL ROSENBERG: Tell me.

JULIUS ROSENBERG: Robbie was asleep and Michael tackles my legs, you know. And then he started to open up a little.

ETHEL ROSENBERG: He did? Tell me.

JULIUS ROSENBERG: This'll kill you. He asked me if we had an *amicus curiae*? An *amicus curiae*. And then he says, did anyone besides Manny

Bloch testify for you? That was it; then he closed right up.

ETHEL ROSENBERG: Well, that's something anyway. Sometimes I can hardly stand to even see them, and they know it. Do you think they understand, Julie?

JULIUS ROSENBERG: I hope so.

ETHEL ROSENBERG: Maybe to them I'm just another mother who runs away. You know for all they know all we have to do is say what the Government wants and we could come home and all be together again. They don't know from history and politics. They're just lonesome. Oh, God—

JULIUS ROSENBERG: You mean they don't know we're heroes? My father the atom spy! (*They both laugh.*) Honey, honey, we've got to live up to the whole thing, a lot of liberals are getting involved in the case, a lot of—

ETHEL ROSENBERG: Do you know something, Julius? I can't even worry about the liberals or anyone else. They'll do what they'll do. I can't even think too much about the children (I know it sounds terrible). But I am not a good German Jew and neither are you, and I'm not going to be. That's what I'm holding on to. I'm—

JULIUS ROSENBERG: That's today. Last week it was "we're innocent and the people will save us." Wait a minute, let me talk, I've got new reasons every day too: the kids, the Jews, world peace, my hate for you know who, etc., etc. Sometimes I can't even picture us ever going back to Knickerbocker Village, know what I mean? Wait, let me finish, we've only got a minute. I love you, that's the reason. I love you. Whoever invented celibacy was insane. I'm making love to you, that's all my reasons.

They talk at once and try again and again to kiss through the screen.

STAGE A

THE COURT: I am again compelled to conclude that the defendants' guilt was established beyond doubt. Neither defendant has seen fit to follow the course of Harry Gold and David Greenglass. Their lips have remained sealed and they prefer the glory which they believe will be theirs for their diabolical conspiracy. The defendants, still defiant, assert that they seek justice, not mercy. What they seek they have attained. Application denied.

STAGE B

A VATICAN DIPLOMAT: I am directed by the Holy See to inform the competent United States authorities that many new demands are being received at the Vatican urging the Holy Father to intervene for clemency in behalf of the Rosenbergs and that leftists' newspapers insist that his Holiness has done nothing. I will be most grateful if you will kindly notify this to the President. There is no doubt that when history returns to this episode, it will seal with a word of highest praise the magnanimous gesture of the Supreme Pontiff.

AN OLD WOMAN: In the name of the family of Colonel Dreyfus, to whom world protest—including the people of America—and French justice assured vindication after a sentence obtained thanks to false testimony, forged documents and so-called confessions, we entreat you to prevent this irremediable act in order that the Rosenbergs be permitted the inevitable review of their trial.

VINCENZINA VANZETTI (*We see an old woman who speaks in Italian.*): Cosi spero fare onore e giustizia alla memoria di mio fratello Bartolomeo Vanzetti che, prima di morire, disse: "Io spero essere l'ultima vittima d'un ingiustizia tanto grande."

VINCENZINA VANZETTI (*simultaneous translation*): I hope thus to honor and render justice to the memory of my brother, Bartolomeo Vanzetti, who, before dying, said "I hope to be the last victim of such a great injustice."

The Screen (simultaneous):
U.S. V. GRUNEWALD, 233 F.2D 556. DECIDED APRIL 10, 1956 (FRANK DISSENT, WHICH THE SUPREME COURT UPHELD):

P. 576 "NO ONE WHO LEGITIMATELY EXERCISES THE CONSTITUTIONAL PRIVILEGE OUGHT TO BE SO PLACED THAT HE MUST SUBSEQUENTLY JUSTIFY IT TO A JURY."

P. 577 "AND AN UNFAVORABLE INFERENCE SHOULD NOT BE DRAWN FROM THE MERE FACT THAT THE FIFTH AMENDMENT PRIVILEGE HAS BEEN INVOKED."

PROFESSOR HAROLD C. UREY: Dear President Eisenhower: Greenglass is supposed to have revealed to the Russians the secrets of the atomic bomb. A man of Greenglass's capacity is wholly incapable of transmitting the physics, chemistry and mathematics of the atomic bomb to anyone. New evidence makes even more plain what was plain enough before, that the prosecution's case has no logic in it, and that it depends upon the blowing up of patently perjured testimony.

Professor Albert Einstein joins me in begging you to spare the Rosenbergs. (Signed) Professor Harold C. Urey

DR. J. ROBERT OPPENHEIMER: I was never requested to be a witness in the trial of Sobell or the Rosenbergs.

STAGE B: RECONSTRUCTION (DREAMS)

A wire screen separates them.

ETHEL ROSENBERG: . . . but I'm not crying so much now. I still have that dream though.

Complete, hollow silence and the faint sound of birds.

THE DOCTOR: Of the boy?

ETHEL ROSENBERG: The scream on the phone when I told him. I'm dreaming about my mother lately, too.

THE DOCTOR: What are your feelings?

ETHEL ROSENBERG: None. That's the point. In one I'm just sitting watching her cook. She doesn't pay any attention to me and I have no feelings one way or another. But there's a lot of smoke, as if something were burning. What's wrong with me that I still think of my mother and Davey as "family"? Why shouldn't I hate them?

THE DOCTOR: Why not?

ETHEL ROSENBERG: Why shouldn't I hate them and love the people who've been more than a family to me? Wait a minute. I have a funny feeling right now. I feel anxiety.

THE DOCTOR: Go ahead.

ETHEL ROSENBERG: I feel frightened, as if my mother could come right here into the prison and get me. Why can't I tell the truth about my feelings?

THE DOCTOR: Try.

ETHEL ROSENBERG: What is there to be afraid of? It's the Government, not my mother, that's killing me. I love Manny Bloch as much as flesh and blood. I'm feeling very frightened now. I'm going to go on—I'm going on—the smoke in the kitchen! It's a smoke screen. I feel love for you, too. Why not? You come all the way out here for nothing. You're kind, you never judge—(*She is more and more emotional.*)—in the kitchen, she'll take the knife and kill me! Doctor—

THE DOCTOR (*He tries to touch her hand*): Ethel, can't you let them go?

ETHEL ROSENBERG (*struggles thought by thought*): I've got to. Who am I to judge anyone? I could save my children if I did what my mother says, "So what would be so bad, what would be so bad?" And Ruthie? So now she's just like my mother. That's what terrifies me—that I'm just like her too. There's only two choices when the Government picks your family out. Maybe if they'd come to us first I'd be Ruth Greenglass and Ruthie would have been Ethel Rosenberg. Listen, I know, I know.

THE DOCTOR: So, can you let them go?

ETHEL ROSENBERG: I'm letting the children go, God help me. There's been enough judging; I'm sick with it. Enough.

THE DOCTOR: Ja, ja.

ETHEL ROSENBERG: Well, what difference does it make now? Who I hate, who I love? But I know that I would have made it. That's true, isn't it?

THE DOCTOR: Before you were—

ETHEL ROSENBERG: Before I was arrested, that summer, there was a real difference. I would have graduated, wouldn't I? (*He laughs. They both laugh. Pause.*) Did you know that I'm the only person in this whole building now?

THE DOCTOR: Is that so?

Pause.

ETHEL ROSENBERG: Listen to the birds. (*Pause.*) Yes, except for the matron. She's really a fine person. I like her very much. Very different backgrounds. In the old life we would never have met. You know New York is really a private little world, isn't it? I think we all miss a lot in life. Even though we think we're free. Was I really free then? I haven't mentioned Julius. I remember him as he looked when he was in college. And I love him truly. But the past is really gone, isn't it? Why should I hate anyone?

THE DOCTOR: The past is still in your dreams.

ETHEL ROSENBERG: But that's because it's gone. I know it's gone; otherwise I wouldn't feel so lonesome.

Screaming headlines, building toward the execution, begin. And the scenes of world protest. Now, through the theater we hear the voices of JULIUS *and* ETHEL ROSENBERG. *As they make their appeal, the slow Ritual of Death begins. Their heads are shorn; their clothes rent. People enter and exit. There are secular and religious figures bending over them.* THE GOVERNMENT AGENT *creeps forward with the open-confession telephone to Washington. They are offered their last food and drink. Absolute silence except for the disembodied voices. Other* PRISONERS *stand frozen and listening. There are whispers everywhere:* "Talk," "Tell us the names." *The transaction becomes ambiguous as figures weave around the victims.* GUARDS *arrange the execution: the slow dance of the technicians. There are the voices; the international films of the mercy throngs; the Death Ritual.*

ETHEL ROSENBERG AND JULIUS ROSENBERG: We, Julius Rosenberg and Ethel Rosenberg, husband and wife, are now confined in the Death House in Sing Sing Prison, awaiting electrocution on June 18, our fourteenth wedding anniversary. . . .

We appealed to you once before. Our sentence, we declared there, violated truth and the instincts of civilized mankind. We told you the truth: we are innocent. The truth does not change. . . .

The guilt in this case, if we die, will be America's. The shame, if we die, will dishonor this generation, and pervade history until future Americans recapture the heritage of truth, justice and equality before the law. . . .

We cannot besmirch our names by bearing false witness to save ourselves. Do not dishonor America, Mr. President, by considering as a condition of our right to survive, the delivery of a confession of guilt of a crime we did not commit. . . .

We submitted proof to show that David Greenglass stole uranium from Los Alamos, in a venture concededly unconnected with us. . . .

We submitted actual physical evidence [the missing console table], never produced in court against us, to show the Greenglasses and the Government collaborated to bring into the trial false testimony that we had in our home an expensive console table, given to us by the "Russians" and equipped for microfilming purposes. It is not a specially constructed table, but one bought by us at R. H. Macy's for about $21 as we testified at our trial. . . .

We ask you, Mr. President, the civilized head of a civilized nation, to judge our pleas with reason and humanity.

DWIGHT D. EISENHOWER: Dear Son: To address myself to the Rosenberg case for a minute, I must say that it goes against the grain to avoid interfering in the case where a woman is to receive capital punishment. But in this instance, it is the woman who is the strong and recalcitrant character, the man is the weak one. If there should be any commuting of the woman's sentence without the man's, then from here on the Soviets would simply recruit their spies from among women. I am convinced that the only conclusion to be drawn from the history of this case is that the Rosenbergs have received the benefit of every safeguard which American justice can provide. . . .

JEAN-PAUL SARTRE (*we see the French philosopher speaking to the audience.*): Maintenant que l'on nous a fait vos alliés, le sort des Rosenbergs pourrait être un avant-coureur de notre propre avenir. Vous, qui prétendez être les maîtres du monde, avez eu l'occasion de prouver que vous étiez d'abord maîtres de vous-mêmes. Mais si vous cédez à votre folie criminelle, cette même folie pourrait vous précipiter demain dans une guerre d'extermination. En frappant les Rosenbergs vous avez tout simplement essayé d'arrêter les progrès de la science au moyen d'un sacrifice humain. Par la magie, la chasse aux sorcières, les autodafés, les sacrifices, nous sommes arrivés maintenant au point ou votre pays est malade de frayeur. Vous avez peur de l'ombre de votre propre bombe. Ne soyez pas étonnés si d'un bout à l'autre de l'Europe, nous crions: Attention! l'Amérique est atteinte de la maladie de la Rage! Rompez tout ce qui nous attache à elle, autrement, nous serons à notre tour mordus et enragés!

JEAN-PAUL SARTRE (*simultaneous translation*): Now that we have been made your allies, the fate of the Rosenbergs could be a preview of our own future. You, who claim to be masters of the world, had the opportunity to prove that you were first masters of yourself. But if you give in to your criminal folly, this very folly might tomorrow throw us headlong into a war of extermination. By killing the Rosenbergs you have quite simply tried to halt the progress of science by human sacrifice. Magic, witch-hunts, autos-da-fé, sacrifices—we are here getting to the point: Your country is sick with fear. You are afraid of the shadow of your own bomb. Do not be astonished if we cry out from one end of Europe to the other: Watch out! America has the rabies! Cut all ties which bind us to her, otherwise we will in turn be bitten and run mad!

In his death costume JULIUS ROSENBERG *steps forward.*

JULIUS ROSENBERG: Dear Manny, Never let them change the truth of our innocence. For peace, bread and roses in simple dignity we face the executioner with courage, confidence and perspective—never losing faith. . . . P.S. All my personal effects are in three cartons and you can get them from the Warden. Ethel wants it known that we are the first victims of American Fascism. All my love—Julie

"CASE SEEN IN PERIL," and an eleventh-hour headline and image chronology begins.

ETHEL ROSENBERG: Dearest Sweethearts, my most precious children, only this morning it looked like we might be together again after all. Now that this cannot be, I want so much for you to know all that I have come to know. Unfortunately, I may write only a few simple words; the rest your own lives must teach you, even as mine taught me. At first, of course, you will grieve bitterly for us, but you will not grieve alone. That is our consolation and it must eventually be yours. Your lives must teach you, too, that good cannot really flourish in the midst of evil; that freedom and all the things that go to make up a truly satisfying and worthwhile life must sometimes be purchased very dearly. Be comforted then that we were serene and understood with the deepest kind of understanding that civilization had not yet progressed to the point where life did not have to be lost for the sake of life; and that we were comforted in the sure knowledge that others would carry on after us. We wish we might have had the tremendous joy and gratification of living our lives out with you. Your Daddy, who is with me in the last momentous hours, sends his heart and all the love that is in it for his dearest boys. Always remember that we were innocent and could not wrong our conscience. We press you close and kiss you with all our strength. Lovingly, Daddy and Mommy

STAGE B

MAN IN THE STREET: Are women more concerned with their facial makeup than their all-around appearance?
ANSWER: No comment.
ANSWER: Yes, too many women fail to check their rear appearance.
ANSWER: No, that's what Lady Astor said. . . .
ANSWER: That's true, a woman's first concern is her face. . . .
ANSWER: No comment.

THE DEFENSE: There was a worldwide reaction to their execution. In Paris, thousands participated in rallies to "save the Rosenbergs." One person was shot and over four hundred arrested as demonstrators clashed with massive police formations. In England, supporters made last-minute attempts to persuade Prime

Minister Churchill to intervene. In Los Angeles, a strange soap-box orator in Pershing Square convinced two lawyers, that I didn't even know, that I had overlooked something. They went to Justice Douglas and he granted the Rosenbergs, *my clients,* a stay of execution! The stay was signed and the court adjourned. Then it came over the wire at 6 P.M.: Attorney General Brownell had ordered Chief Justice Vinson to reconvene the court. *To reconvene* the court—the first time in American history that the court had been asked to convene for the purpose of overthrowing a ruling of one of its own Justices. From all over the country they flew back that night. We went crazy. At the last minute lawyers came into the case from New York. Teams of attorneys went into the homes of judges, they got on their knees; judges were found on golf courses, we pleaded, we begged—they tell me Judge Jerome Frank broke down.

He walks into a new scene.

The Screen (under the action):

U.S. GOVERNMENT BRIEF IN COURT OF APPEALS, 2D CIRCUIT, DOCKET NO. 31259, JUNE 1967.

P. 37 "... IT WAS UNEQUIVOCALLY SPELLED OUT [AT THE TRIAL] THAT THE SKETCH AND THE GREENGLASS DESCRIPTIVE MATERIAL WAS NOT OFFERED AS A 'COMPLETE' OR 'DETAILED' DESCRIPTION [OF THE ATOMIC BOMB], BUT ONLY AS A 'TIP-OFF.' "

THE DEFENSE: Your Honor, I beg you to order a stay until I can complete my presentation. It would be terrible if I could convince your Honor that you should grant the application and it would be too late.

THE COURT: Get along with your argument: The execution has been moved up to 8 P.M. so as not to conflict with the Sabbath.

The Screen:
TELEGRAM

EMANUEL BLOCH
401 BROADWAY NYK

LYONS AND WINCHELL ITEMS FABRICATION MADE OUT OF WHOLE CLOTH—STOP—NEVER REFUSED SERVICE OF RABBI—STOP—NEVER MADE ANY STATEMENTS DIRECTLY OR INDI-

RECTLY ABOUT RABBIS THAT SHOWED ANTI-SEMITISM—STOP—RABBI IRVING KOSLOWE SING SING CHAPLAIN U.S. MARSHAL AND AUTHORITIES HERE CAN VERIFY—STOP—SEE MY LETTERS FEBRUARY 22 AND 23 TO YOU AND FAMILY DECRYING THESE OUTRAGEOUS FRAUDS.

JULIUS ROSENBERG 110649

STAGE B

MAN IN THE STREET: Do you approve of the verdict in the atom spy trial?
ANSWER: Definitely.
ANSWER: Guilty.
ANSWER: They're guilty.
ANSWER: No comment.
ANSWER: No comment.

STAGES A AND B

For the execution there are two DOCTORS, one ELECTRICIAN, three PRISONERS. This group and THE RABBI, PRISONERS and MATRON make up the enactment of the electrocution. The entire remainder of the company, however, are present as witnesses. A UNITED STATES MARSHAL stands, obviously waiting for a sign that JULIUS ROSENBERG will talk. THE MARSHAL stands with a telephone in his hand. JULIUS ROSENBERG stops and confronts the outstretched receiver. THE RABBI speaks as he walks ahead.

THE RABBI: "Yea, though I walk through the valley of the shadow of death, I will fear no evil: for Thou art with me ... "

THE RABBI continues as JULIUS ROSENBERG is strapped in the chair, the cathode is adjusted, the helmet lowered on the head to make contact with the shaven spot, the mask is fixed on. The first charge dims the lights, shakes the chair, sends up a puff of yellow smoke from the head. The second charge, following a three-second release, lasts for fifty-seven seconds; the third, the same. THE DOCTOR approaches, rips the shirt open, listens and speaks.

THE DOCTOR: I pronounce this man dead.

JULIUS ROSENBERG is placed in a guerney and wheeled out. An ORDERLY with a mop and sponge rushes in and cleans the floor and chair. Immediately, THE RABBI, leading ETHEL ROSENBERG, enters; the PRISON MATRON follows.

THE RABBI:
"In thee, O Lord, do I put my trust;
    let me never be ashamed
For I have heard the slander of many:
    fear was on every side:
While they took counsel together against me,
    they devised to take away my life."

Now THE RABBI sings the Hebrew lament for the dead. Smiling softly, ETHEL ROSENBERG starts toward the electric chair. As she passes the PRISON MATRON, she holds out her hand; the older woman grasps it and ETHEL draws her close and kisses her lightly on the cheek. There are the shocks. THE DOCTOR advances.

THE DOCTOR: She is still alive.

The EXECUTIONER runs out from his cubicle.

EXECUTIONER: Want another?

There are two more shocks.

THE DOCTOR: I pronounce this woman dead.

ETHEL ROSENBERG is removed from the stage.

THE CHORUS:
"So when the Rósenbergs lie dead
Wrapped in a shroud of Kremlin-red;
All future traitors should beware
They too will burn within the 'chair.' "

They pause, then exit repeating the last phrase.

"They too will burn with the 'chair.' "
THE DEFENSE: At 7:32 P.M. the White House turned us down for the last time. At 7:45 P.M. Judge Kaufman denied motions for the last time. In New York ten thousand people in Union Square wept and screamed as eight o'clock drew near. (*Pause.*) Three days later Justice Frankfurter made public his dissenting opinion. (*Pause.*) It was the way François Mauriac wrote: After years, the long set of appeals and petitions for mercy ended in this violently lighted lacquered room, furnished with a single chair. The man standing on the threshold would have only one word to say, one sign to make, not to cross it. They did not say the word, they did not make the sign. There was only the cruel telephone wire which the day before the Sabbath linked the white House and Sing Sing and which will link them forever. (*Pause.*) For thirty years I had been an officer of the court. True, I had seen nefarious practices in the criminal courts, but basically I believed in the administration of justice and in the integrity of most officials sworn to uphold it. But how could I dream that officials of the Department of Justice would lend themselves to the perpetration of a complete hoax, like the Jello box business, concocted by these weird characters Gold and the Greenglasses? (*With emotion.*) I was full of fear, too; like the judge and the jury and the man in the street. I suppose that was my biggest mistake, and having those illusions, underestimating the cynicism and power for evil in high places. . . . Maybe that's why I believed to the last minute that they wouldn't dare go through with these executions. I couldn't believe in that much evil. And then not one scientist came forward. I had to accept the Government's word. *They read a list of famous names scheduled as witnesses but they never called them.* You have no idea of how lonely it was. *Nobody came forward; nobody who knew would come forward to help.* (*Pause*) "There was truth and there was untruth and if you clung to the truth even against the whole world, you were not mad."

BLOCH exits.

The Screen:
    EMANUEL BLOCH, DIED JANUARY 30, 1954.

On the first big screen a giant picture of the real JULIUS ROSENBERG comes up. On the second, ETHEL ROSENBERG; and on the third, in the distance, between the parents, the two ROSENBERG CHILDREN. There is no curtain call. After a pause there is a dialogue between the audience and the director, actors, and experts on the period.

END

AFTERWORD

The United States of America v. Julius and Ethel Rosenberg, et al.

Et al.? There were others. Morton Sobell spent a generation as a political prisoner and his wife, Helen, like a creation of Bertolt Brecht, told the story of the outrage up and down the country. There is no room for them in this play. Powerful books by John Wexley and Walter and Miriam Schneir give all the facts that here would have been dramatically unbearable. They are another play: They survived as creative and vital human beings. They lived to see another day. (The actual end of the "age of conspiracy" came, I believe, when Abby Hoffman pole-vaulted into the Brooklyn Navy Yard and announced that he intended to steal the Polaris missile.)

The case went on. The Sobells and their "family" of attorneys pressed the Government for eighteen years. Had the Rosenbergs lived, they would have gone down part of the same long legal road.

1952: Ranking *European* scientists testified against Greenglass's capacity. Exhibit 8 was still impounded so the Sobell defense was severely handicapped, but the concept of "implosion," the scientists testified, was public knowledge and therefore there was *nothing to steal*. At this time, too, the question of pretrial publicity was opened. Like almost every other point in the long years of appeal, the matter of State propaganda during political trials, brought to the courts by Morton Sobell and to the public by his wife, has become a seriously contested public issue.

1953: The evidence itself was shown to be fatally defective. The console table turned out to be a console table. Prop by prop the Government's case was being shredded.

1956: Mr. Sobell had been kidnapped from Mexico, prior to his arrest, by American agents and not deported as the Government had insisted at the trial. In 1956, after long searching, the attorney Marshall Perlin was able to produce firm evidence of the criminal attack in Mexico.

1966: Morton Sobell, a brilliant engineer, a luminous human being, and a model prisoner, was still denied the parole that anyone else might have expected. Now as his mandatory release date approached, the decision was made to go for the very heart of the case. The Government, fighting to the last, finally lost control of Greenglass's cartoon, Government Exhibit 8. When the shocking sketch that had been the predicate for the great witch-hunts appeared in the *New York Times,* the scandal was complete. At the same moment evidence was brought forward that almost certainly proves FBI forgery in the instance of Harry Gold's New Mexico trip. Suddenly the Government began referring to the fatal Greenglass caricature as "The Strawman"; now the sketch was only "a tip-off," "rhinestones . . . instead of diamonds," no longer was it the "secret of the atom bomb itself!"

There is much more but it is, finally, a question of magic against science: *There was nothing to steal;* no secret formulas *belong* to anyone. The State was defeated, but it persisted nastily; Sobell's pretrial "jail time" was granted him only after a final judge, ashamed to continue the persecution any longer, ordered it so.

So they, the Sobells, survived. They are public and creative and a growing inspiration (young people immediately sense a kinship with Mr. Sobell, they are drawn to him; he seems to exist in color, like them, while others from the past are in black and white).

To take a step backward from the case is to see a generation of radicals tortured, and beyond them the silent majority—dumb with fear, numb with guilt, irreparably injured by what the State let loose on them—coming into the 1970s astounded by events and brokenhearted at the end of the American Dream.

The case is alive because the fears and hopes that underlay the time are still alive. Just as the Government told the Sobells, "If you don't work with us, they'll fry, and you will too," and continued to come to him in prison saying, "The Rosenbergs are dead, you can't help them anymore," so the State came to us all and bid us choose, counting on our silence.

It began with the circulation of the transcripts and fact sheets, then meetings, pickets, committees, the poetry and songs and books, and now the plays and films.

The antimyth is nearing completion. It began when the Rosenbergs and Sobells refused to complete the magic ring which, had they done so, would have reached down to this day and might have led to the actual use of the detention camps. It would not have been a matter of a single or simple "confession" but rather of naming hundreds, thousands, of names; and who could have doubted the word of the atom spy masters themselves?

The beginning of the demythologizing process which is rending the country began, in many ways, with their "No!" The "conspiracy" of which they were a real part is just now coming to light: They were the firstlings of the latest and fast-developing American Human Rights Revolution, whose password is always "No!"

CHRONOLOGY OF EVENTS

1945
August 6 — Hiroshima atom bombed. Dead: 80,000 in the first minute.
August 9 — Nagasaki: 75,000 dead.

1949
September 23 — Announcement of Russian atom bomb explosion.

1950
February 3 — Dr. Klaus Fuchs confesses to atomic espionage for Soviet Union.
May 23 — Harry Gold confesses to being Fuchs's American link in spy ring.
June 15 — David Greenglass arrested as Gold's accomplice.
June 25 — Korean War begins.
July 17 — Julius Rosenberg arrested as co-conspirator with Gold and Greenglass.
August 11 — Ethel Rosenberg arrested on the same charges as her husband, Julius.
August 18 — Morton Sobell arrested as coconspirator.

1951
March 6 — Rosenberg-Sobell spy ring trial begins.
April 5 — Julius and Ethel Rosenberg sentenced to death. Morton Sobell sentenced to thirty years.

1953
February 11 — President Eisenhower denies clemency.
June 19 — Many courts and appeals later (the record of the trial was *never* reviewed by the Supreme Court), Julius and Ethel Rosenberg are executed at 8:02 P.M. and 8:08 P.M., respectively.

1969
January 14 — Morton Sobell is paroled.

"The Case and the Myth: *The United States of America v. Julius and Ethel Rosenberg*"*

THE CASE

The Case—what the Government always called "the atom spy ring"—was my political baptism. Whether it was—as Jean-Paul Sartre called it—the start of World War III or not, it certainly was the start for many of us in the fifties of what was to become known in the sixties as "the movement." But in those days the headlines handed down the fateful news of doomsday. It was as if

———
Ed. note: Donald Freed's essay was originally published with the text of his play.

the atom, like Zeus's fire, had been stolen from Heaven, while the Rosenbergs and Morton Sobell played the roles of antiheroes. It was the Government that dominated the stage with its federal agents, lawyers, judges, Congressmen, and armies of functionaries. It was the United States v. the USSR and the "spies" were only attendant lords in the cosmic drama. We in the public received our mythology from the front pages and thousands of people who were later—through dint of hard study of transcripts and evidence—to become either expert in or obsessed with The Case followed from day to day the cartoonlike melodrama of the editorial imagination. At first we all thought them guilty.

What first made some of us suspicious? It was not the "old left" of the day that first cracked my own particular mythology of virtue and patriotism. It was the well-known legal experts who first fascinated me. So they—the "spies"—were all dead or imprisoned before I began to say: "Wait!"

As the years went by I became both expert and obsessed. The dim figures of The Case began to take on definition. The Rosenbergs began to be real and so, too, did the Government. Roy Cohn and Joseph McCarthy were the agents of the Government and the authors of its new religion: anticommunism. Something was rotten. The Cold War froze to zero degree. Books, opinions, journals, authorities from all over the world, were beginning to be univocal about the conduct of the judge, about the plaguelike atmosphere of what was already being called (somewhat unfairly) the "McCarthy Era," about The Case in general. Now The Case was becoming The Scandal.

But there were two reasons why there could be no play then. First, there was the frozen, frightened political climate, and second, in my opinion, there was no coherent aesthetic vocabulary yet available.

THE FUTURE DETERMINES THE PAST

"The future determines the past," Morton Sobell said one night after he was released. After a generation behind bars for "conspiracy to commit espionage." That is, the past becomes received myth unless or until artists and critics begin a re-

vision or demythologization. In a time when the very breathing is poisoned by the ideas of the past it is a part of the burden of the writer, through fact and cruelty, to help in the construction of these new antimyths—whether plays or films or books—that are meant to be a revelation and a therapy.

The antimyth must have a reflexive structure; it is the double of the myth that it is confronting. There are the gods—the gods of the twentieth century—Freud, Marx, Nietzsche, and the chorus is none other than the terrible Man in the Street; the oracle is the media; the song and dance is that of the couch and the court and the street and the barricade. And there is no beginning or middle or end in sight.

LIBERALS, RADICALS, AND REVOLUTIONARIES

For the "liberal," the meaning of a case like *The United States of America v. Julius and Ethel Rosenberg, et al.* does not turn on guilt or innocence, but only on the astounding and unprecedented death penalty exacted by a panic-stricken and twitching majority. The "radical" is obsessed with the innocence of the victims and his is a rage to tell the truth even if the earth opens at his feet. The "revolutionary" assumes the inequity of the trial with the liberal, shares an identification with the victim as does the radical, but for him the innocence of the victim is less weighty than the *guilt of the State*. And he goes for the Government. He demands of the State a quick accounting. The new historians (the "revisionists") and some of the new playwrights of Fact and Cruelty are attempting this. Once man against Fate, now everyman v. the State.

This is existential work, for the public part of America is gone and dead as the Rosenbergs. If it were not gone, then we could change it. We, none of us, can change the past (that is the fact and the cruelty), but we can, if we are sufficiently lucid, *determine* it, given the weight of information that the play intends. These new antimyths do not invoke terror and pity in the old way; rather they try for something like anguish and, perhaps, a radical solidarity.

FROM KAUFMAN TO HOFFMAN

From Irving Kaufman, of the great atom spy trials, to Julius Hoffman, of the trial of the conspiracy of youth and peace and black liberation, it is only a fraction of a second in political time. Jerry Rubin and Bobby Seale are the epigonoi of Morton Sobell as surely as the struggle has moved from the courts into the streets and back to the courts again. That passage is the passage of time. The charge, "conspiracy," is the same; the State's tactics are stereotyped; silence in the face of power is the same now as then. But the critical difference is in the reactions of people. Where once there was guilt and paralysis, now there is rebellion and movement. Once a handful of men and committees could cow millions of people into silence; now the Army has been in the streets and yet the pressure for change goes up by the numbers.

Here is the vocabulary of the myth of the twentieth century: film, tape, trials, technology, confessions—in short, the State and its visible paraphernalia. The infrastructure of the myth is the agony and confrontation between Science and Magic. The Rosenbergs and Morton Sobell were players in this myth. The antimyth to the magic of the State is Theater of Fact. The antimyth to the science of the State is Theater of Cruelty.

The goal of the antimyth is not guilt but another feeling entirely—the one Marx called revolutionary—*shame*.

Guilt is pervasive and equals repetition; shame is specific, rooted in fact and leads to change. Shame is the recognition of choices past and present. Shame posits the reality of *freedom* and thus choice. Shame has as its components elements of fact and cruelty. Shame is the precondition for hope in modern man.

THEATER OF CRUELTY

The two new theaters of Fact and Cruelty provide a grammar, at last, for a popular drama of the twentieth century. All exponential numbers, facts and figures, names and dates and places are necessary even to begin to come close to the phenomena of our time: the death camps, the great purge trials, the Triple Revolution and most of all the atom bomb. But for the interpretation of all these facts it also requires cruelty. The spectator must be given a choice in order to retain any hope that he can influence the monstrosities that lie before him.

The popular idea of this new theater as a grotesque circus holds for *Inquest*. There is the "Man in the Street" chorus. These are the masses ruined, as Tolstoy diagnosed, by the "Government." The folk who twitch to the signals and magic of science like so many Kafkaesque or Dostoyevskian pale criminals. Next, there are the "creatures of the State," as Whittaker Chambers called them. The professional prosecution witnesses condemned to talk and point forever— poor mad monsters (Harry Gold babbled endlessly of black snakes and secret agents; David Greenglass could never stop smiling). Finally, there are the gods of the twentieth century— Marx, Freud, Nietzsche—under whose prophetic gaze the doomsday scenario must be acted out to the end.

The Theater of Cruelty is surreal in one sense, but this is balanced out against the torment of choice and freedom inherent in the will to survive the nightmare. To wake up is, in itself, an act of hope.

For the New York production of this play, Ken Isaacs prepared a series of aural-visual souvenirs ("The Bomb," "The Spy Ring"). The sights and sounds of the Cold War past, from Milton Berle to Joseph McCarthy, can take the audience back in time, jog their memories and make them recall that it all happened. This is what I mean as one kind of Theater of Cruelty: to be made to remember and therefore to want to choose and change the past, but to be unable to because the past no longer exists, and because the past no longer exists (and that is why we feel such pain), to know that we are free.

THEATER OF FACT

The transcripts and memoranda and tapes are there. Every word no matter how bizarre or poisoned can be documented. It all happened. But I do not think the Theater of Fact can stand alone. I believe that the increments must be thrown into a cruel relief and that reconstructions can and should be drawn from them. When we see Ethel and Julius Rosenberg in love, or Ethel talking to her psychoanalyst, or the two of them talking in prison, we have no choice but to reconstruct from the primary sources of letters and conversations, and memories again.

Predictably, there is loud and quick complaint that the "facts" are merely out-of-context abstractions that can be manipulated to prove anything. "Commitment" is branded as rank bias and propaganda. It is true that the technology of film and tape behind this new theater can be perverted—we know that about any technology—but media, when it is authentic, can also explode the myths of the status quo and make rending gaps in the credibility of the "establishment" of lies.

"Without continual freedom of choice, there can be no dramatic conflict." The assertion by Rolf Hochhuth is now and will be in the future the libido of the new theater.

It is for the dramatist to infiltrate the huge historical abstractions of the time and to bring out from the flux recognizable human beings and a confluence of "all too human" motives to sweep us along to the rational and nonrational understandings of otherwise unspeakable events.

When events are so momentous as to be unspeakable, only myth (poetry) or statistics will begin to encompass and abstract what would otherwise be lost to understandings. It is this planned alienation that makes for the aesthetics, or part of them, of the Theater of Fact. But the impact of the Theater of Fact is not purgative like the Theater of Cruelty: The latter is therapeutic, the former didactic.

How to distinguish the Theater of Fact from such earlier twentieth-century genres as Social Realism, Naturalism, and the Living Newspaper? The Theater of Social Realism was a revolutionary and antiromantic attempt to imitate life in a new way. It was a celebration of late nineteenth-century myth, the myth of mass man in everyday life, and the smallest detail would register with a new impact on those who had been "poisoned by romanticism." The plays of Hauptmann, Gorki, Ibsen, the others, took us through the fourth wall into the microcosm of a Berlin or New York street, a Russian country estate, or a Scandinavian bourgeoisie, into the infrastructure of daily life. All this was dubbed Naturalism and that, in any case, was the aim. How shocked the new century was by this analysis of the selected fateful trivia of the everyday—Zola and Freud, chemistry and psychology—how true it all was!

But the Theater of Fact deals not with the banal or quotidian smudges of life. Rather it has to do with the colossal, the overarching new myth of Evil: the titanic symbol of the camps; the assassination of a leader; murder while "good people" look on; mighty nation-states pitted against small scapegoats; 100,000 victims in the first second. This content, then, is, so far, quite different—and its structure is even more so. These plays most closely resemble "histories," in the old terminology, that have begun to bleed through into the media of the man in the street.

THE PLAY

The story of *The United States of America v. Julius and Ethel Rosenberg, et al.* is Theater of Fact in that every word is taken from primary sources. At its most lunatic there is not an invented word in the entire text. The reconstructions ("Love," "Money," "Dreams") are drawn from letters, notes, always memory. But the *mise-en-scène* of the play is Theater of Cruelty. Stage A is the court; Stage B is the psyche and history. There is an incessant dialectic.

We are combining not only media but also the facts of evil with the cruelty of individual choice. What you see really happened; that is fact. Now you must let it happen to you; that is existential or moral cruelty: You who were passive and did not choose when you had the chance must now undergo everything twice, only now it is forbidden you, that choice, by finitude and time.

The new theater is like the old in its drive to penetrate into the springs of existence. The shock of the numbers and images, in a play like *Inquest,* is meant to be therapeutic, for it is as George Orwell said: "There was truth and there was untruth and if you clung to the truth even against the whole world, you were not mad."

These two new forms of drama, which build out of the past, deal with man no longer as if he were made in the image of a machine but as a desperately ill, thousand-year-old mad animal. But a human animal, however ravaged, is not a machine, and there can be hope for recovery. Here the old cathartic function of the performing arts is invoked again, and the aim of the theater of the future in this century may very well be, in the words Weiss gives Marat, to remind the suffering that—

> The important thing
> is to pull yourself up by your own
>   hair
> to turn yourself inside out
> and see the whole world with fresh
>   eyes

Soon it will require courage, once again, to go to the theater as the twentieth century begins—fatefully—to purge itself. Cruelty is its abreaction, and Fact its therapy.

DISENTHRALLMENT

"We must disenthrall ourselves," said Lincoln when the crisis deepened. That is what these theaters of Fact and Cruelty are about. For many, the American Dream has simply become the American Nightmare, but that, too, is, I think, transitory.

In the twentieth century we have begun to frighten ourselves to death with grotesque and mindless abstractions: "the Government," "the masses," "the power structure," "the outsider." These are our myths and—like the ancients—we really believe them. The difference is that their myths were theirs and served them, whereas ours are invented and received and have made us sick. Racial and political myths can best be subverted, perhaps, by those who should know the most about storytelling—the playwrights. So the play is an antimyth; it means to disenthrall.

What, then, shall be the new myths? That is for the real and new people to create; the playwrights will come later. They will write under the sign of Artaud, who, more than McLuhan, in the genius behind the new "Theater of Time" that is coming: We are not free and the sky can still fall on our heads and the theater exists to remind us of that first of all. For now the theaters of Fact and Cruelty are theaters of absurd hope. Just now we are all involved, alike, in making the necessary "myth of the twenty-first century." Oh, gods, grant us credibility.

—DONALD FREED

Peter Cheeseman et al.

FIGHT FOR SHELTON BAR

1974

Fight for Shelton Bar was first performed at the Victoria Theatre Stoke-on-Trent on Tuesday 22 January 1974 (pub. Methuen, 1977) by the company at that time: Nick Darke, John Darrell, Alan Gill, Polly Hemingway, Dave Miller, Graham Padden, Bill Thomas, Dyfed Thomas, Romy Saunders, Polly Warren, Sandy Walsh, Graham Watkins, and Jim Wiggins. The production was directed by Peter Cheeseman and designed by Alison Chitty. The songs were arranged by Stuart Johnson and Jeff Parton, and played and sung by the cast. The research committee consisted of Peter Cheeseman, Romy Saunders, Polly Warren, and Graham Watkins. The production remained in the repertoire until October 1974, and Robert Aldous, Alun Bond, Bob Eaton, Katherine Iddon, Christopher Martin, Ruth Seglow, and Roger Walker joined the company and took over parts from some of the original cast. A short television version was transmitted on BBC-2 in November 1974 in their "Second City Firsts" series, produced by Barry Hanson and directed by Peter Cheeseman.

INTRODUCTION

In the late summer of 1973 I met Ted Smith and Bill Foster, Chairman and Secretary of the Shelton Works Action Committee, with two members of the company—Graham Watkins and Polly Warren, to ask them amongst other things whether they would like us to do our touring Road Show in their canteen. They asked us if we would do one of our documentaries about them. "What good would that do?" I asked. They said it would alert the people of North Staffordshire to the danger to local employment if a large part of Shelton Bar were to close down. Two years of newspaper articles and public meetings seemed to have been ineffective. It would alert the men of Shelton to the danger—they still didn't seem to believe it. It might generate national publicity to add weight to their case with the British Steel Corporation and the Government. Also, they said, it would cheer them up.

The reasons seemed very cogent to me, and I agreed to do it, abandoning previous program plans so that we could start work straight away. We announced the documentary as a show putting the Action Committee's case on behalf of the whole district, which we served as the publicly subsidized theater for North Staffordshire. It was by no means a politically contentious piece here, but a kind of information and propaganda exercise addressed to the district and the world outside. It seemed to do that job very well, acting as a kind of preamplifier, generating more and wider publicity including wide coverage in national newspapers and TV programs. And it certainly cheered up the Action Committee as it went along.

THE TEXT

Fight for Shelton Bar is the seventh theater documentary which I have helped to create and direct at the Victoria Theatre, Stoke-on-Trent.

We are a professional theater in the round seating about 400 people, serving the district of North Staffordshire with new and classical plays, assisted by subsidy from the Arts Council of Great Britain and our major local authorities, particularly Stoke-on-Trent, Newcastle-under-Lyme, Staffordshire, Stafford Borough, and Cannock. We are very close to the M6 Motorway and consequently draw audiences from the Birmingham area to the south, and Manchester and North Lancashire to the north, as well as from our own immediate district.

The techniques we have evolved for creating theater documentaries are set out in detail in the Introduction to *The Knotty,* our fourth documentary, published by Eyre Methuen, and it is unnecessary to describe them in detail here. For readers who do not want to pursue this particular technical matter so far, however, it is important to make one or two basic points only, so that you may appreciate exactly what you are reading.

The Stoke documentaries are, like most film and radio documentaries, collations of the utterances of the people involved in the real events themselves, collected from written records of those events, minutes of meetings, letters, transcripts of speeches, newspaper and other eyewitness accounts, and by means of the tape recorder. The last two documentaries, *Hands Up, For You The War is Ended!* and *Fight for Shelton Bar,* were primarily made from tape-recorded material. In the latter case, for the first time, we were present at many of the events ourselves, and recorded them happening.

The recordings are transcribed and sections of them spoken by the actors in the form in which they were originally spoken. Selections are made from the written material and used in the same way. Only the songs are actually *written* in the conventional sense, though if they can be collected from the participants we use these in preference, but this is rare. (Only "The Man at the Fire" is really in this category in *Fight for Shelton Bar.*)

The process of selection, editing, and structuring the documentary is my responsibility, in cooperation with a small group of actors from the permanent company which works here and who can be spared from rehearsals of another production in advance of the documentary. We also of course seek advice constantly from the participants when we are dealing with contemporary events. I have tried to describe the origins of each scene and song in the Notes which follow the documentary text.

So the words you are about to read were not written by me, or by the actors, but by the men and women who work at Shelton Steelworks, and by some of the workers' wives. I respectfully dedicate this record of our collaboration to them all.

—PETER CHEESEMAN, June 1977

THE STAGE SETTING

The acting area of Stoke is a rectangle twenty-six feet long, twenty-two feet wide, with the audience on all four sides. There are entrances in two corners of the rectangle and one in the center of the opposite side. Gangways through the audience provide additional vantage points for the odd speech. (The Action Committee statement each evening was made from one of these.)

The stage cloth designed by Alison Chitty for *Fight for Shelton Bar* was of unpainted, bleached canvas, stained and dyed with pale gray and rust-colored marks. From the roof above the heads of actors and audience we suspended a cluster of shapes and angles recalling the roof structure of the rolling mill and the blast furnaces. The different locations in the story were suggested by rearranging a small set of guard rails in 2-inch steel angle made for us on the Bar where such rails are a regular feature of the scenery inside and outside. For all the meetings tubular steel and canvas chairs and two small tables were brought on and off and rearranged by the actors.

Between the two corner entrances, up against the audience is a large gray rostrum where the actors can sit to accompany songs. Also, because the documentary is a piece of manifest storytelling, the actors can come and go quietly during the action, sometimes sitting and watching a scene in which they are not involved, or making small costume changes in the auditorium.

Sound effects, recorded at the works, provide a background to all the scenes of steelmaking. The action never seemed to leave the steelworks. The actors frequently addressed the audience directly—the story was told firmly from within the theater.

PART ONE

OPENING SONG

The GIRLS and two ACTORS are on at the beginning, play a short instrumental and sing the first verse of the Song. The rest of the cast come on in ones and twos with each speech and join in the Song till they are all assembled in a wide circle.

SONG (VERSE 1):
   There is a steelworks in this town,
   Its glow you can see from afar,
   We will tell you now how it all began—
   We will tell you the story of the Bar.
FIRST ACTOR (coming on): Josiah Wedgwood moved onto the site at Shelton and built his first factory there in 1776. This man was largely responsible for the organization of industry in North Staffordshire.
SONG (2):
   Etruria Hall was built to house
   A potter named Josiah.
   He lived and died there and in his place
   Lord Granville lit a fire.
SECOND ACTOR (coming on): We moved on to Earl Granville who decided to build five blast furnaces. These were completed in 1841 and used local deposits of iron ore, limestone and coal.
SONG (3) (with banjo now):
   And the railway lines were forged and rolled
   The Knotty was a buyer
   The age of steam and iron was born
   And the country blazed with fire.

THIRD ACTOR: In 1860 three more blast furnaces were added. In 1866 open hearth furnaces were put on the site as well as steel rolling mills.
SONG (4):
   John Summers arrived at Shelton Bar
   From Shotton in the neighboring shire
   He'd come with a mission, a firm intent
   With fuel for that raging fire.
FOURTH ACTOR: In 1919 the Shelton complex, including coal, was taken over by John Summers. It remained a part of John Summers and Son for forty-eight years.
SONG (5):
   Through days of slump depression and strife
   As numbers on the dole rose higher
   The work went on and the legend grew
   Of the men who worked at the fire.
FIFTH ACTOR: By 1939 the John Summers complex comprised the works on the Dee as well as five coal mines, three large blast furnaces and two mills in North Staffordshire.
SONG (6):
   A Kaldo and Concast plant were built
   The North Works of Etruria
   And a Demag mill, the finest in the land
   A gift for the lads at the fire.
SIXTH ACTOR: In 1958 seven million pounds were spent on a new sinter plant. In 1964 we installed the new steel plant and Demag mill, at a cost of 20 million pounds.
SONG (7):
   Nationalization plans were announced
   So farewell John Summers Esquire
   British Steel Corporation took over the Works,
   But who'll call the tune at the fire?
THIRD ACTOR (now as Ted Smith): On August 1st 1967 the steel industry was nationalized. We waited patiently and about twelve months later in 1968 the first major policy statement was announced.
SONG (8) (GIRLS only):
   There is a steelworks in this town
   Its glow you can see from afar,
   Let us tell you now of the men who make the steel,
   Let us tell you the story of the Bar.

General exit leaving MR. BLACK and OSSIE. The lights change.

SINTER PLANT SEQUENCE: THE STOCK BAY

OSSIE and MR. BLACK speak to the audience, indicating where things are. Sound of overhead crane, railway wagons.

MR. BLACK: Well, thi, this is the er, erm, stockbay, where we receive all the material, the iron ore, and so on and so forth, as you can see. (*He turns and points.*) That's scale, and that is foreign ore. They've all got a different chemical analysis, and you have to bled these to get the right type of sinter which we require.

The crane sound increases as the crane moves overhead.

OSSIE: At the present moment we're using this material that this crane's picking up now at fifty ton an hour on the Sinter Plant so—um—as we've—he's loading these wagons and then the chappies that are in the cabin there—they'll label them what materials they are. He takes three of those grabs and then that's about twenty-five ton into the wagon. That's the grab. That's Labrador he's loading now. (*Ore drops into the wagon.*) Labrador. Ore. That's foreign ore, that.

Lights change; they move to one end—wagon sound loud.

OSSIE: On this job we've got three men—there's a crane driver which you see is—er—loading wagons at the top there with a goliath crane then there's—er—the plate-man (*The PLATE-MAN comes on watching the wagons.*)—and—er—an assistant plate-man.

The ASSISTANT PLATE-MAN hurries on with a brake stick following a wagon, crossing close in front of them: a loud sound of a wagon uncoupling and running then knocking the empty wagon off the tippler plate with a crash. A bell rings, very loud.

PLATE-MAN: Er, that's what gives 'im the all-clear to take the wagon up.

The clunk and whine of the tippler plate—the PLATE-MAN lifts his head slowly, watching the wagon up. His ASSISTANT moves forward.

OSSIE (*shouts*): Don't get under that lift.

PLATE-MAN: As soon as I'm ready when I've got the wagon on—press the bell and he knows as it's all clear. He's not supposed to take it up now, unless I give 'em that ring then he knows it's clear this side 'cos he's working blind round there.

Sound of the tippler stopping and the ore tippling out. This fades. They are all in a half circle round the tippler. TED SMITH comes into the circle, which lights up a little.

TED HEARS THE NEWS

TED: Well, in 1968, the first impact hit me in '68, er, the first major policy statement by the Steel Corporation, were the . . . to have five large coastal sites, known as "green field" sites and everything else was wiped out virtually, so that virtually er, I said to meself, well, that's it Ted you've had the sack mate as soon as they build those, you're out of work. (*The tippler lowers, the circle of MEN move back as the wagon drops. TED moves farther into the center.*) It was in the paper, in the Sentinel and it was on television, y'know it was a master plan 'n . . . but largely the majority of people on Shelton, y'know didn't realize the implications to them . . . er, they were still in their snug little hole at Shelton and they'd had 20 million spent on it and they were secure for their lifetime and their son's lifetime, y'know and so on and er, at that time we had er a new Time Keeper in our office er, named Jim Ellis and I was talking one day, 'n I, I came out with this: I said—(*JIM ELLIS comes across, taking his raincoat off. To JIM:*) Well, we've all had the sack haven't we?

JIM: What d'you mean, had the sack?

TED: Well er the Corporation's, they gonna build five green field sites, on the coast well that's . . . us vulnerable, we've had it mate, from here on in. (*To the audience:*) An' I mosied along with this idea er an' he used to ask me every week.

JIM (*has hung his coat on a rail: HE comes back*): Well, Ted, are we all gettin' the sack then?

TED: Look Jim I y'know I'na playing about, I've looked at what they said and what their intentions are gonna be for the steel industry and we've had the sack, mate. All inland sites for me are on borrowed time.

Lights change to the gloom of the Sinter Plant. JIM and TED go off. The PLATE-MEN move the rails about. OSSIE and MR. BLACK move from one pool of light to another. The sound effects move with them from process to process. OSSIE and MR. BLACK have to shout.

INSIDE THE SINTER PLANT

OSSIE: Well anyway, that material has to go unfortunately up the belt there, along the cross-belt and drop down onto and up the five-foot conveyor belt, then it drops down a chute onto Number One conveyor belt—that's Number Two conveyor belt—goes on Number Three conveyor belt—down onto the twenties and—er—goes up ten, over the secondary screen, down onto 148, the rubble goes onto Number Twelve, then it goes er fifteen, sixteen, seventeen, eighteen and that's in your bunker ready for—er—using on the sinter plant. (*Very loud chute noise, then the din of the secondary screens. OSSIE is yellow now:*) We're at um, underneath the secondary screens now. All that we do here is er screen-screening.

Both crouch down to look up at the igniter flames—they are in a big red glow now.

MR. BLACK: Well, this is the actual machine here, y'see.

The roar of the igniter.

OSSIE: All the materials that's going up that belt now is coated with coke same as a sugar bonbon.

MR. BLACK: And it goes underneath the igniter there.

OSSIE: Twenty-two jets on there, air and gas. Methane gas . . . somewhere about fourteen thousand five hundred o' gas.

MR. BLACK: Which ignites the coke, an it's dragged along. As it travels along very slowly it gradually sinters through, burns thro', so when it comes off the end it's completely sintered.

The roar becomes very loud, then fades away. TED SMITH comes on, with representatives from other parts of the works, many in working clothes, some in helmets.

SCENE—CLOSURE OF THE 18-INCH MILL

TED: In the October er, we were all called to a meeting er, in the Hall, in the boardroom, to tell us that they were going to close the 18-inch mill . . . all the staff shop stewards there . . . we were all called to this meeting and Andrew Young, our director-in-charge came down.

Enter ANDREW YOUNG with a BSC press release. He is followed by the Works Manager, DEREK FIELD.

YOUNG: The British Steel Corporation announces its intention to arrange the closure during 1971 of two of its smaller Teesside works and part of a works in Staffordshire. The proposed closures, which affect a total of 1,658 men, are a necessary part of BSC's overall rationalization plans which are designed to cut costs and improve efficiency. The plants involved are: TUBES DIVISION—Cochrane's Spun Iron plant and Iron Foundry, Teesside, with 665 employees. GENERAL STEEL DIVISION—Britannia Works, Teesside, which has 713 employees, also the 18-inch rolling mill and the arch plant at Shelton Works, Staffordshire, affecting 280 men.

There is a silence.

TED: They'd gotta modern plant at Jarrow and er it was only on fifty percent of its capacity through lack of orders and er, they could do all this work better up there than they could on Shelton.

YOUNG (*reading*): The rate of labor turnover at these works and opportunities for redeployment within BSC would help significantly to minimize redundancy. It is envisaged that the closure of the Cochrane's Works and the Number Three and Number Four mills and the associated Number Four primary mill at Britannia Works would take place in six months and that of Shelton at the same time or shortly afterwards.

Silence again: the MEN *are stunned.*

TED: Not one word was said, not one solitary word. It was deathly silence in the room.

DEREK FIELD, the Manager, steps forward.

DEREK FIELD: I'd like to thank Mr. Young for telling us. Although it's sad tidings, it's not un-expected.

TED: They set up an 18-inch mill Closure Committee. Redundancy Committee they called it and I was . . . Joint Staff secretary elected on to that Committee er . . . to see what could be done for the people that were facing the redundancy, y'know, there was 280 men, initially, that were losing their jobs.

MEN have come on with chairs and a table. They are set up as at a meeting. A SECRETARY *takes minutes.* GERALD WILSON *sits at a table facing the* MEN.

MRS. SIDDEL: Second Meeting of the 18-inch mill Committee held on Tuesday 17th November 1970.

DELEGATE (*standing*): Transfers to other Departments. A lengthy discussion took place and it was agreed that it would not be practical to make men redundant in other parts of the plant to create job vacancies for men from the 18-inch mill. This would severely impede production. (*He sits.*)

ANOTHER DELEGATE (*standing*): It was suggested that a private operator might be interested to continue the operation of the 18-inch mill in its entirety. (*He sits.*)

MRS. SIDDEL: Minutes of the Third Meeting, 1st December.

MR. LATHAM (*standing*): Mr. Latham reported that eighteen men had left the 18-inch mill in the six weeks period up to 30th November. Thirteen men have been engaged on a temporary basis. (*He sits.*)

MR. WILSON (*stands up*): Mr. Wilson thought that it might be possible to help redundant personnel to find other employment outside Shelton. We would work closely with the Department of Employment in finding alternative jobs but it was thought that we could go beyond this by advertising in the local press details of men who would become available for work on a certain date.

He sits: there is a pause. All stand. One MAN *goes out slowly.*

MRS. SIDDEL (*quietly*): Minutes of the Fourth Meeting.

MR. WILSON: The Chairman opened the meeting by asking to be put on record this Committee's regret at the passing of Mr. Tommy Davies who had served this Committee since its inception last year and who had done a great deal of work with Mr. Latham in drawing up the priority list for the 18-inch mill redundancy.

TED: The major delegate from the 18-inch mill collapsed and died. Heart attack. Bang.

MR. WILSON: It was agreed by all present that a minute recording the Committee's regrets should be entered.

Pause: all sit.

MRS. SIDDEL: Minutes of the Fifth Meeting, 30th March 1971.

TED: I held me feelings inside me. I never said much on that Committee, y'know, I just observed everything as went on y'know, an' watched the men, an' interviewed men, and had a look at 'em an' I didn't say—it's a question of whether I said half a dozen words in six month.

MR. WILSON (*stands up*): The current situation then is that there are 65 men with less than two years' service, 20 engineering men who will be transferred to the main works and three retirals; a total of 88 men to be deducted from the 212 on the list to show the number of men we must try to accommodate, i.e., 124 men. (*He sits.*)

MRS. SIDDEL (*writing*): It was agreed that the sooner employees are told of the position as it affects them personally, the better.

MR. LATHAM (*stands*): Mr. Latham agreed to see the 124 men that alternative jobs can be found for, to tell them the position: that jobs are available in the main works and that the offer of alternative employment will be made to them in the fairly near future.

The meeting breaks up. MR. WILSON *is left alone by his table, standing facing a* MAN *who has come on and now sits hunched in a chair, his face hidden, his hands slackly between his knees. It is a break in a hopeless conversation.* TED *moves up to the other end and looks at them.*

TED: We sat on this Committee and I saw the men's faces that were involved as 'ad 'ad the sack. And I said to meself then and there. I says, "Well, Edward, if you ever come to that position, mate, you've got to fight." I saw those men as 'ad the sack. They destroyed 'em. Killed 'em, and I mean killed 'em. I'm firmly convinced that men under stress, that there's a door there and it's locked, bolted and barred and there's big question marks all over it. Beyond is the future, and that door is the redundancy staring you in the face. And I've seen men killed by that. They've died through that door being closed. They haven't got a future once they've; that's it. (*BILL FOSTER moves to stand by TED.*) The staff were taken care of largely apart from one bloke, he was a roll turner, he lives quite near to Bill, and they destroyed 'im—he's now—he's an expert, I mean roll turners, they're probably one of the highest qualified craftsmen in the steel industry, y'-know, and er, they couldn't find a job for this bloke on the steel industry. Staggering to me, he'd bin on Shelton, a boy, he was 57, he was 43 years he'd worked on Shelton, all his working life and Bill told me, he said—

BILL: Ted, I've met that bloke out, and for months on end he was moping around and didn't know what to do, an shattered 'im, 'n he'd bin a top craftsman all his life.

TED: I believe he's er insurance collecting now, I mean, he's gorra job eventually, but if we're goin ta to do that to every man, on closures, then, there's summat got be wrong somewhere, y'know. (*The sound of the Sinter Strand fades in.*) Anyway we worked it out the best we could, the best deal possible. In the end we got 221 jobs (on Shelton) for 217 men. So we'd done our work.

SCENE—THE SINTER STRAND

A conversation on the Tannoy penetrates the sound of the burning sinter.

ROY (*on Tannoy*): Hallo Kelvin.
KELVIN (*Tannoy*): Hallo.
ROY (*Tannoy*): Go get you' snappin and then you can take Stuart off after.

KELVIN (*Tannoy*): Okay.

HAROLD THE IGNITER demonstrates the Sinter Strand to the audience. A long red glow stretches up and down the stage.

HAROLD: Anyway, if you imagine the, the sinter bed, as like this, like so, we ignite it there, as it travels along very slowly, it gradually sinters through if any o' you c'n unnerstan that? Burn, burn through, yes. Burn through, so when it comes off the end it's completely sintered, comes off the end—sinter. (*He holds a piece up.*)

OSSIE: That's a piece of sinter.

HAROLD: We'll go that way, an' you can see it actually comin off.

TED and BILL are looking at the strand and inch up as it moves.

OSSIE: And coke, water and limestone and that's the er final mixing from this er what yer call the secondary mixer.

Enter ROY at the top end.

BILL: What does it have to have the water in for?
ROY: Well, er, er, the, it's, it's one o' these things, that gives you permeability.
BILL: Mmmm.
ROY: It's all, openness in there.
BILL: Oh I see.
ROY: You get it, er
HAROLD: You get it too wet, you get too dry.
BILL: What's it like when it's too wet?
HAROLD: Well, if it's too wet, it wunna sinter, will it? It doesn't sinter properly.
BILL: If it's too dry what happens?
HAROLD: You you've got it, you've got it, er just the same as it's too dry, you won't sinter it if it's too dry. You won't make sinter.

THE GEORGE HOTEL

They are still watching the sinter move along the strand.

TED: Andrew Young came down in the following January and met all the Union delegates in the

George Hotel, on January 12th 1971. Main topic revolved around the future, our future, the rest of us, what could er, Mr. Young tell us, y'know. Er he came out with a very definite statement, he said.

ANDREW YOUNG appears in a spotlight in a corner, with a glass of beer.

YOUNG: In June of this year, you will know your future, a master plan is being produced and it will outline the Corporation's strategy and you will know in June of this year. (*He goes off.*)

TED: This is '71, well er, the 18-inch mill closed on June 4th that year and er, after that closure, union delegates—(*A MAN IN A WHITE HELMET crosses. TED turns to him*): We asked, I did actually, we asked our management, I said: Anything forthcoming from what Andrew Young said?

WHITE HAT: Er, I'll find out for you, Ted. (*He goes off.*)

TED: Quite genuinely y'know, our management, course they were as interested as we were y'-know. Anyway, initial one.

WHITE HAT (*pops back on*): It's bin put back till next month. (*He stays listening to TED.*)

TED: That was July, so in July I ask again. It's bin put back till August er, ask again in August like er it's bin put back er either next month or some time early next year, y'see.

WHITE HAT has nodded along with this, and now goes off. BILL and TED are left alone.

BILL: Sometime the working people in this country . . . will have to make a stand. Somebody's got to call a halt and it's got to be called on the shop floor.

The crashing sound of the breakers is heard. The lights narrow down. ROY comes on.

ROY: This is the breaker. This is where, where the big large slabs drop off, o, over, off the end the sinter machine. This is the breaker that breaks them up into smaller pieces for, manageable pieces, shall we say. As it drops off the end of the sinter machine, it's in too large a slabs to 'andle, int it?

ROY goes off. Big noise, then it fades away.

QUEEN'S HALL SEQUENCE: FIRST ACTION COMMITTEE MEETING

DELEGATES come on, in their public platform outfits. They bring chairs.

TED: I called a meeting to see if we could form a committee of some sort to try and highlight our case an' fight for the retention of steelmaking at Shelton y'know. Anyway fifty-three union delegates turned up at that meeting, along with four MPs. (*The MEN start to assemble for the meeting.*) I introduced them, and the first question I put to the meeting was—(*He turns to them: they pause in their setting up of the chairs, to listen*)—Did they think there was a need to form an Action Committee—and there was a unanimous

TED: ⎤ Yes!
ALL: ⎦ Yes!

The instrumental to the Queens Hall song begins quietly under BILL FOSTER's speech. The MEN put their chairs in a wide arc and sit down.

BILL: What's emerged on Shelton in the last two years is that we've got one union. We still belong to the various organizations that we belong to—I'm in the Transport, Ted's in BISAKTA, we've got boilermakers, roll turners all sorts of people DATA, middle-management people, but they all come into this room and decide the strategy for Shelton, *together.*

The instrumental stops.

RAY CAIRNS (*stands*): My name is Ray Cairns and I have worked at Shelton for over 20 years and at present occupy the position of Chief Fuel Engineer. I think most of you probably know Ted Smith our Chairman. He is a Time Clerk in the Etruria North Works and has served the Company well for 17 years. Bill Foster, our Secretary.

BILL (*stands*): Crane section of the Electrical Department—22 years.

RAY (*looking down at his list*): Roy Pepper, Mill Production Department—15 years' total service. Frank Oldacre, the gentleman sitting behind me here. I think he is the wizard of us all . . . (*He turns to FRANK, who stands.*)

FRANK: Assistant Roller—38 years' service in the Rolling Mills at Shelton.

RAY: Tom Timmis, Stock Controller, 15 years' service.

GEORGE: George Johnson, Bricklayers Laborer, Steel Plant—10 years.

RAY: Martin Gray, Steel Plant Bricklayer—12 years' service.

ALBERT: Albert Cooper, Senior Fuel Engineer—14 years.

RAY: Jim Wakelin, Chief Clerk, Ironworks—37 years' service.

ALF: Alf Wakefield, Works Electrical Shift Foreman—24 years.

RAY: Ken Jepson, clerk in the Cost Office—22 years' service.

BILL: Stan Walley, Ore Prep. Plant Process Worker—25 years.

RAY: I can assure you that each member, no matter his job or what level of the Works structure he appears, we all have the same very similar viewpoint "Save our Shelton."

All applaud and stand; the instrumental begins vigorously. The DELEGATES *all move their chairs to make two long lines across one end of the stage, facing the* GIRLS *who sing and play the song sitting on the rostrum.*

BILL: At today's meeting of the Action Committee it was decided to hold a mass meeting at the Queen's Hall, Burslem on 16th April 1972.

The LORD MAYOR—COUNCILLOR ARTHUR CHOLERTON—*comes in and sh akes hands with the* DELEGATES *and MPs.*

GIRLS (*sing*):
  The rumors were spreading for many a year
  That Lord Melchett was thinking of closing
      the Bar,
  So before it's too late, people started to say
  Let's have a mass meeting and get under way.

MEN (*sing*):
  In this world of today
  You must make yourself heard,
  Don't make no delay
  Or they'll give you the bird.

They all sit except the LORD MAYOR. *The instrumental carries on.*

LORD MAYOR: As you heard, Ladies and Gentlemen, outside all the actual people you have already heard tonight there has been a lot of other work done in the background particularly by your MPs. It is with very great pleasure that I call upon Bob Cant MP to say a few words to us.

All applaud. The instrumental stops. BOB CANT *stands and comes forward.*

BOB CANT: The problem about Shelton as I see it is quite simply this, that in itself Shelton with a minimum investment of four million pounds has an assured future; but certain decisions have been made by the British Steel Corporation way up at the top in terms of investment in other much larger plants in Britain, and Shelton may, I say may, be sacrificed to some extent in order to "pull the chestnuts out of the fire" for British Steel, but this is not acceptable, as Ted Smith, Chairman of the Action Committee, has said. We don't want a situation in which we continue producing, to some extent uneconomically, steel at Scunthorpe and Teesside to have this exported to Shelton in order that it can be used in the rolling mills and so on. That is an unacceptable option as far as we are concerned. And this is a point that we have got to keep on making. That as a unit fitted out with Electric Arc Furnaces, Shelton is a viable economic, technical, and financial proposition.

All applaud. The instrumental starts again. The MAYOR *goes to* JACK ASHLEY.

GIRLS (*sing*):
  Our local MPs are the best you could find,
  You need friends like them in disputes of this
      kind,
  Stoke, North, South and Central and New-
      castle too,
  With this team behind us we've got to win
      through.

ALL (*sing*):
  In this world of today
  You must make yourself heard.
  Don't make no delay,
  Or they'll give you the bird.

The instrumental carries on till the end of the LORD MAYOR's *introduction.*

LORD MAYOR: Ladies and Gentlemen, this area usually throws up a type of person, when adversity comes along, that has got a wonderful ability to fight back. Those of you people already know the adversity of Jack Ashley, the member of Parliament for Stoke South, had to undergo. A man who was struck down with total deafness and yet has been able to fight this and remain within the House of Commons and remain one of the most foremost adversaries as far as the Government is concerned. He now would like to speak to you.

All applaud and rise as JACK ASHLEY steps forward, then they sit.

ASHLEY: My Lord Mayor, Ladies and Gentlemen, I think this is one of the most impressive demonstrations that Stoke-on-Trent has ever seen and it certainly needs to be because Stoke-on-Trent is now facing one of the greatest social and economic disasters this City has ever known. I want to conclude with this message—not just to the members of Stoke-on-Trent but to the Steel Board and to the Government—that there is a serious danger that the good will of the people of Stoke-on-Trent can be taken for granted. Stoke-on-Trent has a proud record of good industrial relations. We don't go in for wild demonstrations, flamboyant demonstrations, and sit-ins in factories but I hope that we won't be pushed too far because if this City is to be denied 2,000 jobs and if we are to have mass unemployment then we must say to the Government that we must consider our position and they are gravely and possibly irreparably damaging industrial relations of this City and of the whole area.

All applaud—the song carries on. The LORD MAYOR goes to TED SMITH.

GIRLS (*sing*):
North Staffordshire people have always been
   fair,
To each man his due rights, to each man his
   share.
If you think they are weak dear Lord
   Melchett, they're not,
A very strong rope ties the Staffordshire knot.

ALL (*sing*):
In this world of today
You must make yourself heard,
Don't make no delay
Or they'll give you the bird.

TED SMITH comes forward.

TED: Shelton employs 2,750 people now. Shelton would employ 2,200 people after electric arcs were installed. Shelton would employ 750 people without electric arcs, running the mill on imported cold steel from Scunthorpe, meaning a loss of 2000 jobs. The closure of iron and steelmaking at Shelton would raise the present unemployment rate from 4.1% to over 7% making Stoke a distressed area. Apart from the direct affect on 2,000 families there are 7,000 suppliers bringing raw materials, ranging from limestone to paper clips. Stoke depends on Shelton Works. It is the highest ratepayer. The loss of revenue to the Local Government would mean considerable increase in rates to everyone. Hundreds of shops, garages, services, housing estates, etc. depend upon Shelton's employees for their livelihood. The effect on future generations is unmeasurable.

All rise, applaud and begin to disperse. The MEN join in the song after the first line. The MAYOR leaves.

GIRLS (*sing*):
We're going to London to see the great men.
ALL (*sing*):
To prove that our Shelton is their golden hen,
Our case is as sound as the product we sell.
So we're bound to come back home with good
   news to tell.

In this world of today
You must make yourself heard,
Don't make no delay,
Or they'll give you the bird.

A LONDON MEETING

All the MEN except TED and BILL go off, setting up a table and a ring of chairs at the other end of the stage. TED and BILL have briefcases and coats.

TED: The first major meetin' was at British Steel Corporation to present the case of Shelton Bar to Herbert Morley. Herbert Morley is the 'ead of General Steels Division. Now one of the directors—when we were talkin about social consequences, etc., he did make one or two statements y'know—the Corporation have our interests at heart—they would do everything possible y'know, and er, I noted him makin drawings. And er, at first I thought he was drawing two electric arc furnaces. Because that was what the arguments and the er meeting centered around. Then he put 2 wings on, I thought—Good God, he's gonna fly 'em up t'Shelton. (*He shows the paper to the audience.*) But er, he was in actual fact drawing an airplane. And this is bloody true mate! This is actually true. I mean, this is a social conscience, he's got your bloody dole-queue place earmarked. And that's what it's all about, and these are the people, the blokes that profess to tell us that they know how we feel—they haven't got a bloody faintest idea.

TED sits in some disgust. BILL *comes forward with a letter.*

CHRISTIANA SPIGERWERK

GIRLS (*sing*):
A Norwegian firm with unpronounceable
    name
Are seeking a site in the Midlands to claim
To open a steelworks, we hope they're sincere,
'Cos we've written a letter inviting them here.

BILL (*reads*): Christiana Spigerwerk, Oslo, Norway. Dear Mr. Sommerfelt, We know that you have been seeking a suitable site for some time and it would appear that Shelton would suit you admirably. Land, plant, and labor are all available together with considerable expertise in steelmaking and rolling. We hope that you will agree to have a meeting with local management to explore the considerable opportunities open to us both.

ALL (*sing*):
In this world of today
You must make yourself heard,

Don't make no delay,
Or they'll give you the bird.

TED (*despondently, as the instrumental ends*): Christiana Spigerwerk will not be coming to Stoke. They have been told by the Department of Trade and Industry that an Industrial Development Certificate will not be granted. Stoke-on-Trent does not fall into the appropriate regional development category.

VIC FEATHER

VIC FEATHER crosses the stage with a knot of animated DELEGATES.

BILL: Vic Feather and the Action Committee had an enlightened discussion in the North Stafford Hotel on Tuesday, 8th August. The phrase you will hear was used by Vic Feather and broadcast on BBC radio and TV. He said that he would initiate a meeting with the TUC Steel Committee quickly to discuss Shelton's future.

GIRLS (*sing*):
North Staffordshire people have always been
    fair,

ALL (*sing*):
To each man his due rights, to each man his
    share,
If you think they are weak dear Lord
    Melchett, they're not,
A very strong rope ties the Staffordshire knot.

Everything stops.

VIC FEATHER: Shelton, no lame duck—more a racing pigeon.

He goes off, waving encouragement, the instrumental comes in for the last time.

CHORUS:
In this world of today
You must make yourself heard,
Don't make no delay,
Or they'll give you the bird.

Everyone goes out. The lights go down to a gloomier level, and the deep hissing roar of the blast furnace gradually creeps in to form the undertone to the whole of the next sequence.

BLAST FURNACE SEQUENCE

TED SMITH stays watching: a tapping is not far off, and the blastfurnacemen will soon begin their final routines. In the meantime various VISITORS IN WHITE HATS hover in anticipation of the coming drama. MR. DAVIES, the blast furnace manager, and his assistant, MR. MARKS, watch and discuss.

TED: A blastfurnaceman hasn't got a job win or lose, only thro' electric arc furnaces.

MR. DAVIES: We take mother earth in the way of ores and mak' it into metal in the blast furnace which is then refined in the steel furnace, but electric arc merely melts scrap. Personally I wouldn't find a great deal of satisfaction in melting scrap—I mean ironmaking's a thing that's gone on since the Queen o' Sheba as a occupation and er technically it's very interesting.

MR. MARKS: To the best of my knowledge they've never been out.

MR. DAVIES: It's a continuous process. It's like a power station. Continuous. Never stops. We never close down you know. We can't close down easily . . . these at all. It's a major job to take them off for a long period. And revive them. Y'ave to repair them. It's a continuous process . . . charge at the top. Out thro' the bottom. All the time.

MR. MARKS: There's never been a time when the, when there hasn't been a blast furnace in blast, as they say. The term is "in blast." We tended to have family after family here. We had er, fathers, grandfathers, grandsons, sons, cousins, all working together.

MR. DAVIES: I think it's fair to say iron's been made in this area since 1837—that's, that's fair comment—we made iron long before they made steel.

TED: Ernie Davies, he's one of the senior managers on Shelton. There's only three men who can make iron in North Staffordshire, he's one of them and he treats his blast furnace like some pregnant woman, constantly giving birth. They've gotta be nursed and cajoled and stroked and petted and looked after. . . . He's got tremendous feeling for his job, . . . and what's he's trying to do.

MR. DAVIES and MR. MARKS move nearer to the tapping hole.

MR. DAVIES: Oh yes, they're like a woman . . .

MR. MARKS: They're . . .

MR. MARKS:] like a
MR. DAVIES:] because

MR. MARKS: . . . woman 'cos yer jus' don't know where the' are.

MR. DAVIES: They talk abut, they talk abut 'er, 'er bags, yer know, they talk about—(*Laughing.*) . . . Well, she's got belly pipes . . .

MR. MARKS: Yes.

MR. DAVIES: Goose necks . . .

MR. MARKS: Yes.

MR. DAVIES: An' we always call her "she" . . .

MR. MARKS: Unpredictable, aren't they?

MR. DAVIES: They say they're most unpredictable, an' believe me, they are.

MR. MARKS: And when they're upset, they stay upset.

They laugh and go off 'round to the other furnaces. TED goes too. Now the BLASTFURNACEMEN come on in their voluminous old clothes and silver helmets. Everyone is wary of the tapping hole at one end. JOE brings a barrow with two shovels, LES and SNUFFY take the shovels. The FURNACE KEEPER, TOM BEVINGTON, looks anxiously at the controls on his cabin wall at one side. The men spread sand with their shovels in a long channel from the tapping hole.

TOM: Well, at the present time this is what they call relining the runner for the next casting period.

SAMMY, THE SHIFT FOREMAN, comes in, a towel swathed round his neck against the sweat.

SAMMY: That's it.

They carry on with their jobs, then are still as the lights change, concentrating on TED and BILL FOSTER, together at the far end of the arena.

BILL: In 1972 for April, May, June, and July the whole of the steel industry was in a recession. During this period Shelton made £200,000 profit. We came out of the gloom situation into a boom situation in September. Subsequently every record that ever stood on production was shattered at Shelton. In September the profit was £250,00 for one month. So we did another projection. This information was submitted in a letter to Lord Melchett.

TED (*holding a letter and envelope*): To the Rt. Hon. Lord Melchett, Chairman, British Steel Corporation. My Lord, May we take this opportunity to present to yourself and the Corporation additional evidence in support of our case for the installation of two arc furnaces at Shelton Works. To illustrate our present output figures in terms of length, during the week ending November 11th we rolled sufficient steel to stretch from Shelton Works to your office door in Grosvenor Place. During the following week we would have reached Maidstone. We are now asking for the means to extend our geographical analogy across the Channel and into Europe! Your truly, Ted Smith, Chairman on behalf of Shelton Action Committee.

TED puts the letter in the envelope and goes off with BILL FOSTER. The BLASTFURNACEMEN move to make further preparations. SAMMY looks at the controls through the cabin window and at his watch, goes over to LES and sends him off to look to the slag at the back of the furnace. MR. DAVIES reappears with TOM BEVINGTON.

MR. DAVIES: They're like elephants if they're, if they're well behaved an' looked after. You're OK, but when they er but when they when they get wild, they're very wild, they're really vicious.

TOM: A blast furnace is—

MR. DAVIES: Well, yer get iron coming out all over the place squirting out, blowing out, filling the place full of slag and iron, and er, hell of a mess, an' then yer can 'ave them come up through the top like a roman candle, only about 5000 times as big.]

TOM: They're literally a bomb.]

MR. DAVIES: If yer slag isn't fluid, yer lime can't get through to the bottom 'cos yer iron isn't fluid either—it bursts its way out then you've a hell'v a mess—you cun get a hell 'v a mess with them, yer see. You wished you'd you wish'd you'd been an ice-cream man, instead. (*They laugh. MR. DAVIES moves on somewhere else.*)

The hiss of the blast is suddenly increased, then drops. SAMMY looks at his watch. The MEN move about with their barrow and tools. The lighting alters for an announcement, showing TED, BILL FOSTER, and the MP who makes the announcement, on the stairs among the audience.

BILL: On 21st December 1972 the BSC Government Plans for the future of the steel industry were announced in the House of Commons.

MP: Modernization means fewer jobs, but is essential if the remaining jobs are to be securely based. BSC estimates that full implementation of the new developments and closures in the strategy should more than double average labor productivity and reduce manpower by about 50,000. Closures already announced before the strategy was settled account for over 20,000 of this reduction. The decision on the strategy means an additional 30,000 net job losses, mainly in the second half of the decade.

TED: It gave approximately 75,000 people working in the Industry a lovely Christmas box—the sack.

MP: The effect will be severe in certain places, but the annual impact overall will not be out of proportion with the average rate of reduction in employment since nationalization. (*He goes: TED and BILL move towards each other.*)

BILL: We were told initially by the Corporation that they were using a computer, in Dallas, in Texas, to bring out the plans, and er, that's what we were waiting for. Well, I don't think anybody really believed it at all.

TOM: In Dallas?

BILL: In Dallas, in Texas, they told us that they'd submitted five possible permutations for the computer to sort out, and apparently the British computer industry don't produce anything that can do it and they'd sent it to America. And the five permutations'd been put into the machine and it was going to come up with the answers.

TED: I didn't believe what they said on that, about British computer. I said, the only reason as far as I'm concerned, you couldn't get a British computer to digest human misery and suffering on the scale that was going to be fed into it, like 75,000 steel workers and their families, somewhere in region of half a million people y'know and er, I said, that's the reason you taking it t'America.

BILL: Well, the American computers are used to that.

TED: Correct. (*They go.*)

The lighting changes. The hiss grows a little. TOM BEVINGTON *hurries on.*

TOM: We're goin to check the furnace. An' now this is what we do now. That is—(*He points away beyond the end of the runner.*) that is my stove man, 'e looks after all the stoves. Now this is what we call checking the furnace. You'll notice the flow go down. (*An enormous roar:* TOM *shouts.*) That is, that noise is, instead of the blast goin into the furnace, the blast is goin in the air casin like this. Now 'es blowin up now. Now we 'aven't got a lot on now, we've ony got what you call ten pounds on. (*The roar goes on.*) Not much. That's one! Just imagine that there's ten, of that, goin in.

The roar starts to drop.

SAM: That's hot blast goin in.

TOM: That's hot blast.

SAM: Between eight hundred and nine hundred degrees centigrade.

TOM: That's right. (*Blast of a klaxon hooter, and the roar drops to the permanent hiss.*) Now, then, y'see now now we back on slow wind now.

SAM: The air is literally red-hot. That is why it's called a blast furnace—that's what blast is. Knock her head off, really, yer know.

The BLAST FURNACE WORKERS *move across the arena and go off in the direction of the runner.* TOM *follows.* MR. MARKS *bustles on to see* SAMMY.

SAM: Yer used to 'ave the old keepers, now then, I can refer to old, two old brothers. Er, Dick Seddon an Harold Seddon. Two old-timers. Er, they're retired now, but they'd never refer, they'd never ter, talk against the furnaces, they used to 'ave the comical ways of the furnaces, but they used to look after them. (*Pause.*) You'd get old George Simpson erm, 'e used to talk to 'er just like talkin to 'is wife, 'e said, 'e'd talk to 'er better than 'e'd talk to 'is wife. (*He laughs.*) That's right, int it, that's right, int it, Mr. Marks, true this is. Ar wouldna, Ar wouldnta, Ar wouldn't a coss you duck, but ar'll coss er at whom to put me bloody cheese up again.

MR. MARKS: The old men used to say we tek the virgin oor from the ground and turn it into metal.

JOE *comes on again with a slagging rake and sample spoon and puts them to warm. The other* LABORERS *join him with big mugs of tea.* SAM *has on.* MR. MARKS *doesn't want one.*

SAM: He 'asn't got to 'ave any nerve. He hasn't got to be frightened of heat. He hasn't got to be frightened er er, er, of, well, taking a risk isn't it?]

LES: Not at all]

SAM: He hasn't gotta be frightened of anythin I mean, er er er, if 'e is gonna be frightened, I mean 'e's goin to turn round an' run. I mean, y'ave an occasion when a tuyere goes bump on the furnace, I mean, an' er, instead of men running to see what it is, you'll get p'raps an odd one that's gone. An' he's missin for two 'ours, down the road. And he won't come back until somethin's 'appened.

LES: Ar. Ar've seen a time. Number Three tuyere burnt all the lining. Set fire to down them steps. And everywhere.

SAM: Did it bother you?

SNUFFY: Neow, Onny a big mess. That's ow.

JOE: Cos if you're goin to start being worried or frightened about 't, what's what's going to happen, then it's time t'finish, int't, really you know, 'cos yer getting up be a bag o nerves. You know. See.

SNUFFY *takes the mugs off.* JOE *goes, to get the oxygen lance.* SAM *goes off.*

LES: A'll tell you why Ar'm stickin to it. I did 12 years in the pit. As a lad. N then A was in the building trade 28 years. And A got this arthritis. In me neck. An A got job here. Semi inside what you might say. A've bin a lot better. An that's the only reason A'm 'ere. With it bein warm you know. The heat. Not in this bad weather.

MR. MARKS: Sometimes it's more than warm tho, isn't it?

LES: Ar, but that's, that's good fer mar complaint.

JOE comes on with the oxygen lance, SNUFFY helping to untwist the long tube. They gradually straighten it out and lay it down parallel to the runner.

LES: Better tha cold. Ha ha ha. That's what
MR. MARKS: Yeah]

LES: . . . they give you up the orthopedic—heat treatment.

SAM comes on fast from behind the furnace.

SAM: Tom, we've just 'ad a bit of iron come over.

TOM: Ar.

SAM: Straight though the armchair.

TOM (*shouts*): Watch them tuyeres, Jack! Les!

TOM goes off quickly. LES and JACK follow him. It darkens. SAM reads the board at the window.

SAM: Now then we've casted in the two-twenty. On the 5.35 cast 'e only 'as 29 tons for 45 tons 'e should ave 'ad. I mean I 'aven't picked all the metal up, she doesn't give you all the metal all the time. I mean, sometimes she will give you in abundance. But I mean, we know that she's not yielding the metal—(*He taps the board.*) for the yield that we're expecting out o the sinter burden that's going in at the top.

TOM comes on and goes right down to the guard rail facing the tapping hole.

TOM: Now, first of all this is a this is a the compressed air being put on. (*He presses a control, the sharp hiss of compressed air comes*). Now then, this one moves the boom around . . . (*He moves another control and there is a long hiss as the drill moves over the tapping hole. The MEN move to their casting positions*). Now then, that's that's, down in 'ole see, about er twenty degrees. Now this starts the drill.

He presses another control: The klaxon hoots. The hammering sound of a pneumatic drill starts. LES is alongside the drill position near the tapping hole, and gestures and shouts out as the marks show how far in it's getting.

TOM: See, that's drilling an' going down now in the 'ole. The slide, it's coming down like that into the 'ole. Into that tap—tappin 'ole. Now then, we should drill about six six foot down into the furnace. The casting man as is down there, you'll see him just now go like that—fer one, two, three, four an' so on. . . . Down on there, m, you've got a ruling on, a foot every time it goes down.

TED and BILL appear on either side of the arena in their own lights.

TED: 1st January 1973. Dear Lord Melchett.

BILL: We spent about four to five hours composing the letter to Melchett to get him down here.

LES (*shouts*): One!

TED: You are familiar with the splendid economics of the proposition at Shelton and the recent production and profitability figures which endorse statements previously made by the Action Committee.

BILL: In fact it was a remarkable letter that. It was so phrased that he couldn't actually refuse.

LES (*shouts and gestures back to TOM at the controls*): Two!

TED: Despite our efforts during the last year Shelton is left without a definite answer and it is difficult to reconcile the position to our fellow workers at Shelton. It is obviously difficult for us to contain a situation which defies understanding.

The drilling gets louder as TOM hits a difficulty.

LES (*shouts*): Three!

TED: In view of the apprehension at Shelton brought about by the lack of information we feel that it is imperative that you visit the works now to have open discussion with the Action Committee to amplify the Corporation's viewpoint on Shelton's future.

LES: Four!

TED: You will find when you come to the Works that it is a splendid plant run by reasonable and loyal men and you will be assured of a sincere welcome and a constructive discussion.

LES: Five.

TED: We are all looking forward very much to meeting you.

BILL: He couldn't refuse.

TED: Yours sincerely, Ted Smith.

TOM: Sparks coming away from that 'ole . . . now I'm approaching the iron—see it.

LES waves TOM to get the drill away. Over the next speeches, JOE and SNUFFY get the oxygen lance into position, standing in line alongside the runner and holding it over their heads, turned away in case the iron bursts out. SAMMY comes on with a bit of coal on a shovel. LES takes a piece to put in the tapping hole.

TOM: Now, this is bringing that boom back now. What Les's doing there now is, I've drilled down to the safety margin of that 'ole, but I haven't fetched the iron yet so, what it is now— he's put a piece of coal in there—now, that coal generates heat so when they put the oxygen pipe—the oxygen in to fetch that iron. (*JOE and SNUFFY are in position now. MR. DAVIES stands by.*) Now, they're not so far off the iron an only when . . . well, can yer hear it rumbling? . . . Yer can just hear that—like a rumble, rumble. Also little sparks coming out. The iron'll come very, very soon—but a still like them to burn it so as te get a wider hole. Otherwise if we don't we're goin a have probably . . . what we properly call bleeding—she isn't actually running, 'er's just bleeding.

JOE and SNUFFY suddenly whip the lance away, laying it down alongside the cabin. A great red glow gradually fills the arena, from a bright strip down the line of the runner. Everyone watches it, faces shielded or turned from the heat. It is quieter, with a steady concentration.

TOM: This is iron, it's this as it's as it is now, it's coming out nice. But yer see 'ere? 'Ere? On on the top there? That's a bit of what what we call sponge an a bit of fire. Now, a furnace a furnace'll melt big coke, but when it's only got what they call breeze, small stuff, it doesn't like it—it throws it back at yer. See . . .

MR. DAVIES: Yer see, this is molten iron at 1450.

SAMMY: W', with the movement of it little particles are thrown up—y'see those little . . .

TED: Sparks.

SAMMY: When it comes into contact with the atmosphere.

MR. DAVIES: You you can get that, yer see, with the flow and the movement of the iron—it's very hot, really, it's about 1450 degrees, yer see, centigrade, the melting point of iron—it's 1500—you're close to the melting point of pure iron.

TOM: What now? Well, I always think, well, this is better than Social Security, it's my living. An I, an a, an a . . . well. A mean if if I 'adn't found it to my liking—I'd 'ave left years ago. Well . . . well er, well, a don't say, thu a . . . a mean, for example, me as a keeper. If I think I can come on 'ere, an er, under normal conditions, I can 'ave about 120 ton, a can go on ere an ave a cup of tea an feel proud, as as we've achieved some-ut.

LES takes the casting spoon and carefully fills it from the stream of molten iron. The others watch. He pours it into a cast for testing.

JOE: I don't like it an I don't hate it here—it's like bein in between things y'know. Yer . . . er you get satisfaction when yer get a good cast, y'know, no messing about. I mean yer yer casting twenty minutes an' yer back in the cabin again in half an hour. That's what yer like about it.

LES goes when he's finished his sampling. So do the OTHERS leaving MR. DAVIES and TOM. It gets quieter.

MR. DAVIES: A think it's true to say it's an art because a think despite all the er knowledge of blast furnaces just how and when all the complicated reactions take place an' all that business, at an instance of time nobody can really *know*. They've put isotopes in the furnace to watch the wear, they put cameras in, they put probes in, but, very of'n, when you're in dead trouble, they cut all the computers off an' it's back on the man on the front te say now what's wrong. Yer see, a blast furnace is a miraculous thing that man didn't invent really. He couldn't have even 'ave thought it would 'ave ever worked.

The instrumental to the song begins quietly on banjo.

TOM: I like to know, thut once I've tapped that furnace, I've got it as dry as a can possibly do—

of iron an' slag so that . . . Yer see, these things, they look all right now. I've seen some nasty accidents to em. Well, when a put that clay gun in, this time I got *seven cubic feet in*—nar then, if you don't get no clay in that 'ole, *you've got a weak 'ole,* so therefore, you've got the blast an' everything pushing at that 'ole—if you 'aven't got a dry furnace an' you've got chaps walking about in front o that and 'er opens up . . . There's no such thing as saying goodbye to yer mamma. You've gone.

The sound of the blast furnace ends. The lights change for the song, lighting only the GIRLS who sing it, and the two speakers, playing TED SMITH and GERALD WILSON, sitting higher up opposite one another in the auditorium.

SONG: MICKY DIRKIN'S GHOST

GIRLS (*sing to banjo accompaniment*):
  George Rushton lost his life one working day
  On the Bar
  His head was crushed by a machine
  A blow that could not be foreseen
  And his workmates stood and watched him
      carried away.
SONG (2):
  In '38 Jack Sherlock worked the blast
  On Number One
  The wind went on before its time
  The furnace blew up like a mine
  And the molten iron ran out and buried him
      fast.
TED: At Irlam, thirty-nine 'eart cases in th' 'ospital, an' they were the first to be announced to be closed up, first major closure, this is in Lancashire, out of thirty-nine 'eart cases, thirty-five of 'em were steelworkers.
GERALD: In fact, they'd got their local hospital, one of these emergency intensive care ambulances sor' of solely standing by for the works, because they were called out so often to it.
SONG (3):
  When Aaron Butcher worked up in the mill
  Between the wars
  The danger there he did not note
  A billet caught him by the coat

And drew him through the rollers with the
    steel.
TED: An' I've seen men, while this fight's bin on, die for no apparent reason. Young men as well. Forty-six. What was it attributed to? No reason. He just died of heart failure—He died of a lack of a future.
SONG (4):
  The ghost of Micky Dirkin haunts the Bar
  So men say
  And the other men who lost their lives
  Who left their workmates and their wives
  Are there with Dirkin's ghost on Shelton Bar.

LORD MELCHETT SCENE

The lights now change for the LORD MELCHETT meeting scene: a businesslike atmosphere. The members of the Action Committee come on, briskly and cheerfully, putting their chairs in position in a semicircle facing three chairs and a table for LORD MELCHETT. There is also a table in front of BILL, who takes minutes of the meeting. TED and ALBERT come on first.

TED: The pinnacle of our achievement was the Chairman visiting our plant.
ALBERT: It was at that stage . . .
TED: Y'know this was it . . .
ALBERT: This is what we'd built up to over 2 years to get him down there . . .
TED: Get him down here
  y'know, all the energy ⎤
ALBERT: To get him look ⎦
  at Shelton, what a great plant it were y'know, and we thought we'd convinced him finally on this.

BILL and BERNARD arrive, then STAN WHALLEY and FRANK OLDACRE.

BILL: On the morning when it happened you and I
BILL: were outside early on, because
  we'd got a ⎤
TED: Yeah. ⎦
BILL: sort of . . .
TED: Early on was about the correct word.
ALBERT: Yes, we were there quite early ⎤
BILL: Early on we'd ⎦

gotta sort the meeting
room out hadn't we: ⎤
TED: four o'clock I   ⎦
got up y'know.

BILL: He'd had a sleepless night.
Then we went out to the back of the
meeting room with a cup of coffee.

ALBERT: An' a pair of binoculars

BILL: And it was rather cold. And he was⎤
touring the plant and we sort of gazed in the
general direction of the hall and there was
a huge pall of smoke
rising up into the air. ⎦

ALBERT: Oh yes

TED: He says, "We dinna believe Stan Whalley
but it looks as though it was bloody true. Them
International Socialists—(*Bill laughs.*)—have
moved in."

BILL: That's right . . . International ⎤

BERNARD: That's it.   ⎦

BILL: Socialists, with this pall of smoke.

TED: Aye, they'd blown it up.

BILL: We walked over towards the Hall
didn't we? ⎤

TED: We did.⎦
Because we couldn't actually pin the direction
and then we came down the back of the Hall
here and realized it wasn't the International Socialists had moved in, it was Bernard who had
carried out his threat because it was the Power
Station and Bernard was on.

TED: That was chaos, wan it?

BERNARD: An' he missed it.

BILL: Yeah.

TED: That was our bad day to start off with.
That finished it off.

BILL: That sort of started the day for us, this fire.

BERNARD: And he didn't see it, did he?

BILL: No, he didn't.

BERNARD: He didn't see it.

BILL: But the actual day itself was a tragedy.

TED: Oh it was, ugh! (*A pause: everyone gets a
little more serious.*) Just before then, everybody
in that room was charged with electricity. The
butterflies were there, the tension was there, everybody was nervous. Everybody was looking
round for everybody, for support.

Pause.

ALBERT: We were sort of in a very tense mood, all
of us, trying to make little jokes to sort of pass
the time away until he arrived.

*LORD MELCHETT arrives, with DEREK FIELD, THE
WORKS GENERAL MANAGER, and GERALD WILSON.*

ALBERT: I remember looking at the faces of people coming in, Melchett was first, followed
closely by I think Derek Field. An' I remember,
I looked at Mr. Field's face an' it was sort of
shrunk, it was ashen when he walked in. I
knew from that instant it was bad news y'-
know. Mr. Field looked terrible, he really
looked shocking I thought.

FRANK (*though actually ALF WAKEFIELD's line*):
Looking at Mr. Field's face an' having sketched
that face I know what it can look like, it was
black.

STAN: When Mr. Field came into the room, anybody who looked at him and knew him, might
well have said to themselves, "Allo, we're gettin' the boot."

BILL: I think for the first time we realized that
something was going to happen.

*TED makes the presentation of the Wedgwood
bowl from its box, while STAN and GERALD quietly comment on it. LORD MELCHETT receives it
with real pleasure and puts it on the table in front
of him as he sits down.*

STAN: Well, what happened was that er, Lord
Melchett, er finally came round the table,
shook hands with everyone present. The presentation took place at this point and he replied
suitably. It was a Wedgwood Imperial bowl.

GERALD: They welcomed Lord Melchett as an
honored guest, they weren't an angry bunch of
Trade Unionists, they were calm. They got for
him a Wedgwood bowl and they presented it to
him, and they did that before the meeting
started, so that whatever he had come to say,
and of course no one in that room knew what
he was going to say, that he had had that gesture quite irrespective. He was certainly caught
off his guard by that because he hadn't been
warned that this was going to happen, so he
was at a *slight* disadvantage from the start, but
he was quite clear and sure in his mind that the
case had to be put to them by himself.

All sit down. LORD MELCHETT *opens a folder and refers to it from time to time as he speaks.*

LORD M.: First of all I would like to express my sincere appreciation of the care and effort you have taken in presenting the case for electric arc furnaces. May I also say how very conscious we are of the performance at the Shelton plant. The mill is one of the best in the country—How extraordinarily well everyone has contributed throughout the entire plant. (*He pauses.*) The affairs of the BSC have been affected by an enormous amount of indecision but I am sure you will understand the Government announcement has been a watershed.

ALBERT *speaks quietly to the audience as* LORD MELCHETT *consults* MR. FIELD.

ALBERT: I remember even during the preamble I had a growing sense of doom y'know, I knew what he was coming up to, the way he phrased his talk. Made me know that we were gonna get the chop.

LORD M.: All the places that are most affected are to be visited. Faced with the number of inland medium-sized plants, the key lies in the large coastal plants, with low-cost ironmaking, as efficient as any in the world, which can produce the range of finished products more cheaply. The use of electric arcs is limited. We have a lot already and scrap is getting scarce and expensive. Any further arcs will be mainly for Special Steel production. Northern Europe is changing to basic oxygen with the rising demand for scrap. (*He pauses, looks at his papers for a moment.*)

STAN: I certainly sensed in the meeting, before he actually announced it that we were goin' to get the smack in the face but when it did come there was a stunned silence.

LORD M.: Shelton has a good argument but the scrap situation is the uncertain factor. (*He pauses.*) It is envisaged that steelmaking here will finish by mid-1975 but we are not yet certain. There is a remote possibility that by the end of the 1970s we could consider restoring steelmaking but that is very remote. This would mean phasing out 1,600 jobs at Shelton before the arc furnace decision was taken. (*He looks down for a moment.*)

TED (*quietly*): His words, it was like a deadly voice talking to you. There was no emotion in his voice. He hadn't got to prove a point, he was declaring his intentions y'know. "I am God." It was unreal, was total unreality in the room. It wasn't real what we were doing.

BILL: Well, I just kept writing an listening an' er, I couldn't really feel anything then.

LORD M.: The official notice of closure has yet to be given. Mr. Morley and his advisers will be coming down to discuss what is to happen. Everyone affected will receive individual counseling. It is intended to keep the casting plant in a workable condition. The performance of the large plants will determine the length of time that the Shelton Plant will run. The large plant performance is not yet certain but they could determine the life of steel production at Shelton. The restructuring is to take place in an improving economy and we would be working in an atmosphere which can make the task easier.

BILL: Well, I think everybody felt there wasn't any point in carrying on really, at that stage. (*He puts his pen down.*)

There is a long pause: some quiet consultation between MELCHETT *and* FIELD.

ALBERT: I remember feeling sort of, a dread, if you like, a sort of weight y'know and sort of shrinking down into me chair, because I knew what was coming and when he actually said it, if you could depict sort of twelve blokes sitting round the table, all shattered y'know, really shattered and yet trying not to show this emotion to Melchett and trying to draw theirselves up out their chair so that they could start asking some constructive questions y'know.

BILL (*half rising, addresses a question to* LORD MELCHETT): With the possibility of arc furnaces in the future, what is intended to be done with the steel plant?

LORD M.: It is the intention to maintain the casting plant and buildings in a workable condi-tion until the very end of the decade—probably about 1979 when the decision will be taken about electric arc furnace capacity in the Midlands.

ALBERT (*rises*): If statutory notice was given would the failure of the large plants to meet targets extend the time of closure?

LORD M.: Nothing is yet certain on the buildup of the large plants and this will give more time to talk to you.

FRANK (*rises, suppressing real anger*): When men have gone, never to come back, how can we reopen again afterwards?

LORD M.: It is correct that once a work force has been dispersed, the special skills go. It is also true that we can reopen and train people again, Sheerness is an example. It probably isn't very clever, but we think that reopening is a long shot anyway.

Another pause.

TED: He just completely and utterly destroyed us, y'know, doesn't matter, y'know, we anna int'rested, y'know and that's it.

BILL rises and breaks back out of the semicircle a pace or two to speak quietly to the audience.

BILL: All right so we don't fit in with their plans. But we're not a bankrupt organization here y'know and somebody else should be able to move in and take up this profitable plant and do something with it. I wouldn't have cared if it was the Communist Party of the Soviet Union comin' in, didn't bother me who it was. It could have bin the Americans, the Russians, I wasn't bothered.

ALBERT: Yes in fact it came up I think Bill because you asked Lord Melchett about the possibility of joint ventures.

 . . . This was was a sort of
BILL: Yeap. . . . That was a]
ALBERT: strategy we'd got up our sleeves. Yes.]
BILL: question.]

Pause. BILL *now turns to* LORD MELCHETT. *His answer was:*

LORD M.: We are open to discuss joint ventures and will make approaches to private companies to create additional jobs. The only qualification is that we are not prepared to sell off at low prices to would-be competitors and could not sell off parts of the plant piecemeal. To take bits and pieces would affect the national plan and ultimately destroy it.

BILL (*replies, with growing anger*): I said: I've never bin anywhere and listened to such arro-gance from anybody, who could sit in front of a body of men and say, that "If *we* don't want you, we'll make sure that nobody else *can* have you." I said that is absolute arrogance. I said it's not something that we will accept. To condemn 1,650 men to the dole like that. I said, "You're saying that if er, we wish to make doll's eyes or sausages, you've got no objection but if we wish to make steel, the thing that we're good at, you would oppose it." And he sort of looked down on the floor an' round the walls, to see if there was anywhere where he could get out.

LORD MELCHETT looks down for a moment during this, then replies to BILL *quietly.*

LORD M.: We will look at joint ventures to generate employment. We will clear the land and sell it cheaply, even invest money in suitable concerns that would make use of BSC products.

ALBERT: I remember that Frank Oldacre at one stage then became quite emotional and gave an impassioned plea to Melchett. Frank was particularly good and I think this impressed Melchett. . . .

FRANK gets up during this.

BILL: I think it embarrassed him more than impressed 'im.

FRANK: Shelton's been there as long as my father was a lad y'know, this int a place, it isn't a place where yer . . . Shelton, it's eat sleep and drink Shelton. All her life you've done it an' why should it go out of existence, somebody's er little brain child. Lord Melchett give us a chance. . . . That's all we ask of you, a chance to work and prove to you what a good labor force we have here at Shelton, that's all we ask of you. But I will tell you that if in a few years I am on the dole and walking the streets, I shall think of you men sitting at the bottom end of that table and I shall hate your bloody guts.

LORD M. (*after a pause.*): We are considering improvements to the mill but we still have to deal with the steelmaking problem.

GERALD: But everyone else was quite composed about it.

LORD M.: Full note of all the facts has been taken but because of the overall plans there is no alternative than to phase out iron and steelmaking as announced, although no official notice of closure has been given yet.

Everyone stands. MR. FIELD *gets the bowl.* TED *steps forward.*

GERALD: And even at the very end urm, Ted stood up and thanked his lordship for coming and er, how they realized what a difficult job he had to do and it closed on that note y'know.

LORD MELCHETT shakes hands with all the AC-TION COMMITTEE MEMBERS.

BILL: Serving the death sentence on a Works, in the manner that he put it over, y'know was, I thought, really excellent, it probably his public school upbringing that did that, I don't know, I mean to be actually pleasant about it, knowing full well what you're doing to people, it's not easy to do.

The MELCHETT PARTY *go out. The* ACTION COM-MITTEE *stay where they are. The lights change, isolating each one almost in his own pool of light. The actor playing* STAN WHALLEY *now takes* PE-TER CARTLEDGE's *lines.*

PETER: I remember looking up at the Hall and the bloody flag was flying wan it?

ALBERT: Yes, we put the flag up for him.

PETER: The flag was flying top of the Hall an I thought well why isn't the bloody thing flying at half mast y'know, so that er as a signal or somat like so that everyone can get this information.

ALBERT: A lot of people said that, Pete.

PETER: An' er we were talking in the shop all the lads y'know, what we going do? Shall we bug-ger off home like, we might as well pack it in and er shall we go outside and try and catch him as he's going off and create some kind a demonstration y'know, let him know . . .

BILL: We did care.

PETER: . . . feelings amongst the blokes. I think we could've er, created a bit of disturbance be-cause the feeling was bloody, real mad y'know. The blokes were really angry in our shop at the time when I went in an' told them.

BERN: We've never bin like that Pete, never bin a bunch of chaps who walk about swinging pickax handles. He came at our invite. It was

us who invited him. You can't turn 'round and then start clobbering with pickaxes.

BILL: I think we felt, we probably felt sick on that day, y'know really sick. I didn't feel it much on the day but I felt it the next day.

BERN: I wanted some hole, I did. Crawl into.

A pause.

ALBERT: I remember going home at night and didn't want to go through the door 'cos I knew the wife would know about it by then, an I didn't know really whether to go in and face her with a smile, y'know, think, it's OK, love, y'know, won't worry about that, y'know, I'd, got, felt *sick*. Y'know it was terrible, terrible, having to walk through the door at home and I remember that night um, an old friend of mine rang up, he'd left Shelton and er, he rang to to sort of get my reaction and he was most upset about it even though he'd left Shelton, and it was, choking almost, trying to talk to him on the phone, y'know.

TED moves away slowly, then sits at BILL's table.

TED: I felt the next day that we'd reached the end of the road, y'know, that was it. That's how I felt, the next day.

BILL: We shall never go through that experience again.

TED: What have I spent 2 years of my life for, twenty hours a day, I thought, what have I been doing it for? Where do I go?

The lights change leaving only TED *lit, sitting alone at the table, and a light on* GERALD, *higher up in the auditorium.* GERALD *speaks slowly, de-liberately.*

GERALD: It wasn't until afterwards, an' a long time afterwards, that they started to recover, be-cause after Lord Melchett's visit nothing hap-pened. There was a vacuum for a quite a few months, and a lot of people started leaving the Works, 'cos immediately we got a high labor turnover, at all levels, staff, works, managers, they all started drifting away, looking round, accepting what'd been said as the final word.

Two MEN *come on in red steel-plant helmets with visors up. They move a rail across the set during*

TED's speech, then start to go to him. They stop, and pass without greeting him and go off.

TED: The most shattering thing to me was on payday, where we pay wages out, and I pay wages out, and blokes were coming up to me and their faces were dropping. Blokes I'd known all me life. Friends as I thought I'd got, you know, and they just dropped their head and walked away, you know. Your fault.

The actor playing TED sits alone at the table while the voice of Ted Smith himself is played through the overhead loudspeaker.

TED SMITH'S OWN VOICE ON TAPE: But a tremendous experience took place to me, and I'm telling you. I'm coming work, on the Friday morning, and another friend had died recently, and that was Cliff Toft, a little old man, he were a storekeeper down there. And I was walking down there, and these men that had died . . . and I usually walk down on me own, down past Air Products. . . . I got off the bus and I was thinking to meself, what would they do. . . . And the message came to me they'd fight . . . and fight, and that was the only thing that come across. And I could hear these voices, mate, and loud and clear they were. You know, men, Tommy Cooper, you know, men 'at'd been killed. George Rushton, his head crushed. What would that man do? And this all, you know, goin through me mind. This this, is, you know, on the Friday afterwards, you know. And I came down there and I surged, energy—(TED slowly stands up.)—surged through me, going past Air Products, and I was on me way from that point on, mate. And I thought, the bastards aren't having my job. Those bloody men aren't giving their lives up for me, and me let 'em down? Not on your bloody life. And tears did roll down my bloody cheeks, mate. Unashamed tears of bloody joy, because I, I was prepared to put my bloody life down same as they had then.

MAYDAY SONG

As each group enters to join in the song, they lift up placards with slogans in black letters saying

"SAVE OUR SHELTON" and "WE DEMAND THE RIGHT TO WORK."

FIRST ACTRESS (sings, unaccompanied):
We thought that we were home and dry,
That Shelton Bar would stay,
But Melchett now has sealed our fate,
He's named the closing day.
These people in their offices,
Can't understand our loss,
And with a red pen in their hands,
They can simply strike us off.

The guitar instrumental begins.

FIRST ACTRESS (sings, accompanied):
Who are they, where are they?
What gives them the right,
To interfere with our lives,
And change them overnight?
We're happy in this city.
We're glad to earn our pay,
Why can't they leave us here in peace,
Why can't they let us stay?

The instrumental continues under TED's speech, while he addresses the audience.

TED: On May 1st 1973 we held a day of protest and the whole of the works shut down and we had 1,200 steelworkers out on a march and demonstration in protest against corporation's attitude to Shelton's case. It was the finest day I have ever had in my life. I have never been on strike. That was the first day and marching with your comrades on a march is the most exhilarating feeling I've ever had. It was truly tremendous, the unity and everything else that goes with it. I got butterflies about turning up but I quite enjoyed it.

ALL THE GIRLS (sing):
One hundred and fifty years have passed,
Since Shelton Bar was built,
How can we let our history go,
And not feel any guilt?
Our fathers and our families
Have lived and worked and died,
Their monument is Shelton Bar,
Their legacy is pride.

Three MEN come on with placards.

ALL (*sing*):
> We only need electric arcs
> To bring us to the 'fore,
> But they say we can't have them
> So it's going to cost much more—
> In handing out redundancies,
> And unemployment pay.
> If there's no new industry for Stoke,
> Then they'll make this district gray.

Four more MEN *now come on with placards.*

ALL (*sing*):
> Most people in North Staffordshire,
> They just don't realize,
> So liven your ideas up
> And start to use your eyes.
> You may not work at Shelton Bar,
> But their fight you can't reject
> If we ever let them shut that plant,
> Then we'll all feel the effect!
>
> You people of North Staffordshire,
> Don't let them have their way,
> Don't be pushed around like this.
> Stand up and have your say.
> You may be quiet and peaceful folk,
> But you know wrong from right
> Turn round and tell them face to face,
> That you have joined the fight.

Pause. The cast now leave the stage.

END OF PART ONE

PART TWO

KALDO SEQUENCE

There is at first general lighting all over the stage—four of the ACTION COMMITTEE *come on and indicate as they speak the geography of the steel plant. A loud harsh hooter sounds.*

PETER: Everything this side of the canal—
FOSTER: Is the North Works.
STAN: The North Works.
BILL FOSTER: This is the steel plant. Over there is the mill, sort of way behind it.
PETER: See the iron where we just seen it made comes down and comes into this buildin 'ere.

Another warning hooter sounds twice as the MEN *start to go off. The lights change. Two* STEEL PLANT WORKERS *in red helmets with visors come on and start to put on their protective gloves and get ready to take a sample. They keep their backs to the intense light from a Kaldo vessel at one end. Otherwise it is gloomy now. There is a great row from the vessels, and the two* WORKMEN *shout.*

FIRST MAN: The iron'll be picked up and poured into these vessels.
SECOND MAN: Kaldo convertors—Swedish.
FIRST MAN: Then it's turned the other way, scrap and all additions put it. Back 'ere, blow oxygen on it, spin it 'round, mix it all up, melt it all down . . . slag, the slag'll go out that way, pour the other way, the steel goes out to the casting plant.

The SECOND MAN *walks in a semicircle slowly round in front of the Kaldo vessel, looking into the light, shielding his face from the heat, to inspect the lining. The recorded commentary from a steel plant* FOREMAN *comes over the speakers.*

FOREMAN'S VOICE: What we do with the iron in the Kaldo is to use oxygen to burn away the carbon, the silicon, the phosphorus, and to get rid of the sulphur as well.

The SECOND MAN *pauses in his inspection.*

SECOND MAN: Technically speaking that is incorrect, but it's the best way of putting it.

He now does the same operation in the other direction, still in a semicircle 'round the front.

FOREMAN'S VOICE: We blow oxygen into the vessel which lies at an angle of about 70 degrees and is rotated to agitate the bath. In this way the oxygen reacts more readily with the constituents.

Two blasts of the warning hooter sound.

TANNOY ANNOUNCEMENT: Kaldo Two tilting, stand clear! Stand clear! Kaldo Two tilting.

The background sound now reduces a little, the MEN *on stage go off, the lights change to reveal three* ACTION COMMITTEE MEMBERS *on the stairs in the auditorium, and two of their* WIVES.

SHANGRI-LA

PHIL ROGERS: By reducing the work force on Shelton Bar, they're gonna take a livin from out of my children's mouths, and they're goin to wander in time to come, so I'm goin t'be a split family with probably a son in Glasgow, one in London, and one in Bristol looking for male work.

STAN: This is our home town, our area, and this is where we want jobs, and where we intend to have them.

PHIL R.: The majority of the people of Stoke-on-Trent are local and they stick. You don't find many communities of Stoke-on-Trent people anywhere else in the country, but only Stoke-on-Trent. We're like together, we don't move.

STAN (*speaking* DAVE MATTHIAS's *lines*): What he's trying to say, that Stoke-on-Trent to us is our Shangri-la. Stoke-on-Trent is our Shangri-la.

MYRA: The day that man on the television, Lord Melchett, said that Shelton Iron and Steel were going to close A sat down and cried. Then I thought what y'cryin for? If it's going to happen, it's going to happen.

TOM TIMMIS: You plan, and all of a sudden somebody at a little desk in a bloody office comes 'round an gets a red pencil and says—you've finished.

MRS. WHALLEY: Wasn't it Prince Philip who said—pull your socks up—when people pull their socks up what do they get for their reward?

PHIL R.: None of us are salesmen, none of us want to go on a milk cart, you know, men do 'ave a little bit of pride.

TOM TIM.: This is what we're fighting for—dignity and pride. I've worked all my life and I feel—I think anyway as I've got dignity, I've got me pride, and if I have to go cap in hand to So-cial Security, and bow to these people, I know very well that I wouldn't be able to lift my head up nowhere—at the moment I can do.

Another blast on the hooter, the lights and sound change back to the Kaldo bay, the two MEN *trundle on a metal screen and a long spoon ready to take a sample.*

SAMPLING

FOREMAN'S VOICE (*over the speaker*): Right. When the, the charge is er come to its end in the respect that we've achieved the temperature that we require er this is er achieved by the amount of oxygen that we blow, and when this amount has been blown we slow the rotation down to make the slag into a consistency such that we can penetrate it by a sample spoon, to obtain a sample of the steel in the bath. We check the temperature. (*As the recorded description goes on, the* MEN *take the sample, wheeling the screen in front of the Kaldo vessel, pushing the long spoon through a slot in it into the molten steel, taking it out with great care, one* MAN *supporting it with a steel hook by the bowl while the* OTHER *pours it into a mold.*) If this temperature is satisfactory, normally 'round 1650 degrees centigrade, we take a sample of the steel bath by pushin the sample spoon through the slag, it coats the spoon with a, er, a layer of slag, a spoonful of steel is pulled out of the bath 'n poured into a copper mold.

FIRST MAN: This sample now goes to the laboratories, behind the offices. They analyze it with an electronic analyzer.

The two MEN *carry off the mold and wheel off the screen and the spoon and hook. The warning sounds. The lights change to show* BILL, TED *and* ALBERT *on the auditorium stairs with the blue BSC documents in their hands.* ROMY *speaks for the Vic Research Committee, as it were.*

THE BROCHURE ARRIVES

ALBERT: All steelworks with notice of closure are presented with a brochure giving the economic reasons why it's closing.

BILL: The economic argument for closing Shelton. It isn't enough to say—you're uneconomic, we think you ought to go, to close our works, they've got to prove it to us, y'see.

SECOND ACTRESS: Four copies of the BSC brochure were handed to the Shelton Action Committee at noon on Wednesday 14th November.

TED: Initially, on hearing of the Shelton brochure, and its publication, I awaited breathlessly for it to be delivered. I was expecting a document four foot thick to tell us why we'd got the sack, but they do it in eight pages.

BILL: The hilarity with which we've greeted it has meant that we've been delayed in getting through it. It's not a long document, but it is funny.

ALBERT: It really is amazingly naive. Perhaps they feel that we're too thick to appreciate some of the financial arguments. But . . . words, words really do fail me. They've taken so many suppositions to suit their case.

TED: We shall build a case page by page on a question and answer, y'know, their question, our answer. That's what we shall do.

The hooter sounds. Lights and sound change back to the Kaldo bay again. The two MEN come on with shovels and protective clothing.

TANNOY: Kaldo Two tilting. Stand clear! Stand clear! Kaldo Two tilting.

FOREMAN'S VOICE: We tip the vessel over to the scrap-charging side, we have a ladle, a steel ladle, which will hold a maximum of 80 tons of steel in a carriage on rails underneath the vessel, this is run underneath the vessel. The vessel is tilted er over to the horizontal position and the steel is run over the lip of the er of the vessel.

The two MEN finally tie scarves around their faces, over nose and mouth.

SECOND MAN: You need these, against the fumes.

FIRST MAN (*lifts up the bottom of his scarf*): We anna makin 'Orlicks, you know; we're makin steel.

The two now shovel from a pile of chemical additives left there by a little dumper truck into the mouth of the Kaldo vessel. They run as near as possible, throw in the stuff, dodge away from the heat, and circle back to the pile to keep clear for the other's run.

FOREMAN'S VOICE: Now as we empty the vessel of the steel into the ladle, we add the constituents required to give us the desired analysis in the steel.

SECOND MAN: The crane then picks the ladle up and takes it 70 feet up to the casting plant through a shaft.

The lights alter to a general spread suitable for a meeting room. The two MEN take off their steel plant clothes and get ready for the meeting. All the cast move on with chairs and tables, stopping to sing the choruses. Two of the cast accompany the song on concertina and mouth organ, while two MEN sing the verses. The furniture is arranged for a conventional meeting, top table faced by rows of chairs. It represents the upstairs classroom of the WEA building in Cartwright House, Hanley.

SONG—THANK YOU KINDLY MR. MELCHETT

ALL:
> Thank you kindly Mr. Melchett, we know exactly where we are,
> We don't think your plan is wise and we're going to organize,
> So you'd better keep your hands from off the Bar.

TWO MEN:
> Now gather 'round me mates and a story I'll relate
> Of the Shelton Bar, a plant of great renown,
> Where we could earn our pay, smelting steel by night and day,
> Till Lord Melchett thought, he'd close the foundry down.
> But we said,

ALL:
> Thank you kindly Mr. Melchett, we know exactly where we are,
> We don't think your plan is wise and we're going to organize,
> So you'd better keep your hands from off the Bar.

TWO MEN:
> I've worked here, man and boy for 40 years or nigh,

And I've sweated cobs as black as any coal,
Now the boss sends his regards, says he's sorting out me cards,
And it won't be long before I'm on the dole.
But we said,

ALL:

Thank you kindly Mr. Melchett, we know exactly where we are,
We don't think your plan is wise and we're going to organize,
So you'd better keep your hands from off the Bar.

TWO MEN:

You're the king of BSC, but you break no ice with me,
As a working bloke I'm very proud to say:
I can earn me food and rent and I owe no one a cent,
And what's more it's me who earns your bloody pay!

ALL:

So thank you kindly Mr. Melchett, we know exactly where we are,
We don't think your plan is wise and we're going to organize,
So you'd better keep your hands from off the Bar.

WEA MEETING 15 NOVEMBER 1973

Behind the top table sit TED SMITH *in the chair, flanked by* BILL FOSTER *and* ALBERT COOPER. *The other* DELEGATES *in a mixture of leisure and working clothes sit facing them. As the scene begins,* BILL *is speaking, standing up holding his copy of the BSC Shelton brochure.*

BILL: The other point that I would like to make is that because of the acoustics of the room, try and restrain your laughter in certain parts of the brochure. (*All laugh.*) I mean this seriously. It starts off paragraph 1, page 1: The Strategy. My comment on the strategy is you could have fooled me. But nevertheless, I'll read it to you. (*He reads:*) "The general strategy is the bulk of the Corporation's steel production will be derived through the hot metal route at five major locations, namely, Scunthorpe, Teesside, Rav-

enscraig, Llanwern, and Port Talbot. The balance will be produced by the electric arc furnace route, including one new steel works, based on the arc furnace and continuous casting process which will be built in Scotland. That's Wallside. Estimates of the future availability of scrap supplies *might* have supported the construction elsewhere of a second small arc furnace, but this possible development has been largely preempted by the decision of Guest Keen & Nettlefold to build one at Cardiff as announced on 7th August 1973." I *would* like to point out to you that we are in a nationalized industry. The Act was designed to concentrate the mass of steelmaking within the nationalized sector, although there might be fringes that were covered by some small steelmaking units. Apparently, the 1973 policy of the Steel Corporation is to tailor the nationalized industry to suit what is necessary in the private sector and because Guest Keen and Nettlefold, to name but one, have decided on an arc furnace plant, the Corporation are opting out of the market. That is the strategy, Paragraph 1. So now apparently I would expect when the news leaks out 'round the edges in Parliament, that somebody would want to ask questions in relation to the nationalization of steel. In other words, has the Chairman gone off his head, has the Chairman decided that we are going to cooperate with the private sector to ensure that people like Guest Keen and Nettlefold can make the major profit and that we'll make steel? This is apparent now. We did suggest some time ago that we thought the nationalized sector would make steel, the private sector would make money. They are confirming this in the brochure.

BILL *sits down,* ALBERT *gets up, taking his pipe out of his mouth.*

ALBERT: It says here also in para. one—(*He reads:*) "Estimates of the future availability of scrap supplies might have supported the construction elsewhere of a second arc furnace," and I think what we must ask is whose estimates and where did they get the figures and on what basis are these estimates arrived at? Because we feel that we have an abundance of scrap supplies in this area. (*He sits.*)

BILL (*sitting*): They're telling us that the scrap isn't available at Shelton, you could have fooled me. I thought Andrew Young went down on his knees last week and said "Please can we have some of your surplus scrap. We know it won't affect your operations." In other words, the scrap arising in the Shelton locality will be required to support steelmaking in the Sheffield and Scunthorpe areas. So, you know, we can expect very shortly to have a request from Sheffield and Scunthorpe in line with the one from Scotland, "We're short of scrap, can you send us some." (*He carries on reading from the brochure.*) Paragraph 2 says: "The strategy therefore calls for the closure of the existing iron and steelmaking plant and the continuous casting plant unit at Shelton. The blooms required for the mill will be supplied from Scunthorpe." (*He looks up.*) I just add that because that is really what Melchett said in March.

A pause while the top table look at their brochures, and MEN *in the meeting consult one another. The concertina and a mouth organ play a few bars of the* MELCHETT *song to indicate the passing of time.* BILL *looks up; the instrumental stops.*

BILL: This is rather an interesting little paragraph. "The Scunthorpe capital is already committed and capital charges can therefore be excluded. As are the charges in respect of the capital employed in the existing Shelton configuration. The amount included in respect of the alternative electric arc scheme reflects the normal return required for new capital." So what they're saying, in effect, is because we are asking for £15 million now, and they decided 6 months ago, or 12 months ago, or 18 months ago, to spend 300 million at Scunthorpe *that* doesn't cost anything, the 300 million. But the 5 million has to be paid for by somebody. It's a good theory. It's a theory that an accountant can understand because *their* minds work in peculiar ways.

The MEN *laugh.*

TED: They put £3.84 a ton for us borrowing 5 million. They've put *nothing* in Scunthorpe's figures for borrowing 300 million. And if that's logic, I don't know where to go.

BILL: We are commonsense people, y'know. We think if we borrow money we have to pay for it. The British Steel Corporation if they borrow 300 million, don't have to pay. But if they borrow 5 million, they have to pay through the nose, as their figures illustrate. I don't know who they've got the er, contracts with for borrowing small sums of money (*More laughter.*) but I could do them a better deal at Hanley Trustee Savings Bank.

Loud laughter and applause—a few more bars of music. Then TED *looks up.*

TED: Anyway, paragraph 3. Moving along. The Demag mill will continue to operate with a guaranteed future throughout the decade. Well, you heard what Bill has got to say on this. What do the mill men feel in relation to this paragraph? Do they see a future, an open door, never ending.

FRANK OLDACRE *speaks from the body of the meeting.*

FRANK: We're taking it all in Ted, we like to sit on the fence a bit, see what the Committee have got to say. But as far as the mill's concerned, this is the first time that I've heard that a four-year plan has been submitted, and I don't know what must be in the air.

GEORGE JOHNSON (*stands up*): We'll tell them as they can't have the rolling mill at all, if they're going to take steelmaking and blast furnaces away from us. We'll sit on the rolls and if they're gonna roll us thro' the rollers, we'll block the whatsit as RSJs. (*He sits down to laughter and applause.*)

FRANK (*stands, alarmed*): You've got to go into it thoroughly. I mean, it's no use saying we'll stop . . . sit on the rollers. Yes, I quite agree, this is a good policy. But can we do it for our end, day in day out, week in, week in, year in, year in. This is what it means, you've got to get some strategy. Have you means to stop those blooms coming to the furnace. That seems the only thing that's reasonable to me.

Several DELEGATES *get up at once and speak noisily protesting and supporting* FRANK's *worries.* BILL *talks them down.*

BILL: What we're talking about actually, is the fact that we're very near to a possibility of a crunch situation when people have got to stand up and be counted.

SOMEONE: Hear! Hear!

TED (*rises to get order*): Just one speaker, lads. (*He sits.*)

Another pause. MEN *consult each other animatedly, while the instrumental plays through. Then* BILL *rises.*

BILL: But all we're asking at this meeting and we've done this once before . . .

DELEGATE: Yeah, that's true.

BILL: Have you made your own minds up as to where you stand, so that we know as a body in this room we're all going out preaching the same gospel. Or has anybody got any doubts, because anybody that's sitting in here now that's got any doubts, that door's not locked. And they might as well go through it. (*BILL points to the door.*)

DENNIS *rises from the body of the meeting.*

DENNIS: Well, can I speak as a mill delegate, Mr. Chairman? I've never believed for one second that the mill could roll in isolation to the rest of the steel plant on this, at Shelton. I have never believed it and I never will, so if you want a seconder to the proposal from the mill, then I'll second it by all means.

TED (*rises*): I'd like to now put that proposition to the meeting. Proposed by Tom Playford that we use the mill as an argument against the Steel Corporation. It has been duly seconded. I put it to the meeting, all those in favor of that proposition? (*All except* FRANK *raise their hands.*) Anyone against? (*No one signifies.*) Passed unanimously.

All sing a final chorus as the chairs and tables are moved aside and the standing rails and angles are brought in to build the guard around the Concast machine.

ALL (*sing*):
Thank you kindly Mr. Melchett, we know exactly where we are
We don't think your plan is wise, and we're going to organize

So you'd better keep your hands from off the Bar.

CONCAST SEQUENCE

The lights change. The guard around the Concast machine is a framework about six feet high with sheets of corrugated iron bolted onto it. Through slots in the frame project the long handles that operate the flow of molten steel from the ladle into the tundish on top of the casting machine. A dazzling light shines through the gaps between the iron sheets. The rest of the stage is gloomy. WALTER WATKINS *and two other* MOLD OPERATORS *with red helmets and big visors build the framework. There is a low continuous roaring sound from gas burners heating new tundishes and empty ladles.*

WALT: We're on top of the casting flow, 70 feet above ground level.

SECOND OPERATOR: The Concast machine. (*He points to it.*)

Sound of the overhead crane comes in.

WALT: The crane—(*He points upwards.*)—lifts that ladle full of molten steel up that shaft and drops it onto this casting machine.

SECOND OPERATOR: There's a man up there, he controls the flow of metal of the ladle.

WALT: The steel runs through into a tundish.

SECOND OPERATOR: Then it runs out of the tundish into these three molds.

WALT: That man up there also controls the water flow which cools the mold. So when the steel gets to the ground floor, it's solid.

SECOND OPERATOR: We control the flow of steel out of the tundish into the molds with three rods.

They have completed assembling the frame and rods and move into position, working the long handles.

WALT: We are making one continuous long billet, which is cut off at the bottom to the required lengths. If you like, a kind of sausage machine.

TED *has come on, looking for someone. The guitar and autoharp instrumental to the Rover's*

Song begins.

TED: I never relate a job to wages I don't, funny that, isn't it? Y'know, I wouldn't like to compare our wages with what they get in other industries. I would compare Shelton as a place of worship, not a place of work. Y'know, it's a place to, y'know, you look forward to going, it's not . . . There's companionship there, there's humor, there's everything.

BILL FOSTER has appeared momentarily, like TED in a helmet.

BILL: They're all comedians up 'ere you know.

ROVER'S SONG

The work carries on while the GIRLS sing the song, sitting on the stairs and the orchestra rostrum, with an actor joining the instrumental on a mouth organ.

GIRLS (*sing*):
We know a joker, Bernard Wright,
Been wielding the Power for years
Then he went to work for a stationery firm
And he soon got bored to tears.

MEN (*join in the chorus*):
So take me back, back on the Bar
It's the rover's constant plea
I haven't half missed you while I've been away
So it's back to the Bar for me.

The instrumental carries on.

WALT: The worst problem on here is in summer—the heat. Then you've got winter which is not too bad because you've got the cold, an' it's nice to be in front o' heat. Where in summer, you've got heat an' heat. We've had men here flake out in front of these strands. Just keel over with heat exhaustion. That's how hard it is here, but still we donna get a penny extra for it in summer. Get nothin' extra for this and it's four times harder in summer than it is in winter.

SECOND OPERATOR: That's when we start running for sweat tablets . . .

WALT: Yes, sweat tablets.

SECOND OPERATOR: Have you ever 'ad any o' them?

WALT: Put salt back into us.

SECOND OPERATOR: Y'start running for sweat tablets—y'can always tell a bloke when he's 'ad sweat tablets, can't you—

They all laugh.

GIRLS (*sing*):
There was Eric Burton, an army bloke
An electrical man by trade
When Swinnerton's gave him redundancy pay
He just turned round and said,

ALL (*sing*):
Please take me back, back on the Bar
It's the rover's constant plea
I haven't half missed you while I've been away
So it's back to the Bar for me.

WALT: Um, you've got the sparks, burns er . . . you've got the problem of keepin the strand goin if the stopper end goes. Very often we get badly burned.

SECOND OPERATOR: Yea.

WALT: Oh yes. We've got men that 'av finished on here. We've got one off the shopfloor now, that's 'ad 'is eye er he's finished altogether. Oh we 'ave several burned.

ONE OF THE GIRLS: What can you do to avoid it?

WALT: You've got protective headwear, sometimes er it's just one o' them things, that a spark hits a bit o' cold metal 'n flirts up into y'visor an' y've got it.

GIRL: Is there anything you can do to stop that—any dodges like?

WALT: No, no. Y'get protective clothing, footwear, suit, and er they use what y've got y'self.

The instrumental plays on mouth organ only, as three GIRLS step forward in their own spotlight, as wives of the men.

MYRA: I asked him what they like about Shelton, he comes home, he's filthy, he's dirty, his shoes are meltin, he's workin in horrible conditions.

SHIRLEY: Do you get that horrible brown the red . . .

MYRA: Mmm—yes oh horrible it is, and he comes in, as you get near . . . you just have to brush past 'im, you're covered.

MYRA: Sometimes, I feel, surely there's a better job than this. Something better for 'im and we could have a much better life.

SHIRLEY: There's bin quite a lot that we know that would love to get back.

MYRA: There's one young apprentice. His uncle offered him a job and it'd got all the good prospects so he left, and he'd come back on his knees tomorrow to join 'em at Shelton—so it can't be as bad as it p'raps sounds, y'know.

GIRLS (*sing*):
Geoff Brooks went away for a year or more
To work for the Michelin men,
But he tired of the tires and he came right back
To the steelworks once again.

ALL (*sing*):
So take me back, back on the Bar,
It's the rover's constant plea,
I haven't half missed you while I've been away
So it's back to the Bar for me.

The MOLD OPERATORS finish the cast, the sound of the crane comes in as the ladle is removed, they dismantle the guard and take the pieces away.

WALT: You could come up to me now an' say—I could do with a drink o' water, can y'get us one?—You can't find a drink o'water on this shop floor of a modern steelworks. (*He erupts with irritation.*) I'll tell you where it is an' y'can go an' 'ave a look at it—an tell me if it's adequate. See them offices down there? Behind them, an everybody bloody washes in it—sink what men 'av got to drink out of.

GIRLS (*sing*):
There's an electrician in the mill
And Rasbridge is his name,
Two years he spent in the building trade
But he came back just the same.

ALL (*sing*):
So take me back, back on the Bar
It's the rover's constant plea
I haven't half missed you while I've been away
So it's back to the Bar for me.

The instrumental carries on very quietly as MRS. COOPER steps forward.

MRS. COOPER: To me it's always been the be all and end all of everything, y'know, Shelton Bar's bought my house, Shelton Bar's bought the furniture, Shelton Bar has given me everything that I've got, I mean, everything I've got I owe to Shelton Bar. When you've worked at the Bar

for as long as my family's been there, you sort of, oh I don't know—it's difficult to explain. . . . I feel as if it's home, Shelton Bar's home.

GIRLS (*sing*):
If Shelton Bar was taken apart
And the bits were carted away
Wherever you went all over the world
You'd hear those pieces say

ALL (*sing*):
Oh take me back, back on the Bar
It's the rover's constant plea
I haven't half missed you while I've been away
So it's back to the Bar for me.

The instrumental carries on.

TED: And er, y'know, I say to meself, well, y'-know, my father gave his life for industry. What did he get out of it? He handed his history and his heritage down to me, that he'd fought and worked for. He'd bin crushed and maimed and buried y'know, in a pit . . . y'see, I've got mental pictures of these things and nothing could ever detract from what I'm fighting for, y'know, I've got a mental picture apart from me father, people on Shelton Bar, I've seen 'em with limbs torn off, heads crushed in, and they're marvelous men, and if they had their time all over again they'd do exactly the same these men would.

As the last verse and chorus of the Rover's Song is sung, half a dozen MEMBERS OF THE ACTION COMMITTEE'S SUBCOMMITTEE come on and set up a long table for a conference.

GIRLS (*sing*):
If Shelton Bar were taken apart
And the bits were carted away,
Wherever you went, all over the world
You'd hear those pieces say

ALL (*sing*):
Oh take me back, back on the Bar
It's the rover's constant plea
I haven't half missed you while I've been away
So it's back to the Bar for me.

THE ACTION COMMITTEE BROCHURE

As the MEN, with the Action Committee MINUTES SECRETARY, AUDREY, get ready with their papers,

POLLY steps forward, as herself—we were present at most of these meetings.

FIRST ACTRESS: We started recording on Shelton Bar in the last week of October. Lord Melchett had died suddenly in the summer. Roy Pepper a Mill Foreman on the Action Committee had spoken to the new Chairman Dr. Monty Finniston, at the TUC Conference. He had agreed to visit Shelton. On Tuesday 20 November, the Action Subcommittee met to complete their reply to the BSC brochure before Dr. Finniston's visit in seven days' time.

The MEN are sitting in shirtsleeves. The table is strewn with paper. AUDREY is listening to the discussion, but at the same time sorting through the contents of the Action Committee's brochure, ready for typing it.

BILL: The point being that they haven't got a port at Scunthorpe.
TED: They're eighteen miles from their nearest port and this er, strategy of theirs was based on deep-water port facilities.
PETER: Do the BSC know of our port facilities round here: Longport, Middleport, Westport Lake, Port Vale?
BILL: Unfortunately for the BSC, they've produced more than one brochure, and one has been delivered to East Moors, and discussed with East Moors, and on that table for East Moors, the cost of new capital—You've all got one of these (*They refer to the xeroxed sheets.*)—of the Scunthorpe project, is defined at £11.20 per ton. But when they come to Shelton, they don't want to include it. We can only draw one conclusion to this, the case they're arguing at Shelton will not stand the addition of these charges. The fact that the BSC don't want to include it is only really saying to us, we haven't got a very good case for Shelton. They can't call it new capital at East Moors with reference to Scunthorpe, and come to Shelton and say it's not new capital.
STAN: It also looks as though they might be playing one works agin another. Are yer gonna give them this information or are we gonna bring this in when Finniston comes down.
BILL: No, no. It's gotta go in the brochure.

TED: We shall photostat this and submit it as evidence, as evidence, as in a court of law.
STAN: Aye.
TED: It's a fact, it's, it's reproduced out of the East Moors brochure. They're the BSC figures.

AUDREY finds a sheet she doesn't recognize.

AUDREY: Is this anything I don't know about?
BILL: Yes, well, that's just an illustration really of the type of table we shall produce.
PETER: Can you pass that 'round the table, please?
BILL: And you can have a look at it. We're going to prove in this brochure that we can produce the steel cheaper than they can at Scunthorpe.

FIRST ACTRESS steps forward again, the instrumental to the Rover's Song is played, the tables are rearranged into a round table shape, and a typewriter is brought in for AUDREY.

FIRST ACTRESS: That afternoon, in the conference room of Etruria Hall, Albert Cooper, Bill Foster, Ted Smith and other members of the Action Subcommittee work to finish the final draft for the printers.

Though late November, it is a hot sunny afternoon. AUDREY types the final draft of the brochure as each page is cleared by long slogging arguments between BILL FOSTER, TED SMITH, and ALBERT COOPER. Everyone is getting tired, but there is a firm constructive atmosphere nonetheless.

BILL (*starting again on this topic*): Let's then take the new capital, new investments at Scunthorpe, BSC's figures, not ours.
ALBERT (*who is playing a kind of devil's advocate role, as the last check on figures*): Yes.
BILL: They say at Scunthorpe it's £11.20 per tonne.
ALBERT: Yes.
BILL: They do say at Shelton, it's £3.84 per tonne.
ALBERT: New capital, yes.
BILL: New capital. They define it as new capital on East Moors brochure and all we've done is put it alongside the new capital they say they require at Shelton.
ALBERT: That's right.

BILL: We're comparing like and like. (*He goes over to* AUDREY.) How are y'doing?

AUDREY: Well, I've got to eleven, but I want Albert's statement.

BILL (*looking in his papers*): Eleven—Albert's statement (*To* TED *and* ALBERT.) Are we satisfied?

ALBERT (*dubiously*): Yeah.

TED: I'm satisfied. Sticking £3.84, £11.20.

AUDREY: Have you got a statement after number eleven, Albert?

ALBERT: Yes, yes. (*He passes it to her.*)

AUDREY: Ah, there we are, yes, there y'are Bill, there's that. (*Handing it to* BILL, *who ignores it.*)

BILL (*to* ALBERT *again*): Would you accept that it says on East Moors brochure what it says on ours: 'Cost of new capital"?

ALBERT: Mm hm.

BILL: You accept that?

ALBERT: Yes, that's what I'm saying.

BILL: What's the cost of new capital on Shelton's brochure?

ALBERT: £3.84.

BILL: No, what *is* it? what does it *mean*? What's it referring to?

ALBERT: New plant.

BILL: Are you sure?

ALBERT: Oh yeah. I'm certain. They said it represented an investment of £6.72 million in arc furnaces.

BILL: And they call it new capital. (*Going at him.*) Now what does it say on East Moors' brochure?

ALBERT (*who won't be stampeded*): In a minute, Bill.

AUDREY (*as she types away*): We shall be here till midnight.

BILL: Does it say cost of new capital? What does it *say*?

ALBERT: Are you saying that . . .

BILL: Shall I tell you what I do know?

ALBERT: Yeah.

BILL: I do know that the £11.20 means Scunthorpe and I want to say that unless they speak with forked tongue, the cost of new capital in the East Moors brochure is identical to the cost of new capital in the Shelton brochure.

ALBERT (*conceding*): Yes, that does seem reasonable. They've used £11.20 in the East Moors

brochure, there's no reason why we shouldn't use it in ours.

AUDREY: Can I just break in a minute? Listen, if the costs are going on a separate sheet, can we just progress a few paragraphs, because if we have, you lot can sort these out and I can carry on.

BILL: Yeah.

AUDREY: Come 'round here now, because if I can get through the next few paragraphs you lot can sort out your papers and I can carry on.

BILL *goes over to* AUDREY. ALBERT *addresses the audience.*

ALBERT: We examined the figures in the BSC's brochure that they gave for the cost of steel produced at Scunthorpe for us to roll. To this cost we added several others they'd left out. Principally the cost of Scunthorpe's new plant: £11.20. We calculated how much it would cost us to produce the steel ourselves. We included the cost of new capital—for electric arc furnaces in Shelton's price. The result was this— Scunthorpe's steel: £44.98 per ton. Shelton's steel: £37.05 per ton. Ours was £7.93 cheaper.

TED (*also to the audience as well as to* BILL *and* ALBERT): Look we want the best out of that meeting next Tuesday and we're gonna submit our brochure to Finniston on Thursday direct in Grosvenor Place. Because there's a team got go down on Thursday. We're to submit our case to independent people of Merchant Bankers, to go over the arguments on costs. And when we're down Grosvenor Place, we'll just drop in and say, "There y'are Monty, there's yours."

Lights change now to the gloomy surroundings of the rolling mill, where many processes are controlled and supervised from control rooms and boxes perched high up above the roller. Each scene tends to take place behind a guard rail, some high up in the auditorium. The instrumental of the song "The Man at the Fire" is played on the mandolin.

ROLLING MILL SEQUENCE: REHEAT FURNACE

Enter FRANK OLDACRE (*the Mill Roller*) *to a rail on the stage. There is the sound from the furnace, but subdued.*

FRANK: The production process ends in the rolling mill. Shelton's mill is world famous—the finest mill in Western Europe. First of all the blooms from the Concast are brought back to a high temperature in the reheat furnace. (ROY, *the* REHEAT FURNACEMAN, *comes to* FRANK's *side.*) Years ago, the old furnacemen down the old mill, there was no clocks . . .

ROY: No, they used to work . . .

FRANK: Used to ope the door, ope the door up.

ROY: Yes . . .

FRANK: Looked in the furnace . . .

ROY: Could tell . . .

FRANK: And 'e could tell, well 'e s'posed to tell 'ow.

ROY: By the color o' the bloom, y'know . . .

FRANK: You you still tell can't yer?

ROY: Oh yeh. Well, we 'ad an occasion some time ago. I think I told you about it, didn't I, that er, I 'ad to fetch the fuel department down ter the reheat. The recording of it on the instruments was showin roughly about thirteen twenty. Now, I fetched 'em down, I said, yer got a false reading there. 'E said, it can't be wrong, I said, well it is. 'E said well, what do you say it is? I says, it's about twelve sixty. Anyway the, 'e fetched the, what's that thing they call fer, checking the front . . . anyway they brought another instrument down, they, they take er, er a reading . . .

FRANK: It's a pyrometer.

ROY: Something, somethin like that, yeah, er on that line.

FRANK: It's er on the top o' the bar.

ROY: The, no, no, not that Frank, no, no, this is one as 'e looks through an 'e can tell by . . .

FRANK: Oh is that it?

ROY: 'E can tell by the color o' the wall within, to within ten degrees of the temperature, there, inside that furnace. An' I was right.

FRANK: You was right.

ROY: I was right.

FRANK (*to the audience*): 'E was right . . . bloody 'ell, see the man on the floor again, his er, practical knowledge comes in 'andy . . .

ROY: You can't always.

FRANK: . . . An' instruments . . .

ROY: You can't always . . . 's, I mean, they're a guide, put it that way, 's far as I'm concerned.

Yer don't rely on 'em all the while.

"The Man at the Fire" instrumental now comes in.

FRANK: How near were you, Roy?

ROY: Pardon?

FRANK: When you said twelve sixty, and the thing read thirteen twenty, how near were you?

ROY: Well, the reading 'e took down there was twelve seventy.

FRANK: Well, that was good goin.

ROY: Well, I was ten degrees out.

Lights come up on the mandolin and guitar players accompanying the song. FRANK *and* ROY *move towards them to join in the chorus. Two other* MEN *sing the verses.*

SONG—THE MAN AT THE FIRE

TWO MEN (*sing*):
There are some who forget what experience means.
(They are generally fellows just out of their teens)
And by using pyrometers seem to acquire
A lack of belief in *The Man at the Fire.*

FRANK AND ROY (*joining the two men*):
The Man at the Fire, The Man at the Fire,
A lack of belief in The Man at the Fire.

TWO MEN:
A pyrometer's good when it's kept in its place,
But sometimes you'll find there's a lie on its face,
And then, when the heat's climbing higher and higher,
The man who can tell is *The Man at the Fire.*

ALL FOUR:
The Man at the Fire, the Man at the Fire,
The Man who can tell is The Man at the Fire.

TWO MEN:
Now do not mistake me; I say, by all means,
While you're lacking in skill, put your trust in machines:
But if to be really expert you aspire,
Then study as well with *The Man at the Fire.*

ALL FOUR:
The Man at the Fire, the Man at the Fire.
Then study as well with The Man at the Fire.

TWO MEN:
So when you are learning your job, never heed
Those who tell you that skill is a thing you
      don't need,
For skill and hard work you will surely re-
      quire,
If you hope to compete with *The Man at the
Fire.*

ALL FOUR:
The Man at the Fire, the Man at the Fire,
If you hope to compete with the Man at the
Fire.

*The lights change. It's Winton Square, in front of
Stoke station.*

JOURNEY TO HAMBROS

*TED and BILL, in best suits with macs and brief-
cases, cross the stage. They are accompanied by
BOB CANT MP. One of the GIRLS questions them
from the stairs in the audience.*

GIRL: What's the purpose of this journey today?

TED: Well, to get a second opinion if you like before we meet Finniston that their brochure is
wrong and ours is right.

GIRL: What additional evidence will it give you?

TED: Well, you see we're putting ourselves out on
a limb. These Merchant Bankers could agree
with the Corporation, and destroy our argument. We think that our case is that good that
we're prepared to take a small risk, in our opinion, to gain maximum benefits.

*All three go off to London. The lights change
back to the mill. FRANK and ROY are at a guard
rail at the side of the stage watching a bloom go
through the first set of rolls, following it with
their head movements far away up and down to
left and right of them with each pass. There is the
recorded sound of the process, hisses, rumbles
and clanks. There are nine passes here.*

BREAKDOWN STAND

FRANK: Well they come out the furnace, at the
temperature required for rollin, go down to the
first set of rolls, which are called breakdown
rolls, which breaks the bloom down in t' the required, section or the, form bloom as required
for the other set of rolls y'see.

ROY: This top roll works on the same principle as
the old mangle 'ow yer used to screw yer
springs down, y'know, to give yer pressure on
yer clothes—Works on that principle.

FRANK: It's just they call, what they call a breakdown process, just breaks them down to that,
what we want. It's a matter of er, each section,
we 'ave, probably seven passes, nine passes,
gotta be odd, it's gotta be odd pass, see.

ROY: This one's a nine pass. As the bar goes
through, that's a pass an then the screws come
down, brings it back again 'n that's another
pass. So nine times, for each bar.

FRANK: It's got be odd number of passes y'see,
because it's gotta go that way, see, c'n be either
seven, nine, eleven.

*The long rumble of the bloom rolling away now
to the main stand. They watch it go.*

ROY: An' away it goes. That bar's finished.

Quiet instrumental of "The Man at the Fire."

FRANK: Steel, you know, it's a thing, same as water, it wants to go where that, where it wants to
go itself. The easiest way out . . . you've got to
force it your way, make it go where you want
to go. And this is what we have to do with
what we call "draughtings," either one way or
the other, see, bit more pressure.

*They go off. Lights change to the City of London.
BILL, TED, and BOB CANT come back across the
stage.*

RETURN FROM HAMBROS

TED: First class. We've had a tactical discussion
with experienced qualified men and they've instructed us on a course of tactics that we shall
discuss with our lads when we get back home.

QUESTIONER: Do you feel that the journey down
here was worthwhile?

TED: Oh I do.

QUESTIONER: May I ask you, Mr. Cant, what you
feel about this meeting this morning?

CANT: Well, I think we've taken a very unusual step in the sense that we must be the only Action Committee that has in fact asked for the costings and the financial statement to be scrutinized in the heart of the City of London. We've had to accept certain things, certain bits of advice that have been given to us, but at the same time, many of the points that we put forward have been confirmed and certainly these will be used by the Action.

QUESTIONER: And what are you going to do now?

TED: Well, we're going to BSC to deliver our brochure in person, if possible to Dr. Finniston, to save him worrying about any messenger boys picking it up and having it delivered. (*They go off to Grosvenor Place.*)

The lights change to the mill. FRANK *is standing very high up at a rail overlooking the audience behind one block of seats. He's with another senior roller,* HERBERT SHAW. *There's the general sound of the mill.*

MAIN STAND

FRANK: From the breakdown, comes into the main stand, where it's er, put thro' its processes, the five passes, against the . . . nine up there, and it's got down vertical-wise 'n 'orizontal-wise, that's the, measurements.

HERBERT: But er, that is a 51 kilogram program see. We put that on there and er experience tells yer 'ow much to allow for "Mill-spring." Don't talk to the Management about "Mill-spring," because they're not conversant with it. I mean this is something they 'aven't learnt. No yer, yer know, yer knock a certain amount off because soon ever yer bar enters the rolls, it opens the rolls up see, bang, so we make an adjustment for that and then, as I say, you judge yer, yer speeds on there, yer load, how much work you're doing.

FRANK *now talks through the five passes on the main stand, through the sound of them, each pass longer than the previous one because the bloom is now growing in length with each movement.*

FRANK: Number one pass, comin through the main stand, enterin' the edger, which, 'bout thirty-five foot elongatin' to, forty foot. Number two pass, enterin' the edger stand first, in the main stand, elongatin' . . . ninety . . . between ninety an' 'undred foot. Number three pass comin in the main stand, into the edger, speed matchin correct, elongatin' to 'bout 'undred 'n twenty foot. Fourth pass entr'in' the edger, into the main stand . . . er, elongatin' to approximately 'undred 'n eighty foot, 'undred 'n ninety foot. The last pass comin up, which is Number five, main stand, edger, that's the last pass, elongatin ter two 'undred, two 'undred 'n ten foot, two 'undred 'n twenty foot. (*The section rolls away to the finishing stand.*) An' it goes down to the finishing pair of rolls, which is a finishing process. (HERBERT *goes away.* FRANK *reflects for a moment.*) I realize now— I'm a roller in the finest beam mill in Western Europe, and to me it's an achievement. Well I think so.

He goes. The lights change to the sparely lit inside of the canteen in the mill. MEN *assemble for a meeting. Some are in the green-colored helmets of the mill. Chairs are put out in a group roughly facing a small table where* TED SMITH *and* FRANK OLDACRE *will sit to address them.*

MILL MEETING

HERBERT (*coming in with an Action Committee brochure*): Shelton Works Action Committee. Brochure. (*He thumbs through to page seven and reads:*) "In these, or any circumstances, the Action Committee is not prepared to close the Works piecemeal; the BSC must decide if it wants an integrated works based on electric arc steelmaking or no works at all. The mill will not roll cold steel from Scunthorpe."

The MEN *look troubled and hand 'round the brochure.* DENNIS STORER *speaks to the audience.*

DENNIS: Well if we're to believe what's being said, and we don't know yet, there's a small section of our brochure that appears to upset the people in the Mill, but we don't know yet, we've not spoken to them. Well, we're saying we won't roll the Scunthorpe product, but we did discuss it at the meeting when we were sort of getting the brochure ready, and it was approved at the meeting, you know.

TED and FRANK are now at the table. The MEN listen, some sitting, some standing. FRANK has risen to speak.

FRANK: Now you know as well as I do this as 'ad to come. You've all known the last three years, this. There's nobody taken any notice 'til just recently, you've 'ad the bloody chop when Melchett come down an' nobody's taken any notice, now this is come now—Finniston's come, Andrew Young come down give us the brush off—Finniston's probably come an' finish it off in June. Now you've got the bloody windup—I don't blame you, your future's at stake. I go along with you—I want to work. I've got ten years to go—I want t'finish that off—I've got a future here, the young 'uns 'ave still got a future if we can get the stuff—if that place closes we've all 'ad it—Anyway, I've asked Ted t'come along—he's volunteered, he's not feeling too good, so I'd like Ted just to take over from there—but mark me out, don't let's get the idea that we're sitting pretty in the mill—let's face up to reality.

TED (*gets up, and begins quietly*): Thank you very much Frank—I welcome this opportunity, lads, of addressing you, on a point of communications. I know how you feel, because I'm tied to this mill as well as you are. I've got a job with the mill, when the steel plant closes—what are we doing here fighting for—for the rest of the Works? Because we're charged with a responsibility, for 2,700 steelworkers and their families. 10,000 people in Stoke-on-Trent depend on you. (*He pauses.*) I want to talk about isolation in this address. We are isolated here—as a steel plant, as a mill, as a blast furnace, as a community. Everybody relies on everybody else in a steelworks. We're dependent on the blast furnaces for iron, we're dependent on the steel plant for steel, we're dependent on the mill and the finishing mill for product, and our profitability. (*He pauses again.*) I've only worked here 20 years—it isn't a good while to some of you.

Like Ernie there, and Frank and Jack. But I've watched men give their lives for this industry. We all have. We saw a great mill-fitter—as far as I was concerned he was my best friend mate—a part of me died when he did—that was Tommy Cooper! (*Tommy Cooper's two SONS are amongst the MEN. One looks down at the floor. Another MAN looks across at him, then at TED.*) After Melchett's visit on March 27, George Harris asked me what I thought was happening. I said to him, "It's murder by economics." Well, I've changed me opinion. I've changed it. I now charge the BSC with economic genocide. There's 75,000 steelworkers being destroyed by a master plan. They've never been given the opportunity of proving their value. £3,000 million spent to prove a point. And 15 years from now they'll want another £3,000 million and they'll want those 75,000 steelworkers who they've cut the throats of. I listened to Jo Gormley tonight. He's screaming out for miners and they're on a 39 quid a week. My God, he should be screaming out for 'em for that price. They've driven men out of the mines. They've closed pits down that are uneconomic. And what I would say to you now lads, I'd ask the mill men to show the same red badge of courage as the blastfurnacemen. Go out and spread the gospel—it's our intention to fight for this works as a whole unit. (*TED is now in full flow. He gestures, passionately, to drive home his next points.*) At the moment, you've got a weapon, but come 1978-79 80—you won't 'ave a weapon. You can't say to the Steel Corporation—You bugger off, we're 'avin that mill, we'll roll in that mill—what y'gonna roll with, chewing gum? You can do it now, but you won't be able to do it then. We could use that power now to keep this Works as one unit, but once you stand isolated . . . be alone . . . be apart. (*He makes a gesture of hopelessness, then finishes quietly and very firmly.*) You can show 'em your opinion by saying to the people of Stoke-on-Trent—We are prepared; and to the BSC—we are prepared; and you can show it to Ted Heath and them lads down there—we are prepared. And most of all you can show it to yourself and your family and your children that we are prepared to fight for Shelton Bar.

TED *sits. The* MEN *applaud with sincere enthusiasm.* FRANK *gets up.*

FRANK: You've heard Ted say what he's got to say—I think he's put a damn good case forward, are we go it alone as far as the mill or do we want to back Shelton as a whole to keep it as a small community which to me is sound policy?

ONE OF THE MEN: Wouldn't it have bin a better idea before sending the brochure out, to have a delegates meeting—because I haven't seen that brochure.

TED: The BSC 'ad eight months to produce their brochure we 'ad two days to produce ours, because it'd gotta be ready for next week. The strategy. We're playing 'em at their own game.

HERBERT (*getting up*): But why weren't we told about this Ted?

TED: Well, there were 70 delegates attended that meeting. The vote in principle was taken.

HERBERT: We knew nothing about this 'til er last night.

TED: Well er communications, communications, that's what it is.

HERBERT: Oh.

TED: Its bin produced in rapid quick time, for next Tuesday's meeting.

HERBERT: I'll give you that point Ted, but couldn't it have got around a bit more quickly. I know you haven't got much time . . .

There is a pause.

TED: But yer happier now.

HERBERT: I'm 'appier now, now I've heard the full context of it. (*He sits down.*)

DENNIS STORER *gets up.*

DENNIS: I think we ought to show Ted by a hearty round of applause that we appreciate the fact that he's come to put everything before us.

The MEN *applaud. During the end of this the* GIRLS *have come on, ready to accompany the song.*

SONG—FIGHT FOR SHELTON BAR

Two MEN *sing to banjo and guitar accompaniment. The rest of the* MEN *sing the chorus. The* GIRLS *add a harmony to the choruses—a kind of wordless drone, increasing in volume with each one.*

TWO MEN (*sing*):
We've been making iron at Shelton Bar since 1839,
And through the years of war and strife, we've stood the test of time,
But now they want to turn us out and throw us with the scrap,
They must be bloody barmy if they think we'll stand for that!

ALL (*sing*):
We're Shelton men, we're not afraid, we've got our dignity,
We'll fight and win the battle, boys, against the BSC,
They may be strong and powerful but that won't get them far,
For we are all united now to fight for Shelton Bar!

TWO MEN (*sing*):
The Sinter and Blastfurnace men are with us, every one
They've joined the fight, although for them there's nothing to be won,
Electric arcs don't need them, but they're proud and spirited men,
They'll give all they've got and more, and won't surrender even then!

ALL (*sing*):
We're Shelton men, we're not afraid, we've got our dignity,
We'll fight and win the battle, boys, against the BSC,
They may be strong and powerful but that won't get them far,
For we are all united now to fight for Shelton Bar!

TWO MEN (*sing*):
We know we make a profit, and we know our steel's the best,
Men with money brains and business sense are ready to invest,
We get our orders out on time, we never get complaints,
We're too bloody good to be alive, they ought to make us Saints!

ALL (*sing*):

    We're Shelton men, we're not afraid, we've got
      our dignity,
    We'll fight and win the battle, boys, against
      the BSC,
    They may be strong and powerful but that
      won't get them far,
    For we are all united now to fight for Shelton
      Bar!

TWO MEN (*sing*):

    And now they want to close us with their 10
      year strategy,
    They don't care about the man who has to
      face his family,
    The Kaldo and the Concast men will fight it,
      tooth and nail,
    To save their jobs and keep their pride—we
      know they'll never fail!

ALL (*sing*):

    We're Shelton men, we're not afraid, we've got
      our dignity,
    We'll fight and win the battle, boys, against
      the BSC,
    They may be strong and powerful but that
      won't get them far,
    For we are all united now to fight for Shelton
      Bar!

TWO MEN (*sing*):

    They want to keep our Demag Mill, the finest
      in the land,
    And put the rest in mothballs, just to keep it
      near at hand,
    But we have got another plan, I'm sure you
      will agree,
    Put the BSC in mothballs, and then Shelton
      will be free!

ALL (*sing*):

    We're Shelton men, we're not afraid, we've got
      our dignity,
    We'll fight and win the battle, boys, against
      the BSC,
    They may be strong and powerful but that
      won't get them far,
    For we are all united now to fight for Shelton
      Bar!

*The lights change gradually to flood the stage with
a bluish light. During the next section, the* ACTION
COMMITTEE *and* AUDREY *assemble with their pa-*
pers and with a box containing the present for DR.
FINNISTON. *Everyone is in his best suit. The tables
and chairs are set out in two confronting rows.*

MEETING WITH DR. FINNISTON

*All the following speeches come from the over-
head loudspeakers as everyone assembles. From
time to time everyone listens as they organize.
First it is Tony Inchley, BBC Radio Stoke-on-
Trent's News Editor.*

INCHLEY (*recorded*): "Fight for Shelton Bar"
written by Polly Warren of the Victoria Theatre. It's been released today in a neat sense of
timing on the eve of the crucial visit by Dr.
Monty Finniston, Chairman of the British Steel
Corporation. This afternoon Mr. Ted Smith,
the Chairman of the Action Committee, said he
was now optimistic, optimistic that Dr. Finniston would at least announce the deferment of
closure, coupled with investment in the rolling
mill. And his confidence was shared by the Action Committee Secretary, Bill Foster.

On the stage the OTHERS *look at* BILL *as they
listen.*

BILL (*recorded*): Well, they chose the ground to
play on, and they are supplying their team tomorrow, and, how I look at it, if you're losing
four-none, and there's two minutes to go, there
ain't much chance of winning the game, and
the BSC at the moment are losing four-none.
Every eventuality is called for in the brochure,
except one, and that's the facts. We've provided
the facts. The *fiction* is in the BSC brochure, the
facts are in the Shelton Works Action Committee Brochure.

*It is now the morning of 27 November 1973 in
Shelton Works Canteen.* DR. FINNISTON *comes in
with* HERBERT MORLEY *and another BSC* EXECU-
TIVE. *From the loudspeaker comes the recording
of the actual event. First there are some indistinct
introductions as the BSC* CHAIRMAN *is greeted by*
TED SMITH *and goes along the row of* ACTION
COMMITTEE MEMBERS *shaking hands. Then the
BSC* PARTY *stand aside as* TED *comes forward to
make his presentation.*

TED (*recorded*): I would like now to welcome you on be'alf of two thousand seven 'undred of your loyal workers, at Shelton. In doing so, I would like you to accept a Royal Doulton figure depicting St. George an' Drag, the Dragon on their be'alf. Dr. Finniston.

TED makes the presentation, shaking hands with the CHAIRMAN who looks admiringly at the Royal Doulton figure as the recording proceeds.

DR. FINNISTON (*recorded*): Well thank you very much indeed. Well, Mr. Smith an', err, gentlemen. I can't speak to all two thousand seven hundred of you, but perhaps you'll tell them how er, pleased I am to accept this magnificent gift on behalf of the Corporation. Er, it's a another example of the skill which is shown by the people resident in this area. Ahhh, I think it will grace the Corporation's Board for a long time to come. Er—(*He now moves across to his place at the conference table, with his PARTY, looking across at the ACTION COMMITTEE MEMBERS.*) I've er, I've just got one thing to give you in return, err, following upon the management er, er, er proposal to us, the Board of the Corporation has decided to er, install the the the the stacker which is going to cost us five hundred and fifty thousand pounds. I'm sure this is worth every bit of it and I hope you'll be very happy to have it an' that it'll be a measure of the success for the future that this particular area will deserve.

All onstage now applaud, and the recording with its own applause fades away under this. All sit, and the lights change, to normal bright interior lighting.

AUDREY (*sitting by TED*): Mr. Ted Smith announced the conduct of the meeting.

The scene proceeds coolly, with the speeches half to the other participants, half to the audience.

TED: I said that the brochures would be dealt with paragraph by paragraph with Mr. Cooper reading the BSC one and Mr. Foster reading the Shelton reply. Dr. Finniston would then make his comments. Has Dr. Finniston any new information to add prior to discussion of the brochures?

DR. FINNISTON: Dr. Finniston replied that there was no other news other than the stacker. This proves the future of the mill. I think we should regard this meeting as a consultative one. Any questions can be asked and will be answered by myself, my colleagues or by the Shelton management.

AUDREY: Mr. A. E. Cooper and Mr. W. Foster then commenced to read out the brochures.

ALBERT: Paragraph 1. In reply to this Dr. Finniston said:

DR. FINNISTON: The Corporation must take the view that there is no flexibility in our case at this time. Blast furnaces and Kaldo must go. The question here is arc replacement. The private sector can put their money where they want. Regarding Guest Keen & Nettlefold, the question for the BSC is whether to build in Scotland or Cardiff. The problem is the availability of scrap. There is no way of stopping the private sector if their Board of Directors are prepared to put their money in and they obtain planning permission. They will eat into nationalized industry but the BSC are not reducing their share of the market; we are going for higher quality steels, using scrap and arcs where costs are low.

BILL: Mr. Foster was interested to hear that there was to be "No flexibility." The suggestion that our plant is high cost is not true. We will take that up later. GKN has decided the future of Shelton—as stated in the brochure. We cannot accept this statement. Scrap in Cardiff has no effect on Shelton.

TED: Mr. Smith asked why Scotland needed Midlands scrap. We have just supplied 7000 tonnes to them.

MORLEY: Mr. Morley suggested going through the scrap strategy with the Action Committee. We will remove the *classified* information from the document and it can then be made available for discussion in detail.

A pause.

TED: Mr. Smith said that this was agreeable. Mr. W. Foster referred to the money spent on the 18-inch mill.

BILL: I said, well in relation to that, I said, no doubt you are aware er, that just at your elbow, and he sort of looked to see what was there, there is the 18-inch mill. And while I was speaking, there was a hurried consultation with Mr. Morley who, y'know . . . Would you mind telling me what he's talking about?

The BSC PARTY *behave as described.*

TED: Yeah.

BILL: Because apparently he wasn't aware . . . th . . .

TED: That we had one.

BILL: . . . that just outside the canteen, the 18-inch mill had stood and they'd come along in 1970 and said we're closing it. I said, well in 1970 you undertook considerable expenditure (*more* hurried consultations while I'm speaking) I said, and within two months of this expenditure being carried out, you announce the closure of the mill. I said now I would directly relate that to the present cost of the Demag mill and the £550,000 that you are proposing to spend in there, which is chicken feed . . .

ALBERT: You did say "chicken feed."

BILL: I said "chicken feed," I said (*to the BSC* PARTY): you don't impress *us* with £550,000 that you're spending in there because if we're to look at the two cases, the 18-inch mill and Demag mill, what you could do for the 18-inch mill with *that* expenditure and close it within two months, would suggest to us that the £550,000 spent in the mill wouldn't alter it whatsoever at all.

MORLEY: Mr. Morley observed that the 18 inch mill had closed due to rationalization. The present mill is a different proposition.

DR. FINNISTON: Dr. Finniston asked what the reaction would have been if the BSC did not invest in the mill.

TED: Mr. Ted Smith said that due to the state it was in the mill would have closed itself. And I said, y'know, "We've had all our experts on it, we've had a report from all parts, electricians, fitters, er, production workers that the mill isn't in a fit state to run, without capital expenditure till 1980."

DR. FINNISTON: What amount?

TED: About £1¼ million.

BILL: But Frank came in here.

A light comes up on FRANK *in his boiler suit, high up behind a rail.*

FRANK: I'm a roller, I live down there, mate, I'm down there 8 hours out of every 24, not down Grosvenor Place with a pencil in me hand. The mill's deteriorating rapidly an' the finishing end has been asking for attention for 2½ years, and all you come up with is a bloody sweetener.

BILL: Yeah.

TED: And those were his words.]

ALBERT: Yeah, he said a sweetner.

TED: A *bloody* sweetener, yeah he did. That's what he did say.

DR. FINNISTON: Dr. Finniston admitted that the cost of blooms from Scunthorpe and cost from the arc furnace route are very close together. This was why Shelton was one of the last works on the list to close. The accountant will verify the figures. The argument is based on the fact that, once a plant is built, capital charges no longer apply.

TED: Why have capital charges been included in the East Moors brochure, then?

DR. FINNISTON: In this case the Corporation are trying to decide where the money should be spent.

ALBERT: Mr. A. E. Cooper pointed out that Shelton's plans had been submitted to the Corporation for some years and therefore must be treated in the same way as East Moors to give a consistent approach.

AUDREY: Mr. Smith asked to be compared with Scunthorpe from December 1969 when Shelton's plans for arc furnaces were submitted to the BSC and Scunthorpe was just a dream in some planner's mind.

BILL: Mr. Foster asked if Dr. Finniston had read the letter from Hambros Bank.

DR. FINNISTON: Dr. Finniston replied that he had only been given a copy as he entered the meeting and needed to study it. He would write his reply.

AUDREY: Mr. Smith promised that we will not move in any direction until we received his reply.

DR. FINNISTON: Dr. Finniston thought that the question of costs were very important but they needed to be discussed outside this particular meeting.

AUDREY: He had already agreed that mid-'75 was out and promised two years' notice of closure.

DR. FINNISTON: Dr. Finniston said he would not do anything before mid-June and would see if it could be extended. He wanted to discuss the matter with his colleagues.

TED: Mr. Smith asked the Chairman if it was mutually agreed that the meeting stand adjourned. This was agreed. (*They nod agreement.*)

DR. FINNISTON (*gets up to speak*): Dr. Finniston thanked everyone; he had been treated with the utmost courtesy on entering the meeting and throughout the discussions to the adjournment point.

The BSC PARTY now leave, shaking hands with TED SMITH and other ACTION COMMITTEE MEMBERS. As they do so, BBC Radio Stoke-on-Trent's interview with DR. FINNISTON after the meeting is played over the loudspeaker.

INCHLEY (*recorded*): When you come back next June, or possibly in the autumn, is there a hope that Shelton men could be given a permanent lease of life?

DR. FINNISTON (*recorded*): Well, since I didn't give them an answer, I don't see why I should give you one. (*Laughter.*)

INCHLEY (*recorded*): But is there a possibility, Doctor.

DR. FINNISTON (*recorded*): Well, my responsibility is to the work force. I don't think you should press me on that. Let me deal with them at at er, face to face.

By now the BSC PARTY are leaving the stage and the next speech is gradually faded away and interrupted by BILL before it ends.

INCHLEY (*recorded*): Now, on this question of the economic situation, the financial figures, the British Steel Corporation have been accused by the Action Committee, and I suspect they used these words this morning, of "cooking the books" of fiddling the accounts. How'd you react to that allegation?

The MEN are now relaxing and in an ebullient mood. Some stand near their table, others stretch out in their chairs.

BILL (*with scornful glee*): Mr. Foster asked if Dr. Finniston had read the letter from Hambros Bank.

TED: When we came on to that page, it was utter chaos across the table, mate, they were ready to jump in the Trent out o' the road. It was utter confusion. They couldn't substantiate one single argument as they put forward.

PETER: The thing was, we knew the answers and they bloody well didn't.

TED: Correct. That's true, that is. (*A pause. He now speaks with grim determination.*) The Chairman was warned by me that he was going to reply to Hambros letter in person to me, and I said, I said to him, "I didn't get it off a little tramp at the corner of Euston Station, Mr. Chairman. I got it off men of the City, and I warn you Mr. Chairman, I am *not* going to move until I get that reply, giving you fair chance of fair hearing." Right?

They all stand up now and sing, rowdily, raggedly and unaccompanied, the song POLLY WARREN wrote for them at their request in time for the FINNISTON meeting.

ALL (*sing*):
> We're Shelton men, we're not afraid, we've got our dignity,
> We'll fight and win the battle, boys, against the BSC,
> They may be strong and powerful but that won't get them far,
> For we are all united now to fight for Shelton Bar!

POST MORTEM

Other MEMBERS OF THE ACTION COMMITTEE now return, and a rough meeting is set up. TED and BILL face the rest across the table. ALBERT is at one side of them sucking on his pipe.

TED: Are we right lads? I would welcome everyone now to the 617 Squadron reporting room after a raid on Berlin or Grosvenor Place it should be. And we want your reactions to that meeting this morning. I thought on my own behalf as chairman you were a absolutely superb—brilliant—you were *magnificent*. Albert would you give your conclusions and reactions.

ALBERT: I thought we'd really got them on the run towards the end. They were absolutely confused, there's no doubt about that. I think this business of not *talking* about closure until June next year, that, let's be absolutely clear, that is *a major concession*. That's a guarantee of at least an extra six months' life.

TED: The meeting stands adjourned . . . and the Agenda's not been concluded.

ALBERT: Another thing. We must jump in and *prove* that we can make money because we're on a winning streak. I don't know if you know that last month we made £100,000 and we're sort of coming out the woods now and if we continue at that rate we'll make a million pounds again this year and our plant as it stands is our best advert.

TED: What's your reactions lads?

BILL: What about this morning's meeting? What d'you think?

MICK stands up at the back of the meeting.

MICK: This morning's meeting,
I just want to add—

DEREK: Two to one in our favor.

MICK: —this, that I've seen a poster on the side of a Sentinel van "Shelton Bar," it said, "has made real progress," but what progress *have* we made? We've made none. As far as I can see we're still in the same position as we were six months ago.

TED: Tell the lad. Go on Bill.

BILL: Well let's go *back* six months. Let's go *back* to when Melchett came down here. He said, "You are closing by mid-1975," The bloke this morning said, "You forget about about 1975. That's dead."

MICK: Yes, but we've had these promises before.

TED (*leaps to his feet*): Order—the right of reply is this side of the table. You've had your say.

BILL (*grimly*): The Chairman said this morning, "You forget about 1975. That's gone. There's no possibility of closure." You can shake your head, but if you think that you are closing in mid-1975, I can't—

TED: 75.

BILL: —alter your opinion.

MICK: No, I know, but what I'm saying is, you stated the other day, that we've had that many broken promises, you can't believe anything they say.

BILL: You think we'll close by
mid-1975? Do you?

TED: Mid-1975.

MICK: No, I'm not saying that, no.

BILL: What are you saying?

TED: Look, what's clear to me is have they proved an economic case for closing Shelton Bar?

TOMMY: No.

TED: Right.

TOMMY: But had they before, Ted?

TED (*now disappointedly angry at the criticism, and getting very loud*): No, because it was never discussed before. This is the first time costs have ever entered into the argument of Shelton Bar. We aren't comparing ourselves with Shelton now, we're comparing it with Scunthorpe, that's the difference. And if you think there's no hope out of this morning's meeting, why has it been adjourned and why were all those men in utter confusion around that table? *Don't be so despondent.* You've had a winning day today. When Melchett came down here, everybody in this room including me was shattered and that went on for days, well we're no longer shattered.

TOMMY (*gloomily*): What have we won, Ted?

TED: We've won an extension.

TOMMY: Well, that's some bloody use int it? Six month. Ar, or twelve month. It's only a present, it's just prolonging the agony, isn't it?

TED: Is it prolonging the agony?

TOMMY: I think so, yes.

TED: Well, that's part of our strategy if you'd heard what I'd said.

BILL: Well, I think the boilermakers have made a fair point, it's quite a valid point. All I would ask them now, in relation to this, is, are you satisfied that we should carry on the fight?

MOST MEN: Oh yes, yes.

BILL: No, I'm asking the two lads down there.

MICK: We've gotta put this to the men.

BILL: Of course.

MICK: And it's going to take some knocking in.

BILL: Yep.

TED (*quietly*): That's enough said.

They all go out.

FINISHING STAND

The lights change back to the mill. FRANK comes in to a rail at the side and is joined by HARRY. There are the sounds of the mill and coming up in the foreground the sound of the one long pass at the finishing stand.

FRANK: Just the one pass, a finishing process. Puts the finishing touches to it. Well it's just a . . . so much percentage reduction o the verticals, 'alf as much on the 'orizontal which gives it a finishing pat; for surface; a nice smooth surface.

HARRY: This is the final touch 'ere, this is where we put that special brand on, Shelton Iron an Steel, 'ere y'know.

FRANK: British Steel Corporation.

HARRY: Well it is now, but it was always Shelton Steel before, wan' it?

FRANK: Well, under private enterprise, it was Shelton Iron and Steel, England. But now, it's er, wonder if yer can see it, can yer see it there? (*FRANK points down to the finished section.*) BSC an then, the dimensions of it, err, Britain. There, look, see, the dimensions, what the bar is, Britain. That's all it says an now. But at one time it's Shelton Iron an Steel, err, England.

During this a number of MEN have assembled on chairs at the opposite corner of the stage. One fires a question across at FRANK.

QUESTIONER: What d'yer think about that, Frank?

FRANK: Well . . . I prefer to see Shelton Iron and Steel on.

FINISHING END—MEASURING THE SAMPLE

FRANK now moves across to the adjacent corner. A table is brought on with a set of forms, a pair of callipers and a micrometer. FRANK rakes out his glasses and puts them on. This final scene alter-nates between this corner, as FRANK measures the sample, and the opposite side of the stage, where a group of ACTION COMMITTEE MEMBERS surrounding BILL FOSTER ruminate aloud. There is the distant sound of the finishing end of the mill.

ALF (*sitting down*): Doctor Finishem: that's what they call 'im on the plant.

PHIL (*leaning on a rail*): This Finniston doesn't bother me, 'e's not feeding me or the kids. I mean, the point is if I can keep this steelworks open by goin' private, then we'll go private—never mind the nationalisation, and I'm as Labour as anybody, but, my job comes before nationalisation. It's not good all the country being nationalised if Phil Rogers an' 'is family are on the bloody breadline. I'd rather be bloody go me own or let us go our own.

TED (*who is standing to one side, punches in*): Everybody's criticising nationalisation for Shelton's plight—wrong—it's the men who are running the bloody industry are responsible for Shelton's plight. The senior officials of the British Steel Corporation.

PHILIP D. (*an outsider, like us*): What is the BSC? It belongs to us, have *we* done it then? No, of course we haven't done it because we don't have any control over it.

Our attention is brought across to FRANK's table, by the entrance of MAL with a short piece of a finished section in a pair of tongs. The sample steams from having just been cooled in a bucket of water. MAL puts it on the table in front of FRANK. The others watch.

FRANK: We're measuring the sample now . . . now he gets the micrometer, always go on the drive side first, that's the, that's that side first. They mark it y'see, with a, just 'it it, 'it it with the tongs.

FRANK points to the sample as MAL measures the flange thicknesses with a micrometer, each end as it were, of the H-shaped piece of steel. FRANK writes the measurements on a form as MAL calls them out.

PERCY: One of the tragedies of nationalisation, though, has been, throughout, that it hasn't been done um, to represent the people's interest.

MAL (*top drive flange first*): Seven.

PERCY: And this has been borne out both in mines, railways, and in steel.

MAL (*top off drive flange*): Six-eight.

PERCY: The people should come first, and not any other consideration should be taken. It doesn't matter what to me, same as if they gonna build plants on the coast or the Common Market are taking decisions to me its what matters to these people here.

MAL (*turns the sample over and measures the bottom drive section*): Six-nine.

PERCY: This is where I stand, that nothing, no action should be taken at all without takin' into full consideration the effect that it's going to have on the people, and particularly in our case the people that have got nowhere to go, when the Bar's threatened with closure.

MAL (*measuring bottom off drive flange*): Six-nine.

FRANK (*looks up*): Is that six-nine, Mal?

MAL: Six-nine.

FRANK (*to the audience*): That's all right, you've only got two points, eight eight thou difference there, that's the same er . . .

MAL now turns the sample up and measures the long cross bar of the H—the web thickness — carefully avoiding the brand stamp.

PHILIP D.: The basic reason for this happening is that the people who own the steel industry, have no say in the way it's organised. The people who own the coal mines have no say in the way it's organised. Now then, this is the basic folly of the whole system of nationalisation.

MAL: Five-nine, they're at.

FRANK writes. MAL now measures the flange lengths with the caliper, and a steel 2-foot rule, drive side first, then off drive side.

PHILIP D.: The machinery for the representation of people's views is hopelessly inadequate, and it's as simple as that.

TED: Correct.

FRANK (*looks up*): Now see the flange length. Get it now . . . that should be 101 millimetres.

MAL (*to FRANK*): Just a touch in, nothing too much though, 100 point 5.

MAL now measures the web centres, using a 6-inch and 2-foot rule.

FRANK: Now this is where, this 'as got, yer've got to be right 'ere an there else they wouldn't accept it, see. S'posed to be forty-seven, yer allowed a bit o' course . . . tolerance.

MAL (*the top drive one*): Forty-eight five.

TED: Ask any of our men in here, who they'd rather work for. They aren't bothered, we'll work for anybody. Under nationalisation or otherwise. That's our message. It isn't nationalisation—it's the flaming clowns running it.

MAL (*the top off drive*): Forty-eight. (*He turns the sample over.*)

BILL: It is logical, it is businesslike to put in arc furnaces on a plant where you've spent up to £20 million in development, rather than to scrap it. But of course—rather like the coal board and the other nationalized industries who were in peculiar circumstances after nationalizations—divided loyalties were generated within those corporations as they are in ours.

MAL (*bottom drive*): Forty-seven five.

FRANK: You've got to be spot on there, web centers.

MAL: Web centers.

MAL (*repeats bottom drive measurement*): Forty-seven five. (*Bottom off.*) Forty-eight.

During BILL's next speech MAL measures the length of the chopped-off sample with the calipers and rule, and chalks it on the table.

BILL: Y' can't 'ave senior management who *believe* in private enterprise running nationalised industries. It's taken the coal board up to twenty years to eradicate the last remains of private competition from the minds of their managers, and to get them to accept that nationalisation is the policy, and I don't know how long it's going to take to eradicate it from the minds of the BSC leaders, but it will be eventually, if there's anything left, in the end.

MAL (*as he chalks*): 144 millimetres.

FRANK: Then 'e 'as to weigh 'em now . . . so 'e gets the weight, doesn't matter what, doesn't matter what's length he got, 'e can cut any length. (*MAL goes off with the sample to weigh it.*) He gets the width of the bar first, whatever it is, 144 millimetres or whatever the case may be . . . Errr, it's got to be 25 kilogrammes per metre, but we can get down to that cold. (*MAL comes on again with the sample, puts it on the table, and takes out his slide rule. To the audience*): Slide rule.

MAL: Twenty-four nine, the weight.

FRANK (*who tots them up from his form as he speaks*): We take er one, two, three, four, five, six, seven, eight, nine, ten measurements altogether off the sample (*He now goes to one side and leans across a rail to speak into the Clearcall to the main stand.*) Calling main stand . . . (*To the audience:*) ten measurements altogether.

CLEARCALL (*recorded*): 'Lo Frank.

FRANK (*into the Clearcall*): Bert, come in point two on the horizontals, main an finishin.

TED: We're the nationalised industry. nationalisation should work. We should be part of the Steel Corporation Strategy. That's what *we're* sayin.

CLEARCALL (*recorded*): OK, d'yer hear that, finishin?

FRANK (*picks up the sample and holds it up, placing the web—the crossbar of the H—between his forefinger and thumb to demonstrate*): We've just come in there, point two on the web. It's eight thou, an' it registers, 'l be surprised, that'll come down five point seven next time.

MAL takes off the equipment. FRANK puts the sample down on the table. There is a final burst of the screeching racket from the skids at the finishing end. Then the ACTOR who plays TED SMITH stands up, as HIMSELF now, and turns to the place in the audience where the ACTION COMMITTEE DELEGATE for that evening is sitting.

ACTOR (*who plays TED SMITH*): The meeting with Dr. Finniston was at the end of November, the most recent major event in the Fight for Shelton Bar. I'd now like to ask Ted Smith himself to bring us up to date. Ted, how do things stand today?

ACTION COMMITTEE SPEECH

The ACTORS sit and listen. The GIRLS come on to listen and to prepare for the final song. The lights are changed to dim the stage, with a spotlight on the delegate. This is TED SMITH's speech from the performance on Tuesday 29th January, 1974, the sixth performance of the documentary.

TED SMITH (*himself, standing in the spotlight*): The latest position. You are aware that the meeting with BSC stands adjourned. Before the next meeting certain studies are to be undertaken and discussed. 1. The Economics. Dr. Finniston did reply as promised to the Hambro's analysis. In this reply there has appeared a new set of figures. Hambros, however, are still unconvinced and remain highly suspicious of the BSC arguments. 2. Scrap Availability. An independent survey is being undertaken on our behalf by the Labor Studies group of the North Staffordshire Polytechnic. We hope to challenge the BSC forecast with respect to scrap availability for the arc furnace route at Shelton. 3. The Municipalization Plan. Last week we had further discussions with the Stoke-on-Trent City Council along with Mr. W. H. Summers, who has become involved with our fight. Mr. Summers is the grandson of John Summers, who was the owner of Shelton Bar prior to nationalisation. In the present energy crisis, Shelton shows its value to the BSC and the nation by becoming the most efficient plant within the British Steel Corporation—highlighting yet again the flexibility and the skills of the men of Shelton. At that other famous theater in the round, the House of Commons, on Monday of this week, Mr. Peter Walker, Minister for Industry, gave a reply to a question tabled by Mr. Jack Ashley "about Shelton Bar." The reply: "I have always been worried about going to the theater since Abraham Lincoln went to one on a certain occasion." We would assure the Minister that no assassin is waiting in the wings of the Vic and The Action Committee will guarantee his safety during the performance. This is the latest position—Ladies and Gentlemen, thank you.

TED sits down, and the lights change back to general bright lighting on the stage.

FINAL SONG

The GIRLS assemble by the orchestra position, standing next to the table where the sample is now displayed.

GIRLS (*sing*):
You've seen how steel is made and rolled,

You've listened to Shelton's case,
They want a future for their sons,
Right here in this place.
National plans will come and go,
And if we find they're wrong,
It'll be too late in five years' time,
When Shelton Bar is gone.

ALL (*sing*):
Most people in North Staffordshire,
They just don't realize,
So liven your ideas up,
And start to use your eyes,
You may not work at Shelton Bar,
But their fight you can't reject,
If we ever let them shut that plant,
Then we'll all feel the effect!

The instrumental carries on under BILL's *speech.*

BILL: The people at the Bar can accept this from
the BSC, the closure notice, they needn't be militant, people don' have to be militant, they can
go away, a number of 'em, quite a number of
'em, particularly at the moment anyway, if
things remain as they are, so they could forget
about the Bar and get another job, but they'll
have to face the same situation again, wherever
they go. . . . If people leave the Bar, or anywhere else, and get another job, they'll face the
same situation again and they can keep creeping away into the corner, and saying, "well, I'll
go somewhere else," but in the end there 'ent a
corner to creep into. And I think they've gotta
make their minds up really, you know, when do
you sort of, stand and fight? That's what it
amounts to.

FIRST ACTRESS (*sings alone*):
The working man can run and run,
But there will come a time
When people who have power now
Must answer for their crime,
We can't go on for ever,
Accepting every word,
We've got to call a halt someday,
We must make ourselves heard!

ALL (*sing*):
You people of North Staffordshire
Don't let them have their way,
Don't be pushed around like this,
Stand up and have your say,

We may be quiet and peaceful folk,
But we know wrong from right,
Turn round and tell them face to face
That you have joined the fight.

END OF THE DOCUMENTARY

Notes on the Scenes

PART ONE

Opening Song

When I asked Ted Smith what they would want
the documentary to be about he said "Our history and heritage." I think if we'd put Ted in
charge of the show itself it would have been like
the Wedgwood Bicentennial Pageant in Etruria in
1936. In the end, though we had planned to
spend a little more time on general historical
background, so much time was needed to chart
the story of the Action Committee and the current issues that we reduced the historical background to this one opening song and speeches.

But this is what the fight was for—to preserve a
precious human institution that was harmonious
and industrially efficient. This is the kind of
works where there are often three generations
of the same family working together, and a network of uncles, brothers, grandfathers, sons, sisters and brothers-in-law stretching across its
3,000 workers.

The human continuity and the history and heritage of Shelton Bar is symbolized in its fires.
Since the first blast furnace was blown in in 1841,
a fire has never been out, right through the postwar General Strike, through the Depression,
through the Second World War when great tin
sheets had to hide the tappings from the Nazi
bombers. And the glow from the tapping and
from the tipping of the slag has all this time been
the welcoming beacon for the traveler returning
home to the Potteries, either from a Welsh seaside
holiday or Southern exile. Earth and Fire: Clay
and Coal—that's the Potteries.

When I asked Ted also what music he felt was appropriate to a steelworks he looked at me hard and said "Aïda mate," switched on his cassette recorder and instantly conducted a great chorus from the opera, shouting his own socialist interpretation of the scene through the rich din and between his swinging arms.

Jeff Parton wrote the music for the song, with a kind of elegant and lyrical line that had some of the 18th century in it. John Darrell, Alan Gill, and Polly Warren supplied the words from our research. Sandy Walsh played the treble recorder to make a kind of historical sound, with a mandolin and a guitar and then ultimately the twanging banjo which we used a lot later on.

I wrote the short speeches between the verses—one of only two places where this was the simplest and most economical way of giving a lot of essential information fairly quickly.

Sinter Plant Sequence

Early on in our discussions in the research group, we decided that we must show the whole process of steelmaking in the show. Graham Watkins suggested it. It seemed logical. Throughout the years, day and night, the processes go on, Sundays and Christmas Days, hot nights and New Year's mornings, the blast furnaces cannot go out, or there will be a cold fifty-foot lump of solid slag and iron weighing hundreds of tons to dispose of and an entire furnace to rebuild. They must be tapped regularly with sintered ore and limestone. Throughout the fight, day and night, the works keeps going, through all the meetings. In any case, these men were fighting to enable them to carry on doing this work. It was logical to show it, and appropriate.

It would also, I felt, be possible to place the scenes of each stage in the fight in such a relationship with the production processes, that each one provided imagery for the other.

We reduced the steelmaking process to its five basic production stages: preparation of the ore in the sinter plant, making pig iron in the blast furnaces, converting iron and scrap to molten steel in the Kaldo vessels, casting the steel into blooms (long rectangular billets) in the Concast machine,

and making the final product—steel sections for the building industry—in the rolling mill. We followed these through in their logical order, and interrupted them with scenes from the fight in chronological order. That was the structure.

All the materials for the work sections was recorded on comprehensive preliminary visits to the plant, covering all the processes. These were followed by concentrated visits to each section. Most of the sinter plan scene was recorded on a night shift as we slogged up and down the long ramps and stairways in this vast and dusty rabbit warren behind the tireless Ossie, one of the Senior Foremen. Earlier we had gone round with Ossie and Mr. Black, the Sinter Plant Manager. We interlocked the material from the two visits.

TED HEARS THE NEWS

A great deal of Ted Smith's narrative contribution comes from my first interview with him at his home one Sunday afternoon. This short section is transcribed from that—the first of over 70 tapes we made.

INSIDE THE SINTER PLANT

It is hard to convey the speed with which Ossie delivered the first speech, which gives a glimpse of the complex maneuvres of the iron ores and coke on conveyor belts through the plant, a huge metal-clad building of several stories. The ores are mostly dark red and this earthy dust coats everything and makes it a gloomy dramatic place. Every now and again stands a stoic figure with a shovel in his hand and a joke to greet you. All round the conveyors rattle and rumble and squeak, the motors whine, the screens rattle, the mixing drums clatter, the tannoy bleeps and calls our recorded warnings about sections stopping and starting.

THE SECONDARY SCREENS

The day after the first performance Bill Davidson, the Works Engineer, went into the plant to check the Secondary Screens. "It just shouldn't make a noise like that," he said, and had it repaired.

SCENE—CLOSURE OF THE 18-INCH MILL

This scene combines the minutes of several meetings of the 18-inch mill redundancy committee with extracts from Ted's first interview.

SCENE—THE SINTER STRAND

The Sinter strand is the climax of a visit to the sinter plant. It is a long moving fire-grate where iron ore, coke, and limestone fuse together and then drop off the end with a crash in big slabs, to be cooled and broken up for feeding the blast furnaces. The questions about the water in the sinter were mine but I gave them to the actor playing Bill Foster, who stayed on stage with Ted between one meeting and the next. As Bill and Ted had to spend a lot of time on the works moving about and talking to people in their capacities as Chairman and Secretary of the Action Committee, it seemed appropriate to keep them on stage sometimes between short meeting scenes.

Some of the men's attempts to answer our baffled and often naive questions made it seem even more perplexing, and the sinter plant was a very confusing place. I thought it was a good idea to put in here one of our confusing conversations.

THE GEORGE HOTEL

The George Hotel is in Burslem, one of our Six Towns. (In Arnold Bennett's novels he calls them Five Towns and The George becomes The Dragon.) This speech was quoted by Ted.

Protective helmets on Shelton Bar are color-coded. On the blast furnaces they are Silver; Red on the steel plant; Green in the rolling mill. Managers and executive staff and visitors wear White helmets. The men point out that White Hats seem to be constantly on the increase.

Queen's Hall Sequence

FIRST MEETING OF THE ACTION COMMITTEE

The meeting at the Queen's Hall in Burslem was a big event and stands on its own. The material for the first meeting of the Action Committee comes from Ted Smith's long interview and the transcription made at the time of a recording of the Queen's Hall meeting. The meeting speeches come of course from that transcription, and the words of the song were written by Graham Watkins to a tune by Jeff Parton.

QUEEN'S HALL PUBLIC MEETING

The vigorous participation of our four local MPs (for Stoke-on-Trent and Newcastle-under-Lyme)

was a great support to the Action Committee. The redoubtable Jack Ashley is one of them, but I'm sure none would deny that the steady, penetrating, economic wisdom and advice and constant hard work flowing from our dry Bob Cant (Stoke Central) was the critical factor at most stages of the fight.

A LONDON MEETING

Ted Smith relishes telling this story of an early meeting with BSC Senior Management. This version is from his first taped interview.

CHRISTIANA SPIGERWERK

We kept the almost heady atmosphere of this sequence going with the song to represent the optimistic atmosphere through the ups and downs of this early period, before the blow of the meeting with Lord Melchett. The approach to the Norwegian firm is typical of the way in which the Action Committee explored all kinds of commercial possibilities for the future of their works.

VIC FEATHER

The Action Committee were greatly cheered by meeting Vic Feather, who won headlines for them in the press with his racing pigeon. The search for publicity for their cause was a constant anxiety for a group of men who knew that they would be most likely to slip away, along with their historic works, unheard and unheeded.

Blast Furnace Sequence

The blast furnace routine is a mighty and perpetually recurring drama, culminating in an elemental outburst of spectacular light and heat as the molten iron runs like luminous soup down its channel of sand into the waiting wagons. Sparks fizz and jump out as it hits points of moisture and various impurities oxidize like fireworks. The men shield their faces from the searing heat, standing in extraordinary postures to do so or skipping over the runners to divert a flow into a second or third wagon. All the time the hot air blast which gives the furnaces their name roars away, bells ring, hooters blast, commands are called out.

And the buildup to this climax is a routine of movement and preparation gradually increasing in tempo and anxiety, reflected entirely in the men's movements as they work away between the casts. Their clothes get ruined, like the colliers, but here by sparks which will fill them full of holes, so they wear old stuff under the official protective gear which is of course not always put on (or not always available!). In combination with their silver and visored helmets they often look like a band of ragged medieval soldiery. Above and around them the pipes and brickwork of the old Shelton furnaces, rebuilt dozens of times since 1841 and layered and adapted and codged and extended, look like old farm buildings. The sky appears eventually somewhere through a tangle of metal and a noise as dense as smoke. Steam hisses here and there, a small addition to the ceaseless roar.

The blast furnace drama was tantalizing to me. We spent a lot of one shift with a veteran keeper, Tom Bevington, and I recorded him as he talked me through every phase of it. I stood with him as he swung the hydraulic drill round to pierce the tapping hole in a final roaring rattle, which brought the smoke and the iron gushing out. The transcription of the recording of that tapping forms the basis of the scene, along with several interviews by the devoted Blast Furnace Manager, Ernie Davies, now retired. Overlaid on it are the sequence of events that lead to the distressing meeting with Lord Melchett.

After we had spent a lot of time at the blast furnace, Tom Bevington came into rehearsals to watch our attempts to reproduce the processes, showed the actors carefully how to spread the sand to reline the runner, how to place the tools to warm them before they touched the molten iron, how to take a sample and cast it, how to stand near the furnace.

By gradual reduction as we worked on the scene, all the inessential physical components were removed, so that there wasn't a mass of objects to be got rid of for the next scenes, and more important, so that the action was clear to the audience with only enough visual elements to explain and to stimulate a real imaginative participation in it.

The most important elements are the actors' movements, their costumes, simple and bold lighting effects, bold atmospheric (and absolutely realistic) sound effects. Actual scenery was reduced to two long straight guard rails and two angled ones, with a vague marking on Alison Chitty's floor design (which was actually centered on the line of the runner down which the iron flowed) giving a coherence to the arena. There was a slag rake, a sample spoon and cast, a barrow and two shovels. There was an oxygen lance and a long coil of rubber tubing. But there was no need for sand, for a cabin, for controls on the rails, and for molten iron. So long as the actors learned exactly from observation and advice what the men did, so long as the imagined dials and controls were real to them, the action of the scene was real to the audience.

I must admit that I always find that coming to terms with the way things are actually done, and selecting carefully from it, gives the richest and most exciting results, as well as the truest. People often say to us "Won't you have to, you know, *cheat* some of this, for *theatrical* effect?" We never do, deliberately, and I certainly think it's worth slogging on and trying to find a way of showing what *really* happens.

SONG: MICKY DIRKIN'S GHOST AND HEART ATTACK SPEECHES

Romy Saunders, one of the research committee members, wrote the words for this song from the information recorded by us on accidents at Shelton Bar in the past. Jeff Parton wrote the tune and Romy accompanied it on the banjo.

It is the kind of song that is always difficult to bring off, though conveying information that seemed essential to introduce at this stage. Here was a new kind of industrial hazard to stand alongside the more obvious risks to men's bodies in a dangerous industrial process. But in reflecting the men's attitude to danger, to death and injury, it is easy to slip into melodrama or sentimentality. The men themselves either affect a disregard for such matters (which of course speak for themselves) or understate the seriousness of the events, or most often, joke grimly about them.

Lord Melchett Scene

The material for this scene comes in the main from a discussion recorded between the Action

Committee members in the Shelton Bar conference room in response to our request to describe the Lord Melchett meting in detail, and their own feelings about it. Lord Melchett's speeches are taken from Bill Foster's minutes and turned back into succinct direct speech. Gerald Wilson's descriptive comments come from a separate interview with him. Gerald Wilson is the Works Personnel Manager.

This was for me the most interesting and exciting scene. I have always been fascinated by the possibilities of combining direct speech and narrative in one scene so that many characters have direct access to the audience without apparently interrupting the flow of events. In this way the scene can take place on more than one level and in more than one time scale without, I must add, the audience being aware that this is in fact what is happening. It is after all the way in which we tell stories to one another, combining narrative and enactment one after the other.

In this case it was possible to show what happened and to demonstrate the effect it had on the men as individuals at the same time. It was the climax and turning point of the real events and we felt it should have the same place in the documentary.

Ted Smith's recorded speech which followed it was made at the same discussion as were the individual preceding speeches, in response to a question I asked about their own personal feelings afterwards. Graham Watkins told me some months later that the eyes of one of the toughest of the Action Committee members were full of tears at the end of Ted's speech that afternoon. Ted is a potent and powerful speaker, but I never experienced in any body of men such a richness of imagery and emotion as amongst the Shelton steelworkers.

Ted's bitter reflections on the payday after the Melchett meeting are from his personal interview.

May Day Song

Polly Warren wrote the words of this song to the old ballad tune "King Henry." The song was used to represent the Shelton Works' one-day strike and march through Stoke-on-Trent on May Day 1973, not long after Lord Melchett's visit. We copied

their placards and turned them to the audience at the end. The one thing we hoped for was that we might help to alert our own district to the situation. Part One ended on this defiant, rather emotional, note, as the strength seemed to flow back into the situation. The second part was to proceed in a very determined and businesslike way.

PART TWO

The text of the documentary underwent a lot of changes at the end of its five-week rehearsal period, but also during the weeks immediately following the opening, when we were in the unusual situation for a small permanent company, of having virtually three weeks when we could revise and rerehearse a production just opened, before needing to restock the repertoire with a totally new show. We just had a number of weeks of other shows in hand to keep us going.

So during this period we made substantial alterations and in fact revised entirely the Kaldo and Concast sequences to the form they exist in here.

Very early on, even before the documentary opened, we had to cut two songs written by retired steelmen about Shelton's past, and also a lot of material about the social and domestic impact of the situation, all of which had ended up at this point in the order of events. One song "Farewell Shelton Bar!" lasted a week and then lived on in our Road Show. Some of the social material is left in the Kaldo and Concast sequences, particularly the speeches by the wives. But the main fact was that there was a limit to the length of the show (which ran from 7:30 till just before 10:30, with a 15-minute interval). To do full justice to the complexity of the fight itself took that long.

Kaldo Sequence

One of our visits to the steel plant was on a night shift. The foreman on that occasion, Dennis Robinson, who later came in to supervise our shoveling and inspection routines, watched us marveling at the spectacular dimension the night gave to the many fiery displays in the plant. He said he had been working at the Bar for more than 30 years, and still really looked forward to coming on a night shift to see these amazing things.

All the years I had worked in Stoke I had passed Shelton Bar on my way to Hanley to shop, and thought to myself how lucky I was to be in an exciting and fulfilling job compared to what I imagined was the mucky drudgery of the steelworks. The revelation to me was the attachment that the steelmen had to their jobs, mixed with pride, with real dignity, sometimes even exultation. Around the edge are the inevitable wanderers and drifters. At the core is a total and historic dedication. It is very hard to convey this quality to middle-class people whose understandings are distorted by the shallow philosophies of commerce.

I recorded the commentary for the Concast process myself on one day shift. Despite the tremendous noise the foreman, Bernard Fisher, a Cumberland man, had a clear sharp voice and by keeping the microphone close to him it was possible to get enough clarity to use directly in the theater during performance.

On every visit to the works, always with the portable tape recorder, we were on the lookout for working routines that could be reenacted in our own arena, and conversations that could be reproduced, speeches that could form part of the working or political collage. On the whole works the most striking sight (after the permanent firework display) was the physical relationship between a man and the intense heat, compelling every job performed close to a vessel of molten metal to be done in movements where the whole body and particularly the face was concentrated in a posture of self-protection. The great and constant heat from one direction determined a basic stance or movement. The possibility of a sudden splash or flying spark added to it a balance that would enable a lightning getaway.

In the Kaldo Bay three routines were very striking: the semicircular tour around a 15-foot-or-so perimeter of the revolving vessel tilted down so that the foreman could inspect the brick lining for faults; the cooperative movements of the two-man team who drag in the heavy-metal wheeled screen to sample the molten steel with a long spoon; and the swift lunging of another team shoveling in final additives straight into the Kaldo's white-hot mouth and then circling back to the heap to avoid the next man's rapid forward run. Dennis Robinson and big Phil Rogers from the Action Committee came along to the theater and demonstrated and checked the actors' movements exactly. Any working choreography in the documentary came ultimately from foreman's instructions!

THE BROCHURE ARRIVES

We were involved in and around Shelton Bar during all the events covered in Part Two in the last months of 1973. Lord Melchett's visit was a bitter memory. The meeting with Dr. Finniston was the goal of all efforts. I kept a diary to keep track of the complicated events, and we reserved a series of tapes to record reactions from the men to each major or minor incident. The drama of Part Two rapidly became the story of the Action Committee's reaction to the BSC's statement of their case for closing down most of Shelton Bar, as set out in the BSC brochure, and replied to in the Action Committee's. I managed to arrive with a tape recorder only minutes in the wake of their first reading of the BSC brochure. We recorded these speeches outside for the sake of the *Guardian,* who had arrived to photograph and interview us and the men after we announced we were doing the documentary.

The Action Committee were very anxious for press publicity for their case, but apart from loyal and continuous coverage by our local *Evening Sentinel* (whose industrial correspondent, George Harris, gets a mention from Ted Smith later in the Mill Meeting) and from BBC Radio Stoke-on-Trent, there was no other interest in them till we announced the documentary. Philip Donnellan, who made one of his superb documentary films on the fight—only to have it postponed and then cut and then canceled for quite obscure reasons by the BBC—expressed his anger that they should be so ignored until the comparatively irrelevant chance of a theater doing a show about them. We were sitting over a typically enormous meal in the work canteen. Bill Foster smiled his grim slow smile and said he didn't care how it happened—they'd even been considering using their fighting fund to buy space in the *Financial Times* to get national publicity. We pressed on to the treacle pudding and custard.

Song—Thank You Kindly Mr. Melchett

Don Perrygrove, a Birmingham coach painter and trade unionist who has written a number of songs and sketches for us, contributed the words of this song, sung to the popular and every handy tune of "Tramp, Tramp, Tramp" or "Vote, Vote, Vote." Working against the normal repetitive wording of settings to this music seemed to me to make it delicately biting.

WEA Meeting—15 November 1973

This was the first Action Committee Meeting we recorded in its entirety. It lasted for five hours, though there was a break for lunch. We knew it was going to be very important but quite what stretches of it we would need was not clear until more time had passed and the sequence of events indicated which were the key issues on that day. The difficult position of the rolling mill delegates—all with a job for a while even if the fight failed, was obviously of great importance, however. Here the problem for us was of tact and confidentiality. As our building of the show went on we had to be sure that all those involved approved of what we included, and how we presented it. These visits and inspections by the men, and all our consultations, were an important part of the creative process.

Another major problem was sheer clarity for the audience, after we ourselves had more or less arrived at that happy state. The discussion often focused on working or accounting technicalities. In the end we could not dodge the central issue of dramatizing the comparison of the capital costs of building the Anchor plant at Scunthorpe against the cost of Shelton, attached to the price per (metric) tonne of steel from both works. We just hope it is comprehensible, because it was a key issue in the end. Luckily also, it did emerge as one at the time.

This meeting was the first time in ten years of documentary making that I had recorded the event itself. History was not available to do any editing down to the essentials. Preserving the character and flow of the real event and selecting self-explanatory, completely intact sections to tell the story was the difficult job. I felt it would be a distortion to glue together random speeches from the five hours into a new sequence. In the end it proved possible to take three intact sections and with only a little internal pruning of long speeches join these together by short instrumental interludes. To do justice to the interplay of the personalities, to Ted Smith's authority and passion, to Bill Foster's unflagging dry wit, to the painstaking slog of it all, that was another matter. But all of us in a creative job face human richness with awe, excitement, and a kind of desperate, hopeless, tantalized optimism, praying that something true will emerge from the mess we make.

Concast Sequence

The working sequences ended up focusing around key conversations. On the Concast floor, high up above ground to allow the large steel sausage time and room to cool, it was Walter Watkins who stepped forward to harangue me with good-humored passion about the hazards and shortcomings of the place. We transcribed Walter's remarks from the tape in our normal way and edited in with the other remarks and speeches we'd collected about the Concast, which either came from mold operators or would not be inappropriate in their mouths. Eventually other pieces of material grouped themselves around this cluster.

ROVERS SONG

Early on Ted had suggested a song about "Roving" to the popular folk song and the idea stayed in our minds, then settled here. Then Romy Saunders wrote words describing in each verse the short story of each of the retiring Shelton wanderers we knew. Jeff Parton wrote the tune and it enabled us, as music often does, to cement together the bits and pieces of this sequence.

The wives' material had originally more or less started the documentary, then settled here alongside Walter Watkins' vociferous complaints, Ted's lyrical credo, and the modest remarks by Albert Cooper's wife Glenys, whose family is one of the many closely associated with the Bar.

The Action Committee Brochure

The action of Part One spans a matter of years (130 if we count the opening song) but Part Two is really about a fortnight in November 1973, from the arrival of the BSC brochure on Wednesday 14th to the big meeting with Dr. Finniston on Tuesday 27th.

We attended and recorded all the Action Committee meetings and those of the Subcommittee drafting their brochure during this time. It was a sunny November, with light blazing through the windows at Cartwright House where the big Action Committee meeting was held on Thursday 17th and the first of these two on Tuesday 20th. The second was in the Conference Room at the Shelton Works in the afternoon. The offices are in the grand house that Josiah Wedgwood built opposite his model factory in Etruria (named because his friend Erasmus Darwin told him the Etruscans were great potters). Sunshine and central heating added a special quality to the heady atmosphere as Ted Smith, Bill Foster, and Albert Cooper slogged their painstaking way through the final pages of their brochure. Audrey typed it sheet by sheet as it came from them, treating them with loyal and dedicated amusement. The men argued hard, frankly, and passionately. But the mood was as usual totally constructive, and founded on their great good honor. What's more they knew they had a real case, and an emotional appeal for mercy just didn't come into it.

Any one of these meetings would have made a three-act play. In the end, as usual, when we could see the whole structure, we had to settle for a few key minutes, so that the sequences of meetings told the way the job was done and put the central case.

I felt too it was quite in order to let both Polly and Romy step forward as themselves to make certain key announcements. They had been at the meetings. For once, the actors really did know what they were talking about!

Rolling Mill Sequence

Our final intensive tour of the rolling mill to record the whole process in commentary, observation, and discussion by the men, was on a night shift. A small group of us were taken around by the Senior Roller, Frank Oldacre, whose brother is also a roller at the mill.

The mill rollers are acknowledged by all to be the senior craftsmen on the steelworks. Their hierarchy stands alongside the management structure of foremen and their craftsmanship must be deferred to in many practical matters. There is a roller for each of the three shifts in the 24 hours of the working day, and they spend much time walking up and down the length of the mill—several miles on a shift—checking the massive rollers and their operation, against the actual product that is being squeezed out through the three gigantic mangles: the breakdown stand, the main stand, the finishing stand.

The mill is also a dramatic place to see: a cavernous shed, pierced by long rows of light shafts in the daytime from high windows. It is punctuated by the great bulk of the three roller stands, with their control cabins perched on top of the gantries, straddling the steel as it goes backwards and forwards and then clatters off down to the next one.

At night it has its own appeal like the rest of the works. And this was a rich night for us, in our prospecting work. Often as I was recording the hours of material for the show, I would be excitedly aware that I was recording a scene that would go intact into the documentary. This happened twice that night: in the inspection cabin at the end, and in the reheat furnace control room at the start.

REHEAT FURNACE

Inside a dusty glass cabin within the mill shed is a battery of dials showing temperatures and other physical states inside the furnace where the great steel billets or blooms are brought back to the temperature for rolling. Every now and then the furnace door opens and you get a glimpse of the blindingly hot interior as one of them is nudged along the start of its path to become a steel building beam.

Frank Oldacre asked Roy, in charge there that night, about the accuracy of the dials compared with his own observation, and they had a short conversation on this immortal topic. The men's viewpoint, regarded of course with a kind of patronizing amusement by a lot of graduate technicians, is very important to them, and is a key component in their own attitude to their work.

SONG—THE MAN AT THE FIRE

Halfway through this visit, we were told about a poem hanging on the wall of the office of the Mill Manager, Mr. Billings. We went in straightaway and recorded it into the tape recorder, then someone xeroxed it for us. At this frantic time there always seems to be a chance that a vital piece of material will get overlooked in the rush. Jeff Parton put it to music—a kind of gentle waltz tune. The poem must come from some kind of engineering periodical which we were unable to discover at the time, but its title could well have been the title of the show, and it is one of the best songs I think we have ever performed.

JOURNEY TO HAMBROS

Philip Donnellan recorded these two scenes which were transcribed from the material shot for his film. This one actually took place on the train, but I found it more graphic to bring it back to a sort of walking situation on their way to it. The men rarely wore macs or overcoats except when off the Works and this helped to show that this was a sally into the outside world.

BREAKDOWN STAND

A week or so after the meeting with Dr. Finniston we had to arrive at a basic structure for the documentary. We wrote what seemed to us to be the most important events in the history of the Action Committee up to date along a straight line on a blank sheet of paper. Underneath we wrote the names of the five basic production processes. In the first case the spacing was determined by the time relationship between events, in the second by the length of the names written in capital letters to fill the entire space.

We stuck to the resulting parallels from then on, except that fate and calligraphy placed the May Day sequence in the Kaldo section and it ultimately seemed best to move into the steel plant for Part Two only. However, at the time Ted Smith's office was in a corner of the steel plant, so his bad experiences on the payday after the Melchett meeting we made with men in red helmets.

But it was simply this pedestrian association that placed the final processing of the Shelton Action Committee brochure through all its stages alongside the final processing of the finished steel product in the rolling mill. I cannot say how effective an image this was; it just felt right.

RETURN FROM HAMBROS

This scene was also taken from the BBC tape and was in fact shot in a street in the City of London where the men enjoyed being filmed passing parked Rolls-Royces. Needless to say, the splendid idea of going to Hambros was Bob Cant's, and a donation from the City of Stoke-on-Trent to the Action Committee's funds paid for what turned out to be an invaluable endorsement of their case and a great boost to their confidence at a time when they really needed the strength from the confidence to get through the Finniston meeting.

MAIN STAND

At one of the preliminary visits to the mill with Frank I was very struck by his description of the passage of the steel backwards and forwards as it passes through the rolls, and on the intensive visit I asked Frank to talk each one through, almost like a sports commentary, to describe as exactly as possible to a listener what was happening to the steel—particularly how much longer it got with each mighty squeezing. Here this is placed alongside a description recorded inside a control cabin with Herbert Shaw, another roller, which chimes in splendidly with the theme begun in the reheat furnace and sung about in "The Man at the Fire."

MILL MEETING

This was the great crisis in the last days before the Finniston Tuesday meeting. Would the mill men support that plain challenge in the Action Committee brochure: "The mill will not roll cold steel from Scunthorpe"? For this was the BSC's plan for all that would be left of Shelton. The mill men felt they had not been consulted enough before it was printed. Ted was exhausted and ill over the weekend before the Finniston meeting. He also felt reluctant to talk the mill men out of their troubled state of mind, naturally wanting it to be a kind of spontaneous gesture of support.

In the end, good sense prevailed and Ted decided to do it three times to cover all the shifts. Polly recorded the first one on the Friday evening—a magnificent speech. Three mill shifts gave the Action Committee total backing.

SONG—FIGHT FOR SHELTON BAR

On the Saturday night, at Ted and Bill's request, Polly wrote a "fighting song" for the Action Committee, to a tune we once used in *The Knotty*—a lovely lilting Irish tune, "The Beggarman." She and Jeff Parton sang it to Ted on Sunday night and to the whole Action Committee at the final pre-Finniston meeting on Monday morning. They've all sung it constantly ever since.

It was odd and heartening to see that in these ways we really were being fairly helpful. Barbara Smith told us that our regular recording of Ted helped him to relax when he desperately needed to. There was no doubt that the song brought some positive energy into the situation. At a little ceremony a few minutes before they were to present Dr. Finniston with St. George and the Dragon they gave Polly herself a lovely pottery figure to say thank you.

MEETING WITH DR. FINNISTON

The BSC had agreed in advance that we might record the whole meeting. When it came to the day they demanded the tape recorder be removed as soon as the greetings and presentations were over, including BSC's opening sop of a bit of long-overdue capital expenditure on the mill.

We were able to use this limited recording, plus Tony Inchley's Radio Stoke-on-Trent interviews with Bill Foster and Dr. Finniston to frame the scene. The bulk of it therefore comes from Audrey's minutes and from the interviews we recorded afterwards with Ted, Bill, Albert Cooper, and other members of the Action Committee to fill out the minutes, and provide a nonnaturalistic style that related it to the meeting with Lord Melchett.

The meeting was in the morning in the canteen, followed by a hectic and excited dinner time of noisy interviews over the tables, then Dr. Finniston's short press conference, the Action Committee's formal post mortem, and finally a long emotional debrief between the members of the Action Subcommittee in an office on the works. Ted blew off mighty steam at this, Bill made grim predictions; some of the others teased them both deliberately. It was noisy, nearly violent, and sometimes hilarious. I had to swear solemnly not to use most of the recording, but it was very valuable to be there, as well as a great privilege. It was also quite clear to me then that this was the point at which our documentary should end.

Dr. Finniston's meeting began late and finished late, causing a hungry queue at the canteen door. At about 1:15 the Chairman and his party of well-suited executive colleagues came out. Dr. Finniston himself is a very charming and genuinely friendly Scotsman, and he politely addressed himself to the leaders of the queue, standing in their oily blue overalls. "You can find out all about it now," he said to them as he passed. They were baffled, as they'd only been wondering what was on the menu that day.

POST MORTEM

This was a stormy and dramatic meeting. We were present, and recorded it—putting into the documentary the beginning, the stormy middle, and the conciliatory end as one continuous piece.

Ted and Bill had put so much into the Finniston meeting, and had suffered so much strain, that all they needed at this moment was a vote of thanks, whatever they had achieved. When the cooler assessment inevitably came from the floor, with some rather carping criticism from men who had been on the fringe of events till now, they both found it difficult to respond with Olympian calm. But they succeeded pretty well, even though the meeting didn't survive in the fictional character Ted gave it at the beginning with his announcement of it as a squadron debrief from a wartime film.

Reflecting on it all many times since, I have often thought that their greatest achievement was in many ways a personal one, not just for themselves, but the whole works, and the whole district. They had sat in a meeting with Lord Melchett and lost their jobs, and their dignity and self-respect. Now they had brought the BSC Chairman and his top brass to the conference table, they had fought their own case in accounting and organizational terms, and brought the BSC's plans for the future of Shelton Bar to a halt. There was no appeal to sentiment. They came off the shop floor and politely told the BSC accountants where they were wrong. Shelton Bar now has a future, and two electric arc furnaces are to be installed. But the men had won back their pride and self-respect.

FINISHING STAND

At this end men are actually cutting off the lengths of steel to customers' orders, and the roll puts the Shelton stamp on it, deliberately turned into a virtually anonymous serial number as Frank indicates in the scene. This seems to be the essential genius of the English body corporate. The Chairman gets a knighthood and everyone else gets serially numbered. Even the illusion of feeling important is removed. It will be a great day when human understanding and common sense percolate into the farthest reaches of such bodies.

MEASURING THE SAMPLE

The working scene was recorded on the mill night shift described earlier. Frank Oldacre came into rehearsal and gave the two actors very precise instructions on the taking of the measurements. This part of the scene is exactly as it was recorded that night, and included in performance, for instance, the recording of the main stand's reply to Frank's adjustments.

The reflective discussion which is interleaved with it took place in the theater on the Saturday morning at the end of the first week of the documentary in its original form. About forty members of the Action Committee attended and we asked them "What have we left out? Have we misrepresented anything?"

Their main response was to discuss the way in which nationalisation seemed to be represented as the cause of their problems. As Socialists this bothered them, and they tried to disentangle this issue from what seemed to them to be the true causes, and to define the ways in which they felt nationalisation could be made to work better.

The discussion (which involved Philip Donnellan too) seemed to me to be important enough to be included in a new ending, and this replaced a rather garbled version of the uncensored parts of the emotional debrief I described earlier.

ACTION COMMITTEE SPEECH

The documentary seemed to be complete in itself in concluding with the reflections on the meeting with Dr. Finniston. Apart from the previous scene our major revisions in the weeks after we opened were all geared to improving the way in which we presented material we had already assembled. It was clear to me that a short announcement each evening from a member of the Action Committee would suffice to keep events up to date now that the show presenting their case and the history of their case was complete. They were only too delighted to do this, and it was done on a rota basis by about a dozen members of the Action Committee—all of those who felt brave enough to stand up in a spotlight and address a theater audience of 400 people. The speech was rarely more than two minutes in length, sometimes altered to suit the occasion, as well as the news, on the nights for instance when Jack Ashley MP came along, and ultimately Dr. Finniston himself. It obviously also gave a very special endorsement to the material in the show, and to its impact on the audience.

We have printed here only the speech made on the sixth performance. (At the end also, every night, members of the audience could stay behind to discuss the situation with the Action Committee member, for about 20 minutes.)

Final Song

We closed the case on this deliberately challenging note, adding two more verses to the song sung to "King Henry" at the end of Part One, together with a speech recorded at Bill Foster's personal interview, which graphically indicates one major source of the emotional energy in at least this industrial dispute.

Molly Newman and Barbara Damashek
Music and Lyrics by Barbara Damashek

Quilters

1982

Based on *The Quilters: Women and Domestic Art* by Patricia Cooper and Norma Bradley Allen

Quilters was originally developed and initially produced at the Denver Center Theatre Company, 8 November to 18 December 1982 and subsequently presented at numerous regional theaters. The original production was directed by Barbara Damashek, with set and costumes by Christina Haatainen, and lighting by Allen Lee Hughes. The cast included Georgia Southcotte (Sarah), Marjorie Berman, Charlotte Booker, Shelley Crandall, Audre Johnston, Dorothy Lancaster, and Judy Leavell. *Quilters* was presented by the Denver Center for the Performing Arts, The John F. Kennedy Center for the Performing Arts, The American National Theatre and Academy, and Brockman Seawell at the Jack Lawrence Theatre in New York City on 25 September 1984 for a brief run. It was directed by Barbara Damashek, with setting by Ursula Belden, costumes by Elizabeth Palmer, and lighting by Allen Lee Hughes. The cast included Lenka Peterson (Sarah), Evalyn Baron, Marjorie Berman, Alma Cuervo, Lynn Lobban, Rosemary McNamara, Jennifer Parson, Emily Knapp Chatfield, Melanie Sue Harby, John S. Lionarons, Joseph A. Waterkotte, and Catharine Way.

ACKNOWLEDGMENTS

The authors would like gratefully to acknowledge the inspiration derived from the original quilt design "The Sun Sets on Sunbonnet Sue" as designed and executed by the Seamsters Union Local No. 500 of Lawrence, Kansas, and the inspiration provided by Grace Snyder and Nellie Snyder Yost in their book *No Time on My Hands*.

The authors would also like gratefully to acknowledge the following texts and individuals as invaluable resources in the development of the play: *New Discoveries in American Quilts* by Robert Bishop; *American Quilts and Coverlets* by Robert Bishop and Carleton L. Stafford; Marguerite Ickis; *Letters of a Woman Homesteader* by Elinore Pruitt Stewart; *Our Homes and Their Adornments* by Almon C. Varney; *American Folk Poetry—An Anthology* by Duncan Emrich; *Women's Diaries of the Westward Journey* by Lillian Schlissel; *Aunt Jane of Kentucky* by Eliza Calvert Hall; *Pioneer Women—Voices from the Kansas Frontier* by Joanna L. Stratton; "The Prairie Home Companion," Garrison Keillor, Minnesota Public Radio; *A Little Better Than Plumb* by Henry and Janice Holt Giles; *A Harvest Yet to Reap—A History of Prairie Women* by Linda Rasmussen, Lorna Rasmussen, Candace Savage, and Anne Wheeler; and *Wisconson Death Trip* by Michael Lesy.

Quilters is meant to be produced with a cast of seven actresses who portray Sarah McKendree

Bonham and her six daughters: Jenny, Margaret, Lisa, Dana, Jody, and Jane. Within the "blocks" of the play, these seven actresses transform into the different characters within each scene. These characters are either numbered as Woman One, Woman Two, etc., or, in most cases they have been given names for the benefit of the actresses and director during the rehearsal process. The characters that "Sarah" plays are specified in the text, and the other characters may be divided among the "daughters" at the director's discretion.

SONGS

ACT I

PIECES OF LIVES[1]
ROCKY ROAD
LITTLE BABES THAT SLEEP ALL NIGHT[2]
THREAD THE NEEDLE
CORNELIA
THE WINDMILL SONG
ARE YOU WASHED IN THE BLOOD OF THE LAMB?
  (by E. A. Hoffman)
THE BUTTERFLY
PIECES OF LIVES (reprise)
GREEN GREEN GREEN
THE NEEDLE'S EYE[3]

ACT II

HOEDOWN (traditional)
QUILTIN' AND DREAMIN'
PIECES OF LIVES (reprise)
EVERY LOG IN MY HOUSE[4]
WHO WILL COUNT THE STITCHES?
LAND WHERE WE'LL NEVER GROW OLD (by J. C.
  Moore)
THE LORD DON'T RAIN DOWN MANNA
DANDELION (lyrics by Clara J. Denton)[5]
EVERYTHING HAS A TIME
HANDS AROUND

---

[1]First four lines from "The Quilt by Dorothy MacFarlane.
[2]Lyrics from *Our Homes and Their Adornments* by Almon C. Varney.
[3]Chorus from the lyric of a traditional folk song.
[4]First line by Elinore Pruitt Stewart.
[5]From the poem "Blooming in the Fall".

ACT ONE

JENNY: We were livin' out in the country when we first married and we didn't have much. When the kids started coming along there was lots of quilting to be done. Some folks were doing better than us and they would get together enough material for two quilts. I would piece both of 'em and for my work I got to keep one for nothing. Then, one time Mama come to visit. She saw what I was doin'. She didn't say anything, but later when she went home, she sent me out a great big flour sack stuffed full of scraps with a note sayin', "Jenny, no more piecin' on the halves for any of us." It was a gift that always meant a lot to me. These bags of calico, and denim, and the like have kept cover on our family for generations. (*She reaches into the scrapbag.*) "Oh . . . Margaret look at this. Do you remember it?"
(*Sings.*)
This was a piece of
My wedding dress

DAUGHTERS join.

ALL (*sing*):
Love and laughter
JENNY: Mama kept absolutely everything here. (*SARAH appears.*)
SARAH (*to the audience*): My name is Sarah McKendree Bonham. I've lived a long time and I've made a heap of quilts. But this last one that I'm making, this one's gonna be my best effort ever. It's like a family album. Each block means something special to me. My grandmother's patterns is in this quilt, and my mama's . . . my aunt's, my daughters', my sisters', my friends', and many more. They're all here and so's this great prairie that we all lived on. Like my Papa used to say, "It's not the end of the world but you can see it from here."
JENNY (*sings*):
This was a piece of
My wedding dress
Love and laughter
And tenderness
ALL (*sing*):
Tenderness

JENNY (*sings*):
    And this sprigged muslin
    Color of corn
    I wore right after our John was born
    Wore it after our John was born

All begin dancing with the scrapbags.

CHORUS:
    Pieces of lives
    Patches and tatters
    All of the
    Precious
    The little
    The matter of our lives

    Pieces of lives
    Stitches and secrets
    Pieces of women's lives

    Pieces of lives
    Patches and tatters
    All of the precious
    The little
    The matter of our lives
    Pieces of lives
    Tattin' and trimmin'
    Pieces of women's lives

Music bridge.

    Pieces of lives
    Swatches and notions
    All the unspoken
    Emotion
    Devotion of our lives

    Pieces of lives
    Stitches and secrets
    Pieces of women's
    Women's
    Lives

All freeze.

SARAH: We're gonna put this quilt together block by block. Each block is different, each pattern has a thread of somebody's life runnin' through it. You'll see my thread in there from time to time with all the others . . . my memories, my hopes, my dreams and prayers . . . it's my LEGACY QUILT. (*The DAUGHTERS take out and read their copies of SARAH's letter along with her.*) My Dear Daughters: I know my time is runnin' out and that I am surely piercing my last quilt.

JENNY: I have set out to piecing all the patterns that have some special meaning to me, a different one for every block . . .

MARGARET: . . . and if it be God's mercy to let me complete it, it will belong to you.

LISA: I've been a hard worker all my life . . .

JODY: but most all a woman's work is the kind that "perishes with the usin'" as the Bible says.

JANE: All the work I've got to leave behind me . . .

SARAH: and I've got to leave something behind me

ALL: is just my quilts.

DANA: I hope you will give special care to this last one and use it well.

LISA: I trust that you will be able to read what's written in it.

SARAH AND JANE: In some ways it's our own story. (*WOMAN SIX has removed the "Rocky Road" patch from the oversized hoop which was carried in by WOMAN ONE during the last verse of "Pieces of Lives."*)

WOMAN ONE: BLOCK ONE. (*She folds the hoop in half by snapping it against her knee.*) THE ROCKY ROAD TO KANSAS! (*The COMPANY moves into a standing group carrying hoops and baskets.*)

WOMAN TWO: To Oklahoma!

WOMAN THREE (*Snapping her hoop.*) To Colorado!

WOMAN FOUR: To New Mexico!

WOMAN FIVE (*Snapping her hoop.*) To California!

WOMAN SIX: Where the sun always shines and fruit grows wild. (*The COMPANY sings "Rocky Road":*)
    Rocky road
    Rocky road
    You're a callin' to me
    There's a better life at hand

    O'er the rocky road
    Through the prairie sea
    I am bound for Canaan's land

    Rocky
    Roa . . . d

One at a time, the hoops which have been folded in half are raised over the women's heads, creating the ribs of a Conestoga wagon.

SARAH (*cracking the whip.*): WESTWARD HO!

WOMEN ONE, THREE, and FIVE carry the hoops. WOMEN TWO and FOUR are positioned in between as passengers. WOMAN SIX faces out of the back of the wagon carrying the "Rocky Road" quilt. The wagon begins to move.

WOMAN ONE: Day upon day we moved through the prairie without seein' so much as a tree. Looked like there was nothin' at all up ahead clear to the edge of the earth.

WOMAN TWO: At first it was all grass and sky . . . and then the long stretch of gray dust came. . . . Nothin' but gray and brown, nothin' but dust and tumbleweeds blowin'.

WOMAN THREE: Dust covered everything and everything tasted of dust.

WOMAN TWO: Passed two new graves.

WOMAN FIVE: Then the cold set in . . . the icy rain . . . the hailstones big as rocks and all the big rocks you had to move to make the road. . . . That's what they meant by the Rocky Road West.

WOMAN ONE: Three old graves . . . two new ones.

WOMAN SIX: A baby was born. (*She transforms the quilt into a baby bundle. And turns into the wagon. During the next section, the wagon is slipping or stuck, not really covering ground.*)

WOMAN THREE: The snows came, the footing was treacherous . . . it slowed us down to a crawl, and those winter nights fell down on you as sudden as that . . . and silent.

WOMAN FOUR: Now and again you'd hear somethin' off in the distance . . . coyotes, Indians, anything you were afraid of . . . but there was children with you, so you didn't let on. (*The wagon begins to cover ground again.*)

WOMAN SIX: Seven graves . . .

WOMAN TWO: One marker.

WOMAN ONE: Those nights in the wagon we set to piecin' quilts . . . all of us. . . . We would need as much as we could turn out for the long frost ahead of us.

ALL: Day upon day we moved out of the long stretch of gray into the whiteness. (*The wagon freezes. CHRISTY steps out of the wagon.*)

CHRISTY: When we stopped on this spot, I got out of the wagon to see where our journey had taken us. I took a good long look. As far as the eye could see there was nothing, emptiness, it was so lonely. How could a human endure? Way far off, I thought I could make out some smoke. "People!" I thought.

SARAH: BLOCK TWO! (*The WOMEN break out of the wagon configuration. Jig music underscores SARAH's speech and the setting up of the "Dugout." The WOMAN playing PAPA in the next scene will lie down at this time under another rough hewn quilt or blanket.*) The first home we had out here was a DUGOUT. (*She displays the quilted Kansas "Dugout" patch.*) It was just a large single room dug underground. The funny thing about livin' in that dugout was that I didn't ever get the feelin' that Mama said she had about being closed in down there.

CARRIE (*taking the "Dugout" patch from SARAH.*): To me, being just a little thing, it seemed the safest place in the world, and many a wind got rode out down there. All I can see from way back then is the light playing on the low ceiling, and Mama's back bent over her sewing next to the lamp. I slept with my sister then and she musta' loved me 'cause I can remember on the coldest mornin's she would get out of bed and warm my clothes next to the fire. When they were good and warm, she would stuff them under the quilts next to me so I could dress up warm before getting out of bed. Well, you didn't have much space, but you had your family all around you. (*CARRIE places the "Dugout" patch on top of the quilt which covers PAPA.*) Come to think of it, I don't remember any trouble or distress from those early times, although I know the grown-ups felt it. There was so many stories about rough times when they first settled.

CARRIE, who is now under the quilt, becomes POLLY in the following scene. KATIE enters with a bucket or stool which is transformed into the fireplace. She carries a cup and uses a long wooden spoon to stoke the fire.

KATIE: I had my seventh birthday in a dugout in the dead of winter. (*Blizzard noises begin.*) Papa and sister and me had come west to homestead . . . to kinda make a fresh start after Mama had died. (*KATIE gets under the quilt with PAPA and POLLY and enters the scene.*) When the blizzard hit us it was thirty below. We all slept together under a stack of quilts. Then we piled everything we could find on top of us . . . but you just couldn't get warm. Sister got really bad. One of us, either Papa or me, had to always be tending the fire. (*KATIE moves to the fireplace. The remaining WOMEN with blankets over their backs, play three COWS and a CALF. They enter the scene bleating and moaning silently.*) One night we could hear the cows outside the door bleatin' and moanin' somethin' awful. Then one by one we could hear them dropping. (*PAPA sits up. Blizzard noises. The first two COWS fall. Then the third "MOTHER" COW. The CALF nudges its dead mother's teats gently. Then bleats silently and falls to its knees—its head on its mother's belly. PAPA moves to the door.*) Where ya goin', Pa? Pa?

PAPA opens the imaginary door. Blizzard noises get louder. Then slams it shut. With oversized wooden sewing scissors, PAPA begins skinning the COWS by stabbing them, slitting them up to their throats, and then removing the blanket "skins." The stabbing corresponds to a glottal attack in KATIE's song. The slitting of the throat corresponds to a "yip." KATIE, tucking POLLY in:

KATIE (*sings*):
  Little babes
  That sleep all night

(*First COW is skinned.*) Remember, Mama used to sing that?

  Little babes that sleep all night
  Smile in the face of sorrow

(*The second COW is skinned.*)

  Little birds that sleep all night
  Sing carols on the morrow

(*The third COW is skinned. KATIE goes to the door, looks out, and returns to the fire.*) The cows froze, Polly. All the cows are dead. Papa's

skinnin' 'em now. Don't worry, I'll keep the fire goin' good. (*PAPA throws the first cowhide onto the roof. Loud whump sounds.*) Papa's throwin' the cowhides over the roof to keep out the cold. That should help some. (*PAPA throws the second cowhide.*) I wish I could sleep through all this like you do. Are you thirsty? Want some water? I'll get you some fresh snow to drink. (*KATIE goes to the door with the cup in hand. She opens the door and scoops up some snow. Blizzard noises are loud. She pulls the door shut. She moves to the fire to melt the snow and warm her hands. Then she takes the cup to POLLY.*) Here, Poll. It's prob'ly cold already. Take it, Polly. Please take it. I know you want it. You haven't had nothin' to eat for two days. Take it. I'm afraid to open your mouth. I don't want to catch it. (*No response from POLLY.*) Here, I'll just set it on your chest. (*PAPA throws final cowhide on the roof. The cup overturns.*) Mama! I don't know what to do. Why did you go and leave us, Polly? Why does everyone have to go away all the time? (*She runs to the door and opens it. Screaming.*) Papa! (*No answer. PAPA, unseen by KATIE, is frozen outside the dugout. KATIE closes the door and runs to POLLY. During the next speech she tries to "pound" the life back into her sister by hitting her on the chest and shaking her. The whump sounds continue in rhythm with this action like an accelerated heartbeat.*) Polly . . . Polly . . . Get up! . . . Wake up! . . . Get up . . . Wake up! (*KATIE gives up. The blizzard noises begin to taper off.*) Papa promised just as soon as the storm lets up, we're gonna bury you proper. (*KATIE towers her head over POLLY in the same position as the calf over its mother. A WOMAN'S VOICE sings off in the distance.*)

WOMAN (*singing—gently*):
  Smile in the face of sorrow.

Lights up. A banjo plays.

WOMAN ONE (*singing*):
  Children come . . .
ALL (*sing*):
  Thread the needle . . .

All clap time under SARAH's speech.

SARAH: Way back even before I was old enough to quilt, my mother and older sisters would be quiltin' and us little ones had to keep their needles threaded. We'd be out in the yard playin' and they'd holler out to us . . . (*During the song, "Thread the Needle," the* COMPANY *dances and plays with larger-than-life wooden needles.*)

Children come!
Thread the needle
Thread the needle
Keep 'em all goin'
Thread the needle

Fiddle phrase.

Keep 'em all goin'
Keep 'em all goin'
Keep 'em all goin'
Keep 'em all goin'

CHILDREN *surround the bucketful of needles. Keeping time in a kind of patty-cake.*

Don't break the rhythm of the
Fingers and the stitchin'
Thread up the sharps
And the in-betweens

CHILDREN *pull the appropriate needles out of the bucket, one at a time.*

Sharp!
Sharp!
In-between
Sharp!
In-between
Sharp!
Sharp!
In-between!

CHILDREN *dance with needles clacking.*

Stick 'em in the
Middle of the
Quiltin' frame

And then go out and
Play your games

Then go out and
Then go out and
Play

Children come
Thread the needle
Thread the needle
Children!

Stick 'em in the middle
In the middle
In the middle
Stick 'em in the middle
In the middle
Stick 'em in the middle

Play your games
Play your games

SARAH: BLOCK THREE!
ALL: BABY'S BLOCKS!

SARAH *displays part of a pieced top of "Baby's Blocks." At the end of the dance, all the* COMPANY *have collapsed in sitting positions, leaving* EVELYN *and* SALLY *in the middle of the space.*

SALLY: Remember when we was little we had those dark comforts made from overalls and wool trousers on the bed? Well, sometimes the neighbor women would come in and quilt with Mama; and them quilts was always real pretty.
EVELYN: Once a week when the neighbors came, Teddy would haul Mama's big old bed down from her bedroom and set up the frame in the kitchen—it was quite a job.
SALLY: He never minded it, though.
EVELYN: There was never more than four women working because there was no room for more, and us little ones had to wait outside.
SALLY: We'd be standing in the doorway with our thumbs in our mouths watching them.
EVELYN: Waiting and waiting for them to go home because we were so hungry. But it wasn't proper to ask for food with company in the house.
SALLY: How we envied them pretty bright colored quilts.
EVELYN: Finally I got up my courage to ask Mama could we please, *please* keep some of 'em. And she said we could make do with what we had.
BOTH: Others needed them more.
SALLY: And then you burst into tears.
EVELYN (*to the others*): They took all the pretty quilts to the Baptist Church. They was for the poor people and the foreign missions.

SALLY: And sometimes if somebody lost their house to a fire or a twister, the women would all go with a stack of quilts and say:

EVELYN AND SALLY: These quilts is from the ladies of the First Baptist Church!

THE COMPANY (*sings*):
Children come
Thread the needle
Thread the needle
Children

ONE dances SARAH into the middle to tell her story.

SARAH: I remember like it was yesterday my first quilt. Mama had one of them frames that swung down from over the bed and there was always a quilt in it. She quilted for the public to pay our way. Now we might take one out late one night when it was finished and wait till mornin' to put the next one in. But that was as long as it ever was. Mama was a beautiful quilter. She had the smallest stitches and the smallest feet in the country. Everybody knew it. She never let nobody else touch her quilts. Sometimes when she was through quiltin' for the day on a job that she liked a lot herself she would pin a cloth over the top of the quilt so nobody could look at it till she was done. I always longed to work with her and I can tell you how plain I recall the day she said . . . (*A WOMAN sitting on a stool turns out front as FLORENCE.*)

FLORENCE: Sarah, you come quilt with me now if you want to. (*SARAH enters the playing space as a CHILD. During her speech she removes a five-inch wooden needle from her apron and mimes the sewing through her fingers.*)

SARAH: I was too short to sit in a chair and reach the frame so I got my needle and thread and stood beside her. I put that needle through and pulled it back up again then down and my stitches was about three inches long. Papa come in about that time. (*Another WOMAN on a stool focuses out as PAPA.*)

PAPA: Florence, that child is flat ruinin' your quilt. (*SARAH hears this and starts shortening her stitches.*)

FLORENCE: She is doin' no kind of a thing. She's quiltin' her first quilt.

PAPA: Well you're jest goin' to have to rip it all out tonight.

FLORENCE: Them stitches is going to be in that quilt when it wears out.

SARAH: All the time they was talkin' my stitches were gettin' shorter and shorter.

THE COMPANY (*sings*):
Keep 'em all goin'
Keep 'em all goin'
Keep 'em all goin'
Keep 'em all goin'

ONE of the Company has danced CYNTHIA into the center.

CYNTHIA: When I was about four years old the neighbor's baby died and all the women were called in to help. Mama knew what her part was because right away she took some blue silk out of her hope chest. I remember the silk so well because it was special and I got to carry it. When we got to the neighbors, some of the women was cooking and the men was making the casket. Mama and three other women set up the frame and quilted all day. First they quilted the lining for the casket, and then they made a tiny little quilt out of the blue silk to cover the baby.

THE COMPANY (*sings*):
Children come
Thread the needle
Thread the needle
Children!

SARAH crosses through the space to the area where her scrapbags are stored, beckoning to JANIE who plays a small child.

SARAH: Janie, come sit here by me. It's time I showed you somethin'. Now this here's my scrapbag. It's full of pieces of fabric I've been savin' through the years. All different sizes and colors and textures. Different ones of our family are always appearing out of one of these bags. (*She reaches into a bag and pulls a scrap out.*) Ooh, I haven't seen this one for a while. This here was your great-aunt Mildred's Sunday-Go-To-Meetin'-Dress. Lord but she sang high. You could always pick her voice right out from the choir. You know, the one that's always a little too high? That was Aunt Millie. Well, when I'm making a quilt top, I take these scraps, cut 'em into triangles, and squares and other shapes. They fit together like a puzzle to form the pattern I want. Then I sew them together and that's called . . .

JANIE: Quiltin'.

SARAH: No . . . piecin'. When I've pieced a whole quilt top, I put my bottom lining on the frame, my cotton battin' in between, and my quilt top over all, and sew the three layers together, and THAT'S called . . .

JANIE: "Quiltin'."

SARAH: Right! Now when you're a really good quilter, you'll be able to get eleven stitches to the inch. (*She gives* JANIE *the pieces she has been demonstrating on.*) Would you like to keep that?

JANIE: Yes please.

SARAH: It's yours. There are lots of full scrapbags now and I keep 'em sorted out real neat; so if you ever need to find anything and I'm not here, you should have no trouble. Look, these are all darks. I've always had plenty of darks. I use them if I need a shaded area in a block. The Log Cabin patterns have lots of those. . . . And sometimes, I'll set off my bright patterns with a solid dark block of fabric with no design to it at all. Some call it a plain block—I call it a SHADOW BLOCK.*

CHILDBIRTH SHADOW BLOCK

A solo flute plays. It is the voice of the spirit of the infant struggling to be born. At first the improvised phrase should be short and spare with

---

*The "Shadow Blocks" are essentially nonverbal representations of the darker side of the women's rites of passage. The events depicted are not always tragic, but we should get a sense of the unspoken fears involved and the presence of Mystery and Death. The action is performed with muffled improvised dialogue or in silence. The audience "overhears" it. The "Shadow Block" lighting is a visual motif which sets these blocks apart: a sepia photograph in comparison with the brighter tones of the rest of the piece. The textures of this motif are things which the lighting designer must play with and expand. In Act Two the "Secret Drawer," a fully scripted block, is announced as a "Shadow Block." "Crosses and Losses" can also be thought of as a "Shadow Block."

pauses between them. They should grow more intense as the MOTHER *goes into final contractions and finally build to a celebrative trill as the* MIDWIFE *lifts the* BABY *over her head. We also hear the rhythmic flapping of pieces of muslin. These are the pulse of the contractions of the "labor." They are spare at first and accelerate in the final phases.*

WOMAN ONE *enters the playing area with the childbirth quilt, which she drapes over the* PREGNANT WOMAN. *The* PREGNANT WOMAN *enters the space and lies on the floor under the "Childbirth" quilt. If the director prefers, a birthing stool can be used, which the* PREGNANT WOMAN *brings in with her.* WOMAN ONE *supports the* PREGNANT WOMAN *from behind, mopping her brow and trying to keep her comfortable. The* MIDWIFE *focuses on the abdominal area, speaking to and encouraging the* PREGNANT MOTHER. *A* FOURTH WOMAN *is tending the fire and keeping the water boiling. (We hear the slow flapping of muslin and sporadic flute. The action begins right after a bout of contractions from which the* PREGNANT WOMAN *is trying to recover.)*

After a pause, the PREGNANT WOMAN *begins to bear down for the final contractions. The* MIDWIFE *encourages her to "push."* WOMAN ONE *inserts a cloth "bit" in the* PREGNANT WOMAN'S *mouth and continues to comfort her. (If a birthing stool is used,* WOMAN ONE *should support the* PREGNANT WOMAN *with her back all through the contractions.)*

The contractions quicken. (Accelerate the flapping of muslin and the flute phrases until . . .) The final big push. The NEW MOTHER *moans through the bit. The* MIDWIFE *puts her arm all the way up to the elbow under the mother's skirt and pulls. . . . (Ripping of muslin.) The* MIDWIFE *pulls the baby out. The* MOTHER *moans. (The* BABY *is the nonquilted "Rebel Patch" wrapped in a bundle, wrong side out.)*

The MIDWIFE *lifts the* BABY *and slaps it. (We hear the sound of the slap and then a* BABY *crying.)* WOMAN ONE *supports the* MOTHER *who has collapsed against her. The* MIDWIFE *places the* BABY *on the mother's stomach.*

MOTHER: God Bless this baby.

The MIDWIFE *pulls out scissors from her apron and snips the umbilical cord. (Sound effect for the* snipping.) *The* MIDWIFE *lifts the* BABY *over her head in thanks.* (*The flute crescendoes to a joyous trill and then abruptly cuts off.*)

MIDWIFE (MIZ): BLOCK FOUR . . . THE REBEL PATCH. (MIZ *unrolls and displays the "Rebel Patch." Lively underscoring from the guitar is heard.*)

MIZ: Lord know honey, I never quilted when I was a child. Not me, I was the one ran outside and stayed gone most of the day. The prairie provided us kids with all the toys we could ever want, and with that big playground out there, I couldn't be cooped up in no house.

A whistle is heard. The music stops. CHILD ONE *tumbles into the scene. Her arms are gloved to the elbow in a coarse fabric, the cloth suggestion of a corncob. The Cornelia doll will be constructed on her right hand. The Cornelius doll, on her left. During* MIZ's *speech, the rest of the* COMPANY *has donned short gloves with their finger tips randomly cut off. The* ACTRESS *who does the "Sunbonnet Sue" speech should have a pouch and a rattle. The "Rebel Patch" can be worn by* MIZ *as she enters this scene as a* CHILD, *or the director can decide its use. But somehow it should end up on the Cornelia doll. The image here for the "Cornelia" Song is hand puppets. The hands should also be involved in a kind of visual sign language for the chorus of the song.*)

CHILD ONE (*singing, raising her right hand*):
For my Cornelia corncob doll
ALL (*sing*):
I found the longest cornsilk strands
And made her a
Right fine head of hair

CHILD TWO *puts the hair on.*

And from the husks I made her
Floppy hands

CHILD THREE *puts the hands on.*

CHILD ONE (*spoken*): "Waddya think?"
ALL (*spoken*): It's good!
(*Sing*) I'd sit 'n pretty her up
Till she'd be sittin' pretty
CHORUS:
It was the mornin' and the

Evenin' of the
First day

SARAH *enters as a* CHILD.

For my Cornelia corncob doll
CHILD FOUR (*sings*):
I made a hat of
Dried sunflower
ALL (*sing*):
And then I'd fancy it up
With chicken feathers
CHILD FIVE (*sings*):
I'd be huntin' them for hours
(*She finds a feather, sets it in the hat. Spoken*):
Whaddya think?
ALL (*spoken*): It's good!
(*Sing*) And I'd be paintin' her face
Till she'd be quite the lady
CHILD ONE (*making the hand puppet sing*):
It was the
Mornin' and the
Evenin' of the second day
ALL (*sing*):
It was the mornin' and the
Evenin' of the second day

The skirt is put on.

And then I'd
Fix up a frock from the
Piecin' bag
From the scraps of my Sunday best
And then I'd
Quick

CHILD ONE *raises left hand.*

Whip up a Cornelius
Doll

A cup inverted becomes a hat for Cornelius.

And on the third day
I'd get 'em wedded and blest
And come the mornin'
And the evenin' of the

COMPANY *makes kissing noises.*

(*kiss*) Fourth day and of the
(*kiss*) Fifth day and of the
(*kiss*) Sixth day
There'd be

The COMPANY *raises their hands with the cut off gloves. The "nubbins" are the wiggly fingers.*

Dozens of nubbins
For corncob babies

All fingers wiggling.

And come the seventh
Day
They'd rest

The fingers freeze. CHILD ONE *relaxes her arms.*

CHILD ONE (*spoken*): So much begattin'!
THE COMPANY (*The nubbins droop. Sings.*):
Ahhhhhhhh!

A new cornelia corncob doll
Would be created every fall
And I could pretty much
Make her up pretty

From almost nothin'
Nothin' at all
From almost nothin' at all
And I'd be primpin' her up
Till she'd be tired of primpin'
Throughout the mornin's and the evenin's
Every mornin' every evenin'
Every mornin' every evenin' of the
Win . . . ter's day

La la la la la Cornelia

The COMPANY *exits leaving* ANNIE *alone onstage.*

ANNIE (*to the audience*): My ambition is to become a doctor like my father. I'm my father's girl. My greatest accomplishment was when I was ten years old and was successful in chopping off a chicken's head and then dressing it for a chicken dinner. My mother tries to make me do quilts all the time, but I don't want nothing to do with it. I told her, "Never in my life will I stick my fingers 'til they bleed." Very definitely. My sister Florry is a real good quilter, I guess. Mother says so all the time. Florry's favorite pattern is the Sunbonnet Sue. Mother taught her how to do applique blocks and since then she's made probly a dozen "Sunbonnet Sue" quilt. You've seen 'em, they're like little dolls turned sideways with big sunbonnets on. Florry makes each one different. (*She demonstrates, mimicking* FLORRY.) In one her little foot is turned this way or that, or she'll give her a little parasol, or turn the hat a little bit. People think they're sooo cute. She made one for everybody in the family, so now there are little "Sunbonnet Sue" quilts all over the house. She made a couple of 'em for her friends, and last Spring, when we all got promoted at school, she presented one to our teacher. I nearly died. And she's still at it. Let me tell you, she's driving me crazy with her "Sunbonnet Sues." So I decided to make one quilt and give it to Florry. Like I said, I'm not such a good quilter as her, but I knew just what I wanted to do with this one. It's real small. Twin bed size. I finished it and put it on her bed this morning, but I don't think she's seen it yet. I guess I done some new things with "Sunbonnet Sue." I call it the *Demise of Sunbonnet Sue.* Each little block is different, just like Florry does it. I've got a block of her hanging, another one with a knife in her chest, eaten by a snake, eaten by a frog, struck by lightning, and burned up. I'm sorta proud of it. You should see it. . . . (*A scream from the direction of* FLORRY's *bedroom.*) It turned our real good! (*She exits smiling.* FRANKIE *enters carrying a bucket. The guitar plays a phrase from the* "Windmill Song." SARAH *enters with the* "Windmill" *patch on a pole.*)

FRANKIE: BLOCK FIVE. I'll tell you what held your life in this country.

SARAH (*hoists the flat*): A WINDMILL!

FRANKIE: No life without it. I remember so clear and I was just a little tyke when we moved out near Runnin' Water Draw. That was a funny name for it because Runnin' Water Draw never had no water in it, except once in a great while when we had rain. Then it flooded all over the place.

SARAH: The funny thing about the windmill block is that there aren't any circles in it. The circle is a lot harder to cut and sew than those straight edge pieces. One time I made a Dresden Plate that like to never circled. I had them center edges about a sixteenth of an inch off. I watched my papa build a wooden windmill when I was little and he had the same problem. (FRANKIE *crosses the stage where* JUNE *joins her.*)

FRANKIE: Our daddy decided to dig his well right down in the middle of the draw. He figured that the water wouldn't be so far to reach down there. Up on the high ground he couldn't have dug it by hisself.

JUNE: The water was there, but what he didn't figure on was that the sand down there was kindly like quicksand and kept seepin' back into the well. Even now I don't know if I'm more afraid of quicksand or scorpions.

FRANKIE: When the wind blew, the water was pumped into an old wooden barrel down on the ground. The barrel was always coated with green mossy stuff. I'll never forget the way it smelled, or what my face looked like in the water (*She looks into the water and* JUNE *plays the reflection.* FRANKIE *reaches down, hands cupped, to draw some water. This sets the reflection rippling and* JUNE *splashes water into* FRANKIE's *face.* JUNE *rolls out of this space into her position downstage.*) From the time I was about ten years old my job was to hang a bucket on the spout . . . (*She does so.*) and climb the tower when there wasn't no wind. (*Three* ACTRESSES *get into position as the windmill. Their outstretched arms are the windmill blades.* FRANKIE *climbs the ladder.*) I had to turn the wheel by hand. (*She hangs off the ladder in a precarious position, and reaches with one arm to turn the windmill blades.*)

THE COMPANY (*sing*):
Wheel in the wheel in the
Wheel in the wheel
Way in the middle of the air

Singing continues under JUNE's *speech.*

JUNE: Oh how beautiful the windmill was when Daddy got it finished . . . standing up against the sky. It meant water, you know. But it really just looked pretty by itself . . . tall and with the top turning this way and that . . . . whirring around.

THE COMPANY (*sing*):
Wheel in
The wheel in the wheel
In the wheel in the
Wheel . . .

FRANKIE (*sings*):
Ooo wa ooo wa oo

JUNE (*sings*):
Daddy's hand cut a circle
That cut a circle in the sky
Daddy's hand
Made a windmill
And up in the attic
Where we'd
Lie

FRANKIE *pushes the blades again.*

It seemed
Bigger than the moon

FRANKIE (*sings*):
Or a wagon wheel

JUNE (*sings*):
What a sight for
Our sore eyes

JUNE AND FRANKIE (*sing*):
And we would drift to sleep
To the whirring lullabyes

THE COMPANY (*sing*):
Wheel in the wheel in the
Wheel in the wheel
Way in the middle of the air

JUNE (*sings*):
Ooo wa ooo wa oo

JUNE AND FRANKIE (*sing*):
Little prairie girl

Windmill blades stop rotating and just rock.

JUNE (*sings*):
Let me spin you
In my wooden
Arms . . .

JUNE AND FRANKIE (*sing*):
All around the world

The blades start rotating again.

THE COMPANY (*sing*):
Wheel in the wheel in the
Wheel in the wheel
Way in the middle of the
Way in the middle of the
Air . . .

FRANKIE (*sings*):
Daddy's mill
Made the circle
That joined the wind
To the earth below

Giving life
Pumping water
FRANKIE AND JUNE (*sing*):
And causing all living things to grow . . .

Windmill blades go faster and then stop completely.

FRANKIE (*sings*):
Now me and June
FRANKIE AND JUNE (*sing*):
Snuggling spoons
And oh how many
Tunes it played
And we would drift to sleep
To the
Whirring of the
Blades

Blades rotate again.

THE COMPANY (*sing*):
Wheel in the wheel in the
Wheel in the wheel in the
Wheel
FRANKIE (*sings*):
Come on in I'll
Spin you in a dream
Little prairie girl

Blades stop rotating and rock.

JUNE (*making a rudder with her apron, sings*):
Let me spin you
In my wooden arms
All around the
World

Blades go faster and stop after four measures.

FRANKIE: I've seen a growed man slung thirty feet to the ground if the wind happened to come up while he was on top. Me, I'd just grab aholt and ride the thing round and round till the wind would let me off. (*In this last section the blades will move more quickly than they ever have.* FRANKIE *will be enacting riding the windmill.*)

FRANKIE (*sings*):   BLADES (*holding notes*):
Come on   (1) Come on . . .
In I'll
Spin you in a   (2) Spin
Dream   (3) Dream

JUNE (*sings*):
Let me spin you in my wooden arms

Voices begin to overlap.

FRANKIE (*sings*):
Come on in I'll
Spin you in a (dream)
JUNE (*sings*):
Let me spin you in my wooden (arms)
FRANKIE (*sings*):
Oo wa oo wa o
BLADES (*sings*):
Way in the middle of the air . . .
JUNE (*sings*):
Daddy's hands
Daddy's hands
Daddy's hands
Daddy's hands
FRANKIE AND JUNE (*sing*):
Hands

The spinning windmill transforms into a cradle of arms which rocks JUNE *gently.*

SARAH: I'll tell you what held your life in this country. (*Music pauses.*)
FRANKIE: A windmill! (*Final chord.*) Sometimes the worst happened and the well would bust. (ACTORS *split out from the windmill position.* JUNE *collects the bucket. The windmill flag is taken down.*) Then the whole family would take the milk cans and go borrowin' from the neighbors. Nobody ever asked to be paid back, though. (FRANKIE *exits.* JUNE *is crossing the stage. She reaches into the bucket and pulls out "Robbing Peter to Pay Paul" patch. She gives it to* JOY.)
JUNE: BLOCK SIX.
JOY (*displaying the patch*): ROBBING PETER TO PAY PAUL. My Daddy was a Baptist preacher. I reckon that's how come I'm so ornery today. But I remember the funniest day one time when I was a young girl. Mama was goin' to help me start my quilts for my hope chest. (MAMA *enters with a scrapbag and spreads some pieces on the ground.* JOY *adds the patch to this group.*) She had got the old scrapbag out. We spread 'em all out on the bed and tried to kinda put the colors together right. But the scrapbag was really low. (*To* MAMA.)

Well, Mama, we sure haven't gotten any new scraps in a long time. Seems like everybody in church is usin' their own scraps and none have come our way.

MAMA: Come in to town with me Saturday, and we'll just pick up a few pieces of brighter calico to spruce 'em up a bit.

JOY: Come Saturday, true to her word, we went to town with Papa. (*SARAH as PAPA leads JOY and MAMA into town. The CLERK gets into position behind a sawhorse covered with remnants. Against one of his hands is propped a large bolt of red calico.*) He went over to the feed store and we went to the dry goods. (*PAPA exits offstage.*) We had picked these three pieces of remnant blue and was just fingerin' some red calico.

MAMA: Better jest be plannin' on enough for the middle squares from that honey—you know what your father will say.

JOY: Just then Papa come in behind us and I guess he saw us lookin'. He just walked right up to the clerk like he wasn't with us.

PAPA (*to clerk*): How much is on that bolt?

CLERK: Twenty yards.

PAPA: I'll take it all. (*PAPA mimes paying for it. Lifts it over his shoulder. Leads MAMA into the wagon.*)

JOY: He picked up that whole bolt of red calico and carried it to the wagon. Twenty yards of red. Can you imagine? A Baptist preacher, jest like any other man, likes that red. (*PAPA cracks the whip. JOY tumbles into the wagon. Horse's hooves. . . . They are riding home.*)

PAPA: And I quote Proverbs—Chapter 31, Verse 10. O who can find a virtuous woman? For her price is far above rubies. She seeketh wool and flax and worketh willingly with her hands. She perceiveth that her merchandise is good.

MAMA: Amen! (*JOY has stealthily grabbed hold of the bolt and is caressing it in the back of the wagon. Slowly she unravels the fabric and holds it against her . . . unseen by her father.*)

PAPA: She is not afraid of the snow for her household for all her household are clothed with scarlet.

MAMA AND JOY: Amen!

PAPA: Give her the fruit of her hands and let her own works praise her in the gates.

MAMA AND JOY (*loudly*): Amen! (*PAPA looks at MAMA with a gleam in his eye. They freeze.*)

JOY (*the audience*): We had red for a long, long time after that. (*A bass drum booms. Shadow Block lighting.*) Shadow Block.

SARAH (*as the preacher*): Baptism.

BAPTISM SHADOW BLOCK

Sarah displays a pieced handkerchief with the Baptism design on it. The bass drum booms throughout. MAMA and LISA hold up the childbirth blanket, behind which, JOY strips down to her underwear for the dunking. Four WOMEN unroll the bolt of calico, which when extended, becomes the river.

THE COMPANY (*singing*):
Have you been to Jesus
For the cleansing power
Are you washed in the blood
Of the Lamb?

Are you fully trusting
In his grace this hour
Are you washed in the blood
Of the Lamb?

The COMPANY holds the note and the mmm . . . through the PREACHER's speech. JOY has reluctantly moved down to the water, urged on by her MAMA. The PREACHER has stepped into the river which ripples. "He" beckons JOY to come in. The air is cold. The water is cold. JOY steps in. The river rises to their waists. The PREACHER pinches JOY's nose with the handkerchief and prepares to dunk her.

PREACHER: I Baptize you Joy Lee Davis in the name of Jesus Christ. (*He tries to dunk her. JOY pulls away and struggles downstream.*)

JOY: Mamaaaa!

THE COMPANY (*sing*):
Are you washed
In the blood

The PREACHER goes after her and brings her back.

In the soul cleansing blood of the
Lamb?

COMPANY *holds the last note. The* PREACHER *has a firm grip on the* CHILD. JOY *and the* COMPANY *make a gasping sound.*

PREACHER (*dunking her under the water*): I (*Gasp!*) Baptize you in the name of the Father, the Son and the Holy Ghost. (*He gets carried away and loses his grip on the* CHILD. JOY *does some underwater, slow motion, twisting and turning . . . groping against the current for the* PREACHER. *He reaches about blindly for the* CHILD. *The drum plays the lup dup heartbeat of a panicked child. The* PREACHER *finds her and pulls her up. The* COMPANY *and* JOY *make a huge gasp for breath.*)

THE COMPANY (*sing*):
Are your garments
Spotless
Are they
White as snow

JOY *pushes the* PREACHER *away and runs to her* MAMA.

Are you washed in the blood

JOY *looks back at the* PREACHER *on his knees in water up to his neck.*

Of the Lamb?

The silk river is flipped upward. The PREACHER *exits.* LIZZIE *comes up through the middle. She is carrying a paper bag with a crib quilt in it.*

NURSE: What's your name child?
LIZZIE: I was baptized Elizabeth Mary. My family and friends call me Lizzie. But none of 'em was the name I was born with.
A WOMAN (*holding the river*): BLOCK SEVEN.
ANOTHER WOMAN (*holding the river*): THE BUTTERFLY.

*The next scene will be played in three areas: right—*LIZZIE *and* ROSE, *left—the asylum, and upstage—the road. The silk river is flipped upwards and separates to the sides of the stage.*

LIZZIE: Mama, look what I found!
ROSE: Lizzie, where did you find that?
LIZZIE: Out in the shed. I was lookin' for some tools. Whose is it?
ROSE: Yours.
LIZZIE: Did you make it?

ROSE: No.
LIZZIE: Who did then?
ROSE: It was made by your natural mother, Lizzie. She didn't live long enough to finish it.
LIZZIE: Who was she?
ROSE: No one knew very much about her. Just a few things about the time right before she died.
LIZZIE: Can I know? (*Her* MOTHER *appears upstage, carrying two bundles.*)
NURSE: Admitted March 27th . . . Female . . . Approximately eighteen years of age, destitute . . . Found wandering the roads carrying two infants . . . (SARAH *as* MRS. BONHAM *appears and takes* FEMALE BABY.) Female, approximately nine months old . . . Male, approximately three days old, deceased.
ROSE: There were women called Prairie Nightingales. They helped out because there were so few doctors then. They found her and took her to the hospital. (NURSE *and* LIZZIE'S MOTHER *and* MRS. BONHAM *enter the asylum.*)
NURSE: What's your name child? Where's your people? . . . Can you speak? (MRS. BONHAM *indicates that the* MOTHER *is mute. The* NURSE *reaches to touch her jaw.*) Easy now . . . easy. Jaws are locked. . . . Trauma symptoms.
ROSE: She was silent. Sometimes you'd read about things like that happening. It happened a lot with young mothers havin' too many babies too fast . . .
NURSE: That little one needs some rest. . . . (*Referring to dead child still in her grasp.*)
ROSE: or too many troubles. . . .
NURSE: Give him over. We'll take care of him. Come on now . . . you know you have to. (*She holds out her hands and gets the dead child.* NURSE *and* MRS. BONHAM *then exit.*)
LIZZIE: Did I stay with her in the hospital?
ROSE: She couldn't take care of you. They put you in the county orphanage . . . and they buried the baby.
LIZZIE: My brother.
ROSE: They say she was very beautiful. She had long golden hair.
NURSE: Patient discovered this morning with hair cut off to the scalp. Skirt, petticoats, bedsheets ripped up. Search for the instrument proved inconclusive. I'll stay with her Mrs. Bonham. (MRS. BONHAM *gives* NURSE *the sewing basket.*)

LIZZIE: Mrs. Bonham.

NURSE: The patient is sewing the scraps of her garments together. A close watch is kept until we relieve her of the tools. She works feverishly. . . . (*NURSE begins to sew with LIZZIE'S MOTHER.*) When I first came out west I was carrying my firstborn. Many times I was alone and I'd see a duststorm coming right at me. I'd run inside and light the kerosene lamp. Then that wind would start its wailing. I probably would've lost my mind if it wasn't for the piecing. (*LIZZIE'S MOTHER looks, listening to "Butterfly." Sings.*)

There's a certain yellow light
And suddenly everything's quiet
And the dust came toward you
Rising and rolling
Wanting to wrap you inside it

It was dark and cold
When the sand hit
And you'd wake up buried alive
It was just like bein' dead
If not for my butterfly
If not for my butterfly

Ah . . .
Ah . . .
A . . .
  Goes my butterfly
Ah . . .
Ah . . .
Out of the belly of Sheol to the sky

LIZZIE'S MOTHER tries to speak.

NURSE: What . . . what . . . I see it . . . (*LIZZIE'S MOTHER gestures "yes" and continues to try to get the NURSE to understand.*) Give it . . . Give it to . . . Give it to . . . baby. Give it to the Baby! When you finish it, we will. Lie down now.

OFFSTAGE VOICE (*finishing song*):
Goes my butterfly

LIZZIE'S MOTHER lies down.

NURSE: I have not given up hope that she will tell us what happened. . . . (*She exits.*)

ROSE: A couple of months later she passed on. We heard about it and we asked about you.

They brought you out from the nursery in that quilt . . . an untidy little bundle, big blue eyes starin' right up at us.

LIZZIE: Did she ever speak? Did they ever find out about my father or what my real name was?

ROSE: No.

LIZZIE: How old was I when you got me?

ROSE: About a year . . . we weren't sure really . . . Lizzie.

LIZZIE: Yes Mama.

ROSE: I was gonna tell you real soon. You are no different to us than our own flesh and blood. You know that.

LIZZIE: I know.

ROSE: Look at that quilt. She took four stitches at a time before pullin' the thread through. Sick as she was. Four stitches at a time. All these years I've never had the heart to put my needle to it. (*She exits.*)

LIZZIE: When I was alone I looked hard. It was real worn out, not very pretty. It had a single butterfly up in the corner. Four stitches and a space . . . four stitches and a space. But down near the bottom, the stitches got bigger and started goin' all over the place. I turned it over. . . . (*LIZZIE'S MOTHER sits up with the scissors.*) I could see something printed showing through the lining. . . . I got the idea that there was a secret message for me inside . . . maybe my name was written somewhere . . . or hers. (*LIZZIE begins ripping the quilt. LIZZIE'S MOTHER crosses stage and gives her scissors. SARAH and NURSE appear and watch LIZZIE.*)

MRS. BONHAM:	NURSE:
What your name child?	MELANCHOLIA
	INSOMNIA
Where's your people?	DELIRIUM
	DEMENTIA
	CAUSED BY
	INFANT
	DEATH
What's your name child?	

LIZZIE: CHIPPEWA STATE ASYLUM.

NURSE: SUICIDE. (*All exit except LIZZIE.*)

LIZZIE: A piece of a bedsheet. I'd ripped half the thing up. I didn't want to destroy it. So I stuffed all the batting back in and stashed it. I don't want Mama to find out. . . . Now every day I'm sewing a little bit of it back together . . . four stitches and pull four stitches and pull. . . . It's slow goin'.

Schoolhouse music. The COMPANY *enters carrying their stools to set up the Schoolhouse. One passes out small lap hoops, each containing a pieced Schoolhouse Block.)*

THE COMPANY SING ("PIECES OF LIVES"):
This was a piece of
My history
One room schooldays
And a teacher name Miss Jesse

MISS JESSE *enters ringing a bell.*

MISS JESSE: BLOCK EIGHT! SCHOOLHOUSE!

THE COMPANY (*sing, displaying their hoops*):
Pieces of children's lives

Hoops down, they freeze.

LILY (*to the audience*): I really settled into quilting at the Hunter School. Miss Jesse who taught us all our subjects was very interested in that sort of thing. (*The* CHILDREN *unfreeze.*)

MISS JESSE: I am pleased to announce to you children that I have finally received permission from the school board to add the subject of geography to our course of study. You will be the first students at this school ever to have this opportunity. Before we open that wonderful new door, however, we will be spending the next forty-five minutes, as usual, on needlework. (*All the* CHILDREN *get to work except* CYRUS JOHNSON, *in the back of the classroom, who is visibly unenthusiastic about the activity at hand. He spends most of this scene dealing with a pet snake which he's hidden somewhere and which gets away from him; and is generally disruptive throughout.*)

LILY: She called it needlework, and we each had to make one handmade quilt that year. We had to piece and quilt the whole thing by ourselves, and she was real particular about the color and the stitching. If you couldn't find just the right color, she'd let you look in her piecebag. Seemed like her material was always the best. It meant a little bit of Miss Jesse in your quilt.

MISS JESSE (*singing to the tune of "Oh Tannenbaum"*):
Straight and true oh
Straight and true
CHILDREN (*sing*):
Straight and true and even
MISS JESSE: Those are the guidelines for needlework. It is an art and every art requires effort. Take as much care with your design as if you were painting or drawing, and if it's wrong, rip it out. Millicent, that orange will not do. It is vile.

CHILDREN (*with glee*): Vile!

MISS JESSE: Please go to my piecebag and find something more suitable.

A CHILD: Stop it!

MISS JESSE: Cyrus Johnson, just what has provoked this disturbance? Kindly return to your seat and do your piecing. Clara, that is lovely. (CYRUS *returns to his seat.*) Lily, I can see those stitches from way over here and they are as crooked as the teeth of a jack o' lantern. (*All eyes are on* LILY's *hoop.*) You will remove and redo.

LILY: But Miss Jesse, I'm almost . . .

MISS JESSE: Ah, ah, ah—would you leave that shoddy work there to be shaming you for the rest of your days? (*All eyes are on* LILY. LILY *shakes her head "no!" and begins to rip out the stitches.*) Thank you, Lily. (*A scream from one of the* CHILDREN.) Cyrus Johnson, you have a choice. You may either stop disrupting the class and do your running stitches carefully, or you may do your running homeward right now and deal with your parents. (CYRUS *quickly returns to his seat. Takes an awkward stitch.*) That's better. Now that's the way, Lily! (*Tornado alarm sounds. It is very noisy and frightening. The* CHILDREN *begin to panic and scream.* CYRUS *looks out the window.*)

CYRUS: It's a twister, Miss Jesse, a twister and it's aiming straight at us.

THE CHILDREN (*panicked*): A twister! Miss Jesse, a twister. It's coming.

MISS JESSE (*rings the bell and silences them*): Silence. Everyone down to the cellar. Take your slates and go. Cyrus, lift the trap and see that everyone gets down safely. Calmly, children, calmly. Everyone into the ark two by two. (*All descend to the storm cellar. The* CHILDREN *are terrified.* CLARA, *the youngest, needs to be urged down by* CYRUS. MISS JESSE *lights the imaginary kerosene lamp. The* CHILDREN *collect in a clump on the floor, whining and crying. The tornado alarm which has been ringing throughout becomes softer as the* CHILDREN *arrive below. It sounds intermittently through the scene.*) Where is Clara? Do you all have your slates? (*The* CHILDREN *raise their slates.*) Good. Now since we may have to be here for some time . . .

CYRUS: Forty days and forty nights. (CLARA *bursts into tears. The alarm sounds.*)

MISS JESSE: Clara, come to me. Cyrus Johnson, will you kindly hush. Not all the wind is caused by the weather, young man. We will not let this minor disturbance keep us from our appointed course. We will put this time to good use. I was interested to learn while boarding at your houses that your families have come here from all over this country. What better way to explore the subject of geography than to share that information. Your assignment is to write a composition entitled "Where I was born." When they are completed, we will read them aloud. Please begin. (*The* CHILDREN *start to write and* MISS JESSE *engages* CLARA *in a geography game to distract her.*) Clara, now repeat after me. (*Clapping and reciting.*) Augusta on the Kennebec, Maine.

CLARA: Augusta on the Kennebec, Maine. (*All freeze except* LILY.)

LILY: I knew exactly where I was born. It was about ten miles north of town in a half dugout. Well I was ashamed of that, and I wasn't about to tell them and let 'em laugh at me. (LILY *gets an idea and begins to write. The writing is mimed on the schoolhouse hoops. Intro chords for song, "Green Green Green." All unfreeze.*)

MISS JESSE: Time's up. Lily, let's hear what you've written.

LILY (*sings*):
Where I was born
Was North Carolina
In a great white house
With ivory pillars

CHILDREN *start some vocal skepticism.*

'Bout four or five chimneys
Keeping us warm

CHILDREN *react loudly to* LILY's *lying.*

And acres and acres . . .
CYRUS (*sings*):
And hundreds
LILY (*sings*):
And thousands of acres
Of rolling green lawns
Oh the green, green, green
Of the rolling green lawns.

CHILDREN *react, raising hands trying to get attention.*

MISS JESSE: Hush, listen to her! Now that's the way Lily!

LILY (*sings*):
Where I was born
We had white picket fences
And the lawns went rolling
Clear down to the road
And disappeared

And that great wooden house
Was like a ship
On an ocean of green
And there's no green quite
Like it out here

Oh the green, green, green
Of the rolling green lawns
MISS JESSE AND LILY (*sing*):
Oh the green green green
ALL (*sing*):
Of the rolling green lawns.

LILY *tosses the slate to* CYRUS *who shows it to* MISS JESSE. *They all freeze except* LILY.

LILY (*turning out of the scene*): Many years later my husband crossed the ocean on a real great ship to go to a cattleman's convention in Europe. He wanted me to go too but I'm too Scotch, and anyway they were all goin' on a tour and you had to do just what they told you every minute. (*Underscoring begins.*) I stayed home and quilted all the time . . . made the most beautiful quilt—a colonial lady that could have lived in that great wooden house with the ivory pillars. (*Back in the storm cellar.*)

MISS JESSE (*reading and singing*):
Oh the green green green

LILY (*sits in original stool*):
Of the rolling green lawns

MISS JESSE: Why, Lily, you have written a poem! (*LILY and MISS JESSE beam at each other. Music tags the scene. All unfreeze. "Four Doves in a Window" underscores the following.*)

SARAH (*picking up the next patch*): My mama pieced the "Doves in a Window," set it together, and I quilted it. I wouldn't take nothin' for it. It was the second quilt I made. In the summers, we'd put up the frame on the screened porch and when the work was done for the day, Mama would say, "OK girls, let's go to it." That was the signal for good times and laughin'. We'd pull up our chairs around the frame and anyone that dropped in would do the same, even if they couldn't stitch straight. Course we'd take out their stitches later if they was really bad. But it was for talking and visiting that we put up quilts in the summer. People would get out after the chores in the summertime and oh how the word would fly that we had the frame up. Had to have a screened porch 'cause sometimes you'd quilt and visit till midnight by lamplight with the bugs battin' against the screen. I guess we were the Doves in the Window then. And that's BLOCK NINE—FOUR DOVES IN A WINDOW. (*She displays it. A school bell rings. As SARAH exits, four GIRLS run onstage from different corners of the space. They twitter and coo and dance around each other giggling. They ask each other with great interest and secrecy, almost at once.*)

FOUR GIRLS: Have you? No. Have you? No. (*All have answered "No." They shriek with the anticipation of it all and scurry offstage. The school bell sounds again. The four enter again; only NAN has changed in some small way. She walks instead of running or she affects a womanly posture. All meet again at center, and repeat the questioning as before. After all the other GIRLS have answered "No."*)

NAN: Yes. (*The others shriek in horror and run offstage, leaving NAN alone. She comes downstage and kneels. Praying.*) Dear God, why has this happened to me? They teach us that you're good and loving and forgiving and only punish bad people and sinners. I don't remember doing anything to deserve this. Mama calls it the "curse" and says that all girls get it and have it till they're old. Why would you want to put a curse on all the girls? Lord, it hurts so much sometimes in my stomach and my back, I think there's something wrong inside of me. I'm so afraid, too, that people will see, that it'll show through. It's bad enough that it comes from *there,* but God, why did you have to make it red? And Lord, if it happens to every girl, why did you choose me to be first? All the other girls think I'm . . . awful or somethin'. Please, Lord, what I'm asking of you is, *please,* make it go away. I ask this in Jesus' name. A-men. (*The school bell sounds again. The three other GIRLS enter as before, and meet at center.*)

THREE OTHER GIRLS: Have you? No. Have you? No. Have you?

GIRL TWO: Yes. (*All shriek and run offstage. NAN and GIRL TWO together, embracing. The school bell sounds again. They all enter. GIRL THREE waddles in.*)

ALL (*to BECKY*): Have you?

BECKY: No.

ALL (*to GIRL THREE*): Have you?

GIRL THREE: Yes. (*They shriek in acceptance. NAN, TWO and THREE go off together. BECKY tries to follow. They snub her.*)

BECKY (*kneels*): Lord? Why is this happening to me? Is there something wrong with me? Mother says my time will come, just like all the other girls, but I'm afraid I'm some sort of mistake. I mean, just *look* at me. (*Indicating her chest*). I see everyone staring at me, wondering what's the matter with me. Grandma says it's a gift from you. Well, if you can give it to all the other girls, why can't you give it to me? Lord, I'm askin' this one thing and I'll never ask anything again. *Please* make it come. In the name of the Father, Son, and Holy Ghost. A-men. (*School bell rings. She exits. MRS. PRENTISS and MOLLY enter.*)

MRS. PRENTISS: Dear Friends: I am holding a piecing party at my home on the first Saturday of next month to celebrate the occasion of my son Jamie's twenty-first birthday. We will be making a quilt top for him and would be honored if you would participate. Please bring some swatches or any usable scrap. The colors will be the traditional red, white, and blue. The fabric and pattern may be anything you choose. Following the sewing bee, there will be food and drink and merriment of course. Please let me know if you can come. Sincerely, Margaret Prentiss.

LAVINIA, PRU, ELLY, FELICITY, and SARAH as AUNT MATTIE enter singing and carry their stools into the sewing circle.

ALL (*Singing: "The Needle's Eye"*):
Happy birthday to Jamie
Happy birthday
On the eve of your majority

The jig is played. MRS. PRENTISS *motions them to sit.* MOLLY *passes a sewing basket around from which they extract imaginary needles. All use their actual skirts as the fabric they are "sewing" on. They mime sewing in tempo while singing.*

The needle's eye
It doth supply
The thread that runs so true

There's many a beau
That I let go
Because I wanted you you you
Because I wanted you

All focus down on the next stitch. PRU *turns out.*

PRU: Jamie, I know deep down in my heart that someday in the near future, you will come round and realize, as I do, that we are destined to be together forever. That day will be the happiest day of my life. You have told me many secrets, James Prentiss, but my secret I never told you. My inscription reads simply (*singing*):
Yours
Till the sun grows cold
And the stars are old
And the leaves of the judgment
Book unfold
Pru . . .

The COMPANY *resumes sewing.*

ALL (*sing*):
The needle's eye
It doth supply
The thread that runs so true

There's many a beau
That I let go
Because I wanted you you you
Because I wanted you

All take the next stitch and freeze focused down.

LAVINIA (*turning out*): Jamie, there are hearts hidden in this design. It's supposed to be unlucky to sew 'em before the engagement is official, but I just can't wait. You have to look real hard to see them though. I can't stand that you don't think you should speak with Daddy just yet, 'cause that means I can't tell anybody and I'm just bustin' with the news. But since you want it that way, I will obey you. I may as well get used to obeying you, Sweetheart, 'cause it looks like I'll be doing it for a long time. But Darlin', don't let's wait too long. I'm not that patient. (*Singing.*)
Yours till Wichita Falls
(*Spoken.*) Did you find the hearts? (*Singing.*)
Lavinia Hall

She turns back into the circle.

AUNT MATTIE (*turning out*): James, you've always been my favorite nephew, so I'm not going to mince words. Everyone will be wanting a piece of you . . . so don't spread yourself too thin. (*Singing.*)
With all my love Aunt Mattie
PRU: (*sings, showing her inscription*):
Till the leaves of the judgment
Book unfold . . . (*spoken*) Pru
LAVINIA (*overlapping*):
Lavinia Hall
AUNT MATTIE (*overlapping*):
With all my love
Aunt Mattie
THE COMPANY (*beginning to use their feet in the dance, sing*):
The needle's eye
It doth supply
The thread that runs so true . . .
MOLLY (*turns out, interrupting the song*): How I envy you, Jamie, not belonging to nobody and not havin' nobody tellin' you what to do all the time. Seems like I'm never gonna have my freedom. Everything a girl ever does belongs to someone else, don't you know. Like all the

quilts we get go to our husbands, and I ain't never gettin' married, that's for darn sure. Remember when we was little, and you'd tease me about my freckles and my stringy hair, and I'd try to beat you up and I'd end up tearing all my clothes and getting the punishment? Well, I tried to get a patch off that old skirt I wore then, but it just fell apart in my hands. So I stole a piece of this from Mama's special scrap. Recognize it? It was the first time you ever told me I looked pretty in anything. I wore it when you took me to town. And remember that man thought we was man and woman instead of brother and sister? I saw pictures of some faraway places in town. Sure would like to see 'em someday. Maybe we could go together, seein' as how I ain't never gettin' married. (*Singing.*)
Love ya
Sister Molly

THE COMPANY (*sing*):
There's many a beau
That I told no-o (*Yip.*)

They freeze.

MOLLY: P.S. I like your new girl . . . she has freckles!

THE COMPANY (*sing*):
Because I'm waiting
Here for you
I'm waiting here for you

ELLY: Remember this calico print? You should. You had a hard time keepin' your hands off it. I wore it the time you called on me promisin' to marry and be true. Well we sealed that promise, James Earl Prentiss, and whatever you think, I done what I done all for the love of you. And now I'm practically gone crazy with the shame of it, and waiting for you to come round. What's keeping you from me, Jamie? I thought we really had something special. Well, I'm not gonna beg you. I still have my pride . . . but I'm here. And I'm sewing the Wild Goose Chase pattern into my block because sometimes that's what lovin' you feels like. And I'll tell you somethin' else. If I get near that simp I hear you're fiddlin' with, I'm gonna tear her hair out. You'll always belong to me, Jamie, no matter how free you think you are.

ELLY turns in. FELICITY turns out.

COUSIN FELICITY:
If you are not handsome at 20
Not strong at 30
Not rich at 40
Not wise at 50
You never will be.
Well, James, you got the handsome part down.

PRU: I know deep down in my heart that (*ELLY starts her line.*) we are destined to be together forever.

ELLY: You'll always belong to me, Jamie (*LAVINIA starts her line.*) no matter how free you think you are.

LAVINIA: But darlin', don't let's wait (*MOLLY starts her line.*) too long. I'm not that patient.

MOLLY: Maybe we can go together (*AUNT MATTIE looks up.*) seein' as how I'm never getting married. (*COUSIN FELICITY has watched all the previous lines.*)

COUSIN FELICITY: Good luck. (*Singing.*)
Cousin Felicity

FELICITY turns in. MRS. PRENTISS turns out.

MRS. PRENTISS: My dearest son . . . I am making this centerpiece for the quilt which will simply say. (*Singing.*)
Friendship
(*Spoken.*) May you always be surrounded by as many "friends" as you have now.

One at a time, the COMPANY enters singing their inscriptions. They begin to overlap and finally they sing simultaneously in great cacophony.

THE COMPANY:

Elly		
Friendship		
	Elly	
		Friendship
Yours till Wichita Falls	Yours till the leaves of the	
Lavinia	Judgment book unfold . . . Pru	
With all my love	Lavinia	Love ya sister
Aunt Mattie	Cousin Felicity	Molly

Now they all sing simultaneously.

Pru	Lavinia	With all of my	
Pru	Lavinia	All o my	
Pru	Lavinia	All o my	
Pru	Lavinia	All o my	
Pru	Lavinia	All o my	
Pru	Lavinia	All o my	
Pru	Lavinia	All o my	
Pru	Hall	Love	
Molly	Elly	Felicity	Friendship
Molly	Elly	Felicity	(etc.)
Molly	Elly	(etc.)	
Molly	Elly		
Molly	Elly		
Molly	Elly		
Molly	Elly		
Molly	Elly		

They put the lid on their excitement and sing the last chorus together with a kind of spirited foot movement. A seated dance. Singing.

The needle's eye
It doth supply
The thread that runs so true
There's many a beau
I'll never know
Because of loving you you you

They break their imaginary thread with their teeth.

Because of loving you
Happy twenty-one
James Earl Prentiss
Here's your freedom quilt!

They display their skirts spread out.

BLACKOUT

END OF ACT ONE

ACT TWO

The musicians are discovered onstage playing a lively square dance tune [The Entr'Acte]. Five stools are arranged in a tight circle at center. After the music establishes itself JANIE *comes in with a broom to sweep the stage and* SARAH *is adding some finishing touches to the decoration for the dance. The rest gather in a line, as at a social, waiting for the next dance to be called. The music finishes.*

SARAH: When a girl was thinkin' on marryin', and we all done a lot of that, she had to start thinkin' on gettin' her quilts pieced.
FIDDLER: BLOCK TEN.
ALL THE MUSICIANS: THE LONE STAR.

The GIRLS *excitedly move down to the circle of stools. Each pulls a handkerchief from her pocket which is held between her hand and that of her imaginary male partner. As the "Quiltin' and Dreamin'" instrumental begins, a waltz, all bow to the stools and begin to dance around.* LOU ANN *is the clumsiest of the dancers, bumping and apologizing throughout. At a given point, each* LADY *lifts a stool which becomes her male partner.* LOU ANN *doesn't get one. She stands aside, wallflower style and dances with the broom. At the end of the waltz all the* DANCERS *sashay off to the sides with their stools and sit down.*

SARAH: As a little girl, I remember hearing the saying, "A maid who is quiltless at twenty-one, never shall greet her bridal sun." I started quiltin' for my Hope Chest when I was eleven. Why, a baker's dozen of quilts was often the only dowry you had . . . and a sack of potatoes was what you paid the preacher man with. It took a whole lot of cover to keep warm in one of them old open houses on the plains.
LOU ANN: Now the way I done mine was real nice I think. Papa had laid up a beautiful arbor in the brush he had cleared from the land. It was just set up a ways back of the house. Well, I just went out under that arbor, set up my frame, and went to quiltin' outdoors. (LOU ANN *has set up a quilting frame during this speech.*) Now some thought that was real funny, but I sure thought

it was nice. Mama gave me one real beautiful quilt top, a Lone Star, (*She reveals the "Lone Star" block in her quilting frame.*) that she had done herself. I quilted it and made three by myself that I don't reckon were much to look at, but I was awful proud of them then. And that's what I set out with when I married my sweetheart. Now that's a story. (*Underscoring begins for "Quiltin' and Dreamin.' "*) You won't believe it to look at me now but I married me the finest lookin' young man for three counties around when I was eighteen. And I didn't meet him at no dance neither. I don't reckon I would have stood a chance there. These big size tens were never so graceful. They're just good strong platforms for standin' on. Anyway, what I was doin' was . . . (*sings*)

Setting' there under the quiltin' arbor
Of an afternoon in the spring
It was the fourteenth
Day of April
And the meadowlarks did sing

She begins to quilt.

Thinkin' while quiltin' through
Blue, pink and purple
All the happy colors of
My design
I must've had
The wild prairie flowers
Somewhere in the back of
My mind

CHORUS:
Quiltin' and dreamin' a dream
On every stitch
Conj'rin' up a cowboy for my
Husband to be

ONE *of the COMPANY begins to play the part of Cowboy John. "He" moves around the corners of the stage on a "horse." Rides by the fiddler and removes her cowboy hat, placing it on "his" head.*

Longin' for to see him
The one who'd lie dreamin'
Underneath my lone star
With me

LOU ANN, *lost in her reverie, falls off her stool.*

THE COMPANY (*sing*):
Settin' there under the
Quiltin' arbor
Of an afternoon
In the spring
LOU ANN (*sings*):
Laughin' and blushin'
And prickin' my fingers
Rippin' out some crazy seams
THE COMPANY (*sing*):
Quiltin' and dreamin' a dream
On every stitch
Conj'rin' up a cowboy
Strummin' on a guitar

Dreamin' bout the carin'
When two become one
Sharin' life beneath my lone star
Beneath my lone (star)
LOU ANN (*sings*):
Sharin' life beneath my lone star!
COWBOY JOHN (*steps into her space*): Pardon me, ma'am . . . didn't mean to startle you. But I been seein' you out here every day for weeks and I just got up my nerve to come over and speak to you and see what you were workin' on with such care.
LOU ANN (*to audience*): Lordy now, I married him and as I recall it now that was the longest speech he ever said at one time to this day.
COWBOY JOHN: BLOCK ELEVEN. (LOU ANN *throws another quilted patch at him. He opens it.*)
LOU ANN: DOUBLE WEDDING RINGS. (*Music: "Pieces of Lives." The* COWBOY *displays the block and* LOU ANN *stands next to him behind it in a wedding picture pose. The* COMPANY *behind as* BRIDESMAIDS *and* FAMILY.)
THE COMPANY (*sings*):
This was a piece of
My wedding dress
Love and laughter
And tenderness
LOU ANN (*sings*):
Tenderness
SARAH: I think this is the prettiest one I ever made. (JOHN *calls his "horse" and puts his* BRIDE *in the saddle.*)

THE COMPANY (*sing*):
All of the remnant
The raiment
The moment of a woman's
Life

JOHN and LOU ANN ride off under the wedding canopy which is being held up by the COMPANY, into the sunset. A yip and the canopy is dropped and the COMPANY exits.

CORA (*coming downstage*): There was always lots of soldiers around here then. And they was always lookin' for girls. Sometimes they'd leave signs on their tents.

WOMAN ONE (*peering out from behind the tent flap*): WANTED—LOVEABLE HOUSEKEEPER!

WOMAN TWO (*from behind another tent flap*): WANTED—A GIRL: MUST BE KIND TO DOGS.

CORA: At old Fort McPherson during the Indian Wars they shipped in a whole bunch of Irish girls to be laundresses. Most of them good lookin' girls found themselves married in a day or so. I was one of 'em. They say it took a week or two for the homely ones. (*CORA exits. CLARA enters with chores to do. She is actually setting up the "stove" [a sewing basket set in an inverted stool] and the kitchen area for the next scene.*)

CLARA: I was born on a mountain but I don't hardly remember bein' a girl. I was married to a man when I was not quite fifteen years old. I was figurin' a while back and I reckon he was thirty-two at the time. I suppose I liked him some then. But I was jest like all the rest of the girls on the mountain. We thought if we could get married and leave home we wouldn't have to work so blasted hard. Ha! Little did we know what kind of work we was gettin' into. I had the first baby nine months and eighteen days after we married. (*CLARA exits. The WOMEN in the next scene enter, one at a time, through the hanging quilt, with the utensils they will need in the "Secret Drawer."*)

WOMAN ONE: My first baby we named Glenn. I was just a baby myself when we had him but I couldn't have been prouder.

WOMAN FOUR: My firstborn was Edwin. That little baby was the light of my life.

WOMAN TWO (*to the audience*): Second came Alice. She was no bigger than a minute but she could yell louder than anybody.

WOMAN THREE (*enters carrying the quilted "Secret Drawer" patch, folded up wrong side out*): Our third baby was stillborn. (*WOMAN THREE gives the quilt bundle to SARAH.*) My fourth was Mark. He was dark and slender and smart as a whip. (*WOMAN THREE joins ONE at stove.*)

WOMAN ONE (*to WOMAN THREE*): Begin by boiling in a quarter of water . . . (*The WOMEN freeze as SARAH announces:*)

SARAH: BLOCK TWELVE.

WOMAN TWO: Shadow Block. (*Shadow Block lighting.*)

SARAH (*displaying the block*): SECRET DRAWER.

SECRET DRAWER. SHADOW BLOCK

SARAH exits quickly. This scene will be played with four areas: the kitchen upstage, two separate downstage areas for MABEL LOUISE and HARRIET, and a fourth for the DOCTOR's office. The business at the stove should be underscored with spare musical sound effects. When the WOMEN upstage are not taking their turn at the stove, they should be focused into the distance, keeping a lookout. The litany of their children should be directed to the audience. The recipe, to each other.

WOMAN ONE (*coming to life*): . . . one tablespoon klipsweet and one tablespoon pennyroyal. (*WOMAN THREE empties the imaginary contents of two thimbles into the pot.*) Let it boil for fifteen minutes. (*WOMAN ONE stirs the mixture with a wooden spoon as light come up on HARRIET.*)

HARRIET: Dear Mabel Louise. Another Durham came into the world last month. This one we named Robert Burns Durham. Little Robert gave me quite a scare being born. Andrew was gone loggin' and it was a howlin' norther outside. I broke water and was having too much pain. Feelin' that baby with my hands I knew for certain it was gonna breach. I put the kids to bed to keep warm, and told the older ones to keep the fire goin' no matter what. We got a little room tacked onto the back and I got in there under my quilts and Lordy did I pray for Andrew to come back. He came blowin' in that night. Said he just had a feelin'. I was never so glad to see anyone. He pulled that baby out.

WOMAN ONE (*hands the spoon to* THREE *and moves downstage to join the lookout*): My fifth baby was Jane. She was our first girl and the apple of her daddy's eye. Sixth came Betty. Oh what a little scamp she was.

WOMAN THREE (*stirring*): Let's see, my seventh child we named Benjamin. He was named after his granddaddy because of his pretty wavy hair. Eighth after Ben came Nan. She was always the quiet one.

WOMAN TWO: Add a cup of quinine and continue boiling for five minutes. (*She adds imaginary quinine from a real cup. Lights up on* MABEL LOUISE.)

MABEL LOUISE: Dear Harriet. It seems like it's just been one baby after another. I'm pregnant with number eight and wondering how we'll ever get along with another one. It's like Mama always used to say, "I wouldn't take a million dollars for any of my kids, but I wouldn't give a nickel for another one."

WOMAN TWO (*stirring*): Number nine was Daniel. He was born during the drought and didn't get a proper bath until he was walkin'.

WOMAN ONE: Our ninth baby died when he was just ten days old—the cholera. Ten and eleven were the twins.

WOMAN FOUR: Remove from the fire and add one eighth teaspoon of iron sulphate. (*As* WOMAN TWO *pulls the pot off the stove,* WOMAN FOUR *adds the iron sulphate. They react to its fumes.*)

HARRIET: Dear Mabel Louise. All the children are asleep finally so I'm sitting down to write before I go to sleep myself. The children are keeping me busy all the time. Luckily there's not another one on the way. I'm awful afraid of getting pregnant again and that's put a strain on things between me and Andrew.

WOMAN FOUR (*stirring*): The next miscarried. My eleventh one was Margaret. She arrived almost a month early. Gave us quite a scare.

WOMAN ONE: Take a handful of human hair and snip it into small pieces. When swallowed these will bring on stomach contractions. (*The*

WOMAN *with the longest hair offers hers for cutting.*)

MABEL LOUISE: Dearest Sister. Well, it seems we'll be expecting our twelfth child this winter and I frankly don't know what to do or where to turn. I went to see the doctor to ask him for help. (*Lights up on* SARAH *as* DR. BLAKE. MABEL LOUISE *walks into this space.*)

DR. BLAKE: Yes, Mabel Louise, you surely are pregnant again, but you didn't come all this way for me to tell you that.

MABEL LOUISE: Dr. Blake, please, this'll be number twelve for Caleb and me, and I'm almost thirty-five years old. The last one laid me up for two solid months after the birth. I'm scared of another one. Caleb needs me well and strong. If I have to take to bed again after the birth . . . or if I die . . . I don't know what'll happen to my family. Doctor, I'm askin' for your *help*.

DR. BLAKE: Mabel Louise, believe me, I sympathize with your situation. But if you're askin' me what I think you're askin', you know I can't. My oath forbids taking a life.

MABEL LOUISE: I'm scared for my life and the lives of my children if you don't help me. Please, Doctor Blake, I'm begging ya now for relief. Please

DR. BLAKE (*after a time*): Mabel Louis, I'm gonna forget we ever had this conversation and I suggest you do the same. I'm sorry, but you're just going to have to live with this. There's nothing I can do.

WOMAN ONE: My twelfth was Ellie.

WOMAN FOUR: Miscarried.

WOMAN TWO: My thirteenth was Alan. (*At this point the naming turns into a kind of intoned chant. The* WOMEN *also are involved in a subtle rocking motion.*)

WOMAN THREE: My fourteenth was Matthew.

WOMAN ONE: Miscarried.

WOMAN FOUR: My fifteenth was Luke.

WOMAN TWO: My sixteenth was Samuel.

WOMAN ONE: Miscarried

WOMAN THREE: Miscarried.

WOMAN ONE (*speaking*): Pour the mixture in a cup and allow it to cool slightly.

HARRIET: Dear Mabel Louise. I have come across a recipe that I hope will be the answer to our prayers. A woman I know of knows another woman who has used it herself. My friend guarantees it will relieve you of your problem. The ingredients are simple and I hope available to you. After you've followed the enclosed recipe . . .

WOMAN FOUR: Stir the hair into the mixture. (*This is done.*)

HARRIET: When it has cooled you must drink the whole thing down at once. The taste is unpleasant, but you must drink it all. (*MABEL LOUISE meets WOMAN ONE at center. ONE brings the cup. MABEL LOUISE drinks the potion and goes upstage to lie down on the childbirth quilt which has been laid down for her. The WOMEN move downstage of her and raise their skirts creating a barrier around her—chanting their children's names softly as they go.*) My friend tells me that you are likely to feel quite uncomfortable for a time, but it will all be over in a few hours. You should have time enough after putting Caleb and the children to bed. I wish I could be with you my darling sister. I hate to think of you carrying this burden alone. My thoughts and prayers are with you. Your loving sister, Harriet.

HARRIET:	WOMAN ONE:	WOMAN TWO:
Paul, Peter,	Glenn, Robert,	Andy, Alice
Laura, Robert,	Oscar, Seth,	Donald, Edith,
James,	Jane, Betty,	Gabriel,
Catherine,	Mary, Edward,	Thomas,
Richard,	James, Michael,	Leslie
Belinda,	Donald, Ellie	Timothy
Jenny, Will,		Daniel, Alan,
Dorothy,		Samuel, John
Charlotte		

WOMAN THREE:	WOMAN FOUR:
Eleanor, Mark,	Edwin, Christy,
Kimberly, William,	Theodore, Douglas,
Travis, Benjamin,	Ruth, Gilbert, Isaac,
Nan, John, Martin,	Wilhelmina, Joseph,
Matthew, Jay, Stephen	Margaret, Zachary, Luke

We are aware of violent movement from MABEL LOUISE under the cloth. The chanting builds in intensity. MABEL LOUISE screams. Lights dim. In the darkness the fugue dwindles down until we hear the chanting of only one voice—SARAH's. Lights up.

SARAH: Jenny, Lisa, Jane, John, Jody, we sure went in for those J names, ah, Margaret, Dana, Joseph, and Ted. I quilt right here every day

with all the family pictures up there in front of me. It gives me a good feelin'. Makes me think of the times you kids were little and always crawlin' around under my feet. It doesn't seem so long ago. (*"Log Cabin" block is shown.*) Well, I hope I can keep up and get this quilt finished. My arthritis is slowin' me down again. Gettin' old just never did agree with me. When people ask me where I get so much energy at my age, I tell 'em, "I don't have time to get old—I'm too busy." Sometimes my hands get so bad though I can't do any quiltin' at all and just the simplest piecin'. That's why I like this next pattern—the "Log Cabin." It's just skinny strips sewn one to the other—nothin' fancy but it sure turns out pretty. And you can make this pattern from the tiniest of remnants, the bottom of the barrel—as long as they're the same width. Some of these belonged to my babies and some of them was given to me by my mama, her children's clothes. (*Chord. The MOTHER in "Log Cabin," appears.*)

MOTHER: The apple never falls far from the tree, Sarah.

SARAH: Me and Mama, we never could throw anything away.

MOTHER: One thing about havin' so many children. They could turn the hardest work into fun if they had a mind to. All those months of puttin' up the new house. (*CHILD ONE, the STORYTELLER, climbs onto the upstage ladder and begins clapping rhythmically.*)

CHILD ONE (*Storyteller*): BLOCK THIRTEEN! (*She is answered in rhythm by the four other CHILDREN who are carrying in a stack of large lumber.*)

THE OTHERS: LOG CABIN! (*The rhythmic pulse is augmented by having the bass player "slap" the back of his instrument.*)

ALL (*sing*):
Every log in my house
Straight as a pine can grow

STORYTELLER: All his life my father was a lumberman.

THE COMPANY (*sing*):
Every log in my house
Straight as a pine can grow

STORYTELLER: We lived in a forest near Hot Sulphur Springs. (*This game is a kind of Simon*

Says. The COMPANY *assists by constructing the cabin using ropes and poles.*) He always whistled when he worked.

THE COMPANY (*sing*):

Ooo. . .

STORYTELLER: Sometimes he and Mama would whistle harmony. We all turned to listen to that when it happened. (*They do.*) I was always allowed to choose if I wanted to work outside with Papa or inside with Mama.

THE COMPANY: Outside with Papa!

STORYTELLER: He built our house. (*The COMPANY raises the poles.*) It was a log cabin . . . and it was plenty big. It had a fireplace. . . . *The rope is thrown out. Sawhorses are used.*) . . . It had four rooms. He had plans all laid out to make it bigger. (*Something precarious happens.*) When the family grew and he had time. He put such care in fitting everything just perfect. (STORYTELLER *puts some finishing detail on the construction. Song: "Every Log in My House":*)

THE COMPANY (*singing*):

Every log in my house
Straight as a pine can grow
Every log in my house
Straight as a pine can grow

Every room has a window
And every room has a door
And there's a dandelion carpet
Growing through the floor

Growing through the
Growing through the
Growing through the floor

COMPANY *jumps the rope.*

Jump jump jump
The rocky mountains

Jump jump jump
The rocky mountains

Jump the Rocky Mountains
Jump the Rocky Mountains (*etc.*)

MOTHER: We had that whole house finished except for the floorboards. Now, we'd been told over and over, "You have to lay floorboards in the dark of the moon, otherwise they'll curl up and never fit straight." But we were so anxious to move in and the children were so excited, that we went ahead and laid them floorboards under a waxin' moon. And wouldn't you know it, every last one of them boards warped and shrank up and left huge cracks between 'em. The kids never minded it though; they'd always be jumpin' from one board to the other. Sometimes it would drive you crazy. . . . (CHILD TWO *is jumping around upstage with a container of something in her hand. To* CHILD TWO.) You spill that and there'll be a lickin' lyin' in the salt for you when your Daddy comes home . . . hear?

CHILD TWO: Don't worry, Mama. (*As soon as* MAMA *turns her back,* CHILD TWO *is at it again. The rest of the* KIDS, *ever exuberant, jump into the house.*)

CHILD ONE: The cows are milked.

CHILD THREE: The wood is stacked.

CHILD FOUR: Took care of the chickens.

MOTHER: All right, all right, everyone. Get ready for bed. We have a big day tomorrow. (*The* CHILDREN *move to the middle area with sounds of complaint and begin preparing for bed: warming their clothes by the fire, combing each other's hair, fighting, etc.*)

CHILD TWO: After all living together in one room for so long, our cabin seemed like a palace to us. Mama's room was called the "best room" and it was in the front. In the back was Papa's workroom. We had a lean-to kitchen and all the kids slept off to the sides . . .

MOTHER: . . . most of the time. (*The* KIDS *are lying down, head to toe, tucked in like kittens in a basket or the strips in a "Log Cabin" pattern.*) The first night in we were so tired everyone slept like logs. Now that's a funny expression 'cause soon after, when Papa took the stock off to market and left us all alone, I began to notice that the logs weren't sleepin' at all. (MOTHER *has spread a quilt on the floor and gotten under it. Eerie sounds begin . . . like a squeaky door.* CHILD TWO *sits up and moves to the doorway of* MAMA's *room.*)

CHILD TWO: Mama!

MOTHER: What's the matter, honey? You should be sleepin'.

CHILD TWO: I can't. There's all kindsa strange noises here. Mama? (MOTHER *motions for the*

CHILD *to get in bed with her. She crawls under the covers. Noises begin again. Children* THREE *and* FOUR *wake up.*)

CHILD THREE (*at* MAMA's *doorway*): Mama, can I sleep with you?

CHILD FOUR: Can I? (MOTHER *motions them in. Before she knows it,* ONE *and* FIVE *have scrambled and snuck into her bed. There is a great pulling of the covers which should just barely do the job. All settle down, snuggled together like kittens. Squeaky-door log noises begin again.*)

CHILD TWO: Mama, what's that noise?

MOTHER: It's the logs.

CHILD THREE: How can they make noises if they're dead?

MOTHER (*sleepily*): Well, some of 'em been alive for 150 years . . . guess they ain't gonna stop now. (TWO *and* THREE *are satisfied with the answer. They lie down. More noises. . . . This time pops, and gurgles and hisses join the squeaky-door sounds.*)

CHILD THREE (*whispering to* TWO): Sounds like they're talkin' to each other.

CHILD TWO: What if they're uncomfortable bein' so close together? What if they're havin' a fight?

CHILD THREE: What if they bust apart and the whole house comes tumblin' down?

CHILD FIVE: What if snakes come? (*All shriek with fear, delighting in the shrieking.*)

MOTHER: They won't! Your daddy fit them true. I'm sure they're snug and comfortable. Now go to sleep . . . everyone! (MOTHER *pushes them gently to lie down. . . . They do, like petals of a flower opening. When they land, they snuggle even closer all around* MOTHER's *seated body, heads tucked into necks, etc.* MOTHER *can no longer lie down. She falls asleep propped up by the barrier of bodies. After they settle, noises begin again.*)

CHILD TWO: Mama.

MOTHER (*barely conscious now*): What is it now?

CHILD TWO: If the logs are still alive, ya think maybe the house'll keep growing? (*No answer. Log noises.* CHILD TWO *lies down eyes wide open. A final "pop." Lights change.* COMPANY *strikes the log cabin.* SARAH *enters with the folded "Country Crossroads" block.*)

SARAH: When you get on in years sleep doesn't come all that easy. I don't hardly remember sleepin' a whole night through anymore. If it's not the arthritis that wakes me, it's these fool dreams I'm havin'. There's one where I'm rushin' to finish my quilt . . . and I lost the last pattern. I've had that a coupla times. I set it aside myself, but I can't find where and I can't remember it. Serves me right. I'm an old quilter, but it took Job's patience for me ever to do the same pattern twice. Nowadays I can pick up something I made a while back like this here, and look at it and think, "Was it me that made this? I couldn't figure out that pattern now." It's just like lookin' at the work of a stranger. (SARAH *hands the block to* JANIE, *who hangs it on the clothesline stretched across the upstage area. The clothesline moves on pulleys.*)

JANIE (*hanging the block*): Look at that Mama. That's your work all right. The pictures change, but the feelin's, that's Sarah through and through. BLOCK FOURTEEN . . . COUNTRY CROSSROADS. (JANIE *sends this patch across the stage.* BETTY *hangs a patch on the line while* SARAH *speaks.*)

SARAH: Let me see . . . I figure I've made about one hundred quilts in my lifetime. Not bad. I have one quilt that took me twenty-five years to assemble. And those were twenty-five after-puttin-the-children-to-bed years. My husband used to say to me, "Are you ever gonna put those needles down?" But there I'd be, night after night, deep into the stitches and the midnight oil. Those twenty-five years took me through a lot of changes. Some of 'em not so pretty. I tremble sometimes when I remember what that quilt knows about me.

(*Sings.*): Twenty-five years to make a comfort
That is longer lasting than a life
Twenty-five years I labored gladly
Who will count the stitches?

Sarah the child and child bearer
The wife and woman I was taken for

DAUGHTERS (*sing*):
The stitches tell all of these
And many Sarah's more
Who will count the stitches?

During her speech BETTY *hangs all of the patches revealed earlier onto the clothesline.*

BETTY: Now my husband always helps me with the quiltin'. He ain't ashamed of it. He's good at it. I bet if I showed you quiltin' both of us done, you couldn't tell the different between his stitches and mine. I remember that first time the census taker got out here. Now there wasn't no roads then nor anything but mesquite as far as the eye could see. One day here come this lady riding sidesaddle in a long skirt from out the brush. She had on gloves. She come right up in the yard and says, "I'm the census taker. I like to never found ya." Then she took this big old book out of her saddlebag. My husband asked her, "What's that for?" She said, "To count up all the folks and see what they're doin'." Well, he took that lady aside and showed her all the quilts we made together. And then he tells her, "I only do the quiltin'. The wife there's the artist. . . . She's the one that makes the light shine. Put that down in your book." (*Dulcimer intro.*)

EMILY (*sings*):
I have heard of a land
On a faraway strand
It's a beautiful home of the soul

Built by Jesus on high
Where we never will die
It's a land where we'll
Never grow old

All sing together softly.

Never grow old
Never grow old
In a land where we'll never grow old

Never grow old
Never grow old
In a land where we'll never grow old

KATHERINE: No. I never married. Once, I almost did, but it didn't work out. I was twenty-seven years old. I was quite a go-getter in those days. Very headstrong. I'd been away to teachers college and was very definite about my career. Well, I was sick when I was younger, and I couldn't have children. It didn't bother me though, I was so busy with my teaching and my church work and all. So, anyway this doctor came to town. He was from California. My, he was so handsome. He had a gap-toothed grin that would stop your heart. Well, we just fell in love, you know. I'd never thought about marrying anybody before . . . never met anybody I'd consider spending my life with. But him, well, I thought he was pretty special. Right off, I told him about not being able to have children. I wanted that out in the open right off. I told him I was happy with my work and it didn't make a bit of difference to me. Maybe later on, you know, if I changed my mind, I might want to adopt some kids, but all in all, it suited me just fine. He looked me right in the eye and said it suited him fine too. He said he'd never been so sure about kids himself, and even so, it was me he wanted and that was enough. We had a few months of happiness after that. Oh, he could be so much fun. Then one day he told me he'd made a mistake. He really did want children real bad. I could tell by the way it kinda tore him up that he was real sorry. Shortly after that, a woman he knew from California moved to town and they got married. I taught both their children in school before I retired. Like I said, I never married. Living alone always suited me just fine. (*KATHERINE exits.*)

EMILY (*sings*):
In that beautiful home
Where we'll nevermore roam
We shall be in that sweet by and by

ALL: Happy praise to the king
To eternity sing
It's a land where we never shall die.

CASSIE: My husband I married back in Virginia and he wanted to go out west as soon as he could. He got a job laying track for the first railroad into New Mexico. When that job was done he got put to work inspecting twenty miles of track. He walked it. He could do it in a day easy if there wasn't any repair work. I was home caring for the stock and the kids and I wanted to make something nice for him so I started on a quilt that took me two years to finish. I was always hidin' it before he came in . . . sometimes runnin' when he hit the door . . . or stashin' it in the craziest places . . . like one time in the stove. When it was done, I called in Elizabeth, my oldest to give it to him. He took it and studied it and studied it—I was just thinkin' maybe something' was wrong with it, when he rushed

over to me and wrapped the quilt around me, swung me off my feet and sashayed me all around the kitchen. Both of us laughin' to beat the band. He was some man all right. Next spring, I had wrapped up my work for the day and was piecin' up some scraps to cover the baby that was due in the summer. I had just lit the lamp when we heard a lot of horses comin' up the road and ridin' hard. My heart stopped and I reached way down to get my breath and ran out to the porch. There was five men from the railroad. They were sweatin' and talkin' over one another's words. There was this big bushel basket on the ground in front o' them. Jim Rice thought maybe he fell and hit his head on the tracks. Slim Henson thought maybe the heat had got him. None of 'em could figure out why he didn't hear the train. We never did get a clear reason, but they had to bring him home to us in that bushel basket. They tell me I didn't cry or say a word. I just sat down on the porch kinda in a little ball and started rockin' back and forth—rockin and starin', rockin' and starin'. Course I don't remember much now . . . hardly anything in fact. Just what they tell me. I stayed in the back room . . . never came out. I guess it musta been my momma came in and set a piecin' bag in front of me, a needle, a spool of thread, a pair of scissors. I didn't know what those things were for. But one morning, my hands reached out . . . my hands remembered . . . they grabbed the top piece and sewed it to the next piece and the next—didn't matter what it looked like. I never laid a cuttin' edge to any of 'em. Four months later I had a whole quilt and the baby was born; and my eyes came clear again. (*She launches the company into the song: "The Lord Don't Rain Down Manna," singing:*)
The . . .

THE COMPANY (*sing*):
Lord don't rain down manna
In my yard

The COMPANY moves to the clothesline, each removing one of the hanging pieces. Each folds the piece and holds it Bible-fashion while singing. They have moved into a choir configuration with SARAH above them in the pulpit.

Praise God from whom
All blessings flow

The Lord don't rain down manna
Manna in my yard

Praise him all creatures
Here below

Praise him above ye heavenly (host)

When it rains
Don't it though
Muddy waters overflow

The Lord don't rain
Don't rain down manna
It don't rain manna in my yard

Praise Father Son and Holy Ghost

WOMAN ONE (*opening her Bible to display . . .*): BLOCK FIFTEEN . . . CROSSES AND LOSSES.*

FIRE SHADOW BLOCK

ALL (*spoken*): These quilts is from the ladies of the First Baptist Church.
SARAH: Revelations. Chapter 8. (*All open their Bibles.*) And when he opened the seventh seal, there was silence in heaven for the space of half an hour. (*COMPANY bows their heads for a somewhat shorter silence. LILLIAN looks up.*)
LILLIAN: Later they said it was a spark from the engine of the midday train passing through Tyron that started the fire. There had been no

---

*This Block should be developed in a highly stylized fashion. A cataclysm told in cloth. The company begins in the choir configuration but quickly the narration moves from being "outside" of the experience to being "inside" it. Eventually, everyone steps into the action and is baptized by fire. Fire masks are used. These are different shapes and sizes of cloth, all cut from a uniform, transparent, dark material. Some are hoods, masks, shrouds . . . but every character except Sarah emerges from the scene with dark cloth on them to symbolize their having been touched by the fire. And when they look through this transparent fabric, they should appear as the ghoulish, dazed, white-eyed faces we've all seen in the period photographs of similar disasters. The

rain to speak of that summer and the valley was dry as a tinderbox. (*Distant train whistle*.)

SARAH: And he opened the bottomless pit and there arose smoke out of the pit as the smoke of a great furnace. (*A few of the* WOMEN *begin flapping their Bible cloths*.) And the sun and the air were darkened by reason of the smoke of the pit. (*The* COMPANY *begins to enter the experience*.)

MAUREEN: The wind come up and kept the fire movin' and because of the smoke blowin' so thick you couldn't tell where the fire was. It coulda been twenty miles off or just over the next rise.

LILLIAN (*should be played by the same woman who played* MOTHER *in "Log Cabin"*): My husband Bert told us—

BERT: Plow that strip around the house as wide as you can. Everybody—plow like crazy. I'm ridin' off to meet the fire! (*He exits.* LILLIAN *works furiously through her next speech*.)

LILLIAN: Everybody set to plowin' for all we's worth . . . those fireguards would make the fire split off away from the house but it would keep goin' all right . . . sometimes in all different directions. You couldn't stop it; all's you could do was just send it off somewhere else and pray. (*She collapses*.)

THE COMPANY (*sing*):
Praise him above ye heavenly host

SARAH: Their torment was as the torment of a scorpion when he striketh a man.

THE COMPANY: These quilts is from the Ladies of the First Methodist Church. (*The clothesline

---

event of the fire should actually, to some degree, destroy the set. The business of plowing for example, can be dealt with by actually ripping up the ground cloth and stripping the stage back to a dark wood surface . . . a charred earth. The Bible quilts when flapped will create both the image of fighting off the fire, and the sound of the fire. The musicians should augment the sound throughout. When an actress passes by these flapping quilts, she should move as if moving through clouds of smoke. Two firestrips will be required. The large one, made of silk, is pulled across the stage to block and trap Clarence Cline. A smaller one, attached to a kind of dowel, is moved freely across the space. Both are manipulated by the actress who plays Bert.

falls. CLARENCE CLINE *steps out of the choir. The remaining* WOMEN *huddle together, coughing and flapping their quilts*.)

CLARENCE CLINE: Lots o' people in town on Saturday business were trapped there. I was the county treasurer then and only lived half a mile from the courthouse . . . so I struck out for home on foot. (*He moves through them as if fighting his way through clouds of smoke*.) The smoke was so thick and the sand was blowin' right into my face as I walked. I couldn't see the fire from the town. And then oh God, oh God, suddenly it came roaring at me over the hill . . . (*The large firestrip is pulled across the stage . . . dazzling silken flame*.) . . . and there was only one way to go . . . straight through it. . . . Now!!! . . . (*Explosion sounds. The hanging quilt falls.* CLARENCE *runs into the fire curtain. The moment in time expands.* CLARENCE *is a frenetic, twitching moth caught in a flame*.)

MAUREEN: I saw somethin' comin' at me . . . glowing like a firebrand . . . staggering through that plowed field . . . (*Screaming*). CLARENCE!!! (*She runs to the bucket and dips her dark quilt in the water.* CLARENCE *comes out of the firestrip.* MAUREEN *beats him with the fabric. Her hair catches fire. She beats it out. . . .* CLARENCE *rolls over on the ground and ends up in the bucket in a frozen position.* MAUREEN *goes to him and mimes cutting his boots off*.) When I cut the boots off his feet that night, the skin all the way to his boot tops came off with 'em. (*She turns around, gagging. And eventually wraps a smaller piece of "dark cloth" around her head*.)

PATRICIA *emerges from under the hanging quilt which has fallen on her. She carries small strips of black gauze*.

PATRICIA: I went along with Dr. Cooper to nurse as soon as we heard the fire had struck in Tryon. We set out in the wagon with a stack of quilts that patients had given us in payment for services. Before the day was over, I was cuttin' them up for bandages. (*She begins to wind the gauze around* CLARENCE's *feet—then tries it around her head, covering her eyes*.)

SARAH: One woe is past and behold there come two more woes hereafter.

THE ONE REMAINING WOMAN IN THE CHOIR: These quilts is from the Ladies of the First Lutheran Church. (*She exits. The* ACTRESS *playing* BERT *enters moving through the space and around the soddy area, manipulating the handheld fire strip. She is wearing a black gauze bandana to cover her mouth and nose.*)

SARAH (*moves down from the pulpit area*): I sat in that soddy all alone. For hours. Night came and I could see where the fire was blazing against the sky.... Then I saw it pass right by ... it never touched me. Soon after I heard those terrible sounds ... the horses screaming over at the Nelson's barn. I was wondrin' where my boys were. (MRS. SEELEY *enters in a black cloth shroud that completely covers her body and follows her with a long trail.*)

MRS. SEELEY: The Judge and I were in our seventies then—nobody to help us. We set out to beat back the fire alone. All the livestock got roasted in the corner of the pasture but we fought with wet sacks and buckets to save the buildings ... we fought for our lives. Then we dragged ourselves off to bed. Never got up again. (*The firestrip is carried off. She lies down covering her face completely.*)

LILLIAN (*rising and moving upstage*): To this day I don't know how I got all the babies and the kids out into the field just in time—or even what made me do it. But there we sat all night. When Bert come home the next mornin' and saw how the flames had jumped the fireguard he just sat down and wept. It took three years to put up that house and I helped every step of the way, pregnant or not. (BERT *has reentered.*) And that's the one that burnt right to the ground, that night with all my quilts and books with it. We lost all the kids' things too. My momma's quilts was in there with mine. But we were alive. (SARAH *goes to* LILLIAN *offering her Bible quilt.*) We couldn't do any better than to roll up and sleep right there on the ground till we could take in the damage and start rebuilding. (*She leads the* COMPANY *into the hymn. Singing.*)
Praise ...

ALL (*singing and moving toward the bucket*): God from whom all blessings flow ...

The COMPANY *reaches into the bucket wiping off the smoke ... putting smoke masks inside of it.*

SARAH (*still upstage*): And he showed me a pure river of water of life, clear as crystal proceeding out of the throne of God and of the Lamb.

THE COMPANY (*in quiet response*): And on either side of the river was there the Tree of Life ... and the leaves of the tree were for the healing of the nations.

SARAH: You can't always change things. Sometimes you don't have no control over the way things go. Hail ruins the crop or the fire burns you out. And then you're just given so much to work with in a life, and you have to do the best you can with what you got. The materials is passed on to you or is all you can afford to buy ... that's just what's given to you. Your fate. But the way you put them together is your business. You can put them in any order you like. Piecing is orderly.

THE COMPANY (*singing*):
Praise Father Son and Holy Ghost

SARAH: Know ye that there hath no trouble taken you but is common to all men.

THE COMPANY (*sing*):
A—a—men

SARAH: Okay girls, let's go to it! (SARAH *initiates the work. As the* WOMEN *move into the cleanup, they discover small strips of orange calico, which have been strewn about by the fire. The dandelion strips represent the wild flowers that can be seen on the prairie a matter of days after a prairie fire.*)

TWO WOMEN (*raising the strips, singing*):
Dandelion
Why so late
With your golden crown
With your golden crown?

ALL (*sing*):
All your comrades
Long ago
Laid their splendor down

"Dandelion" is a lusty work song. A community exorcising their demons through hard work. The COMPANY *really throws their back into the task at hand. By the end of the song, all the debris should be cleared off the stage. The soft things should be*

dumped into the ground cloth and as much as possible, carried off in it. The hard things can be struck. The floor will then be stripped to the underlying wood, and we should be able to see clear through to the back wall of the theater.

ALL (sing):
Tho your face smiles bravely up
From the grasses dead

Watching you my heart forgets
The summer's wealth is fled

Blessings blessings
Sunny flower
For your shining grace
Doubly welcome that you deck
Autumn's furrowed face

Dandelion
Like the dauntless heart
You seem
Beneath privations power

Smiling bravely
Though above
The threatening tempests lower

The WOMEN are finishing up the work, and line up to look out over the cleared area.

Blessings blessings
Sunny flower
For your shining grace

Doubly welcome
That you deck
Autumn's furrowed face

SARAH (opening the final block): BLOCK SIX-TEEN—TREE OF LIFE.

Musicians play the "Tree of Life Waltz." SARAH dances with great dignity. She has wrapped the quilted block around her like a bishop's cape. One DAUGHTER dances in circles with her, carrying three wooden hoops. The rest of the WOMEN dance in a line which gracefully snakes downstage. SARAH ends up seated with all the DAUGHTERS at her feet. Only GLADYS remains upstage.

GLADYS: There wasn't no choice about finishing this house. Mr. Thompson and I we worked side by side all these years up until I was sixty-five. He taught me everything I know about building and carpentry. We was more than married, we was partners. When he died, we was in the middle of building this house for ourselves, and after the funeral I come home and put on my overalls and finished it in thirty days. I never looked up till I was through. I lost fifty-seven pounds during that time. Then I took up quilting. I plan my quilts just like I used to plan a house. Folks say, "How come you quilt so good?" I say, "If you make careful plans, it will come out right."

THE COMPANY (sing):
Every log in my house

All turn to SARAH, who sings the song: "Everything Has a Time":

SARAH (sings):
Everything has a time
And early in the mornin' I am
Tending my flowers and grapevines
And when everything's properly done
   It puts me in mind
   To get to my quiltin'
   And let the light shine

THE COMPANY (sing):
Every log in my house
Straight as a pine

ALL (sing):
I've done my portion
Of creatin'
Trimmin' and weedin' and cultivatin'
When everything within its time
Is mended and tended then
   It puts me in mind
   To get to my quiltin'
   And let the light shine

THE COMPANY (sing):
Dandelion carpet

SARAH (sings):
And let the light shine

THE COMPANY (sing):
Dandelion carpet

SARAH (sings):
And let the light shine . . .

THE COMPANY (sing):
Dandelion . . .
Hmmmmm

Shadow Block lighting.

LEGACY SHADOW BLOCK

SARAH: So, my dear daughters, it is said that . . .
ALL (*intoning as* SARAH *speaks, with heads bowed*):
   Man proposes and God disposes

The DAUGHTERS *exit.*

SARAH: I've been hurrying to get this quilt finished. It's almost done, but it looks like the finishing touches are going to be up to you girls. (*The* DAUGHTERS *enter in procession like pallbearers carrying an enormous quilt.*) I leave this the work of my hands, to you, my daughters, with all my love and blessings. May it bring you as much joy and comfort in the using of it, as it has brought me in the making of it. (*She starts to go . . . then turns back.*) And by the way, when you bury me, don't bury me in my best quilt. (*She exits. The* COMPANY *stands still with the quilt on their shoulders.*)
JENNY: I want you, Jenny, my oldest, to take it and keep it . . .
MARGARET: and then pass it along to the next one . . .
LISA: and the next one . . .
JANE: each of you keeping it for one year.
JODY: I hope you will show it to my grandchildren and my great-grandchildren . . .
DANA: and tell them the stories that are in it.
JENNY: Okay, girls . . .
ALL: Let's go to it! (*The* DAUGHTERS *raise the quilt over their heads and lower it to the ground singing . . .*)
ALL (*sing*):
   Pieces of lives
      All the unspoken
         Emotion
         Devotion
      Of our lives . . .

Lights up. Music begins. The ladies prepare to open the "Legacy" quilt. [Note: The quilt should be folded up like a "drop," wrong side out. It will therefore only be revealed on the last move of unfolding.] The COMPANY *begins the song kneeling around it. The ladies unfold the quilt two at a time on the appointed "moves," during the song: "Hands Around."*

ALL (*Move 1, Sing.*):
   Hands all hands around
   Now lay on the healing hands
   With no cross
   There is no crown
   Oh sisters, sisters
   Spread the healing hands
      Around (*Move 2. During accompaniment.*)

   Hands all hands around
   Blest be the tie that binds
   Let all the hope in your working hands
   Bring you sisters
   Sisters bring you
      Peace of mind (*Move 3.*)

   Stretch them out
   Over troubled waters
   Gather their strength
   Daughters of Zion

Holding onto an edge of the quilt.

   Hold fast
   Hold tight

SARAH *reenters.*

SARAH: Give her the fruit of her hands and let her own works praise her in the gates!
ALL (*Move 4—the last unfolding. During final notes, the "Legacy" quilt is revealed and flies upward. The* COMPANY *returns to the Conestoga wagon formation . . . now moving in front of the map of the journey they have made.*)
   At evening time
   There shall be
      Light
   At evening time
      There
      Shall
      Be
      Light
      Light
      Light
      Light
      Light!

END

"Patchwork: The Playwrights Talk about *Quilters*"*

In August of 1981 Molly Newman auditioned for the Denver Center Theatre with a piece excerpted from Patricia Cooper and Norma Bradley Allen's *The Quilters: Women and Domestic Art.* The casting director, taken with the material, sent her to Larry Eilenberg, the Literary Manager, who encouraged her impulse to turn the material into a play. In its first version, handed a month later to Ed McCall, Artistic Director, *Quilters* was little more than a set of one-character monologues.

MN: Barbara and I are so different. I was 26 or 27 years old, born and raised in a small city in Indiana on the Ohio River. I went to the University of Denver. Barbara was born and raised in New York City, was Jewish, went to Yale, was older and had a lot more experience in theater . . . and we probably wouldn't have had much to say to each other were it not for this project. . . .

BD: They [i.e., the Denver Center Theatre] had committed to do it even when Molly had come to them with the non-script, the undigested pieces.

MN: What she brought to it was shaping it, writing the music, finding that armature.

BD: Ed McCall phoned me and I remember Ed saying maybe you need the eighty-year-old women. They had sent me the material over the Christmas break, I think. I was living in Pittsburgh at the time. And I went to a museum, a quilting archive, and looked at quilting magazines from the turn of the century and I started to come across these old poems. They were bad poems, but very simple and unclothed in what their sentiment was about and I started to get some sense of the inner life, of what they had

inside when they were doing the quilts. And they screamed out for music. It was very rich . . . and it started to take shape. By the time Ed called me back, I knew that it needed music and I told him you didn't need the eighty-year-old women.

MN: What I brought to it was a sense of protecting these women and not letting them become something they weren't just to serve our idea of what a play should be. And that's exactly why it worked.

BD: By the time they flew me out there I had constructed one quilt block, the Windmill, and I brought it out and showed it to them as an example of how I would approach the play. During that period of time I met Molly. We shook hands and made an agreement to collaborate together and that agreement still holds. I went home and we had maybe five weeks before we were going to do the lab production [at the Denver Center Theatre, Spring of 1982]. When I went home I wrote a basic working script, lyrics, and two-thirds of the score. And then Molly and I started to collaborate. Molly worked off that. I was writing more music, Molly was creating more blocks, and that continued through the rehearsal process. It was a wonderful way to birth a piece.

MN: One of my favorite parts of the script [was the abortion sequence]. . . . It came from our research and partly from a desire to avoid making the play a valentine. . . . I think the idea for it came from the book *Wisconsin Death Trip,* which Barbara looked at. This was also the source of the butterfly incident, which Barbara pretty much wrote herself. . . . Women had eight and twelve children and we just couldn't imagine it. I researched abortifacients in the University of Colorado Medical School library. . . . 19th-century potions to end pregnancy. . . . Barbara felt she shouldn't drink it at the end and there was this disagreement. But we finally went the whole way and had her drink it.

BD: There were sequences that Molly went off and wrote or that I went off and wrote. I think she wrote the secret drawer, the abortion sequence. . . . But we really did collaborate. And we worked together for a month in the summer. I remember saying I wanted to find one

---

*Excerpted from separate telephone interviews with Molly Newman and Barbara Damashek, 3 June 1994.

character who was a sort of Johnny Appleseed of quilts, and what that was was the search for Sarah. And I found this old book called *Aunt Jane of Kentucky* and it was an entire book about a grandmother who was a master-quilter. . . . We knew basically it was a rite of passage thing we were going for; we knew basically it was the alternative point of view to John Ford's story, "Women, get back in the wagon."

MN: I think the reason *Quilters* was successful was that women in general were hungry to see themselves. I think they recognized themselves and their mothers and sisters and grandmothers. How do women relate to one another, how do they behave in groups? Who are women when they are not in the presence of men? These are the issues that interested me and are why I write to begin with.

BD: There is a feminist spirit informing *Quilters*. When we started working on it I wasn't conscious of it. It formed my consciousness by working on it. It wasn't self-consciously didactic. The political impulse was already there in the material. But in 1982 when we first did it people weren't recognizing it as that.

MN: In the audience we would have radical lesbian feminists sitting next to housewives who had never been to the theater before. . . . It touched something in people. You could look at it and say home and family and sewing, and other people could look it and say this is a metaphor for women's struggles.

BD: One of the problems with docudramas is they [the critics] do not really recognize that they are different kinds of plays. It has something to do with the spoken word. There is some radio sensibility that comes through. . . . And part of the reason it didn't succeed in New York was that it didn't conform either to the idea of a New York musical or a documentary. . . . We had all agreed that for a piece like this to have a life in New York—which is not only documentary-phobic, but regional-phobic—we would go into an off-Broadway venue and to avoid being presented and packaged as a musical. We had sited some theaters that would have given it that sort of home, but those sorts of theaters filled up, so we went into the Jack Lawrence Theatre, which was around the corner from Broadway, and that was the kiss of death.

MN: I learned so much from that experience. I learned so much of what you had to do to write a play. And because it took years, I got more confident about my voice and she became more knowledgeable about the women themselves. We brought parts of ourselves to it as well.

BD: She could have met someone else and it could have gone in a different way. . . .

Emily Mann

EXECUTION OF JUSTICE

1984

Execution of Justice premiered at the Actors Theatre of Louisville 22 February 1984, directed by Oskar Eustis and Tony Taccone. Productions followed at the Empty Space (dir. by M. Burke Walker); Berkeley Rep (Oskar Eustis and Tony Taccone); Arena Stage (dir. by Doug Wager); Center Stage (dir. by Stan Wojewodski, Jr.); Alley Theatre (dir. by Pat Brown); The Guthrie (dir. by Emily Mann); and on Broadway at the Virginia Theatre (dir. by Emily Mann). For the Broadway production, the set was designed by Ming Cho Lee, the costumes by Jennifer von Mayrhauser, and the lighting by Pat Collins. The Broadway cast included John Spencer, Mary McDonnell, Stanley Tucci, Wesley Snipes, Christopher McHale, Lisabeth Bartlett, Adam Redfield, Isabell Monk, Donal Donnelly, Nicholas Hormann, Nicholas Kepros, Peter Friedman, Gerry Bamman, Freda Foh Shen, Josh Clark, Suzy Hunt, Gary Reineke, Jeremy O. Caplin, Earle Hyman, Marcia Jean Kurtz, Richard Riehle, Jon de Vries, and Richard Howard.

CHARACTERS

DAN WHITE
MARY ANN WHITE
COP
SISTER BOOM BOOM

CHORUS OF UNCALLED WITNESSES:
JIM DENMAN, *White's Jailer*
YOUNG MOTHER
MILK'S FRIEND
GWENN CRAIG, *Vice President of Harvey Milk Democratic Club*
City Supervisor HARRY BRITT, *Milk's Successor*
JOSEPH FREITAS, D.A.
MOURNER

TRIAL CHARACTERS:
THE COURT
COURT CLERK
DOUGLAS SCHMIDT, *Defense Attorney*
THOMAS F. NORMAN, *Prosecuting Attorney*
JOANNA LU, *TV Reporter*
PROSPECTIVE JURORS
JUROR #3
FOREMAN
BAILIFF

WITNESSES FOR THE PEOPLE:
CORONER STEPHENS
RUDY NOTHENBERG, *Deputy Mayor, Moscone's Friend*
BARBARA TAYLOR, *Reporter*
OFFICER BYRNE, *Department of Records*
WILLIAM MELIA, *Civil Engineer*
CYR COPERTINI, *Secretary To The Mayor*
CARL HENRY CARLSON, *Aide To Harvey Milk*

RICHARD PABICH, *Assistant To Harvey Milk*
Inspector FRANK FALZON, *Homicide*
Inspector EDWARD ERDELATZ

WITNESSES FOR THE DEFENSE:
DENISE APCAR, *Aide to White*
Fire Chief SHERRATT
Fireman FREDIANI
Police Officer SULLIVAN
City Supervisor LEE DOLSON
Psychiatrists: DR. JONES
DR. SOLOMON
DR. BLINDER
DR. LUNDE
DR. DELMAN

IN REBUTTAL FOR THE PEOPLE:
City Supervisor CAROL RUTH SILVER
DR. LEVY, *Psychiatrist*
RIOT POLICE
ACTION CAMERAMAN

THE TIME:
1978 to the present

THE PLACE
San Fransisco

THE WORDS COME FROM:
Trial Transcripts, Reportage and Interviews

ACT I: MURDER

A bare stage. A white screen overhead. On screen: images of San Francisco. Hot, fast music. Images of Milk and Moscone punctuate the visuals.
PEOPLE enter. A day in San Francisco. A maelstrom of urban activity. Without warning: on screen (video, if possible):

DIANNE FEINSTEIN (*almost unable to stand*): As President of the Board of Supervisors, It is my duty to make this announcement: Mayor George Moscone . . . and Supervisor Harvey Milk . . . have been shot . . . and killed. (*Gasps and cries. A long moment.*) The suspect is Supervisor Dan White.

The CROWD in shock. They cannot move. Then they run. Out of the chaos, DAN WHITE appears. On screen: a church window fades up. A shaft of light. DAN WHITE prays.
On audio: hyperreal sounds of mumbled Hail Mary's. Sounds of a woman's high heels echoing, moving fast. Sound of breathing hard, running. MARY ANN WHITE enters, breathless. WHITE looks up. She approaches him.

WHITE: I shot the Mayor and Harvey.

She crumples. Lights change.

CLERK: This is the matter of the People versus Daniel James White.

Amplified gavel. Lights change.

COP (*quiet*): Yeah, I'm wearing a "Free Dan White" T-shirt (*indicating on shirt "NO MAN IS AN ISLAND"*). You haven't seen what I've seen
—my nose shoved into what I think stinks.
Against everything I believe in.
There was a time in San Francisco when you knew a guy
by his parish.

SISTER BOOM BOOM enters.

COP: Sometimes I sit in Church and I think of those disgusting drag queens dressed up as nuns
and I'm a cop,
and I'm thinkin',
there's gotta be a law, you know,
because they're makin' me think things I don't want to think
and I gotta keep my mouth shut.

BOOM BOOM puts out cigarette.

COP: Take a guy out of his sling—fist-fucked to death—
they say it's mutual consent, it ain't murder,
and I pull this disgusting mess down, take him to the morgue,
I mean, my wife asks me, "Hey, how was your day?"
I can't even tell her.
I wash my hands before I can even look at my kids.

They are very aware of each other, but possibly never make eye contact.

BOOM BOOM: God bless you one.
God bless you all.
COP: See, Danny knew—he believes in the rights of minorities. Ya know, he just knew—we are a minority, too.
BOOM BOOM: I would like to open with a reading from the Book of Dan. (*Opens book.*)
COP: We been workin' this job three generations —my father was a cop—and then they put— Moscone, Jesus, the mayor—Jesus—Moscone put this N-negro-loving, faggot-loving Chief telling us what to do—
he doesn't even come from the neighborhood,
he doesn't even come from this city!
He's tellin' us what to do in a force that knows what to do.
He makes us paint our cop cars faggot blue—
he called it "lavender gloves" for the queers,
handle 'em, treat 'em with "lavender gloves,"
he called it.
He's cuttin' off our balls.
The city is stinkin' with degenerates—
I mean, I'm worried about my kids, I worry about my wife,
I worry about me and how I'm feelin' mad all the time.
You gotta understand that I'm not alone—
It's real confusion.
BOOM BOOM: "As Dan came to his day of reckoning, he feared not for he went unto the lawyers and the doctors and the jurors, and they said, 'Take heart, for in this you will receive not life but three to seven with time off for good behavior.'" (*Closes book reverently.*)
COP: Take a walk with me sometime
See what I see every day . . .
Like I'm supposed to smile when I see two bald-headed,
shaved-head men with those tight pants and muscles,
chains everywhere, French-kissin' on the street,
putting their hands all over each other's asses,
I'm supposed to smile,
walk by, act as if this is RIGHT??!!
BOOM BOOM: As gay people and as people of color and as women we all know the cycle of brutality and ignorance which pervades our culture.
COP: I got nothin' gainst people doin' what they want,
if I don't see it.
BOOM BOOM: And we all know that brutality only begets more brutality.
COP: I mean, I'm not makin' some woman on the streets for everyone to see.
BOOM BOOM: Violence only sows the seed for more violence.
COP: I'm not . . .
BOOM BOOM: And I hope Dan White knows that.
COP: I can't explain it any better.
BOOM BOOM: Because the greatest, most efficient information-gathering and dispersal network is the Great Gay Grapevine.
COP: Just take my word for it—
BOOM BOOM: And when Dan White gets out of jail, no matter where Dan White goes, someone will recognize him.
COP: Walk into a leather bar with me some night —They—they're
there are queers who'd agree with me—it's disgusting.
BOOM BOOM: All over the world, the word will go out.
And we will know where Dan White is.
COP: The point is: Dan White showed you could fight City Hall.
BOOM BOOM (*pause*): Now we are all aware, as I said,
Of this cycle of brutality and murder.
And the only way we can break that horrible cycle is with
love, understanding and forgiveness.
And there are those who were before me here today—
gay brothers and sisters
who said that we must somehow learn to
love, understand and forgive
the sins that have been committed against us
and the sins of violence.
And it sort of grieves me that some of us are not
understanding and loving and forgiving of Dan White.
And after he get out,

after we find out where he is . . . (*Long, wry look.*)
I mean, not, y'know,
with any malice or planning . . . (*Long look.*)
You know, you get so depressed and your blood sugar goes up
and you'd be capable of just about ANY-THING! (*Long pause. Smiles.*)
And some angry faggot or dyke who is not understanding, loving and forgiving—
is going to perform a horrible act of violence and brutality
against Dan White.
And if we can't break the cycle before somebody gets Dan White
somebody will *get Dan White.*
and when they do,
I beg you all to
love, understand and *for-give.* (*He throws a kiss, laughs.*)

Lights fade to black.

CLERK: This is the matter of the People vs. Daniel James White and the record will show that the Defendant is present with his counsel and the District Attorney is present and this is out of presence of the jury.

Court setting up. TV lights.

JOANNA LU (*on camera*): The list of prospective witnesses that the defense has presented for the trial of the man accused of killing the liberal Mayor of San Francisco, George Moscone, and the first avowedly homosexual elected official, City Supervisor Harvey Milk, reads like a Who's Who of City Government (*Looks at list.*) . . . Judges, Congressmen, current and former Supervisors, and even a State Senator. The D.A. has charged White with two counts of first-degree murder, invoking for the first time the clause in the new California capital punishment law that calls for the gas chamber for any person who has assassinated a public official in an attempt to prevent him from fulfilling his official duties. Ironically, Harvey Milk and George Moscone vigorously lobbied against the death penalty while Dan White vigorously supported it. This is Joanna Lu at the Hall of Justice.

Gavel. Spotlight on CLERK.

CLERK: Ladies and gentlemen, this is the information in the case now pending before you: the People of the State of California, Plaintiff, versus Daniel James White, Defendant. Action Number: 98663, Count One.

Gavel. Lights. On screen: JURY SELECTION.

COURT: Mr. Schmidt, you may continue with your jury selection.

SCHMIDT: Thank you, Your Honor.

CLERK: It is alleged that Daniel James White did willfully, unlawfully, and with malice aforethought murder George R. Moscone, the duly elected Mayor of the City and County of San Francisco, California.

SCHMIDT: Have you ever supported controversial causes, like homosexual rights, for instance?

JUROR #1 (*woman*): I have gay friends . . . I, uh . . . once walked with them in a Gay Freedom Day Parade.

SCHMIDT: Your Honor, I would like to strike the juror.

JUROR #1 (*woman*): I am str . . . I am heterosexual.

COURT: Agreed.

Gavel.

CLERK: The defendant Daniel James White is further accused of a crime of felony, to wit: that said defendant Daniel James White did willfully, unlawfully, and, with malice aforethought, murder Harvey Milk, a duly elected Supervisor of the City and County of San Francisco, California.

SCHMIDT: With whom do you live, sir?

JUROR #2 (*man*): My roommate.

SCHMIDT: What does he or she do?

JUROR #2 (*man*): He works at the Holiday Inn.

SCHMIDT: Your Honor, I ask the court to strike the juror for cause.

COURT: Agreed.

Gavel.

CLERK: Special circumstances: It is alleged that Daniel James White in this proceeding has been accused of more than one offense of murder.

JUROR #3: I worked briefly as a San Francisco policeman, but I've spent most of my life since then as a private security guard.

SCHMIDT: As you know, serving as a juror is a high honor and responsibility.

JUROR #3: Yes, sir.

SCHMIDT: The jury serves as the conscience of the community.

JUROR #3: Yes, sir. I know that, sir.

SCHMIDT: Now, sir, as a juror you take an oath that you will apply the laws of the State of California as the Judge will instruct you. You'll uphold that oath, won't you?

JUROR #3: Yes, sir.

SCHMIDT: Do you hold any views against the death penalty no matter how heinous the crime?

JUROR #3: No, sir. I support the death penalty.

SCHMIDT: Why do you think Danny White killed Milk and Moscone?

JUROR #3: I have certain opinions. I'd say it was social and political pressures. . . .

SCHMIDT: I have no jury.

COURT: Mr. Norman?

No response. Fine with him. Gavel.

JOANNA LU (*on camera*): The jury has been selected quickly for the Dan White trial. It appears the prosecution and the defense want the same jury. The prosecuting attorney, Assistant D.A. Tom Norman, exercised only 3 out of 27 possible peremptory challenges. By all accounts, there are no Blacks, no gays, and no Asians. One juror is an ex-policeman, another the wife of the county jailer, four of the seven women are old enough to be Dan White's mother. Most of the jurors are working and middle-class Catholics. Speculation in the press box is that the prosecution feels that it has a law-and-order jury. In any case, Dan White will certainly be judged by a jury of his peers. (*Turns.*) I have with me this morning District Attorney Joseph Freitas, Jr. (*TV lights on FREITAS.*) May we ask, sir, the prosecution's strategy in the trial of Dan White?

FREITAS: I think it's a clear case—We'll let the facts speak for themselves—

CLERK: And the Defendant, Daniel James White, has entered a plea of not guilty to each of the charges and allegations contained in this information.

WHITE enters. MRS. WHITE enters.

COURT: Mr. Norman, do you desire to make an opening statement at this time?

NORMAN: I do, Judge.

COURT: All right. You may proceed.

Lights change. On screen: ACT ONE MURDER. Gavel. All screens go to white.

NORMAN (*opening statement—the prosecution*): Your Honor, members of the jury, and you must be the judges now . . . (*takes in audience*) counsel for the defense: (*To audience.*) Ladies and gentlemen—I am Thomas F. Norman and I am the Assistant District Attorney, and I appear here as trial representative to Joseph Freitas, Jr., District Attorney. Seated with me is Frank Falzon, Chief Inspector of Homicide for San Francisco.

George R. Moscone was the duly elected Mayor of San Francisco. (*On screen: Portrait of MOSCONE.*)

Harvey Milk was the duly elected Supervisor or City Councilman of District 5 of San Francisco. (*On screen: Portrait of HARVEY MILK.*)

The defendant in this case, Mr. Daniel James White, had been the duly elected Supervisor of District 8 of San Francisco, until for personal reasons of his own he tendered his resignation in writing to the Mayor on or about November the 10th, 1978, which was approximately 17 days before this tragedy occurred.

Subsequent to tendering his resignation he had the feeling that he wanted to withdraw that resignation, and that he wanted his job back. George Moscone, it appears, had told the accused that he would give him his job back or, in other words, appoint him back to the Board if it appeared that there was substantial support in District Number 8 for that appointment.

Material was received by the Mayor in that regard, and in the meantime, Mr. Daniel James White had resorted to the courts in an effort to withdraw his written resignation.

It appears that those efforts were not met with much success.

On screen: The defense, DOUGLAS SCHMIDT.

SCHMIDT: Ladies and Gentlemen, the prosecutor has quite skillfully outlined certain of the facts that he believes will be supportive of his theory of first-degree murder.

I intend to present ALL the facts, including some of the background material that will show, not so much *what* happened on November 27th, but WHY those tragedies occurred on November 27th.

The evidence will show, and it's not disputed, that Dan White did, indeed, shoot and kill George Moscone and I think the evidence is equally clear that Dan White did shoot and kill Harvey Milk.

Why then should there be a trial?

The issue in this trial is properly to understand WHY that happened.

On screen: Chief Medical Examiner and Coroner for the City and County of San Francisco. Lights. CORONER sits.

STEPHENS (*holding photo*): In my opinion and experience, Counsel, the larger tattoo pattern at the side of the Mayor's head is compatible with a firing distance of about one foot, and the smaller tattoo pattern within the larger tattoo pattern is consistent with a firing distance of a little less than one foot.

That is: The wounds to the head were received within a distance of one foot when the Mayor was already on the floor incapacitated.

NORMAN looks to jury. On screen: Image of figure shooting man in head from a distance of one foot, leaning down "Coup de Grace."

SCHMIDT: Why? . . . Good people, fine people, with fine backgrounds, simply don't kill people in cold blood, it just doesn't happen, and obviously some part of them has not been presented thus far. Dan White was a native of San Francisco. He went to school here, went through high school here. He was a noted athlete in high school. He was an army veteran who served in Vietnam, and was honorably discharged from the army. He became a policeman thereafter, and after a brief hiatus developed, again returned to the police force in San Francisco, and later transferred to the fire department.

He was married in December of 1976. (*He indicates* MARY ANN WHITE.) And he fathered his son in July 1978.

Dan White was a good policeman and Dan White was a good fireman. In fact, he was decorated for having saved a woman and her child in a very dangerous fire, but the complete picture of Dan White perhaps was not known until some time after these tragedies on November 27th. The part that went unrecognized was since his early manhood, Dan White was suffering from a mental disease. The disease that Daniel White was suffering from is called depression, sometimes called manic depression or uni-polar depression.

NORMAN: Doctor, what kind of a wound was that in your opinion?

STEPHENS: These are gunshot wounds of entrance, Counsel. The case of death was multiple gunshot wounds . . . particularly the bullet that passed through the base of the Supervisor's brain. This wound would cause instant or almost instant death. I am now holding People's 30 and 29 for identification. In order for this wound to be received, Counsel . . . the Supervisor's left arm has to be relatively close to the body with the palm turned away from the body and the thumb towards the body.

NORMAN: Can you illustrate that for us?

STEPHENS: Yes, Counsel. The left arm has to be in close to the body and slightly forward with the palm up. The right hand has to be palm away with the thumb pointed towards the body and the elbow in slightly to the body with the arm raised. In this position, all of these wounds that I have just described in People's 30 and 29 line up.

NORMAN: Thank you.

Freeze on position. Lights.

SCHMIDT (*to* JURY): Dan White came from a vastly different lifestyle than Harvey Milk, who was a homosexual leader and politician. Dan White was an idealistic young man, a working-class young man. He was deeply endowed with and believed very strongly in the traditional American values, family and home; like the District he represented. (*Indicates* JURY.)

Dan White believed people when they said something. He believed that a man's word, essentially, was his bond. I don't think Dan White was particularly insightful as to what his underlying problem was, but he was an honest man, and he was fair, perhaps too fair for politics in San Francisco.

DAN WHITE *campaign speech: Hear sounds of* ROCKY *on audio, crowd response throughout.*

DAN: Do you like my new campaign song? (*Crowd cheers.*) Yeah!

On screen: Live video or slides of WHITE *giving speech, cameras.*

DAN (*to camera*): For years, we have witnessed an exodus from San Francisco by many of our family members, friends and neighbors. Alarmed by the enormous increase in crime, poor educational facilities and a deteriorating social structure, they have fled to temporary havens. . . . In a few short years these malignancies of society will erupt from our city and engulf the tree-lined, sun-bathed communities which chide us for daring to live in San Francisco. That is, unless we who have remained can transcend the apathy which has caused us to lock our doors while the tumult rages unchecked through our streets. Individually we are helpless. Yet you must realize there are thousands and thousands of angry, frustrated people such as yourselves waiting to unleash a fury that can and will eradicate the malignancies which blight our beautiful city. I am not going to be forced out of San Francisco by splinter groups of radicals, social deviates, and incorrigibles. UNITE AND FIGHT WITH DAN WHITE.

Crowd cheers. Lights change. Screens go to WHITE.

SCHMIDT: I think Dan White saw the city deteriorating as a place for the average and decent people to live.

COURT: Mr. Nothenberg, please be sworn.

SCHMIDT: The irony is . . . that the young man with so much promise in seeking the job on the Board of Supervisors actually was destined to construct his own downfall. After Dan White was elected he discovered there was a conflict of interest if he was a fireman and an elected official. His wife, Mary Ann, was a school teacher and made a good salary. But after their marriage, it was discovered that the wife of Dan White had become . . . pregnant and had

to give up her teaching job. So the family income plummeted from in excess of $30,000 to $9,600, which is what a San Francisco supervisor—city councilman—is paid. I believe all the stress and the underlying mental illness culminated in his resignation that he turned in to the Mayor on November 10th, 1978.

On screen: MR. NOTHENBERG, *Deputy Mayor. Lights.*

NORMAN: Would you read that for us?

NOTHENBERG: Dear Mayor Moscone: I have been proud to represent the people of San Francisco from District 8 for the past ten months, but due to personal responsibilities which I feel must take precedent over my legislative duties, I am resigning my position effective today. I am sure that the next representative to the Board of Supervisors will receive as much support from the people of San Francisco as I have. Sincerely, Dan White. It is so signed.

SCHMIDT (*to* JURY): Some days after November the 10th pressure was brought to bear on Dan White to go back to the job that he had worked so hard for, and there was a one-way course that those persons could appeal to Dan White, and that was to appeal to his sense of honor: Basically—Dan you are letting the fire department down, letting the police department down. It worked. That type of pressure worked, because of the kind of man Dan White is. He asked the Mayor for his job back.

NORMAN: Mr. Nothenberg, on or about Monday the 27th of November last year, do you know whether Mayor Moscone was going to make an appointment to the Board of Supervisors, particularly for District No. 8?

NOTHENBERG: Yes, he was.

SCHMIDT: The Mayor said: We have political differences, but you are basically a good man, and you worked for the job and I'm not going to take you to fault. That letter was returned to Dan White.

NORMAN: Do you know whom his appointee to District 8 was going to be?

NOTHENBERG: Yes, I do.

NORMAN: Who was that, please.

NOTHENBERG: It was going to be a gentleman named Don Horanzey.

NORMAN: Thank you.

SCHMIDT: As I said, Dan White believed a man's word was his bond. Mayor Moscone had said: If there was any legal problem he would simply re-appoint Dan White. Thereafter it became: Dan White there is no support in District 8 and un-less you can show some broad base support, the job will not be given to you, and finally, the pub-lic statement coming from the Mayor's office: It's undecided. But you will be notified, prior to the time that any decision is made. They didn't tell Dan White. But they told Barbara Taylor.

Blackout—Audio on phone. Spotlight WHITE *and* TAYLOR.

TAYLOR: I'm Barbara Taylor from KCBS. I'd like to speak to Dan White.

WHITE: Yuh.

TAYLOR: I have received information from a source within the Mayor's office that you are not getting that job. I am interested in doing an interview to find out your reaction to that, Mr. White?

Long pause. Spotlight DAN WHITE.

WHITE: I don't know anything about it.

Click. Dial tone. Lights change.

TAYLOR (*live*): Well, the Mayor's office told me: "The only one in favor of the appointment of Dan White is Dan White himself."

NORMAN: Thank you, Miss Taylor.

SCHMIDT: After that phone call, Denise Apcar, Dan's aide, told Dan White that there were go-ing to be supporters down at City Hall the next morning to show support to the Mayor's office. In one day they had collected 1100 signatures in District 8 in support of Dan White. But the next morning, Denise called Dan and told him the Mayor was unwilling to accept the petitioners.

On screen: DENISE APCAR, *Aide to* DAN WHITE.

APCAR: Yes. I told Danny—I don't remember my exact words—that the Mayor had "circum-vented the people."

NORMAN: Did you believe at that time that the Mayor was going to appoint someone other than Dan White?

APCAR: Oh, yes.

NORMAN: At that time, were your feelings such that you were angry?

APCAR: Definitely. Well the Mayor had told him . . . and Dan always felt that a person was going to be honest when they said something. He believed that up until the end.

NORMAN: You felt and believed that Mr. Milk had been acting to prevent the appointment of Mr. Dan White to his vacated seat on the Board of Supervisors?

APCAR: Yes. I was very much aware of that.

NORMAN: Had you expressed that opinion to Mr. White?

APCAR: Yes.

NORMAN: Did Mr. White ever express that opin-ion also to you?

APCAR: He wasn't down at City Hall very much that week so I was basically the person that told him these things.

NORMAN: Did you call Mr. White and tell him that you had seen Harvey Milk come out of the Mayor's office after you had been informed the Mayor was not in?

APCAR: Yes, I did. Then he called me back and said, "Denise, come pick me up. I want to see the Mayor."

NORMAN: When you picked him up, did he do anything unusual?

APCAR: Well . . . he didn't look at me and nor-mally he would turn his body a little bit to-wards the driver and we would talk, you know, in a free-form way, but this time he didn't look at me at all. He was squinting hard. He was very nervous, he was agitated. He was rubbing his hands, blowing into his hands and rubbing them like he was cold, like his hands were cold. He acted very hurt. Yes. He was, he looked like he was going to cry. He was doing everything he could to restrain his emotion.

NORMAN (*looks to the jury*): Did you ever describe him as acting quote "all fired up" unquote?

APCAR: Yes, yes I—I believe I said that.

NORMAN: Did he mention at that time that he also was going to talk to Harvey Milk?

APCAR: Yes, he did.

NORMAN: Did he ever say he was going to quote "really lay it on the Mayor" unquote?

APCAR: It's been brought to my attention I said that, yes.

NORMAN: When you were driving Mr. White downtown, was there some discussion relative to a statement you made? Quote "Anger had run pretty high all week towards the Mayor playing pool on us, dirty, you know" unquote?

APCAR: I believe I was describing my anger. At the time I made those statements I was in shock and I spoke freely and I'm sure I've never used those terms before.

NORMAN: When you made those statements it was 2 hours and 5 minutes after the killings occurred, was it not?

APCAR: Yes.

NORMAN: Miss Apcar—when you were driving Mr. White to City Hall did you know he was carrying a loaded gun?

APCAR: No. I did not.

NORMAN: Thank you.

SCHMIDT: Yes, Dan White went to City Hall and he took a .38 caliber revolver with him, and that was not particularly unusual for Dan White. Dan White was an ex-policeman, and as a policeman one is required to carry, off-duty, a gun, and as an ex-policeman—well I think it's common practice. And as it's been mentioned Dan White's life was being threatened continuously by the White Panther party and other radical groups. And additionally, remember, there was the atmosphere of terror created by the Jonestown People's Temple Tragedy. (*Screens flood with Jonestown image.*)

Only a week before the City Hall tragedy, 900 people, mostly San Franciscans—men, women, and children—died in the jungle. Rumors surfaced that hit lists had been placed on public officials in San Francisco. Assassination squads. And in hindsight, of course, we can all realize that this did not occur, but at the time there were 900 bodies laying in Guyana to indicate that indeed people were bent on murder.

Screen: OFFICER BYRNE, Department of Records. Lights.

NORMAN: Officer Byrne, do persons who were once on the police force who have resigned their position, do they have the right to carry a concealed firearm on their person?

SCHMIDT: And I think it will be shown that Jim Jones himself was directly allied with the liberal elements of San Francisco politics and was hostile to the conservative elements.

BYRNE: No, a resigned person would not have that right.

SCHMIDT: And so, it would be important to understand that there were threats directed towards conservative persons like Dan White.

NORMAN: Officer, have you at my instance and request examined those particular records to determine whether there is an official permit issued by the Chief of Police to a Mr. Daniel James White to carry a concealed firearm?

BYRNE: Yes, I have.

NORMAN: What have you found?

BYRNE: I find no permit.

NORMAN: Thank you.

Lights.

SCHMIDT: Yes, it's a violation of the law to carry a firearm without a permit, but that firearm was *registered* to Dan White. And indeed, many officials at City Hall carried guns because of this violent atmosphere, including ex-Police Chief Supervisor Al Nelder and the current Mayor of San Francisco, Dianne Feinstein.

COURT: Mr. Melia, please be sworn.

SCHMIDT: Upon approaching the door on Polk Street, Mr. White observed a metal detection machine. Knowing that he did not know the man that was on the metal detection machine, he simply went around to the McAllister Street well door, where he expected to meet his aide. He did not find Denise Apcar there. She'd gone to put gas in her car. He waited for several moments, but knowing that it was imminent, the talk to the Mayor, he stepped through a window at the Department of Public Works. (*Screen: Slide of windows with man in front demonstrating procedure.*) Which doesn't require any physical prowess, and you can step through those windows, and the evidence will show that though now they are barred, previously it was not uncommon for people to enter and exit there. They are very large windows, and are large, wide sills (*Screen shows windows which are the windows he stepped through. They are actually small, high off the ground: Now they are barred.*) and it's quite easy to step into the building through these windows.

On screen: Slide of man in three piece suit trying to get leg up. Screen: WILLIAM MELIA, JR., Civil Engineer.

MELIA: At approximately 10:35 I heard the window open. I heard someone jump to the floor and then running through the adjoining room. I looked up and caught a glance of a man in a suit running past the doorway of my office into the City Hall hallway.

NORMAN: What did you do?

MELIA: I got up from my desk and called after him: "Hey, wait a second."

NORMAN: Did that person wait or stop?

MELIA: Yes, they did.

NORMAN: Do you see that person here in this courtroom today?

MELIA: Yes, I do.

NORMAN: Where is that person?

MELIA: It's Dan White. (*pause*) He said to me: "I had to get in. My aide was supposed to come down and let me in the side door, but never showed up." I had taken exception to the way he had entered our office, and I replied. "AND YOU ARE?" And he replied: "I'm Dan White, the City Supervisor." He said, "Say, I've got to go," and with that, he turned and ran out of the office.

NORMAN: Did you say that he ran?

MELIA: Right.

NORMAN: Uh huh, Mr. Melia—had you ever seen anyone else enter or exit through that window or those windows along that side?

MELIA: Yes, I had. It was common for individuals that worked in *our* office to do that.

NORMAN: Individuals who worked in your office. . . . Were you alarmed when you learned that a Supervisor crawled or walked through that window, or stepped through that window?

MELIA: Was I alarmed?

NORMAN: Yes.

MELIA: Yes. I was . . . alarmed.

NORMAN: Thank you. (*He looks to* JURY.)

SCHMIDT (*annoyed*): I think it's significant at this point—also because the fact that he crawled through the window *appears* to be important— it's significant to reiterate that as Mr. Melia just testified people *often climb through that window,* and indeed, on the morning of the 27th,

Denise had the key to the McAllister Street well door. *So,* Dan White stepped through the window, identified himself, traveled up to the second floor. (*Screen: MRS. CYR COPERTINI, appointment secretary to the Mayor.*) And then approached the desk of Cyr Copertini and properly identified himself, and asked to see the Mayor.

Lights.

CYR: I am the appointment secretary to Mayor Feinstein.

NORMAN: In November of last year and particularly on November 27th, what was your then occupation?

CYR: I was appointment secretary to the elected Mayor of San Francisco, George Moscone. (*WITNESS deeply moved.*)

NORMAN: Mrs. Copertini—were you aware that there was anything that was going to happen that day of November 27th of interest to the citizens of San Francisco, uh . . . I mean, such as some public announcement?

CYR: . . . There was to be a news conference to announce the new supervisor for the Eighth District, at 11:30.

NORMAN: Mrs. Copertini, at approximately 10:30 A.M. you saw Mr. Daniel White, he appeared in front of your desk. . . . Do you recall what he said?

CYR: He said: "Hell, Cyr. May I see the Mayor?" I said: "He has someone with him, but let me go check with him." I went into the Mayor and told him that Supervisor White was there to see him. He was a little dismayed. He was a little uncomfortable by it and said: "Oh, all right. Tell him I'll see him, but he will have to wait a coupla minutes."

I asked the Mayor, "Shouldn't I have someone in there with him," and he said: "No, no, I'll see him alone." And I asked him again. And he said, "No, no, I'll see him alone." And then I went back.

I said to Dan White, "it will be a few minutes."

He asked me how I was and how things were going. Was I having a nice day.

NORMAN: Was there anything unusual about his tone of voice?

CYR: No. I don't think so. He seemed nervous. I asked him would he like to see the newspaper while he was waiting? He said: "No, he wouldn't," and I said: "Well, that's all right. There's nothing in it anyway unless you want to read about Caroline Kennedy having turned 21." And he said: "21? Is that right." He said: "Yeah, that's all so long ago. It's even more amazing when you think that John John is now 18."

Lights change. Music, "Deus Irae" Boy's Choir.

DENMAN: The only comparable situation I ever remember was when JFK was killed.

CYR: It was about that time he was admitted to the Mayor's office.

NORMAN: Did you tell Mr. Daniel White that he could go in?

CYR: Yes.

DENMAN: I remember that in my bones, in my body . . .

NORMAN: Did he respond in any way to that?

DENMAN: Just like this one.

CYR: He said: "Good girl, Cyr."

NORMAN: Good girl, Cyr?

CYR: Right.

DENMAN: when Camelot all of a sudden turned to hell.

NORMAN: Then what did he do?

CYR: Went in.

NORMAN: After he went in there did you hear anything of an unusual nature that was coming from the Mayor's office?

CYR: After a time I heard a . . . commotion.

Lights change.

YOUNG MOTHER: I heard it on the car radio, I literally gasped.

NORMAN: Explain that to us, please.

YOUNG MOTHER: I wanted to pull over to the side of the road and scream.

CYR: Well, I heard—a series of noises—first a group and then one—

YOUNG MOTHER: Just scream.

CYR: I went to the window to see if anything was happening out in the street . . .

YOUNG MOTHER: Then I thought of my kids.

CYR: and the street was rather extraordinarily calm.

DENMAN: I noticed when I looked outside that there was an unusual quiet.

CYR: For that hour of the day there is usually more—there wasn't really anything out there.

DENMAN: I went to the second floor and started walking toward the Mayor's office.

YOUNG MOTHER: I wanted to get them out of school and take them home,

NORMAN: Could you describe these noises for us?

YOUNG MOTHER: I wanted to take them home and (*She makes a hugging gestures with her arms.*) lock the door.

CYR: Well, they were dull thuds rather like—

DENMAN: And there was this strange combination of panic and silence that you rarely see.

CYR: I thought maybe it was an automobile door that somebody had tried to shut, by, you know, pushing, and then finally succeeding.

DENMAN: It was like a silent slow-motion movie of a disaster.

NORMAN: Do you have any recollection that you can report with any certainty to us as to how many sounds there were?

CYR: No. As I stood there I—I thought I ought to remember—(*WITNESS breaks down.*)

DENMAN: There was this hush and aura, people were moving with strange faces, as if the world had just come to an end.

NOTHENBERG (*Moscone's friend*): George loved this city, and felt what was wrong could be fixed.

NORMAN: Do you want a glass of water?

CYR sobs.

DENMAN: And I asked someone what had happened and he said: "The Mayor has been shot."

CYR: I ought to remember that pattern in case it is something, but I—

NOTHENBERG: He knew—it was a white racist town. A Catholic town. But he believed in people's basic good will.

CYR sobs.

COURT: Just a minute. Do you want a recess?

NOTHENBERG: He never suspected, I bet, Dan White's psychotic behavior.

NORMAN: Do you want a recess?

NOTHENBERG: That son of a bitch killed someone I loved. I mean, I loved the guy.

CYR: No. I'm all right.

COURT: Are you sure you are all right?

CYR: Yes.

YOUNG MOTHER: I just thought of my kids.

Pause.

NOTHENBERG: I loved his idealism. I loved his hope.

CYR: Then what happened was Rudy Nothenberg left to tell the press that the conference would start a few minutes late.

NOTHENBERG: I loved the guy.

CYR: And then he came back to me right away and said: "Oh, I guess we can go ahead. I just saw Dan White leave."

NOTHENBERG: I loved his almost naive faith in people.

CYR: So then we went into the Mayor's office and said: "Well, he's not here." And I said: "Well, maybe he went into the back room."

NOTHENBERG: I loved his ability to go on.

CYR: Then he just gave a shout saying: "Gary, get in here. Call an ambulance. Get the police."

NOTHENBERG: See, I got too tired to stay in politics and do it. George and I were together from the beginning. Me, Phil Burton, Willie Brown. Beatin' all the old Irishmen.

DENMAN: I heard right away that Dan White had done it.

NOTHENBERG: But George believed, as corny as this sounds, that you do good for the people. I haven't met many of those and George was one of those. Maybe those are the guys that get killed. I don't know.

CYR crying.

NORMAN: All right. All this you told us about occurred in San Francisco, didn't it?

CYR (*deeply moved*): Yes.

SCHMIDT: Dan White, as it was quite apparent at that point, had CRACKED because of his underlying mental illness. . . .

Screen: CARL HENRY CARLSON, Aide to HARVEY MILK.

CARLSON: I heard Peter Nardoza, Dianne Feinstein's aide, say: Dianne wants to see you and Dan White said: "That'll have to wait a couple of minutes, I have something to do first."

NORMAN: I have something to do first?

CARLSON: Yes.

NORMAN: Do you recall in what manner Mr. White announced himself?

SCHMIDT: There were stress factors due to the fact that he hadn't been notified . . .

CARLSON: He appeared at the door which was normally left open. Stuck his head in and asked: "Say, Harv, can I see you for a minute?"

SCHMIDT: and the sudden emotional surge that he had in the Mayor's office was simply too much for him . . .

NORMAN: What did Harvey Milk do at that time if anything?

CARLSON: He turned around.

SCHMIDT: and he cracked.

CARLSON: He turned around . . .

SCHMIDT: The man cracked.

CARLSON: and said "Sure" and got up and went across the hall . . .

SCHMIDT: He shot the Mayor . . .

CARLSON: to the office designated as Dan White's office on the chart.

SCHMIDT: reloaded his gun, basically on *instinct*, because of his police training, and was about to leave the building at that point . . .

NORMAN: After they went across the hall to Mr. White's office . . .

SCHMIDT: and he looked down the hall.

NORMAN: Would you tell us what next you heard or saw?

SCHMIDT: He saw somebody that he believed to be an aide to Harvey Milk.

CARLSON: A few seconds, probably 10, 15 seconds later, I heard a shot, or the sound of gunfire.

SCHMIDT: He went down to the Supervisor's area to *talk* to Harvey Milk.

COURT: Excuse me. Would you speak out. Your voice is fading a bit.

SCHMIDT: At that point, in the same state of rage, emotional upheaval with the stress of 10 years of mental illness having cracked this man . . .

CORONER (*demonstrates as he speaks*): The left arm has to be close to the body and slightly forward with the palm up.

SCHMIDT: ninety seconds from the time he shot the Mayor, Dan White shot and killed Harvey Milk.

CARLSON: After the shot, I heard Harvey Milk scream "Oh, no." And then the first—the first part of the second "no" which was then cut short by the second shot.

CORONER: The right hand has to be palm away with the thumb pointed towards the body and the elbow in slightly to the body with the arm raised.

NORMAN: How many sounds of shots did you hear altogether, Mr. Carlson?

CARLSON: Five or six. I really didn't consciously count them.

CORONER: In this position all of these wounds that I have just described in Peoples's 30 and 29 line up.

Blackout on CORONER *in position. Pause.*

CARLSON: A few moments later the door opened, the door opened, and Daniel White walked out, rushed out, and proceeded down the hall.

NORMAN: Now, Mr. Carlson, when Daniel White first appeared at the office of Harvey Milk and said, "Say, Harv, can I see you for a minute?" could you describe his tone of voice in any way?

CARLSON: He appeared to be very normal, usual friendly self. I didn't, I didn't feel anything out of the ordinary. It was just very typical Dan White.

Music out, lights change.

GWENN: I'd like to talk about when people are pushed to the wall.

SCHMIDT: Harvey Milk was against the reappointment of Dan White.

GWENN: In order to understand the riots, I think you have to understand that the Dan White verdict did not occur in a vacuum.

SCHMIDT: Basically, it was a political decision. It was evident there was a liberal wing of the Board of Supervisors, and there was a smaller conservative wing, and Dan White was a conservative politician for San Francisco.

Screen: RICHARD PABICH, Legislative Assistant to HARVEY MILK. Lights.

PABICH: My address is 542-A Castro Street.

GWENN: I don't think I have to say what their presence meant to us, and what their loss meant to us—

NORMAN: What did you do after you saw Dan White run down the hall and put the key in the door of his old office, Room 237?

GWENN: The assassinations of our friends Harvey Milk and George Moscone were a crime against us all.

PABICH: Well, I was struck in my head, sort of curious as to why he'd been running.

GWENN: And right here, when I say "us," I don't mean only gay people.

PABICH: And he was—it looked like he was in a hurry. I was aware of the political situation.

GWENN: I mean all people who are getting less than they deserve.

PABICH: I was aware that Harvey was taking the position to the Mayor that Mr. White shouldn't be reappointed. Harvey and I had talked earlier that day . . . that it would be a significant day.

Lights. Subliminal music.

MILK'S FRIEND: After Harvey died, I went into a depression that lasted about a year, I guess. They called it depression, anyway. I thought about suicide, well, I more than thought about it.

SCHMIDT: Mr. Pabich, Mr. Milk had suggested a replacement for Dan White, hadn't he?

PABICH: He had, to my understanding, recommended several people, and basically took the position that Dan White should not be reappointed.

MILK'S FRIEND: I lost my job. I stayed in the hospital for, I would guess, two months or so. They put me on some kind of drug that . . . well, it helped, I guess. I mean, I loved him and it was . . .

SCHMIDT: Was he requesting that a homosexual be appointed?

PABICH: No, he was not.

MILK'S FRIEND: Well, he was gone and that couldn't change.

SCHMIDT: I have nothing further. Thank you.

MILK'S FRIEND: He'd never be here again, I knew that.

COURT: All right. Any redirect, Mr. Norman?

NORMAN: No. Thank you for coming, Mr. Pabich. (PABICH *exits.*)

GWENN: It was as if Dan White had given the go-ahead. It was a free-for-all, a license to kill.

PABICH *with* JOANNA LU. *TV lights.*

PABICH (*on camera*): It's over. Already I can tell it's over. He asked me a question, a clear queer-baiting question, and the jury didn't bat an eye. (*Starts to exit, then:*) Dan White's going to get away with murder.

JOANNA LU: Mr. Pabich.

MILK'S FRIEND: I had this recurring dream. We were at the Opera, Harvey and I. I was laughing. Harvey was laughing. Then Harvey leaned over and said to me: When you're watching Tosca, you know you're alive. That's when I'd wake up.

GWENN: I remember the moment I heard Harvey had been shot—(*She breaks down.*)

MILK'S FRIEND: And I'd realize—like for the first time all over gain—he's dead.

Blackout. Hyperreal sounds of high heels on marble, echoing, moving fast. Mumbled Hail Marys. Fade lights up slowly on SCHMIDT, NORMAN.

SCHMIDT: From here I think the evidence will demonstrate that Dan White ran down to Denise's office, screamed at his aide to give him the key to her car. And he left, went to a church, called his wife, went into St. Mary's Cathedral, prayed, and his wife got there, and he told her, the best he could, what he remembered he had done, and then they walked together to the Northern Police Station where he turned himself in; asked the officer to look after his wife, asked the officer to take possession of an Irish poster he was carrying . . . (*Screen: Slide: Stained glass window, cover of Uris book* IRELAND: A Terrible Beauty.) and then made a statement, what best he could recall had occurred. (*FALZON hands on shoulders.*)

FALZON: Why . . . I feel like hitting you in the fuckin' mouth. . . . How could you be so stupid? How?

WHITE: I . . . I want to tell you about it. . . . I want to, to explain.

FALZON: Do you want a lawyer, Danny?

WHITE: No, Frank I want to talk to you.

FALZON: Okay, if you want to talk to me, I'm gonna get my tape recorder and read you your rights and do it right.

NORMAN: The people at this time move the tape recorded statement into evidence.

FALZON: Today's date is Monday, November 27th, 1978. The time is presently 12:05. We're inside the Homicide Detail, Room 454, at the Hall of Justice. Present is Inspector Edward Erdelatz, Inspector Frank Falzon and for the record, sir, your full name?

WHITE: Daniel James White.

FALZON: Would you, normally in a situation like this, ah . . . we ask questions, I'm aware of your past history as a police officer and also as a San Francisco fireman. I would prefer, I'll let you do it in a narrative form as to what happened this morning if you can lead up to the events of the shooting and then backtrack as to why these events took place. (*Looks at* ERDELATZ.)

WHITE: Well, it's just that I've been under an awful lot of pressure lately, financial pressure, because of my job situation, family pressure because of ah . . . not being able to have the time with my family (*sob*).

FALZON: Can you relate these pressures you've been under, Dan, at this time? Can you explain it to Inspector Erdelatz and myself.

WHITE: It's just that I wanted to serve (*FALZON nods.*) the people of San Francisco well and I did that. Then when the pressures got too great, I decided to leave. After I left, my family and friends offered their support and said, whatever it would take to allow me to go back into office—well, they would be willing to make that effort. And then it came out that Supervisor Milk and some others were working against me to get my seat back on the Board. He didn't speak to me, he spoke to the City Attorney but I was in the office and I heard the conversation.

I could see the game that was being played, they were going to use me as a *scapegoat,* whether I was a good supervisor or not, was not the point. This was a political opportunity and they were going to degrade me and my family and the job that I had tried to do an' an' more or less HANG ME OUT TO DRY. And I saw more and more evidence of this during the week when the papers reported that ah . . . someone else was going to be reappointed. The Mayor told me he was going to call me before he made any decision, he never did that. I was troubled, the pressure, my family again, my, my son's out to a babysitter.

FALZON: Dan, can you tell Inspector Erdelatz and myself, what was your plan this morning? What did you have in mind?

WHITE: I didn't have any devised plan or anything, it's, I was leaving the house to talk, to see the Mayor and I went downstairs, to, to make a phone call and I had my gun down there.

FALZON: Is this your police service revolver, Dan?

WHITE: This is the gun I had when I was a policeman. It's in my room an' ah . . . I don't know, I just put it on. I, I don't know why I put it on, it's just . . .

FALZON: You went directly from your residence to the Mayor's office this morning?

WHITE: Yes, my, my aide picked me up but she didn't have any idea ah . . . you know that I had a gun on me or, you know, and I went in to see him an', an' he told me he wasn't going to reappoint me and he wasn't intending to tell me about it. Then ah . . . I got kind of fuzzy and then just my head didn't feel right and I . . .

FALZON: Was this before any threats on your part, Dan?

WHITE: I, I never made any threats.

FALZON: There were no threats at all?

WHITE: I, I . . . oh no.

FALZON: When were you, how, what was the conversation—can you explain to Inspector Erdelatz and myself the conversation that existed between the two of you at this time?

WHITE: It was pretty much just, you know, I asked, was I going to be reappointed. He said, no I am not, no you're not. And I said, why, and he told me, it's a political decision and that's the end of it, and that's it and then he could obviously see, see I was obviously distraught an' then he said, let's have a drink and I, I'm not even a drinker, you know I don't, once in a while, but I'm not even a drinker. But I just kinda stumbled in the back and he was all, he was all smiles—he was talking an' nothing was getting through to me. It was just like a roaring in my ears an', an' then . . . it just came to me, you know, he . . .

FALZON: You couldn't hear what he was saying, Dan?

WHITE: Just small talk that, you know, it just wasn't registering. What I was going to do now, you know, and how this would affect my family, you know, an', an' just, just all the time knowing he's going to go out an', an' lie to the press an', an' tell 'em, you know, that I, I wasn't a good supervisor and that people didn't want me an' then that was it. Then I, I just shot him, that was it, it was over.

FALZON: What happened after you left there, Dan?

WHITE: Well, I, I left his office by one of the back doors an', I was going to go down the stairs and then I saw Harvey Milk's aide across the hall at the Supervisor's an' then it struck me about what Harvey had tried to do an' I said, well I'll go talk to him. He didn't know I had, I had heard his conversation and he was all smiles and stuff and I went in and, you know, I, I didn't agree with him on a lot of things but I was always honest, you know, and here they were devious. And then he started kinda smirking, 'cause he knew, he knew I wasn't going to be reappointed. And ah . . . I started to say you know how hard I worked for it and what it meant to me and my family and then my reputation as, as a hard worker, good honest person and he just kind of smirked at me as if to say, too bad an' then, and then, I just got all flushed an', an' hot, and I shot him.

FALZON: This occurred inside your room, Dan?

WHITE: Yeah, in my office, yeah.

FALZON: And when you left there did you go back home?

WHITE: No, no, no I drove to the, the Doggie Diner on, on Van Ness and I called my wife and she, she didn't know, she . . .

FALZON: Did you tell her, Dan?

Sobbing.

WHITE: I called up, I didn't tell her on the phone. I just said . . . she was working. I just told her to meet me at the cathedral.

FALZON: St. Mary's?

Sobbing.

WHITE: She took a cab, yeah. She didn't know. She knew I'd been upset and I wasn't even talking to her at home because I just couldn't explain how I felt and she had no, nothing to blame about it, she was, she always has been great to me but it was, just the pressure hitting me an' just my head's all flushed and expected that my skull's going to crack. Then when she came to the church, I, I told her and she kind of slumped an' she, she couldn't say anything.

FALZON: How is she now do you, do you know is she, do you know where she is?

WHITE: I don't know now. She, she came to Northern Station with me. She asked me not to do anything about myself, you know that she, she loved me and she'd stick by me and not to hurt myself.

ERDELATZ: Dan, right now are you under a doctor's care?

WHITE: No.

ERDELATZ: Are you under any medication at all?

WHITE: No.

ERDELATZ: When is the last time you had your gun with you prior to today?

WHITE: I guess it was a few months ago. I, I was afraid of some of the threats that were made an', I, I, just wanted to make sure to protect myself you know this, this city isn't safe you know and there's a lot of people running around an well I don't have to tell you fellows, you guys know that.

ERDELATZ: When you left home this morning, Dan, was it your intention to confront the Mayor, Supervisor Milk, or anyone else with that gun?

WHITE: No, I, I, what I wanted to do was just, talk to him, you know, I, I ah, I didn't even know if I was going to be reappointed or not be reappointed. *Why do we do things, you know, why did I, I don't know. No, I,* I just wanted to talk to him that's all an' at least have him be honest with me and tell me why he was doing it, not because I was a bad supervisor or anything but, you know, I never killed anybody before, I never shot anybody . . .

ERDELATZ: Why did . . .

WHITE: . . . I didn't even, I didn't even know if I wanted to kill him. I just shot him, I don't know.

ERDELATZ: What type of gun is that you were carrying, Dan?

WHITE: It's a .38, a two-inch .38.

ERDELATZ: And do you know how many shots you fired?

WHITE: Uh . . . no I don't, I don't, I, I out of instinct when I, I reloaded the gun ah . . . you know, it's just the training I guess I had, you know.

ERDELATZ: Where did you reload?

WHITE: I reloaded in my office, when I was—I couldn't out in the hall.

Pause.

ERDELATZ: When you say you reloaded, are you speaking of following the shooting in the Mayor's office?

WHITE: Yeah.

ERDELATZ: Inspector Falzon?

FALZON: No questions. Is there anything you'd like to add, Dan, before we close this statement?

WHITE: Yes. Just that I've been honest and worked hard, never cheated anybody and I wanted to do a good job, I'm trying to do a good job and I saw this city as it's going, kind of downhill and I was always just a lonely vote on the board. I was trying to do a good job for the city.

FALZON: Inspector Erdelatz and I ah . . . appreciate your cooperation and the truthfulness of your statement.

Lights change. DAN WHITE *sobbing.* MARY ANNE WHITE *sobbing,* JURORS *sobbing.* FALZON *moved.*

NORMAN: I think that is all. You may examine.

COURT: Do you want to take a recess at this time?

SCHMIDT: Why don't we take a brief recess?

COURT: Let me admonish you, ladies and gentlemen of the jury, not to discuss this case among yourselves nor with anyone else, not allow anyone to speak to you about the matter, nor are you to form or express an opinion until the matter has been submitted to you.

Gavel. House light up. On screen: Recess.

END OF ACT I

ACT II: IN DEFENSE OF MURDER

As audience enters, on screen are documentary images of Milk and Moscone. COMPANY/*audience watch.*

MOSCONE: *My late father was a guard at San Quentin, and who I was visiting one day, and who showed to me, and then explained the function of, the uh, the uh death chamber. And it just seemed inconceivable to me, though I was pretty young at the time, that in this society that I had been trained to believe was the most effective and efficient of all societies, that the only way we could deal with violent crime would be to do the ultimate ourselves, and that's to governmentally sanction the taking of another person's life.

MILK* (*FALZON enters*): Two days after I was elected I got a phone call—the voice was quite young. It was from Altoona, Pennsylvania. And the person said, "Thanks." And you've got to elect gay people so that that young child, and the thousands upon thousands like that child, know that there's hope for a better world. There's hope for a better tomorrow. Without hope, they'll only gaze at those blacks, the Asians, the disabled, the seniors, the us'es, the us'es. Without hope, the us'es give up. I know that you cannot live on hope alone. But without it, life is not worth living. And you, and you, and you, gotta give 'em hope. Thank you very much.

Lights up. Courtroom. FALZON *on witness stand.* DAN WHITE *at defense table sobbing.* MARY ANN WHITE *behind him sobbing. On tape.*

WHITE (*voice*): Just that I've been honest and worked hard, never cheated anybody and I wanted to do a good job, I'm trying to do a good job and I saw this city as it's going, kind of downhill and I was always just a lonely vote on the board. I was trying to do a good job for the city.

Dialogue from The Times of Harvey Milk, *a film by Robert Epstein and Richard Schmeichen.*

FALZON: Inspector Erdelatz and I ah . . . appreciate your cooperation and the truthfulness of your statement.

FALZON switches tape off

NORMAN: I think that is all. You may examine.

Lights change, COMPANY *exits. On screen: IN-SPECTOR FRANK FALZON, witness for the prosecution. Dissolve to on screen: ACT TWO— IN DEFENSE OF MURDER.*

SCHMIDT: Inspector Falzon, you mentioned that you had known Dan White in the past, prior to November 27th, 1978?

FALZON: Yes, sir, quite well.

SCHMIDT: About how long have you known him?

FALZON: According to Dan,
   it goes way back to the days
   we attended St. Elizabeth's Grammar School together,
   but we went to different high schools.
   I attended St. Ignatius, and he attended Riordan.
   He walked up to me one day at the Jackson Playground,
   with spikes over his shoulders, glove in his hand,
   and asked if he could play on the team.
   I told him it was the police team,
   and he stated that he was a new recruit at Northern Station,
   wanted to play on the police softball team,
   and since that day Dan White and I
   have been very good friends.

SCHMIDT: You knew him fairly well then, that is fair?

FALZON: As well as I know anybody, I believed.

SCHMIDT: Can you tell me, when you saw him first on November 27th, 1978, how did he appear physically to you?

FALZON: Destroyed. This was not the Dan White I had
   known, not at all.
   That day I saw a shattered individual,
   both mentally and physically in appearance,
   who appeared to me to be shattered.
   Dan White, the man I knew

prior to Monday, the 27th of November, 1978, was a man among men.

SCHMIDT: Knowing, with regard to the shootings of Mayor Moscone and Harvey Milk, knowing Dan White as you did, is he the type of man that could have premeditatedly and deliberately shot those people?

NORMAN: Objection as calling for an opinion and conclusion.

COURT: Sustained.

SCHMIDT: Knowing him as you do, have you ever seen anything in his past that would lead you to believe he was capable of cold-bloodedly shooting somebody?

NORMAN: Same objection.

COURT: Sustained.

SCHMIDT: Your Honor, at this point I have anticipated that maybe there would be some argument with regard to opinions not only as to Inspector Falzon, but with a number of other witnesses that I intend to call, and accordingly I have prepared a memorandum of what I believe to be the appropriate law. (*Shows memo.*)

COURT: I have no quarrel with your authorities, but I think the form of the questions that you asked was objectionable.

SCHMIDT: The questions were calculated to bring out an opinion on the state of mind and—I believe that a lay person, if he is an intimate acquaintance, surely can hazard such an opinion. I believe that Inspector Falzon, as a police officer, has an opinion.

COURT: Get the facts from this witness. I will let you get those facts, whatever they are.

SCHMIDT: All right, we will try that. Inspector Falzon, again, you mention that you were quite familiar with Dan White; can you tell me something about the man's character, as to the man that you knew prior to the—prior to November 27th, 1978?

NORMAN: Objection as being irrelevant and vague.

COURT: Overruled. (*To* FALZON.) Do you understand the question?

FALZON: I do, basically, your Honor.

COURT: All right, you may answer it.

NORMAN: Well, your Honor, character for what?

COURT: Overruled. (*To* FALZON.) You may answer it.

FALZON: The Dan White that I knew prior to Monday, November 27th, 1978, was a man who seemed to excel in pressure situations, and it seemed that the greater the pressure, the more enjoyment
that Dan had,
exceeding at what he was trying to do.

Examples would be in his sports life,
that I can relate to,
and for the first time in the history of the State of California,
there was a law-enforcement softball tournament held in 1971.

The San Francisco Police Department entered that softball tournament along with other major departments,
Los Angeles included,
and Dan White was not only named on the All Star Team
at the end of the tournament,
but named the most valuable player.

He was just outstanding under pressure situations,
when men would be on base
and that clutch hit was needed.

Another example of Dan White's
attitude toward pressure
was that when he decided to run
for the District 8 Supervisor's seat,
and I can still vividly remember the morning
he walked into the Homicide Detail and sat down to—
announce that he was going to run for City Supervisor.

I said: "How are you going to do it, Dan?
Nobody heard of Dan White.
How are you going to go out there,
win this election?"

He said "I'm going to do it the way the people want it to be done,
knock on their doors, go inside, shake their hands,
let them know what Dan White stands for."

And he said: "Dan White is going to represent them.

There will be a voice in City Hall, you watch, I'll make it."

He did what he said he was going to do, he ran, won the election.

SCHMIDT: Given these things that you mentioned about Dan White, outstanding under pressure, there anything in his character that you saw of him, prior to those tragedies of the 27th of November, that would have led you to believe that he would ever kill somebody cold-bloodedly?

NORMAN: Objection, irrelevant.

COURT: Overruled.

NORMAN: Let me state my grounds for the record.

COURT: Overruled.

NORMAN: Thank you, Judge. It's irrelevant and called for his opinion and speculation.

COURT: Overruled. (*Gavel. To* FALZON.) You may answer that.

FALZON: Yes, your Honor.

I'm aware—I'm hesitating only because there was something I saw in Dan's personality that didn't become relevant to me until I was assigned this case.
He had a tendency to run, occasionally, from situations.

I saw this flaw, and I asked him about it, and his response was that his ultimate goal was to purchase a boat, just travel around the world,
get away from everybody.

He wanted to be helpful to people, and yet he wanted to run away from them. That did not make sense to me.

Otherwise, to me, Dan White was an exemplary individual, a man that I was proud to know and be associated with.

SCHMIDT: Do you think he cracked? Do you think there was something wrong with him on November 27th?

NORMAN: Objection as calling for an opinion and speculation.

COURT: Sustained.

SCHMIDT: I have nothing further. (*Turns back.*) Inspector, I have one last question. Did you ever see him act out of revenge as to the whole time you have known him?

NORMAN: Objection. That calls for speculation.

COURT: No, overruled, and this is as to his observations and contacts. Overruled.

FALZON: The only time Dan White could have acted out in revenge is when he took the opposite procedure in hurting himself, by quitting the San Francisco Police Department.

SCHMIDT: Nothing further. Thank you, sir.

NORMAN: Inspector Falzon, you regard yourself as a close friend to Mr. Daniel White, don't you?

FALZON: Yes, sir.

NORMAN: Do you regard yourself as a *very* close friend of Mr. Daniel White.

FALZON: I would consider myself a close friend of yours, if that can relate to you my closeness with Dan White.

NORMAN: Of course, you haven't known me as long as you have know Mr. Daniel White, have you, Inspector?

FALZON: Just about the same length of time, Counsel.

NORMAN: Inspector Falzon, while you've expressed some shock at these tragedies, would you subscribe to the proposition that there's a first for everything?

FALZON: It's obvious in this case; yes, sir.

NORMAN: Thank you.

NORMAN sits. FALZON *gets up and takes his seat. Beside* NORMAN.

NORMAN: The Prosecution rests.

Blackout. On screen: The Prosecution rests. Commotion in court.

COURT: Order.

Gavel. Lights up. FREITAS *alone.*

FREITAS: I was the D.A. Obviously in some respects, the trial ruined me. This trial . . .

On screen: Dissolve into picture of DAN WHITE as fire hero. Screen: THE DEFENSE. Subliminal music. Lights up.

SHERRATT (*Fire Chief*): Dan White was an excellent fire fighter. In fact, he was commended for a rescue at Geneva Towers. The award hasn't been given to him as yet, uh . . .

FREDIANI (*Fireman*): Dan White was the valedictorian of the Fire Department class. He was voted so by members of the class.

On screen: DAN WHITE as Valedictorian.

MILK'S FRIEND: When I was in the hospital, what galled me most was the picture of Dan White as the ALL-American Boy.

SHERRATT: but a meritorious advisory board and fire commission were going to present Mr. White with a class C medal.

On screen: DAN WHITE as fire hero.

FREDIANI: Everybody liked Dan.

SCHMIDT: Did you work with Dan as a policeman?

SULLIVAN (*Policeman*): Yes, I did.

MILK'S FRIEND: Maybe as a gay man, I understand the tyranny of the All-American Boy.

On screen: DAN WHITE as police officer.

FREDIANI: He loved sports and I loved sports.

On screen: DAN WHITE as golden gloves boxer.

SULLIVAN: Dan White as a police officer,
was a very fair police officer on the street.

MILK'S FRIEND: Maybe because I am so often his victim.

GWENN: I followed the trial in the papers.

SCHMIDT: Having had the experience of being a police officer, is it unusual for persons that have been police officers to carry guns?

SULLIVAN: Uh, pardon me, Mr. Schmidt?

GWENN: I thought then something was wrong with this picture.

SCHMIDT: I say, it is uncommon that ex-police officers would carry guns?

GWENN: Something was wrong, we thought, when the Chief Inspector of Homicide became the chief character witness for the defense.

SULLIVAN: No, it is a common thing that former police officers will carry guns.

GWENN: Why didn't the Chief Inspector of Homicide ask Dan White how he got into City Hall with a loaded gun?

SCHMIDT: Without a permit?

SULLIVAN: Yes.

GWENN: Dan White reloaded after shooting the Mayor. If it was "reflex," police training, why didn't he reload again after shooting Harvey Milk?

SCHMIDT: Is there anything in this character that would have led you to believe he was capable of shooting two persons?

NORMAN: Objection.

COURT: Overruled.

SULLIVAN: No, nothing whatever.

GWENN: And what can explain the coup de grace shots
White fired into the backs of their heads as
they lay there
helpless on the floor?

DOLSON (*City Supervisor*): Dan in my opinion was a person who saved lives.

GWENN: Where is the prosecution?

FREITAS: I mean, I would have remained in politics. Except for this. I was voted out of office.

SCHMIDT (*To* DOLSON): Supervisor Dolson, you saw
him on
November 27th, 1978, did you not?

DOLSON: I did.

FREITAS: In hindsight, you know.
I would have changed a lot of things.

SCHMIDT: What did you see?

FREITAS: But hindsight is always perfect vision.

Slide: DAN WHITE as City Supervisor outside City Hall.

DOLSON: What I saw made me want to cry. . . .
Dan was always so neat.
Looked like a Marine on Parade. . . .

GWENN: What pressures were you under *indeed*?

DOLSON: And here he was, this kid, who was badly disheveled
and he had his hands cuffed behind him,
which was something I never expected to see.
He looked (*sobs*) absolutely *devastated*.

GWENN: As the "VICTIM" sat in the courtroom
we heard of policemen and firemen sporting
FREE DAN WHITE T-shirts
as they raised 100,000 dollars for Dan White's
defense fund,
and the same message began appearing
in spray paint on walls around the city.
FREE DAN WHITE.

DOLSON: I put my arm around him, told him that everything

was going to be all right,
but how everything was going to be all right,
I don't know.

WITNESS deeply moved. MARY ANN WHITE sobs.

GWENN: And the trial was still happening . . .
SCHMIDT (*deeply moved*): Thank you. I have
nothing further.

DOLSON sobs.

GWENN: but the tears at the Hall of Justice are all
for Dan White.

*Gavel. They exit. Lights change. The ex-D.A.
alone in an empty courtroom. Nervous, fidgeting.*

FREITAS: I was voted out of office. (*On screen:
JOSEPH FREITAS, JR., former D.A.*)

Well, I'm out of politics and I don't know
    whether
I'll get back into politics
because it certainly did set back my personal
    ah . . .
aspirations as a public figure dramatically.
I don't know.

You know, there was an attempt to not allow
    our office to
prosecute the case
because I was close to Moscone myself.
And we fought against that.

I was confident—(*laughs*)
I chose Tom Norman because he was the se-
    nior homicide prosecutor
for fifteen years and he was quite successful at
    it.
I don't know. . . .

The was a great division in the city then, you
    know.
The city was divided all during that period.
George was a liberal Democrat and Dick
    Hongisto.
I was considered a liberal Democrat
and George as you'll remember was elected
Mayor over John Barbagelata who was the
    leader
of what was considered the Right in town.
And it was a narrow victory.
So, after his election, Barbagelata persisted in

attacking them
and keeping
I thought—
keeping the city divided.

It divided on emerging constituencies like
the gay constituency.
That's the one that was used to cause
the most divisive emotions more than any
    other.
So the divisiveness in the city was there.

I mean that was the whole point of this politi-
    cal fight
between Dan White
and Moscone and Milk:
The fight was over who controlled the city.

The Right couldn't afford to lose Dan.
He was their Saving vote on the Board of Su-
    pervisors.
He blocked the Milk/Moscone agenda.
Obviously Harvey Milk didn't want Dan
    White on the Board.

So, it was political, the murders.

Maybe I should have,
again in hindsight, possible Tom,
even though his attempts to do that may have
    been
ruled inadmissible,
possible Tom should have been a little stronger
    in that area.
But again, at the time . . . I mean,
even the press was shocked at the out-
    come. . . .

But—
Well, I think that what the jury had already
    bought was
White's background—
Now that's what was really on trial.
Dan White sat there and waved his little
    American flag
and they acquitted him.
They convicted George and Harvey.
Now if this had been a poor Black or a poor
    Chicano
or a poor white janitor who'd been fired,
or the husband of an alleged girlfriend of
    Moscone's

I don't think they would have bought the diminished capacity
defense.
But whereas they have a guy who was a member of a
county Board of Supervisors who left the police department,
who had served in the army, who was a fireman,
who played baseball—
I think that's what they were caught up in—
that kind of person *must* have been crazy to
do this.
I would have interpreted it differently.
Not to be held to a higher standard, but
uh . . .
that he had all the tools to be responsible.

One of the things people said was:
"Why didn't you talk more about
George's background, his family life, etc.?"
Well . . .
One of the reasons is that Tom Norman did
know,
that had he opened up that area,
they were prepared,
yeah—
they were prepared to smear George—to bring
up the incident in
Sacramento. With the Woman—
(And other things).
It would be at best a wash,
so why get into it?

If you know they're going to bring out things
that aren't positive.
We wanted to let the city heal.
We—And after Jonestown . . .
Well it would have been the city on trial.
If the jury had stuck to the facts alone,
I mean, the confession alone was enough to
convict him. . . .
I mean, look at this kid that shot Reagan,
it was the same thing. All the way through
that,
they said, my friends—
"Well, Christ, look at what the prosecutors
went through on that one, Joe."
It's tragic that that has to be the kind of expe-
rience

that will make you feel better.
And then about White being antigay,
well . . .
White inside himself may have been antigay,
but
that Milk was his target . . .
As I say—*Malice was there.*
Milk led the fight to keep White off the Board,
which makes the murder all the more rational.
I know the gay community thinks the murder
was antigay:
political in that sense. But
I think, they're wrong. Y' know, some
people—
in the gay community
—ah—even said I threw the trial.
Before this, I was considered a great friend to
the gay community.

Why would I want to throw the trial
—this trial
in an election year?

Oh, there were accusations you wouldn't be-
lieve. . . .
At the trial, a woman . . .
it may have been one of the jurors—
I can't remember . . .
Actually said—
"But what would Mary Ann White do without
her husband?"
And I remember my outrage.
She never thought,
"What will Gina Moscone do without
George?"

I must tell you that it's hard for me to talk
about a lot
of these things,
all of this is just the—just
the tip of the iceberg.

We thought—Tommy and I—Tom Norman
and I—
We thought it was an open-and-shut case
of first-degree murder.

*Lights. On screen: THE PSYCHIATRIC DE-
FENSE. Lights up on four psychiatrists in conservative dress, in either separate witness stands or a
multiple-stand unit.*

NORMAN: It wasn't just an automatic reaction when he fired those last two shots into George Moscone's *brains* was it, Doctor?

COURT: Let's move on, Mr. Norman. You are just arguing with the witnesses now.

NORMAN: Your Honor—

COURT: Let's move on.

SOLOMON: I think he was out of control and in an unreasonable state. And I think if the gun had held, you know, maybe more bullets, maybe he would have shot more bullets. I don't know.

LUNDE: This wasn't just some mild case of the blues.

SOLOMON: I think that, you know, maybe Mr. Moscone would have been just as dead with one bullet. I don't know.

JONES: I think he was out of control.

DELMAN: Yes.

NORMAN: George Moscone was shot four times, Doctor. The gun had five cartridges in it. Does that change your opinion in any way?

SOLOMON: No. I think he just kept shooting for awhile.

NORMAN throws his notes down.

SCHMIDT: Now, there is another legal term we deal with in the courtroom, and that is variously called "malice" or "malice aforethought" . . . and this must be present in order to convict for murder in the first degree.

JONES: Okay, let me preface this by saying I am not sure how malice is defined. I'll give you what my understanding is. In order to have malice, you would have to be able to do certain things: to be able to be intent to kill somebody unlawfully. You would have to be able to do something for a base and antisocial purpose. You would have to be aware of the duty imposed on you not to do that, not to unlawfully kill somebody or do something for a base, antisocial purpose, that involved a risk of death, and you would have to be able to act, despite having that awareness of that, that you are not supposed to do that, and so you would have to know that you were not supposed to do it, and then also act despite—keeping in mind that you are not supposed to do it. Is that your answer—your question?

SCHMIDT: I think so.

JONES (*laughs*): I felt that he had the capacity to do the first three:
that he had the capacity to intend to kill,
but that doesn't take much, you know,
to try to kill somebody,
it's not a high-falutin' mental state.
I think he had the capacity to do something for a base and antisocial purpose.
I think he had the capacity to know that there was a duty
imposed on him not to do that,
but *I don't think he had the capacity to hold that notion*
in his mind while he was acting;
so that I think that the depression,
plus the moment, the tremendous emotions of the
moment, with the depression,
reduced his capacity for conforming conduct.
In fact, I asked him:
"Why didn't you hit them?"
And he was flabbergasted that I asked such a thing,
because it was contrary to his code of behavior,
you know, he was taken aback, kind of—
hit them seemed ridiculous to him—
because it would have been so unfair,
since he could have defeated them so easily
in a fist fight.

SCHMIDT: Thank you. (*He sits. To* NORMAN): You may examine.

*[NORMAN: Doctor Jones, when let off at City Hall the accused was let off at the Polk Street entrance and then walked a block and a half to Van Ness Avenue. Why wouldn't he just enter City Hall through the main entrance?

JONES: He got towards the top of the stairs, then looked up, saw the metal detector and thought: "Oh, my goodness, I got that gun."

NORMAN: Doctor, why would he care whether there was a metal detector there, and that a gun would have been discovered upon his person?

---

*NOTE: The bracketed section was cut in the Broadway production.

JONES: Well, I would presume that would mean some degree of hassle. I mean, I presume that the metal detector would see if somebody is trying to bring a weapon in.

NORMAN: That is usually why they have it. Did he realize at that time that he was unlawfully carrying a concealable firearm?

JONES: I presume so.]

NORMAN: Dr. Jones, if it's a fact that Dan White shot George Moscone twice in the body, and that when George Moscone fell to the floor disabled, he shot twice more into the right side of George Moscone's head at a distance of between 12 and 18 inches, he made a decision at that time, didn't he, to either discharge the gun into the head of George Moscone, or not discharge the gun into the head of George Moscone?

JONES: If decision means he behaved in that way, then, yes.

NORMAN: Well, didn't he have to make some kind of choice based upon some reasoning process?

JONES: Oh, no, not based on reasoning necessarily. I think—I don't think that I—you know, great emotional turmoil in context of major mood disorder—he was enraged and anxious and frustrated in addition to the underlying depression. I think that after Moscone says "How's your family?" or, "What's your wife going to do?" at that point, I think that it's—it's over.

NORMAN: It's over for George Moscone.

SOLOMON: I think that if you look at the gun as a transitional object, you can see that transitional objects are clung to in—in situations of great—of anxiety and insecurity, as one sees with children.

COURT—*raises eyes, gives up.*

NORMAN: Doctor, are you telling us that a person who has lived an otherwise law-abiding life and an otherwise moral life could not premeditate and deliberate as is contemplated by the definition of first-degree murder?!

SOLOMON: I'm not saying that absolutely. Obviously, it's more difficult for a person who lives a highly moral life. And this individual, Dan White, had, if you want—a hypertrophy complex. Hypertrophy meaning overdeveloped,

morally, rigidly, overdeveloped. In fact, if Mr. White were to receive a light sentence I think there is a distinct possibility he could take his own life.

But I would say in general, yes.

I don't think you'd kill Mr. Schmidt if you lost this case.

NORMAN: It's unlikely.

SOLOMON: You may be very angry, but I don't think you will do it because I think you are probably a very moral and law-abiding citizen, and I think if you did it, I would certainly recommend a psychiatric examination, because I think there would be a serious possibility that you had flipped. (*Pause.*) It's most interesting to me how split-off his feelings were at this time.

LUNDE: Dan White had classical symptoms that are described in diagnostic manuals for depression and, of course, he had characteristics of compulsive personality, which happens to be kind of a bad combination in those sorts of people.

NORMAN (*frustrated*): Dr. Solomon, you are aware that he took a gun with him when he determined to see George Moscone, a loaded gun?

SOLOMON: Yes.

NORMAN: Why did he take that gun, in your opinion, Dr. Solomon?

SOLOMON: I might say that I think there are symbolic aspects to this.

NORMAN: Symbolic aspects, now Doctor . . .

COURT: Let's move onto another question.

NORMAN: Well, Your Honor . . .

COURT: Let's move on.

NORMAN (*frustrated*): All right. Dr. Delman, after he went in the building armed with a gun through a window and went up to see George Moscone, at the time he came into to George Moscone, do you feel that he was angry with George Moscone?

DELMAN: Yes.

NORMAN: When George Moscone told him that he wasn't going to appoint him, do you think that that brought about and increased any more anger?

DELMAN: Yes.

NORMAN: All right. Now there was some point in there when he shot George Moscone, isn't that true?

DELMAN: Yes.

NORMAN: Do you know how many times he shot him?

DELMAN: I believe it's four.

NORMAN: Well, Doctor, do you put any significance upon the circumstances that he shot George Moscone twice in the head?

DELMAN: The question is, "Do I put any significance in it?"

NORMAN: Yes.

DELMAN: I really have no idea why that happened.

NORMAN: Well, Doctor, do you think he knew that if you shot a man twice in the head that it was likely to surely kill him?!

DELMAN: I'm sure that he knew that shooting a man in the head would kill him, Mr. Norman.

NORMAN: Thank you! (*He sits.*)

SCHMIDT: But, it is your conclusion, Doctor, that Dan White could not premeditate or deliberate, within the meaning we have discussed here, on November 27th, 1978?

DELMAN: That is correct.

NORMAN *slaps hands to head.* BLINDER *enters.*

SCHMIDT: Thank you.

BLINDER: I teach forensic psychiatry.

I teach about the uses and abuses
of psychiatry in the judicial system.
The courts tend to place psychiatry in a position
where it doesn't belong. Where it becomes the sole arbiter
between guilt and innocence.
There is also a tendency in the stresses of the adversary system
to polarize psychiatric testimony so that a psychiatrist finds himself trying to put labels on normal stressful behavior,
and *everything* becomes a mental illness.
And I think that is an abuse. (*He refers to his notes.*)

Dan White found City Hall rife of corruption.
With the possible exceptions of Dianne Feinstein and Harvey Milk,
the Supervisors seemed to make their judgments, their
votes,

on the basis of what was good for them,
rather than what was good for the City.

And this was a very frustrating thing for Mr. White:
to want to do a good job for his constituents
and find he was continually defeated.

In addition to these stresses, there were
attacks by the press
and there were threats of literal attacks on Supervisors.
He told me a number of Supervisors like himself
carried a gun to scheduled meetings.
Never any relief from these tensions.

Whenever he felt things were not going right,
He would abandon his usual program of exercise and good nutrition
and start gorging himself on junk foods:
Twinkies, Coca-Cola.

Soon Mr. White was just sitting in front of the TV.
Ordinarily, he reads. (Mr. White has always been an
identifiable Jack London adventurer.)

But now, getting very depressed about the fact he would
not be reappointed,
he just sat there before the TV
binging on Twinkies. (*On screen: The Twinkie Defense.*)

He couldn't sleep.
He was tossing and turning on the couch in the living room
so he wouldn't disturb his wife on the bed.

Virtually no sexual contact at this time.
He was dazed, confused, had crying spells,
became increasingly ill,
and wanted to be left alone.

He told his wife:
"Don't bother cooking any food for me.
I will just munch on these potato chips."

Mr. White stopped shaving and refused to go out of the house to help Denise rally support.

He started to receive information that he would not be reappointed

from unlikely sources.
This was very stressing to him.

Again, it got to be cupcakes, candy bars.
He watched the sun come up on Monday
    morning.

Finally, at 9:00 Denise called.
He decides to go down to City Hall.
He shaves and puts on his suit.
He sees his gun—lying on the table.
Ammunition.
He simultaneously puts these in his pocket.
Denise picks him up.
He's feeling anxious about a variety of things.
He's sitting in the car hyperventilating,
blowing on his hands, repeating:
"Let him tell me to my face why he won't re-
    appoint me.
Did he think I can't take it?
I am a man.
I can take it."

He goes down to City Hall, and I sense that
    time is short
so let me bridge this by saying that as I believe
it has been testified to,
he circumvents the mental [sic] detector,
goes to the side window,
gets an appointment with the Mayor.
The Mayor almost directly tells him,
"I am not going to reappoint you."

The Mayor puts his arm around him saying;
"Let's have a drink.
What are you going to do now, Dan?
Can you get back into the Fire Department?
What about your family?
Can your wife get her job back?
What's going to happen to them now?"

Somehow this inquiry directed to his family
    struck a nerve.
The Mayor's voice started to fade out and Mr.
    White felt
"As if I were in a dream."
He started to leave and then inexplicably
    turned around
and like a reflex
drew his revolver.
He had no idea how many shots he fired.

The similar event occurred
in Supervisor Milk's office [sic].

He remembers being shocked by the sound of
    the gun
going off for the second time like a cannon.

He tells me that he was aware he engaged
in a lethal act,
but tells me he gave no thought to his wrong-
    fulness.
As he put it to me:
"I had no chance to even think about it."

He remembers running out of the building
driving, I think, to church,
making arrangements to meet his wife,
and then going from the church
to the Police Department.

Pause. Exhausted.

SCHMIDT: Doctor, you have mentioned the ingestion of sugar and sweets and that sort of thing.
There are certain theories with regard to sugar
and sweets and the ingestion thereof, and I'd
like to just touch on that briefly with the jury.
Does that have any significance, or could it
possibly have any significance?

BLINDER (*turns to JURY*): First, there is a substantial body of evidence that in susceptible individuals, large quantities of what we call junk food,
high-sugar-content food with lots of preserva-
tives, can precipitate antisocial and even violent
behavior.

There have been studies, for example, where
they have taken so-called career criminals and
taken them off all their junk food and put them
on meat and potatoes and their criminal records immediately evaporate. (*Pause.*)

It's contradictory and ironic, but the way it
works is that for such a person, the American
Dream is a Nightmare. For somebody like Dan
White.

SCHMIDT: Thank you, Doctor.

*Lights fade on PSYCHIATRISTS. Pause. Lights up
on MARY ANN WHITE, blazing white. She is almost
blinded. She comes forward.*

SCHMIDT: You are married to that man, is that
correct?

MARY ANN: Yes.

SCHMIDT: When did you first meet him?

MARY ANN: I met him (*WITNESS sobbing*) . . .

SCHMIDT: If you want to take any time//* just let us know.

MARY ANN (*pulling herself together*): I met him in April, 1976 . . .

SCHMIDT: And you were married// and you took a trip?

MARY ANN: Yes. Yes, we went to Ireland on our honeymoon because Danny just had this feeling that Ireland could be this place could be really peaceful for him. He just really likes—loves—everything about Ireland and so we—(*sobbing*)

SCHMIDT: Excuse me.

MARY ANN: —so we went there// for about five wee—

SCHMIDT: During that period did you notice anything// unusual about his behavior?

MARY ANN: Yes, I mean, you know, when we went I thought—went thinking it was going to kind of romantic, and when we got there, the thing that attracted me most to Danny was his vitality, energy and the fact that he always had the ability to inspire in you something that made you want to do your best like he did, and when we got there, when we got to Ireland . . . it was all of a sudden, he went into like a two week-long mood, like I had seen before, but I had never seen one, I guess, all the way through, because when we were going out, I might see him for a day, and being a fireman, he would work a day, and then I wouldn't see him, and when we got to Ireland . . . I mean, I was just newly married and I thought: "What did I do?"

SCHMIDT: After he was on the Board, did you notice these moods// become more frequent?

MARY ANN: Yes, he had talked to me about how hard the job was on him. You know, from June he started to talk about how it was. Obviously you can sense when you not are sleeping together, and you are not really growing together and he would say, "Well, I can't—I can't really think of anyone else when I don't even like my self." And I said, "It's just him. He's not sat-

isfied with what I'm doing and I don't like myself// and so I can't . . . "

SCHMIDT: Did you see him on the morning of . . . November 27th?

MARY ANN: Yes// I did.

SCHMIDT: And at that time did he indicate what he was going to do// that day?

MARY ANN: It was just, he was going to stay *home*. He wasn't leaving the house.

SCHMIDT: Later that morning, did you receive a call//to meet him somewhere?

MARY ANN: Yes. I did. Yes, I went to St. Mary's Cathedral. I went and saw him.
I could see that he had been crying, and I, I
just kind of looked at him
and he just looked at me
and he said,
he said,
"I shot the Mayor and Harvey."

SCHMIDT (*looks to NORMAN as if to say, "Any questions?" NORMAN nods no.*): Thank you.

DAN WHITE sobs. SCHMIDT puts hand on WHITE's shoulder. MARY ANN WHITE stumbles off the stand to her husband. WHITE shields his eyes. She looks as if she will embrace him.

SCHMIDT: The defense is prepared to rest at this time.

MARY ANN WHITE sobs. Hyperreal sound of a woman's high heels on marble echoing. Mumbled "Hail Marys."

COURT: Let me admonish you, ladies gentlemen of the jury, not to discuss this case among yourselves nor with anyone else, not to allow anyone to speak to you about the case, nor are you to form or express an opinion until the matter has been submitted to you.

Gavel. On screen: The Defense rests. ALL exit.

MILK'S FRIEND (*enters alone*): *We got back from the airport the night of the 27th
And my roommate said:
There's going to be a candlelight march.
By now, we thought it had to have reached City Hall.

---

*(NOTE: //=Overlap . . . Next speaker starts, first speaker continues.)

*Dialogue from *The Times of Harvey Milk,* a film by Robert Epstein and Richard Schmeichen.

So we went directly there. From the airport to
   City Hall.
And there were maybe 75 people there.
And I remember thinking:
My God is this all anybody . . . cared?
Somebody said: No, the march hasn't gotten
   here yet.
So we then walked over to Market Street
which was 2 or 3 blocks away.
And looked down it.
And Market Street runs in a straight line
out to the Castro area.
And as we turned the corner
(*On screen: The screens flooded with candles and
the candlelight march music. Barber's "Adagio."*)
   there were people as wide as this wide street
   As far as you could see.

The entire COMPANY *enters holding candles. After
awhile:*

YOUNG MOTHER: *Thousands and thousands of
   people,
And that feeling of such loss.

Music continues.

GWENN: *It was one of the most eloquent expres-
   sions of a
community's response to violence
that I have every seen. . . .

A MOURNER: (*wearing a black arm band*): I'd like
   to read from the transcript of Harvey Milk's
   political will. (*Reads.*)
This is Harvey Milk speaking on Friday, November 18.
This tape is to be played only in the event of
   my death
by assassination. (*On screen: Pictures of MILK.*)

I've given long and considerable thought to
   this,
and not just since the election.
I've been thinking about this for some time
prior to the election and certainly over the years.
I fully realize that a person who stands for
      what I stand for—
a gay activist—

———
*Dialogue from *The Times of Harvey Milk,* a film by
Robert Epstein and Richard Schmeichen.

becomes the target for a person who is inse-
   cure, terrified,
afraid or very disturbed themselves. (DAN
   WHITE *enters. Stops.*)

Knowing that I could be assassinated at any
   moment
or any time,
I feel it's important that some people should
   understand
my thoughts.
So the following are my thoughts, my wishes,
   my desires,
I'd like to pass them on and have them played
   for the appropriate people.

The first and most obvious concern is that
if I was to be shot and killed,
the mayor has the power,
George Moscone . . . (*On screen: Pictures of
   MOSCONE, the funeral, the mourners,
   the widow.*)
of appointing my successor . . .
to the Board of Supervisors.
I cannot prevent some people
from feeling angry and frustrated and mad,
but I hope
that they would not demonstrate violently.
If a bullet should enter my brain,
let that bullet destroy every closet door.

Gavel. All MOURNERS *blow out candles.* DAN
WHITE *sits. Blackout. On screen: The People's re-
buttal/Dr. Levy Psychiatrist. Lights up.*

LEVY: I interviewed the defendant several hours
   after the shootings of November 27th.
   In my opinion, one can get a more accurate diagnosis
   the closer one examines the suspect
   after a crime has been committed.
   At that time, it appeared to me that Dan
      White had
   no remorse for the death of George Moscone.
   It appeared to me, he had no remorse
   for the death of Harvey Milk.
   There was nothing in my interview which
      would suggest to me
   there was any mental disorder.
   I had the feeling that there was some depres-
      sion but it was not

depression that I would consider a diagnosis. In fact, I found him to be less depressed than I would have expected him to be. At that time I saw him, it seemed that he felt himself to be quite justified. (*Looks to notes.*)
I felt he had the capacity to form malice.
I felt he had the capacity to premeditate.
And . . .
I felt he had the capacity to deliberate, to arrive at a
course of conduct weighing considerations.
NORMAN: Did you review the transcript of the proceeding wherein the testimonies of Drs. Jones, Blinder, Solomon, Delman, and Lunde were given?
LEVY: Yes. I found nothing in them that would cause me to revise my opinion.
NORMAN: Thank you, Dr. Levy (*sits*).

SCHMIDT stands.

SCHMIDT: Dr. Levy, are you a full professor at the University of California?
LEVY: No. I am an associate clinical professor.

SCHMIDT smiles, looks to JURY.

SCHMIDT: May I inquire of your age, sir?
LEVY: I'm 55.
SCHMIDT: Huh. (*Picking up papers.*) Doctor, your report is dated November 27th, 1978, is it not?
LEVY: Yes.
SCHMIDT: And yet the report was not written on November 27th, 1978?
LEVY: No. It would have been within several days// of that time.
SCHMIDT: And then it was dated November 27th, 1978?
LEVY: Yes.
SCHMIDT: Well, regardless of the backdating, or whatever, when did you come to your forensic conclusions?
LEVY: I'd say the conclusions would have been on November 27th.
SCHMIDT: And that was after a two-hour talk with Dan White?
LEVY: Yes.
SCHMIDT: Doctor, would it be fair to say that you made some snap decisions?

LEVY: I don't believe// I did.
SCHMIDT: Did you consult with any other doctors?
LEVY: No.
SCHMIDT: Did you review any of the witnesses' statements?
LEVY: No.
SCHMIDT: Did you consult any of the material that was available to you, save and except for the tape of Dan White on the same date?
LEVY: No. That was all that was made available to me// at that time.
SCHMIDT: Now I don't mean to be facetious, but this is a fairly important case, is that fair?
LEVY: I would certainly think so,// yes.
SCHMIDT: But you didn't talk further with Mr. White?
LEVY: No. I was not requested to.
SCHMIDT: And you didn't request to talk to him further?
LEVY: No. I was not going to do a complete assessment.
SCHMIDT: Well, in fact, you didn't do a complete assessment, is that fair?
LEVY: I was not asked to do a complete assessment.
COURT: Doctor, you are fading away.
LEVY: *I was not asked to do a complete assessment.*
SCHMIDT: Thank you.

Blackout. Commotion in court, JOANNA tries to get interview from LEVY.

SCHMIDT (*in black*): She wants to tell the story so it's not
responsive to the questions.

Lights up. On screen: SUPERVISOR CAROL RUTH SILVER, for the prosecution.

SILVER (*very agitated, speaking fast, heated*): The prosecution asked in what other case did a dispute between Dan White and Harvey Milk arise! And it was the Polk Street closing was another occasion when Harvey requested that Polk Street, which is a heavily gay area in San Francisco, I am sure everybody knows, and on Halloween had traditionally had a huge number of people in costumes and so forth down there and has// traditionally been recommended for closure by the Police Department and—

SCHMIDT: I am going to object to this, Your Honor.

SILVER: It was recommended—

COURT: Just as the next question. Just ask the next question.

SILVER: I am sorry.

NORMAN: Did Mr. Milk and Mr. White take positions that were opposite to each other?

SILVER: Yes.

NORMAN: Was there anything that became, well, rather loud and perhaps hostile in connection or consisting between the two?

SILVER: Not loud but very hostile. You have to first understand that this street closure was recommended by the Police Chief and had been done customarily in the years past// and is, was—came up as a uncontested issue practically.

SCHMIDT: Your Honor, I again—

COURT: Please, just make your objection.

SCHMIDT: I'd like to.

COURT: Without going through contortions.

SCHMIDT: There is an objection.

COURT: All right. Sustained.

NORMAN: Miss Silver, did you know, or did you ever see Mr. White to appear to be depressed or to be withdrawn?

SILVER: No.

NORMAN: Thank you (*sits*).

SILVER flabbergasted, upset.

COURT: All right. Any questions, Mr. Schmidt?

SCHMIDT: Is it *Miss* Silver?

SILVER: Yes.

SCHMIDT: Miss Silver, you never had lunch with Dan White, did you?

SILVER: Did I ever have lunch?

Subliminal music.

NOTHENBERG: George Moscone was socially brilliant in that he could find the injustice.

SCHMIDT: I mean the two of you?

SILVER: I don't recall having done so// but I—

NOTHENBERG: His mind went immediately to what can we do?

SCHMIDT: Did you socialize frequently?

NOTHENBERG: What can we practically do?

SILVER: No, when his son was born// I went to a party at his house and that kind of thing.

SCHMIDT: Did Mr. Norman contact you last week, or did you// contact him?

NOTHENBERG: I was with George registering voters in Mississippi in 1964.

SILVER: On Friday morning I called his office . . .

NOTHENBERG: Y'know, he'd never seen that kind of despair before, but when he saw it he said right out: "This is intolerable."

SILVER: because I was reading the newspaper—

SCHMIDT: Yes.

SILVER: And it appeared// to me that—

COURT: Don't tell us.

NOTHENBERG: And whenever he said: "this is *intolerable*" . . .

SILVER: I'm sorry.

NOTHENBERG: In all the years I knew him, he always *did* something about it.

COURT: The jurors are told not to read the newspaper, and I am hoping that they haven't// read the newspapers.

SILVER: I apologize.

COURT: Okay.

SCHMIDT: Miss Silver—

COURT: I am sorry, I didn't want to cut her off—

SILVER: No, I understand.

COURT: from any other answer

SCHMIDT: I think she did complete the answer, Judge. In any event, you contacted Mr. Norman, did you not?

SILVER: Yes, I did.

SCHMIDT: And at that time, you offered to Mr. Norman to round up people who could say that Dan White never looked depressed at City Hall, is that fair?

SILVER: That's right. Well, I offered to testify to that effect and I suggested that there were other people// who could similarly testify to that fact.

SCHMIDT: In fact, you expressed it though you haven't sat here and listened to the testimony in this courtroom?

SILVER: No, I have never been here before Friday when I was subpoenaed// and spent some time in the jury room.

SCHMIDT: But to use your words, after having read what was in the paper, you said that the defense sounded like "bullshit" to you?

SILVER: That's correct.

DENMAN: I thought I would be a chief witness for the prosecution.

SCHMIDT: Would that suggest then that perhaps you have a bias in this case?

DENMAN: What was left unsaid was what the trial should have been about.

SILVER: I certainly have a bias.

SCHMIDT: You are a political enemy of Dan White's, is that fair?

SILVER: No, that's not true.

DENMAN: Before, y'know, there was a lot of talk about assassinating the Mayor among thuggish elements of the Police Officers Association.

SCHMIDT: Did you have any training in psychology or psychiatry?

DENMAN: And those were the cops Dan White was closest to.

SILVER: No more than some of the kind of C.E.B. courses// lawyers' psychology for lawyers' kind of training.

DENMAN: I think he knew a lot of guys would think he did the right thing and yeah they would make him a hero.

SCHMIDT: I mean, would you be able to diagnose, say, *manic depression depressed type,* or could you distinguish that from *uni-polar depression?*

SILVER: No.

DENMAN: I was Dan White's jailer for 72 hours after the assassinations.

SCHMIDT: Did you ever talk to him about his dietary habits or anything like that?

DENMAN: There were no tears.

SILVER: I remember a conversation about nutrition or something like that. But I can't remember// the substance of it.

SCHMIDT: I don't have anything further.

DENMAN: There was no shame.

COURT: Any redirect, Mr. Norman?

NORMAN: Yes.

DENMAN: You got the feeling that he knew exactly what he was doing and there was no remorse.

NORMAN: Miss Silver, you were asked if you had a bias in this case. You knew Harvey Milk very well and you liked him, didn't you?

SILVER: I did; and also George Moscone.

NORMAN: Miss Silver, speaking of a bias, had you ever heard the Defendant say anything about getting people of whom Harvey Milk numbered himself?

Lights up on MILK'S FRIEND.

SILVER: In the Polk Street debate—

MILK'S FRIEND: The night Harvey was elected, I went to bed early because it was more happiness than I had been taught to deal with.

SILVER: Dan White got up and gave—a long diatribe—

MILK'S FRIEND: Next morning we put up signs saying "thank you."

SILVER: Just a—a very unexpected and very uncharacteristic of Dan, long hostile speech about how gays and their lifestyles had to be contained and we can't// *encourage* this kind of thing and—

SCHMIDT: I am going to object to this, your Honor.

COURT: Sustained, okay.

MILK'S FRIEND: During that, Harvey came over and told me
that he had made a political will
because he expected he'd be killed.
And then in the same breath, he said (I'll never forget it):
"It works, it works . . . "

NORMAN: All right . . . that's all.

MILK'S FRIEND: The system works// . . .

NORMAN: Thank you.

DENMAN: When White was being booked, it all seemed fraternal. One officer gave Dan a pat on the behind when he was booked, sort of a "Hey, catch you later, Dan," pat.

COURT: Any recross?

DENMAN: Some of the officers and deputies were standing around with half-smirks on their faces. Some were actually laughing.

SCHMIDT: Just a couple.

DENMAN: The joke they kept telling was,
"Dan White's mother says to him when he comes home,
'No, dummy, I said milk and baloney, not Moscone!' "

Pause.

SCHMIDT: Miss Silver, you are a part of the gay community also, are you?

SILVER: Myself?

SCHMIDT: Yes.

SILVER: You mean, am I gay?

SCHMIDT: Yes.

SILVER: No, I'm not.

SCHMIDT: I have nothing further.

MOSCONE'S FRIEND: George would have said, "This is intolerable," and he'd have done something about it.

COURT: All right, Miss Silver you may leave.

COURT: Next witness, please.

Lights. SILVER *exits towards door.* JOANNA *with TV lights.*

JOANNA LU: Miss Silver, Supervisor Silver, would you like to elaborate on Mr. White's antigay feelings or hostility to Harvey Milk or George Moscone?

SILVER: No comment, right now.

SILVER *distraught, rushes past.*

JOANNA LU: Did you feel you were baited, did you have your say?

SILVER (*blows up*): I said I have no comment at this time!!!

She exits.

COURT: Mr. Norman? Next witness?

NORMAN: Nothing further. Those are all the witnesses we have to present.

COURT: The People rest?

NORMAN: Yes.

COURT: Does the defense have any witnesses?

SCHMIDT (*surprised*): Well, we can discuss it, Your Honor. I am not sure there is anything to rebut.

Light change. Commotion in court. On screen: The People Rest. Lights up on SCHMIDT. *He is at a podium, a parish priest at a pulpit. Dissolve to on screen: Summations.*

SCHMIDT: I'm nervous. I'm very nervous. I sure hope I say all the right things. I can't marshal words the way Mr. Norman can—but—I believe strongly in things.

Lord God! I don't say to you to forgive Dan White. I don't say to you to just let Dan White walk out of here a free man. He is guilty. But, the degree of responsibility is the issue here.

The state of mind is the issue here. It's not who was killed; it's why. It's not who killed them; but why. The state of mind is the issue here.

Lord God! The pressures.
Nobody can say that the things that happened to him days
or weeks preceding wouldn't make a reasonable and ordinary man
at least mad,
angry in some way.

Surely—surely, that had to have arisen, not to kill,
not to kill, just to be mad, to act irrationally,
because if you kill, when you are angry, or under the heat of passion,
if you kill, then the law will punish you,
and you will be punished by God—
God will punish you,
but the law will also punish you.

Heat of passion fogs judgment, makes one act irrationally,
in the very least,
and my God,
that is what happened at the very least.

Forget about the mental illness,
forget about all the rest of the factors
that came into play at the same time;
Surely he acted irrationally, impulsively—out of some passion.

Now . . . you will recall at the close of the prosecution's case,
it was suggested to you this was a calm, cool, deliberating,
terrible terrible person
that had committed two crimes like these,
and these are terrible crimes,
and that he was emotionally stable at that time
and there wasn't anything wrong with him.

He didn't have any diminished capacity.
Then we played these tapes he made directly after
he turned himself in at Northern Station.

My God,
that was not a person that was calm and collected and cool

and able to weigh things out.
It just wasn't.

The tape just totally fogged me up the first
time I heard it.
It was a man that was, as Frank Falzon said,
broken.
Shattered.
This was not the Dan White that everybody
had known.

Something happened to him and he snapped.
That's the word I used in my opening state-
ment.
Something snapped here.

The pot had boiled over here,
and people that boil over in that fashion,
they tell the truth.

Have the tape played again, if you can't remember what was said.
He said in no uncertain terms:

"My God,
why did I do these things?
What made me do this?
How on earth could I have done this?
I didn't intend to hurt anybody.
My God,
what happened to me?
Why?"

Play the tape.
If everybody says the tape is truthful, play the
tape.
I'd agree it's truthful.

With regard to the reloading and some of
these little
discrepancies that appeared to come up.
I am not even sure of the discrepancies,
but if there were discrepancies,
listen to it in context.
"Where did you reload?"
"I reloaded in my office, I think."
"And then did you leave the Mayor's office?"
"Yes, then I left the Mayor's office."

That doesn't mean anything to me at all.
It doesn't mean anything to me at all.
And I don't care where the reloading took
place!

But listen to the tape.
It says in no uncertain terms,
"I didn't intend to hurt anybody.
I didn't intend to do this.
Why do we do things?"

I don't know.
It was a man desperately trying to grab at
something . . .

"What happened to me?
How could I have done this?"

If the District Attorney concedes that what is
on the tape is truthful,
and I believe that's the insinuation we have
here,
then, by golly,
there is voluntary manslaughter,
nothing more and nothing less. I say this to
you in all honesty.

And if you have any doubts our law tells you,
you have to judge in favor of Dan White.

Now, I don't know what more I can say.
He's got to be punished
and he will be punished.
He's going to have to live with this for the rest
of his life.
His child will live with it
and his family will live with it
and God will punish him
and the law will punish him,
and they will punish him severely.
And this is the type of case where, I suppose,
I don't think Mr. Norman will do it,
but you can make up a picture of a dead man
or two of them for that matter
and you can have them around and say
somebody is going to pay for this
and somebody *is* going to pay for this.
But it's not an emotional type thing.
I get emotional about it
but *you* can't
because you have to be objective about the
facts.

But please, please
Just justice.
That's all.
Just justice here. (*He appears to break for a
moment.*)

Now I get one argument.
I have made it.
And I just hope that—
I just hope that you'll come to the same con-
    clusion
that I have come to,
and thank you for listening to me.

NORMAN: Ladies and gentlemen,
I listened very carefully to the summation just
    given you.
It appears to me, members of the jury,
to be a very facile explanation and rationaliza-
    tion
as to premeditation and deliberation.
The evidence that has been laid before you
screams for murder in the first degree.

What counsel for the defense has done is sug-
    gest to you
to *excuse* this kind of conduct and call it
    something that
it isn't,
to call it voluntary manslaughter.

Members of the jury, you are the triers of fact
    here.
You have been asked to hear this tape record-
    ing again.
The tape recording has been aptly described
as something very moving. We all feel a sense
    of sympathy,
a sense of empathy for our fellow man, but
    you are not to let
sympathy influence you in your judgment.

To reduce the charge of murder to something
    less—
to reduce it to voluntary manslaughter—
means you are saying that this was not mur-
    der.
That this was an intentional killing of a hu-
    man being
upon a quarrel, or heat of passion.
But ladies and gentlemen,
that quarrel must have been so extreme,
at the time
that the defendant could not—
was incapable of forming
those qualities of thought which are
malice, premeditation and deliberation.

But the evidence in this case doesn't suggest
    that at all.
Not at all.
If the defendant had picked up a vase or some-
    thing
that happened to be in the mayor's office
and hit the mayor over the head and killed
    him,
you know, you know that argument for volun-
    tary manslaughter
might be one which you could say the evidence
    admits
a reasonable doubt. But—

Ladies and gentlemen:
THE FACTS ARE:
It was *he*—Dan White—who brought the gun
    to the City Hall
The gun was not there.

It was *he* who brought the extra cartridges for
    the gun;
they were not found there

He went to City Hall and when he got there he
    went
to the Polk Street door.

There was a metal detector there.
He knew he was carrying a gun.
He knew that he had extra cartridges for it.

Instead of going through the metal detector,
he *decided* to go around the corner.
He was capable at that time of expressing an-
    ger.
He was capable of, according to the doctor—
well, parenthetically, members of the jury,
I don't know how they can look in your head
    and tell you
what you are able to do. But—
They even said that he was capable of know-
    ing at that time
that if you pointed a gun at somebody and you
    fired that gun
that you would surely kill a person.

He went around the corner, and climbed
through a window into City Hall.

He went up to the Mayor's office.
He appeared, according to witnesses,

to act calmly in his approach, in his speech.

He chatted with Cyr Copertini; he was capable of
carrying on a conversation to the extent that he was
able to ask her how she was, after having asked to see
the Mayor. (*Looks to* AUDIENCE.)

He stepped into the Mayor's office.
After some conversation,
he shot the Mayor twice in the body.
Then he shot the Mayor in the head twice
while the Mayor was disabled on the floor.
The evidence suggests that in order to shoot the Mayor
twice in the head
he had to *lean down* to do it. (*And* NORMAN *does. Looks to* JURY.)
Deliberation is premeditation.
It has malice.
I feel stultified to even bring this up.
This is the definition of murder.

He reloaded the gun.
Wherever he reloaded the gun, it was *he* who reloaded it!

He did see Supervisor Milk
whom he knew was acting against his appointment
and he was capable of expressing anger in that regard.

He entered the Supervisor's area (a block from the Mayor's
office across City Hall)
and was told, "Dianne wants to see you."
He said, "That is going to have to wait a moment.
I have something to do first."

Then he walked to Harvey Milk's office, put his head
in the door and said
"Can I see you a moment, Harv?"
The reply was. "Yes."

He went across the hall and put three bullets into Harvey Milk's body,
one of which hit Harvey directly in the back.
When he fell to the floor disabled,

two more were delivered to the back of his head.

Now what do you call that but premeditation and deliberation?
what do you call that realistically
but a cold-blooded killing?
Two *cold-blooded executions.*
It occurs to me that if you don't call them that,
then you are ignoring the objective evidence and the objective facts here.

Members of the jury, there are circumstances here
which no doubt bring about anger,
maybe even rage, I don't know,
but the manner in which that anger was felt and was handled
is *socially something that cannot be approved.*

Ladies and gentlemen,
the quality of your service is reflected in your verdict.

He sits. JOANNA LU *at door stops* SCHMIDT. *TV lights.*

JOANNA LU: Mr. Schmidt, do you—
SCHMIDT: Yes.
JOANNA LU: Do you feel society would feel justice is served if the jury returns two manslaughter verdicts?
SCHMIDT: Society doesn't have anything to do with it. Only those 12 people in the jury box.

Gavel.

COURT: Ladies and gentlemen of the jury,
Now that you have heard the evidence,
we come to that part of the trial where you are instructed
on the applicable law.

In the crime of murder of the first degree
the necessary concurrent mental states are:
Malice aforethought, premeditation, and deliberation.
In the crime of murder of the second degree,
the necessary concurrent mental state is:
Malice aforethought.
In the crime of voluntary manslaughter,
the necessary mental state is:
an intent to kill.

Involuntary manslaughter is an unlawful killing
without malice aforethought
and without intent to kill.

The law does not undertake to limit or define
the kinds of passion
which may cause a person to act rashly.
Such passions as desperation,
humiliation, resentment,
anger, fear, or rage
or any other high wrought emotion . . .
can be sufficient to reduce the killings to manslaughter
so long as they are sufficient
to obscure the reason
and render the average man likely to act
rashly.

There is no malice aforethought
if the killing occurred upon a sudden quarrel
or heat of passion.

There is no malice aforethought
if the evidence shows that due to diminished
capacity
caused by illness, mental defect, or intoxica-
tion,
the defendant did not have the capacity
to form the mental state constituting malice
aforethought,
even though the killing was intentional,
voluntary, premeditated, and unprovoked.

*A siren begins to cover the court. On screen: Im-
ages of the riot at City Hall begin to appear. Broken glass, images of cop cars burning, riot police,
angry faces. On audio: Explosions—it is the riot.*

GWENN (*on video*): In order to understand the riots, I think you have to understand that the
Dan White verdict did not occur in a vacuum—

COURT: Mr. Foreman, has the jury reached ver-
dicts// in this case?

GWENN: that there were and are other factors
which contribute to a legitimate rage that was
demonstrated dramatically at our symbol of
Who's Responsible, City Hall.

*On screen: Images of City Hall being stormed.
Line of police in front in riot gear.*

FOREMAN: Yes, it has, Your Honor.

GWENN: The verdict came down and the people
rioted.

COURT: Please read the verdicts.

GWENN: The people stormed City Hall, burned
police cars.

*On screen: Image of City Hall. Line of police cars
in flames.*

FOREMAN (*reading*): The jury finds the defendant
Daniel James White guilty of violating Section
192.1 of the penal code. . . .

GWENN: Then the police came into our neighborhood. And the police rioted.

FOREMAN: voluntary manslaughter, for the slaying of Mayor George Moscone.

*MARY ANN WHITE gasps. DAN WHITE puts head in
hands. Explosion. Riot police enter.*

GWENN: The police came into the Castro and as-
saulted gays.
They stormed the Elephant Walk Bar.
One kid had an epileptic seizure and was almost killed for it.
A cop drove a motorcycle up against a phone
booth
where a lesbian woman was on the phone.
blocked her exit
and began beating her up.

COURT: Is this a unanimous verdict of the jury?

FOREMAN: Yes, it is, Judge.

GWENN: I want to talk about when people are
pushed to the wall. (*Off video.*)

COURT: Will each juror say "yea"// or "nay"?

YOUNG MOTHER: What about the children?

MOSCONE'S FRIEND: I know who George offended. I know who Harvey offended.

JURORS: Yea, yea, yea// yea, yea, yea.

MOSCONE'S FRIEND: I understand the offense.

YOUNG MOTHER: What do I tell my kids?

GWENN: Were the ones who are responsible seeing these things?

YOUNG MOTHER: That in this country you serve
more time for robbing a bank than for killing
two people?

JURORS: Yea, yea, yea// yea, yea, yea.

GWENN: Hearing these things?

MILK'S FRIEND: I understand the offense.

GWENN: Do they understand about people being
pushed to the wall?

YOUNG MOTHER: Accountability?

Yea's end.

MILK'S FRIEND: Assassination.
 I've grown up with it.
 I forget it hasn't always been this way.
LEVY: What do I say?
 That two lives are worth seven years and eight
  months// in jail
MILK'S FRIEND: I remember coming home from
 school in second grade—
 JFK was killed—
 Five years later, Martin Luther King.
 It's a frame of reference.

Explosion.

COURT: Will the Foreman please read the verdict
 for the second count?
DENMAN: It's a divided city.
FOREMAN: The jury finds the defendant Daniel
 James White guilty of violating Section 192.1
 of the penal code, voluntary manslaughter, in
 the slaying of Supervisor Harvey Milk.

*DAN WHITE gasps. MARY ANN WHITE sobs. NOR-
MAN, flushed, head in hands. Explosion. Violence
ends. Riot police do terror control. TV lights.*

BRITT (*on camera*): No—I'm optimistic about
 San Francisco.
COURT: Is that a unanimous decision by the jury?
FOREMAN: Yes, Your Honor.
BRITT: I'm Harry Britt. I was Harvey Milk's suc-
 cessor.
MOSCONE'S FRIEND: If he'd just killed George,
 he'd be in jail for life.
BRITT: Now this is an example I don't use often
 because people will misunderstand it, but when
 a prophet is killed, it's up to those who are left
 to build the community or the church.
MOSCONE'S FRIEND: Dan White believed in the
 death// penalty . . .
YOUNG MOTHER: To this jury Dan White// was
 their son.
NOTHENBERG: He should have gotten the death
 penalty.
YOUNG MOTHER: What are we teaching our
 sons?
BRITT: But I have hope.
MILK'S FRIEND: It was an effective assassination.

BRITT: I have hope. And as Harvey said, "you
 can't live// without hope."
MILK'S FRIEND: They always are.
BRITT: "And you, and you, and you—we gotta
 give 'em hope."

Riot ends.

JOANNA LU (*on camera*): Dan White was examined by the psychiatrist at the state prison. They
 decided against therapy. Dan White had no apparent signs of mental disorder. . . . Dan White's
 parole date was January 6th, 1984. When Dan
 White left Soledad prison on January 6th, 1984,
 it was five years, one month, and eight days since
 he turned himself in at Northern Station after
 the assassinations of Mayor George Moscone
 and Supervisor Milk. Mayor Dianne Feinstein,
 the current Mayor of San Francisco, has tried to
 keep Dan White out of San Francisco during his
 parole for fear he will be killed.
BOOM BOOM (*enters*): Dan White! It's 1984 and
 Big Sister is watching you.
JOANNA LU: Dan White reportedly plans to move
 to Ireland after his release.
NOTHENBERG: What do you do with your feelings of revenge?
 With your need for retribution?
BRITT: We will never forget.

Riot images freeze.

BOOM BOOM: I would like to close with a reading from the Book of Dan. (*Opens book.*) Take
 of this and eat, for this is my defense. (*Raises
 the Twinkie. Eats it. Exits.*)
JOANNA LU: Dan White was found dead of carbon
 monoxide poisoning on October 21st, 1985, at
 his wife's home in San Francisco, California.

Lights change. DAN WHITE faces the court.

COURT: Mr. White, you are sentenced to seven
 years and eight months, the maximum sentence
 for these two counts of voluntary manslaughter. The Court feels that these sentences for the
 taking of life is completely inappropriate but
 that was the decision of the legislature.
 Again, let me repeat for the record:
 Seven years and eight months is the maximum
  sentence for
 voluntary manslaughter, and this is the law.

Gavel. Long pause. WHITE *turns to the audience/*JURY.

DAN WHITE: I was always just a lonely vote on the board.

I was just trying to do a good job for the city.

Long pause. Audio: Hyperreal sounds of a woman's high heels on marble. Mumbled Hail Marys. Rustle of an embrace. SISTER BOOM BOOM *enters. Taunts police. Police raise riot shields. Blackout. On screen:* Execution of justice. *Gavel echoes.*

END OF PLAY

Execution of *Justice*

YOU, THE JURY:
Emily Mann's *Execution of Justice**

Emily Mann writes political plays based on affective response. *Still Life,* produced in 1980, deals with the Vietnam War not directly but through the "traumatic memories," as Mann puts it, of a marine who served there, his wife, and his mistress. "Distilled" from taped interviews conducted by the playwright, these monologues are interwoven in such a way that the play itself becomes Mann's "traumatic memory" of their collective memories. Despite this formalistic structure, the effect is startlingly real: the three "survivors" speak their lines directly to the audience, Mann explains, so that it "can hear what I heard, experience what I experienced." This experience is intensified by Mann's setting—either a "conference room," a "trial room," or three contiguous but separate personal spaces. Not only is the audience meant to share the playwright's traumatic response, it actually seems to participate in the testimonial—as confessor, psychiatrist,

juror, special friend. Political issues may ultimately be raised by *Still Life,* but Mann's central concerns seem to be psychological rather than analytic or didactic: How do individuals respond to political events, especially political violence, on an emotional level; how can an audience be made to participate emotionally in that response? This affective approach to a political subject is again readily apparent in Emily Mann's new play, *Execution of Justice,* which premiered on February 22, 1984, as part of the Humana Festival of New American Plays at the Actors Theater of Louisville.

Consider the prologue. First there are bells, running footsteps, mumbled "Hail Marys." Then, in the darkness, a woman's voice, strained to breaking, announces that two men have been shot and killed—Mayor George Moscone and Supervisor Harvey Milk. "The suspect," she adds, "is Supervisor Dan White." A man's voice calls out: "This is the matter of the People vs. Daniel James White." A gavel sounds. A white cross is projected on a screen upstage. Downstage a man appears. He seems huge, burly; he jerks open his jacket to reveal a T-shirt printed with the words "FREE DAN WHITE." He speaks directly to the audience; his tone is angry, aggressive. He's a third-generation San Francisco cop, a Catholic; he's got a wife and kids; his city has been taken over by "stinkin' degenerates"; the sights he sees every day make him sick and mad. He blames Mayor Moscone and his "Negro-loving, faggot-loving" chief of police. They want him to treat the queers with "lavender gloves"; even the squad cars have been painted "faggot-blue." Dan White "understood" all this, he says; "Dan White proved you *could* fight City Hall."

As the cop speaks, another figure appears, dressed in a nun's habit with grotesque white makeup and spike heels. The audience receives an ice-cold blessing. The voice is male. Solemnly it reads a message from the "Book of Dan": "Not life but three to seven with time off for good behavior." A naked leg appears; the black habit splits open, exposing a slender white male body, a jock strap, a garter belt, a red stone in the navel. The pose is defiant. The voice remains cool, ironic: It speculates on the possibility of equal justice for "gay people, and people of color and

---

*Reprinted by permission from *Theater*, 16, 1 (Fall/Winter, 1984): 55–61.

women" in a culture saturated with violence and brutality. With a mocking tone, the voice begs understanding and forgiveness for the "angry faggot or dyke" who, eventually, in a fit of depression, will "get Dan White." The lights go out.

The scene lasts no more than five minutes. On a dark gray, nearly circular stage, with stepped tiers flanking a black "skene" at the back, the cop and the drag nun could be two malignant Euripidean gods, come out for a moment to set the scene. Clearly they personify hostile points of view in an intense social struggle, one that has led to an atmosphere of anger, frustration and to acts of violence. Clearly too, the impact of Mann's scene, her attack, is primarily emotional, not expository; facts are given, but objectivity seems out of the question. The costumes alone are ciphers of prejudice, designed to offend and polarize, while the true subject of the scene is one of the most emotionally charged issues of the day—"homophobia," the fear and hatred of homosexuals. The cop defends it; the drag nun deplores it; both appeal directly to the audience for support and agreement. The effect is brutal, riveting. Not only that, the debate seems rigged. The two sides are not equally balanced: Mann humanizes the cop and dehumanizes the gay. If the cop seems ugly and threatening, he also seems more personal, more real—he goes to church, he has a family, he's concerned about their welfare. Also, his manner is direct: He's tough but he's honest; his words are simple, concrete, colloquial. When he describes gay sex and public behavior, he chooses the most bizarre examples; they throw his "normalcy" into sharp relief.

The drag nun, on the other hand, is nothing but a grotesque mask. Mann bases the character on a real drag nun—Sister Boom-Boom (aka Jack Fertig), one of the "Sisters of Perpetual Indulgence," a San Francisco media figure and sometime politician. The words come from an actual speech delivered by Fertig a number of times in 1979. Mann's version of the character, however, seems quite different from Fertig's. The original Boom-Boom wears an elaborate habit and heels but his manner is less overtly sexual; his tone more comic than satiric; you see the man behind the make-up. Mann's nun, on the other hand, seems principally designed to shock and offend:

The image is toxic, malevolent; the speech, already built on irony and indirection, assumes an especially remote and malicious tone. Indeed, the character seems less a challenge to the cop's homophobia than an objectification of it (he appears on stage just as the cop is saying, "Sometimes I sit in church and I think of those disgusting drag queens dressed up as nuns"). In short, Mann's prologue not only arouses a profound subjective response in her audience, it seems intended to shape the nature of that response: Specifically, it does more than raise the *issue* of homophobia; it provokes the *feeling* as well.

The significance of this becomes obvious as the first of Mann's three* acts begins. Dan White, of course, was the right-wing politician and ex-cop who, in 1978, shot and killed San Francisco's liberal mayor, George Moscone, and its first openly gay elected official, Harvey Milk. The core of *Execution of Justice* is distilled from the manuscript of the notorious trial that followed five months later. It opens with a short scene in which Defense Attorney Douglas Schmidt manages to seat a law-and-order jury whose backgrounds and values closely resemble those of the defendant himself—white, Catholic, blue collar, conservative. In particular, Schmidt excludes all suspected gays from the jury, as well as anyone who indicates a sympathy for gay rights. Thus while homosexual prejudice against the killer of Harvey Milk is probably eliminated, prejudice against homosexuals probably is not. Mann confirms this assumption with one bold stroke. When the scene ends, no jury is actually placed on stage. Instead, as Prosecutor Tom Norman begins his opening remarks, he looks out at the audience: "You," he says, "are the jury now." The emotions provoked by Mann's prologue click firmly into place. The opening moments of *Execution of Justice,* then, depend on an intense responsive transaction. As in *Still Life,* Mann generates a powerfully affective forcefield around her play and assigns the audience a specific role within it. Moreover, she attempts to make an explicit connection between

---

Ed. note: In the course of its various regional productions the play was shortened from three acts to two.

her audience/jury and the original Dan White jury on a deep psychological level. As a result, Mann encourages her audience not simply to become *a* jury, but rather to assume the role of the *real* jury—to share its point of view, to experience the trial as the original jury *experienced* it. Her methods are complex; the consequences, from a political point of view, disturbing.

As it happened, the defense almost totally dominated the experience of the Dan White jury. Throughout the trial, White—handsome, youthful, if a little overweight—sat impassive, expressionless, a blank screen upon which Doug Schmidt projected an image carefully wrought to mirror the presumed values of *his* jury and designed to tap into those values at the root. Using this persona, Schmidt then developed a narrative myth to explain White's "tragedy." In Schmidt's masterful telling, White became an All-American Boy, driven to self-destructive acts by two unprincipled politicians (one, at least, a gay). Thus, while the motivational defense seemed to focus on White's "diminished capacity" (depression triggered by a "chemical change"), it was really a *political* argument on a profound *emotional* level.

Execution of Justice not only makes this clear, it seems designed to support and heighten the sympathetic appeal of Schmidt's fabrication. For example, Mann's first act works contrapuntally. Unlike Schmidt, Prosecutor Tom Norman avoids interpretation of any kind, psychological or political, and sticks doggedly to the "facts" of the case. As he questions a series of witnesses about the two murders, Mann intercuts relevant fragments of Schmidt's opening remarks and subsequent cross-examination. The technique is ingenious: It maintains, indeed sharpens, the essential thrust of the trial, while laying out a massive amount of factual information simply and concisely. This structural maneuver also produces a remarkable effect: Prosecution testimony and defense interpretation become one story, with Schmidt as storyteller. Not only does his point of view thus seem to carry more weight than it does in the actual transcript, his gradual dominance of the proceedings, and influence over the jury/audience, seems almost preordained; he owns a knowledge of the "truth," the power of an omniscient narrator. Mann's editing does little to sub-

vert this power: Occasionally it adds emphasis, a critical accent or stress, but for the most part, gross inconsistencies slip by unnoticed, unchallenged; discordant ironies are muted; crucial evidence remains unexamined—just as in the trial itself. Indeed a number of Mann's cuts, here and elsewhere, actually seem to bolster the defense position.

Moreover, Act I climaxes with the confession of Dan White—a repetition, in White's words, of the story Schmidt has just told. The playing of this intensely dramatic taped narrative was surely a turning point in the trial, a "traumatic" moment for the murderer and then for the jury. As White, choking back sobs, told of the terrible "pressures" that had led him, a moral public servant (not to mention husband and father), to crack, many in the courtroom, and in the jury box, wept openly. To White's peers, at least, the confession was shattering and decisive; premeditation and malice suddenly became impossible, if not irrelevant. Subsequently, White's confession was much criticized: What of the clearly supportive interrogation, or the unusual narrative format; why were the subtle distortions, discrepancies, and contradictions not pointed out by the prosecution? *Execution of Justice* confronts none of these issues. Nor is White's tape actually played; it is dramatized, and edited (the only time, with one brief exception, Mann actually stages an event anterior to the trial). The cuts are not major, although they do eliminate several of the most patently friendly questions by Inspector Erdelatz (incidentally a member of a group called "Cops for Christ"). The dramatization, on the other hand, is stunningly overt. Though lacking the authenticity of the original tape, Mann's extended flashback nevertheless deepens audience involvement with White. A less representational style might have had an "alienating effect"; instead, the realistic staging, as in *Still Life,* enhances White's credibility while it turns his confession into one of the most theatrically compelling and emotionally involving scenes in Mann's play.

Another remarkable example of the way in which the structure of *Execution of Justice* seems to promote the defense position occurs at the climax of Act II. White's trial aroused a storm of outrage against the use of psychiatric testimony, and this section of the transcript reads like something out of Ionesco. Mann heightens the absurdity by bringing out four of Schmidt's experts simultaneously and interweaving their edited comments. The result is the play's most satiric scene. Then, in a surprising stylistic shift, a fifth psychiatrist, Dr. Blinder, gives his testimony straight, uninterrupted and virtually uncut. While the others come across as buffoons spouting gibberish, Blinder seems decidedly sane and even deeply compassionate. It is he who formulates the notorious "Twinkie defense" (junk food raises blood sugar leading to depression and murder), but, as presented by Blinder (and Mann), this theory becomes a minor, not wholly unreasonable point in yet another long, emotion-charged reprise of Dan White's pathetic tale. In effect, Blinder completely undercuts Mann's earlier attack on forensic psychiatry while reaffirming, from a different angle, the validity of Schmidt's argument. Further, Blinder's monologue is followed by the anguished testimony of White's wife. Strongly reminiscent of *Still Life*, Mary Ann White's tortured revelations about her husband's black moods and sexual inadequacy underscore Blinder's analysis in the strongest way—in deeply personal, human terms.

Other examples might be cited. The point is: Again and again, in different ways, Mann encourages audience identification with the original Dan White jury by intensifying the sympathetic appeal of the case for the defense. There is, however, more to *Execution of Justice* than a distillation of the trial itself. For instance, halfway through Act I, two men and a woman appear at different places on the flanking tiers. As a witness in the central acting area, now the courtroom, describes White's behavior just prior to shooting George Moscone, they too speak out, separately, their words intercut with trial testimony. None, however, refers to or even acknowledges the trial. Instead, each tells the audience of his or her *traumatic response* to the news of Moscone's death. Minutes later, two others appear—a "gay man" and Gwenn, a black lesbian activist—and they register similar emotional reactions to the death of Harvey Milk. Although strongly differentiated, the five make up what Mann calls a "chorus of uncalled witnesses." Together they attempt to impart a sense of the profound emotional impact caused by the murders on the city as a whole, but especially on the friends and supporters of Milk and Moscone; the result is a kind of montage in which Mann's chorus creates an emotional counterpoint to the affective thrust of the trial.

The uncalled witnesses reassemble as the trial comes to an end, about a third of the way into Act III. This time, however, their function seems more complex. As in Act I, each is spatially disconnected and each speaks a separate monologue, broken up and intercut with the lines of the others, and with the last, sharply edited, sections of the trial. At the end, in different ways, all express their shock and outrage at what has happened in court, particularly at the verdict. Again one senses a communal challenge to the impression of the trial which has dominated Mann's first two acts. At this point, however, the chorus members aggressively assert themselves, fragmenting the dramatic field and shifting the focus to the city streets. Their words are not only played against the trial but against a series of projections showing the riots which erupted after the verdict was announced. Finally they stand, mute, as White comes forward to speak the last, ironic line of the play: "I just wanted to do a good job for the city."

This antiphonal climax, however, is also built from strongly disjunctive voices; each, apparently, based on a real individual, and each with a significant personal message. For example, Gene Marine, a friend and political ally of Moscone, offers a glimpse of the dead man's genial personality, his genuine concern for social justice—a welcome, if fleeting, contrast to the devious politician portrayed throughout the trial. At another point, Craig talks briefly about gay history and describes the brutal police attack on a gay bar following the City Hall riot. Most important, perhaps, and certainly most arresting, are the words of Jim Denman, "Dan White's jailer for the 72 hours after the assassinations." As trial witness Carol Ruth Silver vainly attempts to testify to White's antagonism towards gays, Denman talks about the defendant's close connection to "thuggish" elements in the police department (where there was talk of assassinating the mayor), and he recalls White's behavior in jail: "There were no tears; there was no shame; you got the feeling that he knew exactly what he was doing and there was no remorse." Not only are Denman's remarks extremely provocative—strongly implying premeditation and malice, even suggesting conspiracy—they confirm the earlier, abortive, discredited testimony of the lone prosecution psychiatrist; they provide one of the few occasions in *Execution of Justice* when the defense characterization of White is cogently challenged. Why Denman was *not* called to testify is also one of the most pointed political questions raised by the play.

Mann's intention at this point seems twofold: to generate an emotional alternative to the affective thrust of the trial, with its apparent bias in favor of the defense, and, using a kind of vocal collage, to raise a number of specific points pertinent not only to a critique of the trial but to a broader social and political context as well. It is a complex and daring maneuver, one which, unfortunately, does not succeed. Unquestionably the chorus conveys a general impression of the controversy surrounding the conduct and outcome of the trial, but it finally fails to impart, on any deeper level, a sense of the trauma it describes. Oddly for a writer who specializes in affective response to political events, the chorus passages of *Execution of Justice,* not only here but in Act I, seem strangely distanced, indirect, even evasive. Perhaps there are simply too many competing voices in too many disparate registers to create a unified visceral pull; certainly the sharply fragmented structure scatters attention and weakens the impact, both collectively and individually. Or perhaps Mann simply has not experienced this testimony directly or deeply enough herself. Much of it, in fact, has a secondhand ring, and some is easily recognizable from other sources: Craig's monologue, for instance, comes from a speech delivered to the Harvey Milk Gay Democratic Club and later published, while Denman's remarks are quoted almost verbatim from a widely read article by San Francisco journalist Warren Hinckle (*Inquiry,* 10/29/79). Despite vigorous performances, these passages seem to lack the intensity and force, the actuality, of the testimony in *Still Life* or, for that matter, in Mann's version of the trial. Even material which seems

unfamiliar, presumably from interviews Mann conducted herself, has a strange, generalized quality to it (the San Francisco mother, for instance, or the gay man).

More disappointing, the issue raised by Denman and others tends to get lost in a kind of theatrical Babel—and so few questions of this kind are raised at all in Mann's play. Clearly the primary intention of *Execution of Justice* is *not* a detailed critique or analysis of the trial of Dan White, and yet there is a critical undertone, implicit in Mann's title, which rises to the surface from time to time and raises at least some expectations along this line. Craig, for example, has an angry aside in Act II challenging White's supposed irrationality, while a Reporter comes on briefly in Acts I and II with several disturbing comments about the trial and about White's subsequent favorable treatment in prison. Such moments are not only rare, the questions they raise are extremely limited—at least they seem so six years after the fact. It is almost as though Mann would rather avoid such comment and controversy altogether. One waits in vain for any hard evidence of Dan White's homophobia, an issue raised so powerfully in Mann's prologue. None, of course, was produced at the trial—the issue was purposely avoided—but plenty has surfaced since and there are many who believe (Hinckle among them) that this was the chief motivating factor in the murders. In *Execution of Justice,* the question remains oblique, unfocused. Or consider the remarkable monologue of District Attorney Joseph Freitas in Act II. Sandwiched between two extremely sympathetic descriptions of White, Freitas' ghostlike appearance from the future offers an extraordinary opportunity for reaction and analysis. Instead, he simplistically sketches in the political background of the time, attacks the jury for not sticking to the "facts alone," and justifies the prosecution strategy with a stunning evasion: "We thought it was an open-and-shut case of first-degree murder." Although he admits, in retrospect, that the murders were "political," he fails to explain why the prosecution chose to ignore this fact; he simply concedes that "certain issues" probably should have been raised, and concludes that "all of this is just the tip of the iceberg." Freitas' frustrating, equivocal testimony not only symbolizes (rather than explains) the inadequacy of the Dan White prosecution, it typifies Mann's uncritical approach to the trial.

Where, then, does this leave Mann's jury/audience? The convention established in Act I continues to the end of the trial, when a Foreman comes on stage to read the two verdicts—"voluntary manslaughter" in both cases. The court then asks each juror to "say 'yea' or 'nay' "; from different places in the house, the "yeas" ring out. Twelve. Twice. By the end of Act III, however, it is clear that Mann has conceived of two *other* roles for her audience. In addition to sharing the "experience" of the original jury, Mann also seems to want her audience to identify emotionally with the "traumatic" responses of her uncalled witnesses, and at the same time to be intellectually aware of some of the more obvious critical questions raised by the trial itself—to be a kind of super-jury, judging the trial as well as its own subjective response *to* the trial. But this composite counterpoise is never really achieved. Surely Mann accomplishes one thing: *How* the Dan White jury reached its verdict now seems obvious. As Mann develops it, though, this understanding rests principally on an affective identification with the original jury—in other words, it depends on a sympathetic response to the portrait of Dan White created by the defense. Whatever Mann's dialectical intentions may have been, there is little in her play that convincingly challenges, or neutralizes, the power of this portrait. In fact, her treatment of the trial seems calculated to enhance it. In *Execution of Justice,* then, Emily Mann's complex affective strategies have disturbing (and probably to many, disappointing) results: They not only exonerate the Dan White jury, they finally seem to validate the verdict as well.

Dan White was paroled on January 7, 1984, and disappeared into a secret hideout somewhere, it is said, in Los Angeles County. As of this writing, *Execution of Justice* has not yet been performed in the city in which his crimes were committed—although the play was originally commissioned by San Francisco's Eureka Theater, and a production there has been promised "sometime soon."

Perhaps by then revisions will be made; if so, it should be interesting to compare the two versions—and the audience/jury response.

—WILLIAM KLEB

REVIEW from the *Washington Post*

"JUSTICE" FOR ALL:
At Arena, the Many-Sided
Dan White Case*

"Execution of Justice" is a deeply disturbing play, although not for the reason that may spring to mind if you are at all familiar with its subject matter: the Dan White murder trial.

White is the former San Francisco supervisor and ex-cop who shattered his star-spangled image forever in 1978, when he assassinated the city's mayor, George Moscone, and fellow supervisor Harvey Milk, the nation's first openly gay elected politician. After a divisive and inflammatory trial, White was convicted of two counts of involuntary manslaughter and sentenced to seven years and eight months. It was the lightest possible punishment (eventually reduced for good behavior) for what many believed, and still believe, was cold-blooded murder.

Using the words of the actual participants and transcripts from the courtroom, playwright Emily Mann has fashioned a sweeping drama about the trial, the events leading up to it, and its awful aftermath. But if you expect to be unsettled by a blatant miscarriage of justice as you slip into your seat at Arena Stage, you are wrong. Or rather, you are only partially right.

What is extraordinary about this work, which opened last night in a stunning multimedia staging by Douglas C. Wager, is that it doesn't take

*Reprinted by permission from *Washington Post,* 17 May 1985.

one side over another. It takes *all* the sides and forces you to do as much. Just when you believe you've got your feelings in hand and your thoughts sorted out, Mann suddenly introduces an angry voice from the streets, a cry from the heart, a plea of utter bewilderment, and all your certainties are swept right out from under you.

Courtroom dramas do not usually operate in this fashion. While they may have some surprises up their somber black robes, by the evening's end they have revealed them all, made order out of disorder, and brought the deadly motive to light. Mann's play is open-ended. It will leave you with worrisome questions—not about White's guilt, perhaps, of which there is no doubt, but about a society that can produce such profound fissures. It will leave you with the question that White asked himself in his confession, tape-recorded only 90 minutes after the murders: "Why do people do things?" It will leave you, in fact, with a violent mixture of emotions: pity, indignation, befuddlement, and sorrow.

Although White's trial provides the spine of "Execution of Justice," the play has the form of a huge dream. It jumps back and forth in time, juxtaposes courtroom testimony and anguished reactions from the community at large, and sometimes allows the defense and the prosecution to unfold simultaneously. "You have to understand," argues a desperate black lesbian leader (Kim Staunton), "that the Dan White verdict did not happen in a vacuum." Indeed, Mann fills that vacuum with dozens of voices, all screaming for relief.

We hear all the official witnesses. But we also hear what Mann terms "the uncalled witnesses"—those on the fringes whose lives were implicated one way or another by Dan White's actions. A policeman, wearing a 'Free Dan White' T-shirt, expresses his disgust at the sexual depravity he encounters on his daily beat; a young gay man decries "the tyranny of the all-American boy"; a housewife, hearing the verdict over the radio, can only wonder, panic in her eyes, "What are we teaching our sons?"

Frequently as the testimony is unfolding, newsreel footage of the people and incidents in question are unreeling on a four-sided screen above the stage. The media, after all, were players in the trial, and the images they relayed to the world fanned passions already dangerously overheated. Wager doesn't leave it at that, however. He has set up his own TV cameras at Arena; the actors in the bright red square that serves as the witness stand are further exposed in wrenching close-up.

Just as Mann, eschewing easy partisanship, refuses to settle on one point of view, Wager won't let us take a single visual perspective on matters. A spotlight, for example, picks out Milk's friend (John Leonard), who remembers the candlelit march that poured down from the Castro district to the steps of City Hall the night of the murders. As he talks, hauntingly beautiful images of the vigil (from the documentary film "The Times of Harvey Milk") shimmer on the screen. At the same time, the Arena cast members, each carrying candles, are collecting onstage for a vigil of their own. The production is layered throughout with similar double and triple exposures. The mind is troubled even as the eye is torn.

And pain is everywhere. You see it in the brave countenance of White's wife (Gina Franz), struggling to maintain her composure in the courtroom. You hear it damming up the words, as a near-inarticulate White (Casey Biggs) confesses his crime to police officers who were once his buddies. You can see it wracking the body of Cyr Copertini (Tana Hicken), Moscone's secretary, as she recalls for the jurors the day White made his fateful office call, a .38-caliber pistol in his pocket. And you can't discount any of it.

It is rare that an American playwright tackles current events, which have pretty much become fodder for television docudramas of dubious merit. For that alone, "Execution of Justice" is exhilarating. It is theater reasserting its claim on the country's moral conscience. Rarer still, I think, is Mann's refusal to tidy up her subject for drama's sake.

That said, her documentary form carries certain limitations. The sprawl can be frustrating. Few of the actual participants in the case were possessed of verbal eloquence, and "Execution of Justice," relying on their words as it does, can't always escape the inchoateness of their emotions: The dialogue is like a chart of human confusion, not a road map to truth. Some spectators, I suspect, will want the truth distilled for them.

With 44 roles to fill, many of the actors must portray multiple characters, and that contributes another kind of confusion to the evening. We really shouldn't have to ask ourselves who's who, but now and then we do. What galvanizes this welter of material, however, is the urgency, bordering on zeal, that has seized the Arena cast. Biggs' intensity even in stillness is so riveting that when he does crack open, his confession is overwhelmingly powerful. Tom Hewitt, pursing Tallulah-red lips, as Sister Boom Boom, a transvestite "nun" and San Francisco street fixture, turns a plea for tolerance into a subtle call to violence, while Stanley Anderson plays White's defense attorney with slippery, manipulative skill. As White's aide, Sarah Marshall has only a few lines, but she invests them with bristling anger. Her performance is characteristic of the ensemble: Everyone seems to have a fiercely personal stake in what is going on.

Mann is certainly not about to let Dan White off the hook, but she won't let us off the hook, either. "Execution of Justice" puts nothing to rest. Stirring the ashes of the past, it uncovers a bed of coals that never went out.

—DAVID RICHARDS

Sergei Kurginian

COMPENSATION
A Liturgy of Fact

1987

Translated by Carolyn Kelson, with Alex and Helen Prokhorov

Compensation was first produced at the "On the Boards" Theater in Moscow, ca. 15 December 1987. It was intermittently in the home and touring repertory of the theater through 1989. The production was directed by Sergei Kurginian, with lighting and set by L. Dzutseva. The cast included Y. Bardakhchiev, V. Moshev, L. Gulyaeva, O. Lapshina, A. Kudinova, V. Sorokina, M. Mamikonian, and S. Kurginian.

CHARACTERS

VOICE ON THE RADIO
PSYCHOLOGIST
FIRST "LIQUIDATOR" (MALE)
SECOND "LIQUIDATOR" (FEMALE)
THIRD "LIQUIDATOR" (FEMALE)
FOURTH "LIQUIDATOR" (FEMALE)
FIFTH "LIQUIDATOR" (FEMALE)
SIXTH "LIQUIDATOR" (FEMALE)

NOTE ON COSTUME: *All of the "Liquidators" are dressed in white nuclear-power-plant uniforms—radiation-proof, head-to-toe safety suit.*

NOTE ON SET: *Upstage curtains. On the floor, shiny doughnut-shaped discs (approximately 12" diameter), which can be picked up and manipulated by the actors. They represent components of a nuclear reactor.*

PROLOGUE

VOICE ON THE RADIO[1]: In 1988 Moscow psychologist Adol'ph Ul'ianovich Kharash[2] with a group of colleagues surveyed the former residents of the city of Pripiat' . . . or it is probably better to say: the residents of the former city of Pripiat', who were exposed to radiation during the time of the clean up—liquidation—of the consequences of the Chernobyl' catastrophe, by the so called, "Liquidators." My acquaintance with Kharash's materials and conversations with him became the stimulus to write this play, this collage, *Compensation*. The speeches, the words of the characters, are authentic documents and have deliberately not been subjected to artistic interpretation. . . . All of the heroes of *Compensation* are authentic . . . (*A spotlight falls on the* PSYCHOLOGIST.) except for him. He is a figure of the imagina-

---

[1]*Translators' note:* Every Russian apartment used to come with a radio in the wall. It could never be turned off; only the volume could be turned down. It played the official radio station, the voice of the state.
[2]*Translators' note:* This is the Psychologist's real name, so it is merely coincidental that his first name and patronymic recall the names of the two major twentieth century dictators Adolf Hitler and Vladimir Ul'ianov (Lenin).

tion, both fictitious and typical. . . . He might be anyone seated in the theater . . . (*Lights up on house.*) maybe you, for example . . . or you . . . or me . . . anyone who happened to be, so to speak, in this particular place.

PSYCHOLOGIST: A heavy drone broke into the depths of my drowsy dreams and I suddenly regained consciousness, like a man forcibly awakened.

VOICE ON THE RADIO (*interrupts*): Dante. *Divine Comedy.*

PSYCHOLOGIST: And suddenly instead of all of this, a room, like a bathhouse in the country, and there were spiders in the corners. That, and for all eternity.

VOICE ON THE RADIO: Fyodyr Mikhaelovich Dostoevskii.

PSYCHOLOGIST: And therein is hidden the mysterious joy and self-confidence of hell . . . a joyful and self-assured hell; it is not defined, language cannot describe it, it exists only to be, but you cannot find it in the newspaper. . . . "Achieving Glasnost."[3]

VOICE ON THE RADIO: Thomas Mann.

PSYCHOLOGIST: The Child asked, "What is grass?"

VOICE ON THE RADIO: Walt Whitman.

PSYCHOLOGIST: What could I answer the child? . . . What could I answer the child?

VOICE ON THE RADIO: So, well said?

Music.

FIRST: The child asked: "What is grass?" and brought me his handfuls of grass. What could I answer the child?

PSYCHOLOGIST: *Pravda,* 30 May 1988, "Conclusions.[4] They have been and are being drawn. It is important to be informed of the realistic radioactive situation to be able to interpret this information correctly. The leading role in the curative prophylactic measures right now is being played by alternative methods of treatment: psychoemotional exercises, psychotherapy of emotional transgressives, and reflexotherapy."

Music.

EPISODE 1

PSYCHOLOGIST (*reading a letter*): Summer, 1987. "Hi from N-sk! Hello dear Liudochka and Volodia. We send you our best and dearest wishes for a strong, healthy, and long life, peace in the heavens and peaceful life on Earth and in your family. Liudochka, we want to thank you so much for your reply to Brovar: To learn at least a little bit about you, about Kiev, about how things are going over there. We live here. . . . "

VOICE ON THE RADIO: "And we know nothing."

PSYCHOLOGIST: "We live and we know nothing."

VOICE ON THE RADIO: "We only wait."

PSYCHOLOGIST: "Only wait. We did not go to the meeting. You see, Vitya is in the hospital. As they cure him, one part of him, he falls apart in another. And I run back and fourth. . . . In the stores there are lines. Butter, sausages, and mayonnaise were scooped up in a flash. In a word, supplies are betwixt and between. But we don't sit around hungry, we find a way around our situation. Soon the fruit and vegetables will come, we are coming to the time when we can feed ourselves from the land.[5] Some of us "Chernobyl'tsy"—this is what we are called by everyone—we went to a meeting in Kiev and saw people who came from all different regions, but the police were afraid of demonstration. . . ."

VOICE ON THE RADIO: "And others say the demonstration happened. . . . "

PSYCHOLOGIST: "And others say the demonstration happened, and at the same time, we don't know what really happened."[6]

---

[3] *Translators' note:* This phrase was a popular one during the Gorbachev era.

[4] *Translators' note:* "Conclusions" is a regular feature of *Pravda.*

[5] *Translators' note:* Literally, "we are passing into the times of under-foot feedings," a Russian saying implying eating from the grass under one's feet like cattle.

[6] *Translators' note:* This division of the Psychologist's discourse into paragraphs graphically distinguishes the voice of the Psychologist's personal thoughts fitted to the words of the letter from the voice of the Psychologist impartially reading Liuda's letter.

"Yes, Liuda, such a Pripiat'[7] and there never will be, and we are all crying about it. My own husband became so sick, he endures a lot. And there is a sadness throughout the country. Again there is a blizzard with snow. . . . "

VOICE ON THE RADIO: "And cold. . . . "

PSYCHOLOGIST: "And cold. I don't know what's going to happen. Liuda, my dear one, it is awful that they are moving you to Slovutich, which is still very close to Chernobyl'. Though the city is pretty, there is still radiation. But we still want to live! I am so sorry for those innocent people who have been killed and got sick, who work without a thought about themselves and their health. They deserve heroes' medals for this is a second kind of war. This thing pierces right through you, and healing yourself is very hard. Liuda, sweetie, when you have a vacation or when Volodia isn't working, come visit us, come see how we are settling ourselves, how things are in our city. . . .

VOICE ON THE RADIO: "In our boondocks."

PSYCHOLOGIST: " . . . in our boondocks. Vitia is in the Borispol'skii region. They have bought an apartment in a five-story building.[8] My mother was there. She took care of her grandchild and now is home. Iurik, the grandson, was sick. His blood tests were bad and showed radiation in his body, but they said, 'it was normal.' . . . "

VOICE ON THE RADIO: "And what is this 'normal'?"

PSYCHOLOGIST: "And what 'normal' is, no one knows."

VOICE ON THE RADIO: "And what kind of children will be born later?"

PSYCHOLOGIST: "And what kind of children will be born later, if any? Time will tell."

"We also had a blood test, they said 'normal,' but what does normal mean if we feel bad? Anyway. So far we are still alive. We'll re-tire soon. I'll have some rest. You can't take it with you! Liuda, dear, drink wine, it helps expel radiation."

VOICE ON THE RADIO: "That's true. . . . "

PSYCHOLOGIST: "That's true. It's very hard to get wine here. People here drink heavily. Two times I stood in line for wine—they nearly crushed me."

VOICE ON THE RADIO: "I had to do it."

PSYCHOLOGIST: "I had to do it: Guests were coming over. They live close, relatives of mine. An hour and a half, two hours and here you are. They now come over very often. We have no homemade liquor. And you can't satisfy men with tea."

VOICE ON THE RADIO: "Let the women drink tea. . . . "

PSYCHOLOGIST: "Let the women drink tea. . . . Vitia says that. The second they start yapping about Chernobyl', and almost every day they either broadcast about the catastrophe or show a movie about it. I cry and Vitia says to me 'Mother, mother, you didn't get your tea today. . . . Where do all your tears come from, you've cried all the water out of you.' "

VOICE ON THE RADIO: "And I keep crying."

PSYCHOLOGIST: "And I keep crying. Sometimes, he can't hold himself together either. Those poor people, who gave their young lives because of somebody's sloppy work."

VOICE ON THE RADIO: "Well enough. . . . "

PSYCHOLOGIST: "Well, Liuda, my pet, my sweet one, eat more honey and carrots. Liuda, soon there will be watermelon. Eat these day and night. They are pure glucose.[9] Believe in this life, as much as you can. If you want to live. You still have a young son."

VOICE ON THE RADIO: "And a good son."

PSYCHOLOGIST: "And a good son. Say hello to him from us, and to all our friends who are there. Kisses to you both. Write. If you can, come visit."

"Liuda, we will wait for you as long as we live. . . . "

---

[7]Translators' note: Pripiat' is a radioactively flowing river near Chernobyl', which infected all the people who lived near it.

[8]Translators' note: These prefabricated concrete structures were introduced in Russia by Khrushchev to solve the housing crisis in urban areas. Though intended to last for 25 years, virtually all are still in use. They have become the equivalent of slums.

---

[9]Translators' note: All of the watermelons in the Ukraine that year were saturated with radiation, but the people did not know that.

(*Addressing the audience.*) This letter came to my archives in the Winter of 1988, and the very next day I found out that one of my close friends who was closely connected with the events at Chernobyl' tried to smash his kitchen television. . . .

VOICE ON THE RADIO: Color?

PSYCHOLOGIST: Black and white. . . .

(*The remaining actors enter the stage.*)

EPISODE 2

THIRD: At least some compensation.

SECOND (*laughing*): And I smacked this one man right across the face. Really, I am not kidding. We had just moved to a new place. I went out and walked around with my husband. He felt really depressed. We went out; there was one Kievan who said: "Ah, Pripiat. Yes, you'll be dead in two years and we will live in your apartment. . . ." You know, I couldn't hold myself together. I got mad, went up to him and punched him. And he said, "What's with you? What are you, nuts? Crazy or something? What's with you?"

Music.

FIRST: What could I answer the child? I know no more than he does.

PSYCHOLOGIST: And what were they showing on television?

SECOND: Il'in[10] was giving a speech.

FOURTH: And did you watch it?

PSYCHOLOGIST: I watched it.

VOICE ON THE RADIO: And, so . . .

FOURTH: Didn't you notice how his eyes shifted? What kind of psychologist are you then? You saw he was reading. He read it all. He read it all and it wasn't his words. . . . What about Romanenko? He insisted on evacuating all the children from Kiev, but they forced him, and then Amosov, and now Amosov says. . . . How can you believe any of them?

---

[10]*Ed. note:* "Vice President of the USSR Academy of Sciences, the man who is regarded as most responsible for the cover-up," Alma Law (q.v. below).

Music.

FIRST: Maybe grass is the flag of my feelings?

THIRD: As I understand it, you are more interested in our personal experiences.

VOICE ON THE RADIO: It was a Saturday. . . .

EPISODE 3

FIRST: It was a Saturday afternoon. People were walking around. No one knew anything.

SECOND: In the Pioneer camps, the children got hysterical when they found out that they could never return to Pripiat'.

THIRD: One of my most terrible recollections is how children were playing, lowering their arms into the stream which was foamy like a disinfectant solution.

SECOND: All magnetic instruments stopped. And when the director of the factory where I worked brought up the question of evacuation, they called him a panicker and threatened to take away his party card.

FIFTH: All of the local authorities sat there in a bunker, and Fomin and Briukhanov. No one ran away, just as they wrote in the newspapers . . . only nobody said anything about the accident either. They said only that there had been an explosion and that graphite was burning.

PSYCHOLOGIST: The newspaper *Evening Kiev* from the 6th of February 1988. From an interview with the academician Il'in: "Right after the catastrophe it was recommended to residents to shorten the amount of time spent outdoors, not to open windows, and outdoor activities at all children's institutions were forbidden. The medical brigade carried out prophylactic iodine treatment of children. By taking these measures, the people who stayed indoors were exposed to a good deal less influence of gamma rays."

THIRD: Il'in sat right here a week ago, right near us. But it's all the same, it's all lies in the newspapers.

FIFTH: I turned on the radio. I hoped that they would announce if something was wrong.

FOURTH: They believed they won't abandon us. After all, it was sixty thousand people.

SECOND: So we kept reassuring each other: "There are too many of us. Nothing will happen to us. They won't desert us."

FIFTH: They continued to sell ice cream on the streets, the movie theaters stayed open.... That day the beaches were filled, there were crowds of people. Were they warned too?

SIXTH: At the resort I met up with one family. The 26th[11] was their first day of vacation.

Music

FIRST: Maybe it is the flag of my feelings, woven out of green threads—out of the color of hope.

VOICE ON THE RADIO: So; and they went to the beach....

EPISODE 4

SIXTH: ... went to the beach with the whole family. The whole day from early in the morning they sunbathed on the beach. They had a little boat. They sailed on it across the river and relaxed there. They had their own little nook over there.

VOICE ON THE RADIO: The day was warm then?

SIXTH: It was warm, a good day....

VOICE ON THE RADIO: And no one knew anything?

SIXTH: They knew nothing. The husband and the son were fishing, they sat by the water under a crag....

VOICE ON THE RADIO: Thank goodness they were under the crag.

SIXTH: Thank goodness they were under the crag, but the woman with the girl sat in the sun.

VOICE ON THE RADIO: The whole day?

SIXTH: All day. All day they were out in the sun. They took their kitten with them, they took it everywhere with them. So this woman says that she noticed, something was strange with how the kitten carried itself, all the time it seemed like it was looking for somewhere to hide....

VOICE ON THE RADIO: To conceal itself?

SIXTH: Yes, to conceal itself. And only the people in the city had learned that something had happened. And they relaxed near the Red Forest.[12] ...

VOICE ON THE RADIO: Were the children examined?

SIXTH: The children were examined. They said everything was fine. And then ... it was already Autumn, the woman started to get the girl ready to go to kindergarten one morning, and the little girl says: "Mama, you've tied my hair back too tightly. ... "

VOICE ON THE RADIO: "Fix it."

SIXTH: "Fix it." So she took the hair and wanted to pull it up....

VOICE ON THE RADIO: Straighten it out.

SIXTH: Yes, to straighten it up a little. So she took up a clump of hair into her hand, the amount she had gathered up in her hand stayed there. I saw this little girl, I held her in my arms. You know, she has tiny hairs like an infant....

VOICE ON THE RADIO: So fine....

SIXTH: So thin, fine, all the same length. Can I ask you a question, as a psychologist? Why didn't our delegate speak at the Party conference? The thing is, he's a determined man, yes, and in general not afraid of anything. So, why didn't he speak, what do you think? Why?

VOICE ON THE RADIO: You don't know?

PSYCHOLOGIST: I don't know.

Music.

FIRST: Or maybe, it is a handkerchief from God.

EPISODE 5

FOURTH: All this could be repeated. Because the system stays the same. I would advise you not to read the newspapers, don't watch TV. I only read *Murzilka*.[13]

THIRD: I was always for the reading of political literature and newspapers. And now I don't believe anything. I can't look at our leaders, when they appear on TV. I can't ... Maybe it is not

---

[11]*Translators' note:* The Chernobyl' explosion occurred on 26 April 1986.

[12]*Translators' note:* Red Forest is located in the vicinity of the explosion.

[13]*Translators' note:* A children's magazine.

right that I'm saying this to you, maybe I'm prejudicing you, but this is how I feel. . . . Sixty thousand people were sacrificed. Look at our children. It used to be that you couldn't make him go to bed. Now he lies down at 8. They were showing "Seventeen Moments of Spring."[14] I asked, "Will you come watch it? Will you watch it? . . . Will you watch it!!!"

VOICE ON THE RADIO: He refused?

THIRD: He refused.

SECOND: I remember her son, before the "war." He read all the time, even when we were visiting somebody, thick books and till late at night. He used to be lively. And now look at him, he's withered, tired, he almost never goes to school, he's sick all the time.

FIFTH: Out of all our Pripiat' children not a single one has spent less than a month in the Pushe Boditse, in the Radiology Center in Pushcha-Voditsa. They all have swollen thyroids, their livers hurt. And the doctor says that in our century there is a tendency towards early manifestations of hereditary diseases. . . .

SECOND: One of my friends once joked. She came to the doctor and said "Doctor, doctor. I feel dizzy and nauseated all the time. I am probably suffering from hereditary pregnancy. . . . " (*Laughter.*)

Music.

FIRST: Or maybe it is a handkerchief from God.

SIXTH: Can I ask you a question, as a psychologist? If you were the head of the Magate,[15] wouldn't you, probably, also want to avoid a scandal? It doesn't matter that it's an international agency, it's still an agency. And wouldn't you have your own interests? Really, wouldn't you want everything to be kept secret? What do you think?

VOICE ON THE RADIO: You don't know?

PSYCHOLOGIST: I don't know.

Music

FIRST: It is a handkerchief from God, a fragrant handkerchief. . . .

EPISODE 6

SECOND: It turned out that they punished enthusiasm. Human decency was punished. Do you understand? This is very telling.

THIRD: They didn't pay salaries for the first five months, and they didn't say anything about how much they would pay. And everyone worked. For instance, the water pipes had broken. They fixed them, and that was that. Nobody measured how much radiation they got.

VOICE ON THE RADIO: And what could be done?

THIRD: And what could be done? If there is no engine operator, I run to the station. If there is no fuel oil at the pump station, I run and get it. If there is no trackman, locksmith, I run again. There was no fear, although everybody understood. . . .

FOURTH: We worked for twelve hours near the boiler. Radiation measurers came and said "You can stand safely in this spot for one minute."

SECOND: Characteristic of the general situation. In the month of May I was exposed to 13 rem.[16]

THIRD: While I was exposed to 7 rem over two years.

FOURTH: She says: "I repel everything, like a magnet, because of radiation."

FIFTH: This tragedy showed each person's worth.

VOICE ON THE RADIO: Who is who. . . .

EPISODE 7

FIFTH: That's it, who is who. Since the day of the catastrophe, every bigwig has visited us.

VOICE ON THE RADIO: Who's there now, at the station?

FIFTH: Piruev, I think. . . .

VOICE ON THE RADIO: Who's he?

---

[14]*Translators' note:* A very popular miniseries in the former USSR.

[15]*Translators' note:* International Body Responsible for Atomic and Electrostations, called "Magate."

[16]*Translators' note:* "Rem" is the international designation that corresponds to Russian "ber."

FIFTH: I guess, he's a deputy minister. Anyway, every time they creatively . . .

VOICE ON THE RADIO: . . . inform you? . . .

FIFTH: You could say that, inform.

THIRD: I saw with my own eyes, how they erased everything from the children's medical chart. They simply tore the pages from them, leaving just a record of vaccinations.

FOURTH: We went to the country after the explosion. And one time in the evening my kids said to me: "Mama, take us to Kiev, to watch fireworks and salute before we die." And then, we stood on a bridge and the youngest one said, "Let's all throw ourselves into the Dnieper and end all our unhappiness." I am sorry that I am crying, I don't even know myself, why I'm telling you all this. . . .

VOICE ON THE RADIO: Gaps in memory?

FOURTH: Yes, gaps . . . in memory. . . . I wanted to say something important. . . . Yes, temporary lodging, ten years at the nuclear power plant and after all that . . .

VOICE ON THE RADIO: Temporary lodging.

FOURTH: People sneered at us. My one friend reassured me. And I said to him "You live in the Soviet Union, and I don't know where I live, I am a temporary person." Our passport is like a brand.[17] Everywhere there is an open door, but it opens into a glass wall. In our large country, no one needs us. Maybe in Moscow they don't know about this. I went to vote and while voting I thought to myself: what for? No one needs us. I pleaded to God. You just don't know whom else to plead to. We don't believe in anything anymore. Now it's all the same to us. Only when they show accidents on TV now we understand it in a different way. A different way. And sometimes . . . (*Pause.*)

VOICE ON THE RADIO: What, is it too awful to say?

FOURTH: It's too awful to say. You wish . . . (*Pause.*)

VOICE ON THE RADIO: . . . everything had exploded and everyone had been killed. (*Pause.*)

That it should have all exploded and everyone should have been killed? (*Pause.*) Is that what you mean?

Music.

FIRST: . . . as a gift for us to remember. There is a mark somewhere in the corner. . . .

EPISODE 8

FOURTH: You offer help. Give help! Call it what you want, but give help! A man lost his health there, because he didn't run away, do you understand? Because he did his work to the end. There needs to be social justice. If there is justice, then everything will remain calm.

VOICE ON THE RADIO: Deep in the river it is also calm[18] (*Laughter.*)

EPISODE 9

FIFTH: Oh, how lucky we all are that there were people who died, but these people pumped water from the pressure-suppression pond. If they hadn't pumped that water out, then it would have spread from the Urals to Paris. . . . Where do such people come from, I wonder?

SIXTH: My friend participated in the draining of the water from under the pressure-suppression pond. They gave him a bonus of about 80 rubles.

VOICE ON THE RADIO: And that's all?

SIXTH: That's all.

THIRD: There is a constant need to choose between the well-being of your children and, on the other hand, that ten people will remember that you didn't lose your conscience.

VOICE ON THE RADIO: And maybe after a year they will forget?

THIRD: That is very possible, that they'll forget.

Music.

---

[17]*Translators' note:* The Russian is "white ticket," connoting special privileges. E.g., holders of the tickets should have been given work whenever it was available.

[18]*Translators' note:* This is related to the expression "Still waters run deep."

FIRST: . . . and there is a mark, so that when you see them you can identify, whom it belongs to. . . .

SIXTH: I will tell you straight, that what happened after the accident, all those lies, they were far more terrible than the accident itself. Because now they do it deliberately. I'm quite sure about that.

VOICE ON THE RADIO: For instance, Poles'e.[19]

SECOND: Poles'e, 1986. Near the station Vil'cha. In September and August they evacuated the livestock, and brought in the children. How could it be explained to the mothers?

FIFTH: They came to test my child's blood, and I asked them why. And they said honestly, "This is just a formality, just like . . . "

VOICE ON THE RADIO: " . . . just like everything else."

FIFTH: " . . . just like everything else." And I said, "Write down whatever you like, but don't prick the child."

THIRD: My husband took the kids to the clinic and their records somehow ended up in his hands. He looked them over, and in them was written: "Father—drug addict."

VOICE ON THE RADIO: No kidding?

THIRD: No kidding. That is what was written, "Father—drug addict, mother—alcoholic." He took the records, and went to the head of the clinic and he said, "Excuse me, this is a mistake. Tear it up."

VOICE ON THE RADIO: You should have kept the records. . . .

THIRD: Of course, he should have. . . . But he . . .

VOICE ON THE RADIO: Was too shocked?

THIRD: Yes, shocked. . . .

VOICE ON THE RADIO: Did he really give them back to her?

THIRD: He gave them back to her.

VOICE ON THE RADIO: Well, what can I say!

Music.

FIRST: Or, maybe, grass is a child itself?

---

[19]*Translators' note:* A region near Chernobyl'.

EPISODE 10

FOURTH: There are people who suffered a lot in the first hours of the accident. They were severely radiated. Among them, many are now invalids. They compensated them with 46 rubles. Somehow they need to live off of that.

PSYCHOLOGIST: Why 46?

FOURTH: They counted it all up and decided that in 1½ years in that danger zone she, for example, received about 5 roentgens of radiation.

VOICE ON THE RADIO: Conclusions.[20]

SIXTH: Conclusions: There wasn't sickness, just fantasies, radiationphobia.

VOICE ON THE RADIO: Radiationphobia?

SIXTH: Radiationphobia.

FOURTH: And for that you are to receive 46 rubles a month. Oh yes, now that you mention it, children who are still in the danger zone the whole time also receive compensation. The parents get 10 rubles a month for each child. They refer to it as "for the coffins."

VOICE ON THE RADIO: Black humor.

SIXTH: And can I ask you a question? You, as a psychologist? Doesn't it seem to you that someone is taking advantage of our grief, do you know what I'm saying . . . to save money?

VOICE ON THE RADIO: I wouldn't exclude that possibility.

PSYCHOLOGIST: I don't know.

FIRST: The child asked "What is grass?" and brought me handfuls of it. What could I answer the child? I don't know better than he, what is grass.

EPISODE 11

SIXTH: You know, I would now give everything, if only the truth existed in the world. Yes, probably everything. . . .

VOICE ON THE RADIO: What's with you? What are you, nuts?

---

[20]*Translators' note:* Probably a reference to the *Pravda* "Conclusions" mentioned earlier.

EPISODE 12

SIXTH: Why were all the first record tapes lost, the tapes that our husbands had taken on April 26th and 27th?

VOICE ON THE RADIO: What's with you?

SIXTH: Why did my husband get "zeroes"[21] in his records if on the 26th he was there, at the station at the time of the explosion and he did not leave for 12 hours?

VOICE ON THE RADIO: What are you, nuts?

SIXTH: Why did they diagnose him stubbornly as "idiopathic blood clots"? "Idiopathic"—that means from nowhere, spontaneous. The thing is, my husband carried away firemen at the station, who put out the fire. He was only wearing a sleeveless shirt and without his head gear, he only called home at 8 P.M., he said "Shut the doors and windows." He hadn't had any time till then. He saw the cloud, how it . . .

VOICE ON THE RADIO: What are you, nuts?

SIXTH: Why is it that, after the October Revolution, after 70 years of Soviet Power . . .

VOICE ON THE RADIO: What's with you?

PSYCHOLOGIST: SHUT UP!

SIXTH: When my husband was in the hospital, representatives came from the Supreme Soviet and the Council of Ministers. They read out loud all the decrees which awarded them damages.

PSYCHOLOGIST: Among them was the doctor.

SIXTH: Yes, and they asked the patients, "Aren't these decrees good?"

PSYCHOLOGIST: And the doctor answered, "Yes these decrees are good, but who will be able to make use of them?"

VOICE ON THE RADIO: Your patients will?

PSYCHOLOGIST: "Excuse me."

SIXTH (addressed to the audience): It was the doctor who told them that. . . .

PSYCHOLOGIST: "Excuse me most sincerely, but Gus'kova[22] gave us instructions, that we were not to write about this in the medical records. So that only a small handful of people could make use of these privileges. And all the others would not be allowed." Whom are you fooling?

SIXTH: Us?

FIRST: YOU!

EPISODE 13

SIXTH (altering delivery[23]): Liudasia, you know my memory has become like a chicken's, I'm always forgetting, first the day, yes and oh now the date has just fallen out. Yes and my health is just so-so.

FIFTH: Just a little bit of work left until my pension, and forget it. These two years are overloading me. In general nothing is good.

FOURTH: They don't turn on hot and cold water. They bring it in big trucks.

THIRD: Liuda, you hold onto that apartment in Kiev. Slovutich is too close to the plant, and you've caught enough radiation already. Come see us, we're waiting.

SECOND: Liuda, excuse my handwriting, if it isn't right. My head makes noises and then the words are lost. I've started to notice, you can't get something for nothing.

Music.

FIRST: And maybe the grass is a hieroglyph, eternally, one and the same. Eternally, one and the same.

EPISODE 14

SIXTH: What is going on? Where do we live, after all?! I'm scared. I, sometimes, when I'm reflecting on it, I get so scared. I remember the words of my husband, how he used to say—

VOICE ON THE RADIO: If something should happen to me, the state will help you.

SIXTH: And I don't believe it.

SECOND: Nor I.

THIRD: Nor I.

---

[21]*Translators' note:* Zero radiation.
[22]*Translators' note:* Gus'kova is a government official.

---

[23]*Translators' note:* In this episode, all the "liquidators" take on the role of the letter writer. They return to their own characters in the next episode.

FOURTH: Nor I.

FIFTH: And I don't also. No, I don't believe it.

SIXTH: I'm sure that everyone who at that time acted like my husband did, who didn't think of himself, now starts to think about it. I think, they think "Aha and what will happen to me? And what will happen to my family?"

FOURTH: Go to Slovutich? La, la-la! Don't go too close to the trees, don't sit on the grass, put a plastic bag on the ground before you sit down. . . . This is absurd! You need to say to a seven-year-old child, "Take your plastic bag with you?!"

FIRST: The grass is a hieroglyph, and it signifies, "I spring up everywhere, where I must, I accept everyone equally, I accept everyone equally, everyone. . . . "

EPISODE 15

SECOND: On the 26th of April everyone in Clinic Number Six wanted to see their comrades, who are over there at the cemetery. And what happened? Well, they promised a bus, they promised everything.

VOICE ON THE RADIO: And suddenly . . .

SECOND: And suddenly on the 25th they said, "Anyone who leaves the Clinic building will not be permitted to return for treatment for having violated the regime."

FOURTH: They organized a fair on the October Revolution Square. It was raining. And police . . .

THIRD: You could murder someone—no police, but there, there were so many . . . practically a policeman for each person.

FIFTH: As soon as somebody starts complaining, well, well, you're all schizophrenics, you all need to be put in a psychiatric ward.

SIXTH: I have an 18-year-old son. "Look," I say, "at Dad, how he acted. You shouldn't do that. You don't want to always be in the front or the back. Stay in the middle."

VOICE ON THE RADIO: And how did he reply? Your son, I mean, how did he answer?

PSYCHOLOGIST: He answered, "No, mom, I want to act in exactly the same way as my father."

Music.

EPISODE 16

SIXTH: You know, I came home, and my daughter was crying. It turns out that in her kindergarten, the kids pushed her off the swing. They said, "You damn Chernobyl'ka, when are you getting out of here?"

FIFTH: What a big surprise! My daughter is in fifth grade and she comes home from school and says, "The Kievans said to me straight: 'When are you getting out of here?' " Almost every day. I'm telling you, almost every day they ask her this. (*She exits.*)

FOURTH: My husband and I were given an apartment, we got our keys first of anyone in the house. We couldn't get in yet. The lock sat in my husband's pocket, he'd bought it a month ago, but didn't have the tools to install it and take out the old lock. We desperately wanted something to drink, and a nearby house was already occupied. I ran over there, a man stood by himself. I say, "Sir, please give me a can of water." And he says: "What's with you? Are you from Chernobyl'? Get the hell out of here!" I thought he was joking. I knocked on a second door. . . .

VOICE ON THE RADIO: And no one gave it to you?

FOURTH: No one. They wouldn't give me a can of water. Then I say, "However many years I live, I will always remember this." (*She exits.*)

THIRD: I need a refrigerator. Excuse me, naturally, I just need to tell somebody. I went to the store—to buy a refrigerator. So, I say I need a refrigerator. How they jumped on me in the line, they began to yell and scream at me: "What's with you, can't you live without a fridge?"

VOICE ON THE RADIO: "They'll give it to you all the same. . . . "

THIRD: "All the same," they said, "they'll give it to you! Let all the Chernobyl'tsy choke." (*She exits.*)

SECOND: And you know what happened then? Some children would not acknowledge their parents. If they were from the zone, they said they were "dirty." (*She exits.*)

SIXTH: When they were evacuating, the slogan they carried was "Your life is in your own hands." (*She exits.*)

EPISODE 17

VOICE ON THE RADIO: That's probably enough.

PSYCHOLOGIST: Let him have his say.

VOICE ON THE RADIO: Enough.

FIRST: Many times I accompanied people to their apartments. . . . You know they come off the bus. . . . The city is overgrown . . . weeds . . .

VOICE ON THE RADIO: Enough, I said. . . .

FIRST: Grass is growing, sticking straight up out of the asphalt. As they're walking from the bus, they laugh, joke. . . . They go into their apartments and suddenly, shock. If it is a woman, next come the hysterics. . . . I am forgetting about radiation I can get. Women have to be calmed so that they don't faint . . . because there is radiation everywhere . . . they need to sit somewhere "clean." They calm themselves down. I've already gotten used to it. . . . I don't show anyone how I feel. . . . "Let's go," I say, "take away your documents or whatever you need there, and get out quickly. . . . " In short, I got used to it . . . but when I got to my apartment, these devices hanging there, bags filled with water—you could only drink mineral water, and then I walked in, and I was in the same . . . stupor. . . . I gasped . . . these toys lying on the floor of the house, everything literally, like when I left. You can never understand what it means to lose your home . . . so that absolutely nothing is left for you . . . as if you were pulled out of your microcosm and deprived of everything. . . . You're 35, but it's as if you never had been born. You have children, but you cannot prove that they are yours.[24] . . . I grabbed all our photographs . . . I can't say it. . . . I didn't want anything else. . . . I had everything—a three-room apartment . . . furnished, 11 years I lived there. . . . I was all set . . . and I didn't need anything. . . . Only photographs . . . so that there would be a history . . . in order to remember. . . . What kind of compensation could there be for this? What was I talking about?

Music.

———
[24]*Translators' note:* Implying having to leave behind irradiated documents.

PSYCHOLOGIST: Tufty grass. You look like the uncut hair of graves to me. . . .

FIRST: Maybe—

PSYCHOLOGIST: Maybe you grow out of the chest of young men. . . .

FIRST: Maybe—

PSYCHOLOGIST: Maybe if I had known them, I would have loved them. . . .

FIRST: Maybe—

PSYCHOLOGIST: Maybe you grow out of old men or infants, only just torn away from their mothers' bosoms. . . .

FIRST: Maybe—

PSYCHOLOGIST: Maybe you are that mother's bosom. . . .

FIRST: Maybe—

PSYCHOLOGIST: This grass speaks. . . . This grass speaks. . . . This grass speaks. . . .

FIRST: To die, it's not at all what you thought it was, but better. . . . (*Music.*) You come home, it's so pleasant, the children are there. The children walk around the house. It's a little bit soothing. But there it's like during a war. You walk through the forest, and add things up. . . . Here you can stay for some time, there you should pass through quickly. And from here you should take people away as soon as possible. Death is everywhere. In the grass, in the water, in the trees . . . everywhere death. You know, I went with my family to the Caucasus. We happened upon a glade . . . an alpine glade. . . . There was such grass there . . . a heap of color . . . and all of it was nonradioactive, "clean." We lay there and gasped from it all. My soul was ready to split apart. There is still life!

PSYCHOLOGIST: To die, it's not all that you thought, but better, it's not quite all that you thought. . . .

Music.

VOICE ON THE RADIO: For no particular reason there were already no walls in the room, long plank beds. Close together slept some soldiers. They slept heavily, they were tired. Their faces in sleep were very young.

PSYCHOLOGIST: Some of them were also childlike. . . .

VOICE ON THE RADIO: There were some childlike faces there still untouched by a razor.

PSYCHOLOGIST: Are they alive?

FIRST: I don't know. I am only able to show those who were killed before me. Like him, for instance, or him, or him.

VOICE ON THE RADIO: The soldiers sleep. As they dream their faces are calm.

FIRST: They were killed early in the morning in an attack.

PSYCHOLOGIST: And you?

FIRST: I was also killed in an attack, on the next day, early in the morning. There was a heavy rain that night.

PSYCHOLOGIST: Were you scared?

FIRST: Yes, I was. In the forest, you never know where the shooting is coming from.

PSYCHOLOGIST: You knew you were killed?

FIRST: No, I threw my face in the wet grass. I thought I would survive. Then I understood I would not. Others ran farther. I don't know who survived.

VOICE ON THE RADIO: They were silent, looking each other in the eyes.

PSYCHOLOGIST: Then I would like to. . . .

FIRST: Don't!

PSYCHOLOGIST: "And what I do?"

VOICE ON THE RADIO: Asked Sergei.

FIRST: "Live!"

VOICE ON THE RADIO: Answered the soldier.

PSYCHOLOGIST: "How?"

VOICE ON THE RADIO: Asked Sergei. . . . The soldier stood up and looked around.

FIRST: "How old are you?"

VOICE ON THE RADIO: Asked Sergei.

PSYCHOLOGIST: I don't know.

VOICE ON THE RADIO: I just can't remember what film it is, we're quoting right now.

PSYCHOLOGIST: *I'm Twenty.*[25]

VOICE ON THE RADIO: Then I understand . . .

PSYCHOLOGIST: What?

VOICE ON THE RADIO: . . . why I can't remember. . . . Memory repression. . . .

PSYCHOLOGIST: What?

VOICE ON THE RADIO: I said memory repression. Exactly like Freud described it. And you don't know what it means, repression?

PSYCHOLOGIST: I don't know.

VOICE ON THE RADIO: What kind of a psychologist are you?

PSYCHOLOGIST: And who told you I am a psychologist?

VOICE ON THE RADIO: Then what are you?

PSYCHOLOGIST: I don't know. By the way, don't you remember in what year this film came out?

VOICE ON THE RADIO: I believe it was '63 or '64. I don't exactly remember. And what?

PSYCHOLOGIST: Much water has flowed under the bridge since then. . . .

VOICE ON THE RADIO: Where to?

PSYCHOLOGIST: What?

VOICE ON THE RADIO: I asked you where it has flowed. You also don't know?

PSYCHOLOGIST: I know. That, perhaps, is the only thing I do know exactly.

VOICE ON THE RADIO: From the paper *Pravda* on 13 November 1988. "Enough about that. Speaking about psychology, the only thing worth mentioning is that there is a lot of data about the rise in frequency of emotional tension among the intelligentsia, especially the creative intelligentsia."[26] What's with you?

---

[25]Translators' note: *I'm Twenty* is a well-known Russian film directed by Marlen Khutsiev. The original title of the film was *Lenin's Guard (Zastava Il'icha).* "Khrushchev attacked this unfinished film. . . . He explicitly objected to a scene where the hero asks his father, killed in the war, for advice. The dead father appears to the young boy: 'I was younger than you are now, when I died. How can I give you any advice.' Khrushchev considered this scene as an open attack on the wisdom of the fathers. . . . Toward the end of 1964 (three months after Khrushchev's fall) Khutsiev's film, retitled *I'm Twenty,* was shown in movie theaters, having been partly reshot, reedited by Gerasimov, and finally completed under extremely difficult conditions." Mira and Antonin J. Liehm, *The Most Important Art: Soviet and East European Film after 1945* (Berkeley: University of California Press, 1985), 216.

[26]Translators' note: The term "creative intelligentsia" designates people working in arts: artists, writers, actors, etc. Sometimes scholars are also included in the "creative intelligentsia." The argument among native speakers of Russian as to whether scholars are a part of "creative intelligentsia" or not is based on the myth that scholars discover "objective" laws of nature and society, as opposed to those people whose "findings" arise from an "unscientific" font of "subjective inspiration": "creative intelligentsia."

PSYCHOLOGIST: In the stores there are lines. They snatched up sweet butter, sausages, and mayonnaise. Everyone wants to live, Liuda, Liudochka, drink wine. It expels radiation a bit.

FIRST: It's true.

PSYCHOLOGIST: People drink an awful lot here. Two times I stood in line for wine, they almost crushed me.

FIRST: I had to do it.

PSYCHOLOGIST: Yesterday, another of my acquaintances.

FIRST: It wasn't you?

PSYCHOLOGIST: I don't know.

FIRST: The television was black and white?

PSYCHOLOGIST: Color.

THE END

"Compensation: A Liturgy of Fact"*

"On April 26, 1986, at 1:24 A.M., massive explosions ripped through the Chernobyl Nuclear Power Plant, one of the newest and most powerful nuclear power plants in the U.S.S.R. A ball of flame, accompanied by clouds of black smoke rose into the sky. The wind carried the deadly cloud, 10 times more radioactive than the atomic bomb dropped on Hiroshima, to the northwest, sowing panic in the Soviet Union and Western Europe alike."[1]

Only now, four years later, is the Soviet government beginning to disclose fully the tragic scope of this nuclear disaster, both in terms of the size of the contaminated area and the number of people directly affected by Chernobyl's fallout, now estimated to be as many as 3 to 4 million, most of whom are still living in dangerously contaminated regions of the Ukraine and Byelorussia.

For audiences who have attended performances of Compensation since it opened a year ago in January 1989, at the Moscow Theater-Studio "On the Boards" (Na doskakh), these new revelations will come as no surprise, For this production, subtitled "A Liturgy of Fact," presents in very human terms the terrible consequences of the nuclear disaster at Chernobyl. Contrary to the frequently expressed opinion that political theater is a dead issue in the Soviet Union now that glasnost allows virtually any subject to be aired in the press, this production—and the audience response to it—suggests that there is still plenty of room for an unflinching examination on the stage of important political and social questions.

Headed by Sergei Kurginyan, a self-styled wunderkind with degrees in math and physics as well as theater, "On the Boards" has made a speciality of staging controversial productions that leave few audience members indifferent. Their program, aimed at what Kurginyan calls the "lumpen intelligentsia" proposes "silent meditation" between stage and auditorium in the context of "poor" theater, seeing it as a counterbalance to the extravagant spectacle of the professional theater. And to insure that he attracts a serious audience, Kurginyan refuses to sell his tickets through the theater kiosks located around Moscow. If one wants to attend a performance one must go to the theater itself, presently located in the club attached to the Moscow Conservatory on Malaia Gruzinskaia Street near the zoo.

The performance of Compensation that is described in the following account took place on March 4, 1989.

By 7:00 P.M. curtain time, all seats in the auditorium are filled, extra chairs have been brought in, and there are people standing along the sides. Prior to the beginning of the performance, Sergei Kurginyan speaks to the audience, explaining that the production is called "a liturgy of facts." He adds, "It's not so much about what happened at Chernobyl as what its meaning is." The performance runs for one hour and twenty minutes.

"There will then be a brief intermission," Kurginyan announces, "during which the audience members can watch a video documentary on

---

*Reprinted with permission from Soviet and East European Performance, 10, 2 (Summer 1990).

[1]Pytor Mikhailov, "The Chernobyl Syndrome," Soviet Life, May 1990, p. 34.

Chernobyl out in the lobby. Following the intermission there will then be a discussion with the audience." He goes on to explain that Adolf Kharash, the psychologist whose material—interviews and psychological studies—on Chernobyl forms the basis of the production,[2] will be present for the discussion along with a journalist and a medical specialist on radiation sickness who examined the firemen after they were brought to Moscow following the blaze at Chernobyl.

The cast consists of a Psychologist-narrator and five "liquidators" garbed in white from head to foot. The performance takes place on a starkly bare set. In the center is a table on which is lying one of the victims of Chernobyl. The floor is covered with shiny metallic discs which in the finale will be gathered up as part of the ritual. To one side is a doll, an "angel" with a candle, also dressed in white. The music for the performance is that of a church liturgy, its beauty providing a striking counterpoint to the stark horror of the facts presented.

The narrator begins speaking, setting the context for the liturgy by quoting from Dostoevsky, Thomas Mann, Walt Whitman. The man on the table rises up[. . . .]

After the intermission the radiation specialist is the first to speak. "How much did Chernobyl cost?" someone asks. "150 billion rubles," he answers. He goes on to say that Chernobyl affected nearly half of Byelorussia, in all, several million people. Worst of all, it's a region of young people.

"When Mikhail Sergeevich [Gorbachev] went to the Ukraine earlier this month, there was not a single medical question, no doctors were along, not even the Minister of Health."

"Ilin and Co. [Leonid Ilin—Vice President of the U.S.S.R. Academy of Medical Sciences, the man who is regarded as the most responsible for the cover-up] are now trying to hold back *Threshold* (*Porog*), a film made about Chernobyl. It's time for glasnost."

"What about Moscow?" someone asks.

"The radioactive cloud went to the west and north, bypassing Moscow," the specialist answers. A woman in the audience asks, "Is it safe to have children?"

The specialist answers, "Such a nuclear catastrophe doesn't pass without effect. Mutations have already begun to appear. They will increase."

The specialist tells how "Ilin and Co." allowed the refugees from Chernobyl to take with them family photographs and whatever mementos they wanted, even though these things were radioactive. Thus the radioactivity spread by indirect means. He tells of one official coming to Moscow and of the clothes he was wearing being tested for radioactivity. They were contaminated and had to be destroyed. The official objected, "No, I'll take them to the dry cleaners." " I had to explain to him that those clothes would then touch and contaminate clothing belonging to other people, including children."

Someone asks about the hazards of atomic testing. The specialist answers, "I'm not allowed to say."

Kharash takes the floor. He begins by addressing the question of radiation phobia observing that one of the main causes of it was the "factor of the unknown." He goes on to express his concern that it's also being used as a cover-up for social problems. "Many sacrificed their health in vain," he says. "One-fifth of the population stayed behind until June 5. They knew nothing of their fate."

By the time it's the journalist's turn to speak, the audience is totally engaged. Someone brings up the cover-up of the Cheliabinsk catastrophe. "It was only years later that the public began to learn the truth.[3] If Chernobyl hadn't been discov-

---

[2]See the two-part article by Kharash: "Zagadochnyi sindrom, ili Chego boytsia chernobyl'tsy?" *Nauka i religiia*, No. 9, 1988, pp. 26–30; *Nauka i religiia*, No. 10, 1988, pp. 18–21.

[3]This person probably had in mind the Urals nuclear disaster in autumn 1958 which occurred in the Cheliabinsk *oblast*. Reports of it first began turning up in the West within a year. But it was the account by exiled Soviet biochemist Zhores Medvedev in 1976 that really brought to the attention of the West the full scope of this catastrophe. By then, although information had still not been published in the Soviet press, according to Medvedev, "everybody in Russia knew about it." See James E. Oberg, *Uncovering Soviet Disasters: Exploring the Limits of Glasnost* (New York: Random House, 1988), pp. 211–28.

ered by Western monitoring stations [and a big point is made of the fact that the West knew well before the Soviet people were told], would it also have been covered up?"

A man raises the question of the Crimean Atomic Plant. When the medical specialist explains that the Soviet experts have pronounced it safe and that now a committee of Western experts are to look at it, the response he gets is very heated. "Why should we trust the Western experts? . . . The West has their own political program. . . . How do we know that their answer isn't a way of sabotaging us?"

From this it's only a short step to questioning whether experts in general can be trusted. Someone quotes Einstein, "The history of science is one of experts' mistakes." "Can we trust what the government tells us?" another voice asks. A chorus of voices responds, "Shouldn't the people be the ones to decide?" One man shouts out, "Why don't they put an atomic plant on Red Square if they're so safe!"

Someone in the back of the room stands up and starts defending atomic energy. Kurginyan asks him to identify himself. It turns out he's an engineer from the Atomic Energy Commission. (I'm told later that they've begun sending someone to each performance to defend their position.) A wave of laughter runs through the audience. The specialist jumps up and asks, "Why did six firemen die? Because the cement burned! That was your responsibility!" Again the question of inviting foreign experts comes up.

Kurginyan leaps in. He gets very excited and at one point calls the A.E.C. fellow "a coward," words he later apologizes for using. Kurginyan broadens the focus of the discussion by expressing his overall concern about middle-level bureaucrats, cautioning that as the level of competency drops, cruelty and indifference to human concerns will increase.

The audience is quiet as it walks out. For many, the evening has given them much to think about.

—ALMA LAW

Theater of Cultural Aggression: "Sergei and Masha Kurginian Talk about *Compensation*"*

SK: [After the psychologist Adolph Kharash came to Kurginian with transcripts of interviews with Chernobyl' victims] I went to Kiev and interviewed people on videotape. We psychoanalyzed these interviews. Because of my connection [to Kharash] I was given access to certain closed sources I would not have been able to talk to on my own.

Then he [Kharash] decided at one point that he wanted to write the play himself. It went back and forth; there were a lot of emotions around it. In the end I told him it could only work one way: He would give me the materials and I would write the play.

I used a Voice that asked questions. The answers to these questions are the documentary. This material allowed me to make something that was not purely documentary; it raises the spiritual, mystical sense of the documentary. I can't use materials that have no spiritual connection.

MK: The Voice is like the voice of the devil. Not the devil really, but he is this kind of persuader. He is heard over a loudspeaker, and while he listens to all this tragedy, he is heard to be drinking tea, having a light lunch. He is at peace while this suffering happens in front of him. He is a pig; he is all of us who sat back and did nothing. He takes the facts to mean what he wants them to. He watches these ordinary people achieve the extraordinary and is unmoved.

SK: I have an audience discussion after every performance and have for the past fifteen years. It

*Excerpted from interviews conducted by Carolyn Kelson on 18 November 1993 (Sergei) and 20 April 1994 (Masha).

is my type of theater. I talk to my public and answer their questions for one or two hours after every performance. The most common reaction [to *Compensation*] was disbelief: "I don't want to know. I don't want to believe. I don't want to be open to this type of information." It is dangerous all over the world, and it is dangerous in Russia. After Chernobyl' and now, too, after every event people just want to feel comfortable; even after the events of this October [i.e., the attempted overthrow of Boris Yeltsin].

I work in the parapolitical, not the political. But the parapolitical with a deep connection to culture. I think of my theater as Theater of Cultural Aggression.

MK: [At Chernobyl'] . . . something happened. Not just a technical tragedy, not just a catastrophe of our time—a catastrophe with religious meaning. Many people in our country did not comprehend the religious meaning in this. These liquidators took away radioactive material; they sacrificed themselves. They wanted to be accepted and remembered for this and they were forgotten. They gave and they were outcast. There was no compensation that could be given for the work they did. Russia has a very strong tradition in Christianity. Socialism also appeals to this Christian center. Money has never been important. What could money compensate them? Money has always been secondary in Russia, which is why there are so many problems in this transition to the market economy—so many thieveries.

These people who gave their lives under the pressure-suppression pond . . . these people didn't do that work for any amount of money. They were corpses. They were paid for something which cannot be repaid—these people who believed in Christian ethics, and were turned against.

It is easy to put the blame on other people, to claim that the government is at fault, the state, the doctors, the scientists who built a bad reactor. But we are all guilty of not understanding and not accepting these people who gave their lives, and more than that for not wanting to understand. This was an uncomfortable thought. Comprehension would cause us to reorganize our way of thinking, the structure of our thoughts. And we didn't want this. We wanted to remain comfortable, to ignore and carry on with our lives. Silence created our guilt. The simple people didn't understand. The collective of the USSR didn't comprehend, and the government in power did not pay it the proper attention.

People thought it [i.e., the play] would be very hard for the Chernobyl'tsy to see, but for them it was far easier than the silence. In a way, it was like a group therapy.

Every time we do a documentary text, we try to find something new to unveil about it. Our actions have often run counter to the text. I think it would be quite boring to always have the actions match the text. We mix the dry text with the psychological thought. This is what the theater docs. This is not our goal before each play, but it seems to happen—although each in a different manner.

SK: Theater is an instrument of science, an investigation. I use this instrument to take psychology, knowledge, history and make it nonverbal nonsemantic, and thereby look for signs of the future. I am not a person of art but a person of science. . . . I create special kinds of investigations using color, words, sounds, historical investigation. One type could be writing a [historical] paper; my method is using the stage for this investigation. Videotapes of my plays should be in the category of new science, not old theater, not new theater.

Mame Hunt
(Conceived by Larry Eilenberg)

UNQUESTIONED INTEGRITY:
The Hill/Thomas Hearings

1993

Unquestioned Integrity was first performed at the Magic Theatre in San Francisco, 17 February through 28 March 1993. It was directed by Ellen Sebastian; set and lighting by Jeff Rowlings; costumes by Kim Porter. The cast included Leo Downey (The Senator), Artis Fountaine (Judge Thomas) and Margo Hall (Anita Hill).

CHARACTERS

THE SENATOR: (*The character of the Senator is actually a compilation of several members of the Senate Judiciary Committee. Impersonations of individual Senators should be avoided. No accents; their way of speaking distinguishes facets of the personality and strategic shifts of this one very powerful white man.*)

JUDGE CLARENCE THOMAS.

PROFESSOR ANITA HILL.

There is no intermission.

AUTHOR'S NOTE

The Clarence Thomas–Anita Hill Senate hearings took place over three days, from October 11 to the 13th, 1991. In the year following the highly publicized, thoroughly televised hearings, the tide of public opinion about the Senate, sexual harassment in the workplace, and the incredibly complex issues of race and gender that were brought to the surface during those three days shifted dramatically. In 1992, women were elected to Congress in unprecedented numbers; Carol Mosely Braun has been chosen to be the first African-American woman to serve in the United States Senate. Clarence Thomas is now serving a life appointment as Associate Justice of the Supreme Court.

While I have condensed and re-choreographed portions of the transcripts for this dramatic presentation of the event, every word is taken directly from the transcripts of the hearings. So, while the gender issues of the hearings rise to the emotional and intellectual surface of the play rather easily, the issues of race remain, unfortunately, as underspoken in the play as they were in the hearings themselves. The Committee's avoidance of race, and the tenacious subtext of it, is not as revealed in this dramatization as I'd like, but given my own chosen restriction to use transcripts only, I leave it to audiences to investigate these issues on their own.

SCENE 1

A hearing room in the Senate Office Building. Across one end of the room stretches a very long table. Old money elegance. There is a collage of sound: people milling in the hearing room, an NPR-type voice describing the first day of the hearing. The stage light comes up on the SENATOR and PROFESSOR HILL. The sound of a gavel, then . . .

THE SENATOR: Welcome, Professor Hill. Perhaps if I may explain what the procedure will be. What we will do is I will begin by asking you some questions, and then the Senator from Pennsylvania will ask you some questions, and then the Senator from Vermont will ask you some questions. And then I assume it will be the Senator from Pennsylvania again, but I am not certain of that. And, again, welcome. We're happy that you are here. Let us stand and be sworn, if you will.

PROFESSOR HILL stands as the stage light dips, flashbulbs fire. The lights slowly come back to their original level.

THE SENATOR: So at the Department of Education, your sole immediate supervisor was Judge Thomas?

MS. HILL: Yes.

THE SENATOR: Can you describe to us how it was that you came to move over to the EEOC with Judge Thomas?

MS. HILL: It was a very tough decision, because his behavior had occurred. However, at the time that I went to the EEOC there was a period—or prior to the time we went to the EEOC there was a period where the incidents had ceased. And so after some consideration of the job opportunities in the area as well as the fact that I was not assured that my job at Education was going to be protected, I made a decision to move to the EEOC.

THE SENATOR: Now, when you went to EEOC, what were your duties? Did you have as much occasion to interact personally with Judge Thomas at EEOC as you had with him at the Department of Education?

MS. HILL: No. No. We were much busier. We were all much busier. And the work that we did was work that did not necessarily require as much interaction.

THE SENATOR: Who was your immediate supervisor at EEOC?

MS. HILL: At the EEOC initially, Clarence Thomas was my immediate supervisor.

THE SENATOR: Who prepared your performance evaluations?

MS. HILL: Judge Thomas prepared the performance evaluations.

THE SENATOR: Did the chief of staff, to the best of your knowledge, have the power to fire you?

MS. HILL: Not to my knowledge.

THE SENATOR: Who had the power?

MS. HILL: Judge Thomas.

Again, the stage light dips as flashbulbs fire. The light slowly comes back to its original level.

MS. HILL: Well, I recall specifically that the incident about the Coke can occurred in his office at the EEOC.

THE SENATOR: And what was that incident again?

MS. HILL: The incident with regard to the Coke can that's spelled out in my statement.

THE SENATOR: Would you describe it once again for me, please?

MS. HILL: The incident involved his going to his desk—getting up from a work table, going to his desk, looking at this can and saying, "Who put pubic hair on my Coke?"

THE SENATOR: Was anyone else in his office at the time?

MS. HILL: No.

THE SENATOR: Was the door closed?

MS. HILL: I don't recall.

THE SENATOR: Let's go back to the first time that you alleged Judge Thomas indicated he had more than a professional interest in you. Do you recall what the first time was and, with as much precision as you can, what he said to you?

MS. HILL: As I recall, it either happened at lunch or it happened in his office when he said to me very casually, "You ought to go out with me some time."

THE SENATOR: You ought to, or you are to?

MS. HILL: You ought to.

Once more, the stage light dips, flashbulbs, light slowly returns.

MS. HILL: The pressure to go out with him I felt embarrassed about because I didn't—I had given him an explanation that I thought it was not good for me as an employee working directly for him to go out. I thought he didn't take seriously my decision to say no and that he did not respect my having said no to him.

I—the conversations about sex I was much more embarrassed and humiliated by. The two combined really made me feel sort of helpless in a job situation because I really wanted to do the work that I was doing.

THE SENATOR: Professor, one of your press conferences, you said that the issues that you raised about Judge Thomas, you referred to as an "ugly issue." Is that how you viewed these conversations?

MS. HILL: Yes, they were very ugly. They were very dirty and they were disgusting.

THE SENATOR: Were any of these conversations repeated more than once?

MS. HILL: The reference to his own physical attributes was repeated more than once, yes.

THE SENATOR: Now again, for the record, did he just say, "I have great physical capability and attributes," or was he more graphic?

MS. HILL: He was much more graphic.

THE SENATOR: Can you tell us what he said?

MS. HILL: Well, I can tell you that he compared his penis size, he measured his penis in terms of length, those kinds of comments.

Slight pause.

THE SENATOR: Professor Hill, I do not regard this as an adversary proceeding.

MS. HILL: Thank you.

THE SENATOR: My duties run to the people who have elected me, and in the broader sense as a United States Senator, to constitutional government and the Constitution. And my purpose, as the purpose of the hearing generally, is to find out what happened.

MS. HILL: Certainly.

THE SENATOR: I think this hearing is very important to the Senate and to this Committee because by 20–20 hindsight we should have done this before, and obviously it's of critical importance to Judge Thomas and you, whose reputations and careers are on the line.

It's not easy to go back to events which happened almost a decade ago to find out what happened, very, very difficult to do. I would start, Professor Hill, with one of your more recent statements, at least according to a man by the name of Carlton Stewart, who says that he met you in August of this year, ran into you at the American Bar Association convention in Atlanta, where Professor Hill stated, quote, "How great Clarence's nomination was and how much he deserved it," unquote. "We went on to discuss Judge Thomas and our tenure at EEOC for an additional 30 minutes or so. There was no mention of sexual harassment or anything negative about Judge Thomas stated during that conversation."

My question is, did Mr. Stewart accurately state what happened with you at that meeting?

MS. HILL: As I recall, we did discuss the nomination. Carlton Stewart was very excited about the nomination and said—I believe that those were his words—how great it was that Clarence Thomas had been nominated. I only said that it was a great opportunity for Clarence Thomas. I did not say that it was a good thing, that this nomination was a good thing.

THE SENATOR: So then Mr. Stewart is simply wrong when he says—and this is a quote—that you said specifically, how great his nomination was and how much he deserved it. He's just wrong.

MS. HILL: The latter part is certainly wrong. I did say that it is a great opportunity for Clarence Thomas. I did not say that he deserved it.

THE SENATOR: You referred to the, quote, "oddest episode I remember," and then talked about the coke incident. When you made your statement to the FBI, why was it that that was omitted, if it was so strong in your mind and such an odd incident?

MS. HILL: I spoke to the FBI agents, and I told them the nature of the comment and did not tell them more specifics. I refer to the specific comments that were in my statement.

THE SENATOR: Well, when you talked to the FBI agents, you did make specific allegations about specific sexual statements made by Judge Thomas.

MS. HILL: Yes.

THE SENATOR: So that your statement to the FBI did have specifics.

MS. HILL: Yes.

THE SENATOR: And my question to you, why, if this was such an odd episode, wasn't it included when you talked to the FBI?

MS. HILL: I don't know. When the FBI investigation took place, I tried to answer their questions as directly as I recall. I have—I was very uncomfortable talking to the agent about that, these instances. I am very uncomfortable now. But I feel that it is necessary.

THE SENATOR: Professor Hill, I can understand that it's uncomfortable, and I don't want to add to that, and if any of it is something you want to pause about, please do.

You testified this morning that the most embarrassing question involved—this is not too bad—women's large breasts—that's a word we use all the time. That was the most embarrassing aspect of what Judge Thomas said to you?

MS. HILL: No, the most embarrassing aspect was his description of the acts of these individuals, these women, the acts that those particular people would engage in. It wasn't just the breasts; it was the continuation of his story about what happened in those films with the people with this characteristic—with this physical characteristic.

THE SENATOR: With the physical characteristic of?

MS. HILL: The large breasts.

THE SENATOR: Well, in your statement to the FBI, you did refer to the films, but there's no reference to the physical characteristic you described. But I don't want to attach too much weight to it, but I had thought you said that the aspect of large breasts was the aspect that concerned you, and that was missing from the statement to the FBI.

MS. HILL: Then I have been misunderstood. It wasn't the physical characteristic of having large breasts. It was the description of the acts that this person with this characteristic would

do, the acts that they would engage in, group acts, acts with animals, things of that nature involving women.

THE SENATOR: Well, now, did you decline to discuss with the FBI anything on the grounds that it was too embarrassing?

MS. HILL: Senator, at the time of the FBI investigation, I cooperated as fully as I could at that time, and I cannot explain why anything in specific was not—was not stated.

THE SENATOR: But—point of clarification. Have you ever seen the FBI report?

MS. HILL: No, I have not.

THE SENATOR: Would you like to take a few moments and look at it now?

MS. HILL: Yes, I would.

NPR voice-over attempts to describe this first round of questioning.

THE SENATOR: Professor Hill, now that you have read the FBI report you can see that it contains no reference to any mention of Judge Thomas's private parts or sexual prowess or size, et cetera. And my question to you would be on something that is as important as it is in your written testimony. . . . Why didn't you tell the FBI about that?

MS. HILL: Senator, in paragraph 2 on page 2 of the report it says that he liked to discuss specific sex acts and frequency of sex. And I'm not sure what all that summarizes, but his sexual prowess, his sexual preferences could have—

THE SENATOR: Which line are you referring to, Professor?

MS. HILL: The very last line in paragraph 2 of page 2.

THE SENATOR: Well, that says, quote—this is not too bad, I can read it—"Thomas liked to discuss specific sex acts and frequency of sex," closed quote. Now are you saying in response to my question as to why you didn't tell the FBI about the size of his private parts and his sexual prowess and Long John Silver that that information was comprehended within the statement, quote, "Thomas liked to discuss specific sex acts and frequency of sex?"

MS. HILL: I am not saying that that information was included in that. At the time of the investigation I tried to cooperate as fully as I could to answer the questions that they asked.

THE SENATOR: Professor Hill, you said that you took it to mean that Judge Thomas wanted to have sex with you, but in fact he never did ask you to have sex, correct?

MS. HILL: No, he did not ask me to have sex. He did continually pressure me to go out with him, continually, and he would not accept my explanation as being valid.

THE SENATOR: So that when you said you took it to mean we ought to have sex that that was an inference that you drew?

MS. HILL: Yes, yes.

THE SENATOR: Professor Hill, did anybody ever tell you that by providing the statement that there would be a move to press Judge Thomas to withdraw his nomination?

MS. HILL: I don't recall any story about using this to press anyone.

THE SENATOR: Well, but was there any suggestion, however slight, that these serious charges would result in a withdrawal so that it wouldn't have to be necessary for your identity to be known or for you to come forward under circumstances like these?

MS. HILL: There was no—not that I recall. I don't recall anything being said about him being pressed to resign.

THE SENATOR: Well, this would only have happened in the course of the past month or so—

MS. HILL: Yes.

THE SENATOR: —because all this started just in early September.

MS. HILL: I understand.

THE SENATOR: You've testified with some specificity about what happened ten years ago—

MS. HILL: Uh-huh.

THE SENATOR: I would ask you to press your recollection as to what happened within the last month.

MS. HILL: And I have done that, Senator. But I really—I have to be honest with you—I cannot verify the statement that you are asking me to verify.

THE SENATOR: Well, Professor Hill, when you talk about the withdrawal of a Supreme Court nominee, you're talking about something that is very, very vivid—stark, and you're talking

about something that occurred within the past four or five weeks. And my questions goes to a very dramatic and important event, if a mere allegation would pressure a nominee to withdraw from the Supreme Court, I would suggest to you that that's not something that wouldn't stick in a mind for four or five weeks, if it happened.

MS. HILL: Well, Senator, I would suggest to you that for me these are more than mere allegations, so that if that comment was made . . . This is the truth to me. These comments are the truth to me. And if it were made, then I may not—I may not respond to it in the same way that you do.

THE SENATOR: Professor Hill, the next subject I want to take up with you involves the kind of strong language which you say Judge Thomas used.

And my question is, understanding that you're 25 and that it's your—you're shortly out of law school and the pressures that exist in this world, and I know about it to a fair extent. I used to be a district attorney and I know about sexual harassment and discrimination against women, and I think I have some sensitivity on it. But even considering all of that, the whole purpose of the civil rights law is being perverted right in the office of the Chairman with one of his own female subordinates—what went through your mind, if anything, on whether you ought to come forward at that stage? What went on through your mind? I know you decided not to make a complaint, but did you give that any consideration, and if so how could you allow this kind of reprehensible conduct to go on right in the headquarters without doing something about it?

MS. HILL: Well, it was a very trying and difficult decision for me not to say anything further. I can only say that when I made the decision to just withdraw from the situation and not press a claim or charge against him, that I may have shirked a duty, a responsibility that I had. And to that extent I confess that I am very sorry that I did not do something or say something, but at the time that was my best judgment. Maybe it was a poor judgment but it wasn't dishonest, and it wasn't a completely unreasonable choice that I made, given the circumstances.

THE SENATOR: There is a report in the *Kansas City Star* of October 8th, 1991, which says in an August interview with the *Kansas City Star,* Anita Hill offered some favorable comments regarding Clarence Thomas and some criticism. And then further on it says, quote—quoting you, "Judicial experience aside, the Clarence Thomas of that period," referring to his days in EEOC early, "would have made a better judge on the Supreme Court, because he was more open-minded."

Well, when you say he would have made a better judge at one point, are you saying that there is not an explicit recommendation or statement that as you said earlier on the basis of his intellect, aside from the personal information, which you decided not to share, that he would have been a better Supreme Court Justice?

MS. HILL: I'm sorry, would you rephrase that?

THE SENATOR: Sure. Isn't the long and short of it, Professor Hill, that when you spoke to the *Kansas City Star* reporter that you were saying that at one point in his career he would have been okay for the Supreme Court?

MS. HILL: No.

THE SENATOR: My red light is on. Thank you very much, Professor Hill. We will adjourn until 2:15.

The chaos of people leaving for lunch, news analysis. Lights fade.

SCENE 2

THE SENATOR: Good afternoon, Professor Hill.

MS. HILL: Good afternoon, Senator.

THE SENATOR: What ultimately—what was the final thing that made you decide that you must go public, knowing that all this would occur?

MS. HILL: Well, I was presented with the information by a newspaper—

THE SENATOR: The information you had submitted—

MS. HILL: —I mean, a reporter.

THE SENATOR: —to me, and I had distributed to the Committee?

MS. HILL: Yes.

THE SENATOR: You were presented with that information—

MS. HILL: Over the telephone, it was read to me verbatim by a member of the press.

THE SENATOR: Now, the thing that was read to you verbatim was the statement that you had submitted and asked me to distribute to The Committee?

MS. HILL: Yes.

THE SENATOR: So, in your view, you're here as a result of some unexpected events?

MS. HILL: Definitely.

THE SENATOR: Events that turned out not to be within your control?

MS. HILL: Definitely.

THE SENATOR: And you do not, therefore consider yourself part of some organized effort to determine whether or not Clarence Thomas should or should not sit on the bench?

MS. HILL: No. I had no intention of being here today. I did not think that this would ever—I had not even imagined that this would occur.

THE SENATOR: Is this what you anticipated?

MS. HILL: This? *(Laughs).* No. Not at all. Not in my—I would have never even dreamed this up. I just can't imagine . . .

THE SENATOR: Is it reasonable to state—say—that it was your hope and expectation that it would not come to this?

MS. HILL: It was exactly what I was trying to—really, very difficult—I made great effort to make sure that it did not come to this, and I was meticulous. I was making every effort to make sure that this public thing did not happen. I didn't talk to the press. I was called by the press on July 1st. I did not talk to the press. I—this is exactly what I did not want.

THE SENATOR: And is it fair to say that attitude prevailed up until the moment a press person called you and read you your statement?

MS. HILL: It prevails even today.

THE SENATOR: Well, we're beyond that point, as you know.

MS. HILL: Yes, we're beyond that point . . .

Pause.

THE SENATOR: Professor Hill. I, and I suppose every member of this committee, have to come down to the ultimate question of who's telling the truth. My experience as a lawyer, judge, is that you listen to all the testimony and then you try to determine the motivation for the one that is not telling the truth. Now in trying to determine whether you are telling falsehoods or not, I've got to determine what your motivation might be.

Are you a scorned woman?

MS. HILL: No.

THE SENATOR: Are you a zealot civil rights believer that progress will be turned back if Clarence Thomas goes on the Court?

MS. HILL: I—no, I don't. I think that civil rights will prevail no matter what happens with the Court.

THE SENATOR: Do you have a militant attitude relative to the area of civil rights?

MS. HILL: No, I don't have a militant attitude.

THE SENATOR: Well, do you see that coming out of this you can be a hero in the civil rights movement?

MS. HILL: I don't like all of the attention that I am getting. Even if I liked the attention I would not lie to get attention.

THE SENATOR: Do you have a martyr complex?

MS. HILL (*Laughs.*): No, I don't.

THE SENATOR: Well, the issue of fantasy has arisen. You have a degree in psychology from the University of—Oklahoma State University.

MS. HILL: Yes.

THE SENATOR: What do you—what are the traits of fantasy, as you remember?

MS. HILL: As I remember, it would have—it would require some other indication of loss of touch with reality other than one instance. There is no indication that I'm an individual who is not in touch with reality on a regular basis.

THE SENATOR: Did you take all steps that you knew how to take to prevent being in that witness chair today?

MS. HILL: Yes, I did. Everything I knew to do I did.

THE SENATOR: There may be other motivation. . . . Are you interested in writing a book?

MS. HILL (*With a laugh.*): No, I'm not interested in writing a book.

Gavel restores order in the room. Pause.

THE SENATOR: I'm shifting now, Professor Hill, to a key issue regarding your testimony that you

moved with Judge Thomas from the Department of Education to EEOC, because you needed the job. That is your testimony, correct?

MS. HILL: Well, I think that's your summary of my testimony.

THE SENATOR: Well, is my summary accurate?

MS. HILL: Well, I said that I moved to EEOC because I did not have another job. I was not sure whether I would have a position at the Department of Education. I suppose that could be translated into I needed the job.

THE SENATOR: Okay. Professor Hill, did you make any effort to find out that as a Class A attorney you could have stayed on at the Department of Education?

MS. HILL: No. I relied on what I was told.

THE SENATOR: Sorry. I didn't hear you.

MS. HILL: I relied on what I was told by Clarence Thomas. I did not make further inquiry.

THE SENATOR: And what are you saying that Judge Thomas told you?

MS. HILL: The indication from him was that he could not assure me of a position at Education.

THE SENATOR: Did you make any inquiry of his successor, Mr. Singleton, as to what your status would be?

MS. HILL: No, I did not. I am not even sure that I knew who his successor would be at the time.

THE SENATOR: Well, was Mr. Singleton on the premises for about four weeks in advance of Judge Thomas's departure as the—

MS. HILL: I don't—

THE SENATOR: May I finish the question?

MS. HILL: I don't—oh, I'm sorry.

THE SENATOR: May I finish the question?

MS. HILL: I'm sorry.

THE SENATOR: Was Mr. Singleton on the premises for about four weeks prior to Judge Thomas's departure for transition?

MS. HILL: I don't recall.

THE SENATOR: Did you make any effort at all with anybody in the Department of Education to find out whether you could stay on in a job there?

MS. HILL: As I said before, I did not make any further inquiry.

THE SENATOR: Professor Hill, there has been disclosed into the public milieu the records of certain telephone logs. And you were quoted in the *Washington Post*, quote, Ms. Hill called the telephone logs, quote, "garbage," unquote, and said that she had not telephoned Thomas, except to return his calls. Did you in fact say that you had not telephoned Thomas except to return his calls?

MS. HILL: No, I did not say that.

THE SENATOR: The *Washington Post* is in error on that statement attributed to you?

MS. HILL: Well, I think there was a miscommunication in the entire interview.

THE SENATOR: Did you call the telephone log issue, quote, "garbage"?

MS. HILL: I believe the issue is garbage when you look at what seems to be implied from the telephone log. Then, yes, that is garbage.

THE SENATOR: Have you seen the records of the telephone logs, Professor Hill?

MS. HILL: Yes, I have.

THE SENATOR: Do you deny the accuracy of these telephone logs?

MS. HILL: No, I do not.

THE SENATOR: Then you now concede that you had called Judge Thomas 11 times?

MS. HILL: I do not deny the accuracy of these logs. I cannot deny that they're accurate, and I will concede that those phone calls were made, yes.

THE SENATOR: So they're not garbage.

MS. HILL: Well, Senator, what I said was the issue is garbage. Those telephone messages do not indicate that which they are being used to indicate, that is, that somehow I was pursuing something more than a cordial relationship, professional relationship. Each of those calls were made in a professional context.

So, the issue that is being created by the telephone calls, yes, indeed, is garbage.

THE SENATOR: Well, the issue which was raised by Senator Danforth, who disclosed this log in a press conference, was done so on the point that you had made repeated efforts to contact Judge Thomas, which bore on the issue as to whether he had sexually harassed you, that if he had victimized you by sexual harassment you would not be calling him so many times.

Now my question to you is, since those calls were in fact made, as you now say, doesn't that have some relevance as to whether the committee should accept your statements about Judge Thomas's sexual harassment in the context of your efforts to call him this many times over that period of time?

MS. HILL: No.

THE SENATOR: Okay.

MS. HILL: I want to back up and say something here. In my statement to you, I never alleged sexual harassment. I had conduct that I wanted explained to the Committee. My sense was—my own personal sense was that yes, this was sexual harassment. But I understood that the Committee with their staff could make that evaluation on their own.

So, I didn't have any doubts. But I wanted to talk with someone who might be more objective.

THE SENATOR: Well, you did call it sexual harassment in your extensive news conference on October 7th, even though you did not so characterize it to the FBI or in your statement to this Committee. You did not tell the FBI that Judge Thomas was guilty of sexual harassment, did you?

MS. HILL: I don't recall telling them he was guilty of sexual harassment, no, I didn't tell them that.

THE SENATOR: But you didn't characterize his conduct as sexual harassment?

MS. HILL: I did or did not?

THE SENATOR: You did not characterize Judge Thomas's conduct as sexual harassment when you gave the statement to the FBI, correct?

MS. HILL: Senator, I guess I'm not making myself clear. I was not raising a legal claim in either of my statements. I was not raising a legal claim. I was attempting to inform about conduct.

THE SENATOR: But you did raise a legal claim in your interview on October 7th.

MS. HILL: No, I did not raise a legal claim then.

THE SENATOR: Well, I will produce the transcript which says that it was sexual harassment.

MS. HILL: Well, I would suggest that saying that it is sexual harassment and raising a legal claim are two different things. Were I filing a claim—if I were filing a complaint in court, this would be done very differently. But this does not constitute a legal complaint.

THE SENATOR: So that you are not now drawing a conclusion that Judge Thomas sexually harassed you?

MS. HILL: Yes, I am drawing that conclusion. That is my—

THE SENATOR: Well, then, I don't understand.

MS. HILL: Pardon me?

THE SENATOR: Then I don't understand.

MS. HILL: Well, let me try to explain again. (*PROFESSOR HILL stands, crosses to THE SENATOR*) I did not bring the information to try to establish a legal claim for sexual harassment. I brought it forward so that the committee could test the veracity of it. The truth of it. From there on, you could evaluate the information as to whether or not it constituted sexual harassment or whether or not it went to his ability to conduct a job as Associate Justice of the Supreme Court. (*She returns to her seat.*)

Pause.

THE SENATOR: You . . . left EEOC in 1983; is that correct?

MS. HILL: Yes.

THE SENATOR: Judge Thomas left EEOC in 1990; is that correct? Approximately seven years in there. . . .

MS. HILL: Yes.

THE SENATOR: If you count up the phone calls that are shown on those phone logs, assuming that they're accurate, that amounts during the seven years to what, a dozen phone calls?

That's about 1½ a year. You weren't exactly—you weren't exactly beating down the doors with phone calls there, were you?

MS. HILL: I was not at all.

THE SENATOR: Now, did anybody tell you that you could stay and have a job at the Department of Education?

MS. HILL: Nobody told be that.

THE SENATOR: Had President Reagan pledged and campaigned on a pledge that he would do away with the Department of Education if elected?

MS. HILL: Yes, he had.

THE SENATOR: And President Reagan was then President.

MS. HILL: Yes, he was.

THE SENATOR: Ms. Hill, I just—if I can—I won't be very much longer. The concern I also have is when you were at the Department of Education and these—and my term is "God-awful" things occurred, grotesque, ugly, I don't know how else I can depict them, and obviously they were extremely offensive to you, and you obviously did not want them to continue, and you attempted to inform the person that you didn't want that. I have a difficult time understanding—and it's obviously because I'm not a woman and have not had that kind of personal experience—I have a difficult time understanding, even though you didn't have another job or anything out there, how you could tolerate that.

And I realize that's part of the whole problem of sexual harassment in the job place, is because women tolerate it.

And maybe you explained this sufficiently, but if you wouldn't mind repeating to me what went through your mind, why, number one, you would stay there after this happened several times, and number two, even though it ceased for a few months, why you would proceed on to another job with someone that hadn't just asked you out and pressed you, but had gotten into the explanations and—expletives and the anatomy and what have you that you pointed out to us today.

MS. HILL: Well, I think it is very difficult to understand, Senator. And in hindsight it is even difficult for me to understand. But I have to take the situation as it existed at that time. At that time, though, staying seemed the only reasonable choice. At that time staying was . . . a choice that I made because I wanted to do the work. And that's what I wanted to do. And I did not want to let that kind of behavior control my choices. So I attempted to end the behavior, and for some time the behavior did stop.

And so the choice to continue with the same person to another agency involved a belief that I had stopped the behavior that was offensive.

THE SENATOR: Is there anything you would change, either in your statement or your answers that you have given us today, about the kinds of conversations that you had with Judge Thomas that you say were so offensive?

MS. HILL: No, sir, I would not change anything.

THE SENATOR: And my last question. Would your life be simpler, quieter, and far more private had you never come forth at all?

MS. HILL: Yes. Norman, Oklahoma is a much simpler, quieter place than this room today.

JUDGE THOMAS enters. They see each other. JUDGE THOMAS sits at the witness table.

JUDGE THOMAS: Senator, I would like to start by saying unequivocally, uncategorically, that I deny each and every single allegation against me today that suggested in any way that I had conversations of a sexual nature or about pornographic material with Anita Hill, that I ever attempted to date her, that I ever had any personal sexual interest in her, or that I in any way ever harassed her.

A second, and I think more important point, I think that this today is a travesty. I think that it is disgusting. I think that this hearing should never occur in America. This is a case in which this sleaze, this dirt, was searched for by staffers of members of this Committee, was then leaked to the media, and this committee and this body validated it and displayed it at prime time over our entire nation. How would any member on this Committee, any person in this room, or any person in this country, like sleaze said about him or her in this fashion? Or this dirt dredged up and this gossip and these lies displayed in this manner? How would any person like it?

The Supreme Court is not worth it. No job is worth it. I'm not here for that. I'm here for my name, my family, my life, and my integrity. I think something is dreadfully wrong with this country when any person, any person in this free country would be subjected to this.

This is not a closed room. There was an FBI investigation. This is not an opportunity to talk about difficult matters privately or in a closed environment. This is a circus. It's a national disgrace. And from my standpoint as a black American, as far as I'm concerned, it is a high-tech lynching for uppity blacks who in any way deign to think for themselves, to do for themselves, to have different ideas, and it is a message that unless you kowtow to an old order, this is what will happen to you. You will be lynched, destroyed, caricatured by a Committee of the U.S. Senate rather than hung from a tree.

THE SENATOR looks down the table to his left, then looks down the table to his right.

THE SENATOR: We will have—yes? (*Pause. He taps the gavel somewhat absentmindedly.*) Judge, just because we take harassment seriously doesn't mean we take the charges at face value.

When a respectable, reasonable, upstanding person, professor of law, someone with no blemish on her record, comes forward, this Committee has the obligation to do exactly what you would have done at EEOC, investigate the charge.

Because this is being investigated, you are making a mistake if you conclude that before all the evidence is in, the conclusion has been reached by this committee . . .
    By me and by my colleagues. . . .
    You've told us things that are new. . . .
    We have to figure this out. . . .
    So do not in your anger, tomorrow, refuse
        to tell us more.
    This is not decided.
    We wish you a good night's rest and . . .
    we look forward to seeing you. . . .
        Well.
    We'll reconvene at 10:00.

Without looking at PROFESSOR HILL, and in a very businesslike manner, JUDGE THOMAS and THE SENATOR leave the stage. PROFESSOR HILL is left alone at the table. Lights fade. News, chaos; it becomes Saturday.

SCENE 3

At rise, all three are onstage. Silence.

THE SENATOR: Now, you, I suppose, have heard Ms.—Professor Hill's—Ms. Hill—Anita F. Hill testify today.
JUDGE THOMAS: No, I haven't.
THE SENATOR: You didn't listen?
JUDGE THOMAS: No, I didn't. I've heard enough lies.
THE SENATOR: You didn't listen to her testimony at all?
JUDGE THOMAS: No, I didn't.

THE SENATOR: On television?

JUDGE THOMAS: No, I didn't. I've heard enough lies. You spent the entire day destroying what it has taken me 43 years to build, and providing a forum for that.

THE SENATOR: Well, Judge Thomas, you know, we have a responsibility, too. And as far as I'm involved, I had nothing to do with Anita Hill coming here and testifying. We're trying to get to the bottom of this, and if she is lying, then I think you can help us prove that she was lying.

JUDGE THOMAS: Senator, I am incapable of proving the negative. It did not occur.

THE SENATOR: Well, if it did not occur, I think you are in a position to testify to in effect to try to eliminate it from people's minds.

JUDGE THOMAS: Senator, I didn't create it in people's minds. This matter was investigated by the Federal Bureau of Investigation in a confidential way. It was then leaked last weekend to the media. I did not do that. And how many members of this Committee would like to have the same scurrilous, uncorroborated allegations made about him, and then leaked to national newspapers, and then be drawn and dragged before a national forum of this nature to discuss those allegations that should have been resolved in a confidential way.

THE SENATOR: Well I certainly appreciate your attitude toward leaks. I happen to serve on the Senate Ethics Committee, and it's been a sieve.

JUDGE THOMAS: Well, but it didn't leak on me. This leaked on me and it is drowning my life, my career, and my integrity and you can't give it back to me and this Committee can't give it back to me and this Senate can't give it back to me. You have robbed me of something that can never be restored.

THE SENATOR: Judge Thomas, one of the aspects of this is that she could be living in a fantasy world. I don't know. We're just trying to get to the bottom of all of these facts. But if you didn't listen and didn't see her testify, I think you put yourself in an unusual position. You in effect are defending yourself and basically some of us want to be fair to you, fair to her, but if you didn't listen to what she said today, then that puts it somewhat in a more difficult task to find out what the actual facts are relative to this matter.

JUDGE THOMAS: The facts keep changing, Senator. When the FBI visited me, the statements to this Committee and the questions were one thing. The FBI's subsequent questions were another thing, and the statements today, as I received summaries of them, were another thing. It is not my fault that the facts changed. What I have said to you is categorical; that any allegations that I engaged in any conduct involving sexual activity, pornographic movies, attempted to date her, any allegations, I deny. So, the facts can change, but my denial does not.

THE SENATOR: Judge, if you are on the bench and you approach a case where you appear to have a closed mind and that you are only right, doesn't it raise issues of judicial temperament?

JUDGE THOMAS: Senator, Senator, there is a big difference between approaching a case objectively and watching yourself being lynched. There is no comparison whatsoever.

THE SENATOR: All right sir. (*Slight pause.*) Let me make sure I understand one thing. Do you believe that interest groups went out and got Professor Hill to make up a story, or do you believe Professor Hill had a story, untrue from your perspective, that groups went out and found? Which do you believe?

JUDGE THOMAS: Senator, I believe that someone, some interest group, I don't care who it is, in combination, came up with this story and used this process to destroy me.

THE SENATOR: Got Professor Hill to say—to make up a story?

JUDGE THOMAS: I believe that, in combination, this story was developed or concocted to destroy me.

THE SENATOR: With Professor Hill? Ms.—critical question—are you saying with Professor Hill, that a group went—?

JUDGE THOMAS: That's just my view, Senator.

THE SENATOR: I know, I'm trying to make sure I understand it.

JUDGE THOMAS: I'm not—there's no details to it or anything else. The story . . . I do not believe the . . . The story is not true.

    The allegations are false and my view is that others put it together and developed this.

THE SENATOR: And put it in Professor Hill's mouth?

JUDGE THOMAS: I don't know. I don't know how it got there. All I know is that the story is here, and I think it was concocted.

THE SENATOR: Well, Judge, I know you believe that, and I am not here to be able to or attempt to, at this moment, refute that. There has been an assertion that has just been made, and I wanted to know whether you had agreed with it, that—it's important for us to keep our eye on the ball here. Either Professor Hill had a story that she told someone and it was taken advantage of by being leaked—that's one thing; she says that—and the other story that seems to be being painted now—not by you; I'm asking if you believe—is that a group sat down, decided to make up a story, and found a willing vessel in Professor Hill and got her to say it.

JUDGE THOMAS: Senator, those distinctions are irrelevant to me. The story is false, the story is here, and the story was developed to harm me.

THE SENATOR: Thank you.

Blackout.

SCENE 4

As the lights come up, PROFESSOR HILL *is alone onstage. She is not speaking to the Committee now, but is speaking from her bewilderment and the bittersweetness of her appearance here.*

MS. HILL: I would have never dreamed this up. I just . . . can't . . . imagine. (*Slight pause.*)

I made great effort to make sure that it did not come to this. And I was meticulous. I was making every effort to make sure that this public thing did not happen. I—this is exactly what I did not want. And I thought that if I were cautious enough, I could . . . control it so that . . . it would not get to this point. But I was mistaken. (*Slight pause.*)

I don't like all of the attention that I am getting. Even if I liked the attention I would not lie to get attention.

I'm not interested in writing a book.

I have nothing to gain. No one has promised me anything.

I have nothing to gain here. This has been disruptive of my life and I've taken a number of personal risks. (*Pause.*)

I've been threatened. (*Slight pause.*) And I have not gained anything except knowing that I came forward and did what I felt that I had an obligation to do, and that was to tell the truth.

The lights fade.

SCENE 5

THE SENATOR: Judge, there are a lot of things that just don't make sense to me in Anita Hill's testimony. I liked her personally. I thought she presented herself well. There's no question she's a very intelligent law professor. She has graduated from one of the finest schools in the land, law schools, that is, and her undergraduate work was exemplary. She clearly is a very intelligent woman and I think everybody who listened to her wants to like her and many do.

But Judge, it bothers me because it just doesn't square with what I think is—some of it doesn't square with what I think is common experience and just basic sense, common sense. I hesitate to do this again, but I think it's critical and I know it outrages you as it would me, as it would anybody who was accused of these types of activities. (*Pause.*)

Yesterday, Hill appeared before this Committee and in her statement yesterday, her written statement of which I have a copy that was distributed to everybody else, she said "His conversations were very vivid. He spoke about acts that he had seen in pornographic films involving such matters as women having sex with animals and films showing group sex or rape scenes. He talked about pornographic materials depicting individuals with large penises or large breasts involved in various sex acts. On several occasions Thomas told me graphically of his own sexual prowess."

But Judge, you know, I mean Judge Thomas, anybody who made those statements, if you take one of them out of context they're so graphic, and so crude, and so outrageous, and I think so stupid, that would be enough in my opinion to find sex harassment against anybody. If it happened.

But the person who would do something like that over a period of time, really a short period of time according to her—that person, it seems to me, would not be a normal person. That person, it seems to me, could be a psychopathic sex fiend or a pervert.

Now Judge, you've had to have thought about this. I know you're outraged by it and you've denied all these things, and you've said these things did not happen, they are simply untrue. And you've had an evening to think about it. Do you have anything further to say about it?

JUDGE THOMAS: Senator, one of the things that has tormented me over the last two and half weeks has been how do I defend myself against this kind of language and these kinds of charges, how do I defend myself? Well, the difficulty also was that, from my standpoint, is that in this country when it comes to sexual conduct we still have underlying racial attitudes about black men and their views of sex. And once you pin that on me I can't get it off. That is why I'm so adamant in this committee about what has been done to me. I made a point at EEOC and at Education not to play into those stereotypes. At all. I made it a point to have the people at those agencies, the black men, the black women, conduct themselves in a way that was not consistent with those stereotypes. And I did the same thing myself.

THE SENATOR: Now I want to ask you about this intriguing thing you just said. You said some of this language is stereotype language. What does that—

JUDGE THOMAS: Senator—

THE SENATOR: —mean? I don't understand.

JUDGE THOMAS: —language throughout the history of this country and certainly throughout my life, language about the sexual prowess of black men, language about the sex organs of black men and the sizes, et cetera, that kind of language has been used about black men as long as I've been on the face of this earth, and these are charges that play into racist, bigoted stereotypes, and these are the kind of charges that are impossible to wash off.

THE SENATOR: Well, I saw—I didn't understand the television program. But there were two

black men. I might have it wrong. But as I recall it, there were two black men talking about this matter, and one of them said "She trying to demonize us." I didn't understand it at the time. Do you understand that?

JUDGE THOMAS: Well, I understand it, and any black man in this country—Senator, in the 1970s, I became very interested in the issue of lynching, and if you want to track through this country in the 19th and 20th century the lynchings of black men, you will see that there is invariably or in many instances a relationship with sex and an accusation that that person cannot shake off. That is the point that I'm trying to make, and that is the point that I was making last night, that this is high-tech lynching. I cannot shake off these accusations because they play to the worst stereotypes we have about black men in this country.

THE SENATOR: This bothers me. It bothers me—

JUDGE THOMAS: It bothers me.

THE SENATOR: Let—let me—I hate to do this, but let me—let me ask you some tough questions. You've talked about stereotypes used against black males in this society. In this first statement: "He told her about his experiences and preferences, would ask her what she had liked or if she had ever done the same thing." Is that a black stereotype?

JUDGE THOMAS: No.

THE SENATOR: Okay. Hill said that "he discussed oral sex between men and women." Is that a black stereotype?

JUDGE THOMAS: No.

THE SENATOR: Okay. "Thomas also discussed viewing film of people having sex with each other and with animals." What about that?

JUDGE THOMAS: That's not a stereotype about blacks.

THE SENATOR: Okay. "He told her that he enjoyed watching the films and told her that she should see them." Watching X-rated films or pornographic films, is that a stereotype?

JUDGE THOMAS: No.

THE SENATOR: "He never asked her to watch the films with him. . . . Thomas liked to discuss specific sex acts and frequency of sex."

JUDGE THOMAS: No, I don't think so. I think that that could—the last—frequency—could have to do with black men supposedly being very promiscuous or something like that.

THE SENATOR: So it could be partially stereotypical then?

JUDGE THOMAS: Yeah.

THE SENATOR: In the next statement, she said, "His conversations were very vivid. He spoke about acts that he had seen in pornographic films involving such things as women having sex with animals and films involving group sex or rape scenes. He talked about pornographic materials depicting individuals with large penises or breasts involved in various sex acts." What about those things?

JUDGE THOMAS: I think the—certainly the size of sexual organs would be something.

THE SENATOR: Well, I'm concerned. "Thomas told me graphically of his own sexual prowess," the third statement.

JUDGE THOMAS: That's clearly stereotypical.

THE SENATOR: Clearly a black stereotype.

JUDGE THOMAS: Clearly.

Blackout.

SCENE 6

Lights fade up on JUDGE THOMAS, *who speaks to the audience.*

JUDGE THOMAS: Think about who you're talking to. I have been a public figure for ten years. I have been confirmed four times. I've had five FBI background checks. I have had stories written about me. I've had groups that despised me looking into my background. I've had people who wanted to do me great harm.

You're talking about a person who ran an agency—two agencies to fight discrimination; who, if he did anything stupid like this, gross like this, had everything to lose. It just seems as though I'm here to prove the negative, in a forum without rules and after the fact. (*Slight pause.*) I expected it to be bad. And I expected awful treatment throughout the process. I expected to be a sitting duck for the interest groups. I even expected personal attempts on my life.

I did not expect this circus. I did not expect to lose my name, my reputation, my integrity, to do public service.

I don't think any American, whether that person is homeless, whether that person earns minimum wage or is unemployed, whether that person runs a corporation or a small business, is black, white, male, female, should have to go through this for any reason.

I did not ask to be nominated. I did not lobby for it. I did not beg for it. I did not aspire to it.

I'd rather die than withdraw from the process. Not for the purpose of serving on the Supreme Court, but for the purpose of not being driven out of this process. I've never run from bullies. I never cry uncle and I'm not going cry uncle today, whether I want to be on the Supreme Court or not.

Lights Fade.

SCENE 7

All three, somewhere. Stormy.

THE SENATOR: Do you think that Anita Hill is lying?

MS. HILL: I have no personal vendetta against Clarence Thomas. I seek only to provide the committee with information which it may regard as relevant.

JUDGE THOMAS: It's just that—it's just that it's incredible. I can't believe it.

MS. HILL: I was 25. I had just turned 25 when I started the job.

THE SENATOR: Judge Thomas, do you think Anita Hill is lying?

MS. HILL: It would have been more comfortable to remain silent.

JUDGE THOMAS: Senator, I know that what she is saying is untrue. I have thought about why she would say these things, why she would come here, why it would keep changing. I don't know. . . .

MS. HILL: If you start to look at each individual problem with the statement, then you're not going to be satisfied that it's true. I think the statement has to be taken as a whole. There is nothing in my background, nothing in my statement—there is no motivation that I would make up something like this.

THE SENATOR: See, we in the committee have a responsibility to figure out if she is not telling the truth, why?

JUDGE THOMAS: I think you have more than an obligation to figure out why she would say that. I think you have an obligation to determine why you would allow uncorroborated, unsubstantiated allegations to ruin my life.

MS. HILL: He said that if I ever told anyone of his behavior that it would ruin his career.

JUDGE THOMAS: Senator, I know that what she is saying is untrue.

THE SENATOR: But we're still faced with the fact, Judge, that if she's lying, why?

JUDGE THOMAS: Senator—

THE SENATOR: If she's telling a falsehood, what is the motivation? Now, we've watched her testify today, and she's a meek woman.

JUDGE THOMAS: Anita would not be considered a meek woman. She was an aggressive debater. She stood her ground.

MS. HILL: It was almost as though he wanted me at a disadvantage—to put me at a disadvantage so that I would have to concede to whatever his wishes were.

THE SENATOR: You think that he got some pleasure out of seeing you ill at ease and vulnerable?

MS. HILL: I think so, yes.

THE SENATOR: Was this feeling more so than the feeling that he might be seeking some type of dating or social relationship with you?

MS. HILL: I think that he wanted to see me vulnerable, and that if I were vulnerable, then he could extract from me whatever he wanted, whether it was sexual or otherwise—that I would be at his—under his control.

JUDGE THOMAS: When—I took it as a sign of immaturity, perhaps, that when she didn't get her way that she would tend to—reinforce her position and get a bit angry. I did not see that as vindictiveness.

MS. HILL: I can say that I felt that he was using his power and authority over me.

JUDGE THOMAS: I remember Anita as aggressive, strong, and forceful in advocating the positions that she stood for.

MS. HILL: I think it was the fact that I had said no to him that caused him to want to do this.

Sound . . . Lights Fade.

SCENE 8

THE SENATOR: And here we are. You've been before us for 105 days. We've seen everything, known everything, heard every bit of dirt, as you call it so well.

And what do we know about Professor Hill? Not very much. I'm waiting for 105 days of surveillance of Ms. Hill, and then we'll see, you know, who ate the cabbage, as we say out in the Wild West. This is an impossible thing.

And now I really am getting stuff over the transom about Professor Hill. I've got letters hanging out of my pocket, I've got faxes, I've got statements from her former law professors, statements from people that know her, statements from Tulsa, Oklahoma, saying "Watch out for this woman." But nobody's got the guts to say that, because it gets all tangled up in this sexual harassment crap.

I believe sexual harassment is a terrible thing. I had a bill in a year ago doubling the penalties on sexual harassment. I don't need any test, don't need anybody to give me the saliva test on whether one believes more or less about sexual harassment. It's repugnant, it's disgusting in any form.

And if we're really going to do it right—we're all mumbling about how do you find the truth. I'll tell you how you find the truth, you get into an adversarial courtroom and everybody raises their hand once more and you go at it with the rules of evidence and you really punch around in it. And we can't do that. It's impossible for us to do that in this place.

So if we had 104 days to go into Ms. Hill and find out about her character, her background, her proclivities and all the rest, I'd feel a lot better about this system.

I said at the time this would be destructive of her. And some said, "Well, isn't that terrible, a menacing threat." It wasn't menacing, it was true, that she would come forward and she would be destroyed. She will, just as you have been destroyed. I hope you can both be rehabilitated. (*Slight pause.*)

Angela Wright will soon be with us—we think. But now we're told that Angela Wright has what we used to call in the legal trade "cold feet." Now, if Angela Wright doesn't show up to tell her tale of your horrors, what are we to determine about Angela Wright? Did you fire her? And if you did, what for? You said that . . .

JUDGE THOMAS: I indicated, Senator, I summarily dismissed her. And this is my recollection. She was hired to reinvigorate the public affairs operation of EEOC. I felt her performance was ineffective and the office was ineffective. And the straw that broke the camel's back was a report to me from one of the members of my staff that she referred to another male member of my staff as a faggot.

THE SENATOR: As a faggot.

JUDGE THOMAS: And that's inappropriate conduct and that's a slur and I was not going to have it.

THE SENATOR: And so you just summarily discharged her?

JUDGE THOMAS: That's right.

THE SENATOR: That was enough for you?

JUDGE THOMAS: That was more than enough for me.

THE SENATOR: That's kind of the way you are, isn't it?

JUDGE THOMAS: That's the way I am with conduct like that, whether it's sex harassment or slurs or anything else. I don't play games.

THE SENATOR: Well, you know all of us have been through this stuff in life, but never to this degree. I've done my old stuff about my past and shared that. I won't get into those old saws, but I tell you I do love Shakespeare. Shakespeare would love this. This is all Shakespeare. This is about love and hate and cheating and distrust and kindness and disgust and avarice and jealousy and envy—all those things that make that remarkable bard read today. But, boy, I tell you one came to my head and I just went and got it out of the back of the book, "Othello." Read "Othello" and don't ever forget this line. "Good name in man and woman dear, my Lord"—remember this scene—"is the

immediate jewel of their souls. Who steals my purse steals trash, T'is something, nothing. T'was mine, t'is his and has been slave to thousands. But he that filches from me my good name robs me of that which not enriches him and makes me poor indeed."

What a tragedy! What a disgusting tragedy!

Blackout.

SCENE 9

The lights come up slowly throughout the following. The light is constantly moving, and it's never very bright. As the fade-up reaches its conclusion halfway through, it begins to decline again. It is a moment of calm.

MS. HILL:
My name is Anita F. Hill, and I am a professor of law at the University of Oklahoma.

I was born on a farm in 1956. I am the youngest of 13 children.

JUDGE THOMAS:

My earliest memories are those of Pinpoint, Georgia. As kids, we caught fiddler crabs in the marshes and skipped shells across the water.

In 1955, my brother and I went to live with my mother in Savannah. We lived in one room in a tenement. Our mother only earned $20 every two weeks as a maid, not enough to take care of us, so she arranged for us to live with our grandparents later in 1955. Imagine two little boys with all their belongings in two grocery bags.

I had my early education in Okmulgee County.

I attended segregated parochial schools and later attended a seminary near Savannah.

My father, Albert Hill, is a farmer, My mother's name is Irma Hill. She is also a farmer and a housewife. My childhood was one of a lot of hard work and not much money, but it was one of solid family affection, as represented by my parents.

I attended Yale Law School. Yale had opened its doors, its heart, its conscience to recruit and admit minority students. I benefited from this effort.

I was reared in a religious atmosphere in the Baptist faith, and I have been a member of the Antioch Baptist Church in Tulsa, Oklahoma, since 1983. It is a very warm part of my life at the present time.

But for the efforts of so many others who have gone before me, I would not be here today. It would be unimaginable. Only by standing on their shoulders could I be here.

The light has gone out.

SCENE 10

THE SENATOR: Well, I think you have presented yourself and your testimony in an extraordinary way. (*Slight pause.*)

I thought of my daughter—my rainbow of life. And I would be outraged if such alleged conduct occurred directed to her. And then I've had the terrible pain of also thinking of my sons, raised by a very enlightened mother, responsive, still kiss their old man goodnight and things like that, and rather expansive, stalwart boys—and where that kind of conduct could leave them. Very troubling for me because all we heard for 103 days is about a most remarkable man, and nobody has come forward, and they scoured his every shred of life, and nobody but you and another witness apparently who is alleging no sexual harassment has come forward.

And so, maybe—maybe it seems to me you really didn't intend to kill him, but you might have. And that's pretty heavy—I don't care if you're a man or a woman—to know that 43 years or 35 years of your life or 60 years of your life where no one has corroborated what is a devastating charge, kind of a singular torpedo blow below the water line, and he sinks.

And, you know, leave out who leaked what to who or what media person let it out. If what you say this man said to you occurred, why in God's name, when he left his position of power or status or authority over you, and you left it in 1983, why in God's name would you ever speak to a man like that the rest of your life?

MS. HILL: I have suggested that I was afraid of retaliation. I was afraid of damage to my professional life. And I believe that you have to understand that this response—and that's one of the things that I have come to understand about harassment—this response, this kind of response, is not atypical.

And I can't explain. It takes an expert in psychology to explain how that can happen. But it can happen, because it happened to me.

Sound. . . . JUDGE THOMAS and PROFESSOR HILL look at each other. Blackout.

END OF PLAY

"UNQUESTIONED INTEGRITY QUESTIONED"

Examining the structure, manipulation of source material, and the reconstruction and interpretation of historical events in Mame Hunt's *Unquestioned Integrity* (*UQ*) provides insight into the concerns which are unique to documentary theater. The basis of this inquiry will be an intertextual comparison of the script and the hearing transcripts from which it is drawn (*Nomination of Judge Clarence Thomas*, Senate Judiciary Committee hearings [Washington D.C.: Government Printing Office, October 11–13, 1991])—both as texts and historical documents—and a telephone interview (11 April 1994) with the playwright.

Hunt offers a few clues as to why she deemed it appropriate to dramatize the hearings, which, she reminds us, were both "widely publicized" and "thoroughly televised" (*UQ*). In her "Author's Notes," Hunt states that in the year after the hearings, several issues became prominent in the public debate, including "the tide of public opinion about the Senate, sexual harassment in the workplace, and the incredibly complex issue of race and gender." She cites that in 1992 "women were elected to Congress in unprecedented numbers," and the election of Carol Mosely Braun as the first African-American woman to serve in the United States Senate (*UQ*), suggesting that these important events be considered as direct results of the hearings and the public debate that they sparked.

In conversation, Hunt provided additional reasons for her decision to dramatize the hearings and why she felt it was particularly suited to the stage. First, she maintained that she is "not a playwright, but a dramaturg," and that she approached the project as a "huge dramaturgical process." She related that the original idea was Larry Eilenberg's—her predecessor as Artistic Director of the Magic Theatre—when she served as

Literary Manager/Company Dramaturg. She ultimately decided to undertake the project because "at the time [of the hearings], we had so much information regarding what was or what may have happened that I felt the need to bring the events to some conclusion." She was quick to point out, however, that she wanted to present the information "objectively" so as to let the "audience make their own decisions" regarding the event itself (and the aftermath): the truth regarding the sexual harassment claim and the "underspoken" issue of race.

As to why the hearings were particularly conducive to theatrical representation, Hunt recalled the experience of an actress friend, who related that because she was initially exposed to the hearings not on television but on the car radio, she felt isolated, with neither a "social or emotional outlet." Hunt remembered that she felt similarly isolated at the time of the hearings and that this was probably the experience "of many others." Hunt's decision to dramatize the hearings, therefore, followed from her idea that the theater is a unique medium in that it "can provide such an outlet" as well as the opportunity to "listen more carefully . . . unmediated by news commentary and hype."

While dramatizing the hearings, however, Hunt necessarily engaged in a process of mediation, even at the most elemental level of editing out those portions of the testimony she chose not to include. In this respect, Hunt not only pared down the material to a manageable length but also "condensed and rechoreographed portions of the transcripts . . . [with] every word . . . taken directly from the transcripts of the hearings" (*UQ*). In the interview, she added that in selecting the material, of particular interest were those moments that were either "highly dramatic in themselves" or "particularly conducive" to theatricalization. In the selection process, therefore, Hunt privileged the material that she felt would sustain interest, tension, and dramatic "effect."

In regard to the play's structure, Hunt acknowledged Clarence Thomas's "high-tech lynching" speech as the moment in the hearings which proved to be the most significant in deciding on a dramaturgical strategy, because she felt that it was at that moment that "the logic of the whole proceeding began to break down." Hunt elaborated that the pretense for the hearing—"the fact-finding mission . . . the idea that an absolute truth could ever be found, as if there is an absolute truth"—and the resultant surfacing of "very explosive ideas" all "fell apart" at the moment of Thomas's speech in which he "changed all of the rules." Consequently, it is this moment in the play where the "linear logic of the structure also breaks down." She recalled that in the original Magic Theatre production directed by Ellen Sebastian, this dramaturgical shift was accompanied by changes in the theatrical sign-systems, as the "set began to crumble and break apart," and the lighting became "more surrealistic and extreme." Further, Hunt believes that the play works better and "productions are better reviewed" when the director capitalizes on the surreal elements as opposed to those which attempt a more "purely documentary style."

Examining the text for this linear progression and its ultimate breakdown yields some interesting results. On the basic structural level, Hunt constructed the play in ten scenes, the first two centering on Anita Hill's direct examination by the fourteen Senate Judiciary Committee members, here distilled to one composite character—the Senator. It should be noted that although Hunt begins the play with Hill's testimony, Thomas was in fact given the opportunity to appear before the committee to answer the charges of sexual harassment prior to the examination of Hill (Hrg. 5–11). Moreover, it was in these preliminary remarks that Thomas first alluded to the surrealistic turn the Committee investigation had taken (which had already been in progress for some months throughout the summer of 1991) by referring to the process as "Kafka-esque" (Hrg. 8). Thomas concluded his opening statement by foreshadowing the "high-tech lynching" speech, commenting that he would "not provide the rope for my own lynching or further humiliation" (Hrg. 11).

These distinctions become significant in relation to Hunt's dramaturgical move toward structural and narrative disintegration, since it highlights her own subjectivity in regard to the moment when the hearing itself disintegrated. It is, after all, Hunt's opinion that it was following Hill's testimony that the illogical components of the process became apparent, when in actuality, Thomas seemed to have already "changed the rules" before Hill took the stand. This illuminates a major issue facing the documentary playwright and her audience, specifically, that the truth-telling enterprise is necessarily mediated at the moment that interpretation becomes a factor in the presentation of historical events. What "New Historicists" would add to this is that all acts of history writing are similarly mediated, and that even the most seemingly objective historical documents converge to some degree with literary formations in the historiographical process. In this regard, the documentary drama form appears to be the apotheosis of the New Historicists' position. Compounding this is the further consideration that the documentary play is not necessarily intended as a historical document per se, but has, as its ultimate outcome, performance. The implications of the performative means and mechanisms inscribed in Hunt's play, as well as additional mediations involved in the truth-telling enterprise in light of performative ends, are examined in what follows.

It is noteworthy that in the first speech of the play—spoken by the composite character of the Senator (in the hearing itself by Chairman Joseph Biden)—Hunt changed not only the actual words and syntax of Biden's speech, but also the names of Senators Specter and Leahy to "the Senator from Pennsylvania" and "the Senator from Vermont" (*UQ*; Hrg. 30). While this may have been necessary to conventionalize the strategy whereby the composite "Senator" comes to represent fourteen, this does qualify Hunt's claim that "every word is taken directly from the transcripts of the hearings" (*UQ*).

Returning to the structural organization of the play, particularly the narrative linearity in the presentation of material prior to Thomas's speech, and its subsequent dissolution, cross-referencing the script and the transcripts reveals that Hunt engaged in a process of editing not only extraneous questions and responses, but also specific words within lines. It also reveals that Hunt did in fact present the material in the first two scenes dramatizing Hill's testimony sequentially, the primary dramaturgical functions consisting of selecting and editing.

Hunt also interpolated three significant ruptures within the narrative progression in the first two scenes: the inclusion of "the NPR voiceover [that] attempts to describe this first round of questioning"; the "chaos of people leaving for lunch, new analysis, etc." to indicate the break between morning and afternoon session; and the entry of Clarence Thomas at the end of Hill's testimony, wherein "they see each other" prior to Thomas's speech (*UQ*). These events, which are not recorded in the hearing transcripts, elide the break of more than an hour between Hill's testimony and Thomas's speech (Hrg.157), and serve in the play both to suggest that the hearings were indeed arbitrated by the media (specifically reportage and hype), and to create visceral tension by the contiguity of the two main players in her drama.

While Thomas's "high-tech lynching" speech was recorded faithfully by Hunt (Hrg.157–8), she eliminated the subsequent thirty pages of testimony, and instead, jump-cut to the Chair's adjournment of the evening session of October 11. This moment, which closes Scene Two, is rendered by Hunt in the progressively broken syntax of the Senator's speech, apparently to reflect the communicative breakdown of the hearing process, as well as to what Hunt referred to as the breakdown of the logic underlying the proceedings following Thomas's speech. This narrative disintegration is reinforced in the next scene, which should begin "on Saturday," as suggested by the Senator's fragmented remarks concluding Scene Two, but which is contradicted by the Senator's first question of Thomas at the top of Scene Three:

> SENATOR: Now, you, I suppose, have heard Ms.— Professor Hill's—Ms. Hill—Anita F. Hill testify today (*UQ*).

The scene is actually comprised of portions of Thomas's examination on Friday and Saturday. Scene Three, therefore, initiates the erosion of a chronological narrative as it exists in the transcript, and accents the structural technique wherein Hunt "re-choreographed" her source material. Scene Four, for example, finds Hill alone on stage, her speech actually a composite of fragmented statements abstracted from portions

of Hill's testimony prior to Thomas's second appearance and before the events presented in Scene Three. Hunt followed this in Scene Five by returning to the examination of Thomas, and in Scene Six by presenting Thomas, who "speaks to the audience" portions of testimony culled from the opening statements (prior to Hill's testimony) and thus, prior to the opening scene of the play.

Scene Seven is a montage of statements made by Hill, Thomas and the Senator(s) sifted from all phases of hearings, and takes place, according to the stage direction, "Somewhere. Stormy" (*UQ*). By contextualizing these remarks in an indeterminate place (as opposed to the Senate chambers), and in a storm, Hunt seems to register the relativity underlying the fact-finding enterprise of the hearings, as well as the elusiveness of any recoverable truth regarding the charges. This theatrical device underscores the dramaturgical strategy of deconstructing the linear narrative progression once Thomas's testimony begins in the play, and is reinforced (and the thematic issues it raises further entrenched) in the subsequent scene (Eight), which contradicts the "official" position of the Senate disapproving of sexual harassment, particularly in the Senator's quote from *Othello* which implies that Judge Thomas's character has been assassinated. Here, Hunt seems to be responding to the irony of the Senator's empathic response to Thomas's situation in the same moment that he invoked a dramatic character (Iago) loaded with racist and sexist connotations of which he is apparently ignorant, and which furthermore seems to serve as a metaphor for the whole proceeding. The Senator's folly, therefore, shapes the play and the story it tells not as a tragedy but as a surreal comedy—one foreshadowed by Thomas's remarks and Hunt's dramaturgical techniques. Additionally, the muddled posturing of the Senator at this moment (and all through the dramatization) is consistent with Hunt's choice of a composite Senator to represent "one very powerful white man" (*UQ*). When viewed from the perspective of race, which Hunt admits was "underspoken" in both the hearings and the play, this strategy makes both Thomas and Hill victims of a racist legislative body. Alternatively, when viewed from the perspective of gender difference—the issue which is dramatized more preponderantly by

Hunt, and which she felt more at ease with given the "restriction to use transcripts only"—the Senator's ironic display of empathy with Thomas shifts the object of victimization solely to Hill.

By creating the hegemonic and monolithic character of the Senator ("one very powerful white man"), Hunt related that she was able to foreground that "race and gender are the most divisive issues of our time." At the same time, she noted her goal of not making all the decisions in regard to who was telling the truth even if she could, since that "is not the way to move the culture forward"; rather, she felt her task was to "ask the questions . . . [which was] a political decision in itself." Hunt's "political decision," however, engages not only the social issues raised in the hearings, but questions regarding agency and responsibility in the truth-telling enterprise.

—DAVID PELLEGRINI